Key to map symbols

⊕	British Rail station
⊖	Underground station
🚂	Private railway station
⬤	Bus or coach station
Ⓗ	Heliport
◆	Police station (may not be open 24 hours)
✚	Hospital with casualty facilities (may not be open 24 hours)
☐	Post office
+	Place of worship
◾	Important building
P	Parking
174	Adjoining page indicator
✕	No adjoining page
═══	Motorway
═══	Dual carriageway
───	Main or through road
A27	Road numbers (Department of Transport)
─┬─	Gate or obstruction to traffic (restrictions may not apply at all times or to all vehicles)
─ ─ ─	Path, bridleway, byway open to all traffic, road used as public path, dismantled railway etc.
═══	Track

The representation in this atlas of a road, track or path is no evidence of the existence of a right of way

Amb Sta	Ambulance Station	LC	Level crossing
Amb Dpo	Ambulance Depot	Liby	Library
Coll	College	Mus	Museum
FB	Footbridge	Acad	Academy
F Sta	Fire Station	Sch	School
Hospl	Hospital	TH	Town Hall or Town House

0	¼	½	¾	1 mile
0	250m	500m	750m	1 Kilometre

The scale of the maps is 3½ inches to 1 mile (1:18103)

The small numbers around the edges of the maps identify the 1 kilometre National Grid lines

Key to map pages

Place names: DUNBLANE, BRIDGE OF ALLAN, STIRLING, ALLOA, ALVA, TILLICOULTRY, Tullibody, Menstrie, Fallin, Cowie, Bannockburn, Plean, Cambusbarron, Cambuskenneth, Cauldhame, Killearn, Drymen, Gartocharn, Loch Lomond, River Forth, Arden, HELENSBURGH, ALEXANDRIA, Cardross, Rhu, COVE, Blairmore, GOUROCK, GREENOCK, PORT GLASGOW, Langbank, Bishopton, Old Kilpatrick, DUMBARTON, Bonhill, Duntocher, Kilmacolm, Bridge of Weir, Kilbarchan, Howwood, Lochwinnoch, JOHNSTONE, PAISLEY, Houston, RENFREW, ERSKINE, CLYDEBANK, BEARSDEN, MILNGAVIE, Strathblane, Lennoxtown, Milton of Campsie, KILSYTH, Twechar, KIRKINTILLOCH, Murhead, Stepps, Bishopbriggs, GLASGOW, RUTHERGLEN, Newton, BARRHEAD, Neilston, Bankhock, DENNY, Dunipace, Larbert, Stenhousemuir, FALKIRK, GRANGEMOUTH, Airth, Bonnybridge, CUMBERNAULD, Greengairs, Plains, AIRDRIE, COATBRIDGE, Glenboig, Glenmavis, Calderbank, Holytown, Caldercruix, Avonbridge, Slamannan, Shieldhill, California, ARMADALE, Blackridge, Eastfield, Westfield, Harthill, Fauldhouse, Shotts, Salsburgh, Cleland, Allanton, Newmains, MOTHERWELL, Chapelhall

Road numbers: A977, A91, A907, A905, M876, M9, M80, A803, A809, A811, A81, A875, A84, A873, A9, A82, A814, A83, A821, A815, A880, A78, A770, A760, A737, A761, A8, A726, A736, A724, A725, A749, A71, A73, A89, A74, A807, A891, M73, M8, A9

Grid numbers:
1, 1b, 2, 3, 4, 5, 6, 7, 8, 9, 10, 11, 12, 13, 14, 21, 22, 23, 24, 38, 39, 40, 41, 42, 63, 64, 65, 66, 85, 86, 87, 105, 106, 107, 125, 126, 127, 145, 146, 147
15, 16, 17, 18, 19, 20, 25, 26, 27, 28, 29, 30, 31, 32, 33, 34, 35, 36, 37, 43, 44, 45, 46, 47, 48, 49, 50, 51, 52, 53, 54, 55, 56, 57, 58, 59, 60, 61, 62
67, 68, 69, 70, 71, 72, 73, 74, 75, 76, 77, 78, 79, 80, 81, 82, 83, 84
88, 89, 90, 91, 92, 93, 94, 95, 96, 97, 98, 99, 100, 101, 102, 103, 104
108, 109, 110, 111, 112, 113, 114, 115, 116, 117, 118, 119, 120, 121, 122, 123, 124
128, 129, 130, 131, 132, 133, 134, 135, 136, 137, 138, 139, 140, 141, 142, 143, 144

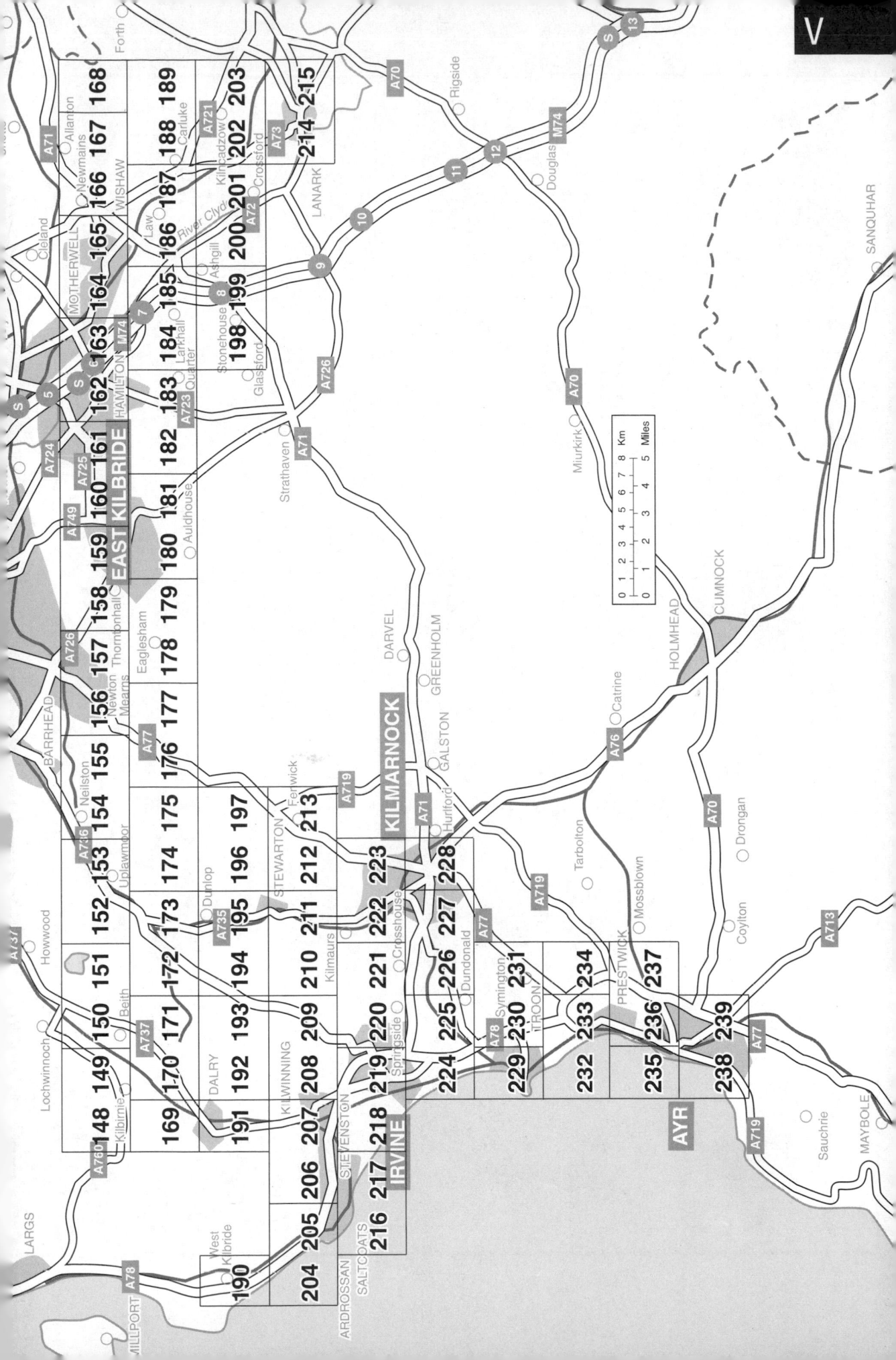

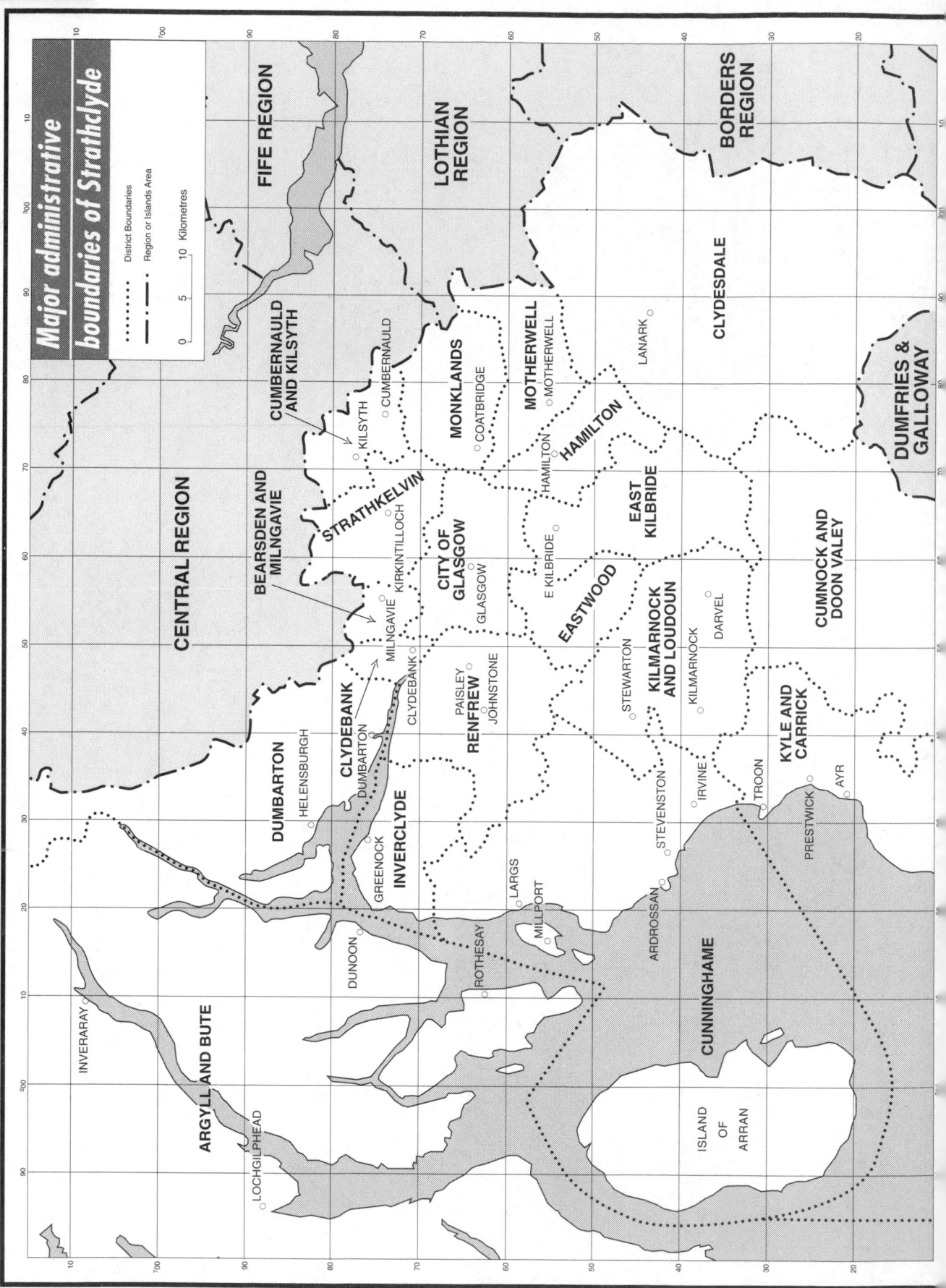

Major administrative boundaries of Strathclyde

District Boundaries
Region or Islands Area

0   5   10 Kilometres

FIFE REGION

LOTHIAN REGION

BORDERS REGION

CENTRAL REGION

CUMBERNAULD AND KILSYTH

KILSYTH

CUMBERNAULD

MONKLANDS

COATBRIDGE

MOTHERWELL

MOTHERWELL

HAMILTON

HAMILTON

LANARK

CLYDESDALE

DUMFRIES & GALLOWAY

BEARSDEN AND MILNGAVIE

STRATHKELVIN

KIRKINTILLOCH

MILNGAVIE

CITY OF GLASGOW

GLASGOW

E KILBRIDE

EAST KILBRIDE

EASTWOOD

KILMARNOCK AND LOUDOUN

DARVEL

KILMARNOCK

CUMNOCK AND DOON VALEY

CLYDEBANK

CLYDEBANK

DUMBARTON

DUMBARTON

HELENSBURGH

PAISLEY

RENFREW

JOHNSTONE

STEWARTON

INVERCLYDE

GREENOCK

STEVENSTON

IRVINE

TROON

KYLE AND CARRICK

PRESTWICK

AYR

DUNOON

ROTHESAY

LARGS

MILLPORT

ARDROSSAN

ARGYLL AND BUTE

INVERARAY

CUNNINGHAME

ISLAND OF ARRAN

LOCHGILPHEAD

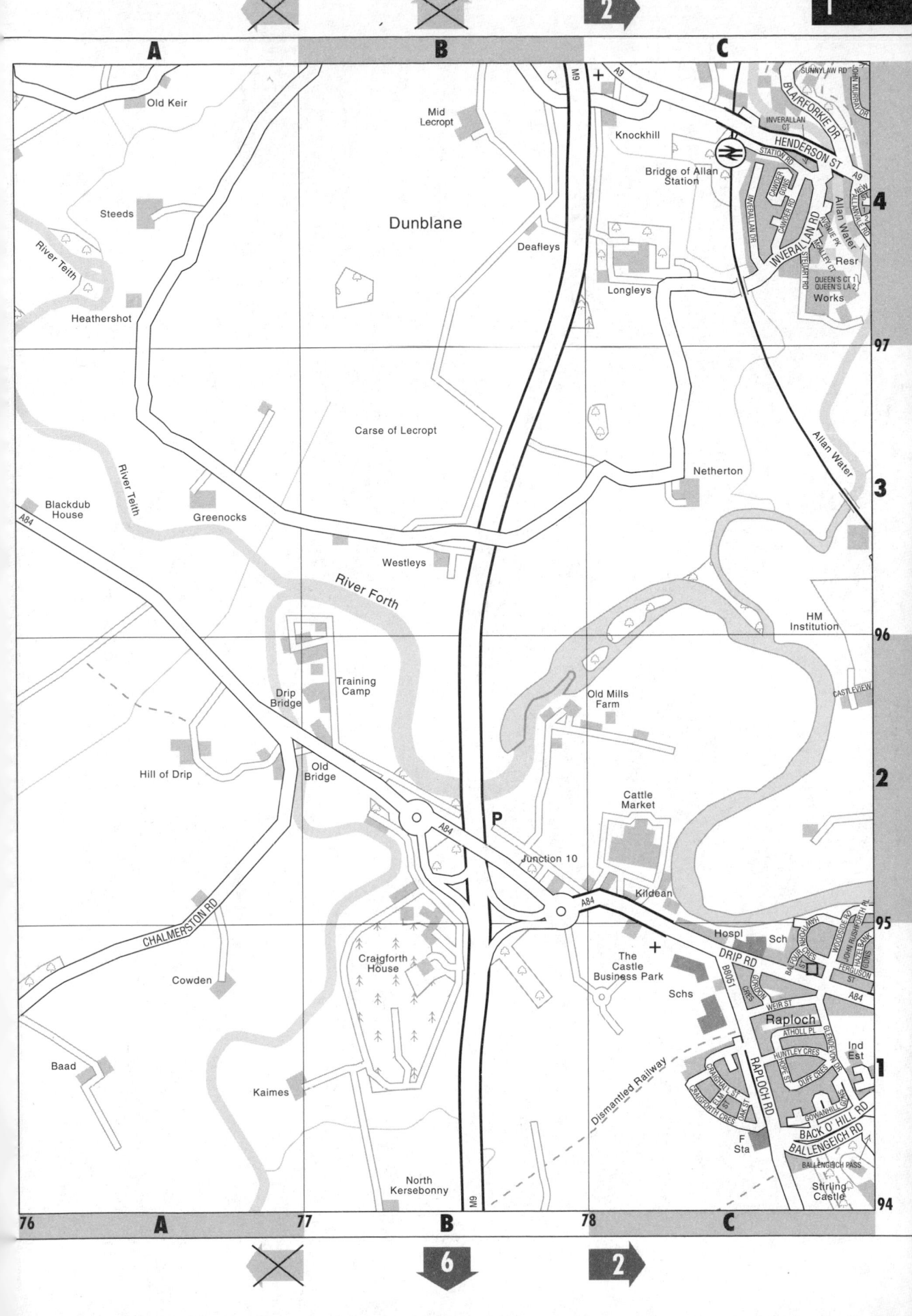

Dunblane

Old Keir

Mid Lecropt

Knockhill

SUNNYLAW RD

JOHN MURRAY DR

BLAIRFORKIE DR

INVERALLAN CT

HENDERSON ST

STATION RD

Bridge of Allan Station

Steeds

Deafleys

Longleys

CAWDER GDNS

CAWDER RD

AVENUE PK

HEALEY RD

STUART RD

INVERALLAN DR

Allan Water

NEW ALLANWATER

Resr

QUEEN'S CT 1
QUEEN'S LA 2

Works

River Teith

Heathershot

97

Carse of Lecropt

Allan Water

River Teith

Blackdub
House

Greenocks

Netherton

3

Westleys

River Forth

HM
Institution

96

CASTLEVIEW

Drip
Bridge

Training
Camp

Old Mills
Farm

Hill of Drip

Old
Bridge

2

Cattle
Market

P

Junction 10

Kildean

A84

Hospl

Sch

95

CHALMERSTON RD

DRIP RD

Cowden

Craigforth
House

The
Castle
Business Park

Schs

WOODSIDE RD

JOHN RUSHFORTH PL

RIVERBANK

FERGUSON

BALFOUR CRES

HIGHLAND DYKE

Raploch

WEIR ST

ATHOLL PL

GLENGARRY

GLEN TYE

HUNTLEY CRES

CLIFF CRES

GOWANHILL

Ind
Est

Baad

Kaimes

Dismantled Railway

BACK O' HILL RD

CRAIGS VALE

CRAIGHALL ST

CRAIGFORTH CRES

RAPLOCH RD

F
Sta

BALLENGEICH RD

BALLENGEICH PASS

Stirling
Castle

1

North
Kersebonny

94

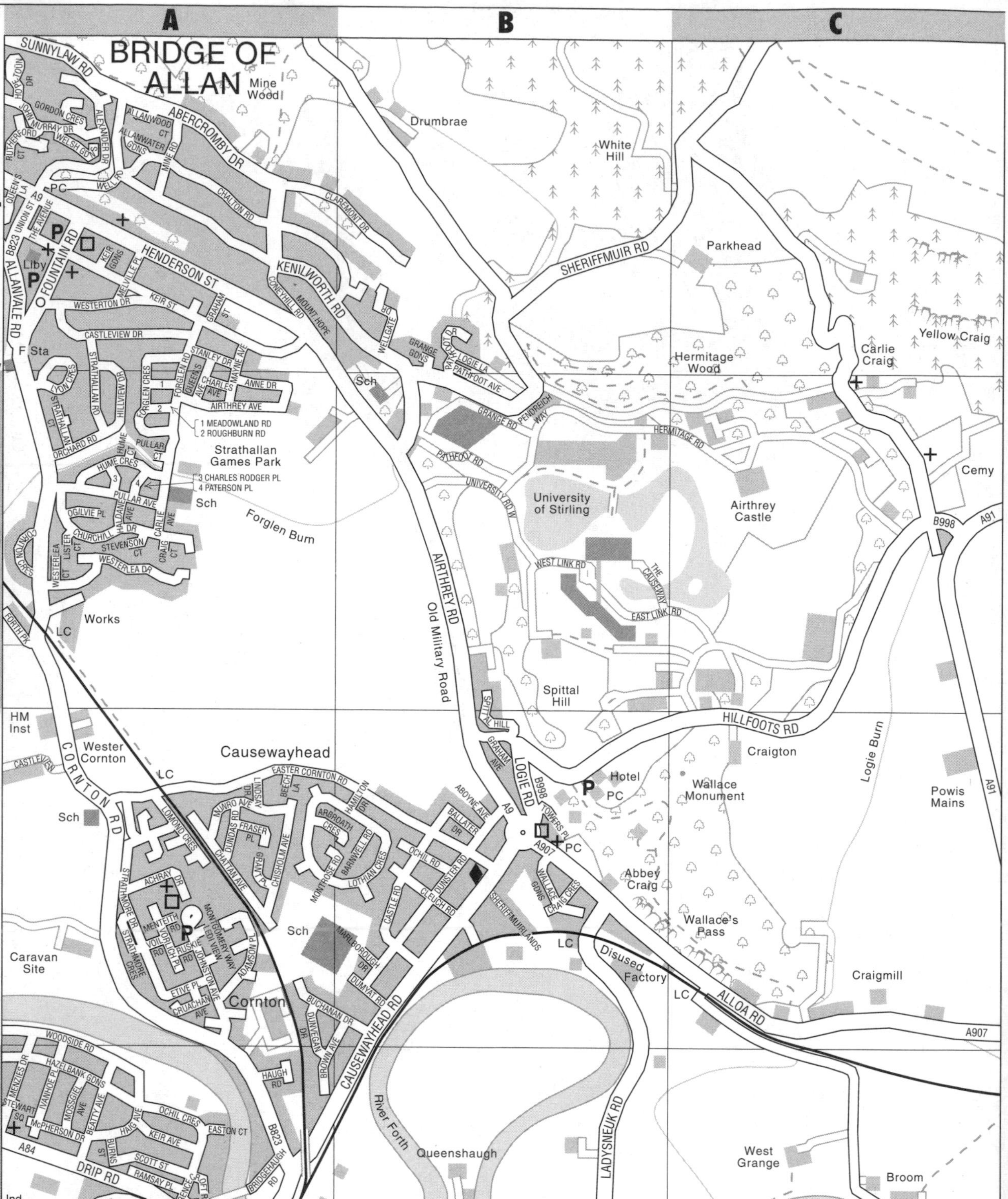

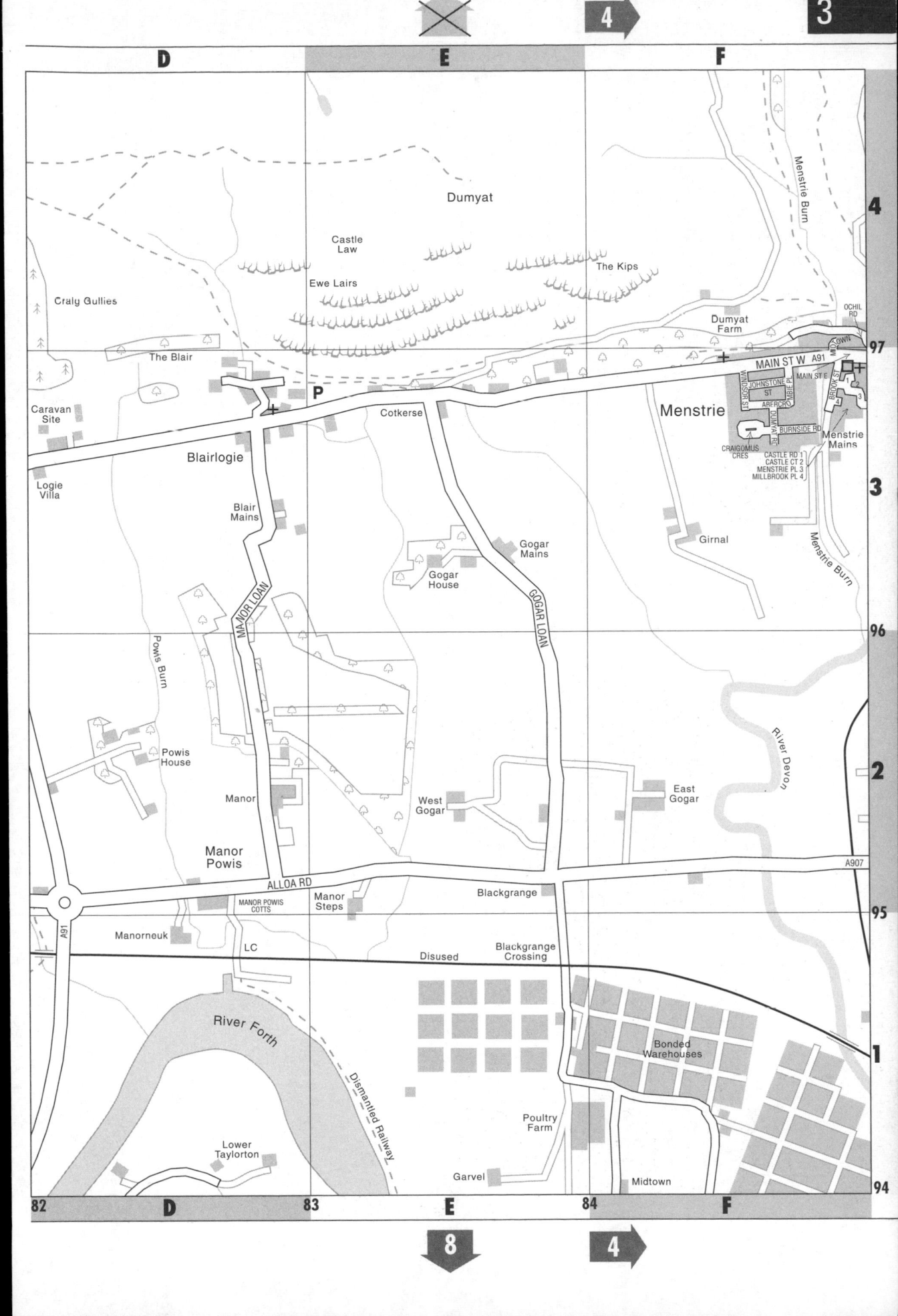

Dumyat

Castle
Law

The Kips

Ewe Lairs

Craig Gullies

Dumyat
Farm

OCHIL
RD

MIDTOWN

The Blair

MAIN ST W A91

Menstrie

97

P

WINDSOR ST

JOHNSTONE ST

AFFR CRO

DUMYAT RD

BROOK ST

MAIN ST E

Caravan
Site

Cotkerse

BURNSIDE RD

Menstrie
Mains

Blairlogie

CRAIGOMUS
CRES

CASTLE RD 1
CASTLE CT 2
MENSTRIE PL 3
MILLBROOK PL 4

Logie
Villa

Gogar
Mains

Girnal

3

Blair
Mains

Gogar
House

MANOR LOAN

GOGAR LOAN

Powis Burn

96

Powis
House

River Devon

West
Gogar

East
Gogar

2

Manor

Manor
Powis

A907

ALLOA RD

Blackgrange

A91

MANOR POWIS
COTTS

Manor
Steps

95

Manorneuk

LC

Disused

Blackgrange
Crossing

River Forth

Bonded
Warehouses

1

Dismantled Railway

Lower
Taylorton

Poultry
Farm

Garvel

Midtown

94

82 D 83 E 84 F

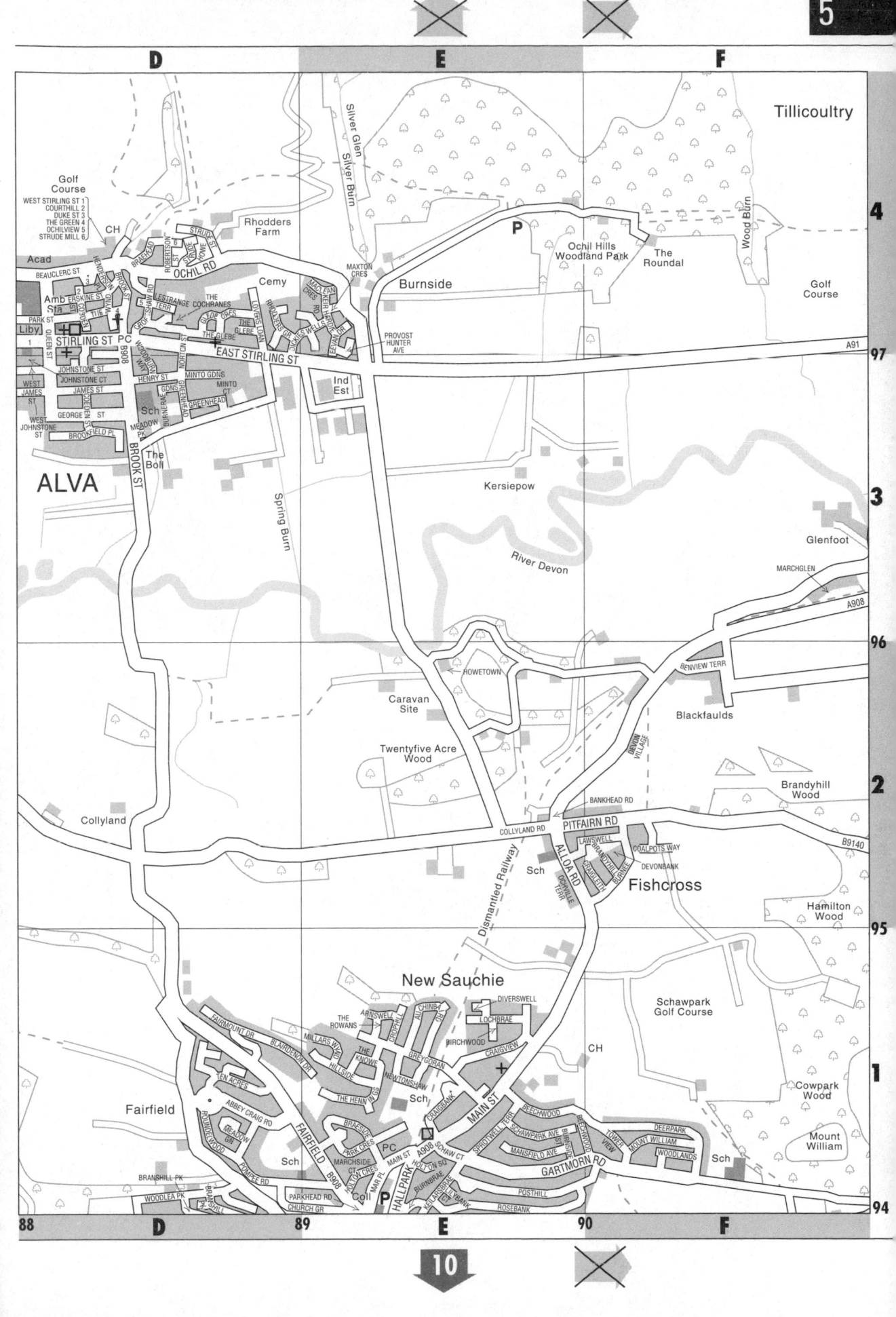

Tillicoultry

Golf Course
WEST STIRLING ST 1
COURTHILL 2
DUKE ST 3
THE GREEN 4
OCHILVIEW 5
STRUDE MILL 6

CH
Acad
Rhodders Farm

Silver Glen
Silver Burn

Wood Burn

P
Ochil Hills
Woodland Park
The Roundal
Golf Course

BEAUCLERC CT
Amb Sta
ERSKINE ST
PARK ST
Liby
QUEEN ST
WEST JAMES ST
WEST JOHNSTONE ST
George St
JOHNSTONE ST
JOHNSTONE CT
JAMES ST
HENRY ST
BROOKFIELD PL
SCH
MEADOW PK
The Boll

STIRLING ST
OCHIL RD
ROBERTSON ST
STRUDE ST
STRUDE HOWE
BRECKEAD
OCHIL RD
PC
Cemy
LESTRANGE TERR
THE COCHRANES
RHODDERS LOAN
JAMES WELLS
EAST STIRLING ST
THE GLEBE
LOVERS LOAN
MACLEAN CRES
MAXTON CRES

Burnside

A91
97

MINTO GDNS
GREENHEAD
MINTO CT
Ind Est

ALVA

BROOK ST
Spring Burn
Collyland

River Devon
Kersiepow

Glenfoot
MARCHGLEN
A908
3

Howetown
Caravan Site
Twentyfive Acre Wood

BENVIEW TERR
Blackfaulds
96
Brandyhill Wood

Collyland Rd
Collyland
Dismantled Railway

BANKHEAD RD
PITFAIRN RD
LAWSWELL
COALPOTS WAY
Sch
DEVONBANK
ALLOA RD
CRAIGEITH
DEVONALE TERR
Fishcross

B9140
2
Hamilton Wood

New Sauchie
DIVERSWELL
ARNSWELL
CHOPHILL
ALTCHINBA
LOCHBRAE
BIRCHWOOD
CRAIGVIEW
THE ROWANS
THE KNOWE
HILLSIDE
MILLARS WYND
BLAIRDENON DR
FAIRMOUNT DR
GREYGORAN
NEWTONSHAW
CH

95

Schawpark Golf Course

Fairfield
TEN ACRES
ABBEY CRAIG RD
MEADOW GR
ROUNDELWOOD
THE HENN
BRAESIDE
PARK CRES
FAIRFIELD
MARCHSIDE
ALTON CRES
Sch
POMBSE RD
BRANSHILL PK
WOODLEA PK
PARKHEAD RD
CHURCH GR
Coll
PC
P
B908
MART PL
MAIN ST
SCHAW CT
ALTON SQ
BURNBRAE
HOLTON SQ
NEWARTHILL
LILYBANK
ROSEBANK
POSTHILL
Sch
CRAIGBANK
MAIN ST
SPROTWELL TERR
SCHAWPARK AVE
MANSFIELD AVE
BEECHWOOD
BIRCHWOOD
TOWER VIEW
MOUNT WILLIAM
DEERPARK
WOODLANDS
GARTMORN RD
Sch

Cowpark Wood
Mount William

1

94

A | **B** | **C**

River Forth
Dismantled Railway
Falleninch
M9
DUMBARTON RD
King's Knot
A811
B8061 RAPLOCH RD
4
A811
Polrogan Bridge
Bankend
White House
South Kersebonny
King's Park Farm
Golf Course
CH
BALMORAL PL
QUEEN'S RD
THE HOMESTEADS
King's Park
B8061
93
Hollandbush
Raploch Burn
ST THOMAS'S WELL
Hayford House
Cemy
BROOMHILL PL
ST THOMAS'S
DOUGLAS TERR
SNOWDON PLACE LA 1
SNOWDON PL 2
PC
PARK AVE
KING'S PK RD
Hillhead
Johnny's Bridge
PARK DYKE
PARK PL
TOUCH RD
MILL RD
Cambusbarron
NORTHEND
STEWART ST
DONALDSON PL
HAYFORD PL
BIRKHILL RD
GRAMPIAN RD
CONEY PARK
DALMORGLEN PK
Batterflatts
Torbrex
LAURELHILL GDNS
Johnny's Burn
3
GRIEVESON
MILL HILL BRAE
THE BRAE
COWAN
GRAMPIAN RD
SPRINGWOOD AVE
QUARRY RD
PARK TERR
CAULDHAME CRES
THE YETTS
Sch
MURRAY PL
WOODSIDE CT
Liby
UNDERWOOD RD
Polmaise Farm
POLMAISE RD
DEVERON PL
Hospl
SYCAMORE PL
ABERDEEN GR
Old Drove Rd
THOMSON PL
UNDERWOOD COTTS
BRUCE TERR
GILLIES HILL
WALLACE PL
ST NINIAN'S RD
KENNINGKNOWE RD
BIRCH AVE
CEDAR AVE
ASH TERR
Gartur
Cambusbarron Quarry
TORBREX LA
TORBREX FARM RD
ST VALERY DR
92
Murray's Wood
Gillies Hill
Bearside
TORBREX RD
WELL PARK CRES
Touchadam Craig
Polmaise Castle
POLMAISE RD
Coxet Hill
CULTENHOVE CRES
CAMPBELL CT
2
Fir Park
CULTENHOVE PL
Murrayshall Quarry
Haggs Wood
GATESIDE
Castlehill
Murrayshall Farm
GRAYSTALE RD
91
Graystale
Sauchie Craig
Wallstale
Moor Burn
Chartershall House
1
Middlethird Wood
Bannock Burn
Chartershall Farm
Cultenhove
CHARTERSHALL RD
90
76 | **A** | 77 | **B** | 78 | **C**

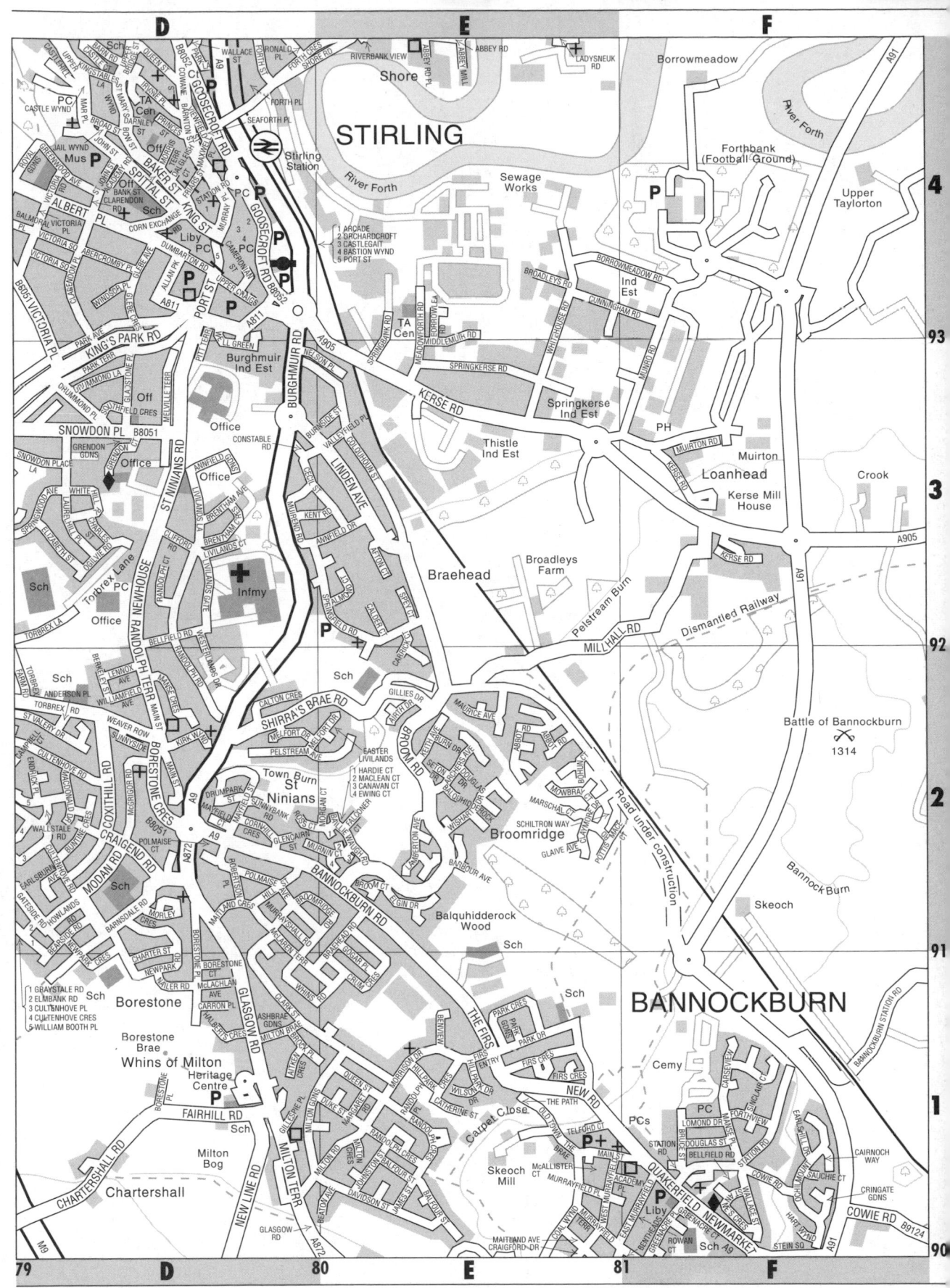

D E F

STIRLING

Shore

Borrowmeadow

RIVERBANK VIEW

ABBEY RD

LADYSNEUK RD

River Forth

Forthbank
(Football Ground)

Upper
Taylorton

P

Sewage
Works

4

BROADLEYS RD

Ind
Est

BORROWMEADOW RD

CUNNINGHAM RD

MUNRO RD

Stirling Station

1 ARCADE
2 ORCHARDCROFT
3 CASTLEGAIT
4 BASTION WYND
5 PORT ST

TA
Cen

SPRINGKERSE RD

93

Springkerse
Ind Est

PH

MUIRTON RD

Muirton

Crook

Loanhead

Kerse Mill
House

KERSE RD

3

Thistle
Ind Est

A905

Office

SNOWDON PL B8051

CONSTABLE
RD

Braehead

Broadleys
Farm

Sch

Infmy

P

Pelstream Burn

MILLHALL RD

Dismantled Railway

92

Braehead

Battle of Bannockburn
1314

2

Town Burn
St
Ninians

1 HARDIE CT
2 MACLEAN CT
3 CANAVAN CT
4 EWING CT

Broomridge

Road under construction

Bannock Burn

Skeoch

Balquhidderock
Wood

Sch

91

Borestone

1 GRAYSTALE RD
2 ELMBANK RD
3 CULTENHOVE PL
4 CULTENHOVE CRES
5 WILLIAM BOOTH PL

BANNOCKBURN

Borestone
Brae
Whins of Milton
Heritage
Centre

Cemy

THE FIRS

PARK CRES

NEW RD

PC

1

Skeoch
Mill

McALLISTER
CT

QUAKERFIELD
NEWMARKET

Liby

COWIE RD B9124

FAIRHILL RD

Sch

Milton
Bog

CHARTERSHALL RD

Chartershall

GLASGOW
RD

MILTON TERR

90

A   **B**   **C**

River Forth

Bolfornought

Dismantled Railway

Poultry Farm

Bonded Warehouses

Haugh Cottage

4

Refuse Tip

Haugh of Blackgrange

Bannock Burn

93

Steuarthall Farm

Steuarthall

The Kennels

A905

Sewage Works

River Forth

3

Sch

Dykes

POLMAISE CRES

BRUCE DR

92

Redhall

Dismantled Railway

HARDIE CRES

HAWTHORN DR

LAMONT CRES

OAK DR

ARM RD

HAWTHORN CRES

GRACIE CRES

CLAIR

Alton

HILLVIEW PL

BANNOCK RD

WOODSIDE PL

FORTH ST

WALLACE ST

WEIR ST

BANDEATH RD

BAXTER ST

STIRLING RD

HILTON TERR

KING ST

THE SQUARE

Liby

P.C.

Drypow

South Cockspow

MOSS RD

QUEEN ST

Bandeath House

CASTLE VIEW

Fallin

2

Hartsmailing

Spoil Heap

PH

Burnbank

91

KERSIE RD

Newmills

Wester Moss

Lower Greenyards

Craig Moss

1

Burnhead

BANNOCKBURN STATION RD

Bankhall Kennels

COWIE RD

B9124

MAIN ST

+

90

82   **A**   83   **B**   84   **C**

D   E   F

DEVON PL

P

Cambus Farm

STATION RD
FORTH ST
MAIN ST
SOUTH ST

PH

Cambus

A907

Arnsbrae

Gean House

INGLEWOOD

DUNMAR DR

KENT RD
CROWN RD
TULLIBODY RD
WLOBIE
TIMVEA

Golf Course

GEAN RD
WDS GR

Acad Sch

INGLEWOOD CRES
CLAREMONT
LORNSHILL CRES
WINDSOR GDNS
CASTLE
CHURCH ST
CHARLES ST
OBERON GDNS
LAWSON
PAVILION VIEW

Disused

4

STIRLING RD

A907

CARSE TERR
ACADEMY ST
COWIE
NORWOOD AVE
NORWOOD CRES
CARSE GR

LC

93

Orchard Farm

Orchard House

MITCHELL CRES
DIRLETON LA
DIRLETON GDNS
GRANGE RD

Pier

SMITHFIELD LOAN

BELLEVUE RD
STANTON AVE
FORBES ST
SHIRE WAY
MACNEILL
CALEDONIAN GDNS

Works

Sch

Works

CALEDONIAN RD
TOWNS CRES

KELLIEBANK

Longcarse

Tullibody Inch

Rhind Rack

Dismantled Railway

Longcarse Reach

KEVIEKAE
MUNRO PL
KELLIEBANK
CRAIGWARD

3

Bandeath Ind Est

92

Rhind

Inch

Throsk House

FERRY RD

Works

Pier

South Alloa

2

Throsk

KERSIE RD

A905   KERSIE RD

River Forth

Kersie Mains

KERSIE TERR

91

Mains of Throsk

Poppletrees

Kersie Bridge

Dismantled Railway

Willowbank

Meadowfield

South Kersie

1

South Mains

A905

90

85   D   86   E   87   F

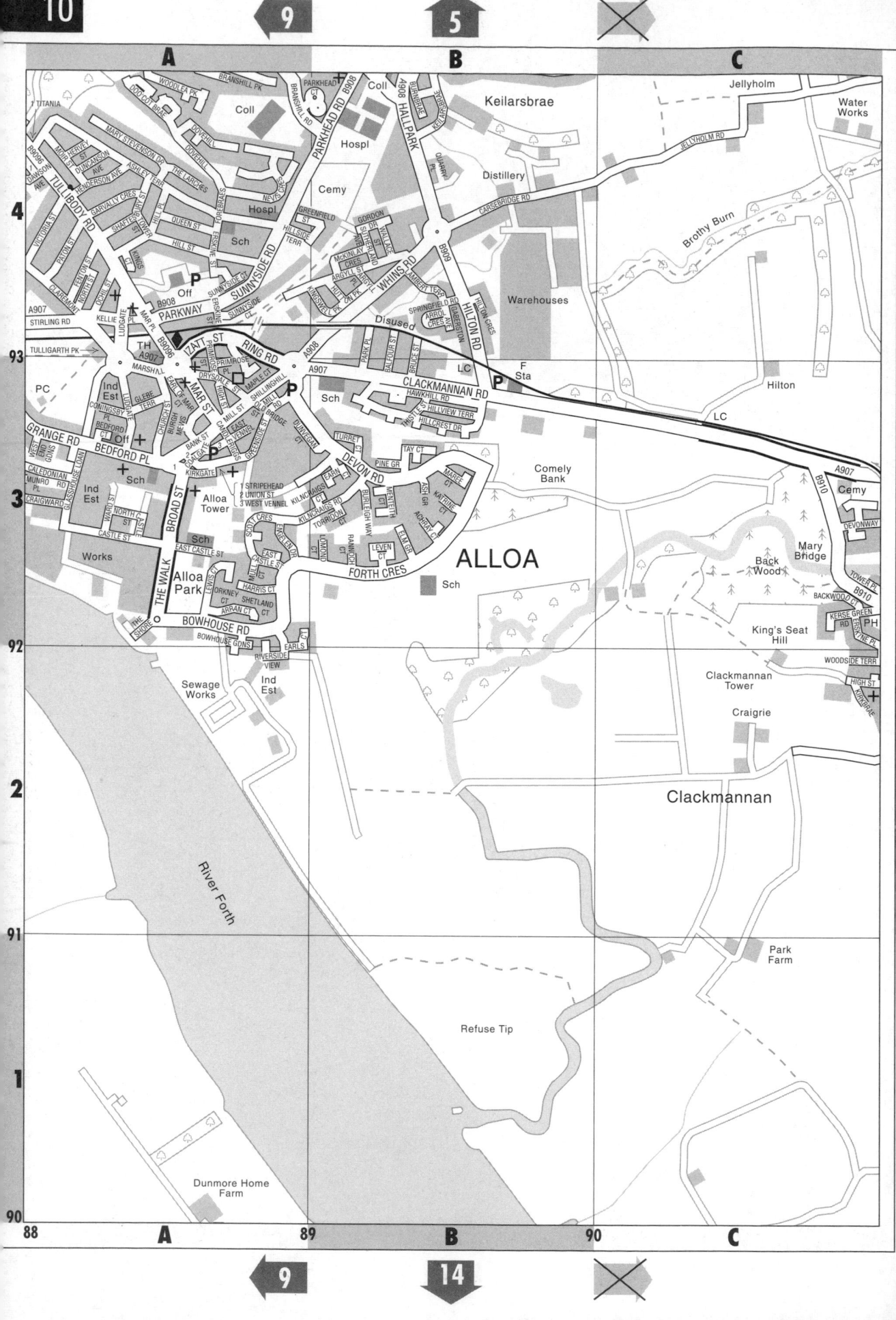

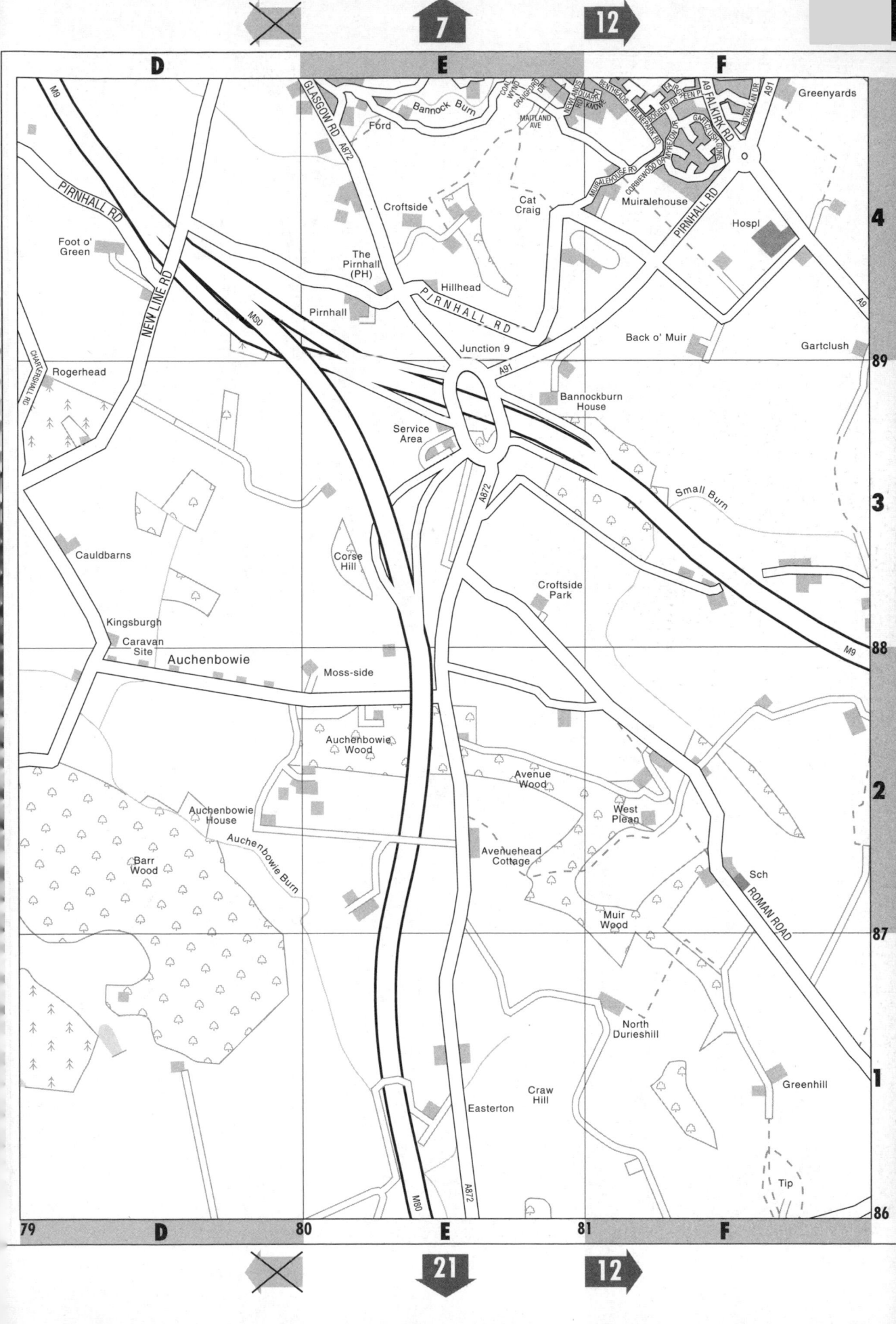

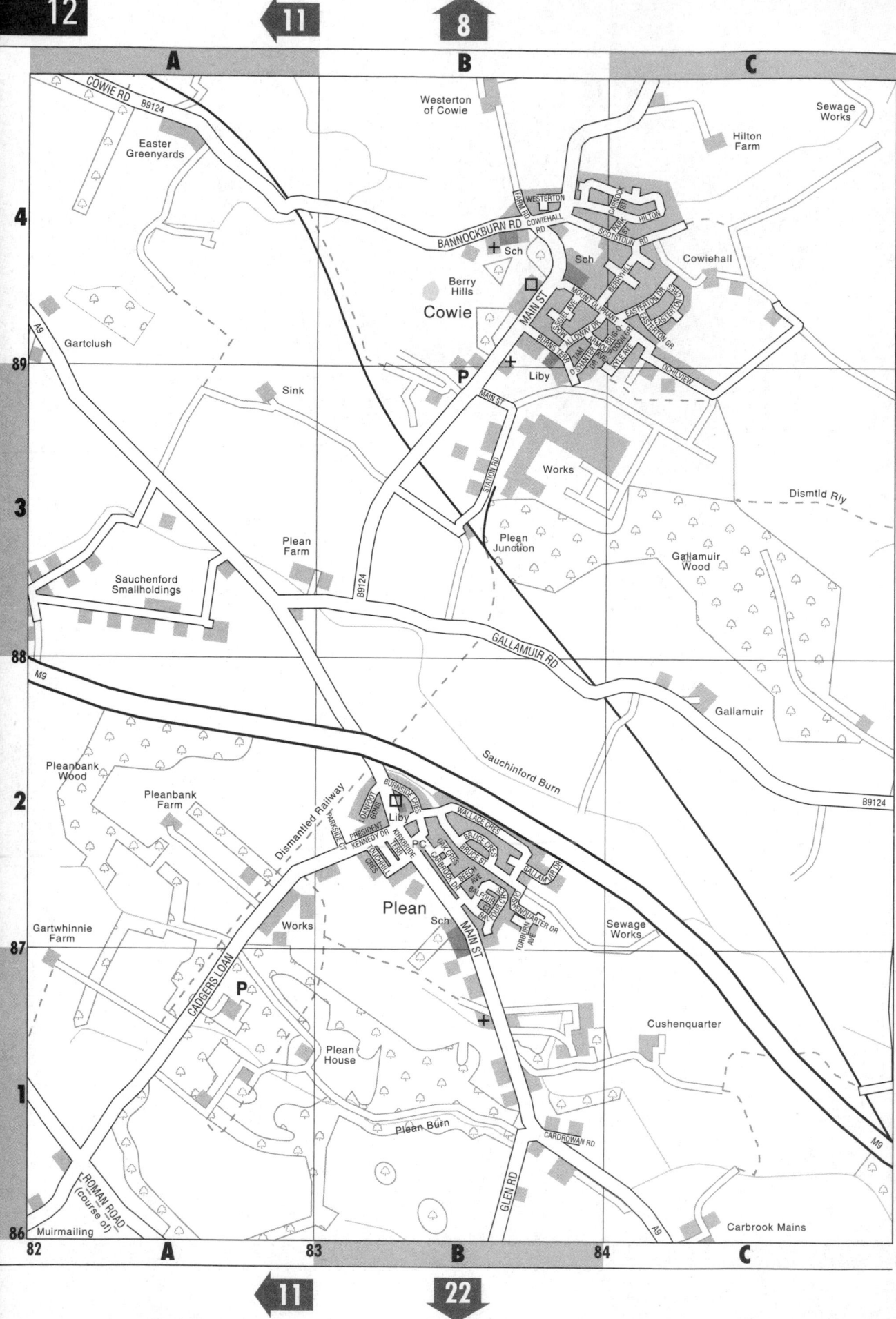

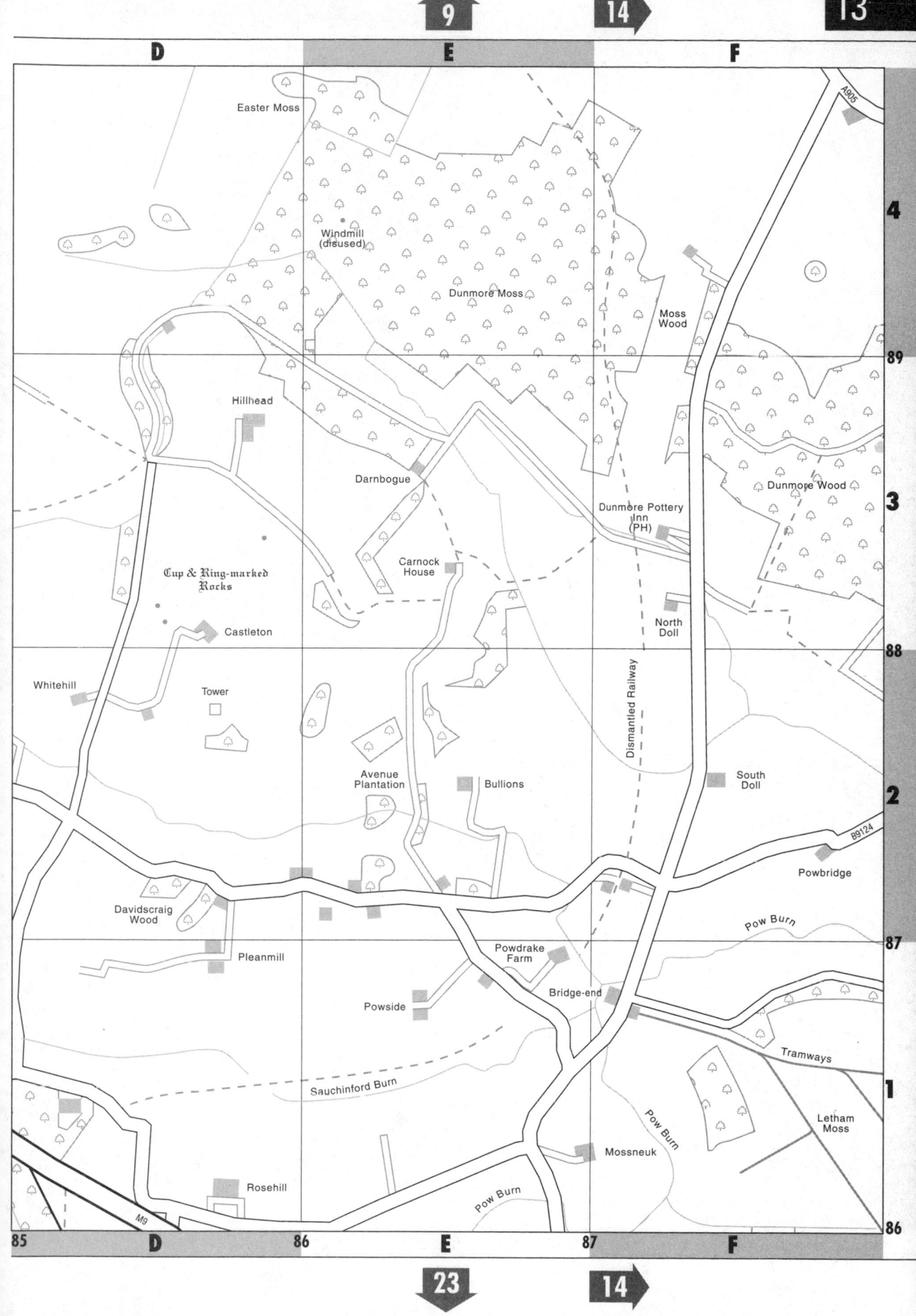

Easter Moss

Windmill (disused)

Dunmore Moss

Moss Wood

Hillhead

Darnbogue

Dunmore Wood

Dunmore Pottery Inn (PH)

Cup & Ring-marked Rocks

Carnock House

North Doll

Castleton

Whitehill

Tower

Dismantled Railway

Avenue Plantation

Bullions

South Doll

Powbridge

Davidscraig Wood

Pow Burn

Pleanmill

Powdrake Farm

Powside

Bridge-end

Tramways

Sauchinford Burn

Letham Moss

Pow Burn

Mossneuk

Rosehill

Pow Burn

M9

A905

B9124

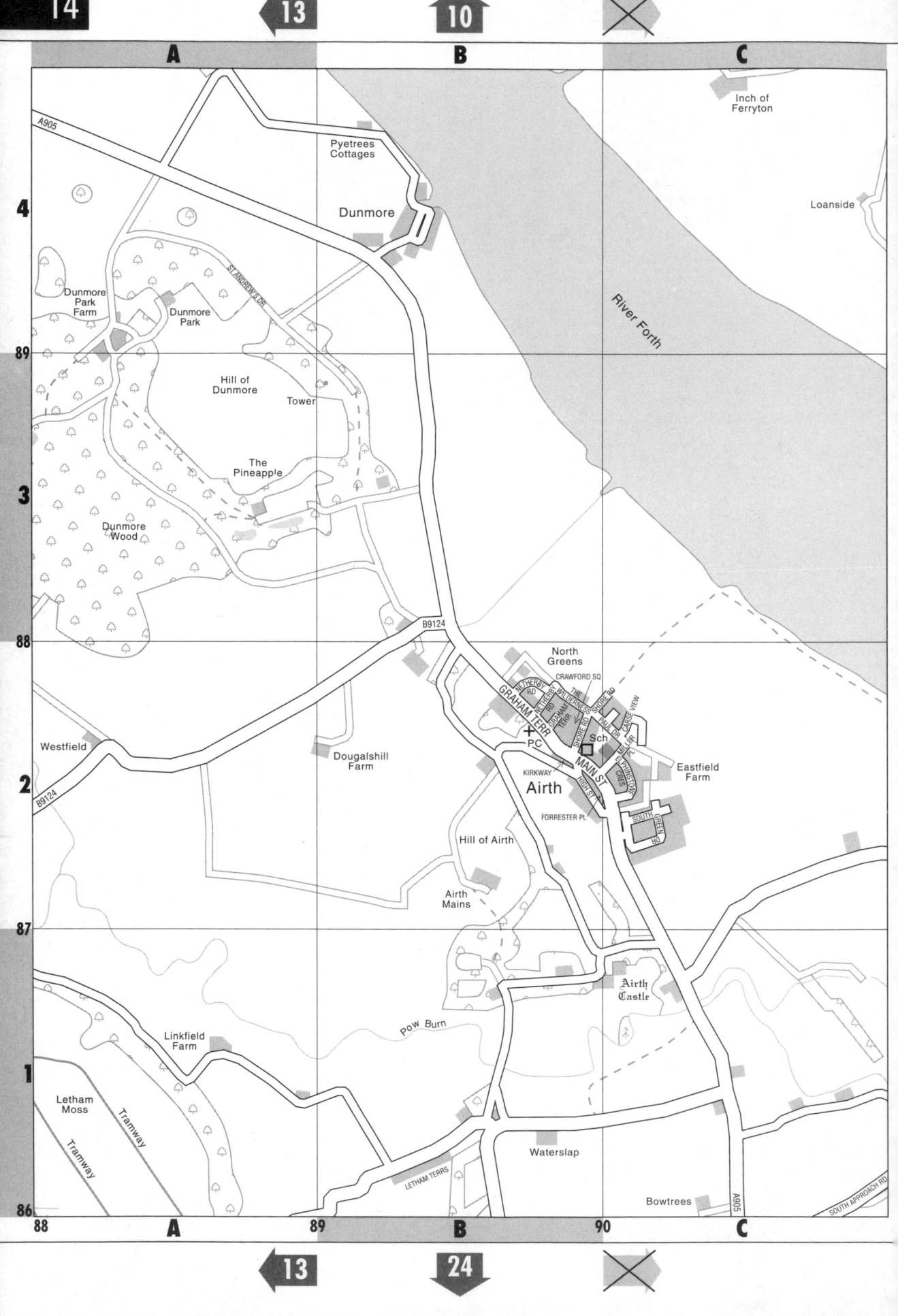

A   B   C

A905

Pyetrees
Cottages

Dunmore

Inch of
Ferryton

4

Loanside

Dunmore
Park
Farm

Dunmore
Park

ST ANDREWS DR

Hill of
Dunmore

Tower

River Forth

89

The
Pineapple

3

Dunmore
Wood

B9124

88

North
Greens

CRAWFORD SQ

Westfield

Dougalshill
Farm

GRAHAM TERR

WETHERBY RD
THE WILDERNESS
SHORE RD
STORE RD
PAUL DR
CARSE VIEW

Sch

Eastfield
Farm

2

B9124

KIRKWAY

Airth

MAIN ST
HIGH ST

PC

+

CHRISTIE CRES

Hill of Airth

FORRESTER PL

SOUTH GREEN SQ

Airth
Mains

87

Airth
Castle

Linkfield
Farm

Pow Burn

1

Letham
Moss

Tramway

Tramway

Waterslap

Tramway

LETHAM TERRS

A905

SOUTH APPROACH RD

Bowtrees

86

88   A   89   B   90   C

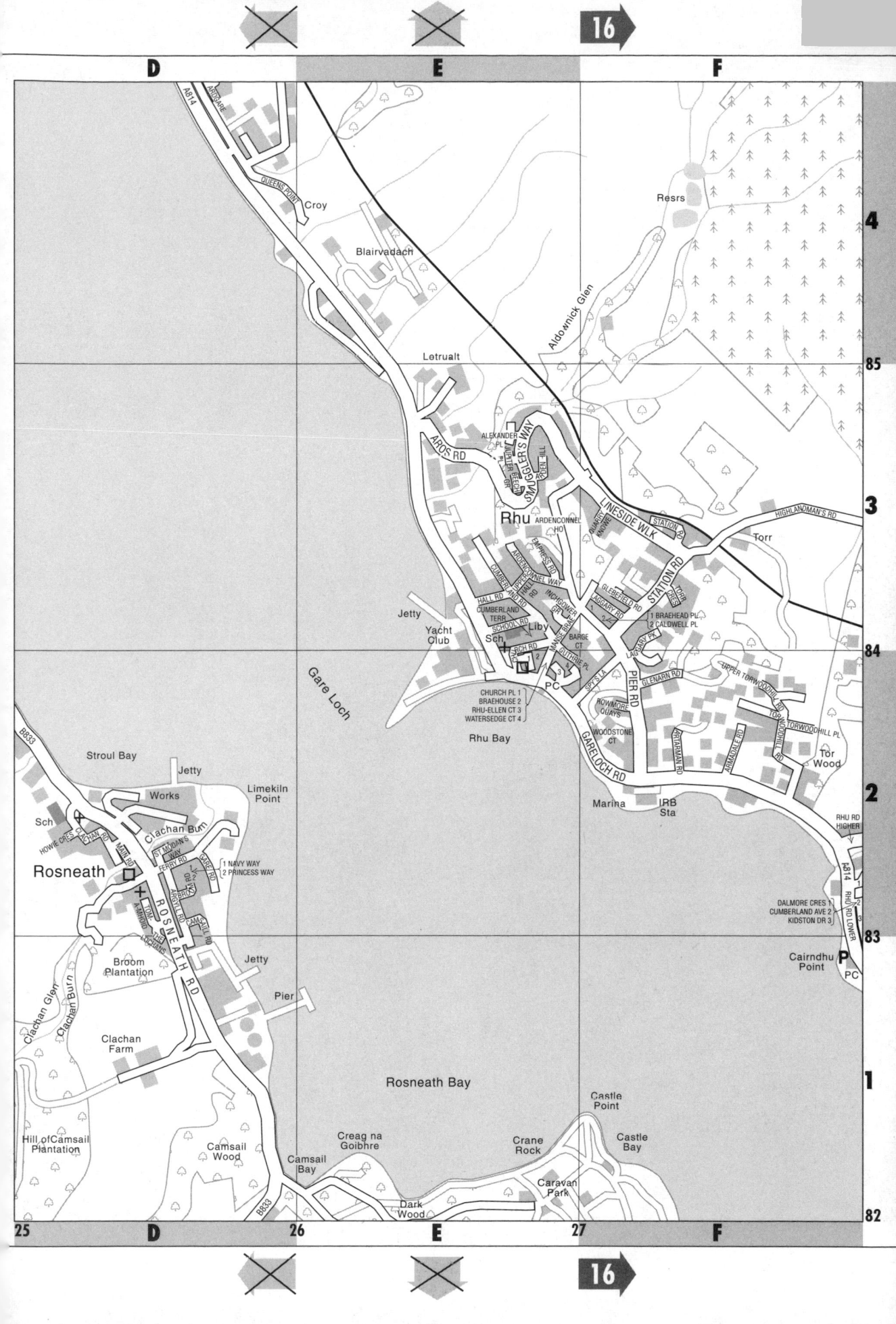

D E F

4

Resrs

Croy

Blairvadach

Aldownick Glen

85

Letrualt

AROS RD

ALEXANDER
PL

RAVEN HILL

JUBILEE BECH

SMUGGLER'S WAY

Rhu

ARDENCONNEL
HO

LINESIDE WLK

STATION 2

HIGHLANDMAN'S RD

3

Torr

EMPRESS'S WAY

ALBERT KNOWE

TORR CRES

STATION RD

Jetty

ARDENCONNEL WAY

CUMBER-
LAND RD

HALL RD

INCHGOWER RD

GLEBEFIELD RD

LAGGARY RD

1 BRAEHEAD PL
2 CALDWELL PL

Yacht
Club

Sch

CUMBERLAND
TERR

SCHOOL RD

MANSE BRAE

BARGE
CT

1 2

Liby

LAGARY PK

UPPER TORWOODHILL

84

SCH RD

GUTHRIE PL

SPEY S LA

GLENARN RD

TORR TORWOODHILL PL

PC

1
3

ROWMORE
QUAYS

PIER RD

TORWOODHILL RD

Gare Loch

CHURCH PL 1
BRAEHOUSE 2
RHU-ELLEN CT 3
WATERSEDGE CT 4

WOODSTONE
CT

ARMADALE RD

ARTARMAN RD

Tor
Wood

Rhu Bay

GARELOCH RD

2

Stroul Bay

Jetty

Marina

IRB
Sta

RHU RD
HIGHER

Works

Limekiln
Point

Sch

Clachan Bum

HOWIE CRES

ST MODAN'S

MAIN RD

FERRY RD

1 NAVY WAY
2 PRINCESS WAY

DALMORE CRES 1
CUMBERLAND AVE 2
KIDSTON DR 3

83

Rosneath

ARGYLL RD

ROSNEATH RD

CAMSAIL RD

Cairndhu
Point

P

PC

Broom
Plantation

Jetty

Clachan Glen

Clachan Bum

Pier

Clachan Farm

Hill of Camsail
Plantation

Rosneath Bay

1

Castle
Point

Camsail
Wood

Creag na
Goibhre

Crane
Rock

Castle
Bay

Camsail
Bay

Caravan
Park

Dark
Wood

B833

82

HELENSBURGH

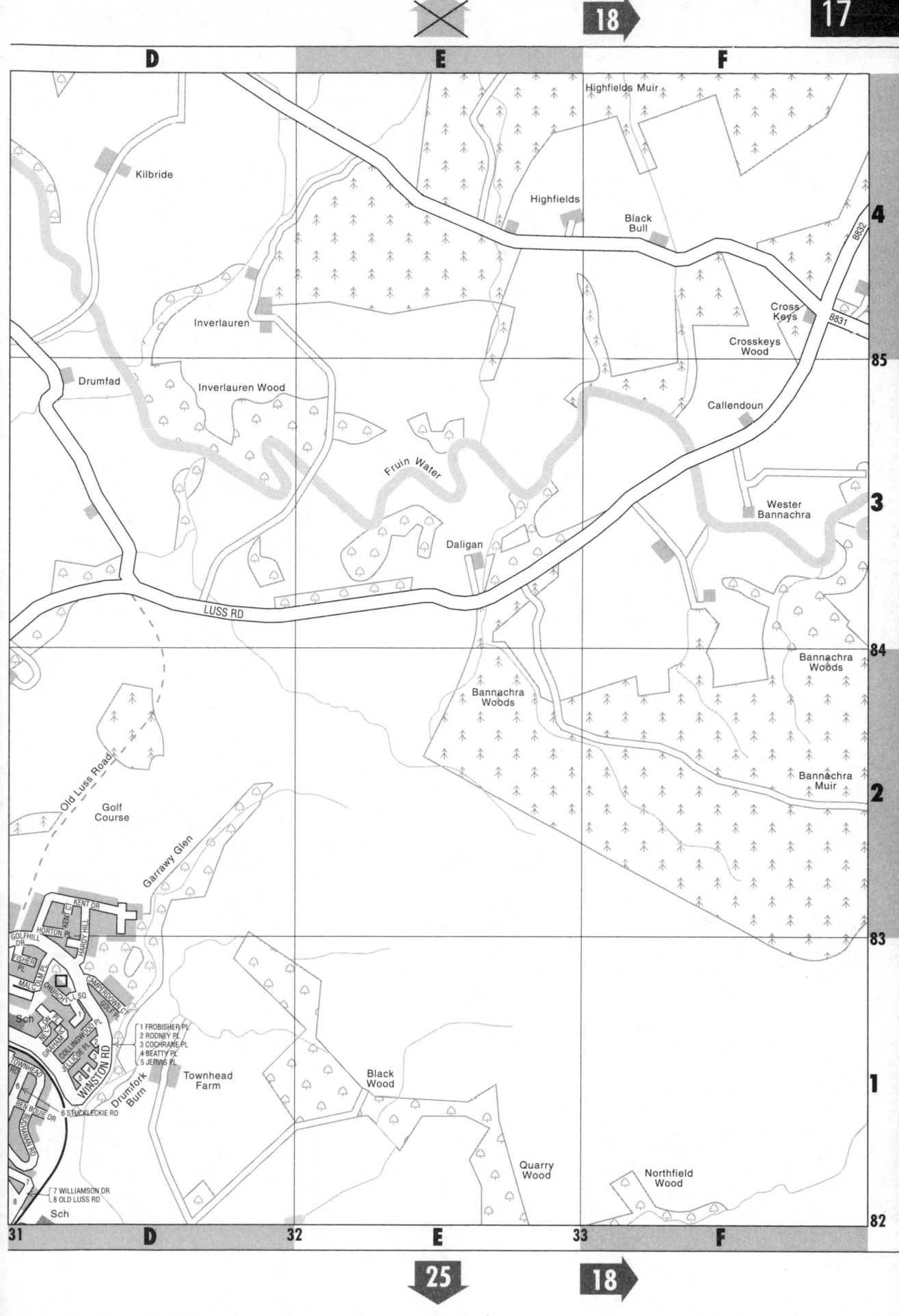

Highfields Muir

Kilbride

Highfields

Black
Bull

Inverlauren

Cross
Keys

Crosskeys
Wood

Drumfad

Inverlauren Wood

Callendoun

Fruin Water

Wester
Bannachra

Daligan

LUSS RD

Bannachra
Woods

Old Luss Road

Bannachra
Woods

Golf
Course

Bannachra
Muir

Garrawy Glen

KENT DR

KENT CT

HORTON PL

GOLFHILL
DR

HARDY HILL

FISHER
PL

MALT PL

CHURCH L SQ

CAMPERDOWN CT

BOX PL

Sch

1 FROBISHER PL
2 RODNEY PL
3 COCHRANE PL
4 BEATTY PL
5 JERVIS PL

GRAHAM

JELLICOE PL

COLLINGWOOD PL

WINSTON RD

Townhead
Farm

Black
Wood

TOWNHEAD
RD

Drumfork
Burn

6 STUCKLECKIE RD

BEN BOUIE DR

BUCHANAN RD

Quarry
Wood

Northfield
Wood

7 WILLIAMSON DR
8 OLD LUSS RD

Sch

A B C

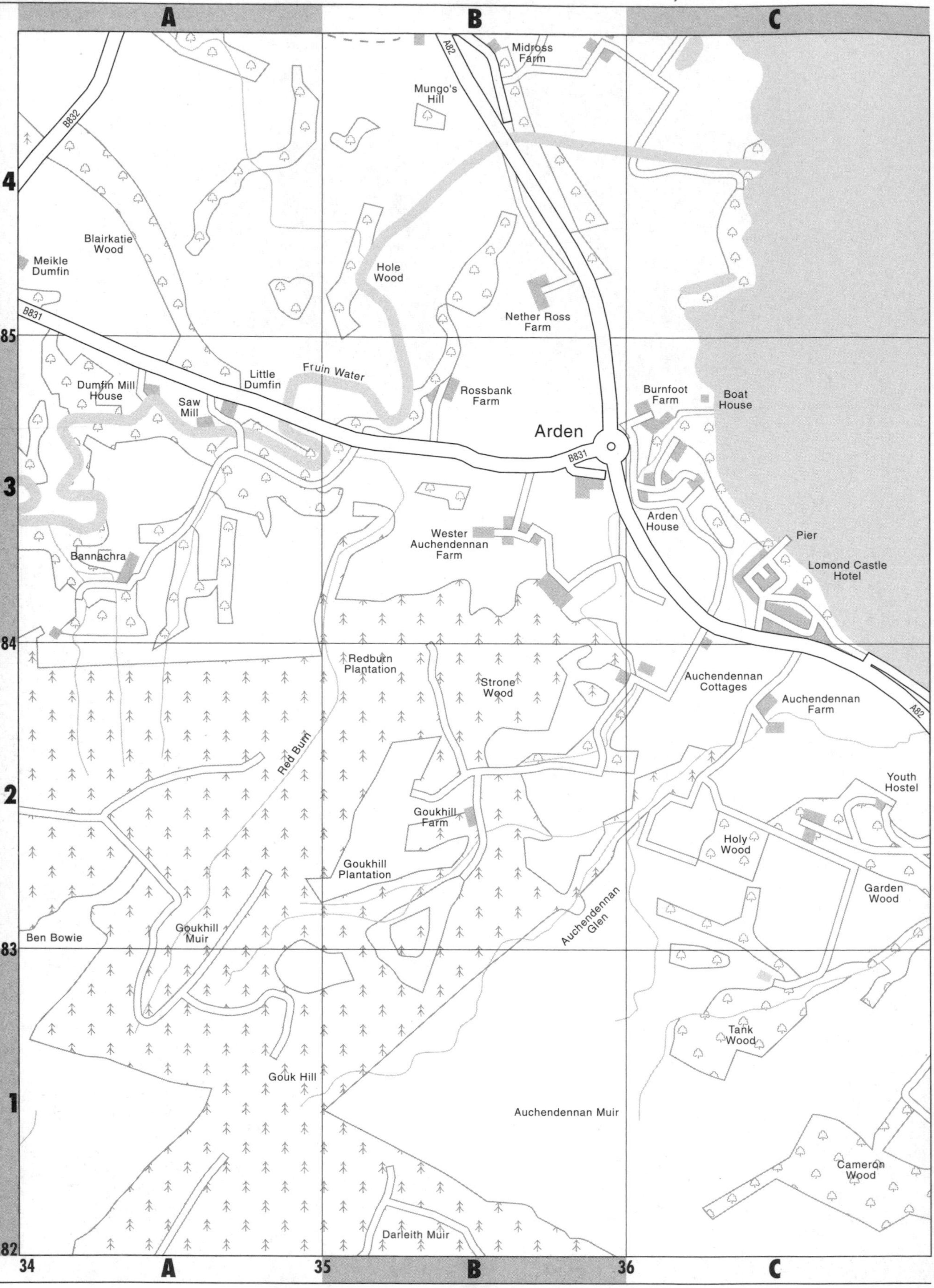

4

Mungo's
Hill

Midross
Farm

Blairkatie
Wood

Hole
Wood

Meikle
Dumfin

Nether Ross
Farm

85

Dumfin Mill
House

Little
Dumfin

Fruin Water

Rossbank
Farm

Burnfoot
Farm

Boat
House

Saw
Mill

Arden

3

Bannachra

Wester
Auchendennan
Farm

Arden
House

Pier

Lomond Castle
Hotel

84

Redburn
Plantation

Strone
Wood

Auchendennan
Cottages

Auchendennan
Farm

Red Burn

Youth
Hostel

2

Goukhill
Farm

Holy
Wood

Garden
Wood

Goukhill
Plantation

Auchendennan
Glen

Ben Bowie

Goukhill
Muir

83

Tank
Wood

Gouk Hill

1

Auchendennan Muir

Cameron
Wood

82

Darleith Muir

34 A 35 B 36 C

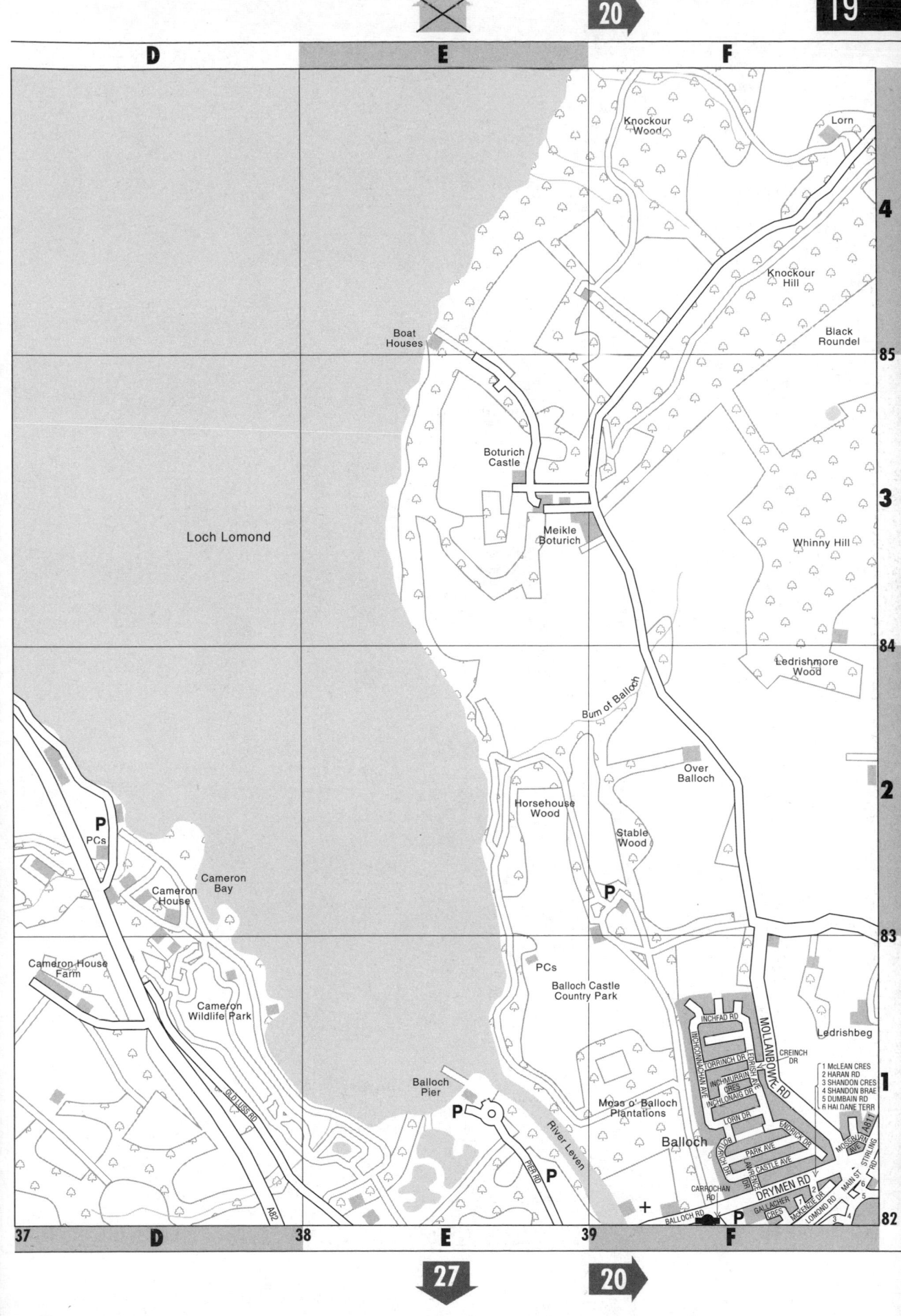

D
E
F

4

85

3

84

2

83

1

82

Knockour
Wood

Lorn

Knockour
Hill

Black
Roundel

Boat
Houses

Boturich
Castle

Meikle
Boturich

Whinny Hill

Loch Lomond

Ledrishmore
Wood

Burn of Balloch

Over
Balloch

Horsehouse
Wood

Stable
Wood

P

P
PCs

Cameron
Bay

Cameron
House

Cameron House
Farm

Cameron
Wildlife Park

PCs

Balloch Castle
Country Park

Ledrishbeg

CREINCH
DR

INCHFAD RD

MOLLANBOWIE RD

1 McLEAN CRES
2 HARAN RD
3 SHANDON CRES
4 SHANDON BRAE
5 DUMBAIN RD
6 HAI DANE TERR

INCHMURRIN AVE

TORRINCH DR

INCHMOAN AVE

LEDRISH AVE

INCHMURRIN CRES

INCHLONAIG DR

Balloch
Pier

P

P

P

River Leven

PIER RD

Moss o' Balloch
Plantations

LORN DR

PARK AVE

CASTLE AVE

ENDRICK DR

LAWRENCE DR

MOSSHEAD

STIRLING

MAIN ST

Balloch

DRYMEN RD

CARROCHAN
RD

GALLAGHER
CRES

MCKENZIE DR

LOMOND RD

BALLOCH RD

P

+

A82

GLENUSK RD

A82

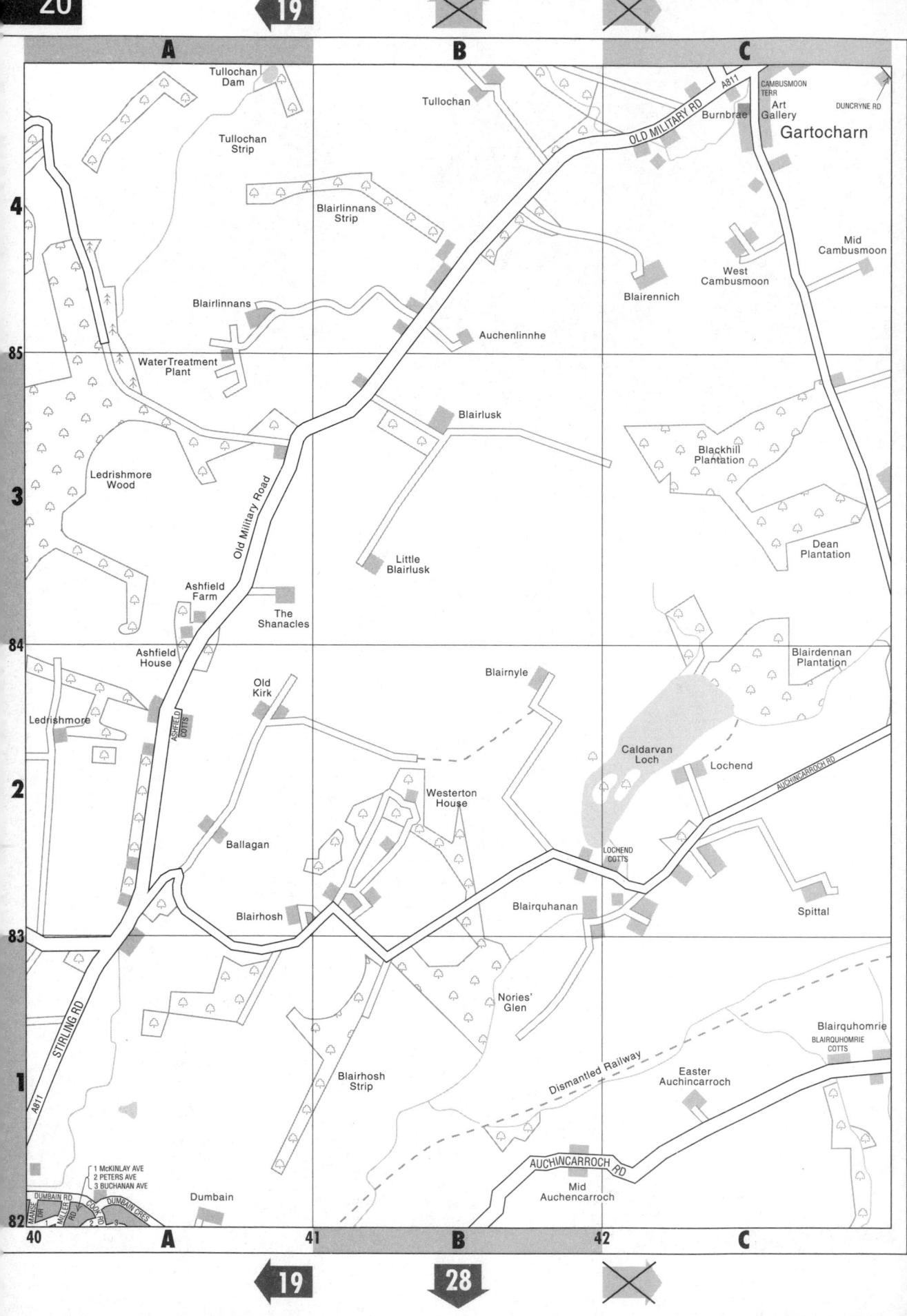

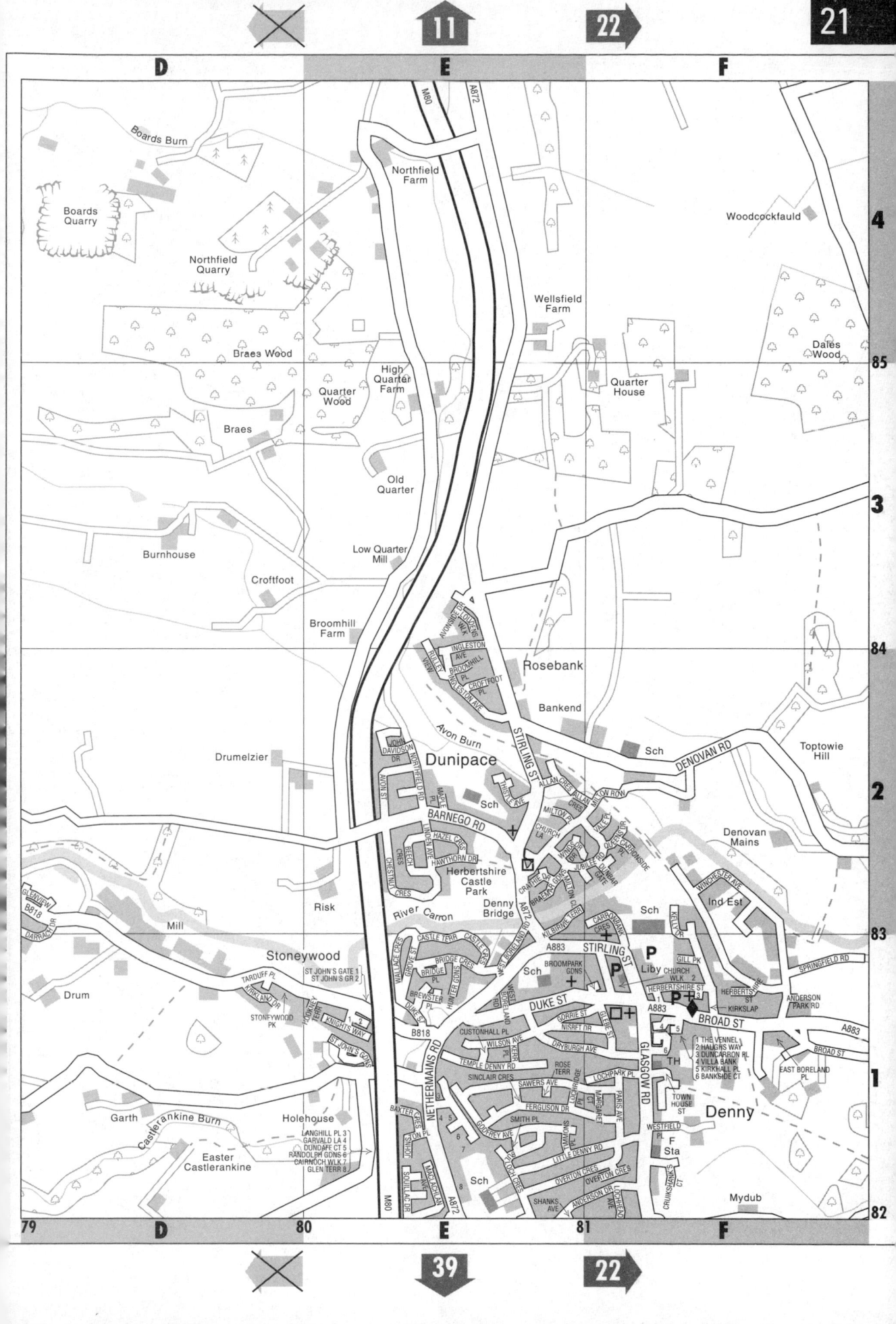

Boards Burn

Boards
Quarry

Northfield
Quarry

Northfield
Farm

Woodcockfauld

Braes Wood

Wellsfield
Farm

Dales
Wood

High
Quarter
Farm

Quarter
Wood

Quarter
House

Braes

Old
Quarter

Burnhouse

Croftfoot

Low Quarter
Mill

Rosebank

Bankend

Sch

Broomhill
Farm

DENOVAN RD

Toptowie
Hill

Drumelzier

Avon Burn

STIRLING ST

Dunipace

Sch

Denovan
Mains

BARNEGO RD

Sch

Herbertshire
Castle Park

Ind Est

Risk

River Carron

Denny
Bridge

Sch

Mill

Stoneywood

A883

STIRLING ST

Liby

Springfield Rd

Drum

St John's Gate 1
St John's Gr 2

Broompark
Gdns

P

P

P

Anderson
Park Rd

DUKE ST

A883

BROAD ST

B818

NETHERMAINS RD

TH

1 THE VENNEL
2 HALLNS WAY
3 DUNCARRON RL
4 VILLA BANK
5 KIRKHALL PL
6 BANKSIDE CT

GLASGOW RD

BROAD ST

EAST BORELAND
PL

Garth

Castlerankine Burn

Holehouse

Temple Denny Rd

Sinclair Cres

Rose
Terr

TOWN
HOUSE
ST

Denny

Easter
Castlerankine

LANGHILL PL 3
GARVALD LA 4
DUNDAFF CT 5
RANDOLPH GDNS 6
CAIRNOCH WLK 7
GLEN TERR 8

Baxter Dr

Smith Pl

Ferguson Dr

WESTFIELD
PL

F
Sta

Sch

Overton Cres

Mydub

SHANKS
AVE

ANDERSON DR

M80

A872

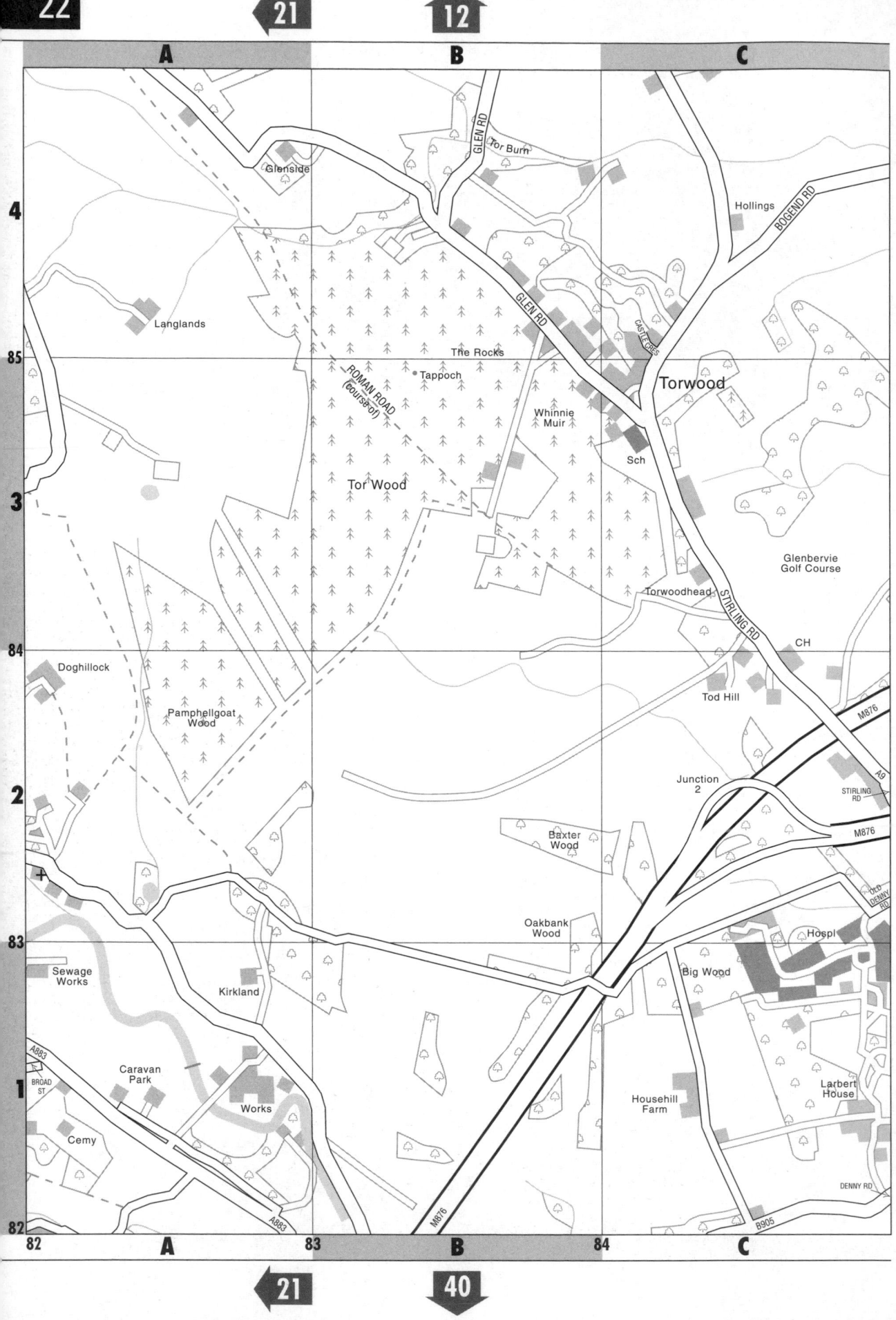

A   B   C

4

Glenside

GLEN RD

Tor Burn

Hollings

BOGEND RD

Langlands

85

The Rocks

Tappoch

GLEN RD

CASTLE CRES

Torwood

ROMAN ROAD (course of)

Whinnie Muir

Sch

Tor Wood

3

Glenbervie Golf Course

STIRLING RD

Torwoodhead

CH

84

Doghillock

Tod Hill

M876

Pamphellgoat Wood

A9

Junction 2

STIRLING RD

2

Baxter Wood

M876

OLD DENNY RD

Oakbank Wood

83

Hospl

Sewage Works

Big Wood

Kirkland

A883

BROAD ST

Caravan Park

Household Farm

Larbert House

1

Works

Cemy

DENNY RD

82

A883

M876

B905

82   83   84

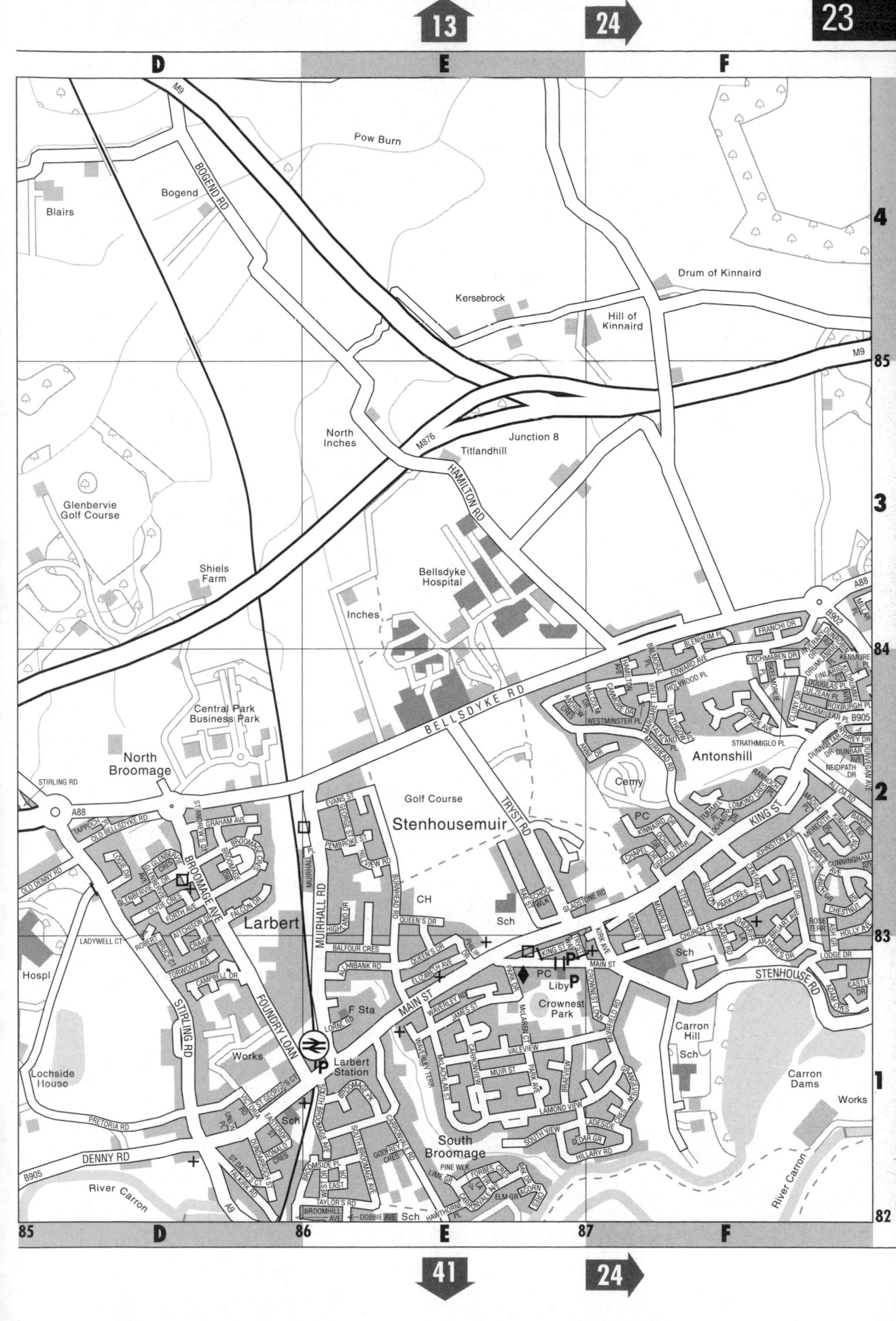

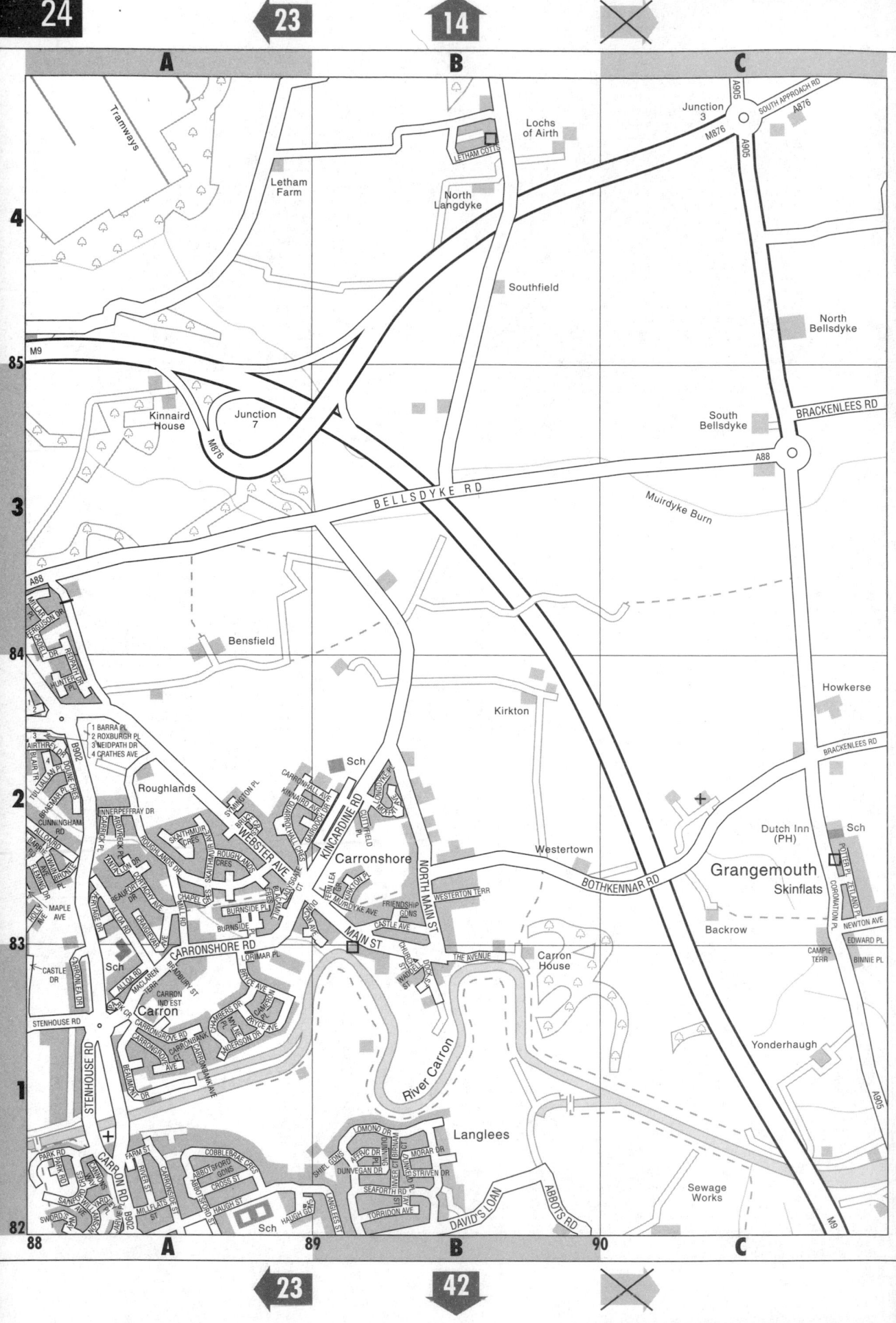

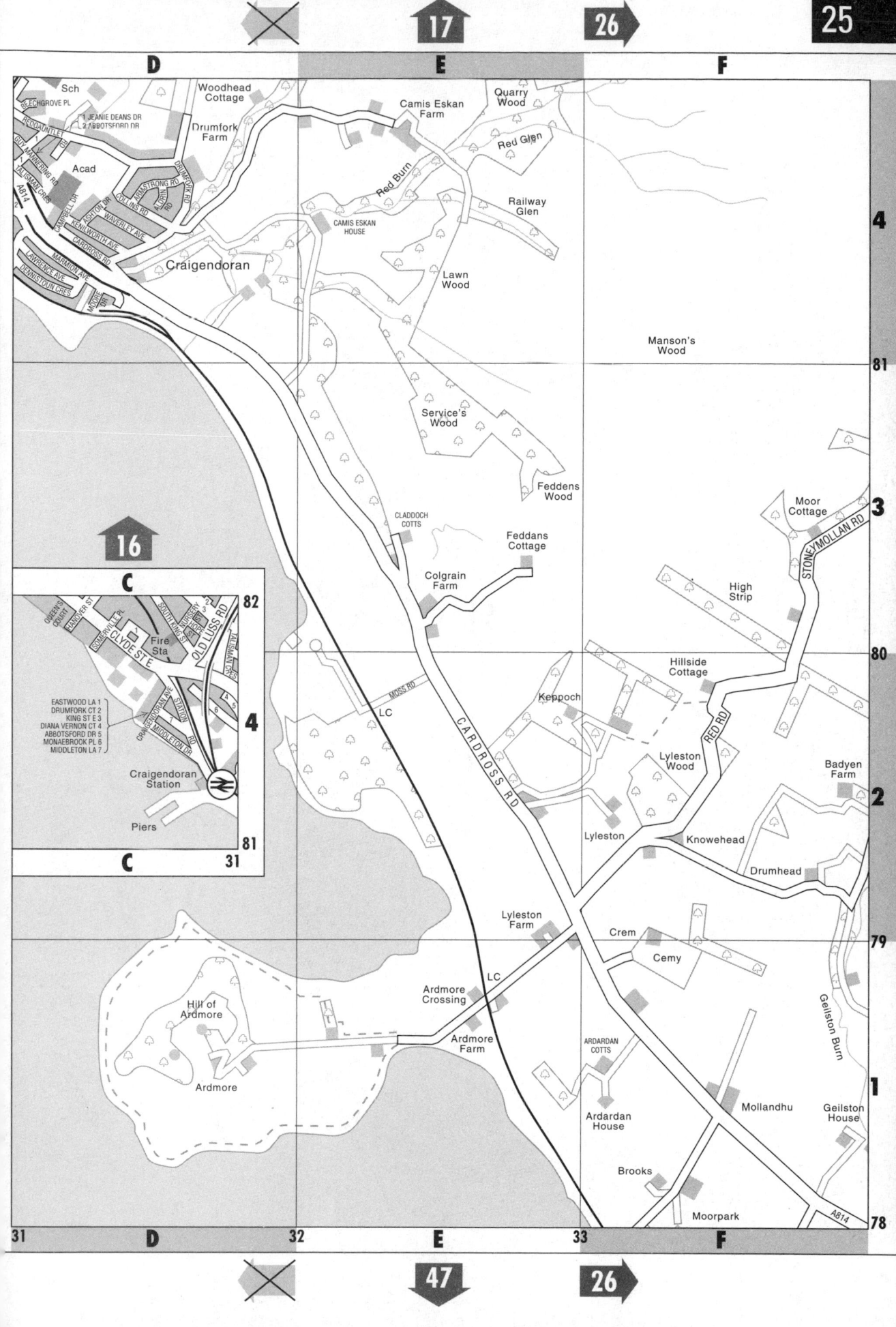

17
26

D E F

Sch
BEECHGROVE PL
1 JEANIE DEANS DR
2 ABBOTSFORD DR
Woodhead
Cottage
Camis Eskan
Farm
Quarry
Wood
REDBOURNTREE
Drumfork
Farm
Red Glen
Red Glen
GILMARTIN LING RD
TALISMAN CRES
Acad
CAMPBELL DR
ASHTON DR
ROLLINS RD
ALTAIR RD
DRUMFORK RD
Red Burn
Railway
Glen
KENILWORTH AVE
CARDROSS RD
WAVERLEY AVE
CAMIS ESKAN
HOUSE
LAWRENCE AVE
MARMION AVE
A814
Craigendoran
DENNISTOUN CRES
MOSS DR
Lawn
Wood
Manson's
Wood

Service's
Wood

Feddens
Wood

16

CLADDOCH
COTTS

Feddans
Cottage
Colgrain
Farm

Moor
Cottage
STONEYMOLLAN RD

C

QUEEN'S
COURT
HANOVER ST
ISOAMPIVILLE PL
SOUTH KING ST
NURSERY
82
OLD LUSS RD
TALISMAN CRES
High
Strip

Fire
Sta
CLYDE ST E

EASTWOOD LA 1
DRUMFORK CT 2
KING ST E 3
DIANA VERNON CT 4
ABBOTSFORD DR 5
MONAEBROOK PL 6
MIDDLETON LA 7
CRAIGENDORAN AVE
STATION RD
MIDDLETON DR
4
80
Hillside
Cottage
Keppoch
RED RD
MOSS RD
LC
Lyleston
Wood
Badyen
Farm

Craigendoran
Station

Lyleston

Knowehead
Drumhead

81
C 31

2

79
Lyleston
Farm
Crem
Cemy

Geilston Burn

Hill of
Ardmore

LC
Ardmore
Crossing

Ardmore
Farm
ARDARDAN
COTTS

Ardmore

Ardardan
House
Mollandhu
1
Geilston
House

Brooks

Moorpark
A814
78

31 D 32 E 33 F

47 26

3
81
4
80
3
2
1

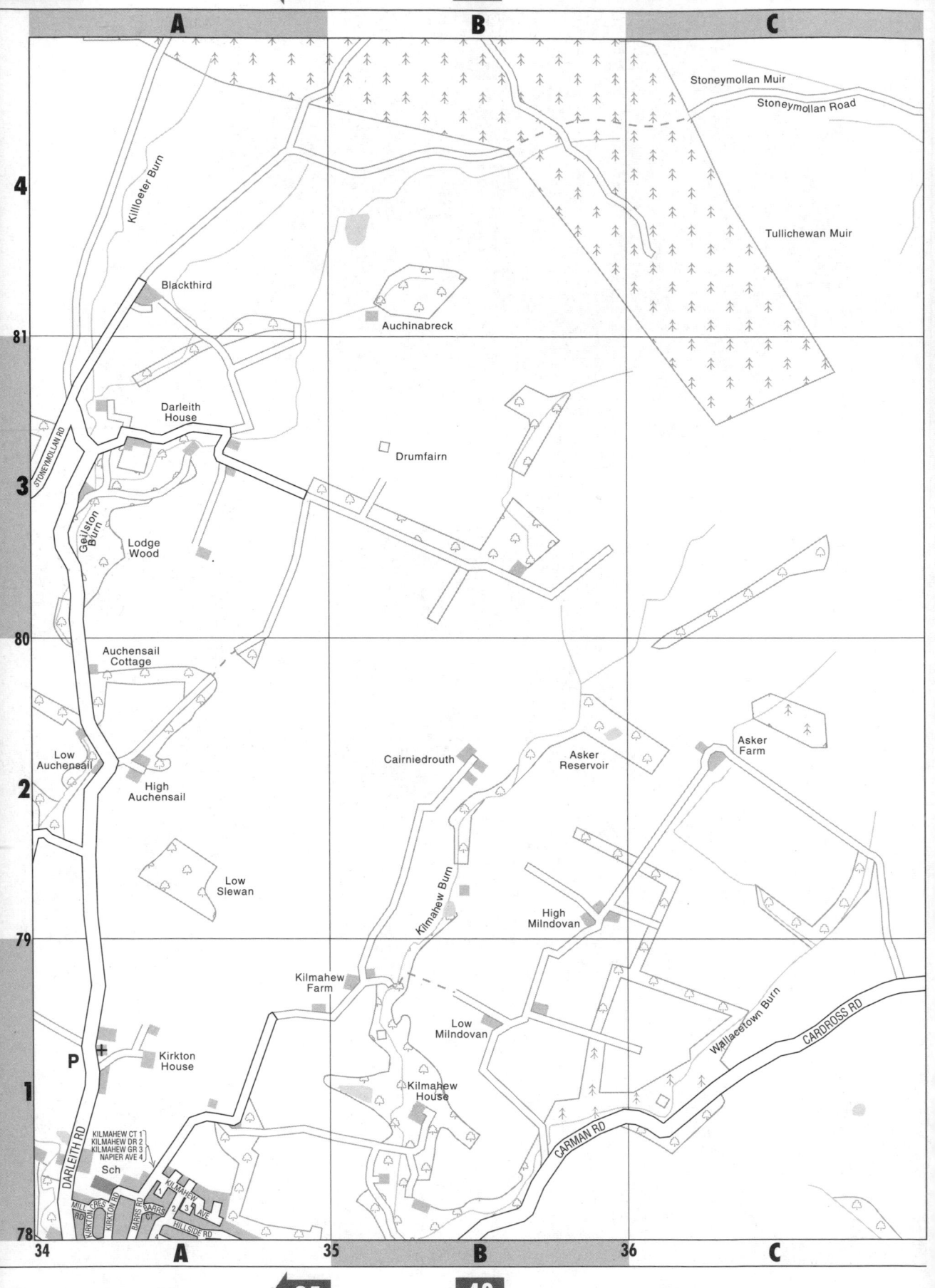

A B C

Stoneymollan Muir

Stoneymollan Road

4

Killoeter Burn

Tullichewan Muir

Blackthird

81

Auchinabreck

STONEYMOLLAN RD

Darleith House

Drumfairn

3

Gelston Burn

Lodge Wood

80

Auchensail Cottage

Low Auchensail

Asker Farm

Cairniedrouth

Asker Reservoir

2

High Auchensail

Low Slewan

High Milndovan

Kilmahew Burn

79

Kilmahew Farm

Wallacetown Burn

CARDROSS RD

Low Milndovan

P +

Kirkton House

1

Kilmahew House

CARMAN RD

KILMAHEW CT 1
KILMAHEW DR 2
KILMAHEW GR 3
NAPIER AVE 4

Sch

DARLEITH RD

78

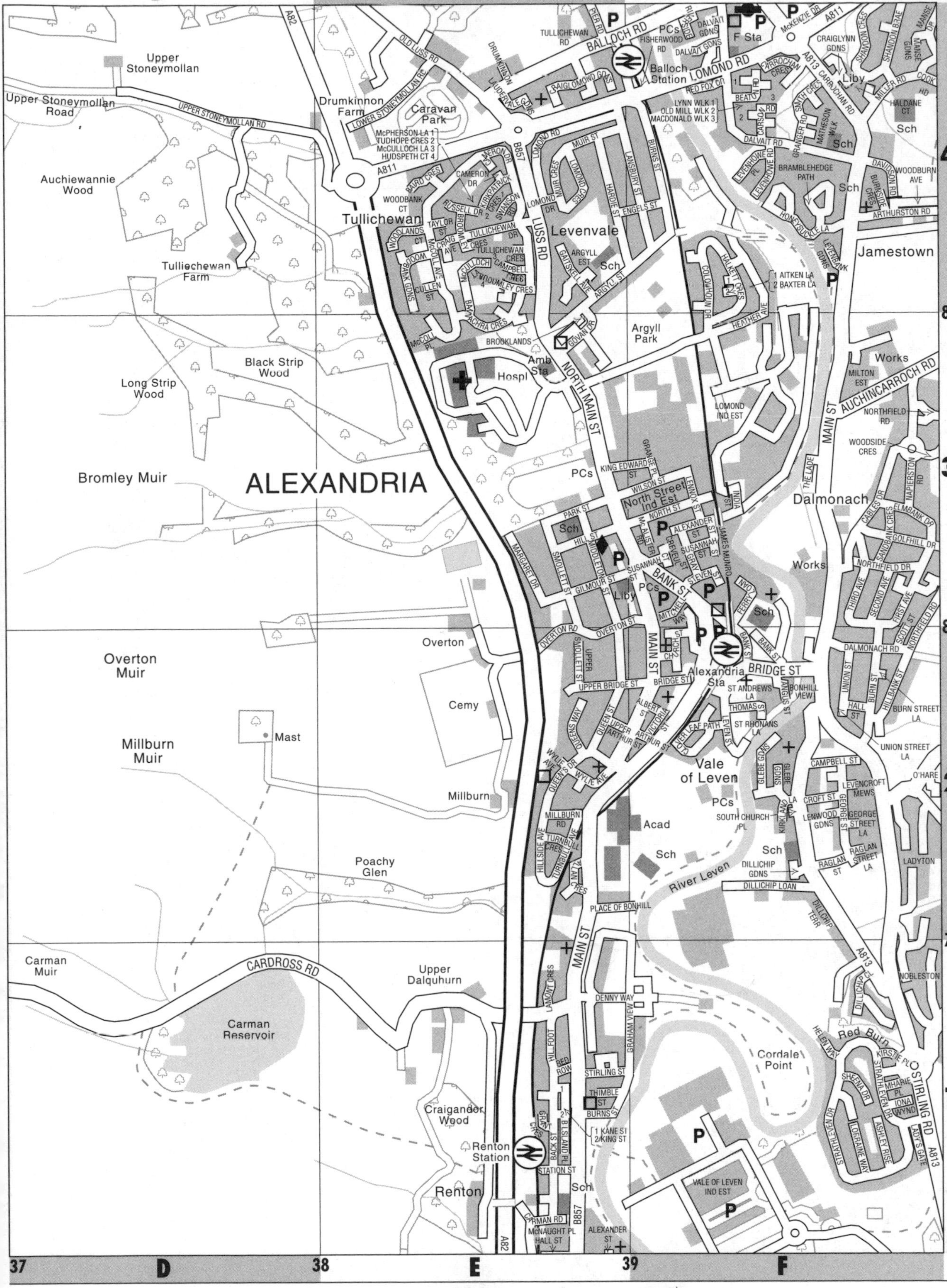

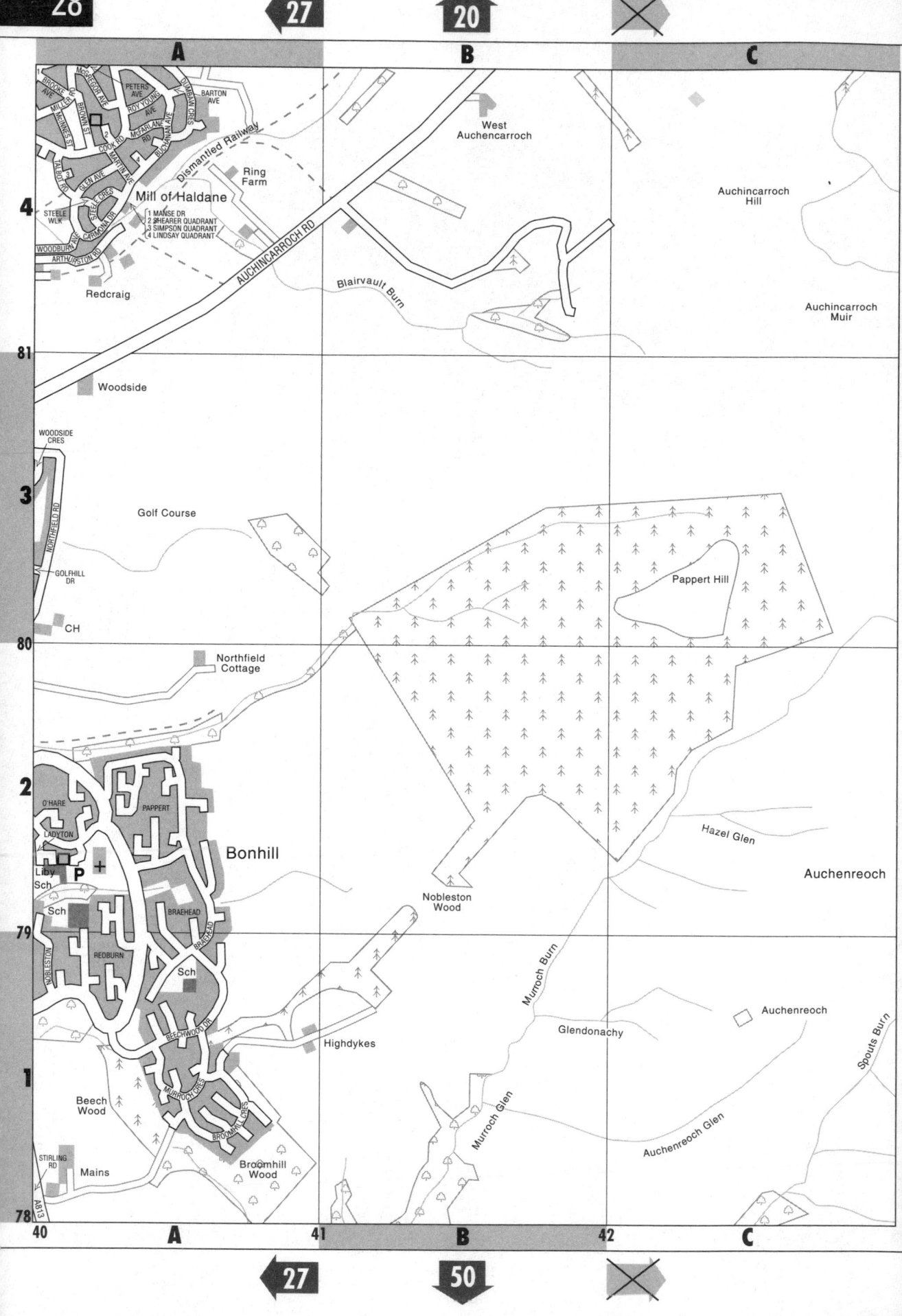

A   B   C

4

Mill of Haldane

1 MANSE DR
2 SHEARER QUADRANT
3 SIMPSON QUADRANT
4 LINDSAY QUADRANT

BROOKS AVE
MORRISON AVE
MILLER ST
McINNES ST
BROWN ST
PETERS AVE
ROY YOUNG AVE
DUNBAN CRES
BARTON AVE
BARTON CRES
TALBOT RD
GLEN AVE
STEELE CRES
COOK RD
MARTIN AVE
McFARLANE AVE
BUCHANAN AVE
STEELE WLK
WOODBURN
CARMONA DR
ARTHURSTON RD

Ring Farm

Barton Cres

West Auchencarroch

Auchincarroch Hill

Dismantled Railway

AUCHINCARROCH RD

Redcraig

Blairvault Burn

Auchincarroch Muir

81

Woodside

3

WOODSIDE CRES

NORTHFIELD RD

Golf Course

GOLFHILL DR

Pappert Hill

CH

80

Northfield Cottage

2

O'HARE

PAPPERT

LADYTON

Bonhill

Hazel Glen

Liby
P +
Sch

Auchenreoch

Sch

BRAEHEAD

Noblestown Wood

79

NOBLESTON

REDBURN

BRAEHEAD

Sch

Murroch Burn

Auchenreoch

Glendonachy

BEECHWOOD DR

Highdykes

1

MURROCH CRES

Beech Wood

BROOMHILL CRES

Murroch Glen

Auchenreoch Glen

Spouts Burn

STIRLING RD

Mains

Broomhill Wood

A813

78

40   A   41   B   42   C

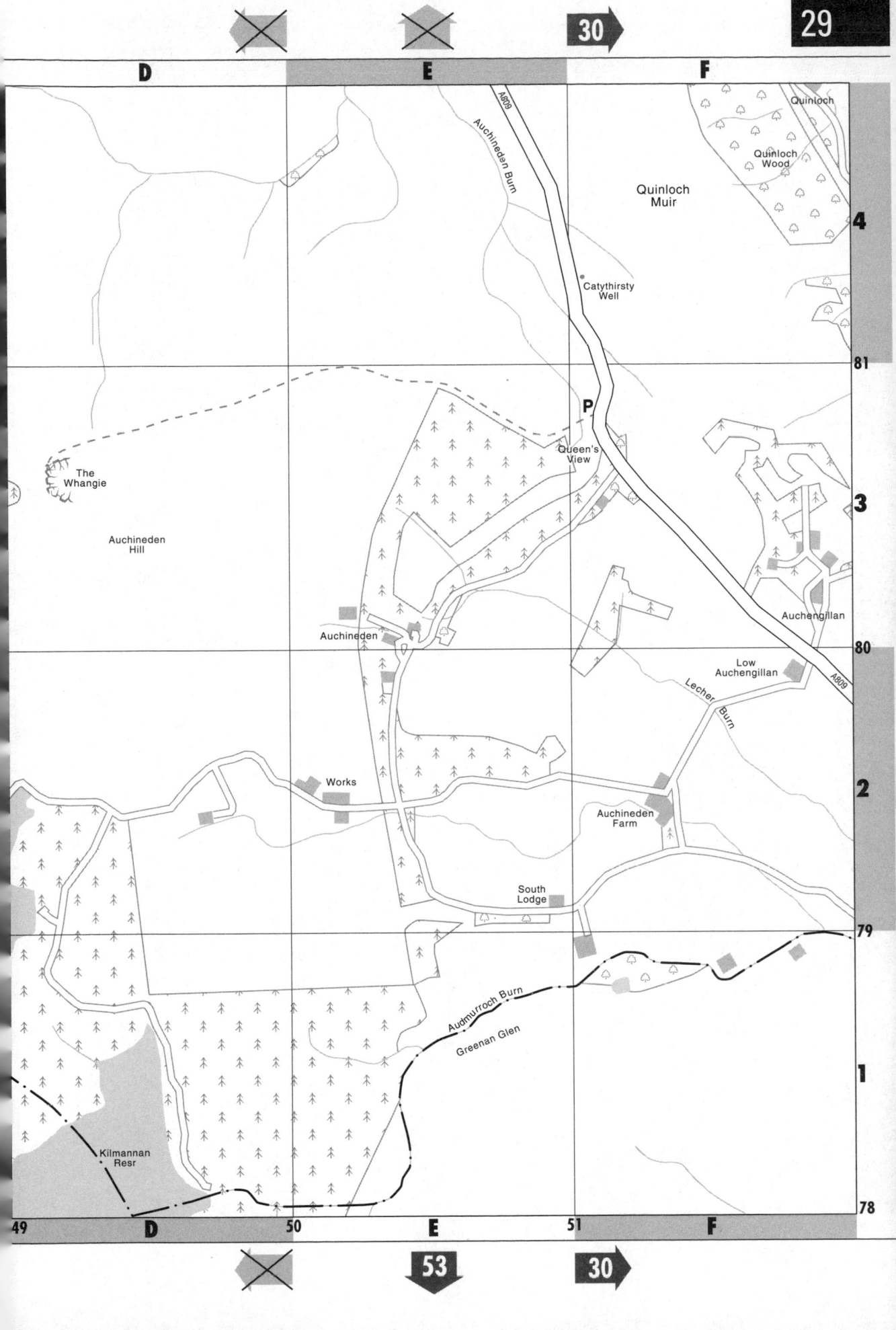

D   E   F

Quinloch

Quinloch
Wood

Quinloch
Muir

4

Catythirsty
Well

81

P

Queen's
View

The
Whangie

3

Auchineden
Hill

Auchengillan

80

Auchineden

Low
Auchengillan

Lecher Burn

A809

2

Works

Auchineden
Farm

South
Lodge

79

Audmurroch Burn

Greenan Glen

1

Kilmannan
Resr

78

49   D   50   E   51   F

A   B   C

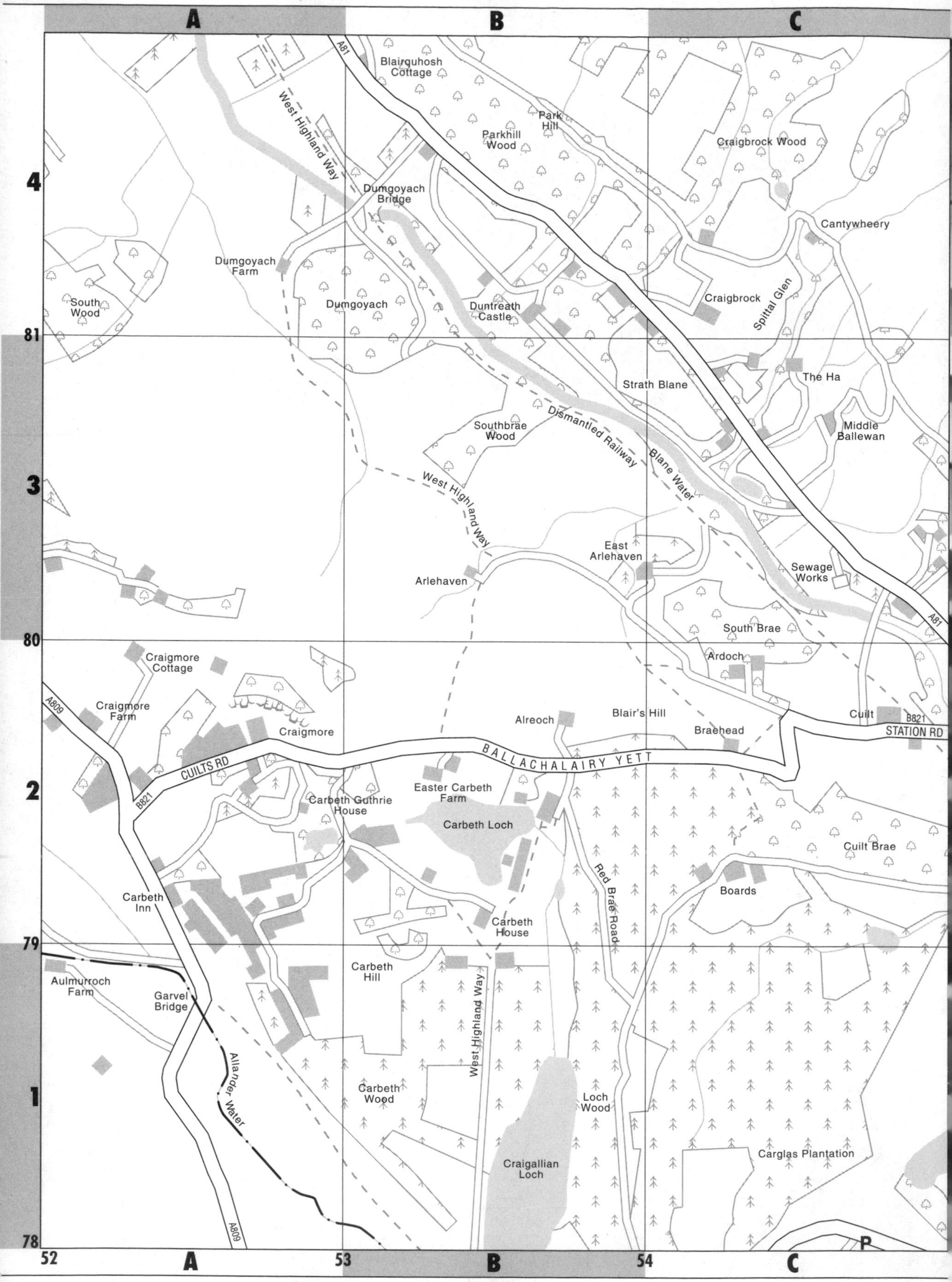

Blairquhosh Cottage

Park Hill

Parkhill Wood

Craigbrock Wood

West Highland Way

Cantywheery

Dumgoyach Bridge

Dumgoyach Farm

Dumgoyach

Duntreath Castle

Craigbrock

Spittal Glen

South Wood

4

81

Strath Blane

The Ha

Southbrae Wood

Dismantled Railway

Blane Water

Middle Ballewan

3

West Highland Way

East Arlehaven

Arlehaven

Sewage Works

South Brae

80

Craigmore Cottage

Ardoch

Cuilt

Craigmore Farm

Alreoch

Blair's Hill

Braehead

STATION RD

B821

Craigmore

BALLACHALAIRY YETT

CUILTS RD

2

Carbeth Guthrie House

Easter Carbeth Farm

Carbeth Loch

Cuilt Brae

B821

Boards

Carbeth Inn

Red Brae Road

Carbeth House

79

Carbeth Hill

Aulmurroch Farm

Garvel Bridge

West Highland Way

1

Carbeth Wood

Loch Wood

Allander Water

A809

Carglas Plantation

Craigallian Loch

78

52   A   53   B   54   C

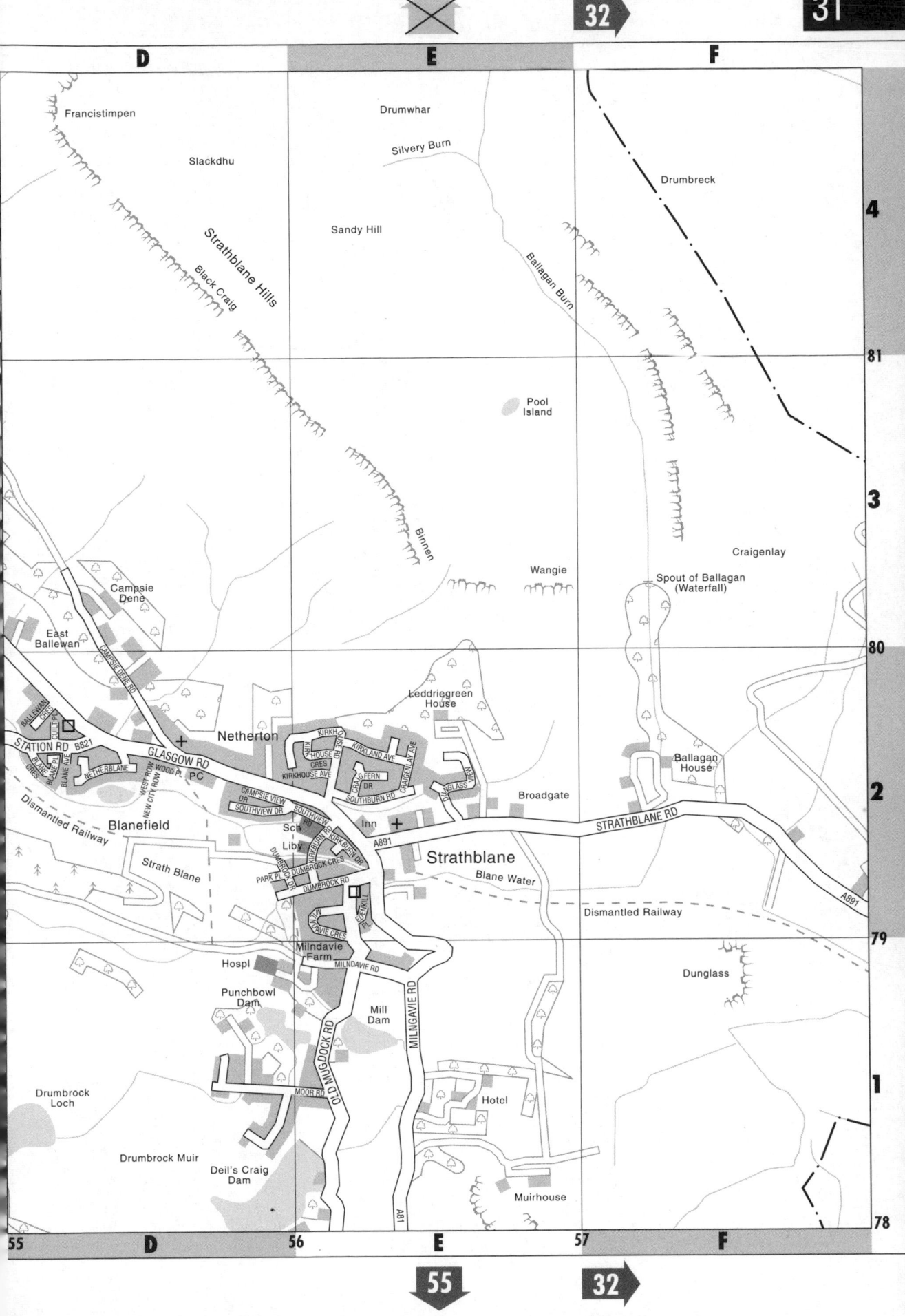

32

D   **E**   **F**

Francistimpen

Drumwhar

Slackdhu

Silvery Burn

Drumbreck

4

Strathblane Hills

Sandy Hill

Black Craig

Ballagan Burn

81

Pool
Island

3

Binnen

Craigenlay

Wangie

Spout of Ballagan
(Waterfall)

Campsie
Dene

Leddriegreen
House

80

East
Ballewan

Ballagan
House

Netherton

KIRKH
HOUSE RD

KIRKLAND AVE

CRAIGENLAY AVE

STATION RD

B821

GLASGOW RD

NETHERBLANE

WEST POW
WOOD PL

NEW CITY ROW

PC

KIRKHOUSE
CRES

KIRKHOUSE AVE

CRAIG FERN
DR

SOUTHBURN RD

DUNGLASS AVE

Broadgate

2

Dismantled Railway

Blanefield

CAMPSIE VIEW
DR

SOUTHVIEW DR

SOUTHVIEW
RD

Sch

Liby

KIRKBURN DR

Inn

A891

Strathblane

STRATHBLANE RD

A891

Strath Blane

DUMBROCK
LN

PARK PL

DUMBROCK CRES

DUMBROCK RD

Blane Water

Dismantled Railway

79

MILDAVIE CRES

BEECH PL

Milndavie
Farm

Dunglass

Hospl

MILNDAVIE RD

Punchbowl
Dam

MOOR RD

OLD MUGDOCK RD

Mill
Dam

MILNGAVIE RD

1

Drumbrock
Loch

Hotel

Drumbrock Muir

Deil's Craig
Dam

A81

Muirhouse

78

55   **D**   **56**   **E**   **57**   **F**

	A	B	C

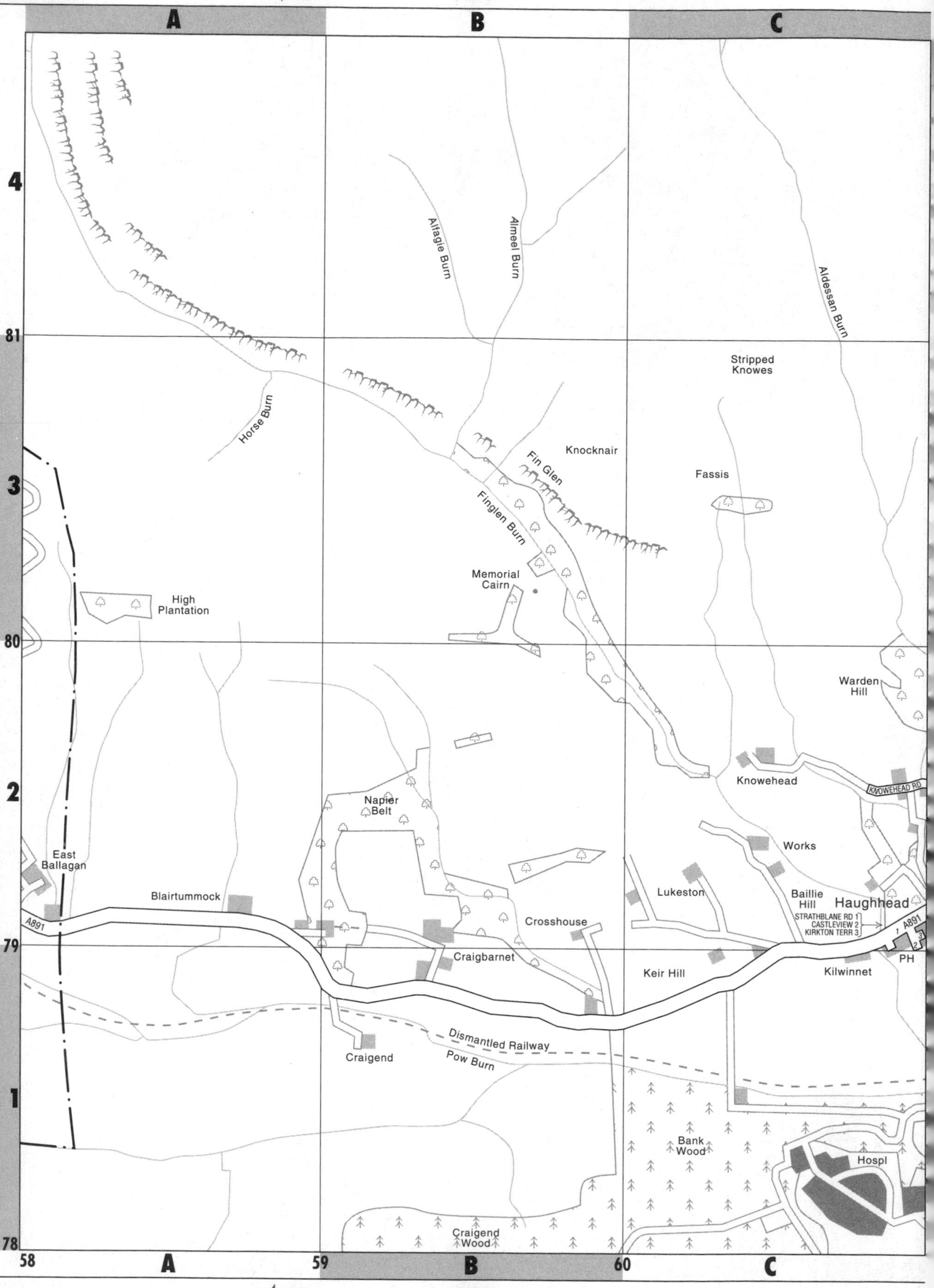

4

Alfagie Burn

Almeel Burn

Aldessan Burn

81

Horse Burn

Stripped Knowes

Knocknair

Fin Glen

Fassis

Finglen Burn

3

Memorial Cairn

High Plantation

80

Warden Hill

2

Napier Belt

Knowehead

KNOWEHEAD RD

Works

East Ballagan

Blairtummock

Lukeston

Baillie Hill

Haughhead

STRATHBLANE RD 1
CASTLEVIEW 2
KIRKTON TERR 3

A891

Crosshouse

A891

79

Craigbarnet

Keir Hill

Kilwinnet

PH

Dismantled Railway

Craigend

Pow Burn

1

Bank Wood

Hospl

78

| 58 | A | 59 | B | 60 | C |

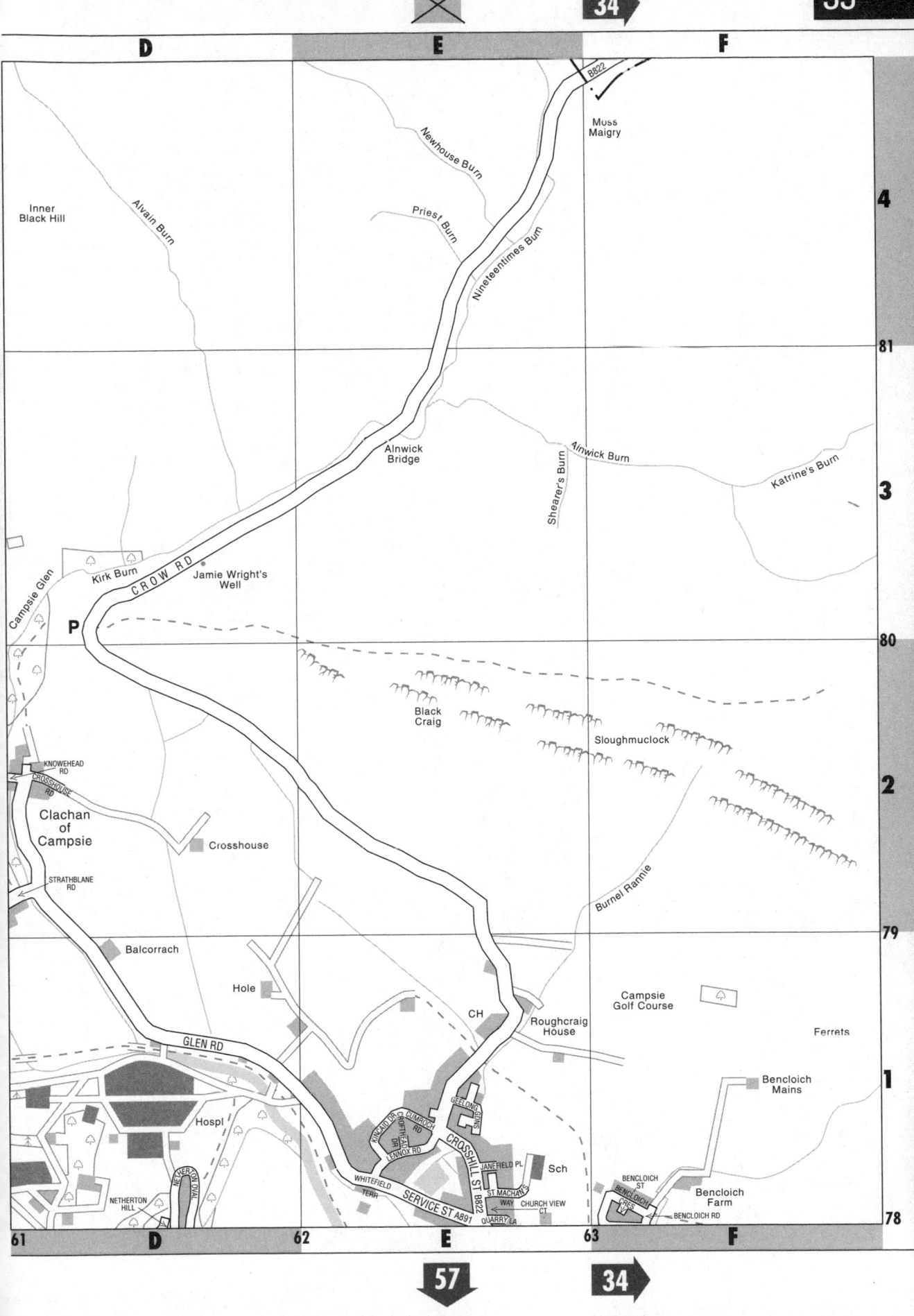

D   E   F

4

81

Moss
Maigry

B822

Newhouse Burn

Inner
Black Hill

Alvain Burn

Priest Burn

Nineteentimes Burn

3

Alnwick Bridge

Shearer's Burn

Alnwick Burn

Katrine's Burn

Campsie Glen

Kirk Burn

C R O W R D

Jamie Wright's
Well

P

80

Black
Craig

Sloughmuclock

KNOWEHEAD
RD

2

CROSSHOUSE
RD

Clachan
of
Campsie

Crosshouse

Burnel Rannie

STRATHBLANE
RD

79

Balcorrach

Hole

Campsie
Golf Course

Ferrets

CH

Roughcraig
House

Bencloich
Mains

GLEN RD

1

Hospl

NETHERTON OVAL

KINKAID DR

CUMROCH RD

CROFTHEAD DR

GEELONG GDNS

LENNOX RD

CROSSHILL ST B822

JANEFIELD PL

Sch

BENCLOICH ST

BENCLOICH CRES

Bencloich
Farm

NETHERTON
HILL

WHITEFIELD
TERR

SERVICE ST A891

ST MACHAN
WAY

CHURCH VIEW
CT.

QUARRY LA

BENCLOICH RD

78

61   D   62   E   63   F

A | B | C

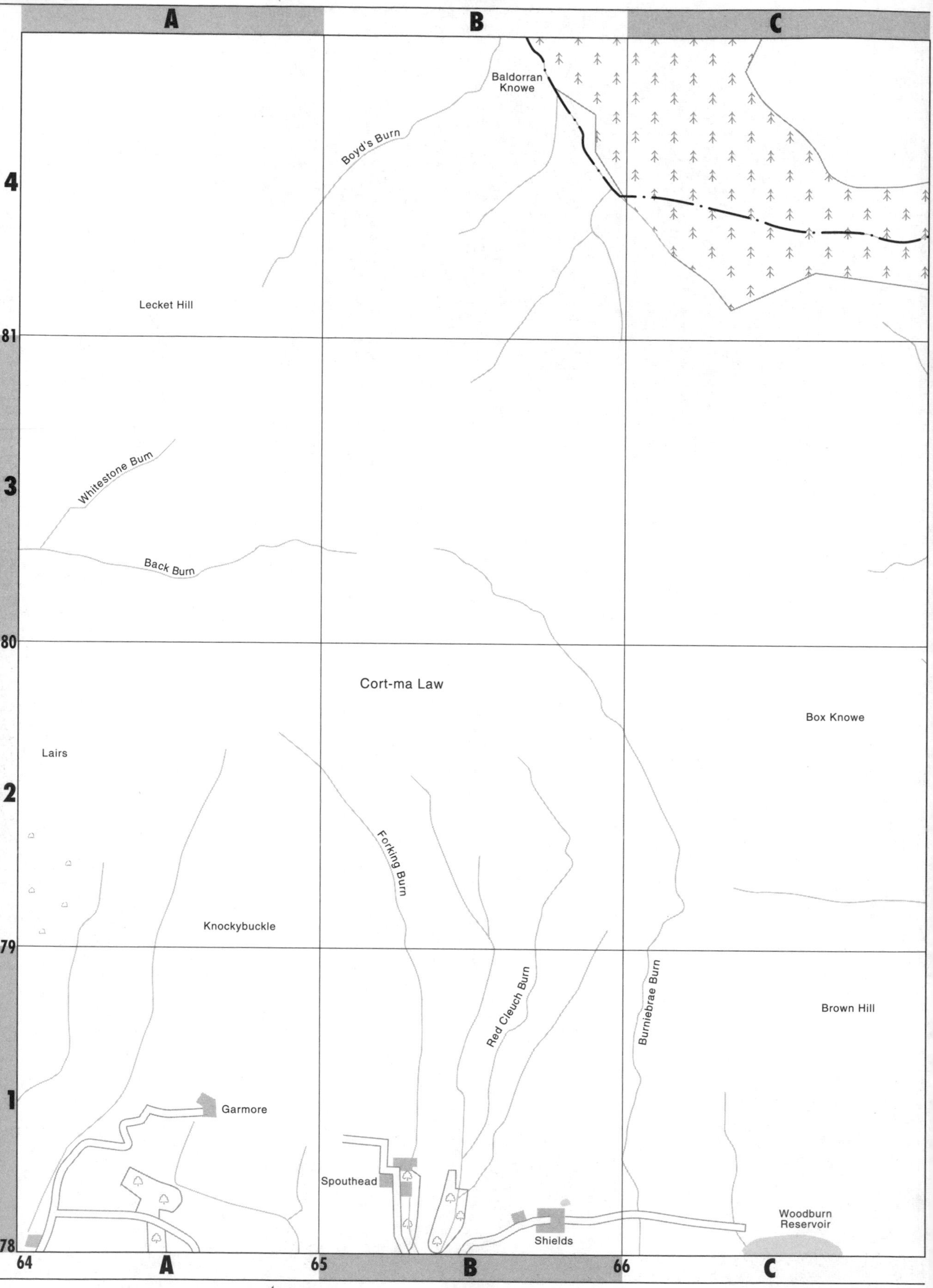

Baldorran Knowe

Boyd's Burn

4

Lecket Hill

81

Whitestone Burn

3

Back Burn

80

Cort-ma Law

Box Knowe

Lairs

2

Forking Burn

Knockybuckle

Red Cleuch Burn

Burniebrae Burn

79

Brown Hill

1

Garmore

Spouthead

Woodburn Reservoir

78

Shields

64 | A | 65 | B | 66 | C

D   E   F

4

Black Hill

81

Birkenburn
Reservoir

Lunch Knowe

Plea Muir

Birken Burn

3

Laird's Hill

Gray Mare

Kilsyth Hills

White Craig

80

Hallstane Burn

2

The Banns

Corrie
Plantation

Mast

Corrie

79

Drumheldric

Corrie Burn

Stoneree Glen

Cairnbog

1

Burnhead
Farm

Dykehead

78

WHIN LOAN

DYKEHEAD RD

35

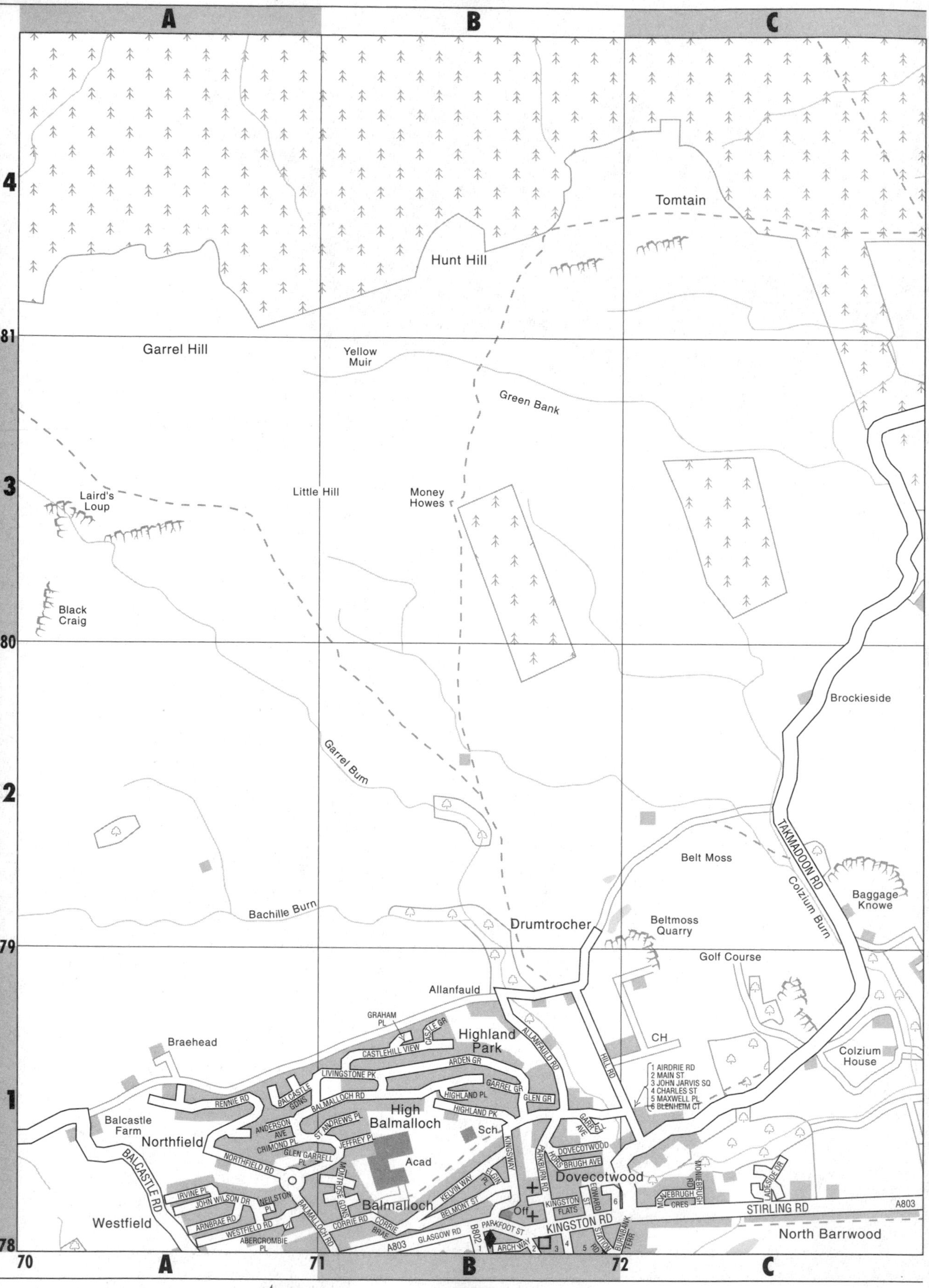
A
B
C
4
Tomtain
Hunt Hill
81
Garrel Hill
Yellow Muir
Green Bank
3
Laird's Loup
Little Hill
Money Howes
Black Craig
80
Brockieside
Garrel Burn
2
TAKMADOON RD
Belt Moss
Colzium Burn
Baggage Knowe
Bachille Burn
Drumtrocher
Beltmoss Quarry
79
Golf Course
Allanfauld
GRAHAM PL
CASTLE GR
Highland Park
Braehead
CASTLEHILL VIEW
ARDEN GR
ALLANFAULD RD
CH
HILL RD
Colzium House
1 AIRDRIE RD
2 MAIN ST
3 JOHN JARVIS SQ
4 CHARLES ST
5 MAXWELL PL
6 BLENHEIM CT
LIVINGSTONE PK
GARREL GR
BALCASTLE GDNS
BALMALLOCH RD
HIGHLAND PL
GLEN GR
RENNIE RD
HIGHLAND PK
1
High Balmalloch
Balcastle Farm
ANDERSON AVE
ST ANDREWS PL
GARRELL AVE
Northfield
CRIMOND PL
JEFFREY PL
Sch
DOVECOTWOOD
GLEN GARRELL PL
KINGSWAY
HORSBRUGH AVE
NORTHFIELD RD
Acad
PARKBURN RD
MONIEBRUGH RD
BALCASTLE RD
MONTROSE GDNS
ELGIN PL
Dovecotwood
LADESIDE DR
IRVINE PL
NEILSTON PL
KELVIN WAY
JOHN WILSON DR
Balmalloch
BELMONT ST
KINGSTON FLATS
EDWARD ST
MONIEBRUGH CRES
STIRLING RD
A803
ARNBRAE RD
Off
Westfield
WESTFIELD RD
BALMALLOCH RD
CORRIE RD
CORRIE BRAE
PARKFOOT ST
KINGSTON RD
STATION RD
BURNBANK TERR
North Barrwood
ABERCROMBIE PL
GLASGOW RD
B802
A803
ARCH WAY
78
70
71
72

35

60

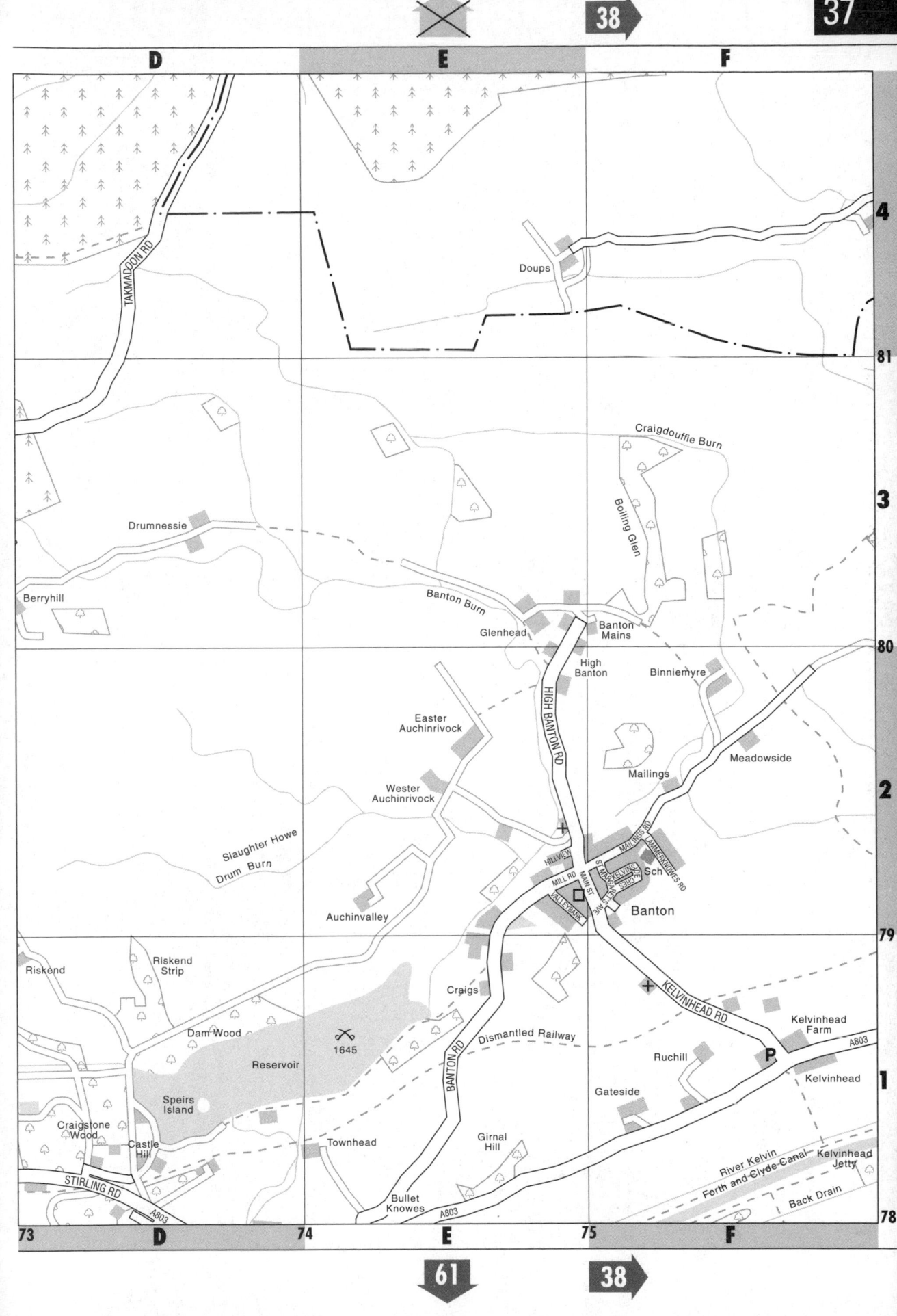

D　　　　　　　**E**　　　　　　　**F**

TAKMADOON RD

Doups

4

81

Craigdouffie Burn

Boiling Glen

3

Drumnessie

Berryhill

Banton Burn

Glenhead

Banton Mains

80

High Banton

Binniemyre

HIGH BANTON RD

Easter Auchinrivock

Mailings

Meadowside

2

Wester Auchinrivock

Slaughter Howe

Drum Burn

HILLVIEW

MILL RD

MAIN ST

MAILINGS RD

LAMMERKNOWES RD

ST MACHANS BRAE

KELVIN DR

Sch

Banton

PAILEYBANK

Auchinvalley

79

Riskend

Riskend Strip

Craigs

Kelvinhead Rd

+

Riskend

Dam Wood

1645

Reservoir

BANTON RD

Dismantled Railway

Ruchill

Kelvinhead Farm

P

A803

Speirs Island

Gateside

Kelvinhead

1

Craigstone Wood

Castle Hill

Townhead

Girnal Hill

River Kelvin

Forth and Clyde Canal

Kelvinhead Jetty

STIRLING RD

A803

Bullet Knowes

A803

Back Drain

78

73　　　**D**　　　**74**　　　**E**　　　**75**　　　**F**

A | B | C

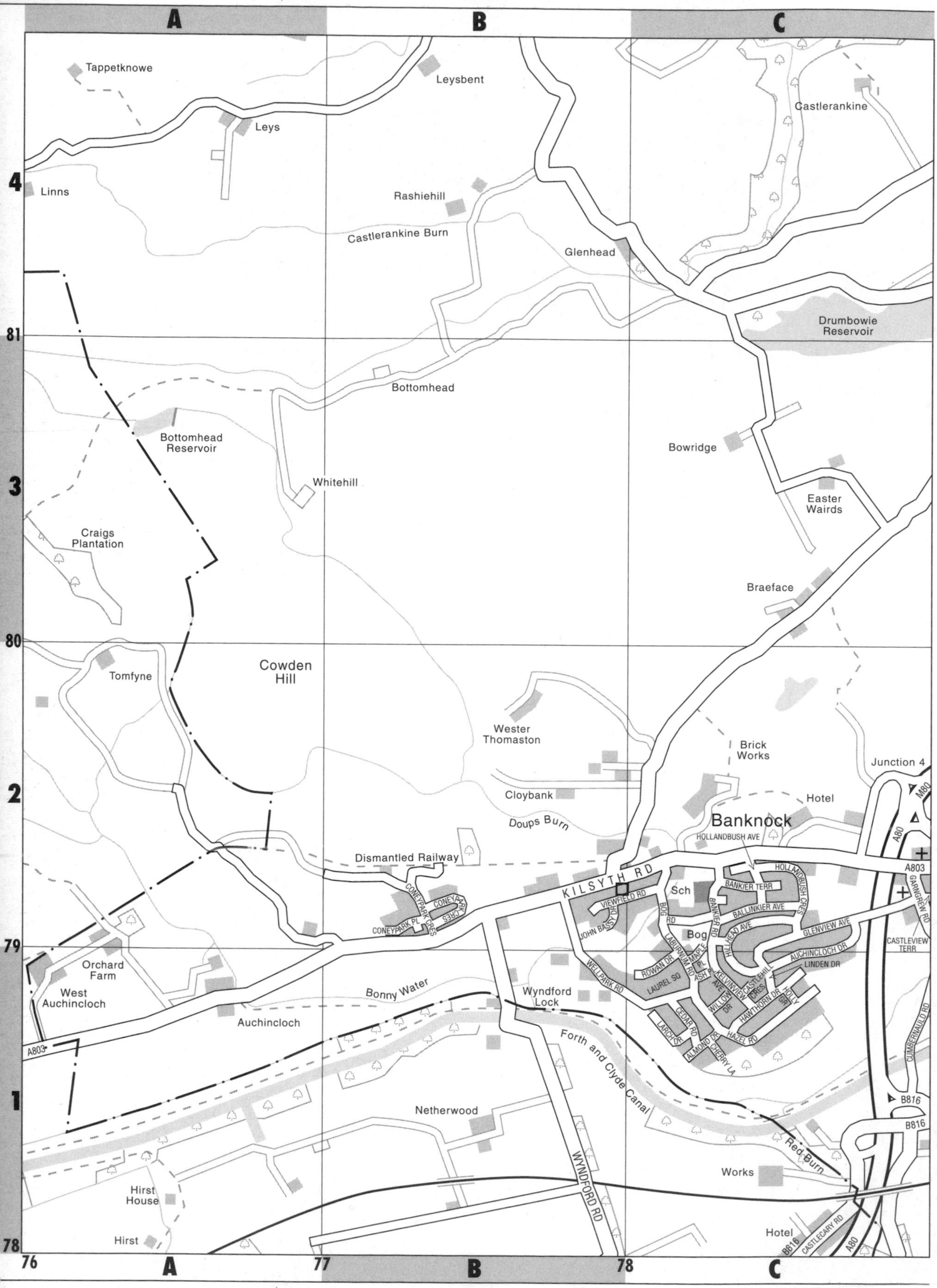

Tappetknowe

Leysbent

Leys

Castlerankine

4

Linns

Rashiehill

Castlerankine Burn

Glenhead

Drumbowie
Reservoir

81

Bottomhead

Bottomhead
Reservoir

Bowridge

Easter
Wairds

3

Whitehill

Craigs
Plantation

Braeface

80

Tomfyne

Cowden
Hill

Wester
Thomaston

Brick
Works

Junction 4

A80

A803

2

Cloybank

Doups Burn

Hotel

Banknock

HOLLANDBUSH AVE

HOLLANDBUSH CRES

Dismantled Railway

CONEYPARK CRES

KILSYTH RD

Viewfield Rd

Sch

BANKIER TERR

BALLINKIER AVE

GLENVIEW AVE

A803

GARNGROW RD

CONEYPARK PL

CONEYPARK S RD

John Bass

BOG RD

Bog

BANKIER PL

HILLHEAD AVE

AUCHINCLOCH DR

LINDEN DR

Castleview
Terr

79

Orchard Farm

WELLPARK RD

BOWAN DR

LAUREL SQ

MAPLE PL

ASH PL

KESTING CRES

EASTERHILL CRES

WILLOW DR

HAWTHORN DR

BIRCH

West
Auchincloch

Auchincloch

Bonny Water

Wyndford
Lock

CEDAR RD

LARCH DR

ALMOND DR

CHERRY LA

HAZEL RD

Forth and Clyde Canal

B816

B816

1

Netherwood

WYNDFORD RD

Works

Red Burn

Hirst
House

Hotel

CASTLECARY RD

B816

A80

78

76 | 77 | 78

A | B | C

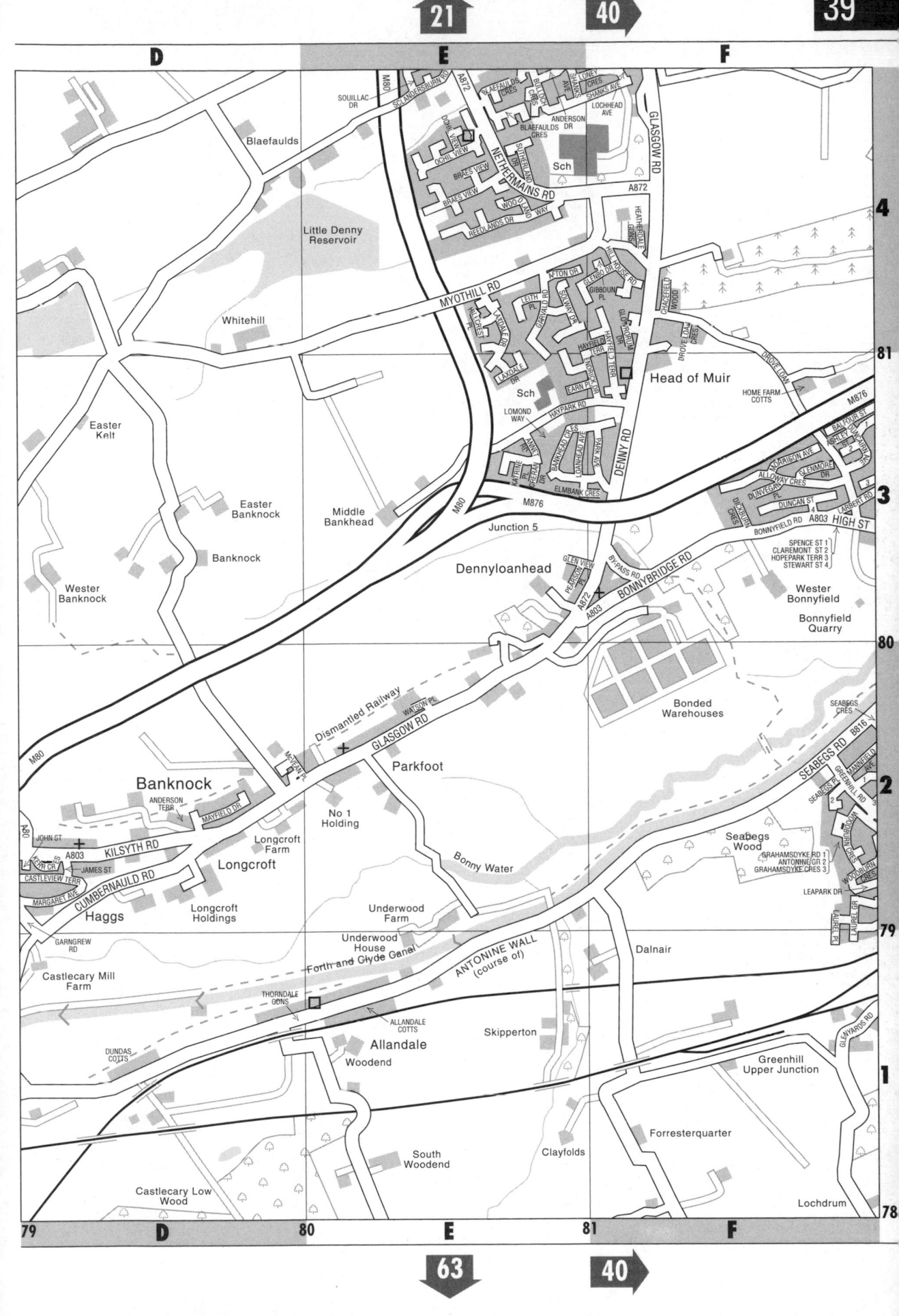

A **B** **C**

Cuthelton

Chacefield Wood

Junction 1

Nursery

Cemy

Hills of Dunipace

River Carron

4

CH

Bonnybridge Golf Course

Dismantled Railway

Bogton Farm

A883

PRIMROSE ST
FAIRWAYS PL
NORWOOD AVE
ROBERTSON AVE
DRUMMOND PL
FERGUSON GR
ROSE ST
HIGHLAND DYKES
BONNYVIEW GDNS
GREENFIELD ST

Sewage Works

Bonny Water

Wester Carmuirs

81

M876
FIR CRES
BALFOUR ST
SPENCE ST
KENT ST
COWAN ST
HOPEPARK TERR
DUNURE TERR
CHACEFIELD ST
WHEATLANDS AVE
HIGHLAND WAY
LARBERT RD
FAIRFIELD AVE
PEATHILL RD
MAIN ST
WELLPARK TERR
FORD RD
Sch

THORNTON AVE
GATESIDE AVE
GATESIDE AVE
THORNTON AVE
NORTH ST
PATERSON ST
FALKIRK RD
Park
Hospl

Works

A803

West Carmuirs Loam

Rowan Tree Burn

3

A803
HIGH ST
PC
DUNURE CRES
BRIDGE ST
MARCH ST
ANDERSON ST
BARLEYHILL
PRINCESS ST
MAIN ST

Forth and Clyde Canal

Bonnybridge

P PC
Liby

Cowden Hill

BONNYSIDE RD

Bonnyside Farm

FOUNDER RD

Antonine Wall

80

SEABEGS RD
Sch
Murnin Road Ind Est
MANNFIELD AVE
BALFOUR ST
B816
SEABEGS CRES

Chattan Ind Est

BROOMHILL RD

Sch
Sch

Works

2

GRAHAMSDYKE RD
ROMAN RD
Milnquarter

PARK ST
NORTH ST
WAVERLEY CRES
MILLAR PL
LOCHINVAR PL
CHURCH ST
HILL ST
NEW RD

B816

1 GRAHAMSDYKE CRES
2 LEAPARK DR
3 BANTON PL
4 LAURELBANK AVE

REILLY RD

Works

BONNYHILL RD

Works

LEAPARK DR
LAUREL DR
GREENHILL RD

BROOMSIDE RD

High Bonnybridge

79

Greenhill

GLENYARDS RD

Margreta

Bonnyhill Farm

Howierig

1

Wester Drum

Drum Wood

Greenrig

78

82 **A** 83 **B** 84 **C**

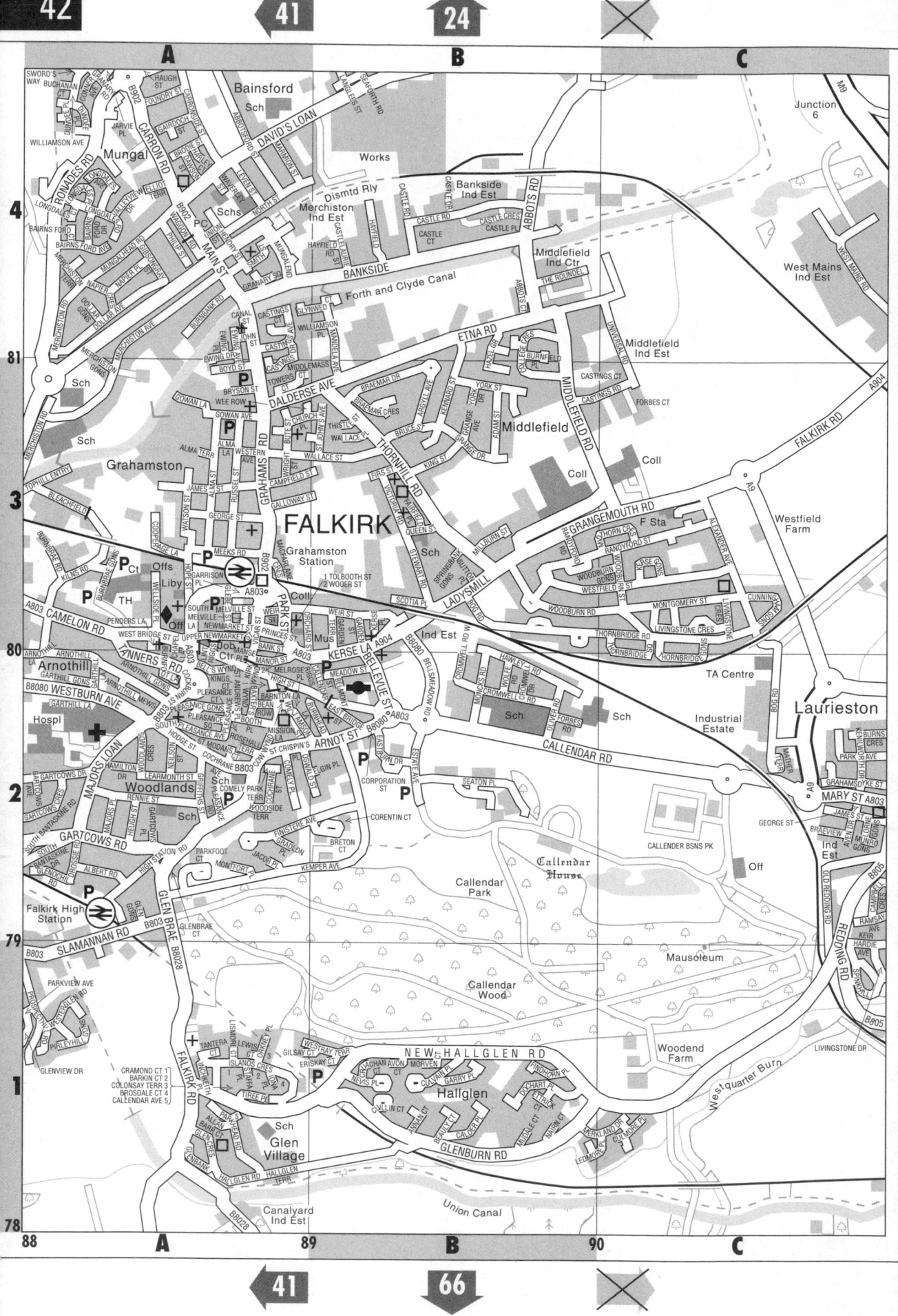

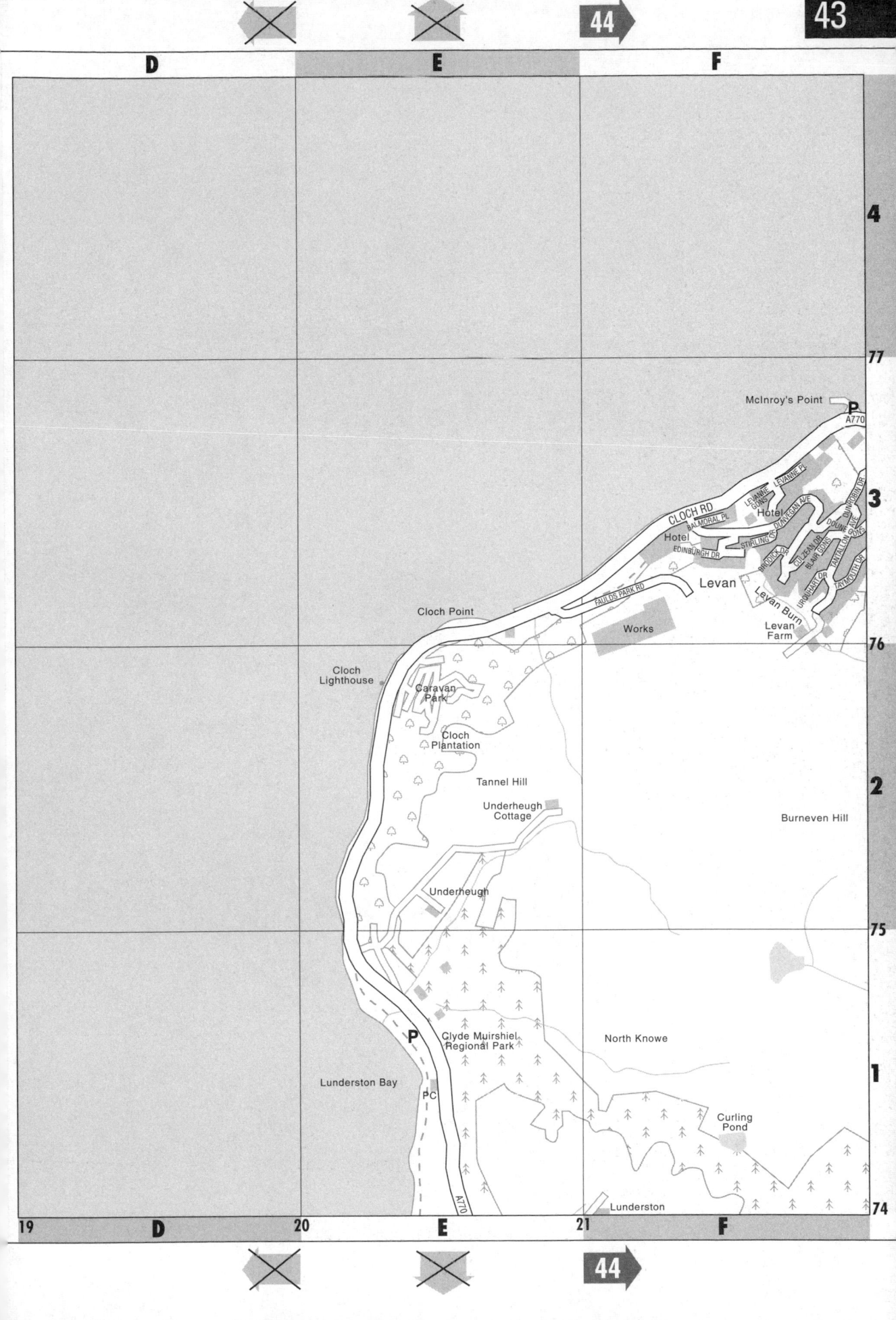

A   B   C

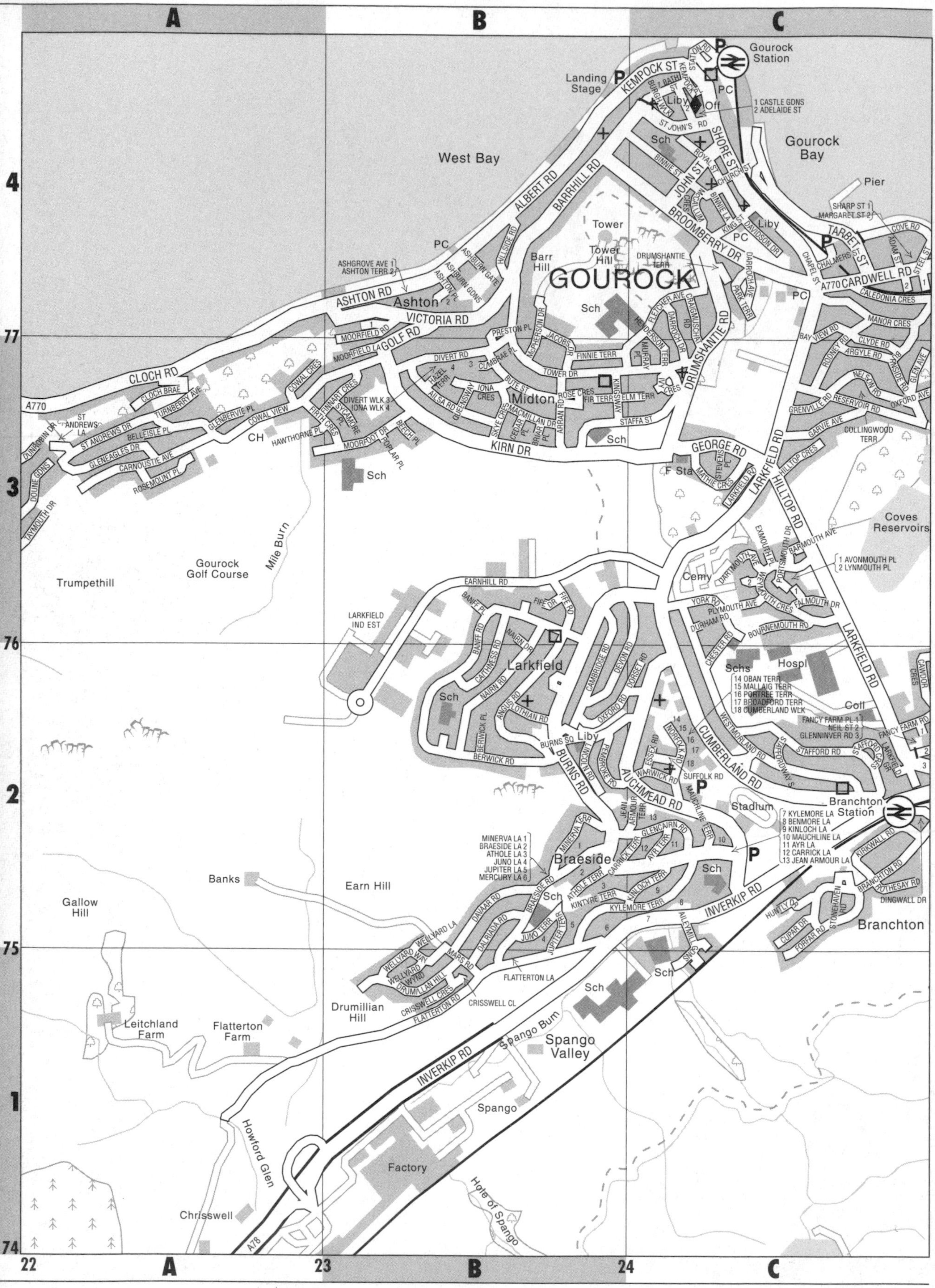

GOUROCK

West Bay

Gourock Station
Landing Stage
KEMPOCK ST
SHORE ST
Gourock Bay
Pier
1 CASTLE GDNS
2 ADELAIDE ST
SHARP ST 1
MARGARET ST 2
COVE RD
ADAM ST
STEEL ST
TARRET ST
A770 CARDWELL RD
CALEDONIA CRES
MANOR CRES
BAY VIEW RD
CLYDE RD
ARGYLE RD
NELSON ST
GLEN AVE
OXFORD AVE
RESERVOIR RD
GRENVILLE RD
GARVIE AVE
COLLINGWOOD TERR

ALBERT RD
BARRHILL RD
Tower
Tower Hill
Barr Hill
DRUMSHANTIE TERR
Sch
BROOMBERRY DR
DARROCH DR
JOHN ST
BINNIE ST
St JOHN'S RD
CHURCH ST
ROYAL ST
KING ST
DAVIDSON DR
CHALMERS ST
DARROCH PARK TERR
PC
Liby
Off
Sch
PC

ASHGROVE AVE 1
ASHTON TERR 2
ASHTON RD
Ashton
VICTORIA RD
PC
ASHTON LA
WILSIDE RD
ASHBURN GDNS
MOORFIELD RD
GOLF RD
Midton
Preston Pl
Divert Rd
CAMBRAE ST
BUTE ST
Finnie Terr
Rose Cres
FIR TERR
ELM TERR
TOWER DR
STAFFA ST
ARRAN PL
GEORGE RD
DRUMSHANTIE RD
LARKFIELD RD
HILLTOP RD
HILLTOP CRES

CLOCH RD
A770
CLOCH BRAE
TURNBERRY AVE
St ANDREWS LA
DOUNE GDNS
BELLEISLE PL
GLENEAGLES DR
CARNOUSTIE PL
ROSEMOUNT LA
TAYMOUTH DR
DVNDONAN DR
COWAL VIEW
GLENBERVIE PL
SYCAMORE
MOORFOOT DR
POPLAR PL
BEECH PL
HAWTHORNE PL
IONA WLK 3
IONA WLK 4
DIVERT WLK 3
DIVERT WLK 4
FIRTH CRES
TINNART CRES
SAFE END
QUEENSWAY
MACMILLAN PL
BRAE PL
IONA CRES
AILSA RD
HAZEL TERR
KIRN DR
Sch
CH
Sch

Trumpethill
Gourock Golf Course
Mile Burn

Cemy
EXMOUTH
DARTMOUTH AVE
PORTSMOUTH AVE
YARMOUTH AVE
1 AVONMOUTH PL
2 LYNMOUTH PL
Coves Reservoirs

EARNHILL RD
LARKFIELD IND EST
BANFF RD
FIFE RD
FIFE DR
MALLN DR
NAIRN RD
CALTHNESS RD
ANGUS RD
CAMBRIDGE RD
DEVON RD
DORSET RD
LITHIAN RD
OXFORD RD
BERWICK RD
BERWICK PL
BURNS Sq
Liby
BURNS RD
Larkfield
Sch
York Rd
PLYMOUTH AVE
DURHAM RD
CHESTER RD
BOURNEMOUTH RD
FALMOUTH DR
WESTMOORLAND RD
STAFFORD RD
Schs
Hospl
14 OBAN TERR
15 MALLAIG TERR
16 PORTREE TERR
17 BROADFORD TERR
18 CUMBERLAND WLK
FANCY FARM PL 1
NEIL ST 2
GLENNINVER RD 3
Golf
FANCY FARM PL
LARKFIELD RD
CAWDOR CRES

Gallow Hill
Banks
Earn Hill

MINERVA CRES
MINERVA LA 1
BRAESIDE LA 2
ATHOLE LA 3
JUNO LA 4
JUPITER LA 5
MERCURY LA 6
Braeside
Sch
JEAN ARMOUR TERR
GLENCAIRN RD
CARRICK TERR
KINTYRE TERR
KYLEMORE TERR
JUPITER TERR
AUCHMEAD RD
CUMBERLAND RD
SUFFOLK RD
Stadium
Branchton Station
7 KYLEMORE LA
8 BENMORE LA
9 KINLOCH LA
10 MAUCHLINE LA
11 AYR LA
12 CARRICK LA
13 JEAN ARMOUR LA
INVERKIP RD
Sch
Branchton
KIRKWALL RD
BRANCHTON RD
ROTHESAY RD
DINGWALL DR
STONEHAVEN
CUPAR DR
FORFAR RD
HUNTLY DR

Leitchland Farm
Flatterton Farm
Drumillian Hill
WELLYARD LA
WELLYARD
WELLYARD WYND
DALRIADA HILL
DRUMILLAN HILL
BATAVIA PL
FLATTERTON LA
CRISSWELL CRES
FLATTERTON RD
CRISSWELL CL
Sch
Sch

Spango Burn
Spango Valley
Spango

Howford Glen
Chrisswell
A78
Factory
Hole of Spango

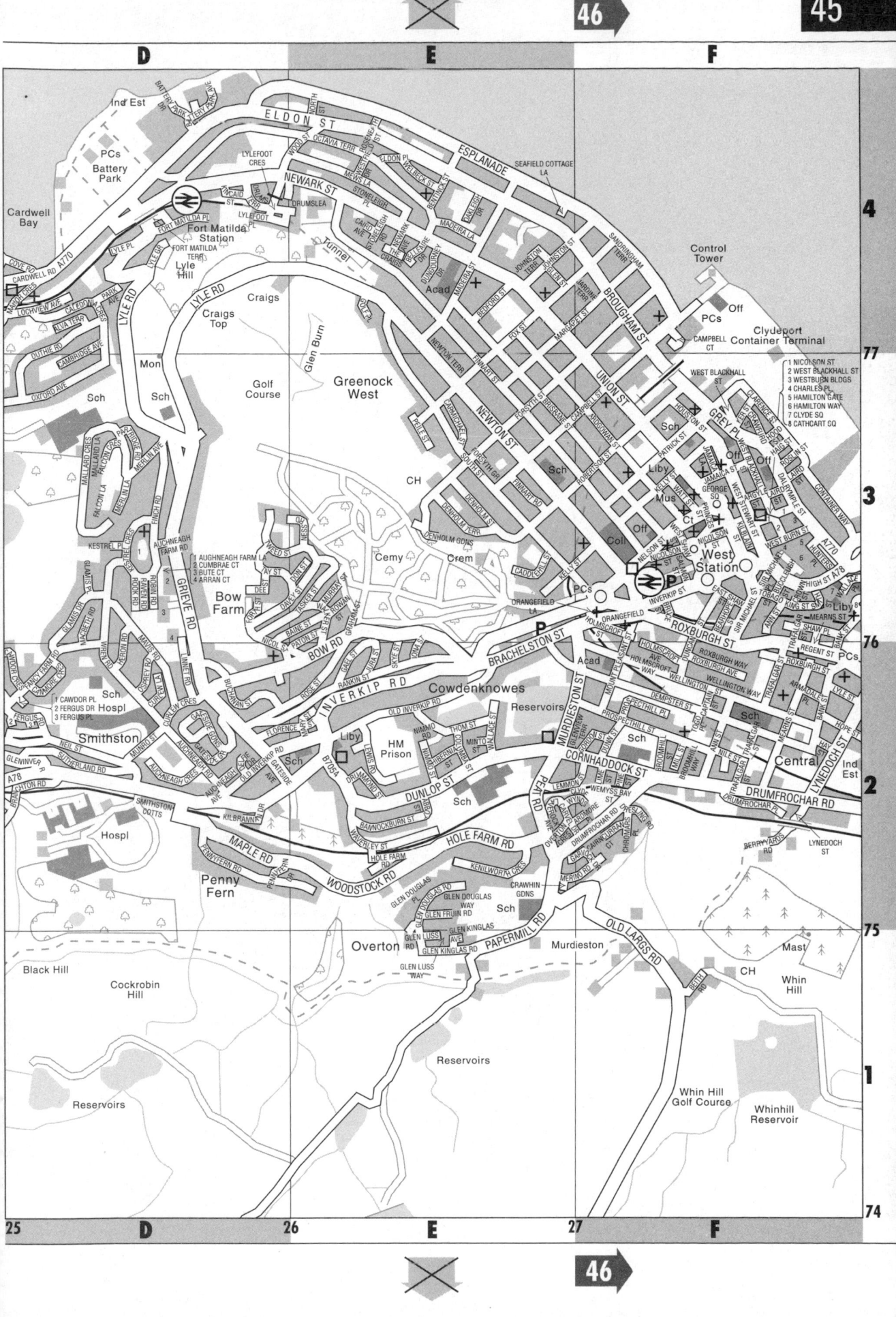

A   B   C

4

Firth of Clyde

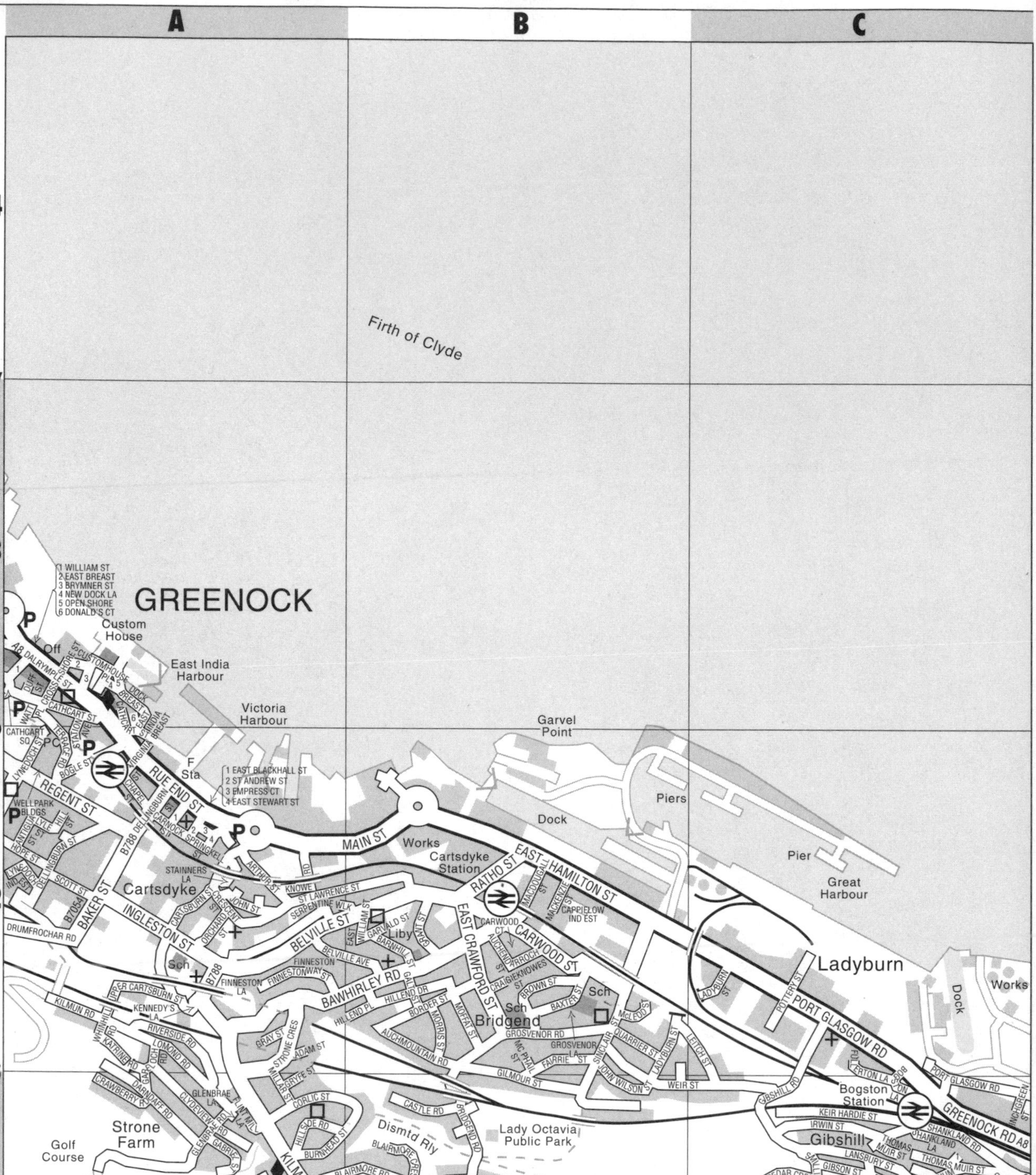

77

3

1 WILLIAM ST
2 EAST BREAST
3 BRYMNER ST
4 NEW DOCK LA
5 OPEN SHORE
6 DONALD'S CT

GREENOCK

Custom
House

East India
Harbour

Off

CUSTOMHOUSE

A8 DALRYMPLE ST

Victoria
Harbour

Garvel
Point

76

CATHCART
SQ   SPC

CATHCART
TERRACE

BOGLE ST

WATT
STATION

DUNCAN ST

REGENT ST

DRUMFROCHAR RD

F
Sta

1 EAST BLACKHALL ST
2 ST ANDREW ST
3 EMPRESS CT
4 EAST STEWART ST

RUE END ST

B788 DELINGBURN

Piers

Dock

Pier

WELL PARK
BLDGS

HOPE ST

LYLE ST

SCOTT ST

BAKER ST

INGLESTON ST

Cartsdyke

STAINNERS
LA

KILBLAIN ST

NICOLSON ST

ANN ST

ROXBURGH ST

ARTHUR ST

JOHN ST

ORCHARD ST

KNOWE

ST LAWRENCE ST

SERPENTINE WLK

MAIN ST

Works

Cartsdyke
Station

RATHO ST

EAST HAMILTON ST

CARWOOD

CAPRIELOW IND EST

Great
Harbour

Ladyburn

2

Sch

BELVILLE ST

BELVILLE AVE

GARVALD ST

BARBHILL

CARLUNG ST

LIby

FINNESTON ST

FINNESTON
LA

FINNESTONWAYS

HILLEND DR

HILLEND PL

EAST CRAWFORD ST

CARWOOD ST

PRIBOCH

CRAIGIEKNOWES

BROWN ST

BAXTER ST

Sch

Sch

MCLEOD

LADYBURN ST

PORT GLASGOW RD

Dock

Works

KILMUN RD

KENNEDY'S
LA

RIVERSIDE RD

LOMOND RD

BAWHIRLEY RD

GRAY ST

STRONE CRES

ADAM ST

HILLEND RD

BORDER ST

JAMES MORRIS ST

AUCHMOUNTAIN RD

Bridgend

GROSVENOR RD

MAC PHAIL

FARRIE

QUARRIER ST

SINCLAIR

JOHN WILSON ST

WEIR ST

Bogston
Station

KEIR HARDIE ST

IRWIN ST

75

CRAWFURBY RD

WHINHILL ST

KATHRINE ST

GLENBRAE
LA

CLYDEVIEW

NEILL
ST

CORLIC ST

GARVEL RD

CASTLE RD

BRIDGEND RD

GILMOUR ST

GIBSHILL RD

PORT GLASGOW RD

GREENOCK RD A8

THOMAS
MUIR
LA

SHANKLAND
LA

SHANKLAND RD

THOMAS MUIR ST

Gibshill

Golf
Course

**Strone
Farm**

GABRIEL

BURNHEAD

KILMACOLM RD

CLYDE RD

Dismtd Rly

BLAIRMORE RD

BLAIRMORE DR

CASTLE RD

KILCREGGAN VIEW

CARDROSS CRES

Lady Octavia
Public Park

Strone

CEDAR CRES

FIR ST

GIBSON ST

LANSBURY ST

BELL ST

DALMALLY

GOBHAM ST

POPLAR ST

LABURNUM
RD

THOMAS MUIR RD

WHITELEES RD

MITCHELL ST

EAST ST

Works

**Auchmountain
Glen**

ABERFOYLE RD

KILLERN

FINTRY RD

BALLOCH RD

KENDRICK RD

TORRANCE
RD

LEVEN RD

BLAIRMORE RD

SHANDON PL

KILMACOLM PL

CLYNDER RD

CARDROSS CRES

Sch

Sch

Strone

• Mast

THOMAS MUIR LA 1
LILYBANK RD 2
FARQUAR RD 3
BROADSTONE AVE 4

**Knocknairs
Hill**

BALMORE RD

LUSS AVE

LUSS PL

RENTON RD

DALTON

ARDMORE RD

DALMOAK RD

ARDEN RD

AUCHMOUNTAIN RD

B788

Craigieknowe Burn

1

74

28   **A**   29   **B**   30   **C**

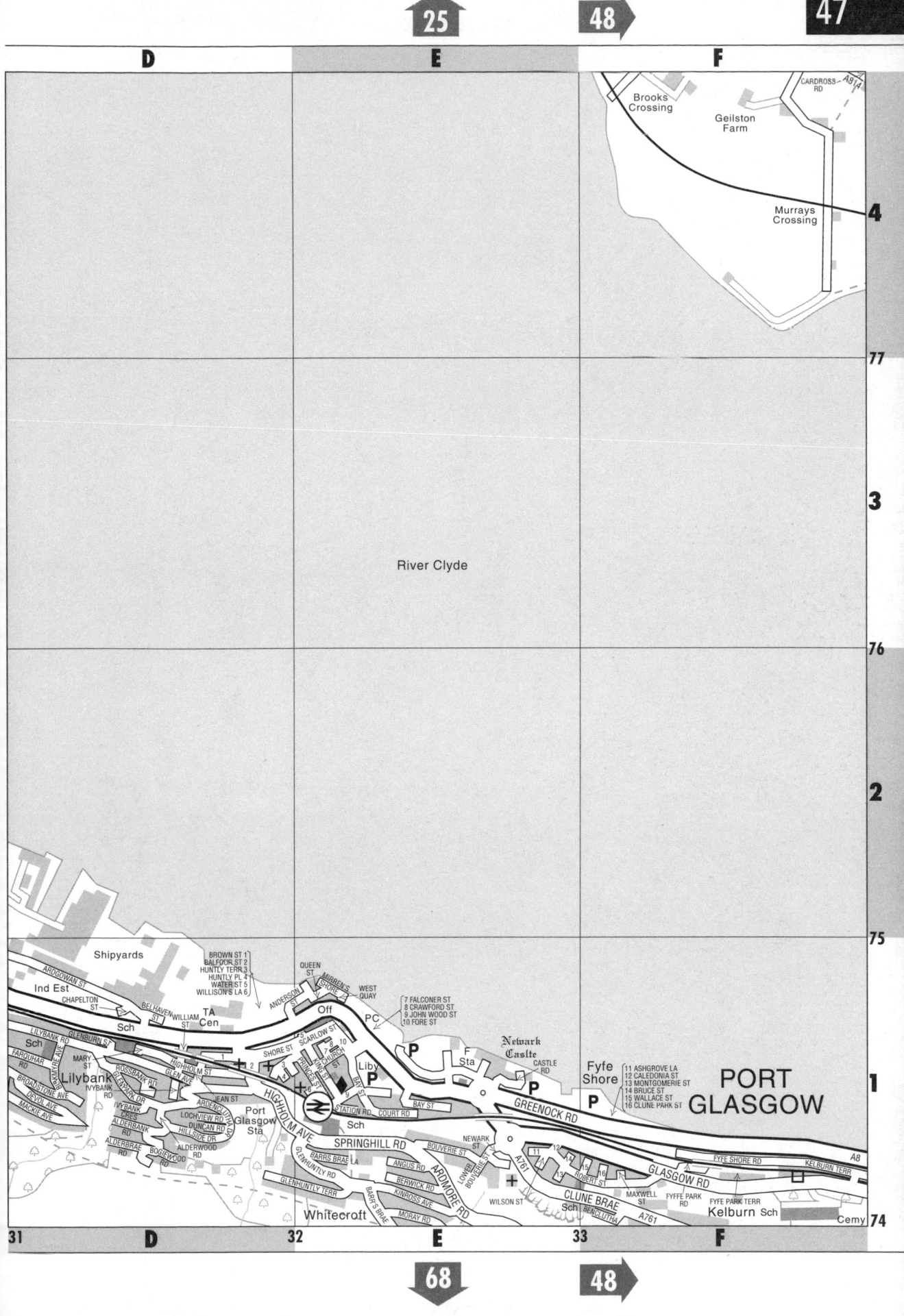

4

77

3

River Clyde

76

2

75

1

Brooks Crossing

Geilston Farm

CARDROSS RD

A814

Murrays Crossing

Shipyards

Ind Est

AROGOWAN ST

CHAPELTON ST

BELHAVEN

WILLIAM ST

Lilybank

Sch

GLENBURN ST

LILYBANK RD

FARQUHAR RD

MARY ST

BROADSTONE AVE

ORCHARD AVE

IVYBANK RD

MACKIE AVE

DEVOL AVE

ROSSBANK RD

HIGHHOLM ST

GLEN AVE

ARDENCRAIG DR

LOCHVIEW RD

DUNCAN RD

HILLSIDE DR

ALDERBANK RD

ALDERBRAE RD

BOGLEWOOD RD

ALDERWOOD RD

JEAN ST

Port Glasgow Sta

HIGHHOLM AVE

BARRS BRAE LA

GLENHUNTLY RD

GLENHUNTLY TERR

BARR'S BRAE

Whitecroft

SPRINGHILL RD

ARDMORE RD

Sch

ANGUS ST

BERWICK RD

KINROSS AVE

MORAY RD

WILSON ST

BROWN ST 1
BALFOUR ST 2
HUNTLY TERR 3
HUNTLY PL 4
WATER ST 5
WILLISON'S LA 6

QUEEN ST

MIRREN'S SHORE

WEST QUAY

ANDERSON ST

Off

PC

SCARLOW ST

SHORE ST

Liby

BAY ST

STATION RD

COURT RD

Sch

TA Cen

Sch

7 FALCONER ST
8 CRAWFORD ST
9 JOHN WOOD ST
10 FORE ST

P

P

F Sta

Newark Caslte

CASTLE RD

P

Fyfe Shore

P

11 ASHGROVE LA
12 CALEDONIA ST
13 MONTGOMERIE ST
14 BRUCE ST
15 WALLACE ST
16 CLUNE PARK ST

GREENOCK RD

NEWARK ST

LOWER BOUVERIE ST

A761

BOUVERIE ST

ROBERT ST

CLUNE BRAE

BENCLUTHA

A761

Sch

Kelburn Sch

MAXWELL ST

FYFFE PARK RD

GLASGOW RD

FYFE SHORE RD

FYFE PARK TERR

KELBURN TERR

A8

Cemy

PORT GLASGOW

74

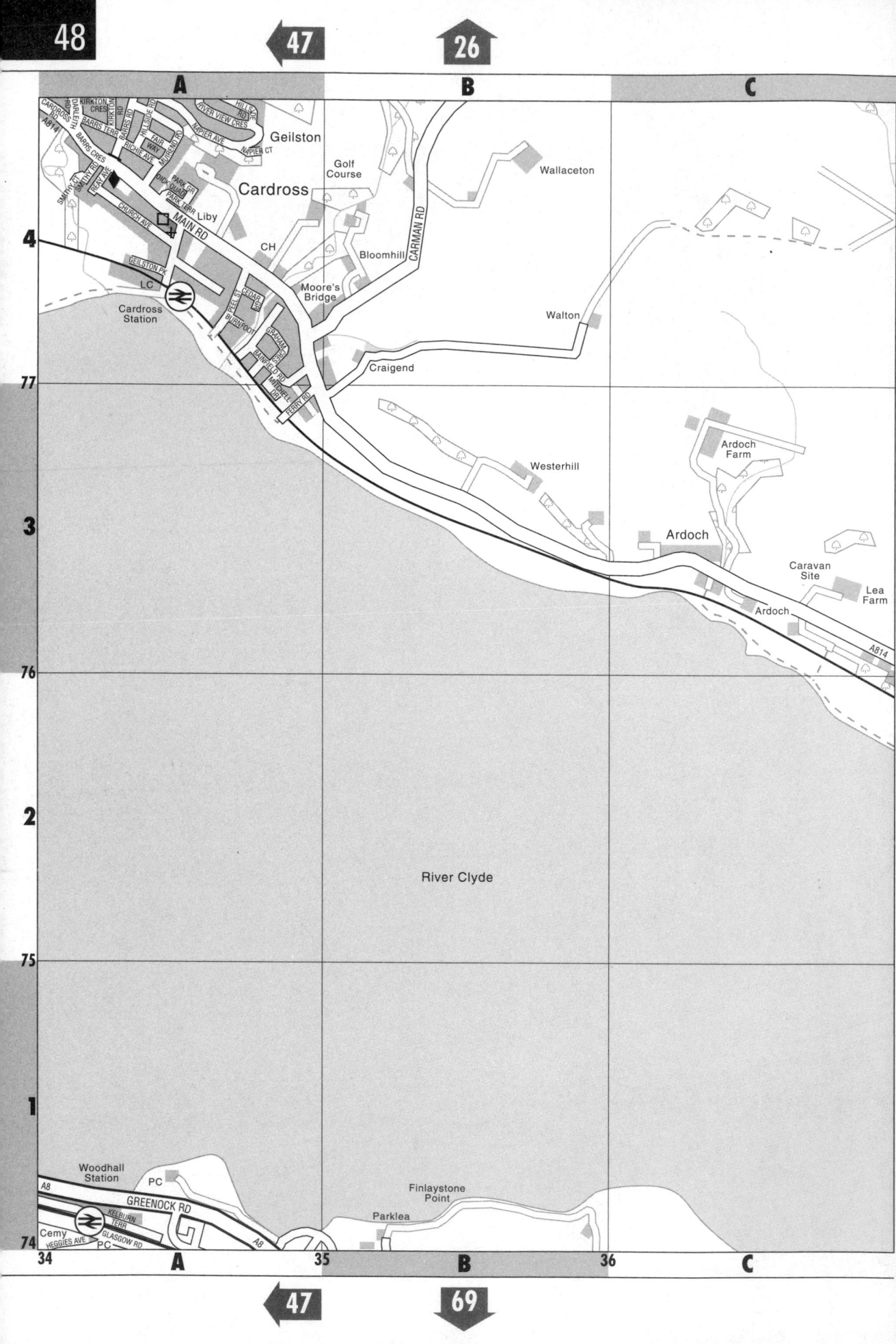

Geilston

Cardross

Golf
Course

Wallaceton

CARMAN RD

Bloomhill

Moore's
Bridge

Walton

Cardross
Station

LC

CH

Liby

MAIN RD

CHURCH AVE

GEILSTON PK

Craigend

Westerhill

Ardoch
Farm

Ardoch

Caravan
Site

Lea
Farm

Ardoch

A814

River Clyde

Woodhall
Station

PC

Finlaystone
Point

GREENOCK RD

KELBURN
TERR

GLASGOW RD

Parklea

Cemy

HEGGIES AVE

PC

A8

A8

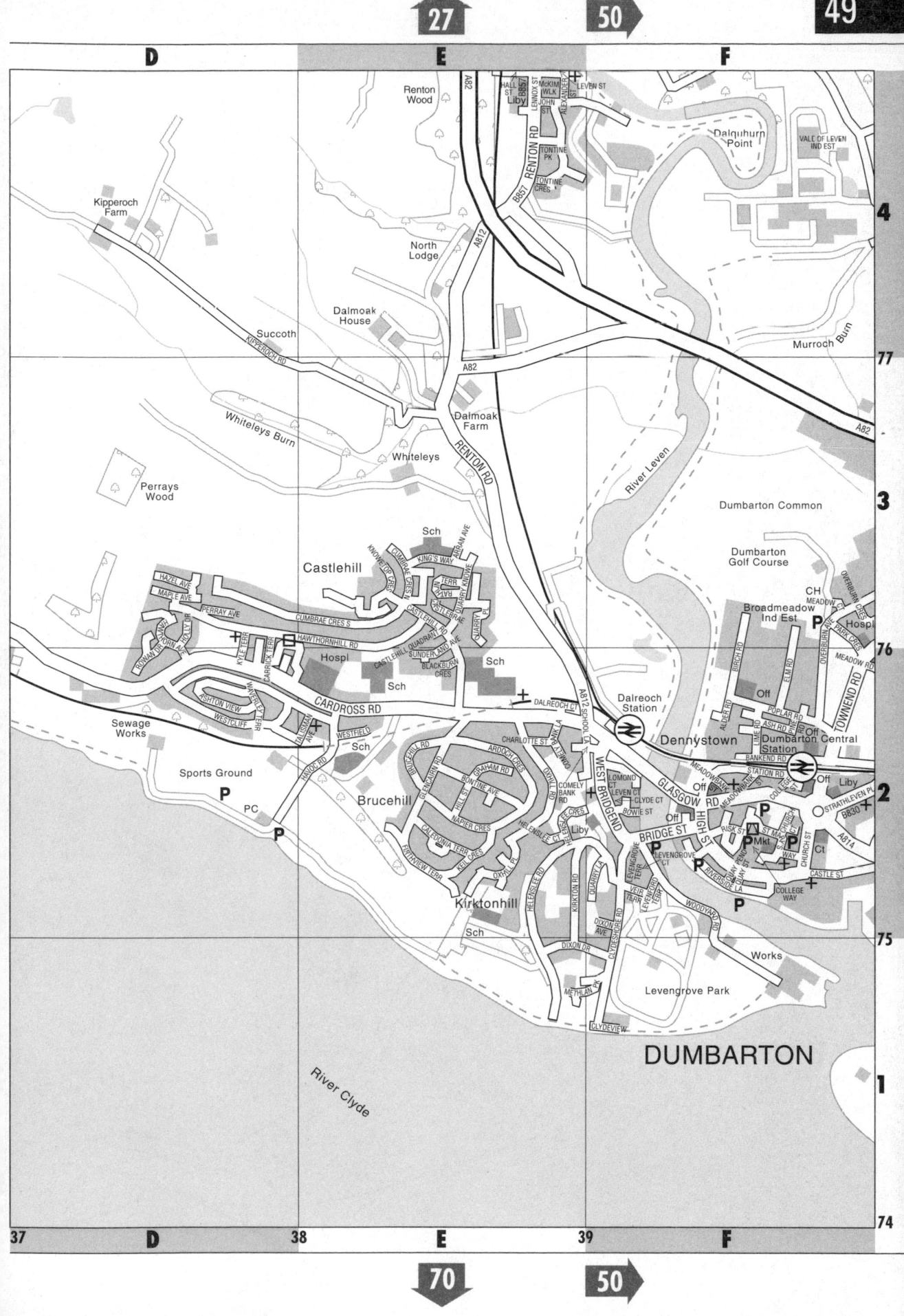

D
E
F

4

77

3

76

2

75

74

Renton Wood

Kipperoch Farm

Succoth

KIPPEROCH RD

North Lodge

Dalmoak House

Whiteleys Burn

Perrays Wood

Dalmoak Farm

RENTON RD

Whiteleys

A82

A812

B857 RENTON RD

Liby

HALL ST
LENNOX ST
B857
McKIM WLK
JOHN ST
LEVEN ST
ALEXANDER
TONTINE PK
TONTINE CRES

Dalquhurn Point

VALE OF LEVEN IND EST

Murroch Burn

A82

River Leven

Dumbarton Common

Dumbarton Golf Course

Castlehill

Sch

KNOWE TOP CRES
CUMBRAE CRES
King's Way
ADRIAN AVE
HAY
KILTEARN
TERR
QUARRY KNOWE
QUARRY PL

HAZEL AVE
MAPLE AVE
PERRAY AVE
HOLM VIEW
HOLLY AVE
CUMBRAE CRES S
CASTLEHILL RD
CASTLEHILL QUADRANT
SUNDERLAND AVE
BLACKBURN CRES

ROWAN TERR
THORN AVE
KYLE TERR
CARRICK TERR
HAWTHORNHILL RD

CH
MEADOW
Broadmeadow Ind Est
P
Hospl

BIRCH RD
ELM RD
POPLAR RD
ASH RD
ALDER RD
OVERBURN RD
PARK CRES
MEADOW RD
TOWNEND RD

Hospl

Sch

Sch

CARDROSS RD

ASHTON VIEW
WESTCLIFF
WAVERLEY TERR
HALDANE AVE
HAVOC RD

Sewage Works

Sports Ground

P

PC

P

Sch

Westfield

Dalreoch Station

Dalreoch

A813 SCHOOL RD
DALREOCH CT

Off

Dennystown

Dumbarton Central Station

Off
Off
Liby

Brucehill

BRUCEHILL RD
GLENGAIRN RD
GRAHAM RD
HILL ST
BONTINE AVE
ARDOCH CRES
CHARLOTTE ST
PARK LA
LENNOX
OXHILL RD

CALEDONIA TERR
NAPIER CRES
FAIRVIEW TERR
KEIL CRES
OXHILL

HELENSLEE RD
HELENSLEE CRES

Comely Bank Rd

WEST BRIDGEND

LOMOND
CT
LEVEN CT
Clyde Ct
BOWIE ST

Liby

BRIDGE ST

GLASGOW RD

HIGH ST

MEADOWBANK
STATION RD
BANKEND RD

RISK ST
Off

MEADOW AVE
St MARY
CHURCH
COLLEGE ST
STRATHLEVEN PL
B830
A814

P
Off
Mkt
P
P
Ct

LEVENGROVE TERR
LEVENGROVE
CT

RIVERSIDE LA

CLAY ST
QUAY ST

COLLEGE WAY

WAY

CASTLE ST

P

Kirktonhill

KIRKTON RD
QUARRY RD

DIXON
AVE
DIXON DR

CLYDESHORE RD

VETS TERR
LEVENSIDE TERR
WOODYARD RD

Sch

METHLAN PK

CLYDEVIEW

Levengrove Park

Works

River Clyde

DUMBARTON

1

A   **B**   **C**

Murroch Burn

Murroch

Square
Wood

4

Black
Wood

Barr
Wood

Maryland

STIRLING RD

77

Bellsmyre
Cottage

Bellsmyre

Sch

Garshake Burn

A82

Sch

Garshake
Reservoir

Overtoun Burn

3

Garshake

Overburn
Ave

Water
Works

TOWNEND RD

Cemy

Spardie
Linn

Hospl

76

Townend
Sch

Off

Tom's
Seat

BONHILL RD

ROUND RIDING RD

P

Silverton

P

Police
HQ

Barwood
Hill

Barnhill

2

Acad

Sch

Gruggies Burn

Off
1 BANKEND RD
2 STRATHLEVEN PL

Loch
Bowie

Middleton

Off

Dumbarton
East
Station

STIRLING RD

Northwood

Dumbowie

GREENHEAD RD

Sch

75

Castlegreen
La

Knoxland
Sq

Milton
House

MILTON BRAE

GLASGOW RD

Sta
Greenhead
Ave

KNOXLAND ST 1
BURNSIDE PL 2
BURNSIDE ST 3
EASTFIELD PL 4

Milton
Hill

Milton

Sch

1

P

Works

Hotel

Dumbuck

PC

DUMBARTON RD

A814

A82

River Clyde

74

40   **A**   41   **B**   42   **C**

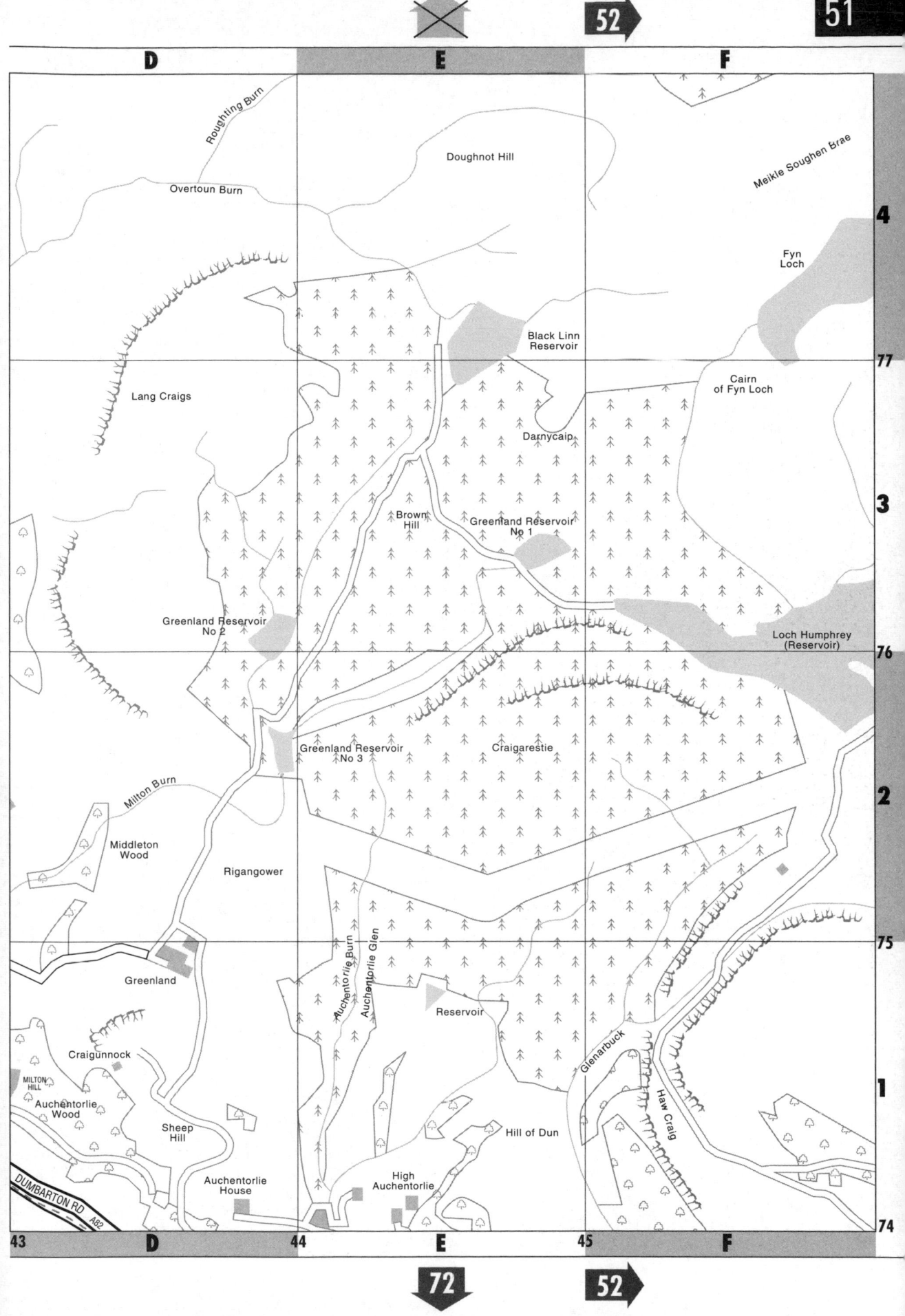

D   E   F

Roughting Burn

Doughnot Hill

Meikle Soughen Brae

Overtoun Burn

4

Fyn Loch

Black Linn Reservoir

77

Lang Craigs

Cairn of Fyn Loch

Darnycaip

3

Brown Hill

Greenland Reservoir No 1

Greenland Reservoir No 2

Loch Humphrey (Reservoir)

76

Milton Burn

Greenland Reservoir No 3

Craigarestie

2

Middleton Wood

Rigangower

Auchentorlie Burn

Auchentorlie Glen

75

Greenland

Reservoir

Craigunnock

Glenarbuck

MILTON HILL

Haw Craig

1

Auchentorlie Wood

Sheep Hill

Hill of Dun

Auchentorlie House

High Auchentorlie

74

DUMBARTON RD A82

51

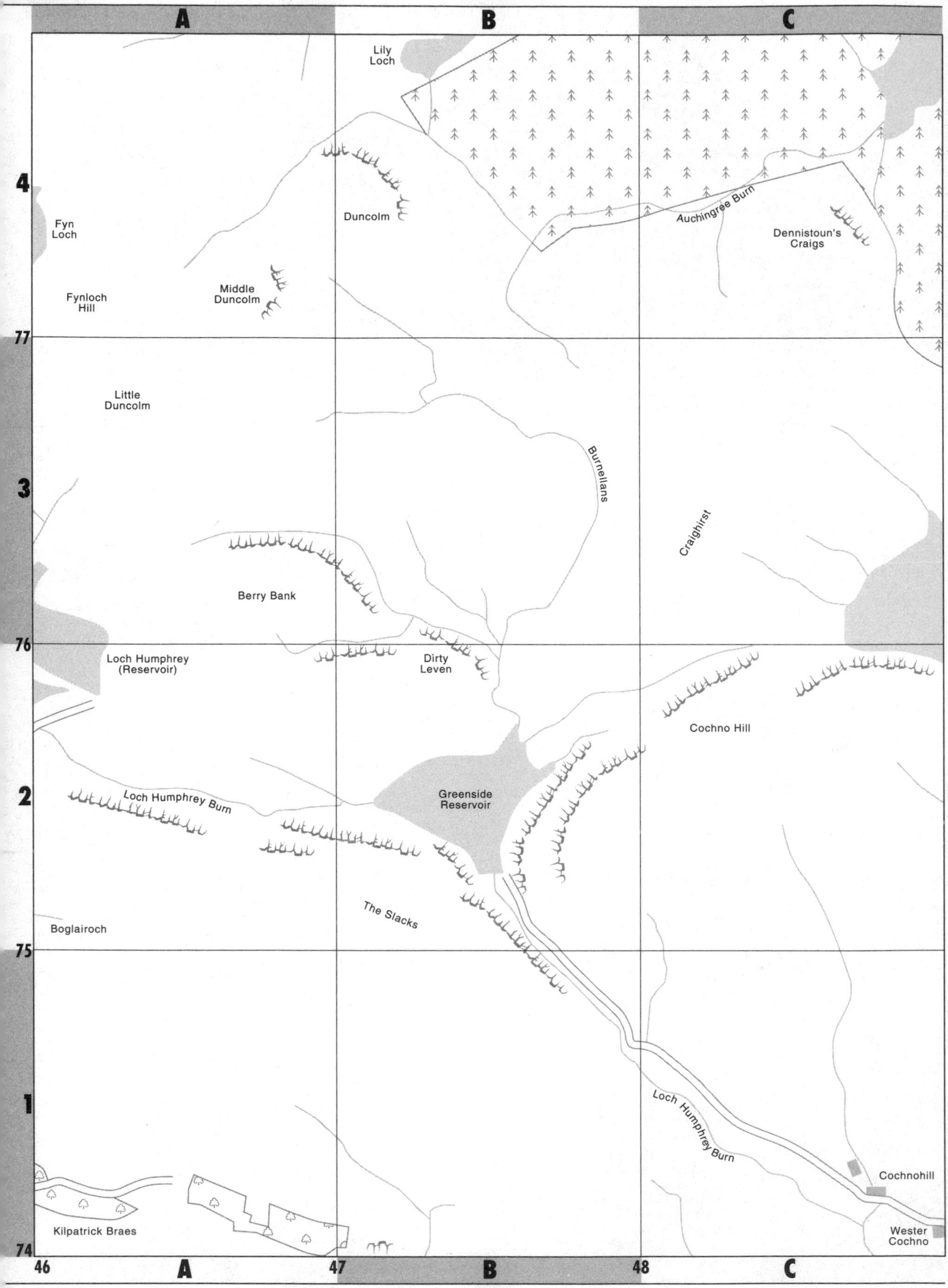

A　　　　　　B　　　　　　C

Lily
Loch

4

Fyn
Loch

Duncolm

Auchingree Burn

Dennistoun's
Craigs

Fynloch
Hill

Middle
Duncolm

77

Little
Duncolm

Burnellans

3

Craighirst

Berry Bank

76

Loch Humphrey
(Reservoir)

Dirty
Leven

Cochno Hill

2

Loch Humphrey Burn

Greenside
Reservoir

The Slacks

Boglairoch

75

1

Loch Humphrey Burn

Cochnohill

Kilpatrick Braes

Wester
Cochno

74

46　　　　A　　　　47　　　　B　　　　48　　　　C

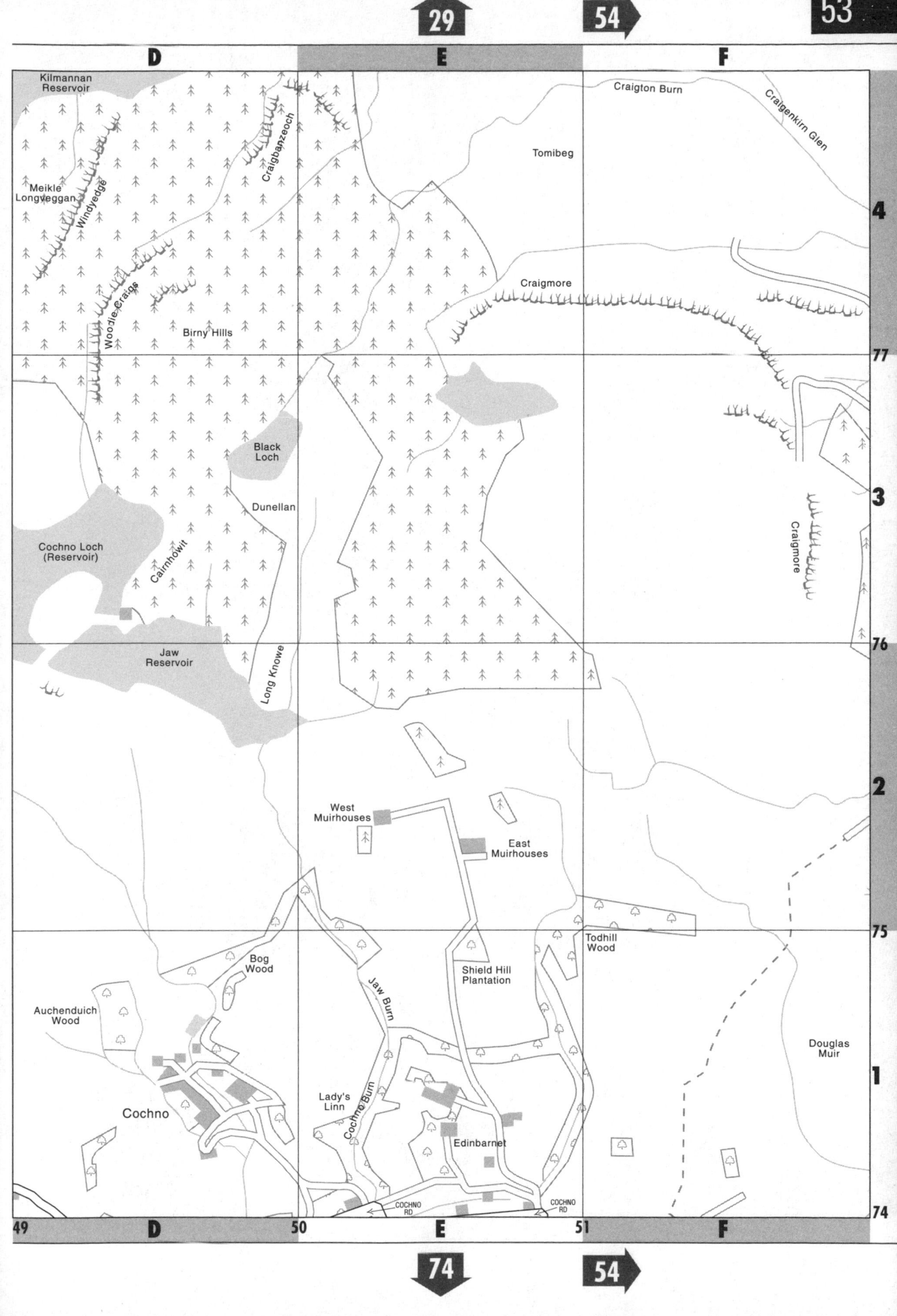

Kilmannan
Reservoir

Craigton Burn

Craigenkirn Glen

Craigbanzeoch

Tomibeg

Meikle
Longveggan

Windyedge

Woozle Craigs

Craigmore

Birny Hills

Black
Loch

Dunellan

Craigmore

Cochno Loch
(Reservoir)

Cairnhowit

Jaw
Reservoir

Long Knowe

West
Muirhouses

East
Muirhouses

Todhill
Wood

Bog
Wood

Shield Hill
Plantation

Auchenduich
Wood

Jaw Burn

Douglas
Muir

Cochno

Lady's
Linn

Cochno Burn

Edinbarnet

COCHNO
RD

COCHNO
RD

A   B   C

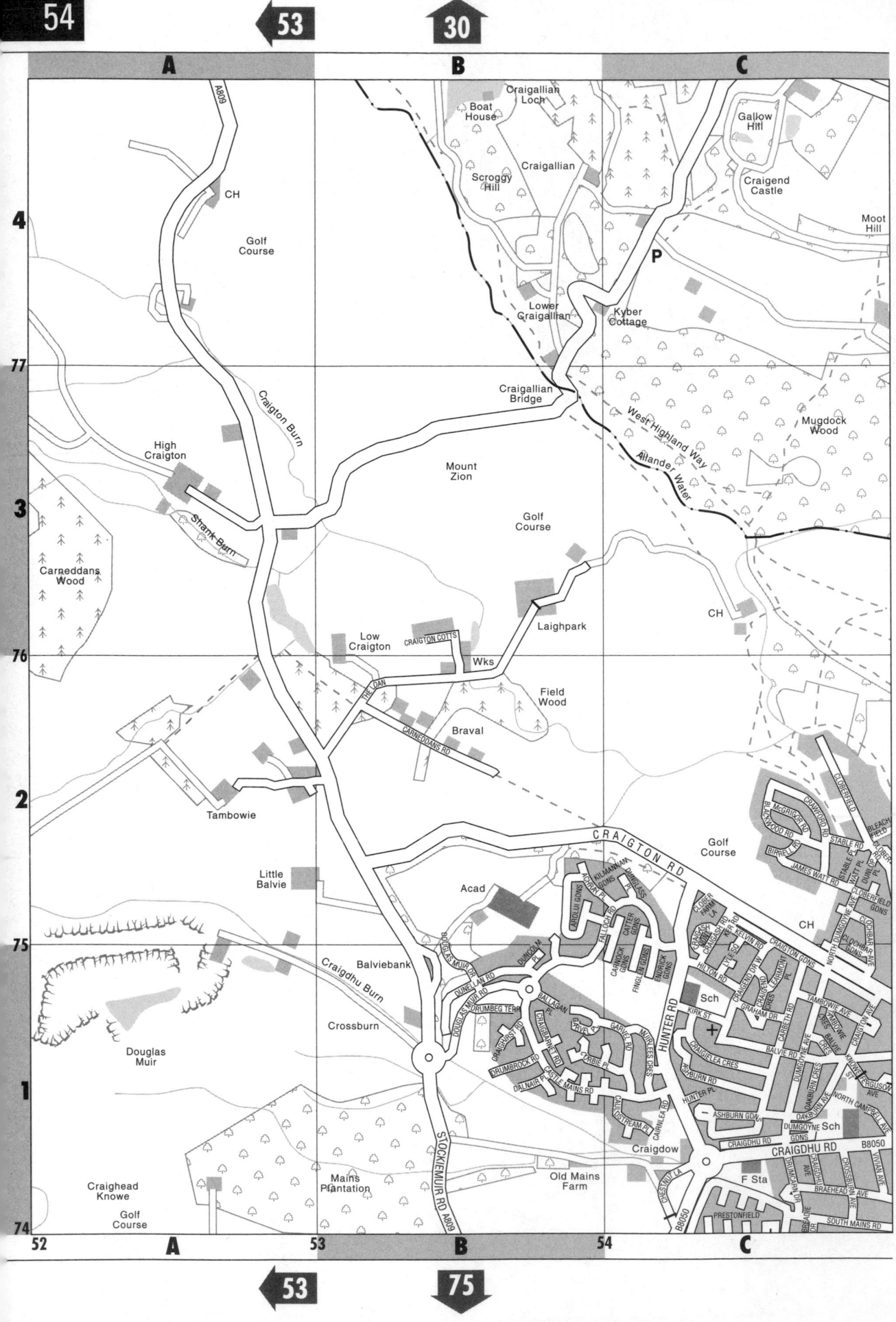

4

Craigallian Loch

Boat House

Craigallian

Gallow Hill

Scroggy Hill

Craigend Castle

Moot Hill

CH

Golf Course

P

Lower Craigallian

Kyber Cottage

77

Craigton Burn

Craigallian Bridge

West Highland Way

Mugdock Wood

High Craigton

Mount Zion

Allande Water

Shank Burn

3

Golf Course

Carneddans Wood

CH

Low Craigton

Laighpark

CRAIGTON COTTS

76

Wks

THE LOAN

Field Wood

CARNEDDANS RD

Braval

2

Tambowie

Golf Course

CRAIGTON RD

Little Balvie

Acad

CH

75

Balviebank

Sch

Craigdhu Burn

Crossburn

Douglas Muir

1

HUNTER RD

Sch

Craighead Knowe

Mains Plantation

STOCKIEMUIR RD A809

Old Mains Farm

Craigdow

CRAIGDHU RD B8050

F Sta

Golf Course

Prestonfield

74

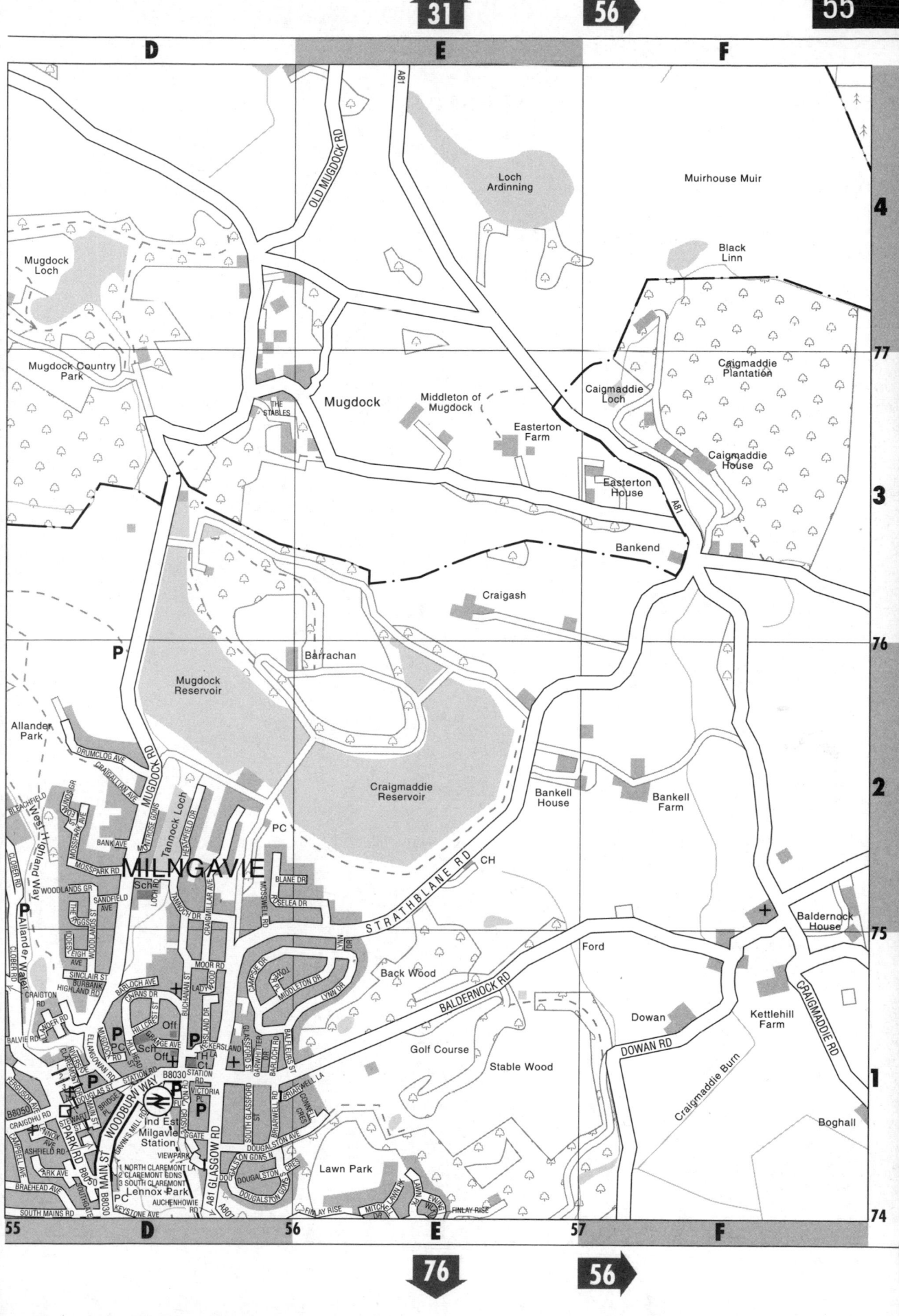

D   E   F

4

Loch
Ardinning

Muirhouse Muir

Mugdock
Loch

Black
Linn

77

Mugdock Country
Park

Mugdock

THE
STABLES

Middleton of
Mugdock

Caigmaddie
Loch

Caigmaddie
Plantation

Easterton
Farm

Easterton
House

Caigmaddie
House

3

A81

Bankend

Craigash

76

P

Barrachan

Mugdock
Reservoir

Allander
Park

DRUMCLOG AVE
CRAIGALLIAN AVE
MUGDOCK RD
MONTROSE GDNS
HEXFIELD DR

Craigmaddie
Reservoir

Bankell
House

Bankell
Farm

2

BLEACHFIELD
West Highland Way
MOSSPARK RD
WOODLANDS GR
BANK AVE
MOSSPARK RD
Tannock Loch

BLANE DR
ROSELEA DR

PC

CH

Baldernock
House

75

MILNGAVIE
Sch

STRATHBLANE RD

+

P

Allander Valley
CLOBER RD

CRAIGALLIAN AVE
CRAIGDHU RD
HIGHLAND RD
SINCLAIR ST
BURBANK

BARLOCH AVE
CAIRNS DR
BUCHANAN ST
LADY'S
MIDDLETON DR

CAMPSIE DR
TOUR
LYNN DR

Back Wood

BALDERNOCK RD

Ford

Dowan

Kettlehill
Farm

CRAIGMADDIE RD

+
P
PC
Sch

BALVIE RD
ELLANGOWAN RD
HILLHEAD ST
HILLCREST ST
KIRKLAND DR
BALFLEURS ST

STATION
RD
VICTORIA

Off
Off

Golf Course

Stable Wood

DOWAN RD

Craigmaddie Burn

1

B8050
CRAIGDHU RD
LENNOX
AVE
ASHFIELD RD
PARK RD
MAIN ST
MAIN ST B8030
DOUGLAS ST
BRIDGE ST
PARK RD

P
PC

WOODBURN WAY

Ind Est
Milgavie
Station
VIEWPARK
B8030
A81 GLASGOW RD
STATION
RD
CROFT
GATE
SOUTH GLASSFORD
BRIARWELL RD
BRIARWELL LA
BRIARDENE
GARRVANT
BRIAR CONNEL
CRES

Lawn Park

Boghall

South Mains Rd
B8030
BRAEHEAD AVE
AUCHENHOWIE
KEYSTONE AVE
PC
1 NORTH CLAREMONT LA
2 CLAREMONT GDNS
3 SOUTH CLAREMONT
Lennox Park
DOUGLASTON AVE
DOUGLASTON GDNS N
DOUGLASTON CRES
FINLAY RISE
MITCH
LYNN
WOOD
FINLAY RISE

74

A

B

C

Pattie's Bughts

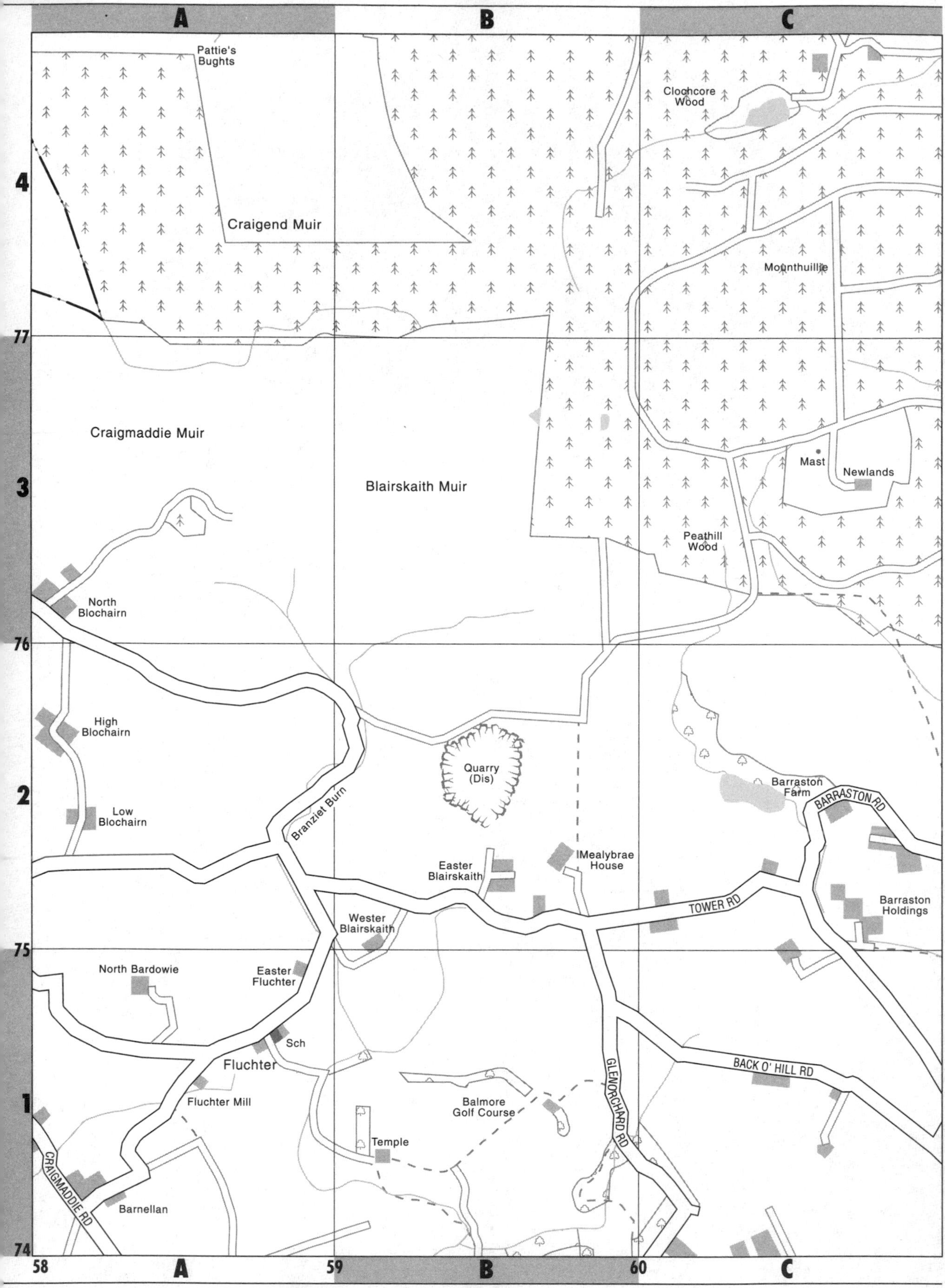

Clochcore Wood

4

Craigend Muir

Mounthuillie

77

Craigmaddie Muir

Mast

Newlands

3

Blairskaith Muir

Peathill Wood

North Blochairn

76

High Blochairn

Quarry (Dis)

Barraston Farm

BARRASTON RD

2

Branziet Burn

Low Blochairn

Easter Blairskaith

Mealybrae House

TOWER RD

Barraston Holdings

Wester Blairskaith

75

North Bardowie

Easter Fluchter

Sch

BACK O' HILL RD

GLENORCHARD RD

Fluchter

1

Fluchter Mill

Balmore Golf Course

CRAIGMADDIE RD

Temple

Barnellan

74

58

A

59

B

60

C

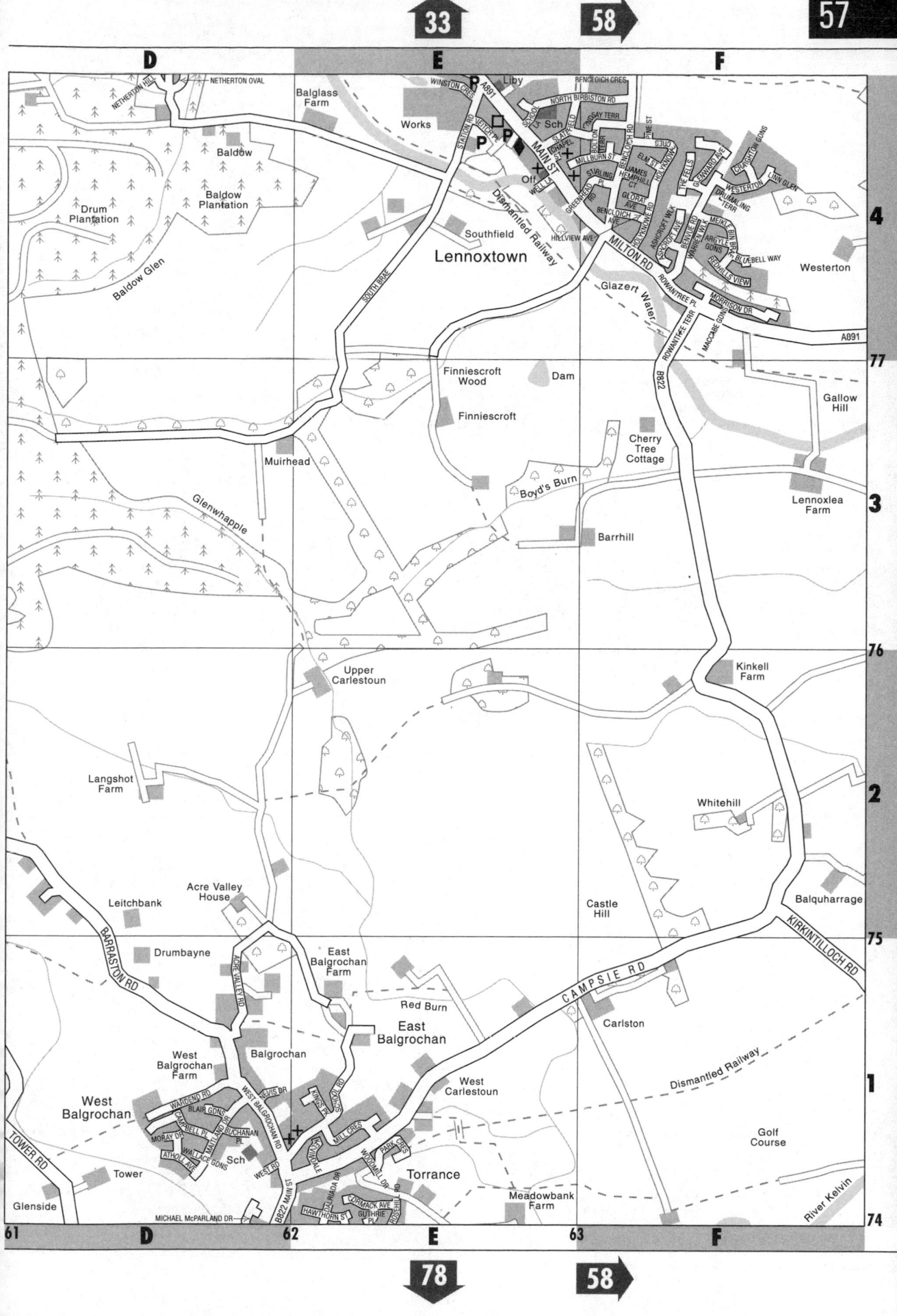

D | E | F

NETHERTON HILL — NETHERTON OVAL

Balglass Farm

Works

WINSTON CRES

Liby

North Birbiston Rd

BENCLOICH CRES

P

Baldow

STATION RD

VEITCH PL

A891

MAIN ST

LS Sch

CHAPEL

NORTH BIRBISTON RD

SLEAFIELD

BOLTON

SAY TERR

ELM ST

JAMES HEMPHILL CT

THE FELLS

CRICHTON GDNS

WESTERTON

LINN GLEN

Drum Plantation

Baldow Plantation

P

P

Off

WELL

Millburn St

GREENHEAD RD

STIRLING

GLORAT AVE

ASHCROFT WLK

BEVUE RD

ROY KNOWE

MEIKLE BIN BRAE

DRUMALING TERR

GLENYARD AVE

ARGYLE GDNS

HARRIET WAY

BLUEBELL WAY

Westerton

Southfield

HILLVIEW AVE

MILTON RD

REDHILLS VIEW

Baldow Glen

Lennoxtown

Glazert Water

ROWANTREE PL

MORRISON DR

MACRAE GDNS

A891

4

Finniescroft Wood

Dam

ROWANTREE TERR

B822

Gallow Hill

77

Finniescroft

Cherry Tree Cottage

Muirhead

Boyd's Burn

Lennoxlea Farm

3

Glenwhapple

Barrhill

Upper Carlestoun

Kinkell Farm

76

Langshot Farm

Whitehill

2

Acre Valley House

Leitchbank

Castle Hill

Balquharrage

KIRKINTILLOCH RD

75

Drumbayne

East Balgrochan Farm

BARRASTON RD

ACRE VALLEY RD

Red Burn

CAMPSIE RD

Carlston

Dismantled Railway

1

West Balgrochan Farm

Balgrochan

East Balgrochan

West Carlestoun

Golf Course

West Balgrochan

WARDEND RD

BLAIR GDNS

CAMPBELL PL

MORAY DR

ATHOL AVE

WALLACE GDNS

BUCHANAN PL

WEST BALGROCHAN RD

LEVIS DR

KING ST

SCHOOL RD

MILL CRES

WINDYDALE

PARK CRES

Sch

TOWER RD

Tower

WEST RD

B822 MAIN ST

KILMADA DR

WINDMILL DR

HAWTHORN ST

CORMACK AVE

GUTHRIE PL

Torrance

West Carlestoun

Meadowbank Farm

River Kelvin

Glenside

MICHAEL McPARLAND DR

74

A | B | C

Stratford Cottage

Woodburn Reservoir

Ashenwell Dams

Spouthead Burn

Shields Cottage

Water Works

Girdle Hill

4

Alloch Dam

Cowies Glen

Burniebrae Farm

Mount Dam

A891

LOCHABER WLK

77

Newmill

CAMPSIE RD

VALLEYFIELD

MOUNT PLEASANT CRES

Works

Sch

Liby

SCHOOL LA

Milton of Campsie

Antermony Loch

NEWLANDS TERR

GRETA MEEK LA

B757

FERGUSSON TERR

Wattry Burn

Alton Holdings

Lochmill Farm

MARGUERITE PL

ARCHIBALD TERR

JAMES LEESON CT

BEECHER TERR

MURRAY GDNS

ANTERMONY RD

A891

Lochmill

3

MARLEY WAY

LABURNUM DR
IRVINE GDNS
CHESTNUT CT

HILLSIDE TERR

CAIRNVIEW RD

MONTGOMERY TERR

LON CRES

GLENBURN CRES

Alton Farm

Alton Holdings

LINDEN LEA

KINCAID CRES

BLAIR DR

KINCAID FIELD

REDMOSS RD

KINDEL DR

Redmoss

GLAZERT PL

VIEWFIELD AVE

MUNRO DR

MAPLE AVE

HAWTHORN WAY

WILLOW

POPLAR

76

ROWAN AVE

SYCAMORE WAY

JUNIPER DR

HAZEL BANK

Hospl

BIRDSTON RD

Glazert Water

Sewage Works

2

Wetshod

Birdstonbank Farm

Birdston

Dismantled Railway

Inchbelle Farm

Birdston Farm

A803

75

Dismantled Railway

Inchbelly Bridge

B8023

Kirkintilloch Golf Course

Hospl

PC

Forth and Clyde Canal

ALLOWAY TERR

ATLSA DR

Ind Est

Goyle Bridge

Amb Sta

ARRAN

BROOMHILL FARM MEWS

Cleddans

ALLOWAY GDN

LOCH LEA

MOSSGIEL GDNS

DOON LA

KIRKINTILLOCH RD

CH

Springfield

MILTON RD B757

KELVINDALE

KILSYTH RD

5 MILTON CT
6 ALTON CT
7 HARDMUIR GDNS

AFTON VIEW

1

ROCHDALE PL 1
BROADCROFT 2
BROADCROFT RD 3
PETER D.STIRLING RD 4
HOPKIN'S BRAE 5

Works

BANKS RD

GRAHAMSDYKE

LANGMUIR AVE

Hayston House

River Kelvin

Ind Est

Ind Est

HILLHEAD RD

1 HIGHFIELD GR
2 ROSEBANK AVE
3 HIGHFIELD RD
4 LENNOX CT

Schs

P

CAMPSIE RD

A803 GLASGOW RD

WASHINGTON RD 1
GLASGOW RD 2

P

Liby

WEST HIGH ST

EAST HIGH ST

EASTSIDE

LION BANK

REDBRAE RD

MEIKLEHILL RD

HIGHFIELD

Merkland

PEEL BRAE

COWGATE

Mus TH

WATERLOO GDNS

74

64 | A | 65 | B | 66 | C

D
E
F

Drumairn

Lossit

Old Place
Farm

Kierhill

DYKEHEAD RD

WHIN LOAN

ANDERSON CRES
HILLCREST RD
MEADOWSIDE RD
DUMBRECK TERR
A803

Sch
Gallow
Hill

KILSYTH RD
PH
Queenzieburn

Ind
Est

Dyke
Farm

Woodburn

Queenzieburn
Farm

Gavell
Farm

Gavell

GAVELL RD

Gavell

4

77

MILL RD

Sewage
Works

Queenzie Burn

Inchwood
Farm

Cast Burn

Netherinch
Farm

ANTERMONY RD
Roitfair

AUCHENREOCH

Wood Burn

Dismtd Rly

3

A891

Burnside
Cottage

Works

76

Twechar
Farm

B8023

MAIN ST

River Kelvin

GLEN SHIRVA RD
MERRYFLATS

1 HILLVIEW COTTS
2 MELROSE GDNS
3 SHIRVA LEA
4 WHITELAW TERR

ALEXANDER AVE
WINDY
SUNNYHILL
PARK AVE
ANNIESTON
BURNBRAE
BARHILL
LA

Shirva
Board Burn

2

Sewage
Works

Twechar

ANTONINE WALL
(course of)

Auchendavie
Farm

DAVIDSON CRES
MACDONALD
CRES

Sch

KELVIN
TERR
KELVIN VIEW
JOHNSTONE TERR
DIXON
GARTSHORE CRES

Bridgend
Farm

75

Forth & Clyde Canal

Mine
(dis)

Easterton Moss
Plantation

Easterton

1

ALLOWAY
TERR
ALLOWAY
ALLOWAY DR
ELLIGLAND DR
ELLISLAND
AUCHENDAVIE RD
TINTOCK RD
EASTMAINS
KINGSWAY
ANTONINE
MAUCHLINE AVE

DICK CT
KILWINNING
CLARINDA
CRES
ST FLANAN RD

Tintock

Castle
Hill

East
Gartclash

East
Lodge

Harestanes
DOON RD
BURNS DR
BLAIRS RD
MAUCHLINE CT
KYNTYRE AVE
GONNACHIE
STRATHALLAN RD
KINROSS
KINTYRE
KINNAIRD
ATHOLL CT

Sch

APPIN CT
CLYDE CRES
RAVENOCH RD
CUPAR PL
LANGMUIR RD

MERKLAND DR
GRAY
DAER

HARESTANES
GDNS
ARMOUR CT
FOSSIL GR
MOIDART
MORAY
Langmuir
CAVAL CRES
KINNAIRD
GAIRLOCH
GDNS

1 ARMOUR GDNS
2 ALLOWAY QUADRANT
3 ARMOUR PL
4 GLENCONNER WAY
5 MERKLAND PL
6 MERKLAND CT

Saddles Brae
Farm

West
Gartclash

B8048

B8048

74

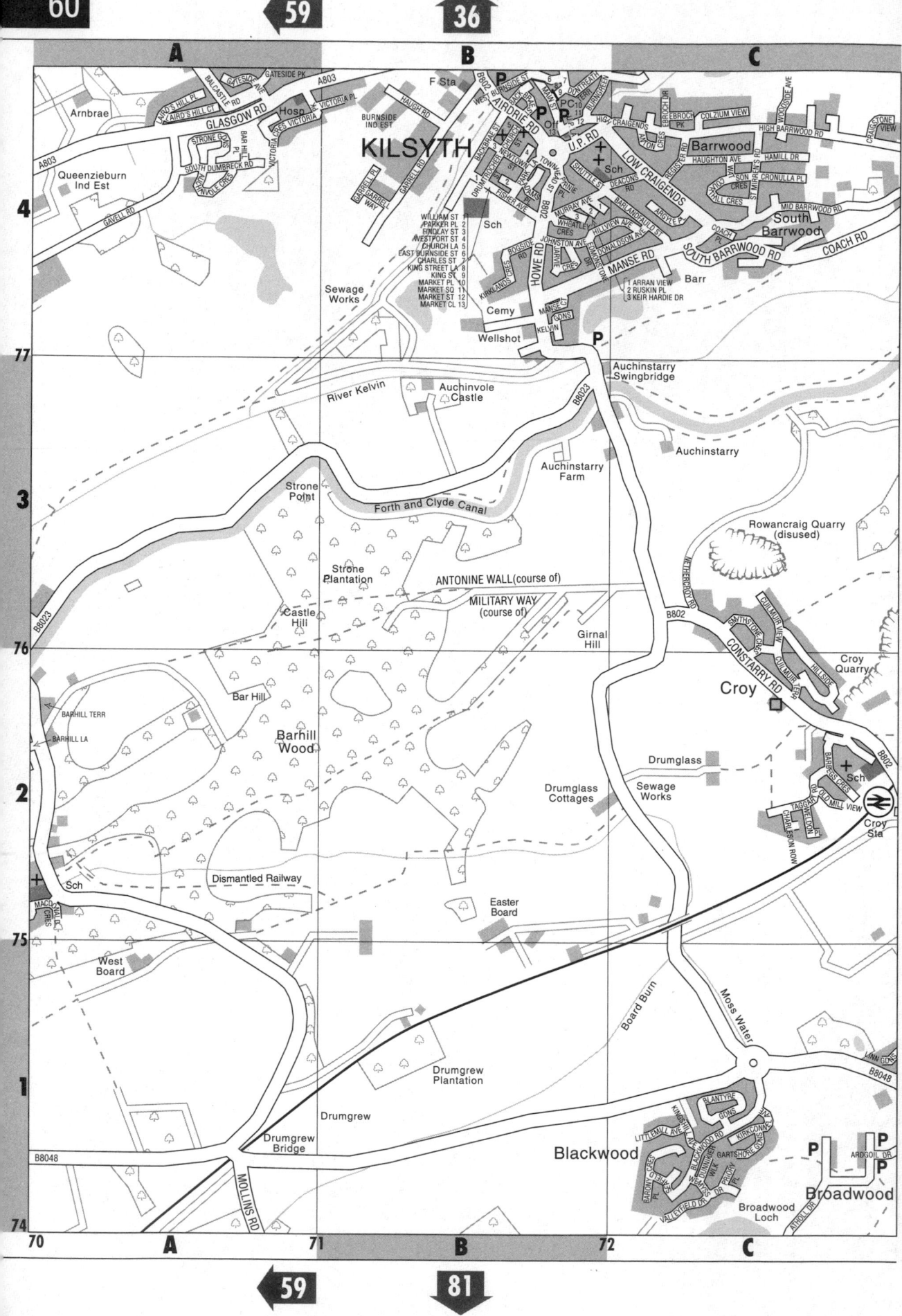

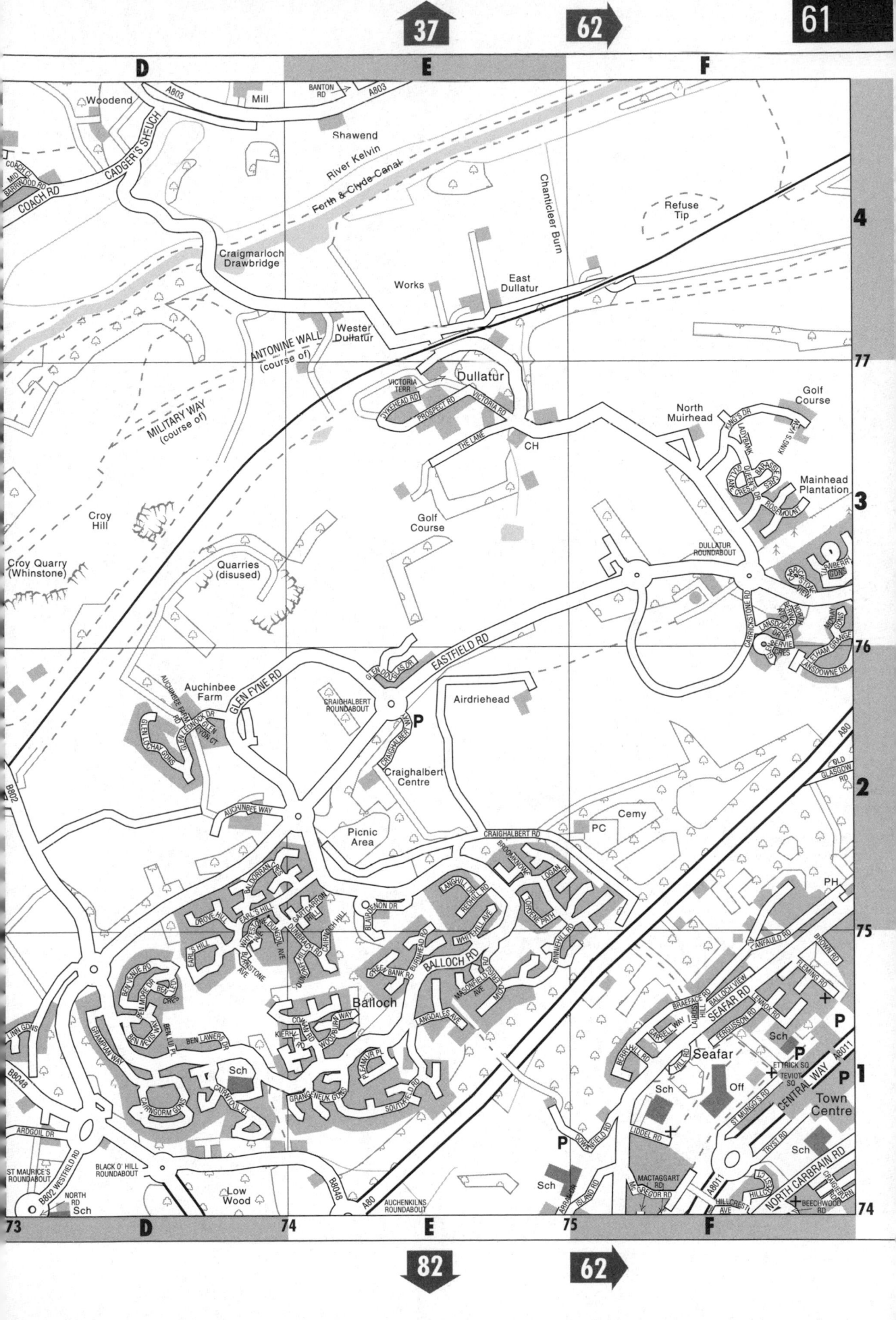

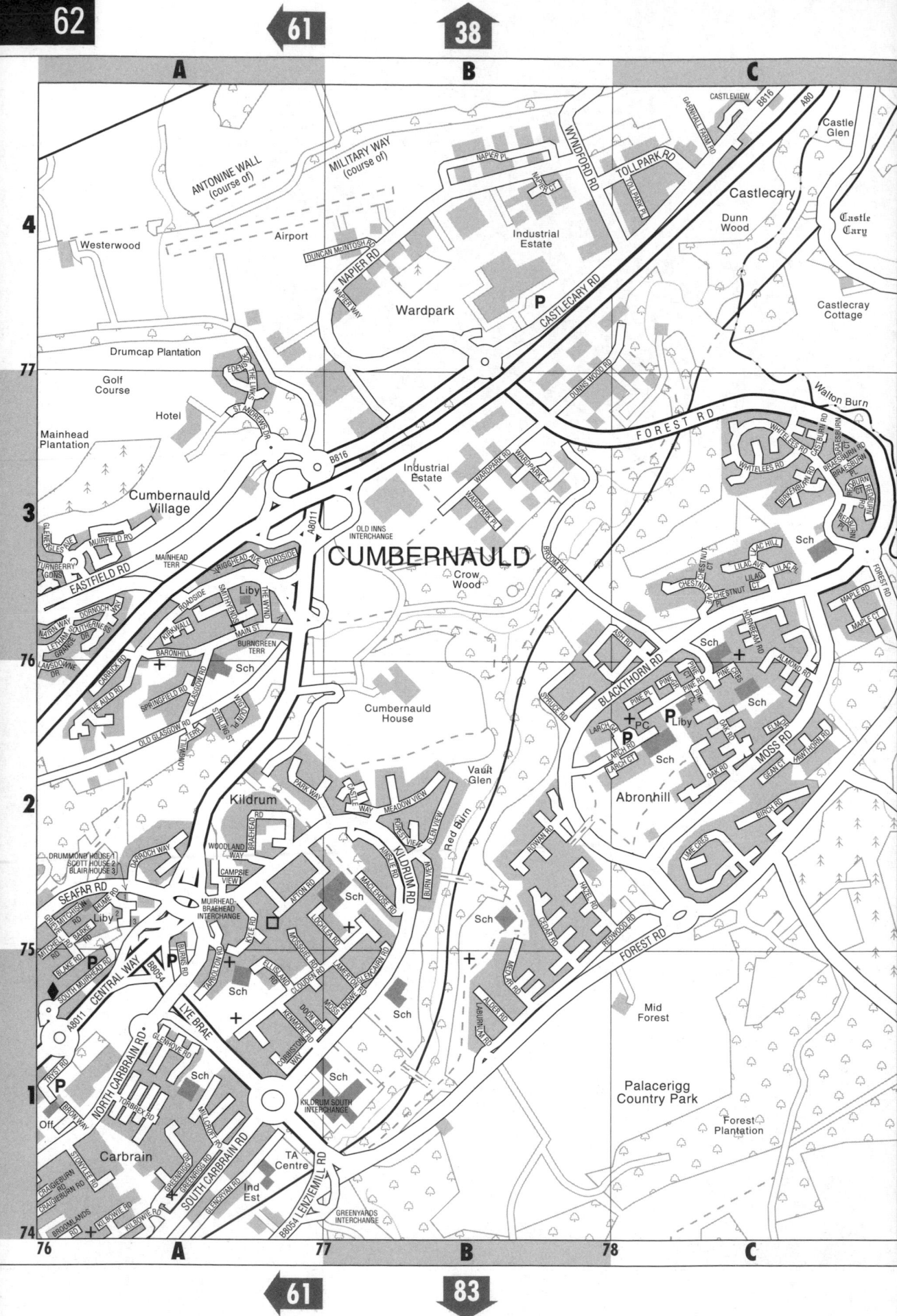

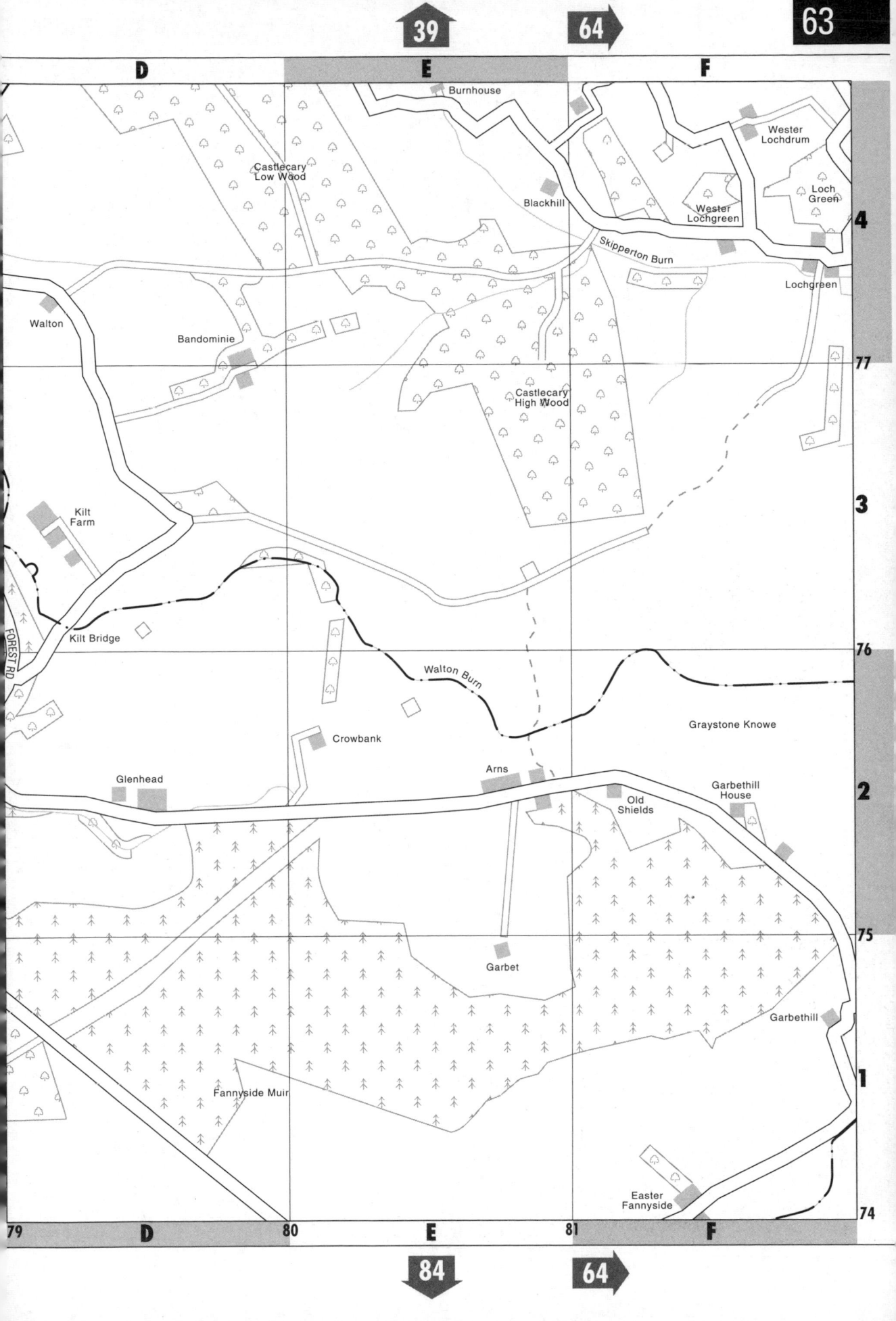

D
E
F

Burnhouse

Wester Lochdrum

Castlecary Low Wood

Blackhill

Wester Lochgreen

Loch Green

4

Skipperton Burn

Lochgreen

Walton

Bandominie

77

Castlecary High Wood

3

Kilt Farm

FOREST RD

Kilt Bridge

76

Walton Burn

Graystone Knowe

Crowbank

Glenhead

Arns

Garbethill House

Old Shields

2

75

Garbet

Garbethill

1

Fannyside Muir

Easter Fannyside

74

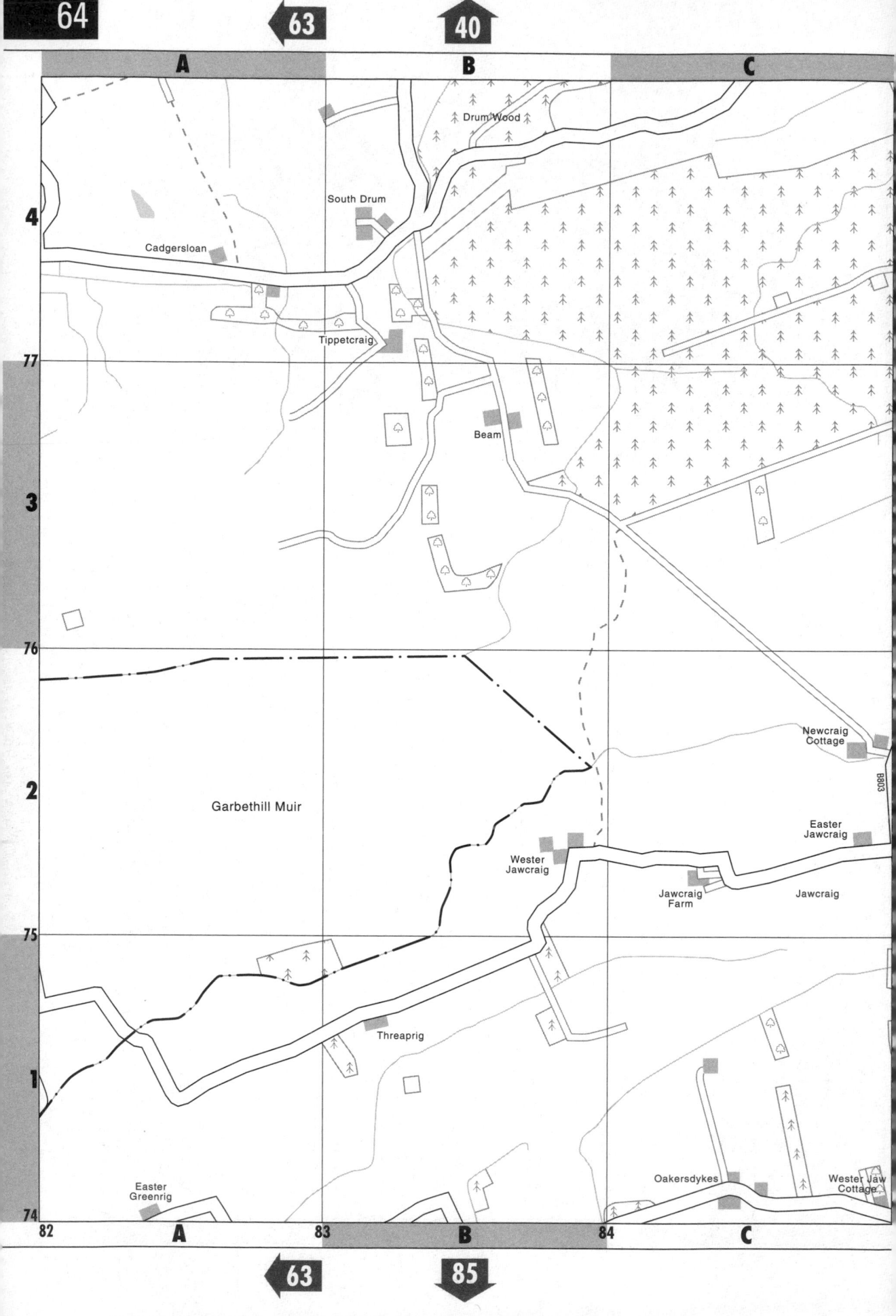

A
B
C

4

South Drum

Cadgersloan

Drum Wood

Tippetcraig

77

Beam

3

76

Newcraig
Cottage

B803

Garbethill Muir

2

Easter
Jawcraig

Wester
Jawcraig

Jawcraig
Farm

Jawcraig

75

Threaprig

1

Easter
Greenrig

Oakersdykes

Wester Jaw
Cottage

74

82   A   83   B   84   C

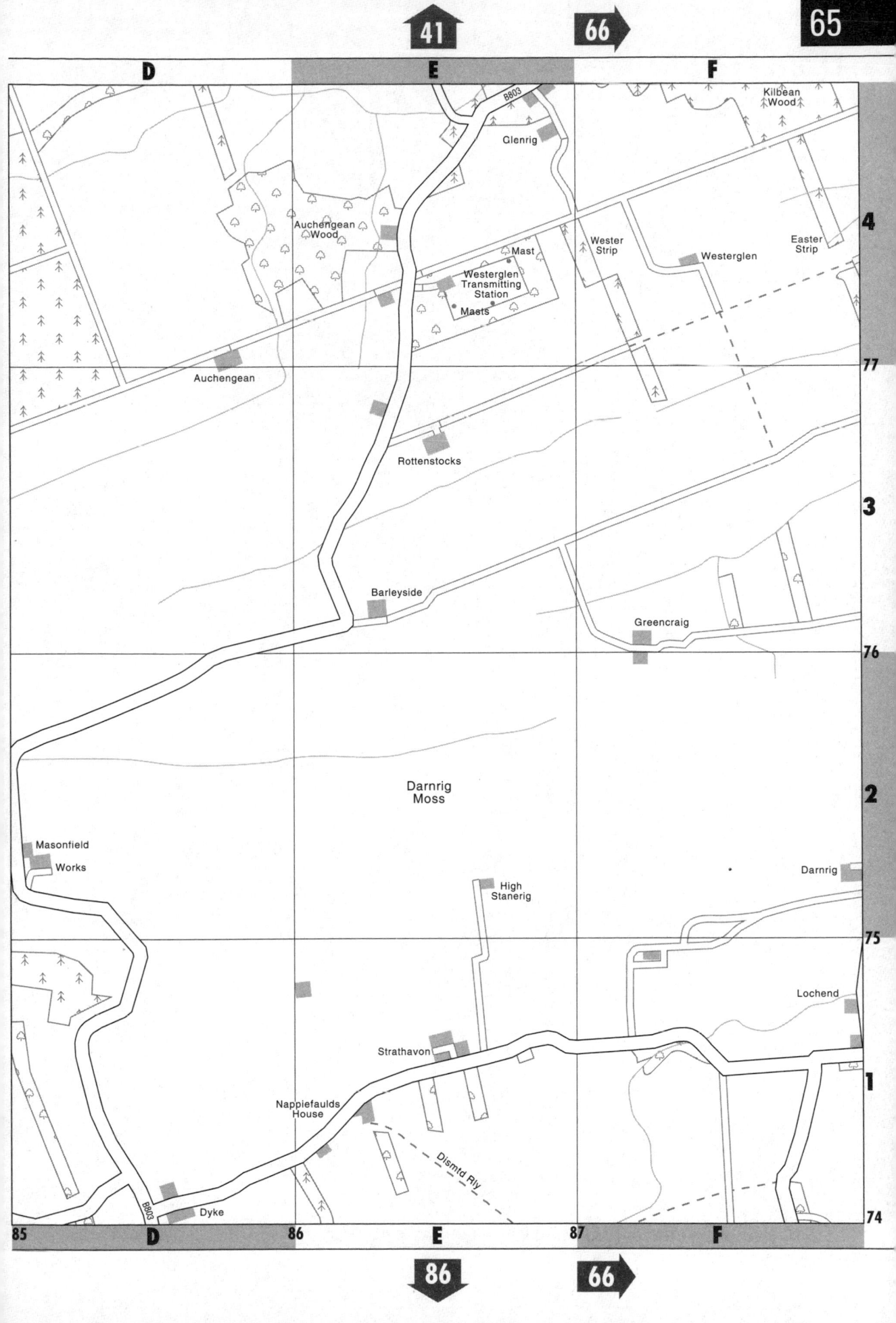

D E F

4

77

3

76

2

75

1

74

Kilbean
Wood

Glenrig

B803

Auchengean
Wood

Mast

Westerglen
Transmitting
Station

Masts

Wester
Strip

Westerglen

Easter
Strip

Auchengean

Rottenstocks

Barleyside

Greencraig

Darnrig
Moss

Masonfield

Works

High
Stanerig

Darnrig

Lochend

Strathavon

Nappiefaulds
House

Dismtd Rly

B803

Dyke

85 D 86 E 87 F 74

65 42

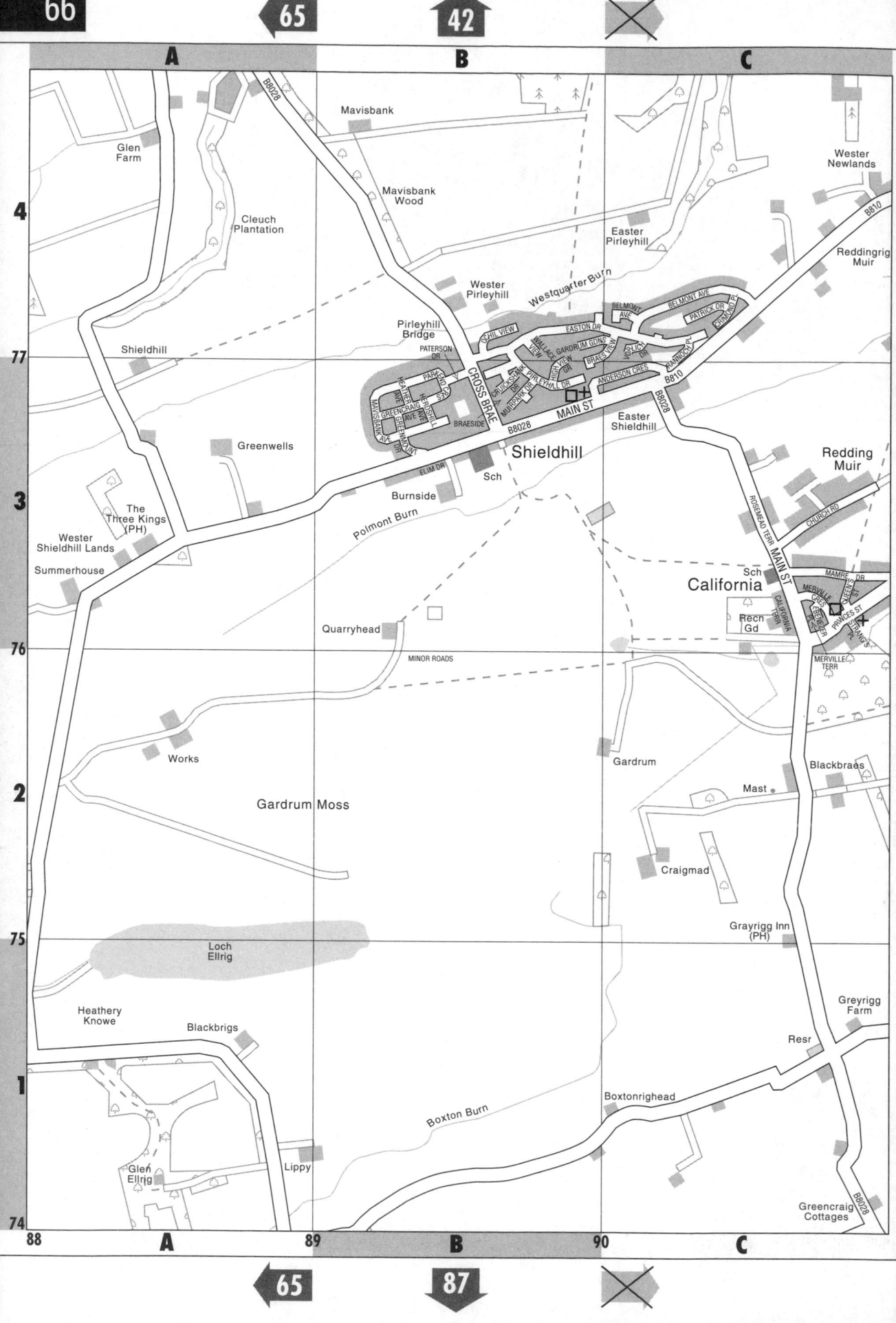

A
B
C

4

Glen Farm

Mavisbank

Wester Newlands

Cleuch Plantation

Mavisbank Wood

Easter Pirleyhill

B810

Reddingrig Muir

Westquarter Burn

Shieldhill

Wester Pirleyhill

Pirleyhill Bridge

PATERSON DR

SHIL VIEW

BELMONT AVE

BELMONT AVE

PATRICK DR

ORMOND PL

77

PARKHOL ST

EASTON DR

WALLACE VIEW

GARDRUM GDNS

BRAES VIEW

HOLICH DR

RANNOCH PL

HEATHER AVE

GREENCRAIG AVE

HERSHILL AVE

GREENMINT AVE

CROSS BRAE

BRUCKSFIELD

MURPARK DR

PIRLEYHA

HORSEVIEW GR

ANDERSON CRES

B810

MAVISBANK AVE

BRAESIDE

MAIN ST

B8028

Shieldhill

Easter Shieldhill

B8028

3

The Three Kings (PH)

Greenwells

ELIM DR

Burnside

Sch

Redding Muir

CHURCH RD

ROSEMEAD TERR

Wester Shieldhill Lands

Polmont Burn

Sch

MAIN ST

California

MAMRE DR

MELVILLE CRES

GREENACRE CRES

Summerhouse

CALIFORNIA TERR

Recn Gd

QUEEN'S CT

PRINCES ST

HASTINGS

Quarryhead

MINOR ROADS

MERVILLE TERR

76

Works

Gardrum

Blackbraes

Mast

2

Gardrum Moss

Craigmad

Grayrigg Inn (PH)

75

Loch Ellrig

Greyrigg Farm

Heathery Knowe

Blackbrigs

Resr

1

Boxtonrighead

Boxton Burn

Glen Ellrig

Lippy

Greencraig Cottages

B8028

88
A
89
B
90
C
74

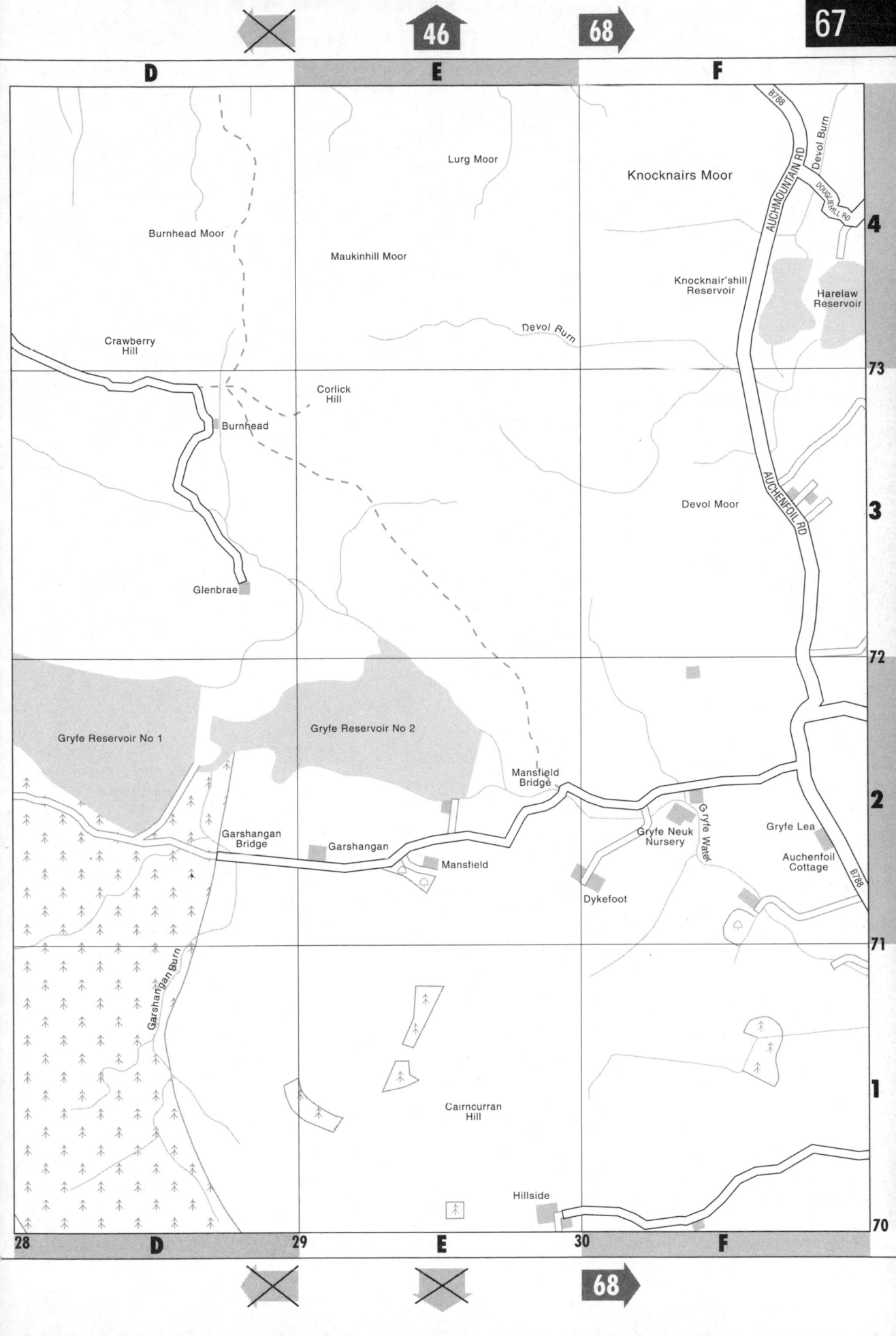

D
E
F

4

Burnhead Moor

Lurg Moor

Knocknairs Moor

B788

AUCHMOUNTAIN RD

Devol Burn

DOUGRALL RD

Maukinhill Moor

Knocknair'shill
Reservoir

Harelaw
Reservoir

73

Crawberry
Hill

Devol Burn

Corlick
Hill

Burnhead

Devol Moor

AUCHENFOIL RD

3

Glenbrae

72

Gryfe Reservoir No 1

Gryfe Reservoir No 2

Mansfield
Bridge

2

Garshangan
Bridge

Garshangan

Mansfield

Gryfe Neuk
Nursery

Gryfe Lea

Gryfe Water

Auchenfoil
Cottage

B788

Dykefoot

71

Garshangan Burn

1

Cairncurran
Hill

Hillside

70

28
D
29
E
30
F

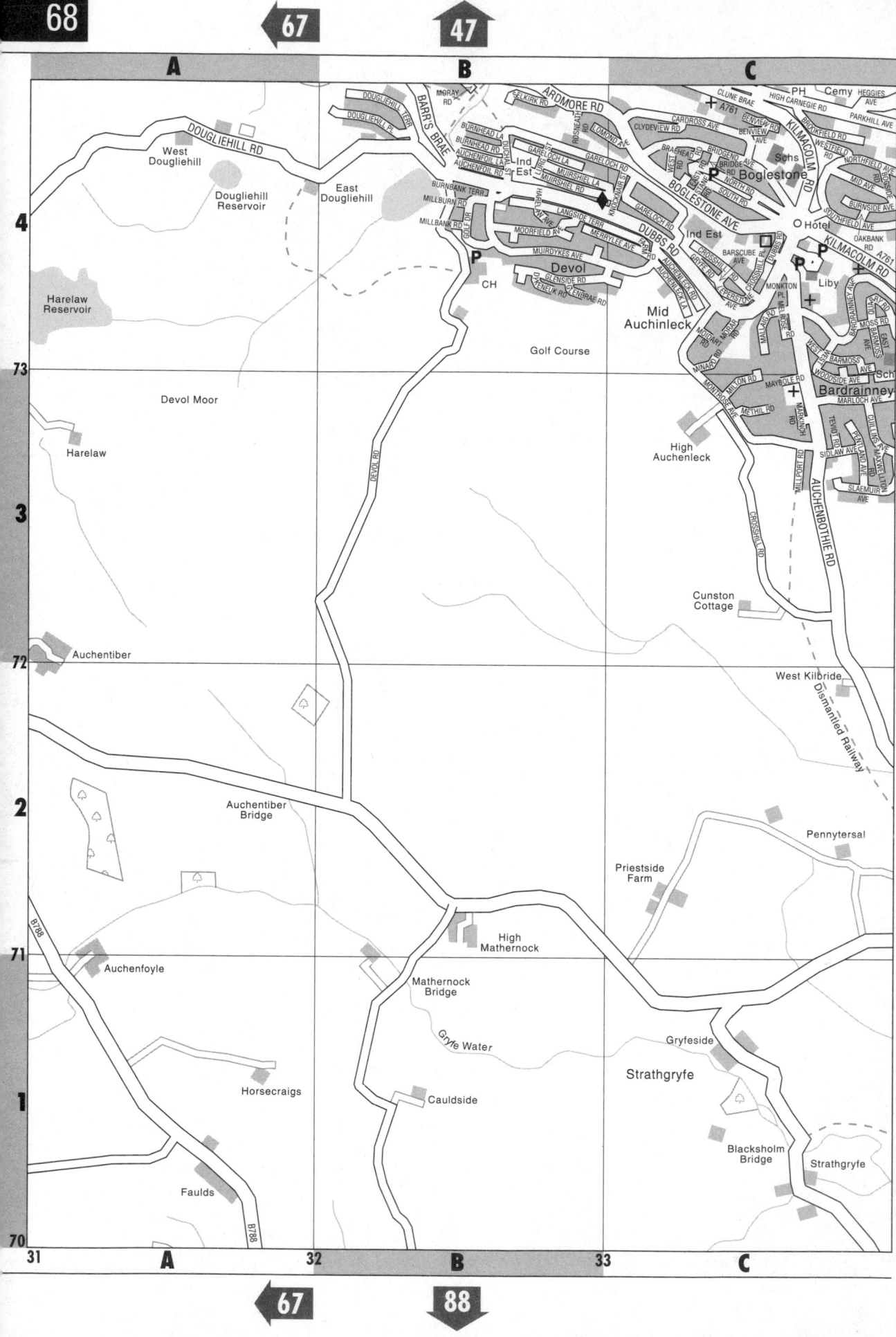

A
B
C

DOUGLIEHILL RD

West Dougliehill

Dougliehill Reservoir

East Dougliehill

MORAY RD

DOUGLIEHILL PL
DOUGLIEHILL TERR
BARR'S BRAE
ARDMORE RD
SELKIRK RD
DUCHAL RD
ROSNEATH RD
LOMOND AVE
CLUNE BRAE
HIGH CARNEGIE RD
PH
Cemy
HEGGIES AVE
A761
BENVIEW RD
CARDROSS AVE
BROOKFIELD RD
PARKHILL AVE
CLYDEVIEW RD
BENVIEW AVE
WESTFIELD RD
NORTHFIELD AVE
BRAEHEAD
BRIDGEND
MID AVE
BURNSIDE AVE
STURFIELD AVE
KILMACOLM RD

BURNHEAD LA
BURNHEAD RD
AUCHENFOIL LA
AUCHENFOIL RD
Ind Est
GARELOCH LA
GARELOCH RD
MUIRSHIEL LA
MUIRSHIEL RD
BURNBANK TERR
MILLBURN RD
MILLBANK RD
GOLF DR
HARELAW AVE
LANGSIDE TERR
MOORFIELD AV
MERRYLEE AVE
MUIRDYKES AVE
DUBBS RD
GARELOCH RD
GRYFE RD
CRYEBERSTONE
BARSCUBE AVE
CROSSHILL RD
LONGHEAD
AUCHENLECK LA
LOVIBES RD

P

Schs

BOGLESTONE AVE

Boglestone

P

Ind Est

O Hotel

OAKBANK RD

P

P

Liby

KILMACOLM RD
A761

Devol

P

CH

Mid Auchinleck

GLENSIDE RD
DYKENEUK RD
GLENBRAE RD

Golf Course

MOTEART RD
MINART RD
WALLACE RD
MONTROSE RD
MILTON RD
MAYBOLE RD
WOODSIDE AVE
METHIL RD
MARKINCH RD
MONKTON PL

High Auchenleck

MAYBOLE RD
MARLOCH AVE
Bardrainney
Sch

CROSSHILL RD

73

Devol Moor

DEVOL RD

Harelaw

Harelaw Reservoir

4

73

3

72

Auchentiber

Cunston Cottage

West Kilbride

Dismantled Railway

AUCHENBOTHIE RD

SIDLAW AVE
PENTLAND AVE
TEVIOT AVE
CULLINS AVE
MAXWELTON
PHILLIPS AVE
SLAEMUIR AVE

CROSSHILL RD

2

Auchentiber Bridge

Pennytersal

Priestside Farm

71

1

Auchenfoyle

High Mathernock

Mathernock Bridge

Gryfe Water

Gryfeside

Strathgryfe

Horsecraigs

Cauldside

Blacksholm Bridge

Strathgryfe

Faulds

B7788

B7788

70

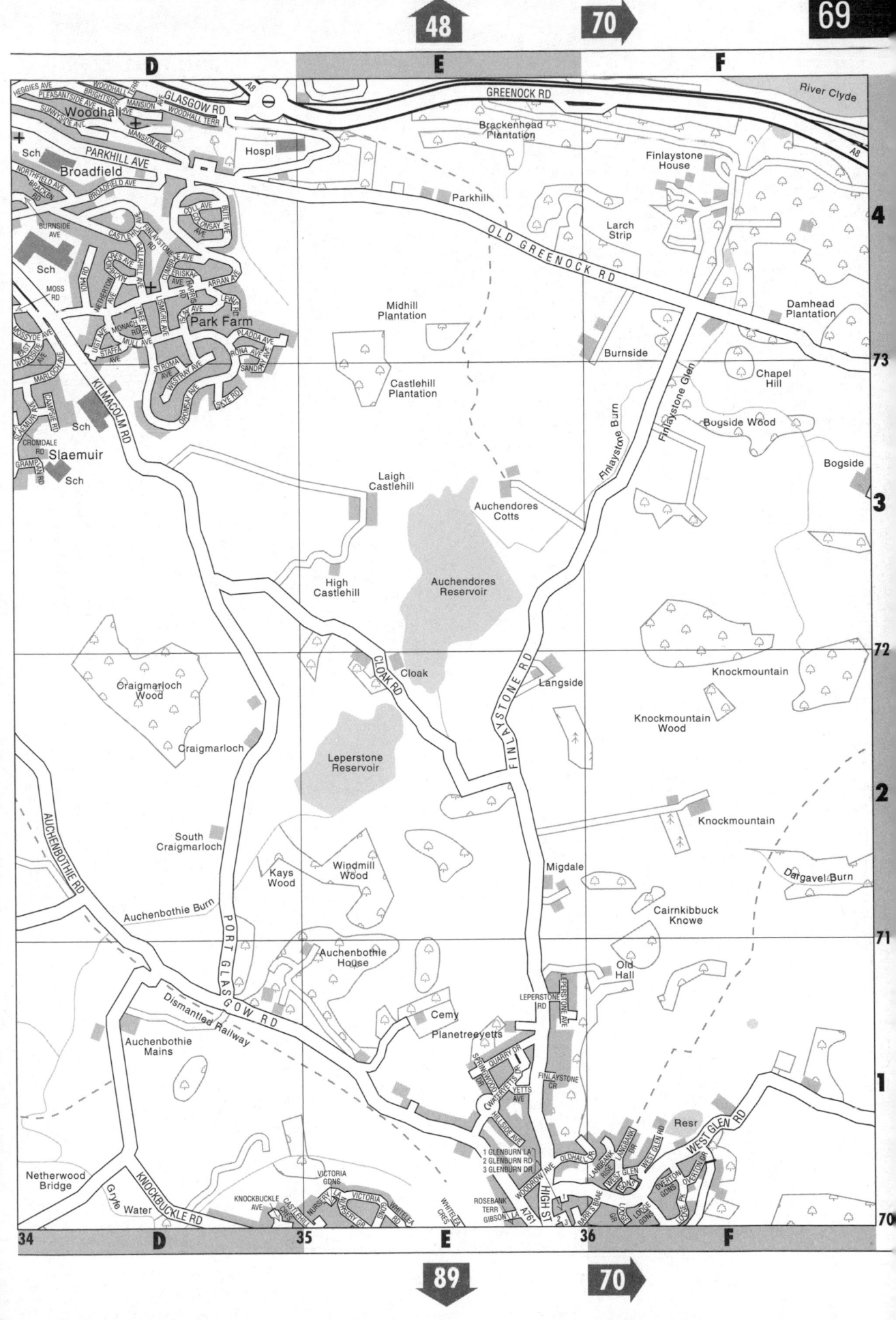

D E F

River Clyde

GLASGOW RD
Woodhall
Hospl
Sch
Broadfield
PARKHILL AVE
Sch
MOSS RD
Park Farm
Sch
Slaemuir
CROMDALE RD
Sch
KILMACOLM RD

GREENOCK RD

A8

Brackenhead Plantation

Finlaystone House

Parkhill

Larch Strip

OLD GREENOCK RD

Midhill Plantation

Burnside

Damhead Plantation

Chapel Hill

Castlehill Plantation

Boyside Wood

Laigh Castlehill

Auchendores Cotts

Bogside

Finlaystone Burn

Finlaystone Glen

High Castlehill

Auchendores Reservoir

Knockmountain

Craigmarloch Wood

CLOAK RD
Cloak

Langside

Knockmountain Wood

Craigmarloch

Leperstone Reservoir

FINLAYSTONE RD

Knockmountain

AUCHENBOTHIE RD

South Craigmarloch

Kays Wood

Windmill Wood

Migdale

Dargavel Burn

Cairnkibbuck Knowe

Auchenbothie Burn

PORT GLASGOW RD

Auchenbothie House

Old Hall

LEPERSTONE AVE

LEPERSTONE RD

Dismantled Railway

Cemy
Planetreeyetts

Auchenbothie Mains

FINLAYSTONE CR

QUARRY DR

YETTS AVE

HILLSIDE AVE

Resr

WEST GLEN RD

Netherwood Bridge

KNOCKBUCKLE RD

Gryfe Water

VICTORIA GDNS

KNOCKBUCKLE AVE

VICTORIA CRES

WHITELEA CRES

1 GLENBURN LA
2 GLENBURN RD
3 GLENBURN DR

ROSEBANK TERR
GIBSON LA

HIGH ST

A761

LODGE GDNS

OVERTON DR

4

73

3

72

2

71

1

70

34 D 35 E 36 F

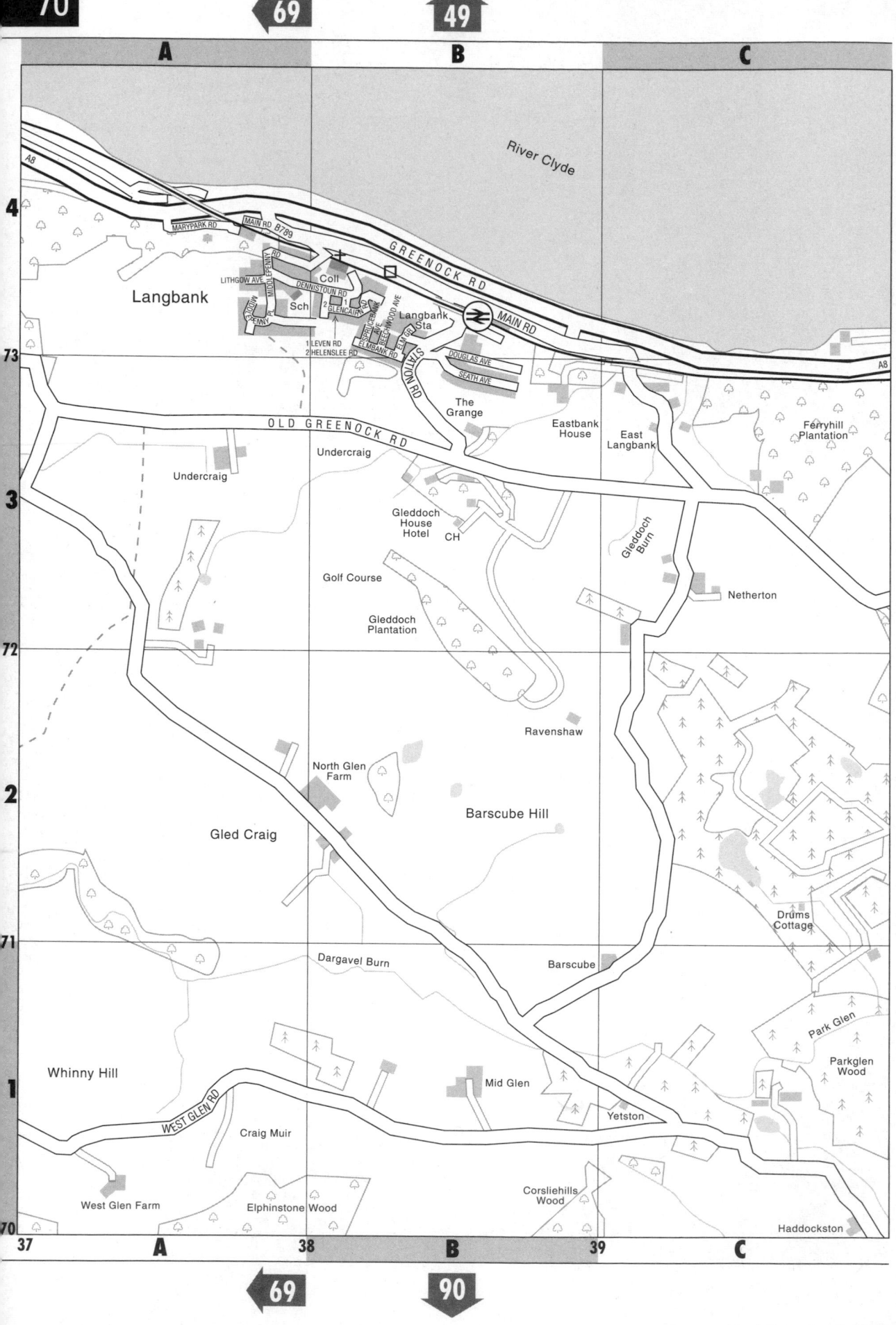

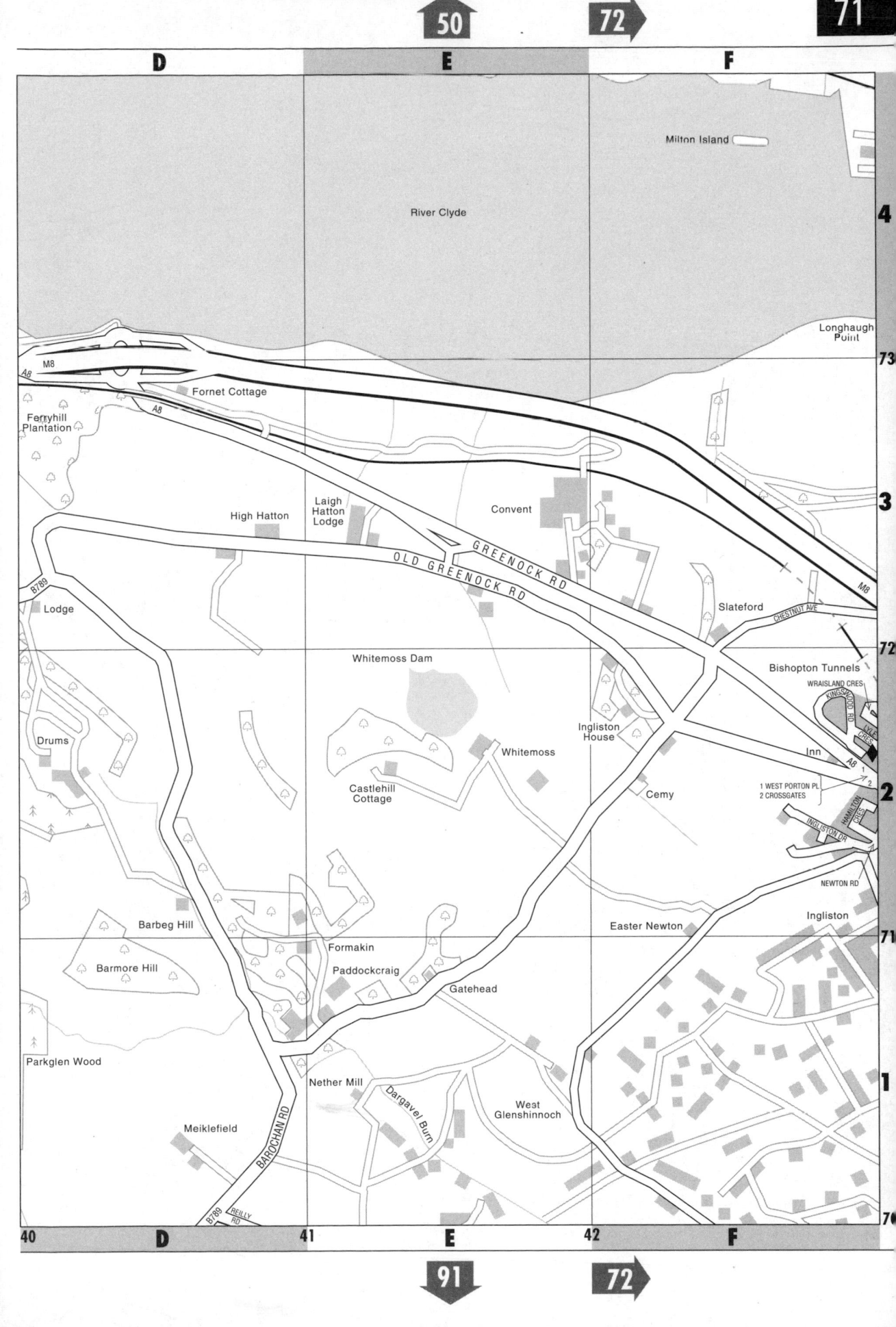

D E F

Milton Island

River Clyde

4

Longhaugh Point

M8
A8
Fornet Cottage

73

Ferryhill Plantation

A8

Laigh Hatton Lodge

Convent

High Hatton

Slateford

3

OLD GREENOCK RD

GREENOCK RD

M8

B789

Lodge

CHESTNUT AVE

72

Whitemoss Dam

Bishopton Tunnels

WRAISLAND CRES

Drums

KINGSWOOD RD

LYLE CRES

Whitemoss

Ingliston House

Inn

A8

Castlehill Cottage

1 WEST PORTON PL
2 CROSSGATES

Cemy

2

HAMILTON CRES

INGLISTON DR

Barbeg Hill

NEWTON RD

Easter Newton

Ingliston

71

Barmore Hill

Formakin

Paddockcraig

Gatehead

1

Parkglen Wood

Nether Mill

West Glenshinnoch

BAROCHAN RD

Dargavel Burn

Meiklefield

B789

REILLY RD

7

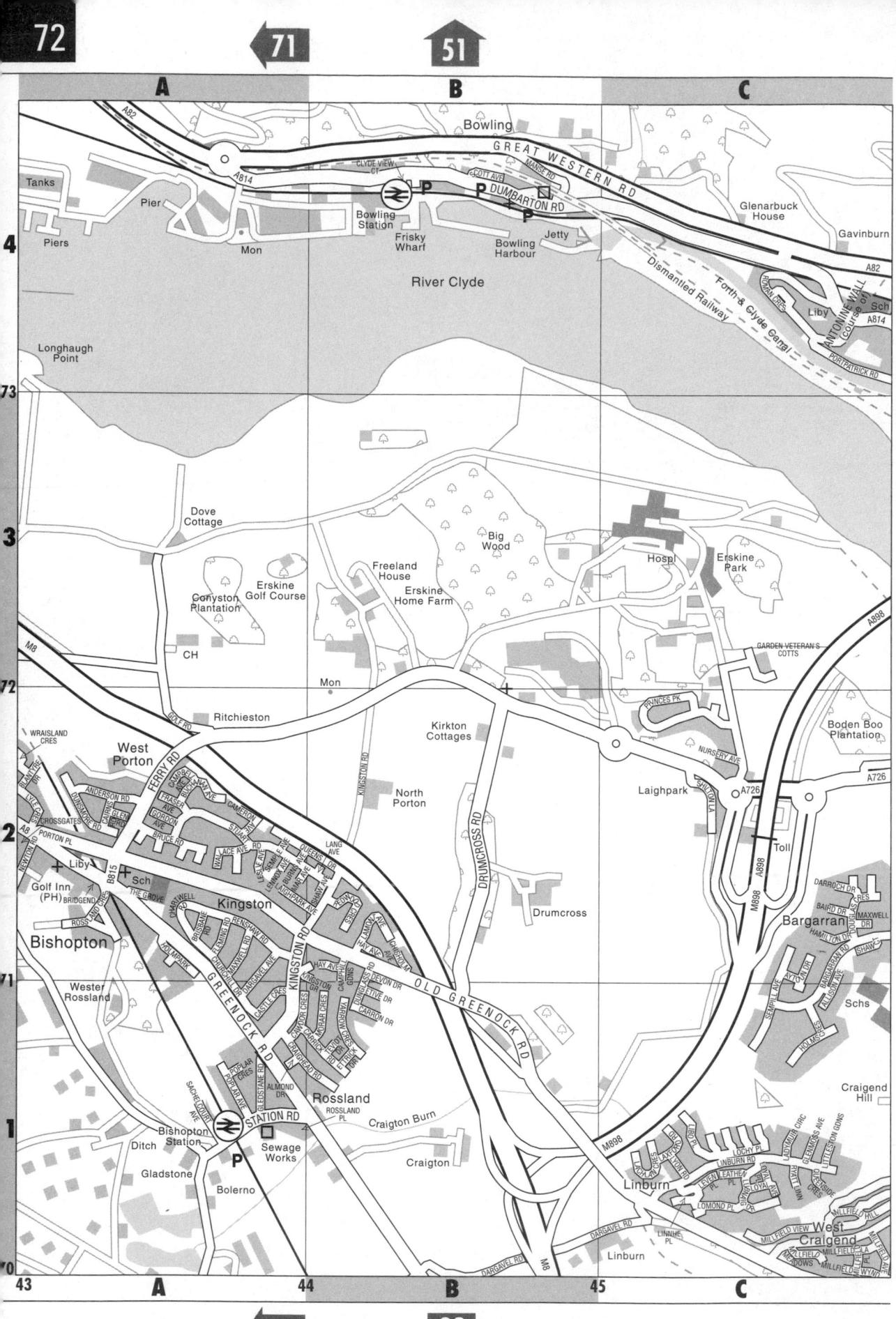

A B C

4

73

3

72

2

71

1

70

43 A 44 B 45 C

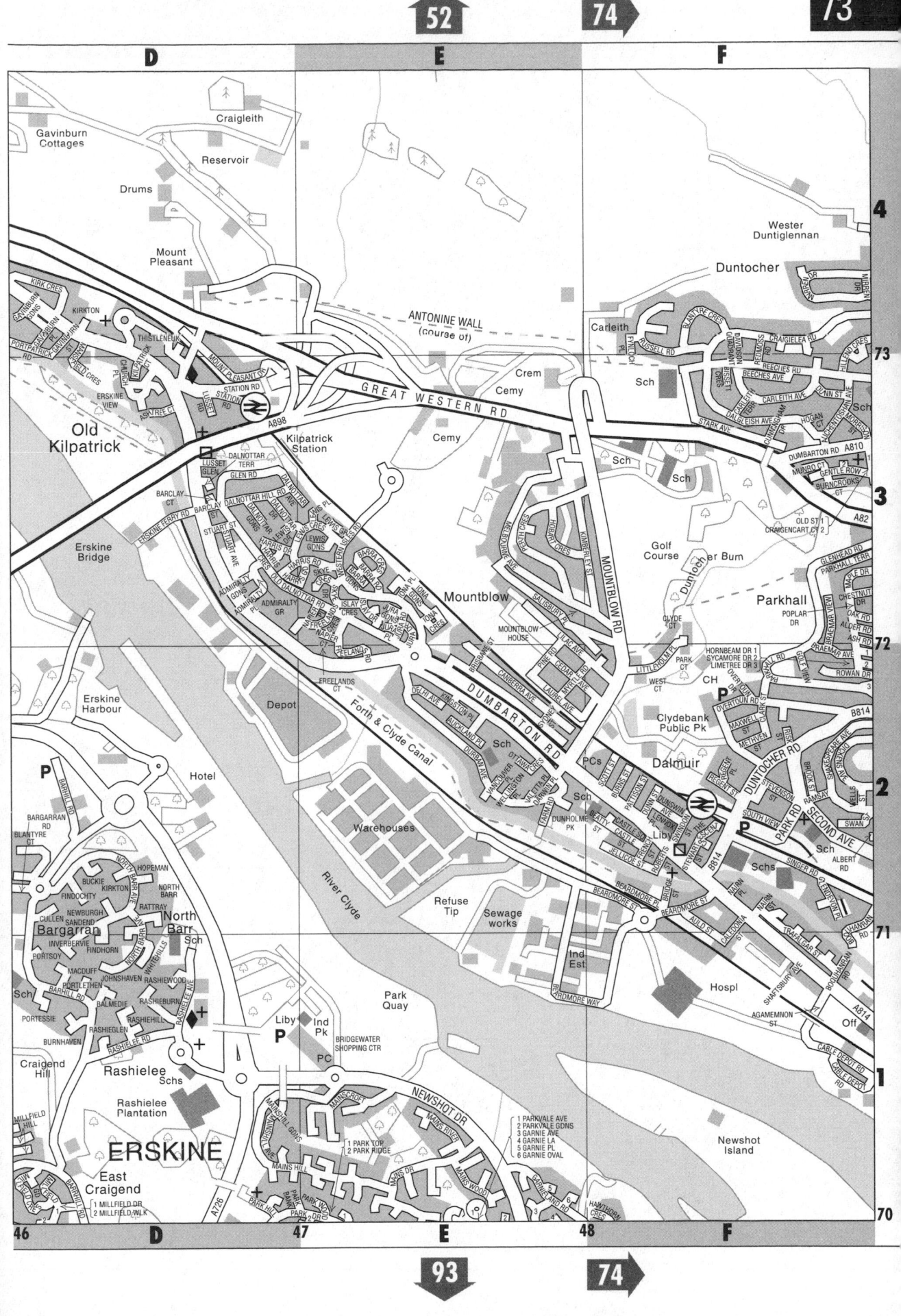

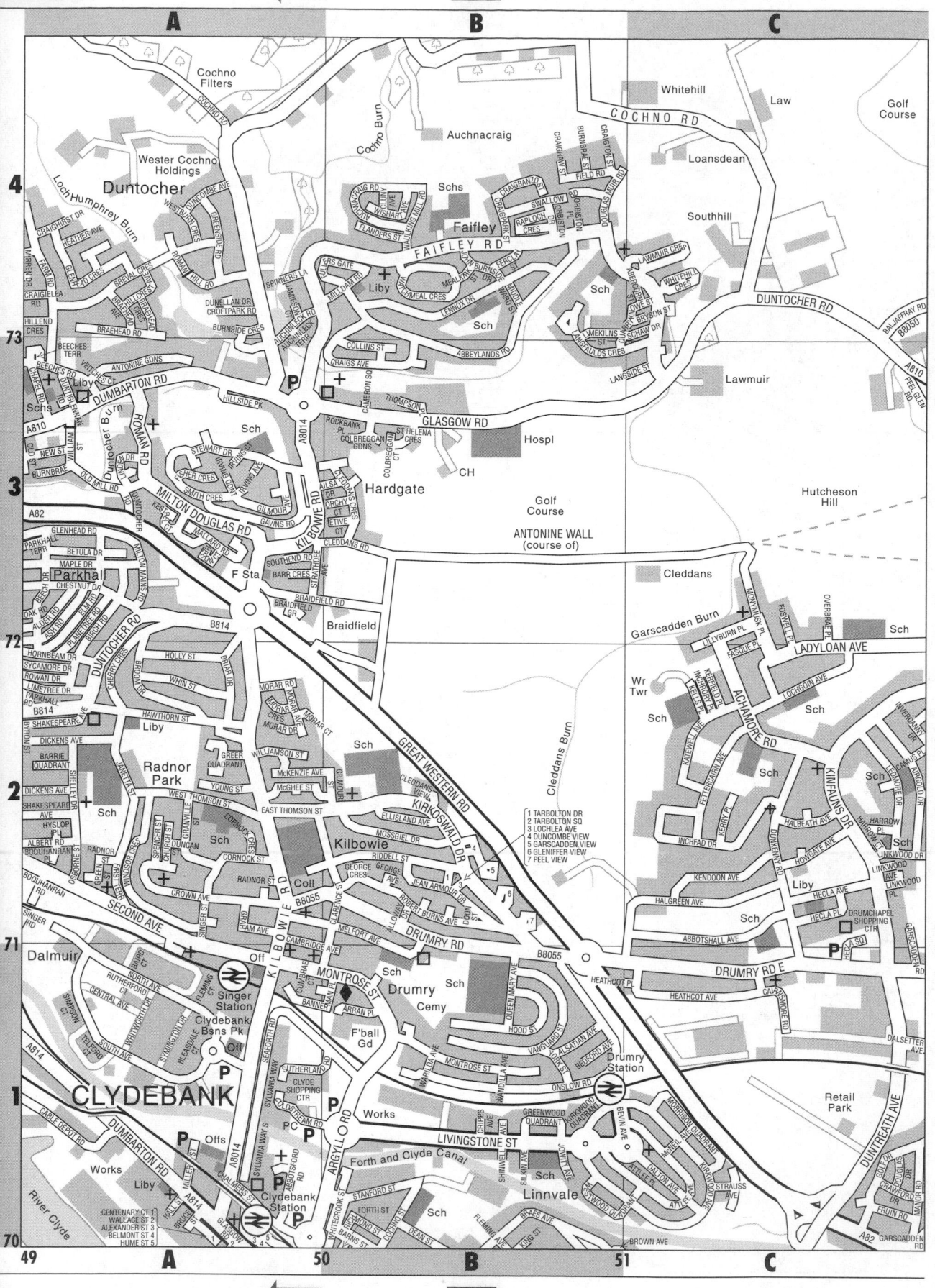

A   B   C

Cochno Filters

Whitehill

Law

Golf Course

COCHNO RD

Auchnacraig

Loansdean

4

Wester Cochno Holdings

Duntocher

Loch Humphrey Burn

Schs

Faifley

Southhill

FAIFLEY RD

DUNTOCHER RD

B8050

73

Sch

Lawmuir

A810

Hardgate

GLASGOW RD

Hospl

CH

3

A82

ANTONINE WALL
(course of)

Golf Course

Hutcheson Hill

MILTON DOUGLAS RD

F Sta

Cleddans

LADYLOAN AVE

72

Parkhall

Braidfield

Garscadden Burn

ACHAMORE RD

B814

Liby

Sch

Wr Twr

Sch

GREAT WESTERN RD

Radnor Park

Sch

Kilbowie

Sch

Sch

Liby

2

Sch

KINFAUNS DR

1 TARBOLTON DR
2 TARBOLTON SQ
3 LOCHLEA AVE
4 DUNCOMBE VIEW
5 GARSCADDEN VIEW
6 GLENIFFER VIEW
7 PEEL VIEW

Sch

Sch

DRUMRY RD E

Coll

DRUMRY RD

B8055

Liby

DRUMRY RD

HECLA PL

DRUMCHAPEL SHOPPING CTR

P

71

Dalmuir

SECOND AVE

Singer Station

MONTROSE ST

Drumry

Sch

Cemy

HEATHCOT PL

Drumry Station

HEATHCOT AVE

Singer Rd

Clydebank Bsns Pk

F'ball Gd

Retail Park

A814

P

1

CLYDEBANK

Clyde Shopping Ctr

PC

P

Works

LIVINGSTONE ST

A82

DUMBARTON RD

A8014

Offs

Clydebank Station

P

Forth and Clyde Canal

Linnvale

Sch

River Clyde

Works

Liby

Sch

70

CENTENARY CT 1
WALLACE ST 2
ALEXANDER ST 3
BELMONT ST 4
HUME ST 5

BROWN AVE

A82 GARSCADDEN

49   A   50   B   51   C

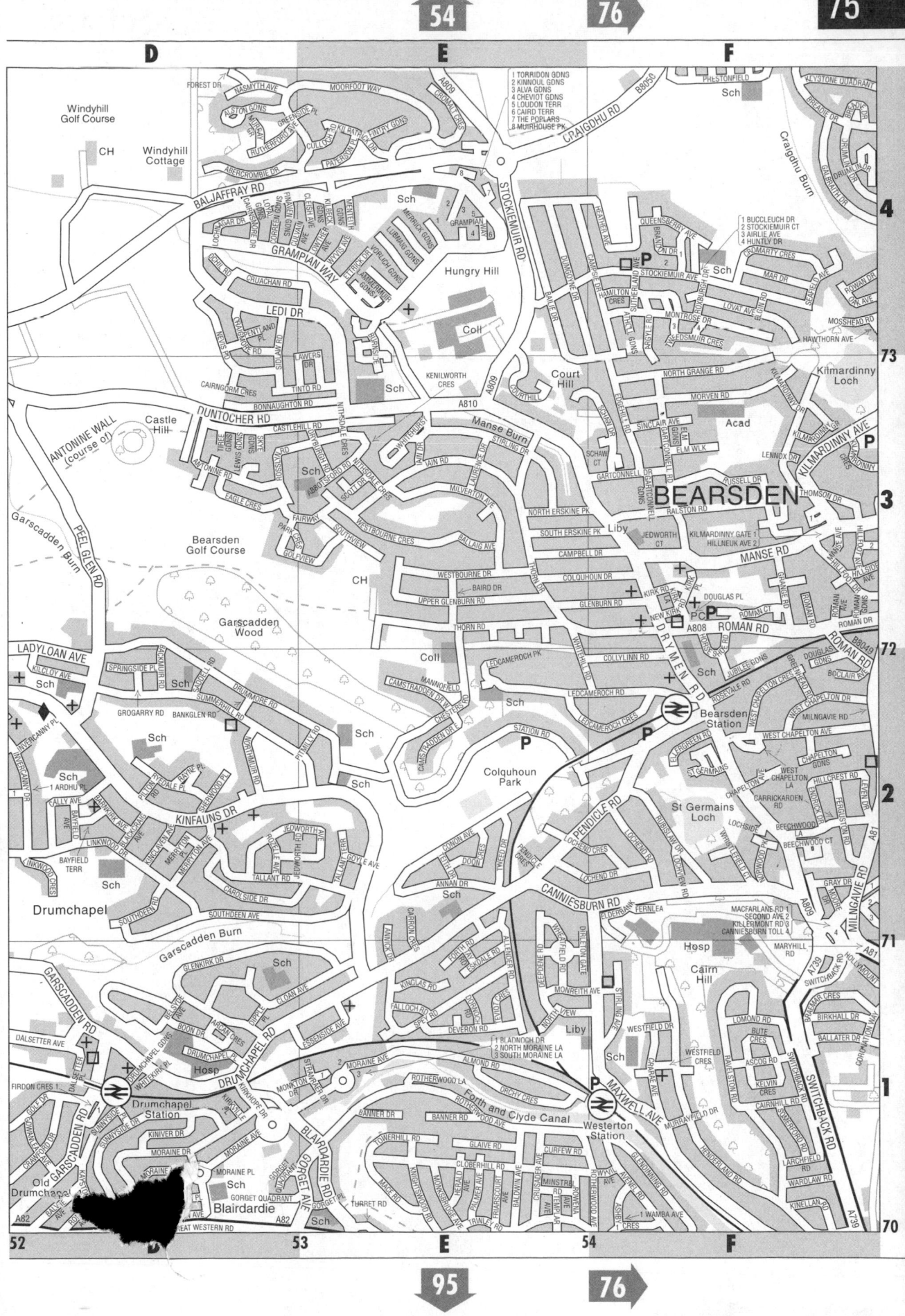

A   B   C

BREADIE DR
KEYSTONE AVE
KEYSTONE QUADRANT
BRAEFOOT AVE
B8030
KEYSTONE RD
QUEEN'S CT
MAIN ST
A807
GLASGOW RD
A81

The Jaw
Bardowie Mains
Bardowie Castle
Bardowie Loch

AUCHENCRUIVE
ALAN PL RISE
OSWALD WLK
BRIDGEGAIT
DUNMORE WLK
DUNMORE
EWING WLK
MURDOCH DR
COCHRANE CT

Dougalston Loch
Beech Wood

Langbank Holdings
DOWAN RD

4

SHAW RD
DRUMLIN DR
NETHERMAINS RD
ROWAN DR
HAZEL AVE
MOSSHEAD RD
OAK AVE
BEECH AVE
HAWTHORN AVE
GALBRAITH
BURNBRAE AVE

Craigdhu Burn
Sewage Works

Sports Centre

AUCHENHOWIE RD

Pow Burn

Langbank Farm

Hayhill

BALMORE RD
A807

73

KILMARDINNY AVE
CARSEVIEW DR
KILMARDINNY CRES
REID AVE
PARK CRES
DOUGLAS PARK CRES

Manse Burn

Allander Water

B8049
A879

3

MANSE RD
HILLNEUK AVE
Cemy
CH
1 HILLSIDE AVE
2 HILLFOOT DR
3 ROMAN DR

Boclair
Crow Hill

Douglas Park Golf Course

ANTONINE WALL (course of)

Temple of Boclair

Summerston Farm
BALMORE RD

Liby
Hillfoot Station
BIRCH VIEW
TYNDRUM RD
STATION RD
A81

BOCLAIR RD

West Millichen
East Millichen

72

B8049
BOCLAIR CRES
BUSHMAN DR
CLAITHA AVE
AVIEMORE GDNS
KINNAIRD CRES
DURNESS RD
GLENAIRD CRES
DUNKELD DR
INVERNAN DR
KENMORE GDNS
LEONS DR
BROOK AVE
MELTHVIN AVE
BIRNAM CRES

Off

MILLICHEN RD

Balmuildy Bridge
A879

2

Acad
GLENDARUEL AVE
GREENWOOD DR
BRORA DR
ETIVE AVE
EARN RD
AVON AVE
ORONSAY CRES
AFTON CRES
HANNOCK DR
KESSINGTON DR
BORLAND RD
POLLOCK RD
CAMERON DR
SPEIRS RD
Sch
KILLERMONT CT
ALBERT DR
ARSAIG DR
GLENFINNAN DR

Kessington

Templehill Wood

Dismantled Railway

71

HOLLYMOUNT
CLUNY DR
SECOND AVE
FIRST AVE
KILLERMONT RD
GARRY AVE
HUTCHISON DR
ALEXANDER RD
WOODVALE AVE

Killermont Golf Course

River Kelvin

Blackhill Farm

BLACKHILL RD

1

MACFARLANE RD
MAR WEST
ADRIAN RD
BALMORAL DR
BALLATER DR
BANCHORY CRES
MARYHILL RD
KILLERMONT AVE
KILLERMONT VIEW

Garscube Bridge

Acre

CH

CARNOCH ST 11
ARDESSIE ST 12
GEARY ST 13
CARBOST ST 14
LEWISTON DR 15
LEWISTON PL 16
FORRES ST 17

Cawder Cuilt

Summerston

MILOVAIG AVE
LETTERFEARN RD
DUICH GDNS
SHIEL BRIDGE
HAWTHORN
HOPETOUN
KERKIRK DR
BROUGHTON GDNS
INVERSHIEL RD
Sch

Acad

ACRE RD
ACRE DR
A81
Univ

DRUMLAKEN AVE 1
DRUMLAKEN CT 2
ROTHES PL 3
LITTLETON DR 4
DRUMLAKEN PL 5
ARROCHAR PATH 6
DRUMLAKEN PATH 7
MULLARDOCH ST 8
CRAIGBO DR 9
CRAIGBO AVE 10

CALDERCUILT RD
TORRIN RD
MILO ST
VAIG ST
TORGYLE ST
ELPHIN ST
HARRIS RD
STONEFIELD
ARROCHAR ST
CHATON
LEWISTON RD
Sch
GLENBERVIE PL
LITTLETN ST
ROTHES DR

FOXHILLS PL
HOYLAKE
DOUGLASTON RD
HOLMSWELL RD
LYTHAM
PENCAITLAND PL
NEWSTEAD GDNS
LYNNE DR
TOLSTA ST
CALLAN DR
ALDRICH DR
Cemy

70

55   A   56   B   57   C

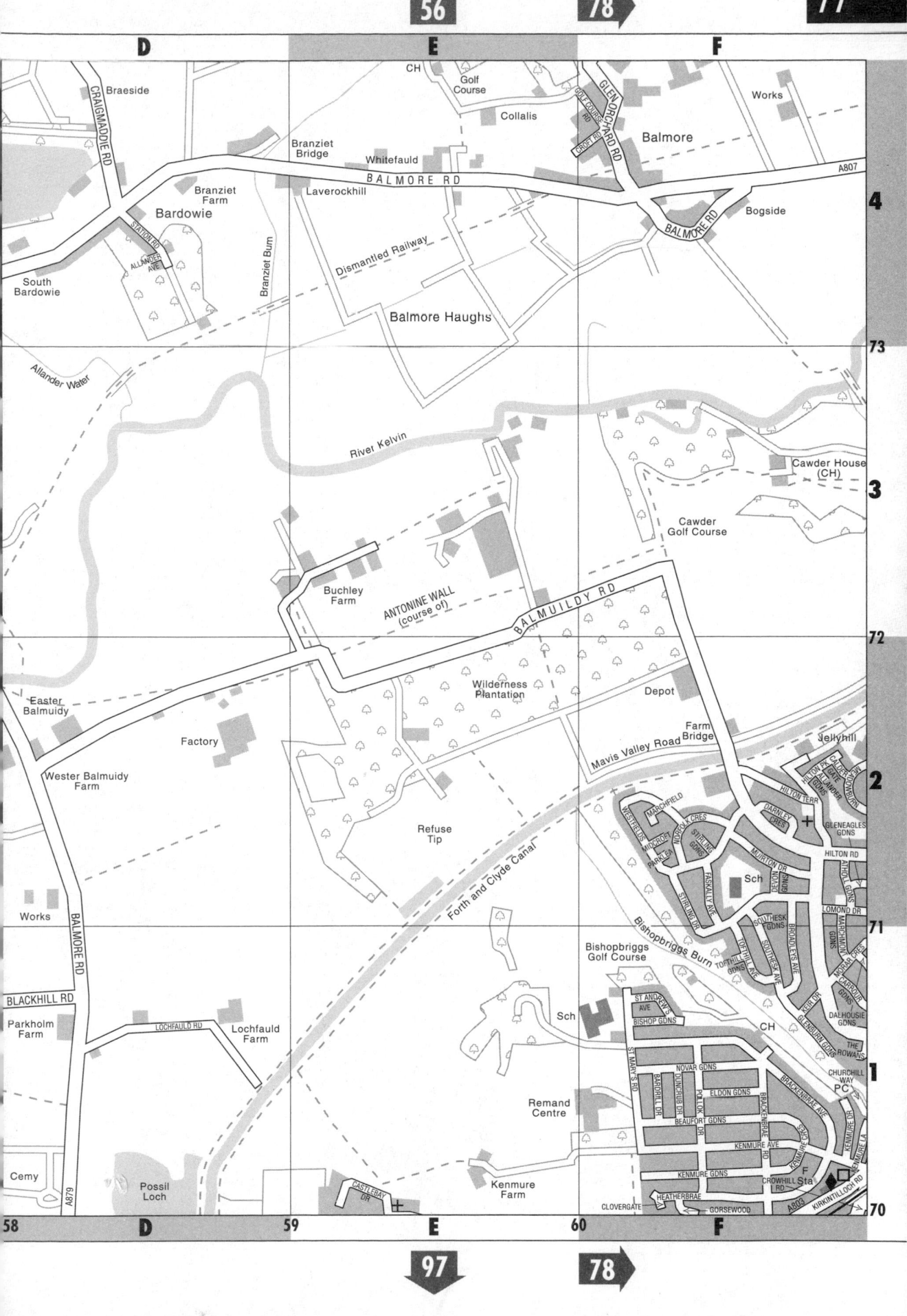

D   E   F

CH
Golf Course
Collalis
Works
Balmore
Braeside
CRAIGMADDIE RD
Branziet Bridge
Whitefauld
GOLF COURSE RD
GLEN ORCHARD RD
CROFT RD
BALMORE RD
A807
Branziet Farm
Laverockhill
Bardowie
BALMORE RD
Bogside
4
STATION RD
ALLANDER AVE
Branziet Burn
Dismantled Railway
South Bardowie
Balmore Haughs
73

Allander Water
River Kelvin
Cawder House (CH)
3
Cawder Golf Course

Buchley Farm
ANTONINE WALL (course of)
BALMUILDY RD
72

Easter Balmuidy
Wilderness Plantation
Depot
Farm Bridge
Jellyhill
HILTON PK GATE
GLANDER
RD
Factory
Mavis Valley Road
HILTON TERR
2
Wester Balmuidy Farm
MARCHFIELD
NORFOLK CRES
BARNLEY CRES
GLENEAGLES GDNS
WESTFIELD
MIDCROFT
PARKLEA
STIRLING
MORTON DR
MORVEN
DEVON
HILTON RD
Sch
DALSETTER
LOMOND DR
Works
FASKALLY AVE
SOUTHESK GDNS
MATCHMAN
Refuse Tip
Forth and Clyde Canal
STIRLING RD
BROADLEAS AVE
SOUTHESK AVE
CARNOCK GDNS
KEIR AV
MOT CAIRN
71
BALMORE RD
Bishopbriggs Golf Course
Bishopbriggs Burn
TOPHILL GDNS
TOPHILL LAV
GLENBURN GDNS
DALHOUSIE GDNS
THE ROWANS
BLACKHILL RD
Sch
CH
Parkholm Farm
LOCHFAULD RD
Lochfauld Farm
BISHOP GDNS
ST ANDREW'S AVE
CHURCHILL WAY
PC
1
NOVAR GDNS
BARDRILL DR
DUNCHUB DR
ELDON GDNS
BRACKENBRAE RD
BRACKENBRAE AVE
KENMURE DR
ST MARY'S RD
PIKETON
BEAUFORT GDNS
Cemy
Possil Loch
Remand Centre
Kenmure Farm
KENMURE AVE
KENMURE RD
Crowhill Sta
A879
CASTLEBAY DR
KENMURE GDNS
CROWHILL RD
KIRKINTILLOCH RD
A803
70
CLOVERGATE
HEATHERBRAE
GORSEWOOD

A **B** **C**

Dismtd Rly
TOWER RD
JOHN McEWAN WAY
CRAIGMADDIE GDNS
SMEATON AVE
DUNDAS AVE
FORTH RD
ALLANDER DR
CRAIGBARNET AVE
CRAIGMARLOCH AVE
MAIN ST
VIOLA PL
ROSEHILL RD
KELVIN VIEW
FIRBANK AVE
QUEEN'S WAY
B822
PH
Meadowbank House
River Kelvin
Sandy Knowes
Sewage Wks

A807 BALMORE RD
Sewage Wks
Torrance Bridge
KELVINBRIDGE ROUNDABOUT
Bogton

4

TORRANCE RD
Easter Cadder
The Stables (PH)
A803

73
Hungryside Bridge
A807
ANTONINE WALL (course of)
P
Glasgow Bridge
Meiklehill Farm

Keir Golf Course
Forth & Clyde Canal

Bishopbriggs Burn

3
Cawder Golf Course
CADDER RD
Cadder
Wks
Cemy
HM Prison
CROSSHILL RD
Bearhill Farm
Park Burn

HIGH ROW
CADDER WYND
CADDER RD
KIRKINTILLOCH RD
B819
Low Moss Ind Est
Low Moss Plantation
Wester Boghead Holdings

72
KIRKSTALL GDNS
KIRKRIGGS AVE
CADDER CT
INVERARAY DR
LANCASTER CRES
WELLINGTON RD
RICHMOND DR
ELAMIS GDNS
Lochgrog
B819

2
BONAWE PL
CANDER RIGGS
MEADOWBURN
CROFTHILL
BARNARD
GDNS
RANSBROOKE
CUNNIGAR DR
MAXTON
LINDSAY
CAIRNGORM
CROFTBANK
LYLE
LINDALE
PINEGRAIL
VALLAFIELD
DALKEITH RD
LIV KEITH RD
FRIAR AVE
CLOAN CRES
Sch
ASHTED
CRAYFIELD
Works
WESTERHILL RD
Cadder Yard

F Sta
HILTON RD
HILTON CT
High Moss Plantation
BISHOPBRIGGS
Depot
Rushyhill

GLENEAGLES GDNS
GLENGARRY
LOMOND DR
COWDEN DR
P
PARK AVE
BURRA GDNS
RONALDSAY DR
COLLA
MONTYMUSK GDNS

71
MORAR CRES
MELVILLE
KELVIN DR
STANLEY DR
BIRNAM GDNS
BIRNAM AVE
BIRKHILL AVE
BIRKHILL GDNS
TWEEDSMUIR
MOORFOOT
DORNOCH PL
LORNE
CROMARTY AVE
BEAULY PL
PITMEDDEN RD

VALLOUISE
CARROUR GDNS
BALMUILDY RD
HILLSIDE DR
PARK RD
MYBIE
MAILING AVE
ALLSOP
KENMORE RD
WESTER CLEDDENS RD
Sch
KNITTESACK GDNS
GRAING
Westerhill
B812
ROBROYSTON RD

1
THE ROWANS
Liby
BOCLAIR AVE
BOCLAIR CRES
CLENDENS CT
SOUTH CROSSHILL RD
Sch
CARRON CRES
RANNOCH AVE
KARRIEMUIR RD
CLAIR RD
CARESTON PL
CORTACHY PL
NEWTYLE PL
DUNNICHEN GDNS

NESS GDNS 1
MAREE GDNS 2
LOCHY GDNS 3
RANNOCH GDNS 4

CHURCHILL WAY
KENMURE LA
P
A803
THE LEYS
SPRINGFIELD RD
EMERSON RD
HANOVER GDNS
KATRINE AVE
LINNHE AVE
RIVEN AVE
RANNOCH GDNS
CARNOUSTIE CRES
MURRIN AVE
CARRICK RD
FALKLAND CRES
CATES GDNS
AUCHINAIRN RD
B812

1 YOUNGER QUADRANT
2 ARNOLD AVE
3 EMERSON RD W
4 CALLIEBURN RD
5 WOODFIELD AVE
6 ELM BANK

ETIVE CRES
WOODHILL RD
HAZEL AVE
ST CYRUS RD
CRINAN PL
FETTERCAIRN GDNS
MORVEN RD
FINTRY CRES
INTO RD

70

61 **A** 62 **B** 63 **C**

A   B   C

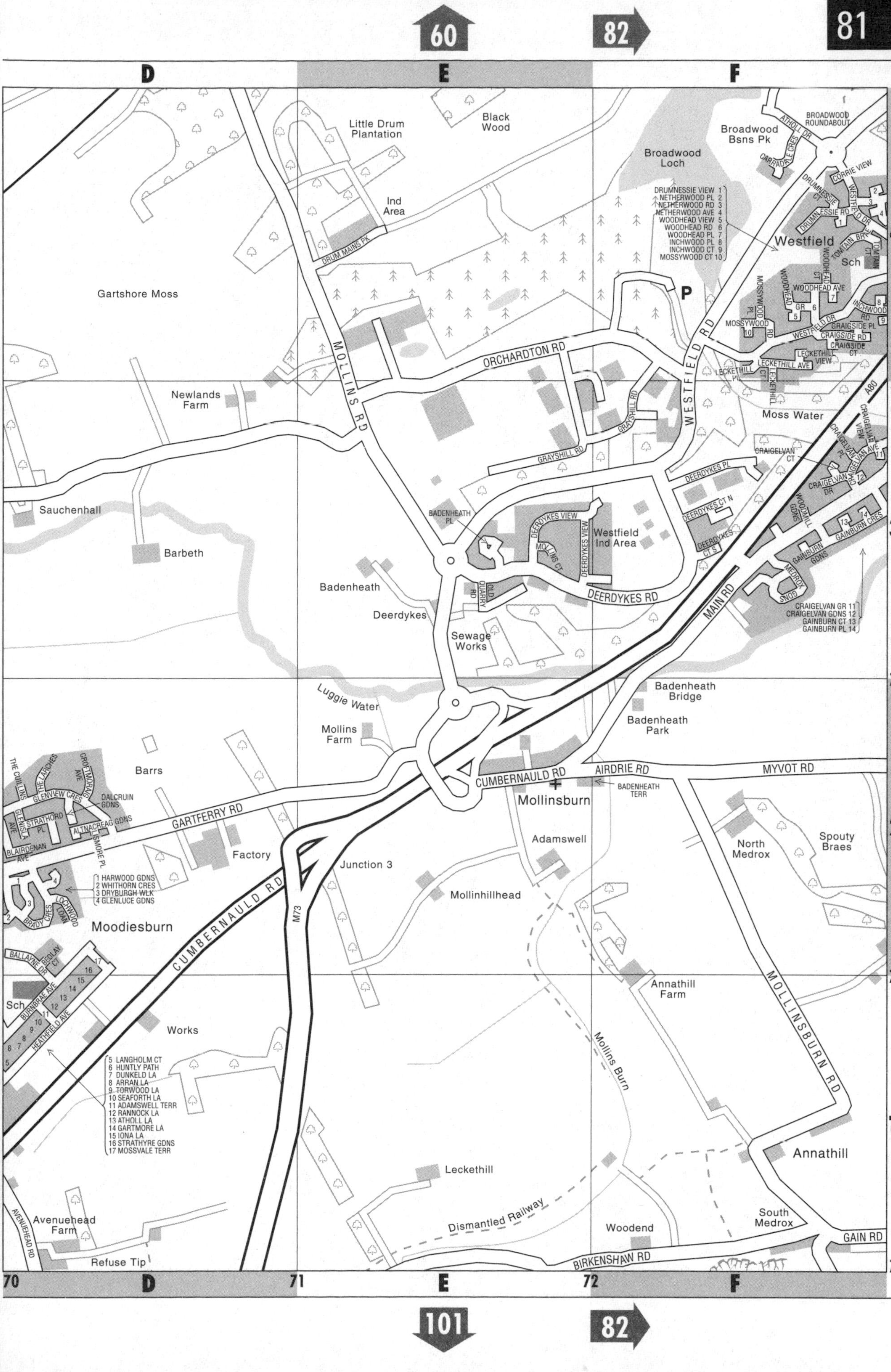

60
82

D | E | F

Little Drum Plantation

Black Wood

Ind Area

Broadwood Bsns Pk

BROADWOOD ROUNDABOUT

Broadwood Loch

ATHOLL DR

CARRADALE CRES

CORRIE VIEW

DRUMNESSIE VIEW 1
NETHERWOOD PL 2
NETHERWOOD RD 3
NETHERWOOD VIEW 4
WOODHEAD VIEW 5
WOODHEAD RD 6
WOODHEAD PL 7
INCHWOOD PL 8
INCHWOOD CT 9
MOSSYWOOD CT 10

DRUMNESSIE CRES

WESTFIELD RD

DRUMNESSIE RD

TOM MAIN BRAE

TOWN HEAD

Westfield

Sch

4

Gartshore Moss

DRUM MAINS PK

MOLLINS RD

P

ORCHARDTON RD

MOSSYWOOD PL

WOODHEAD DR

WESTFIELD DR

WOODHEAD AVE

GR

CRAIGSIDE PL

INCHWOOD RD

MOSSYWOOD

CRAIGSIDE RD

CRAIGSIDE CT

Newlands Farm

GRAYSHILL RD

WESTFIELD RD

LECKETHILL PL

LECKETHILL AVE

LECKETHILL VIEW

LECKETHILL

73

GRAYSHILL RD

Moss Water

A80

Sauchenhall

DEERDYKES PL

CRAIGELVAN VIEW

CRAIGELVAN CT

CRAIGELVAN DR

Barbeth

BADENHEATH PL

DEERDYKES VIEW

Westfield Ind Area

DEERDYKES CT N

CRAIGELVAN GDNS

WOODMILL GDNS

CRAIGELVAN DR

GAINBURN CRES

73 74

3

Badenheath

MOLLINS CT

DEERDYKES CT S

MEDROX

GAINBURN GDNS

Deerdykes

OLD QUARRY RD

DEERDYKES RD

MAIN RD

CRAIGELVAN GR 11
CRAIGELVAN GDNS 12
GAINBURN CT 13
GAINBURN PL 14

Sewage Works

Luggie Water

72

Mollins Farm

Badenheath Bridge

Badenheath Park

Barrs

THE CHILINS

THE LASTORES

CROFTMARTAG AVE

GLENVIEW CRES

DALCRUIN GDNS

STRATHORD PL

ALTNACREAG GDNS

ELSMORE PL

BLAIRDENAN AVE

LOCHWOOD

CUMBERNAULD RD

AIRDRIE RD

MYVOT RD

BADENHEATH TERR

North Medrox

Spouty Braes

2

1 HARWOOD GDNS
2 WHITHORN CRES
3 DRYBURGH WLK
4 GLENLUCE GDNS

GARTFERRY RD

Factory

Junction 3

Mollinsburn

Adamswell

Mollinhillhead

MOLLINSBURN RD

Moodiesburn

CUMBERNAULD RD

M73

BALLANTAY

BIGLAW

CT

BUCHBRAE AVE

HEATHFIELD AVE

16
17
15
14
13 12 11 10 9
8 7
6

Sch

71

Annathill Farm

Works

5 LANGHOLM CT
6 HUNTLY PATH
7 DUNKELD LA
8 ARRAN LA
9 TORWOOD LA
10 SEAFORTH LA
11 ADAMSWELL TERR
12 RANNOCK LA
13 ATHOLL LA
14 GARTMORE LA
15 IONA LA
16 STRATHYRE GDNS
17 MOSSVALE TERR

Mollins Burn

Annathill

1

Leckethill

Woodend

South Medrox

GAIN RD

Avenuehead Farm

AVENUEHEAD RD

Refuse Tip

Dismantled Railway

BIRKENSHAW RD

70

101
82

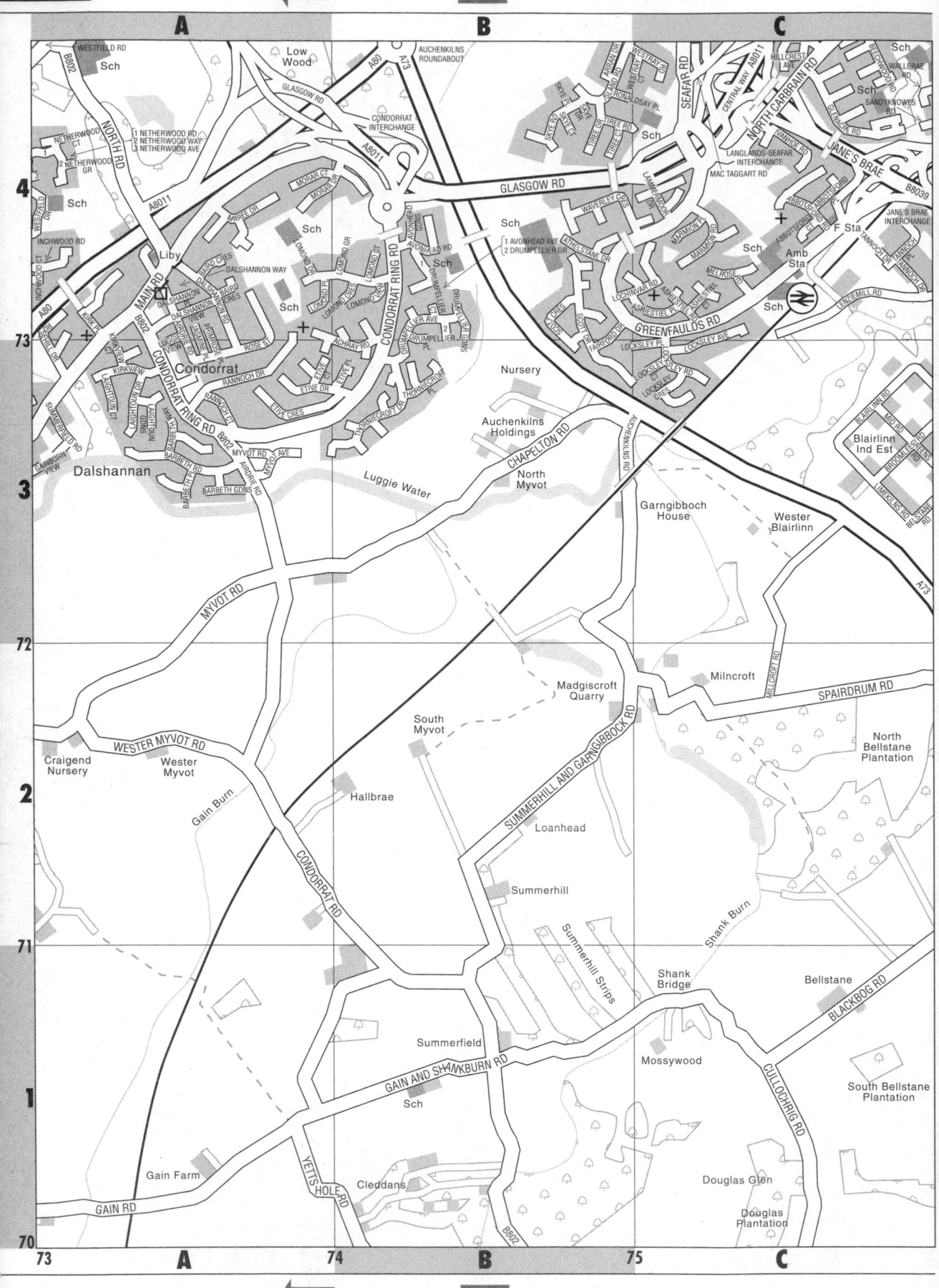

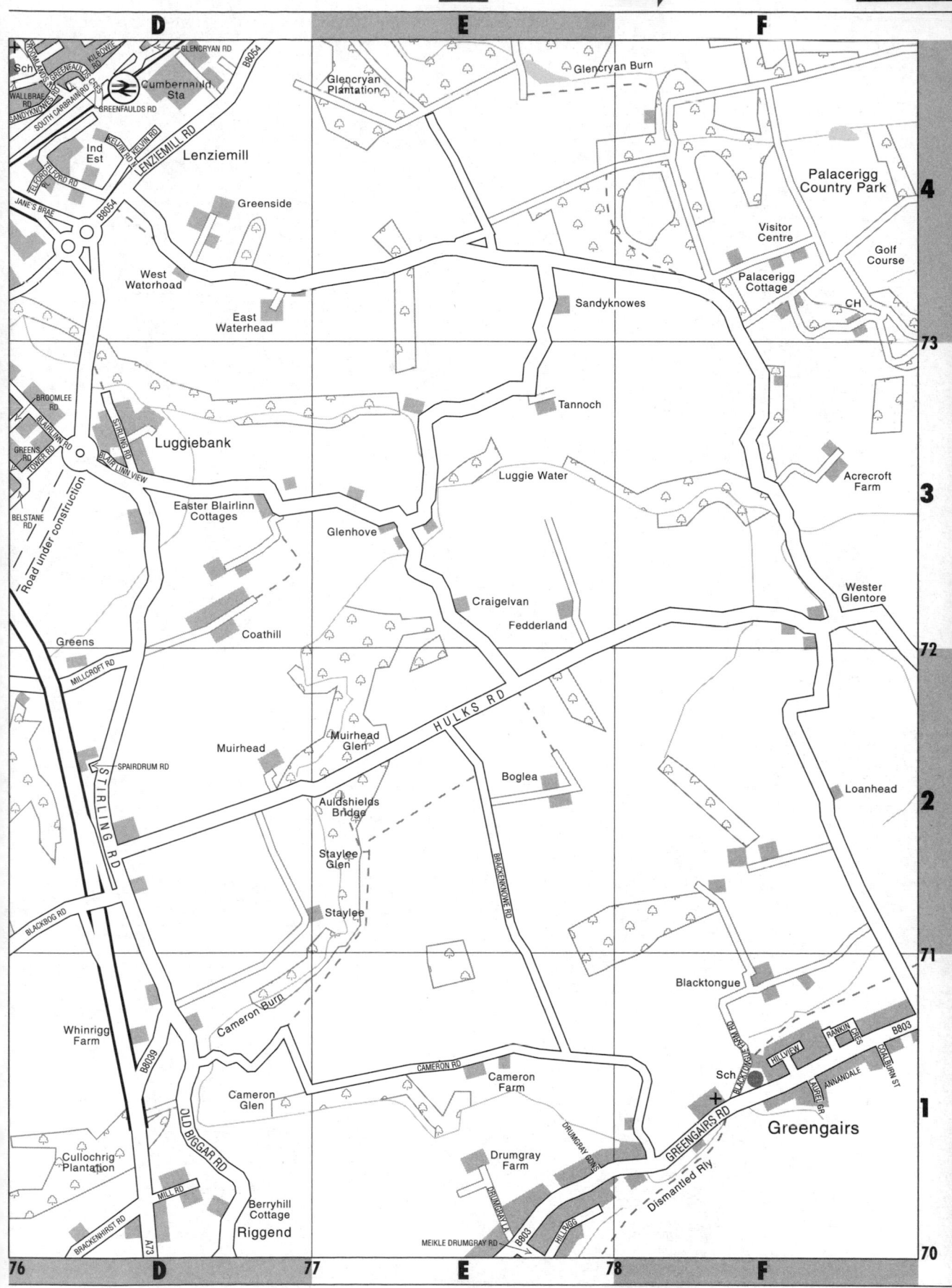

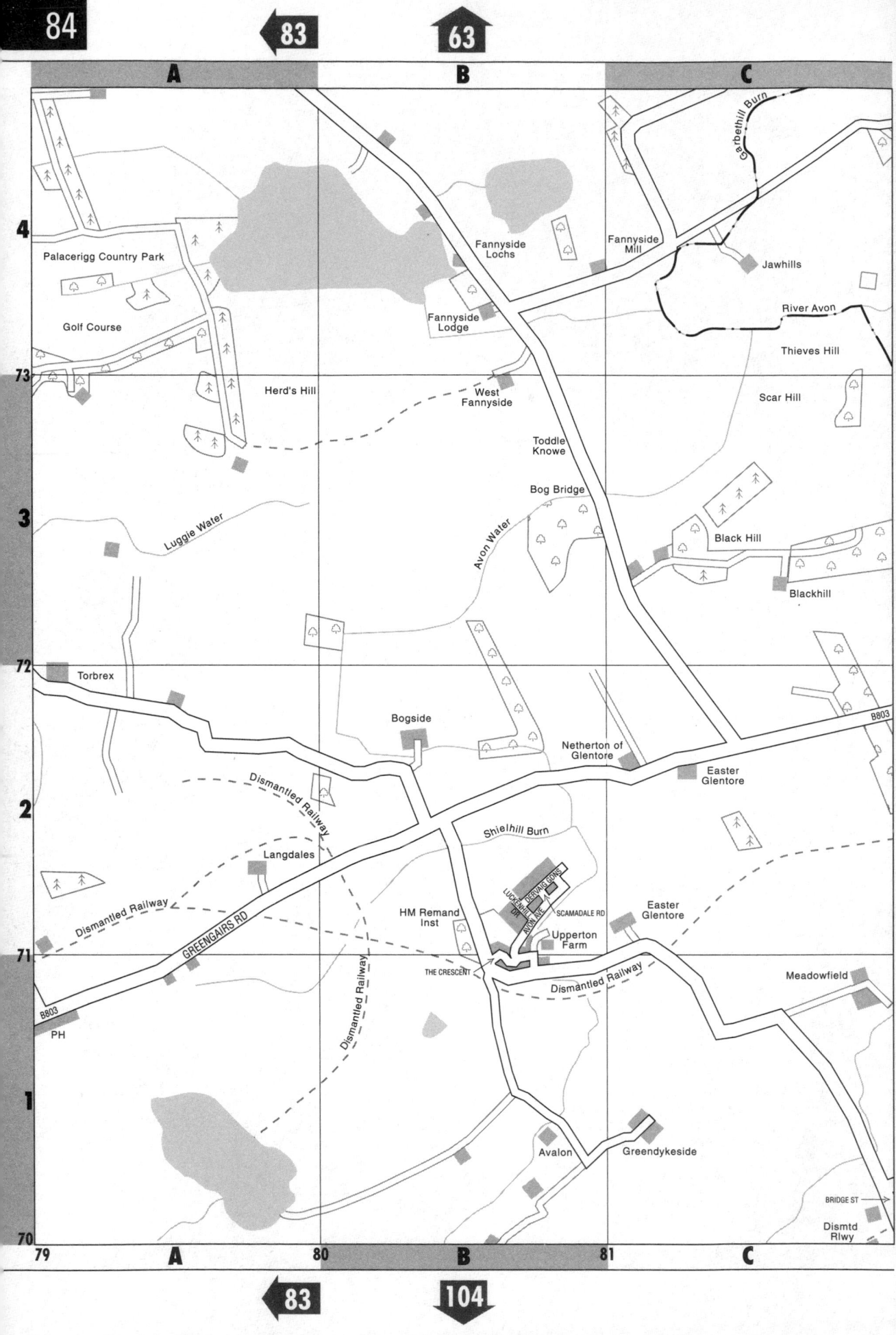

A B C

4

Palacerigg Country Park

Golf Course

Fannyside Lochs

Fannyside Lodge

Fannyside Mill

Jawhills

River Avon

Thieves Hill

73

Herd's Hill

West Fannyside

Scar Hill

Toddle Knowe

Bog Bridge

Black Hill

3

Luggie Water

Avon Water

Blackhill

72

Torbrex

Bogside

Netherton of Glentore

Easter Glentore

B803

2

Dismantled Railway

Shielhill Burn

Langdales

Dismantled Railway

GREENGAIRS RD

HM Remand Inst

LUCKENHILL DR

DERVAIG GDNS

AVON AVE

SCAMADALE RD

Upperton Farm

Easter Glentore

71

Dismantled Railway

Dismantled Railway

THE CRESCENT

Dismantled Railway

Meadowfield

B803

PH

1

Avalon

Greendykeside

BRIDGE ST

Dismtd Rlwy

70

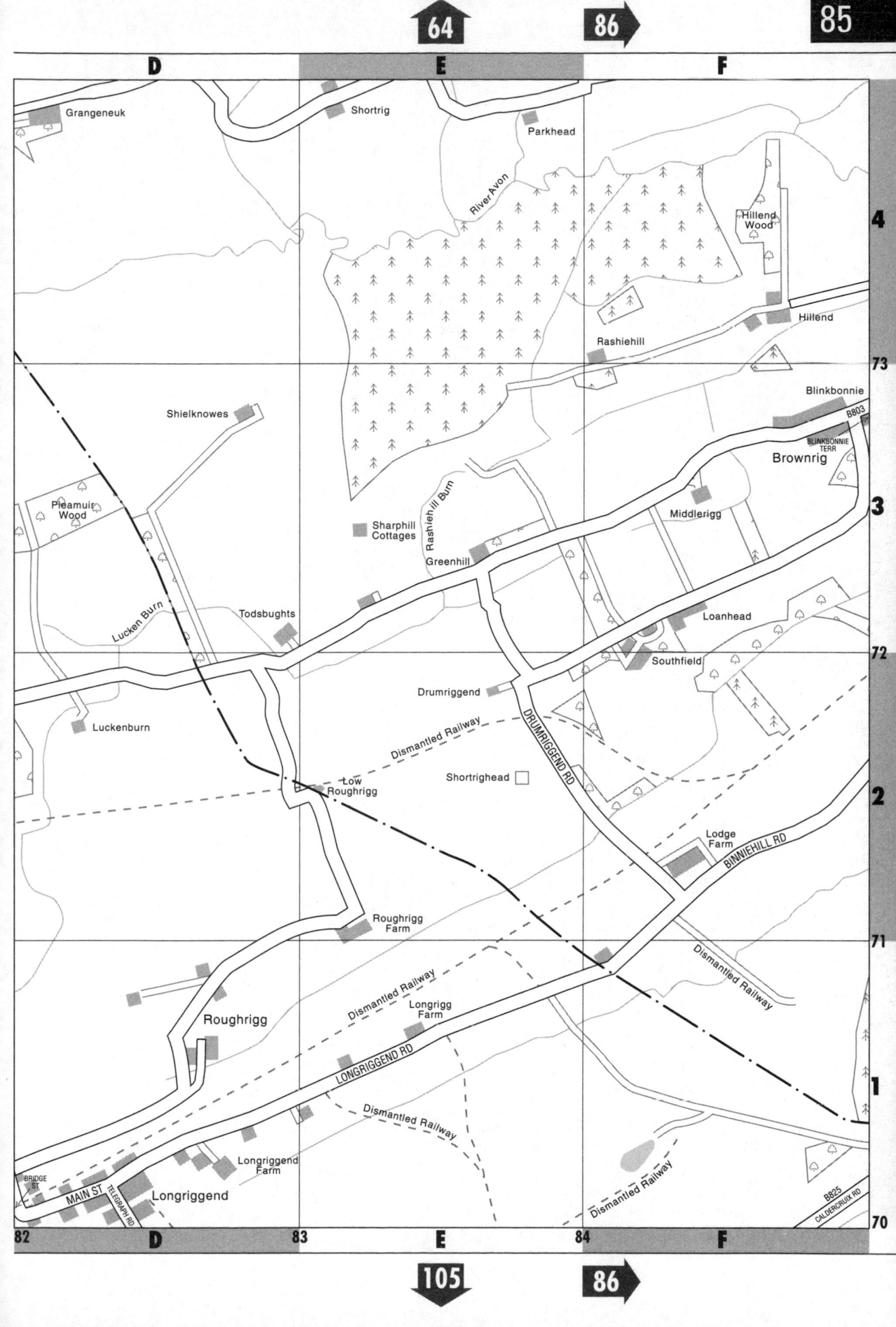

A | B | C

4

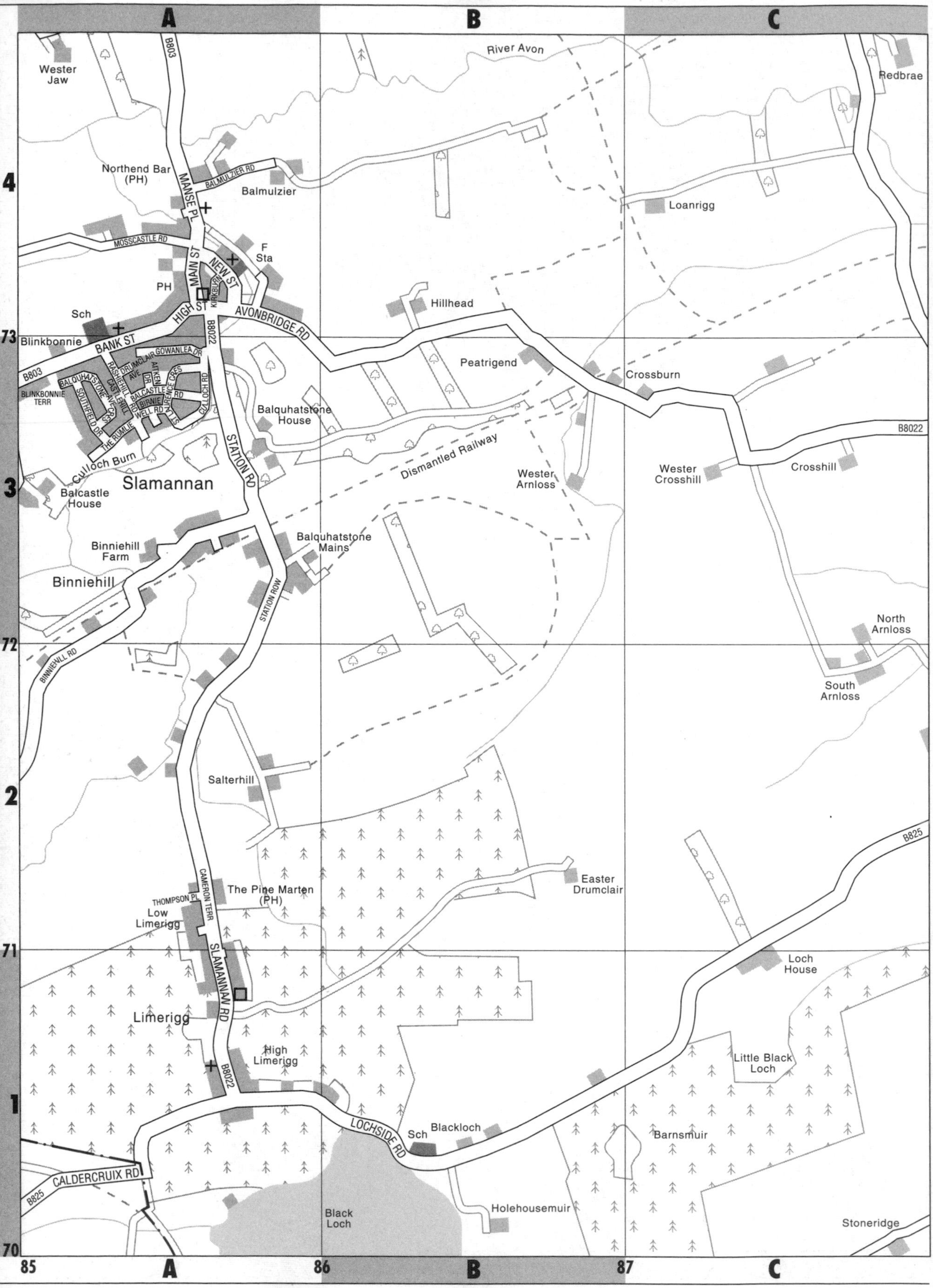

Wester Jaw

B803

River Avon

Redbrae

Northend Bar (PH)

MANSE PL

BALMULZIER RD

Balmulzier

Loanrigg

MOSSCASTLE RD

NEW ST

REDBRAE

F Sta

PH

HIGH ST

B8022

AVONBRIDGE RD

Hillhead

73

Sch

Blinkbonnie

BANK ST

B803

BLINKBONNIE TERR

BALQUHATSTONE CRES

SOUTHFIELD

THE REMILTY

DRUMCLAIR AVE

GOWANLEA DR

BIRNIE

BALCASTLE

WELL RD

DR HOTT'S

Balquhatstone House

Peatrigend

Crossburn

Wester Crosshill

Crosshill

B8022

Dismantled Railway

3

Balcastle House

Culloch Burn

Slamannan

STATION RD

Balquhatstone Mains

Wester Arnloss

North Arnloss

Binniehill Farm

Binniehill

STATION ROW

72

BINNIEHLL RD

South Arnloss

Salterhill

2

The Pine Marten (PH)

CAMERON TERR

Easter Drumclair

B825

THOMPSON PL

Low Limerigg

71

SLAMANNAN RD

Loch House

Limerigg

High Limerigg

B8022

Little Black Loch

1

LOCHSIDE RD

Sch

Blackloch

Barnsmuir

CALDERCRUIX RD

B825

Black Loch

Holehousemuir

Stoneridge

70

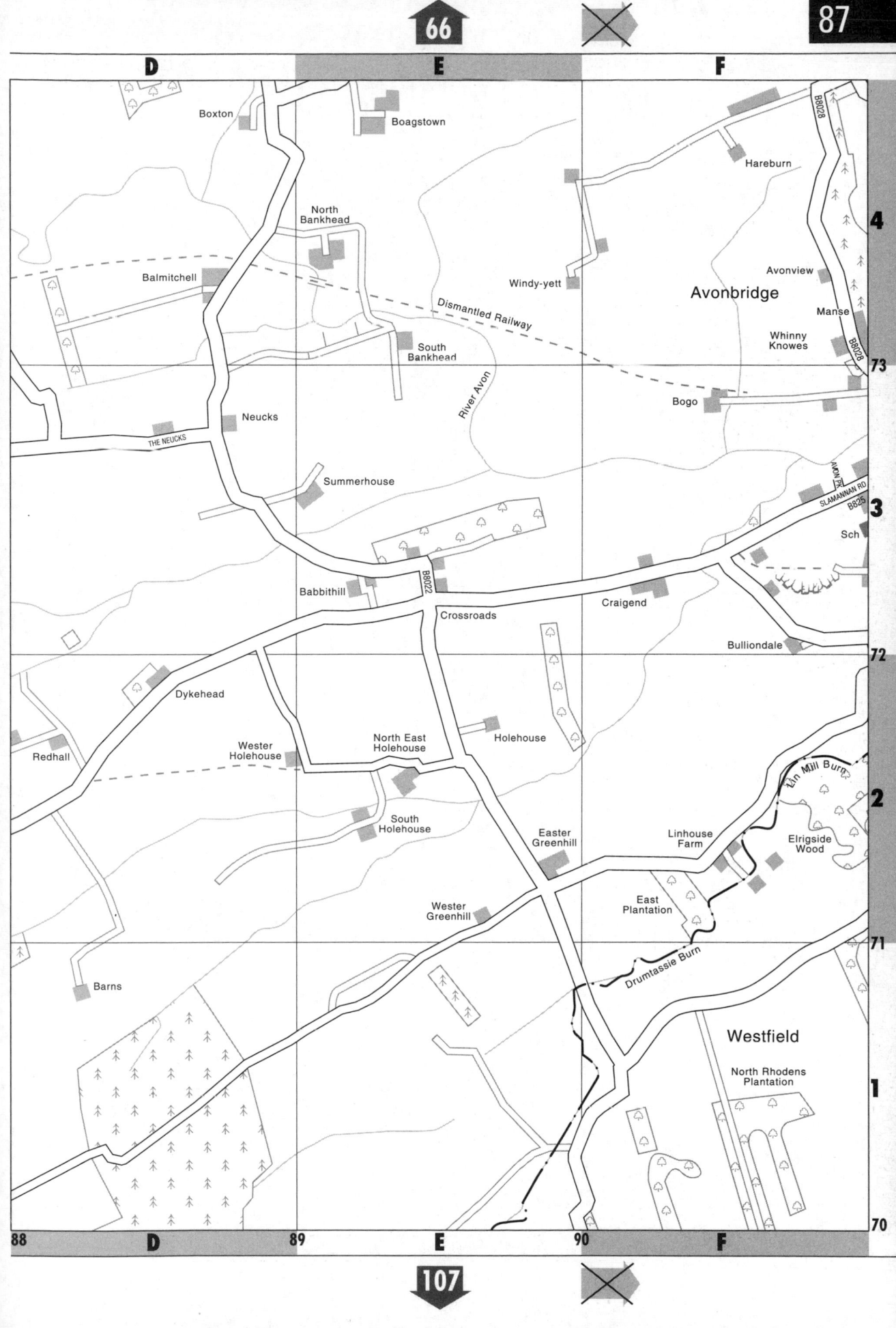

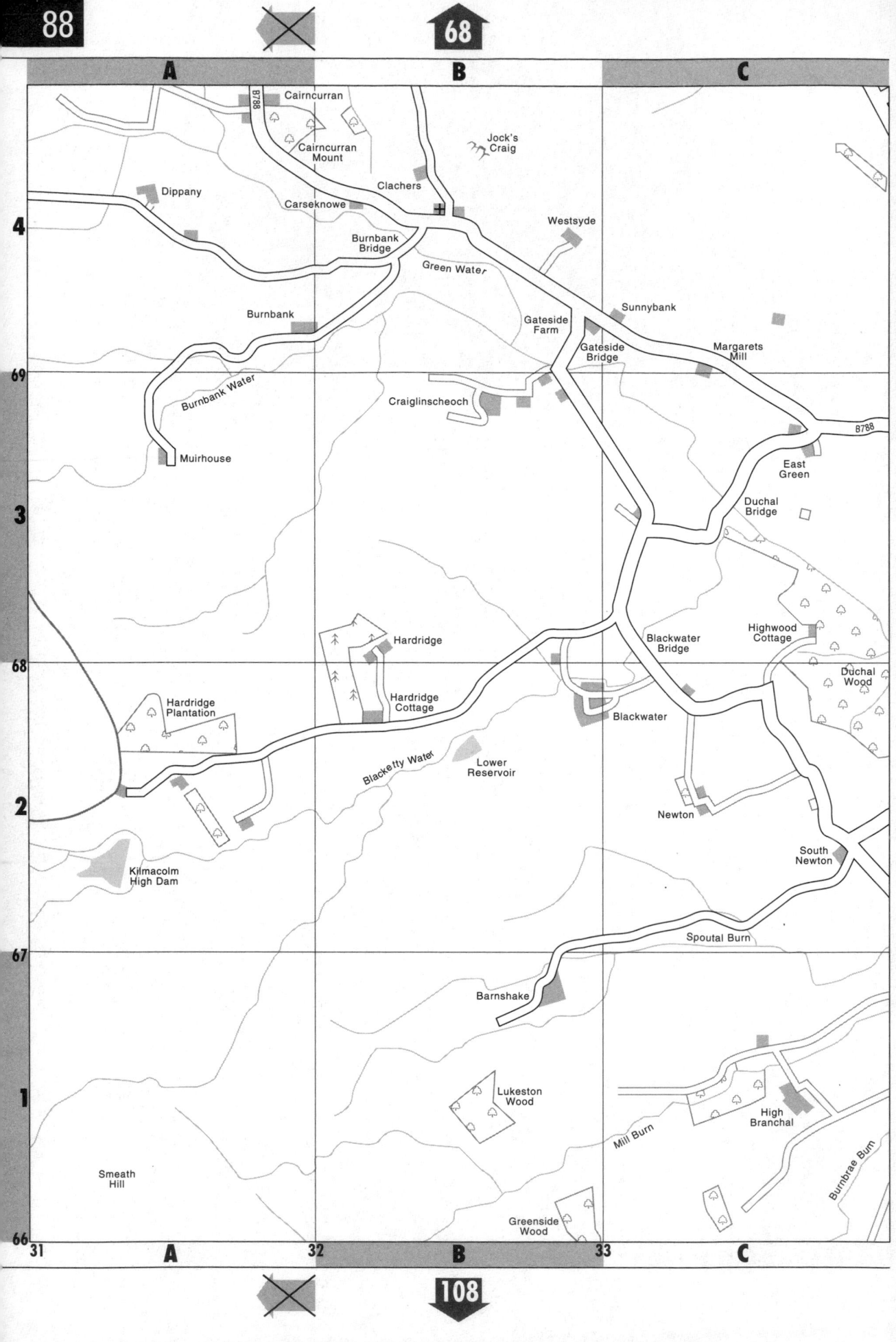

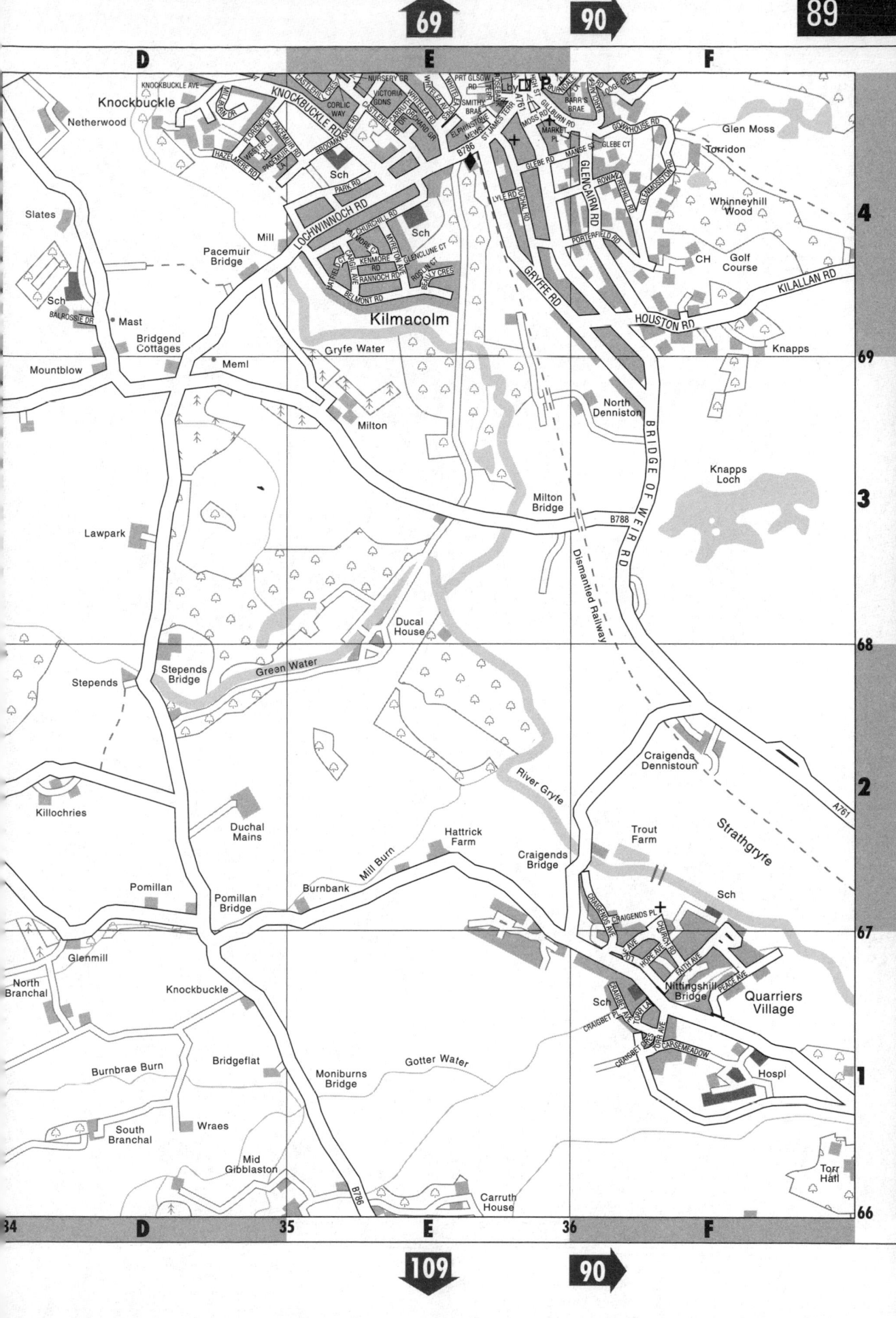

D   E   F

Knockbuckle
Netherwood

Slates

Mountblow

KNOCKBUCKLE RD
KNOCKBUCKLE AVE
Sch

HAZELMERE RD
FLORENCE DR
WRIGHTFIELD
PACEMUIR RD
PACEMUIR LA
BROOMKNOWE RD
PARK RD
LOCHWINNOCH RD
Mill

Pacemuir
Bridge

CASTLEHILL CRES
CORLIC WAY
CASTLEHILL RD
CARRUTH DR
VICTORIA GDNS
WHITELEA AV
CHURCHILL RD
MORE RD
KENMORE RD
CARGILL AVE
HATFIELD RD
RANNOCH RD
BELMONT RD
RANNOCH RD
GLENCLUNE CT
ROSLIN CT
BEARLY CRES

NURSERY GR
WHITELEA RD
PORT GLSGW RD
Sch
B786
Lyle RD
DUNN RD

ELPHINSTONE RD
ST JAMES TERR
Sch

Kilmacolm

Gryfe Water

Meml

Milton

PRT GLSGW RD
Lby P
SMITHY BRAE
MKTG
MARKET PL
MOSS RD
GLEBE RD
MANSE ST
GLEBE CT

GOWK HOUSE RD
Glen Moss
Torridon

Whinneyhill
Wood

GLENCAIRN RD
ROW RD
FREELAND RD
GLEAMOSS TON
PORTERFIELD RD
CH
Golf
Course

KILALLAN RD
GRYFE RD
HOUSTON RD
Knapps

Bridgend
Cottages
Mast

Balrossie Dr
Sch

North
Denniston

BRIDGE OF WEIR RD

Knapps
Loch

Lawpark

Milton
Bridge
B788

Dismantled Railway

Ducal
House

Green Water
Stepends
Stepends
Bridge

Craigends
Dennistoun

A761

River Gryfe

Strathgryfe

Killochries

Duchal
Mains

Mill Burn

Hattrick
Farm

Trout
Farm
Sch

Pomillan

Pomillan
Bridge

Burnbank

Craigends
Bridge

CRAIGENDS AVE
CRAIGENDS PL
CHURCH RD
FAITH AVE
HOPE AVE
Sch

Glenmill

North
Branchal

Knockbuckle

Burnbrae Burn

Bridgeflat

Moniburns
Bridge

Gotter Water

B786

South
Branchal

Wraes

Mid
Gibblaston

Carruth
House

CRAIGBET PL
CRAIGBET AVE
TORR LA
TORR AVE
Sch
Nittingshill
Bridge
BEACH AVE
Quarriers
Village

CARSEMEADOW
Hospl

Torr
Hatl

34   D   35   E   36   F

4

69

3

68

2

67

1

66

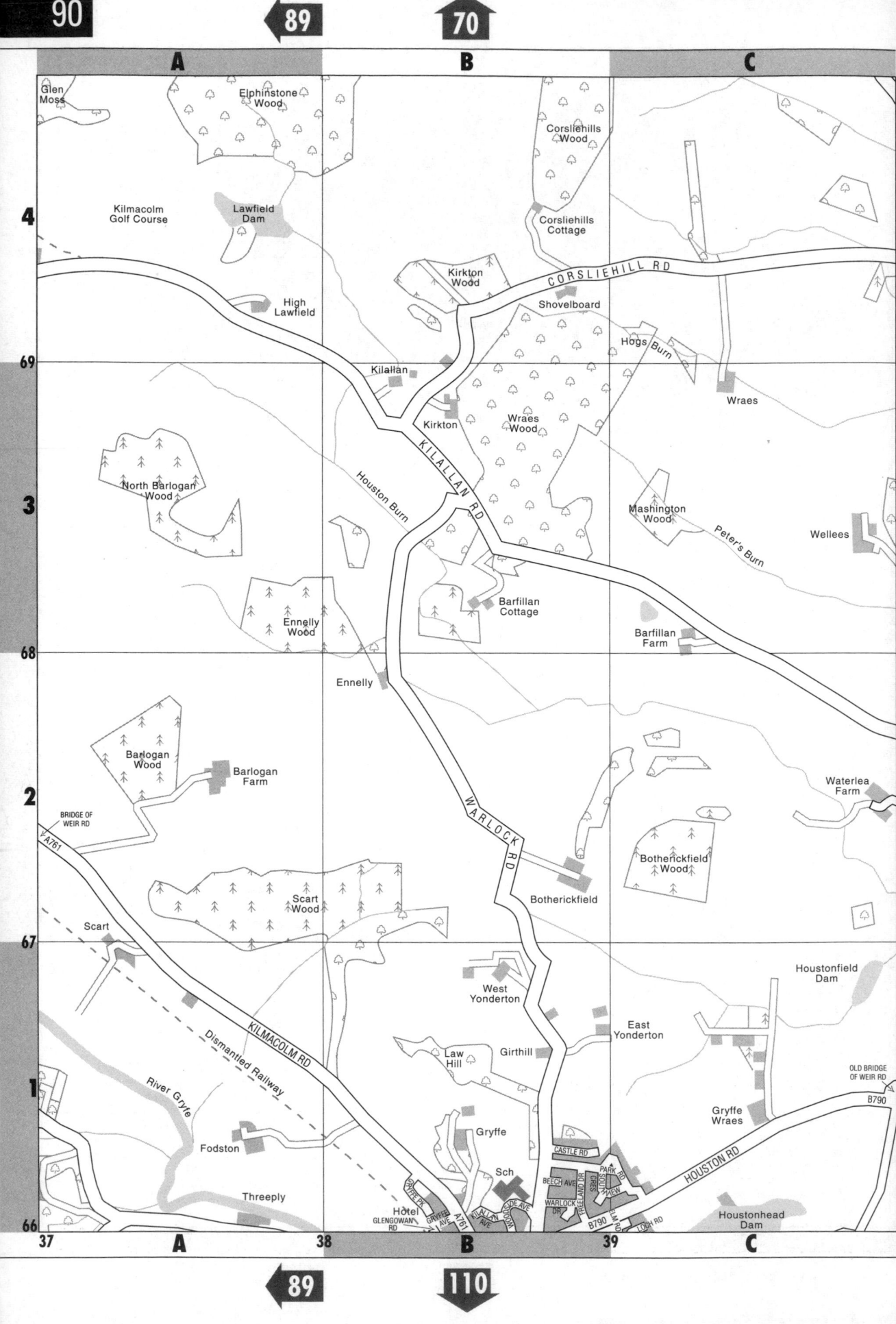

A   B   C

Glen Moss

Elphinstone Wood

Corsliehills Wood

4 Kilmacolm Golf Course

Lawfield Dam

Corsliehills Cottage

CORSLIEHILL RD

High Lawfield

Kirkton Wood

Shovelboard

Hogs Burn

69

Kilallan

Wraes

Kirkton

Wraes Wood

Houston Burn

KILALLAN RD

3 North Barlogan Wood

Mashington Wood

Peter's Burn

Wellees

Ennelly Wood

Barfillan Cottage

Barfillan Farm

68

Ennelly

Barlogan Wood

Barlogan Farm

Waterlea Farm

2 BRIDGE OF WEIR RD

A761

WARLOCK RD

Botherickfield Wood

Scart Wood

Botherickfield

Scart

67

West Yonderton

Houstonfield Dam

KILMACOLM RD

East Yonderton

Dismantled Railway

Law Hill

Girthill

OLD BRIDGE OF WEIR RD

1 River Gryfe

B790

Gryffe Wraes

HOUSTON RD

Fodston

Gryffe

Sch

CASTLE RD

BEECH AVE

PARK RD

SOUTH VIEW

Threeply

Hotel

GLENGOWAN RD

GRYFFE AVE

A761

KILALLAN AVE

ESDE AVE

WARLOCK DR

B790

LOGH RD

Houstonhead Dam

66

37   A   38   B   39   C

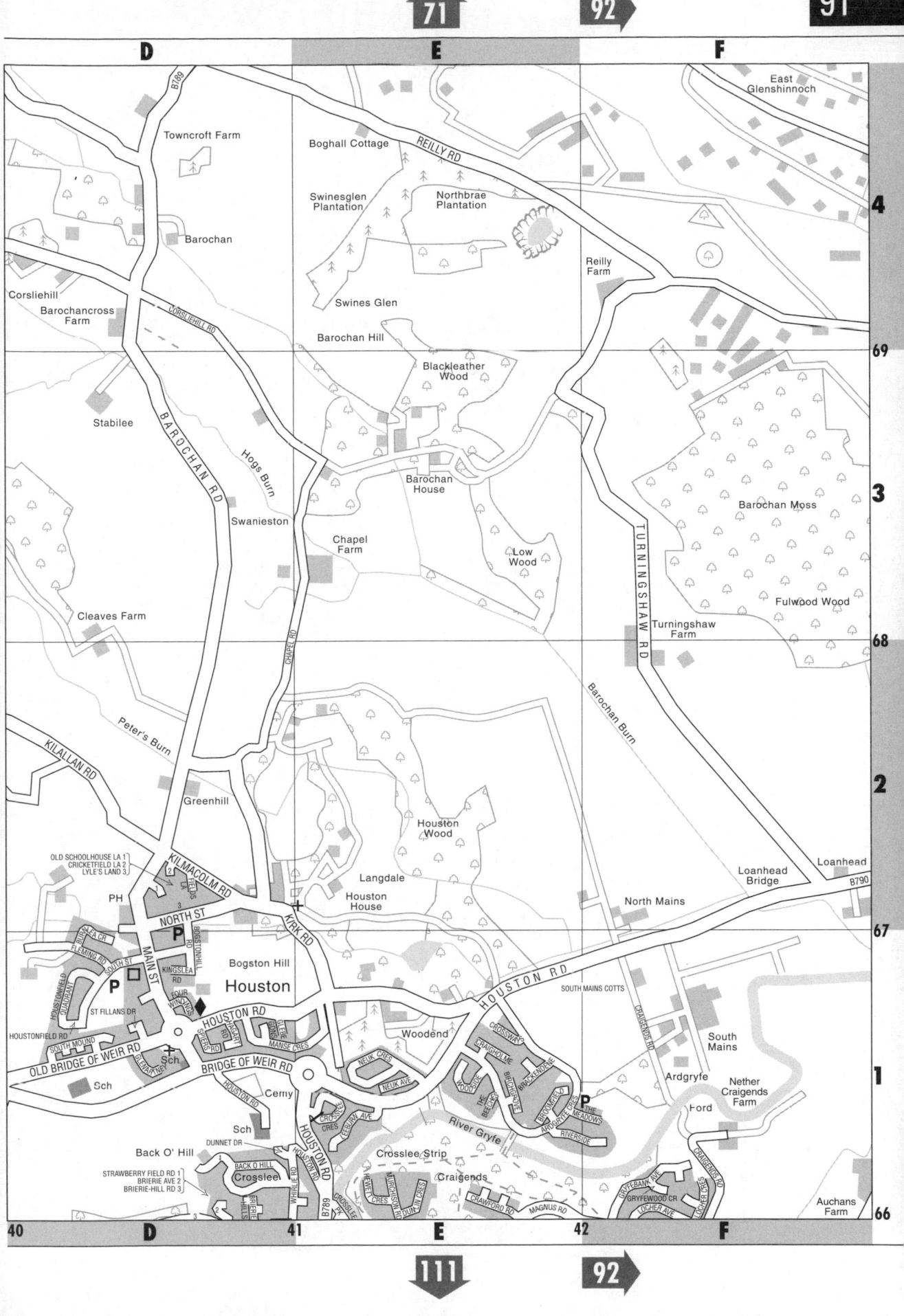

D E F

East Glenshinnoch

Towncroft Farm

Boghall Cottage

REILLY RD

4

Swinesglen Plantation

Northbrae Plantation

Barochan

Reilly Farm

Corsliehill

Barochancross Farm

CORSLIEHILL RD

Swines Glen

69

Barochan Hill

Stabilee

Blackleather Wood

BAROCHAN RD

Hogs Burn

Barochan House

Barochan Moss

3

Swanieston

Chapel Farm

Low Wood

TURNINGSHAW RD

Fulwood Wood

Cleaves Farm

CHAPEL RD

Turningshaw Farm

68

Peter's Burn

Barochan Burn

KILALLAN RD

2

Greenhill

Houston Wood

Loanhead Bridge

Loanhead

B790

OLD SCHOOLHOUSE LA 1
CRICKETFIELD LA 2
LYLE'S LAND 3

KILMACOLM RD

Langdale

Houston House

North Mains

PH

NORTH ST

KIRK RD

67

BRIDSTONHILL RD

P

Bogston Hill

HOUSTON RD

SOUTH MAINS COTTS

MAIN ST

KINGSLEA RD

Houston

South Mains

P

ST FILLANS DR

FOUR WINDS

Woodend

CRAIGENDS RD

Ardgryfe

Nether Craigends Farm

HOUSTONFIELD RD

SOUTH MOUND

HOUSTON RD

MANSE CRES

Craigholme

BRACKENDENE

BROOMFAULD

Ford

1

OLD BRIDGE OF WEIR RD

Sch

BRIDGE OF WEIR RD

NEUK CRES

NEUK AVE

THE BEECHES

ARDGRYFE CRES

THE MEADOWS

RIVERSIDE

P

Sch

Cerny

HOUSTON RD

FEEBRIN AVE

River Gryfe

Back O' Hill

Sch

DUNNET DR

CROSSLEE CRES

Crosslee Strip

Craigends

Auchans Farm

STRAWBERRY FIELD RD 1
BRIERIE AVE 2
BRIERIE-HILL RD 3

Crosslee

BACK O' HILL

WHIRLIE RD

HOUSTON RD

B789

CROSSLEE RD

HEWEL CRES

MITCHISON RD

DUNN CRES

CRAWFORD RD

MAGNUS RD

GRYFEBANK AVE

GRYFEWOOD CR

LOCHER AVE

LOCHER CRES

66

40 D 41 E 42 F

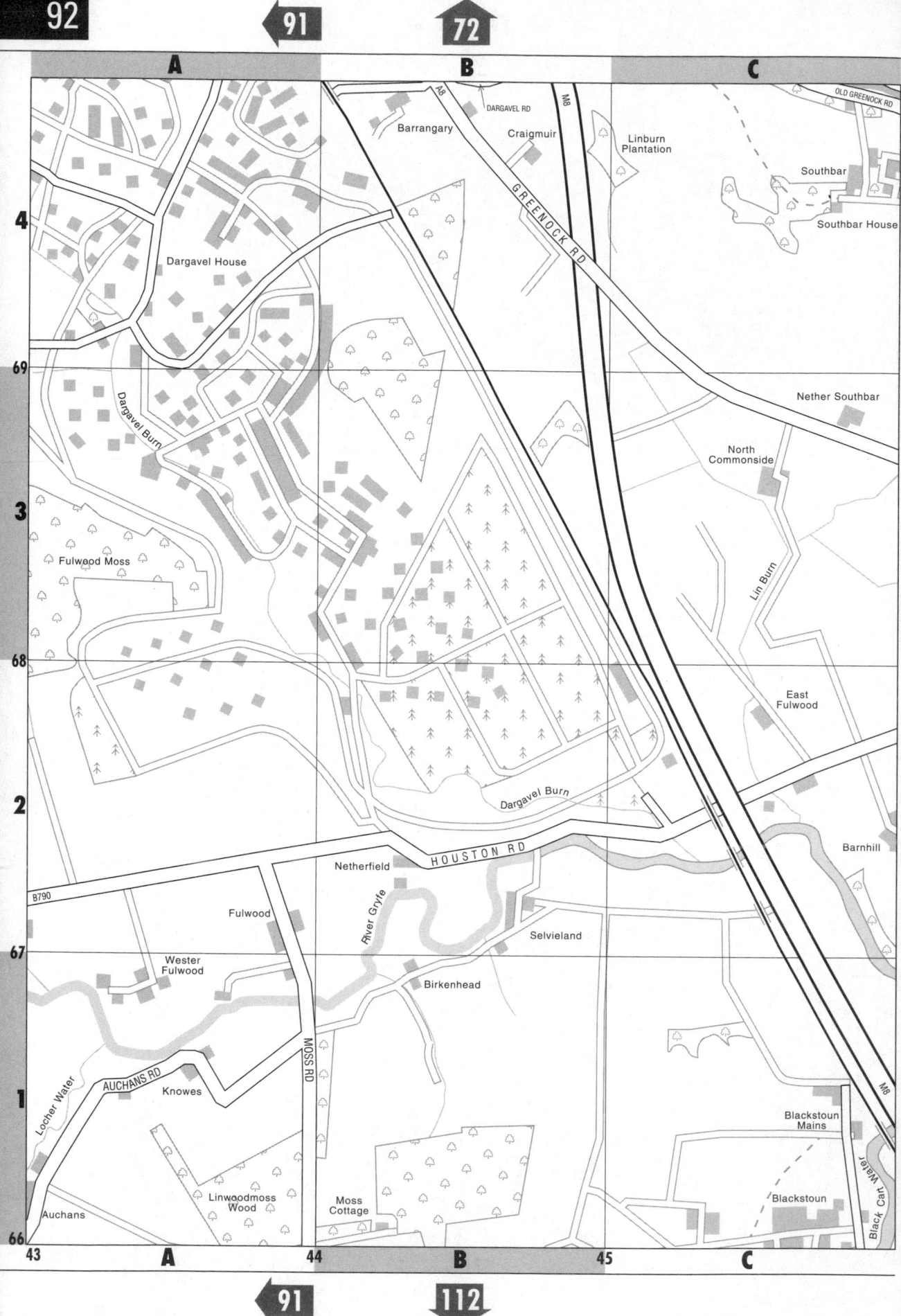

OLD GREENOCK RD

DARGAVEL RD

Barrangary

Craigmuir

Linburn
Plantation

Southbar

Southbar House

GREENOCK RD

Dargavel House

Nether Southbar

4

69

Dargavel Burn

North
Commonside

3

Fulwood Moss

Lin Burn

68

East
Fulwood

2

Dargavel Burn

Barnhill

HOUSTON RD

Netherfield

Selvieland

B790

Fulwood

River Gryfe

Birkenhead

67

Wester
Fulwood

Locher Water

AUCHANS RD

Knowes

MOSS RD

1

Blackstoun
Mains

Linwoodmoss
Wood

Moss
Cottage

Blackstoun

Black Cart Water

Auchans

66

D   E   F

1 HAWTHORN WAY
2 HAWTHORN RD

OLD GREENOCK RD

MILLFIELD WYND
1 MILLFIELD WLK
3 MILLFIELD DR

PARKWAY

Park Mains

Freeland

Sch

Sch

Cemy

Sandieland Wood

Northbar House

Inchinnan

Teucheen Wood

Florish

BEARDMORE COTTS

PH

4

69

GREENOCK RD

Town of Inchinnan

Broom Hill

3

New Mains

Nursery

Allands Holdings

NEWMAINS AVE

Inchinnan Ind Est

Works

HOUSTON RD

B790

TA Centre

Mast

Ind Est

Brownsfield

Black Cart Water

68

Camp (dis)

Easter Yonderton

Wester Yonderton

2

Barnsford Bridge

BARNSFORD RD

Easter Walkinshaw

WALKINSHAW RD

67

Glasgow Airport

ABBOTSINCH RD

White Cart Water

Works

F Sta

Blackstone Mains

ARRAN AVE

Mill

WRIGHT ST

1

Douglas Terr

Sewage Wks

CLYDESDALE AVE 1
SOMERLED AVE 2

Wester Walkinshaw Farm

M8

A726

ST ANDREW'S CRES

CALEDONIA WAY

BUTE RD

St Andrew's Dr

NEVIS WAY

P

P

P

Hotel

P

ARGYLL AVE

St Andrew's Dr

66

46   D   47   E   48   F

Dock
Works
BON ACCORD SQ
Whitecrook
Recn Gd
FORTH ST
BARNS ST
EAST BARNS ST
Sch
GLASGOW RD
Dock
SOUTH DOUGLAS ST 1
SOUTH BANK ST 2
SOUTH ELGIN PL 3
SOUTH ELGIN ST 4
NORTH ELGIN PL 5
PC
Yoker Sta
Sch
Ian Smith Ct
GARSCADDEN RD S 1
ARCHERHILL TERR 2
ARCHERHILL SQ 3
Sports Ground
4 LADHOPE PL
5 SOLLAS PL
6 PORTSOY AVE
7 WYVIS PL
Sports Ground
FULWOOD PL 1
MUIRHILL CRES 2
DUNWAN PL 3
YOKER MILL RD
ALDERMAN RD
Yoker
Sch
HALLEY SQ
HALLEY DR
KELSO ST
Sch
Hospl
1 BOUVERIE ST
2 LASSWADE ST
3 TWEEDVALE PL
SOUTHINCH AVE
4 YETHOLM ST
5 LADY ANNE ST
Works
Old Mains
Black Cart Water
Portnauld
River Clyde
Renfrew Golf Course
Blythswood
Ind Est
LONDON ST
Ferry (foot)
DUMBARTON RD
Dismtd Rly
A814
SANDHOLM PL 6
BLAWARTHILL ST 7
CH
GRYFFE AVE
Dismtd Rly
SIMONS CRES
Hospl
Off
FERRY RD
KING'S INCH RD
The King's Inch
Swing Bridge
Hotel
P
WEST LODGE RD
INCHINNAN RD
Off
STATION RD
White Cart Bridge
ABBOTSINCH RD
LEVEN SQ
KIRKLANDNEUK RD
CRERAN DR
Sch
TH
P
P
P
EDWARD AVE
ANDREW AVE
1 DUNLOP ST
2 DUNLOP CRES
Sch
1 MILLBURN AVE
2 MILLBURN DR
3 MILLBURN WAY
KING'S INCH RD
Kirklandneuk
VENNACHER RD
DUNVEGAN QUADRANT
ARD RD
Netherton
White Cart Water
Robertson Park
PC
Loanhead
HIGH ST
GLEBE ST
Off
A877
MERLINFORD WAY
MERLINFORD CRES
Works
OLD GOVAN RD
FINDHORN AVE
RENFREW
Hotel
GLASGOW RD
ETTRICK AVE
Porterfield
P
Sch
Works
PAISLEY RD
F Sta
Liby
PC
Moorpark
SANDY RD
DEAN PARK RD
Playing Field
PC
Dean Park
1 CLAIRINCH GDNS
2 HERALD WAY
3 ARGOSY WAY
4 LANCASTER WAY
5 WELLINGTON WAY
6 ANSON WAY
7 HALIFAX WAY
8 STIRLING WAY
9 LYSANDER WAY
10 CARAVELLE WAY
11 HAMPDEN WAY
Sch
1 TIRRY WAY
2 NETHY WAY
Victory Gardens
Sch
JESSIMAN SQ 1
BARCLAY SQ 2
METHUEN RD
B791
COCKELS LOAN
A741
COCKELS LOAN
M8
Junction 26
3 MONTROSE AVE
4 KELVIN AVE
MOSSLAND RD
NAPIER RD
A736

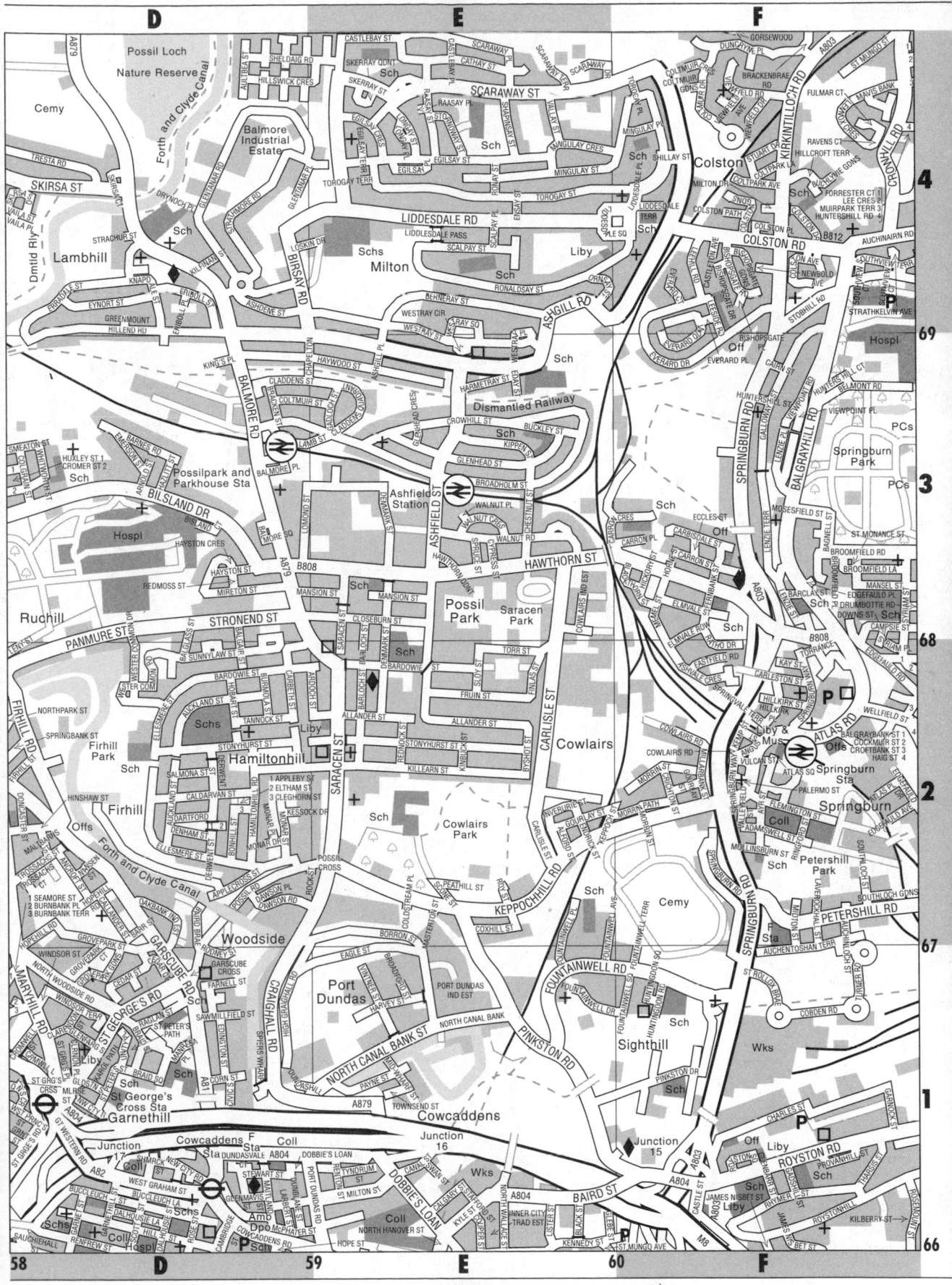

D   E   F

Arronhill
Plantation

Langmuirhead
Farm

LANGMUIRHEAD RD   Cardyke Farm

Cult Burn

Auchengree
Farm

4

Hornshill

Glen
Plantation

Saughs

Garnkirk Burn

Whitehill
Farm

Gateside

69

Recreation
Ground

Hotel

CUMBERNAULD RD   A80

Buchanan CT

Buchanan BSNS PK

Stepps

3

Sch

Stepps
Railway
Station

F Sta

Sch

Dismantled   Railway

Millerston

Frankfield
Loch

Craigendmuir

68

Caravan and
Camp Site

MOSSBANK
DR

ROYSTON RD

Molendinar Burn

Cardowan
Moss

2

Hogganfield
Loch

Bird
Sanctuary

Hogganfield
Park

Sch

GLENRAITH
PATH

Sch

Blackfaulds
Farm

B806

67

Golf
Course

Craigend

Garthamlock

Sch

Ruchazie
Junction 11

GARTLOCH RD   B765

B806

Auchinlea
Park

Provan
Hall

P

Auchinlea
Retail
Park

P

1

66

99
80

A   B   C

Drumsack Plantation

Garnkirk Burn

RICHMOND GDNS
BARCALDINE AVE
THE EVERGLADES

Glen Cottage

CH

Crow Wood Golf Course

Crow Wood

Chryston

Schs

Liby

MAIN ST
LINDSAYBEG RD
CLOVERHILL PL
PARK RD

MORAY

MILLBRK

BOTHLYN RD

CHRYSTON RD

SOUTH LOAN

HILLCREST

Cemy

Bothlin Burn

Holms

GLENTNEY RD
GREENLEA RD
LANRIG RD

B819 LINDSAYBEG RD

B819

CUMBERNAULD RD

A752

A80

A752

DRUMCAVEL RD

Muirhead

CHURCH

ELMIRA RD

STATION RD

Sch

P

GREENLEA RD
CROW WOOD TERR

WOODHEAD TERR

LAUREL BANK RD

QUARRY WOOD GR

MOORPARK AVE 1
STENHOUSE AVE 2

POTASSELS RD

LILYBANK AVE

MOSS RD

NEUK AVE

Garnkirk Moss

DRUMCAVEL RD

Glaudhall Farm

HOLMS PL
QUEENSPARK
AVE

SOUTHVIEW PL

CORONATION
AVE

BOTHLIN
SLAKIEWOOD
AVE

LOCHEND AVE

Mount Ellen

Lochend House

LOCHEND RD

A80

Highpit Plantation

Woodhead Farm

Garnkirk

WOODHEAD

Heathfield Moss

STATION RD

Heathfield Farm

Johnston Loch

B804

LOCHVIEW TERR

LOCHEND
CH

MOWBRAY AVE

MANOR RD

JOHNSTON RD 1
LOCHSIDE 2
WOODNEUK TERR 3
BEARD CRES 4
JARDINE TERR 5
WOODNEUK LA 6

Gartcosh

KIRKHILL RD

LOCHEND

WOODNEUK RD

Depot

OLD GARTLOCH RD

ALLISON PL

Sch

B806

MT73

COATBRIDGE RD

A579

West Cottages

Gartloch Farm

Mid Cottages

GARTLOCH RD

Gartloch Cottages

Lochview Cottages

Bothlin Burn

B806

Hospl

Bishop Loch

Lochwood Cottages

Lochwood Farm

Baillie Moss Wood

Lochwood Plantation

SKELBO PATH

MYROCH PL

Sch

AUCHINGILL RD

LOCHEND RD

LOCHDOCHART RD

Craigend Wood

BALCURVIE RD
GARDYNE ST
BALGLUE
WHITSLADE ST
DUFFUS ST
AUCHINLEA RD
BIRGIDALE ST
BRUNSTANE RD

CONISBOROUGH RD

Sch

Sch

BOGBAIN RD

BALDRAGON RD

CARNBROOK RD

DUBTON ST

FORGLEN ST

COLFIN ST

STRIB RD

CALGARY ST
INCHLEE ST

CALGARY ST
LIFE PL

DALILEA
RD

Sch

Sch

TWINLAW ST

ABBERCREEN

WESTERHOUSE RD

A   B   C

67   68   69

99
120

D E F

4

69

3

68

2

67

1

66

70 D 71 E 72 F

Refuse Tip
Drumcavel Lodge
DRUMCAVEL RD
Dismantled Railway
AVENUEHEAD RD
M73
Bothlin Burn
Shankramuir
GLENBOIG RD
Mount Ellen Golf Course
CH
JOHNSTON RD
Croftfoot
Johnston
BLADE CT
LOCHSIDE
BEARD CRES
BEECH GR
Recn Gd
EASTGATE
KIRKHILL RD
WOODNEUK RD

Sch
South Medrox St
CHESTNUT GR
GLENBURN GDNS
CHAPMAN AVE
THE OVAL
EASTER
GARTSHERRIE RD
GAYNE DR
MARNOCH DR
CENTRE

CARMICHAEL PATH 1
EASDALE PATH 2
BALLATER WAY 3
RUTHVEN LA 4
McGREGOR PATH 5
STRONE PATH 6
CARSAIG LOAN 7
INVERCREE WLK 8
GLENELG PATH 9
EAGLESHAM PATH 10

GLENBOIG RD
DYNTRA PL

Garnqueen Farm

Works

PH

Refuse Tip

Gartcloss Farm

Woodend

Woodend Loch

Lochend Cottages

GARTCOSH RD
A752
P
Pursuit Centre

Lochend Loch

Drumpellier Country Park
Golf Course

TOWNHEAD RD

COATBRIDGE RD

BIRKENSHAW RD
Inchneuk Farm
Dismantled Railway
Marnoch
HILLSIDE COTTS
INCHNEUK RD
MAIN ST
CARRICK VIEW
CARRICK PL
PH
Garnqueen

GLENBOIG FARM RD
GLENBOIG NEW RD
Medrox Quarry (disused)
MOLLINSBURN RD
Glenboig Farm
Glenboig
Ramoan
COATBRIDGE RD
GARTSHERRIE AVE
VIEWBANK AVE
WHITELAW AVE
MUIRDYKE RD

Gartliston Farm

Gartsherrie Holm Farm

LC

Heatherbell

GARTLISTON RD

Gartsherrie Wood
B804
Gartsherrie Burn
Blacklands
HOLLANDHURST RD
Hollandhurst
Freightliner Terminal
HORNOCK RD
HOLLANDHURST RD
Gartsherrie Ind Est

GARTGILL RD

Sch
DUDLEY DR
DOVER ST
GARTCLOSS RD
GARTGREEN PL
MERRYLAND RD
DOCHART DR
DERWENT DR
THORNTON ST
SELBY ST
LEVEN ST
WILTON ST
WITCHWOOD CT
LOMOND RD
OCHVIEW RD
TAY ST
TANTALLON DR
DEE ST
KATRINE PL
ALMOND PL
WYE ST
LEVEN RD
Sch
BELMONT ST
CRINAN PL
DEVERON ST
ACHRAY PL
DUNVEGAN PL
AVON PL
IONA PL
RANNOCH
DOUNE TERR
MOBAR CRES
COLT AVE
DEVERON ST
LOMOND PL
CH
Witch Wood
Sch

A   B   C

Callochrig

CULLOCHRIG RD

Gaindydykehead

East Lodge Wood

B802

Foot o' Loan Wood

East Gartmillan

Shank Burn

LC

4

GLENBOIG NEW RD

Greenfoot

West Gartmillan

Glenmill Wood

Drumbowie Farm

MOLLINSBURN RD

Ardaryth

BRACKENHIRST RD

Dismtd Rly

69

Haggmuir

MOLLINSBURN RD

CONDORRAT RD

Refuse Tip

Brackenhirst

YETTS HOLE RD

Gas Storage Depot

3

MUIRDYKE RD

Gartverrie Burn

Ryden Mains

New Monkland

Cemy

68

BURNLIP RD

Palace Farm

PC Sch

Dismantled Railway

RYDEN MAINS RD

ST BRDAN'S VIEW

QUARRYSIDE ST

KIRKSTYLE PL

B802

B803

LOCHBUIE LA

ALTON WYND

MELDRUM MAINS

Rochsales

HAWKWOOD RD

RAEBOG RD

CRATHIE DR

Gartverrie Farm

Copse Wood

2

MACARTHUR AVE

GLEN VIEW ST

GLENWELL ST

PH

Glenmavis

Blackwalk Plantation

Cromlet

Braidenhill

Dryflat

Golf Course

STRATHMUNGO CRES 1
STAINEYBRAES PL 2

67

COATBRIDGE RD

CH

GLENMAVIS RD

Virtuewell Glen

Sch

DYKEHEAD RD

BALLOCHNEY LA

Kippsbyre

Burnfoot

1

Kipps

North Burn

Kipps

Laggan Quadrant

LAIDON RD

Acad

WHINHALL RD

BALLOCHNEY ST

Works

Coatbridge Ind Est

Greenhill

COLTSWOOD RD B804

B804 GARTLISTON RD

NORTHBURN RD

WAVERLEY ST

BURNSIDE ST

CHASSELS ST 1
BRUCE ST 2

GREENSIDE ST

BURNBANK ST

CAMERON ST

CAEND RD

Sch

COMMONHEAD ST

WILSON ST

WHINHALL AVE

B802

ARRAN DR

66

73   A   74   B   75   C

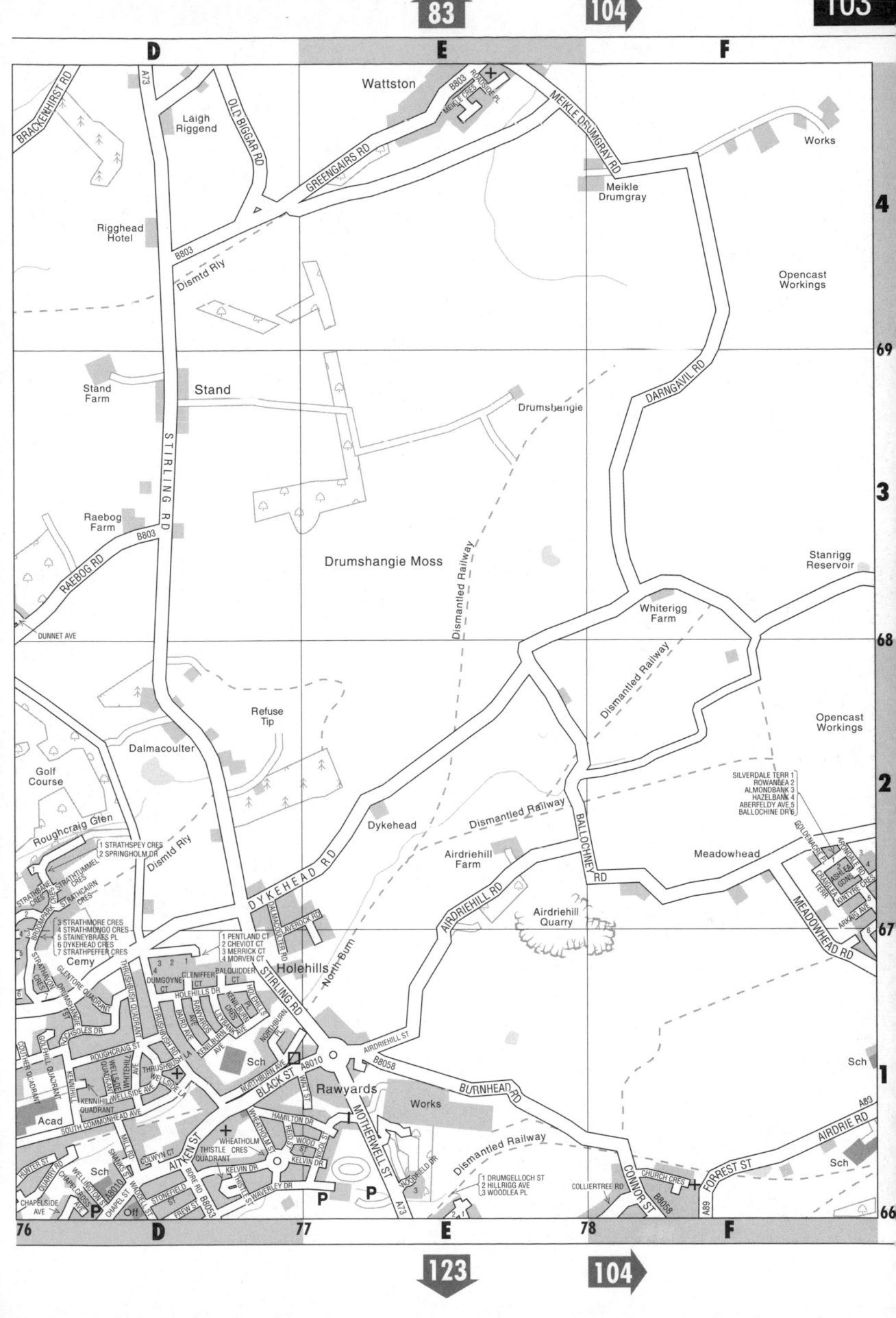

Wattston

BRACKENHIRST RD

A73

OLD BIGGAR RD

Laigh
Riggend

MEIKLE CRES

B803

ROADSIDE PL

MEIKLE DRUMGRAY RD

Works

GREENGAIRS RD

Meikle
Drumgray

4

Rigghead
Hotel

B803

Dismtd Rly

Opencast
Workings

STIRLING RD

Stand Farm

Stand

Drumshangie

DARNGAVIL RD

69

Raebog
Farm

B803

RAEBOG RD

Drumshangie Moss

Dismantled Railway

Stanrigg
Reservoir

3

DUNNET AVE

Whiterigg
Farm

68

Golf
Course

Refuse
Tip

Dalmacoulter

Dismantled Railway

Opencast
Workings

SILVERDALE TERR 1
ROWANLEA 2
ALMONDBANK 3
HAZELBANK 4
ABERFELDY AVE 5
BALLOCHINE DR 6

2

Roughcraig Glen

1 STRATHSPEY CRES
2 SPRINGHOLM DR

Dismtd Rly

Dykehead

Dismantled Railway

BALLOCHNEY RD

Meadowhead

GOLDENACRE TERR

ASH LA
GDNS
KINTYRE CRES

ARKAIG AVE

MEADOWHEAD RD

STRATHBRAAN CRES
STRATHUMMEL CRES
STRATHCAIRN CRES

Airdriehill
Farm

AIRDRIEHILL RD

3 STRATHMORE CRES
4 STRATHMUNGO CRES
5 STAINEYBRAES PL
6 DYKEHEAD CRES
7 STRATHPEFFER CRES

Cemy

DYKEHEAD RD

KILMACOLM

1 PENTLAND CT
2 CHEVIOT CT
3 MERRICK CT
4 MORVEN CT

KILMACOLM RD

Airdriehill
Quarry

67

THRUSHBUSH QUADRANT

DRUMSHANGIE

GLENTORE QUADRANT

DUMGOYNE CT

GLENIFFER CT

BALQUIDDER CT

HOLEHILLS DR

Holehills

North Burn

STIRLING RD

AIRDRIEHILL ST

BRANCHAL

STRATHAVON CRES

GOLFHILL QUADRANT

THRUSHBUSH QUADRANT

ROUGHCRAIG ST

THRUSHBUSH LA

BAIRD AVE

RAWYARDS AVE

KENILBURN AVE

LILYBANK AVE

HOLECROFT

NORTHBURN AVE

B8058

Sch

BLACK ST

A8010

Rawyards

WATT ST

BURNHEAD RD

Sch

A89

1

Acad

KENNIHILL

WELLSIDE AVE

SOUTH COMMONHEAD AVE

KENNIHILL QUADRANT

HAMILTON DR

Wheatholm CRES

THISTLE Quadrant

WOOD ST

MOTHERWELL ST

Works

Dismantled Railway

AIRDRIE RD

A89

Sch

HUNTER ST

QUARRY RD

WELLINGTON ST

B8010

Sch

Acad

CHAPEL CROSS

MILL RD

SHANKS ST

COLWYN CT

AITKEN ST

WADDELL ST

STONEFIELD ST

BORE RD

B8063

FREW ST

WAVERLEY DR

KELVIN DR

WADDELL ST

KELVIN DR

P

P

A73

MOTHERWELL ST

WOODFIELD DR

1 DRUMGELLOCH ST
2 HILLRIGG AVE
3 WOODLEA PL

COLLIERTREE RD

CONNOR ST

CHURCH CRES

B8058

FORREST ST

Sch

A89

CHAPELSIDE
AVE

P

Off

66

4

69

3

68

2

67

1

66

Avon Water

Avonhead Cottage

Head of Avon Water

Dismantled Railway

Easterton

Easterton Cottage

Midtown

Arden Glen

West Arbuckle

Sewage Wks

North Calder Water

Bleachfield Cottages

Dismantled Railway

AIRDRIE RD

Sch

PROGRESS DR

HILL ST

MILL ST

MOSS AVE

BEECH

GLEN RD

ROSELEA 1
SPRING LA 2

DRUMFIN AVE

ALDER AVE

STATION RD

PARK LEA 3
MILLSTREAM CRES 4

MAIN ST
CHURCH PL

LIMELANDS QUADRANT

A89

Ballochney Farm

ARBUCKLE RD

BALLOCHNEY RD

Outdoor Pursuits Ctr

Braefoot Farm

Moffat Hills

ABERFELDY AVE

KINTYRE CRES

MEADOW VIEW

EAST

MOFFAT VIEW

Plains

Ford Bridge

LEARGIE RD

MILL LAND DR

Wks

Stepends Farm

NORTHBURN ST

STATION RD

JARVIE AVE

WALLACE ST

PH

Anns Hill

BALLOCHNIE DR

VICTOR ST

ST MAC LA

ARDEN ST

MARLC LA

MAIN ST

Anneshill

STEPENDS RD

Annies Hill

MEADOWHEAD RD

Sch

AIRDRIE RD

A89

Sch

Sewage Wks

Browns Burn

BROWNIESIDE RD

Easter Moffat Farm

Berrieswalls

Briarfield

DUNTILLAND RD

Greystones

CH

Easter Moffat Golf Course

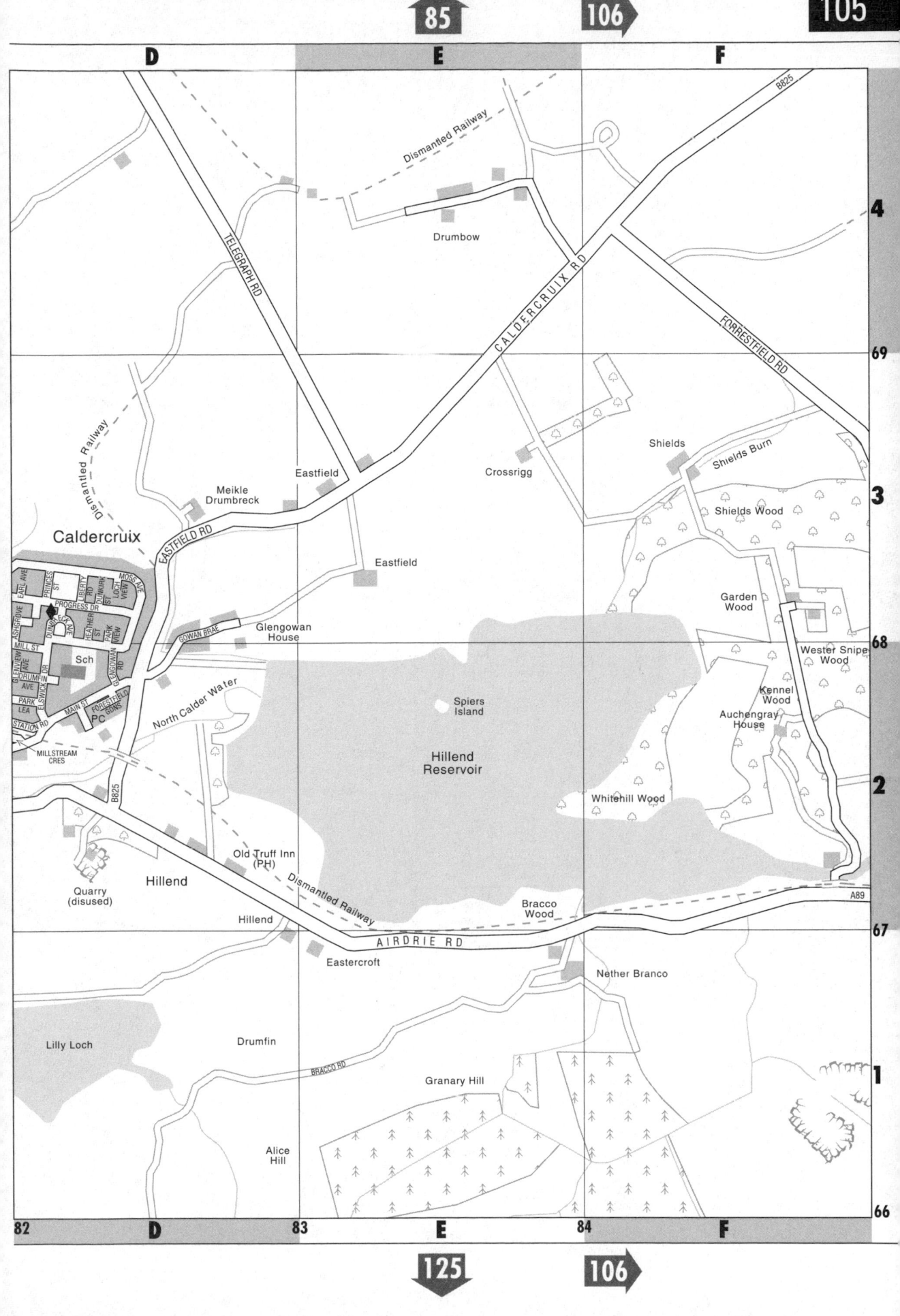

D E F

Dismantled Railway
B825

Drumbow

CALDERCRUIX RD

FORRESTFIELD RD

4

69

Dismantled Railway

Shields
Shields Burn

Eastfield

Meikle
Drumbreck

Crossrigg

Shields Wood

3

EASTFIELD RD

Caldercruix

MOSS AVE
EARL AVE
PRINCES ST
DUNKIRK ST
LOCH VIEW
PARK VIEW

Eastfield

Garden
Wood

ASHGROVE
LIBERTY ST
HEATHER ST
PROGRESS DR
DUNBECK RD

68

Wester Snipe
Wood

MILL ST
Sch
GLENGOWAN RD
DRUMFIN AVE
ELSWICK DR

Glengowan
House

GOWAN BRAE

Spiers
Island

Kennel
Wood

PARK LEA
MAIN ST
FORRESTFIELD GDNS
Pc
STATION RD

North Calder Water

Auchengray
House

MILLSTREAM CRES

Hillend
Reservoir

Whitehill Wood

2

B825

Old Truff Inn
(PH)

Dismantled Railway

A89

Quarry
(disused)

Hillend

Bracco
Wood

67

Hillend

AIRDRIE RD

Eastercroft

Nether Branco

Lilly Loch

Drumfin

BRACCO RD

Granary Hill

1

Alice
Hill

66

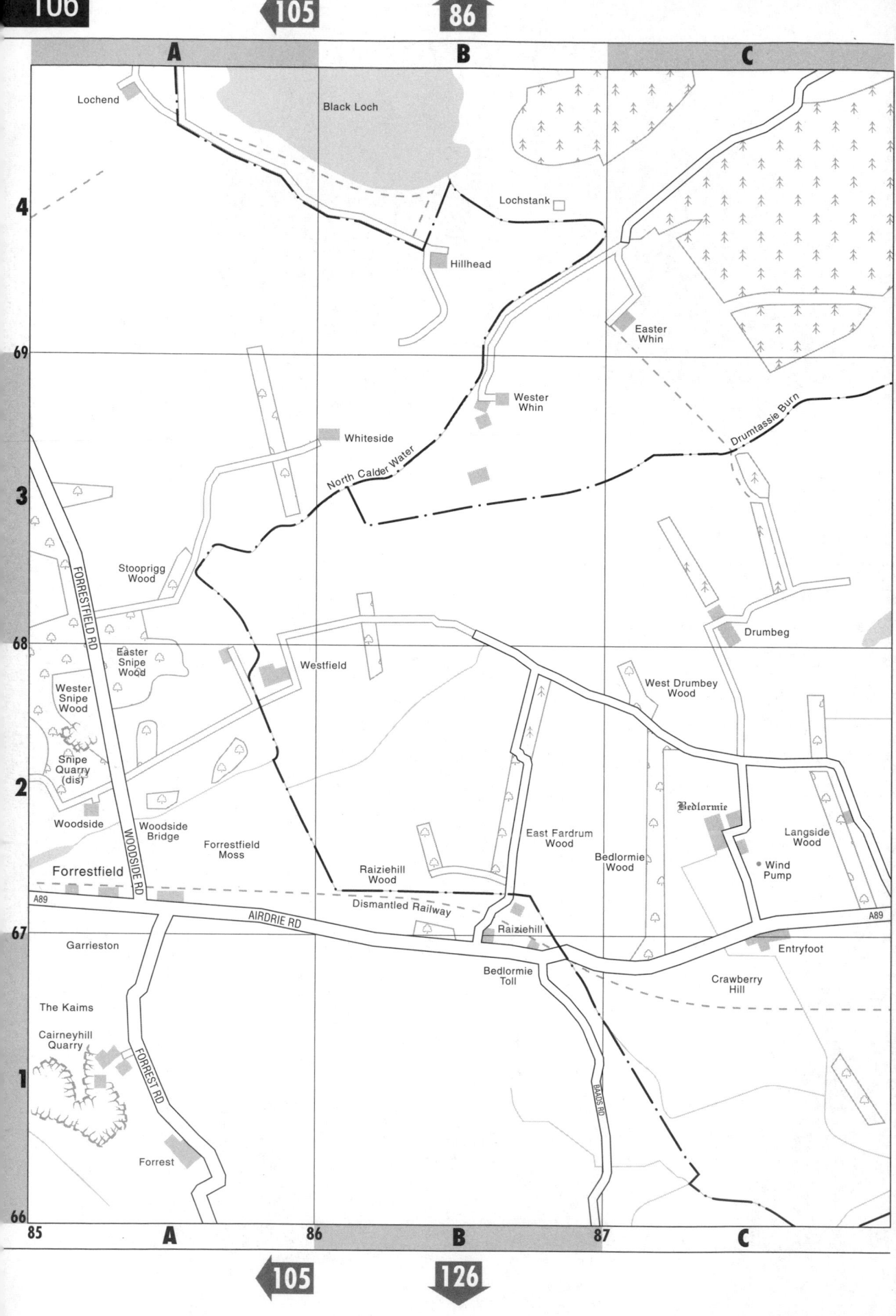

Lochend

Black Loch

Lochstank

4

Hillhead

Easter
Whin

69

Wester
Whin

Whiteside

Drumtassie Burn

North Calder Water

3

Stooprigg
Wood

Drumbeg

68

Easter
Snipe
Wood

Westfield

West Drumbey
Wood

Wester
Snipe
Wood

Snipe
Quarry
(dis)

Bedlormie

Langside
Wood

2

East Fardrum
Wood

Wind
Pump

Woodside

Woodside
Bridge

Forrestfield
Moss

Bedlormie
Wood

Forrestfield

Raiziehill
Wood

A89

FORRESTFIELD RD

WOODSIDE RD

AIRDRIE RD

Dismantled Railway

A89

67

Garrieston

Raiziehill

Entryfoot

The Kaims

Bedlormie
Toll

Crawberry
Hill

Cairneyhill
Quarry

FORREST RD

BAADS RD

1

Forrest

66

85   A   86   B   87   C

D   E   F

4

69

3

68

2

67

1

66

Burnhead
Moss

Burnhead

Wester Burnhead
Wood

Drum Park
Plantation

Croft
Plantation

Heights

Tawnycraw
Hill

West Rhodens
Plantation

Armadale

Drumtassie Burn

Opencast
Workings

Drumelzie

East Backmuir
Wood

Blawhorn Moss

Reservoir

Eastcraigs
Hill

Crowns
Hill

Blawhorn
Wood

Barn
Wood

Wester
Redburn

Heatherhouse
Wood

Bedlormie
House

Easter
Redburn

Blackridge

Craigs

Westcraigs
Hill

1 CRAIGHILL VIEW
2 BLACKHILL RD
3 SUNNYDALE RD

GREENHILL
RD

SUNNYDALE
DR

PARK RD

CRAIG ST

Westrigg

A89

FARQUHAR
SQ

Sch

LANDSIDE
DR

WOODHILL RD

DRUMMOND
PL

HEIGHTS RD

HILLSIDE DR

FLEMING PL

+PH

MAIN ST

MACLEAN TERR

CRAIGINN TERR

PC

WESTCRAIGS
PK

LOUBURN

Liby

BEDLORMIE DR

OGILFACE
CRES

REDBURN RD

B718

WESTCRAIGS RD

Mosshouse

Dismantled Railway

Standhill
Farm

STATION
RD

HARTHILL RD

Spoil
Heap

WHITELAW ST

Dismantled Railway

Bogend
Farm

Torrance
Farm

B718

88   D   89   E   90   F

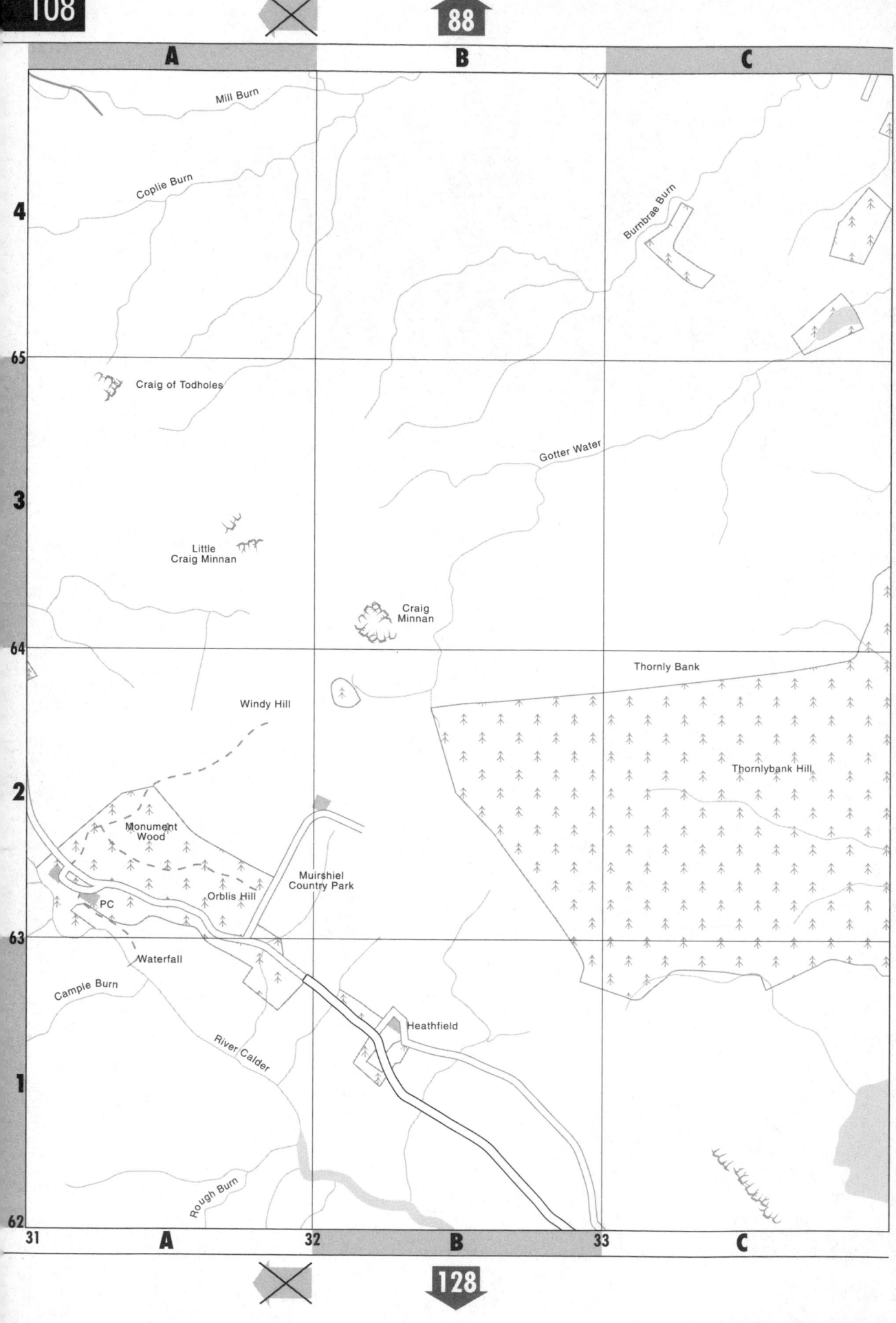

A

B

C

Mill Burn

Coplie Burn

4

65

Craig of Todholes

Gotter Water

3

Little
Craig Minnan

Craig
Minnan

64

Burnbrae Burn

Thornly Bank

Windy Hill

Thornlybank Hill

2

Monument
Wood

Muirshiel
Country Park

Orblis Hill

PC

63

Waterfall

Cample Burn

Heathfield

River Calder

1

Rough Burn

62

A **B** **C**

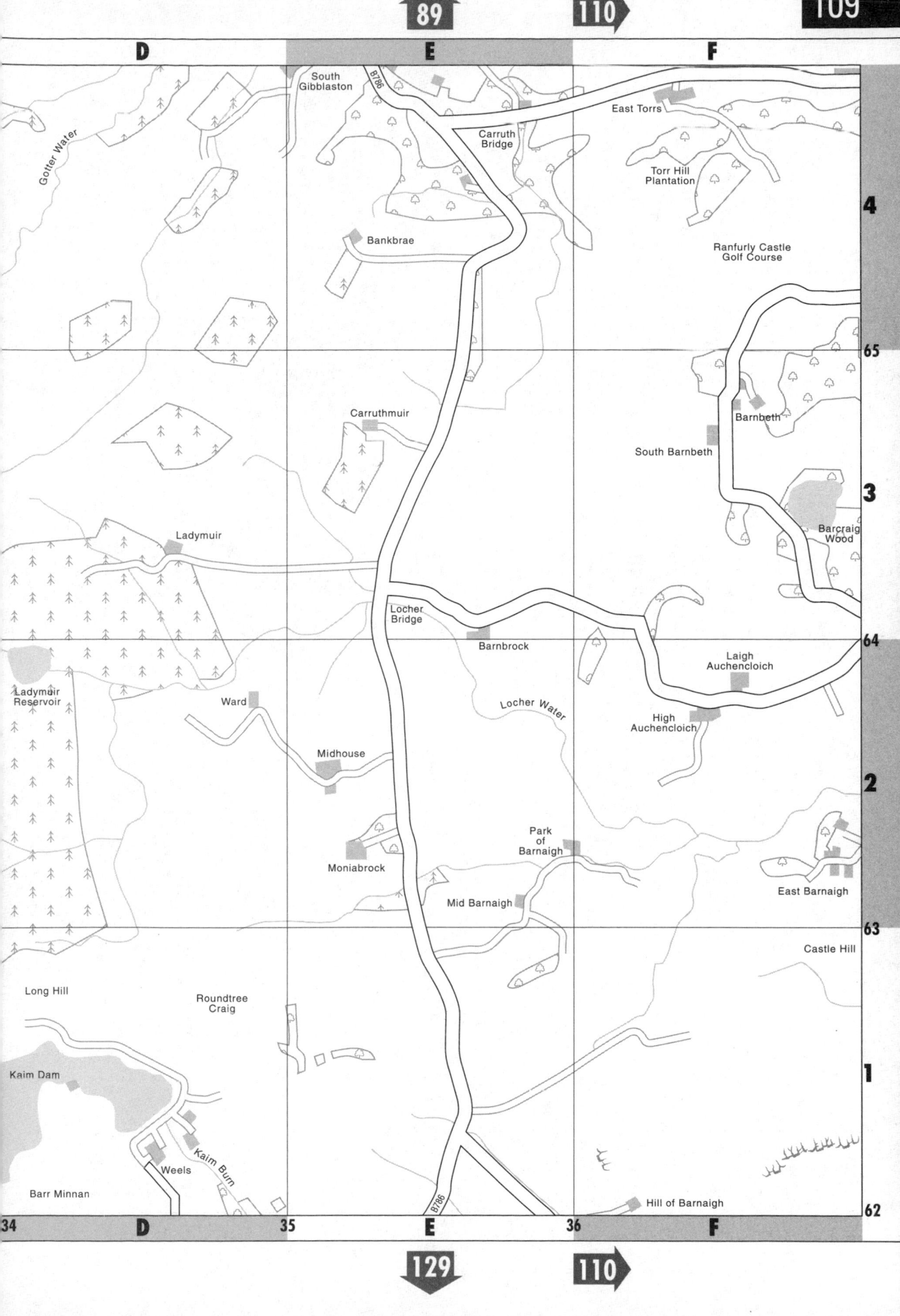

D

E

F

4

Gotter Water

South
Gibblaston

Carruth
Bridge

East Torrs

Torr Hill
Plantation

Ranfurly Castle
Golf Course

Bankbrae

65

Carruthmuir

Barnbeth

South Barnbeth

3

Ladymuir

Barcraig
Wood

Locher
Bridge

64

Barnbrock

Laigh
Auchencloich

Ladymuir
Reservoir

Ward

Locher Water

High
Auchencloich

2

Midhouse

Moniabrock

Park
of
Barnaigh

East Barnaigh

Mid Barnaigh

63

Castle Hill

Long Hill

Roundtree
Craig

1

Kaim Dam

Kaim Burn

Weels

Barr Minnan

Hill of Barnaigh

62

34

D

35

E

36

F

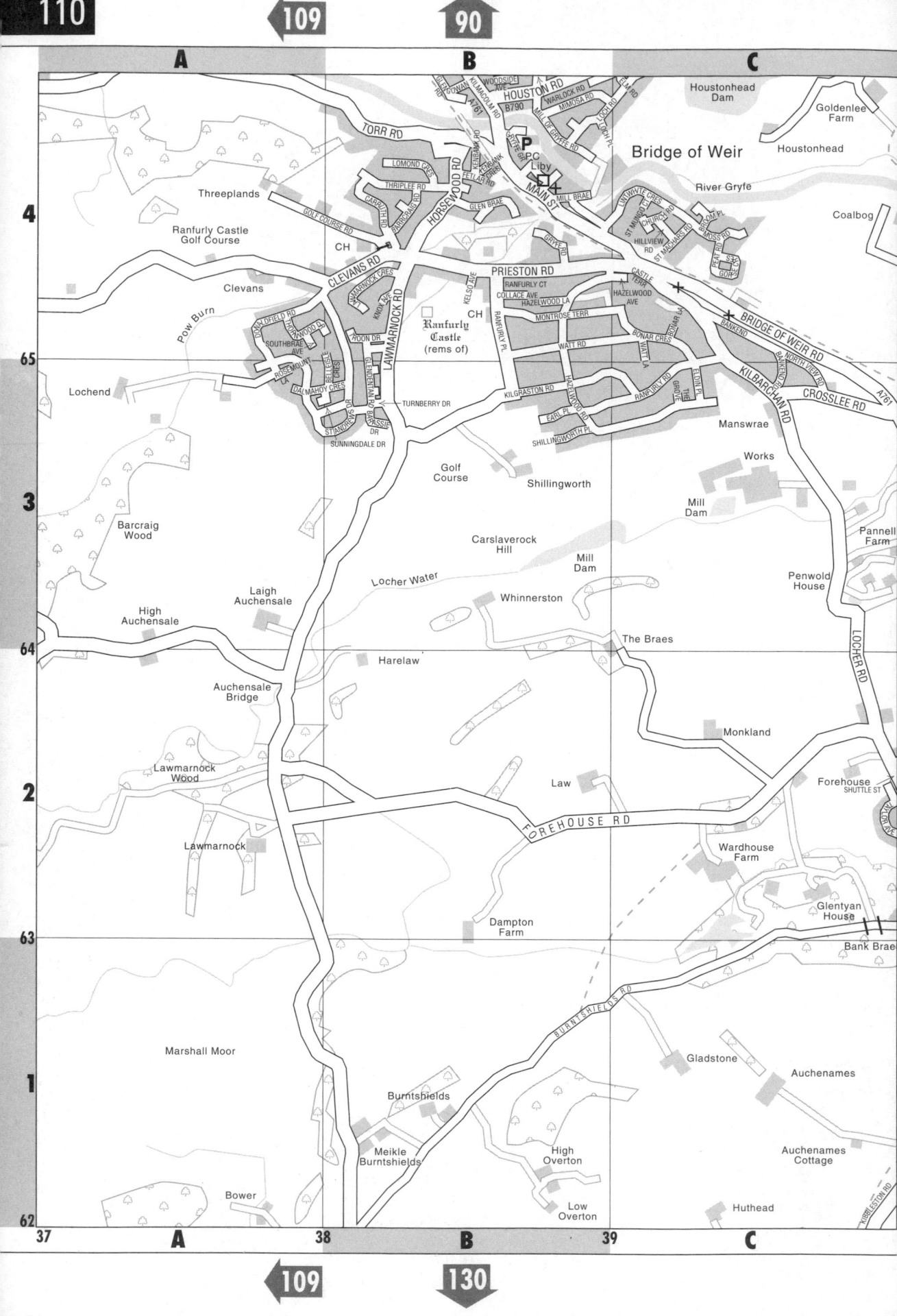

A   B   C

Houstonhead
Dam

WOODSIDE AVE
HOUSTON RD
WARLOCK RD
MIMOSA RD
A761
B790
ELM RD
LOCH RD

KILMACOLM RD
MILL OF GRYFE RD

Goldenlee
Farm

TORR RD

Bridge of Weir

LOMOND CRES

Houstonhead

P
P C
Liby

HORSEWOOD RD

THRIPLEE RD

KEILBANK

FETLAR RD

River Gryfe

Coalbog

Threeplands

4

Ranfurly Castle
Golf Course

GOLF COURSE RD

CARRUTH RD

BARCRAIG RD

GLEN BRAE

MAIN ST

Mill Brae

ST MUNGO'S RD
ST MIRREN'S RD
CHURCH RD
LINTWHITE CRES
BROOM PL
CROSS RD
HILLVIEW RD

CH

CLEVANS RD

LAWMARNOCK CRES

KNOX RD

KELSO AVE

PRIESTON RD

Ranfurly Ct
COLLACE AVE
HAZELWOOD LA

CASTLE
TERR
HAZELWOOD
AVE

+

+

Clevans

CH

BRIDGE OF WEIR RD

Pow Burn

DALINFIELD RD
HAZELWOOD LA
SOUTHBRAE
AVE
ROSE MOUNT
BELLFLAT
DALMAHOY CRES
GLENORCHY DR
BASSIE
DR
ST ANDREWS DR
SUNNINGDALE DR

LAWMARNOCK RD

Ranfurly
Castle
(rems of)

RANFURLY PL

MONTROSE TERR

WATT RD

BONAR CRES

WATT LA

KILBARCHAN RD
BANKEND
NORTH VIEW RD
BANKFIELD RD

A761

65

Lochend

TURNBERRY DR

KILGRASTON RD

HAZELWOOD RD

EARL PL

RANFURLY GRO
THE GROVE
ELDIN PL

CROSSLEE RD

Manswrae

Works

SHILLINGWORTH PL

Golf
Course

Shillingworth

Mill
Dam

Pannell
Farm

3

Barcraig
Wood

Carslaverock
Hill

Mill
Dam

Penwold
House

Laigh
Auchensale

Locher Water

Whinnerston

LOCHER RD

High
Auchensale

The Braes

64

Harelaw

Auchensale
Bridge

Monkland

Lawmarnock
Wood

Law

Forehouse
SHUTTLE ST

2

FOREHOUSE RD

Wardhouse
Farm

Lawmarnock

Glentyan
House

Dampton
Farm

BURNTSHIELDS RD

Bank Brae

63

Marshall Moor

Gladstone

Auchenames

1

Burntshields

Meikle
Burntshields

High
Overton

Auchenames
Cottage

KIBBLESTON RD

Bower

Low
Overton

Huthead

62

37   38   39

A   B   C

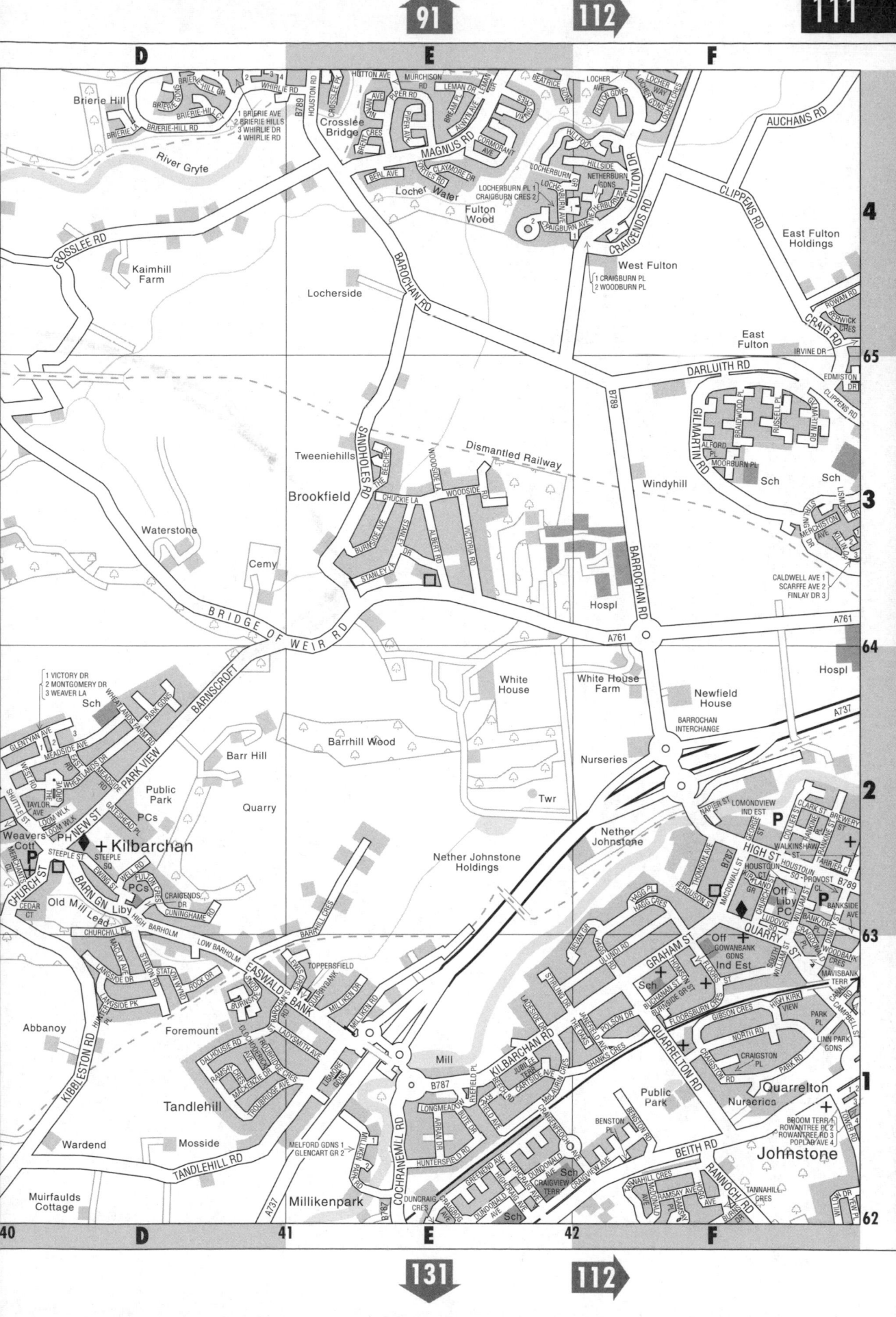

D E F

Brierie Hill
BRIERIE LA
BRIERIE-HILL GR
BRIERIE-HILL RD
1 BRIERIE AVE
2 BRIERIE HILLS
3 WHIRLIE DR
4 WHIRLIE RD
WHIRLIE RD

River Gryfe

Crosslee Bridge

HUTTON AVE
MURCHISON AVE
PIPER RD
LEMAN DR
BEATRICE...

HOUSTON RD
CROSSLEE CRES

MAGNUS RD
Locher Water

BERL AVE
CLAYMORE DR

CORMORANT AVE

Fulton Wood

LOCHERBURN PL 1
CRAIGBURN CRES 2
CRAIGBURN AVE

LOCHER
LOCHER AVE
FELTON GDNS
HILLSIDE
LOCHERBURN GR
NETHERBURN GDNS
NETHERBURN AVE
LOCHERBURN...

FULTON DR
CRAIGENDS RD

AUCHANS RD

CLIPPENS RD

East Fulton Holdings

West Fulton
1 CRAIGBURN PL
2 WOODBURN PL

ROWAN RD
BERWICK CRES
CRAIG RD

CROSSLEE RD

Kaimhill Farm

BAROCHAN RD

Locherside

East Fulton
IRVINE DR
EDMISTON DR

65

DARLUITH RD

B789

GILMARTIN RD
BRADWOOD PL
RUSSELL PL
ALFORD PL
MOORBURN PL

GLYN MARTIN RD
CLIPPENS RD

Sch

Sch

Dismantled Railway

Tweeniehills
SANDHOLES RD
BEECHES

Windyhill

MERCHISTON AVE
LISMORE DR
KILN LA

3

Brookfield
CHUCKIE LA
WOODSIDE RD
WOODSIDE RD
BURNSIDE AVE
STANLEY DR
STANLEY AVE
ALBERT RD
VICTORIA RD

CALDWELL AVE 1
SCARFFE AVE 2
FINLAY DR 3

Waterstone

Cemy

Hospl

BAROCHAN RD

A761 A761

BRIDGE OF WEIR RD

A761

64

1 VICTORY DR
2 MONTGOMERY DR
3 WEAVER LA
Sch
GLENTYAN AVE
MEADSIDE AVE
WEST RD
WHEATLANDS FARM RD
WHEATLANDS DR
PARK GDNS

BARNSCROFT

White House

White House Farm

Newfield House

Hospl

BAROCHAN INTERCHANGE

A737

Barr Hill

Barrhill Wood

Nurseries

2

PARK VIEW

Public Park
PCs

Quarry

Twr

Nether Johnstone

NAPIER ST
LOMONDVIEW IND EST
COLLIER ST
CLARK ST
BREWERY
WALKINSHAW ST
TARTER CT
PROVOST CL
B789
BANKSIDE AVE

P

TAYLOR AVE
SHUTTLE ST
LOOM WLK
GATESHEAD DR

Weavers Cott
P
CHURCH ST
STEEPLE ST
STEEPLE SQ
NEW ST
WELL RD
FULTON GR
PCs

+ Kilbarchan

Nether Johnstone Holdings

HIGH ST
HOUSTOUN SQ
HOUSTOUN
HOLLAND GR
LUDOVIC SQ
Off Liby
PC
MACDOWALL ST
FERGUSON ST
P
BANK...
WOODBANK

Off
GOWANBANK GDNS
Ind Est

QUARRY
MAVISBANK TERR

BARN GN
Old Mill Lead
HIGH BARHOLM
CRAIGENDS DR
CUNINGHAME
CHURCHILL PL
LANGSIDE AVE
LANGSIDE DR
LANGSIDE PK
LOW BARHOLM

BARRHILL CRES

63

Cedar Ct

GRAHAM ST
Sch
BUCHANAN ST
BURNSIDE GR
FLOORSBURN CRES
SOUTH WILLIAM ST

CAMPBELL PL

KIBBLESTON RD

Abbanoy

Foremount

KILBARCHAN RD
JUBILEE TERR
CARTSIDE AVE
LADYSMITH AVE
MILLIKEN RD

Mill
B787

GIBSON CRES
NORTH RD
CRAIGSTON PL
HIGH KIRK VIEW
PARK PL
LINN PARK GDNS

Quarrelton
Nurseries

EASWALD BANK
TOPPERSFIELD
DALHOUSIE RD
RAMSAY AVE
MACKENZIE AVE
TROMBRIDGE AVE

ROCK DR

Tandlehill

Wardend Mosside

MELFORD GDNS 1
GLENCART GR 2

LONGMEADOW
ARRAN DR
HUNTERSFIELD RD

Mill

BENSTON PL

Public Park

BROOM TERR 1
ROWANTREE PL 2
ROWANTREE PL 3
POPLAR AVE 4

1

Muirfaulds Cottage

TANDLEHILL RD

A737

Millikenpark

COCHRANEMILL RD
DUNCRAIG CRES

CRAIGVIEW TERR
CRAIGVIEW AVE
DUNDONALD AVE
Sch

GREENEND AVE
Sch

BEITH RD

Johnstone

RANNOCH RD
TANNAHILL CRES

62

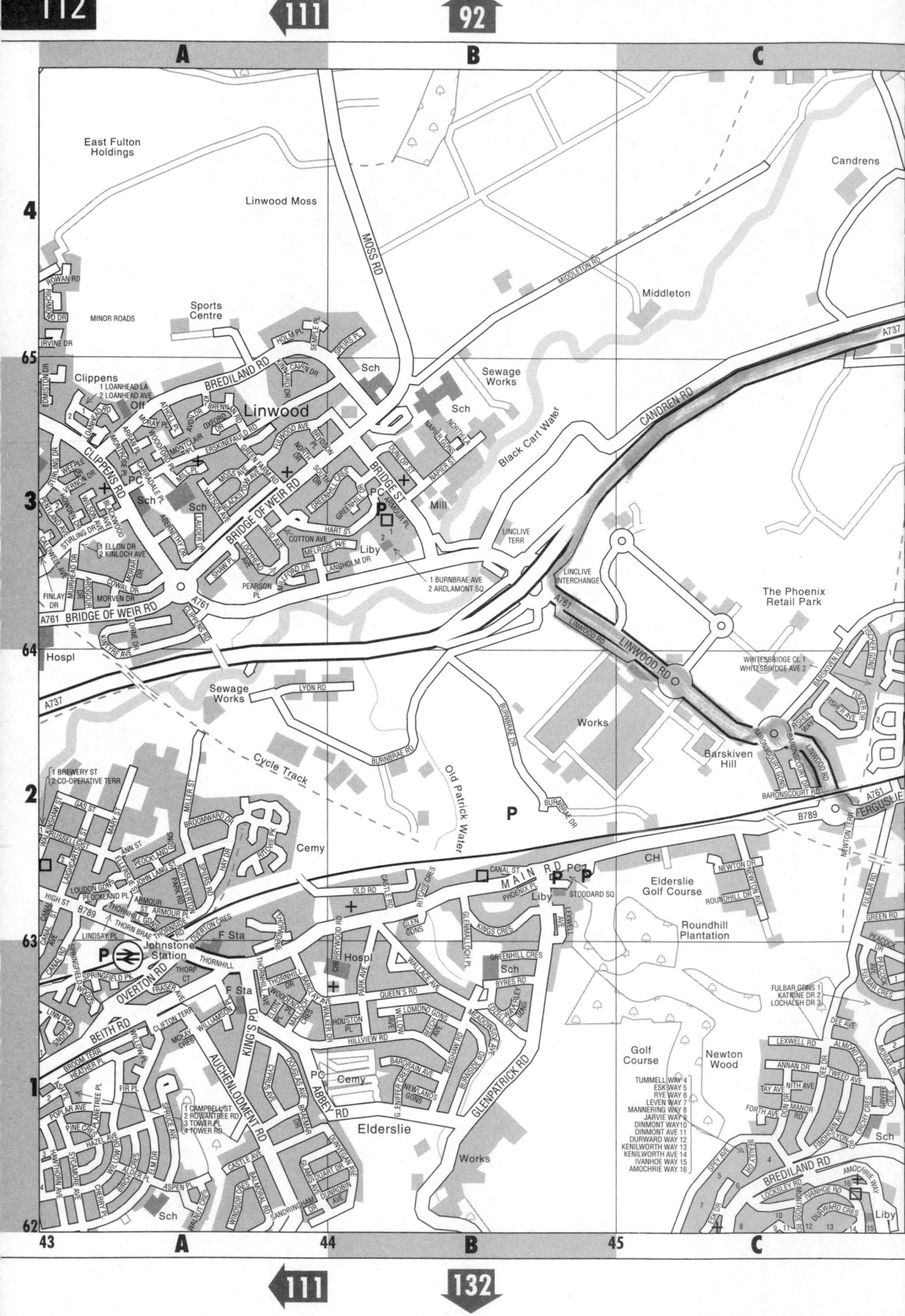

East Fulton Holdings

Linwood Moss

Candrens

MOSS RD

MIDDLETON RD

Middleton

A737

4

Sports Centre

Sewage Works

Black Cart Water

CANDREN RD

65

Clippens
1 LOANHEAD LA
2 LOANHEAD AVE

BREDILAND RD

Sch

Off

Linwood

CAIRN DR

SPIERS PL

HOLM PL
SEMPLE PL

Sch

PC

CLIPPENS RD

BRIDGE OF WEIR RD

BRIDGE ST

Mill

LINCLIVE TERR

The Phoenix Retail Park

3

PC

Liby

LINCLIVE INTERCHANGE

1 BURNBRAE AVE
2 ARDLAMONT SQ

LINCLIVE INTERCHANGE

A761

LINWOOD RD

64

Hospl

A761 BRIDGE OF WEIR RD

A761

WHITESBRIDGE CL 1
WHITESBRIDGE AVE 2

A737

Sewage Works

LYON RD

BURNBRAE DR

Works

Barskiven Hill

LINWOOD RD

BARONSCOURT RD

2

1 BREWERY ST
2 CO-OPERATIVE TERR

GAS ST

Cycle Track

Old Patrick Water

P

BURNBRAE DR

B789

FERGUSLIE

A761

Cemy

BURNBRAE RD

P

CANAL ST

MAIN RD PC

CH

Elderslie Golf Course

NEWTON DR

63

Johnstone Station

OVERTON RD

F Sta

Thornhill

F Sta

OLD RD

CASTLE RD

Liby

STODDARD SQ

Roundhill Plantation

Hospl

BEITH RD

KING'S RD

ABBEY RD

AUCHENLODMENT RD

Cemy

GLENPATRICK RD

Golf Course

Newton Wood

FULBAR GDNS 1
KATRINE DR 2
LOCHALSH DR 3

LEXWELL RD

ANNAN DR

1

PC

Elderslie

1 CAMPBELL ST
2 ROWANTREE RD
3 TOWER PL
4 TOWER RD

Works

TUMMELL WAY 4
ESK WAY 5
RYE WAY 6
LEVEN WAY 7
MANNERING WAY 8
JARVIE WAY 9
DINMONT WAY 10
DINMONT AVE 11
DURWARD WAY 12
KENILWORTH WAY 13
KENILWORTH AVE 14
IVANHOE WAY 15
AMOCHRIE WAY 16

BREDILAND RD

Sch

AMOCHRIE WAY

Liby

62

43   A   44   B   45   C

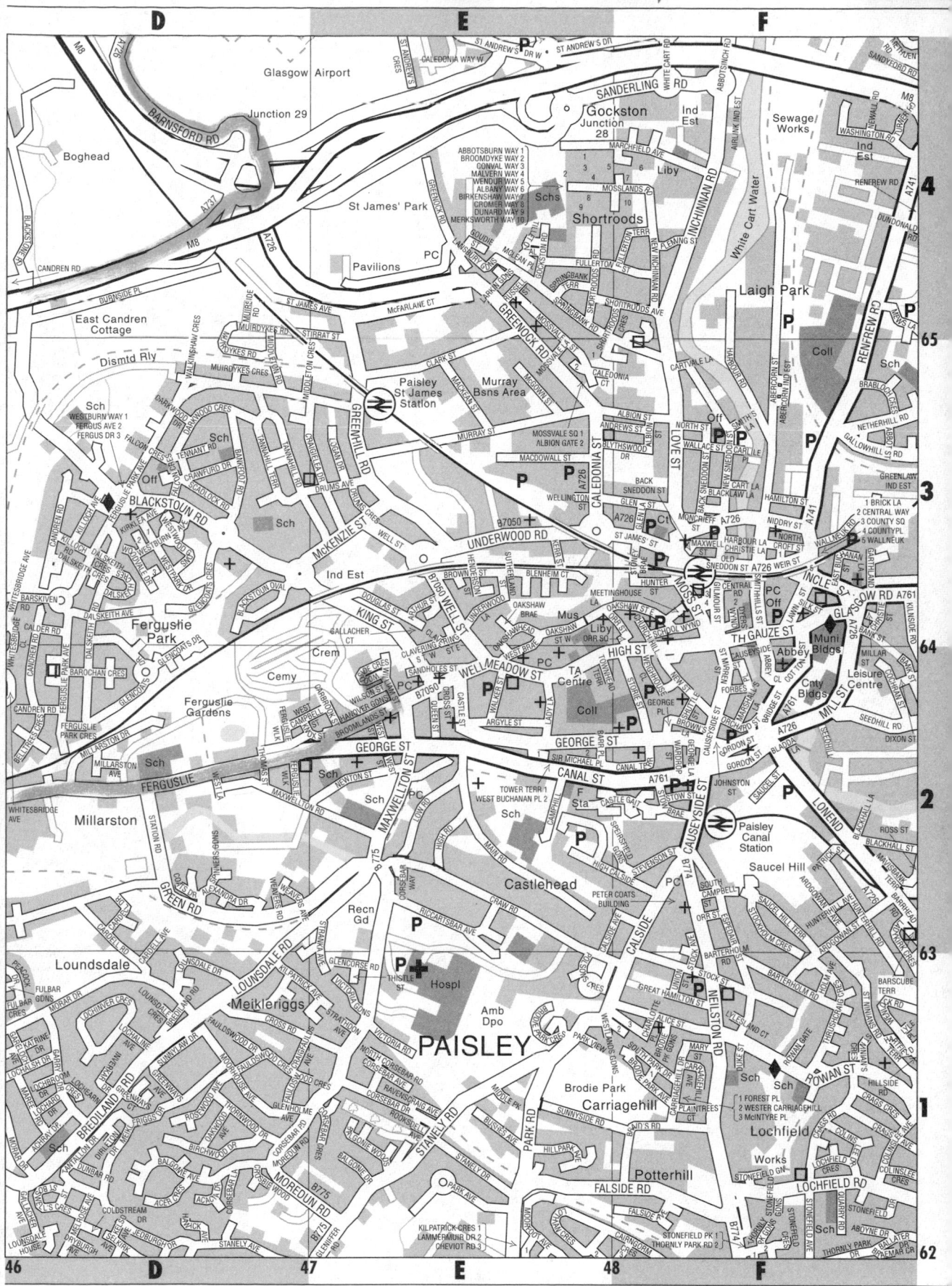

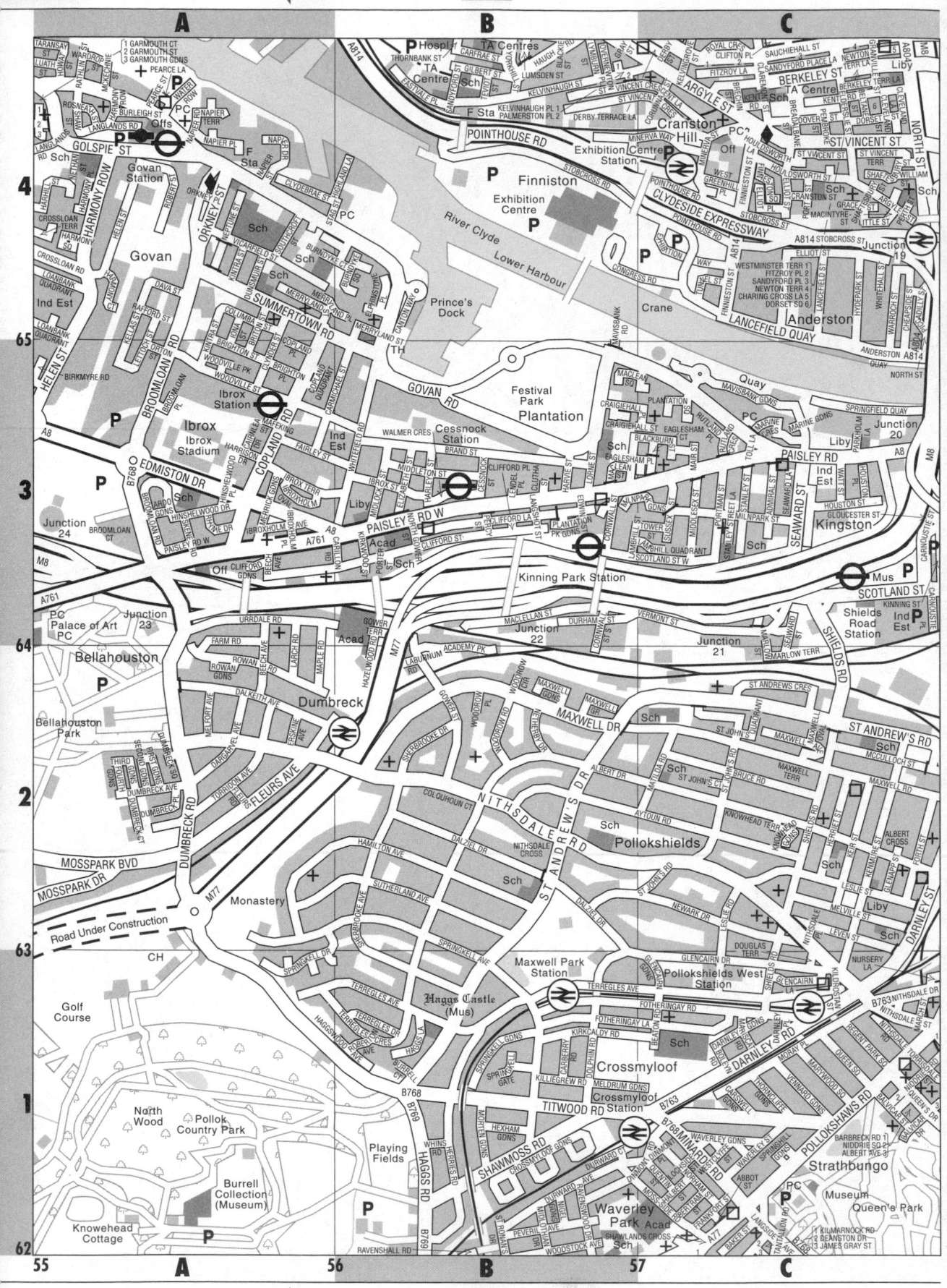

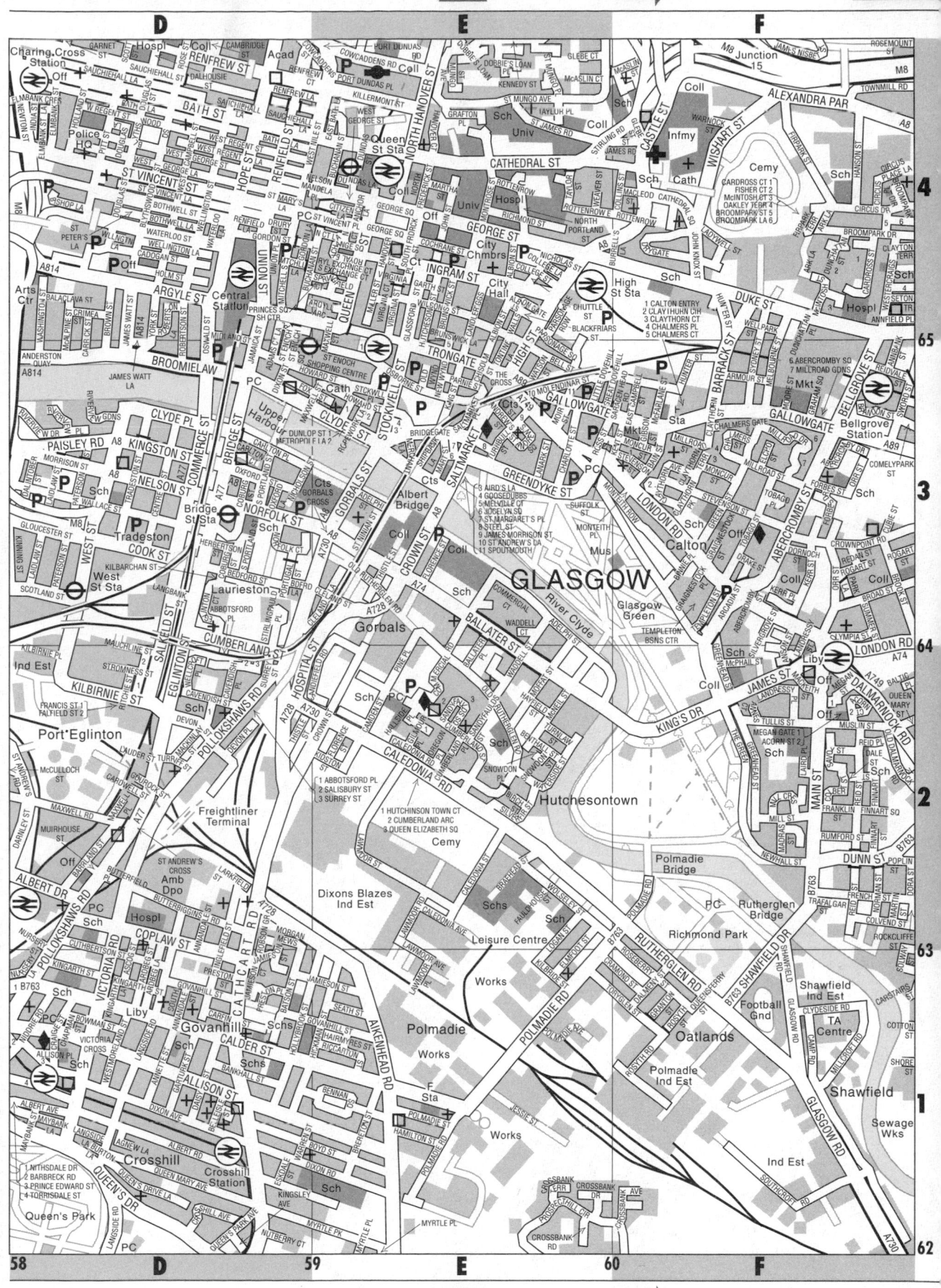

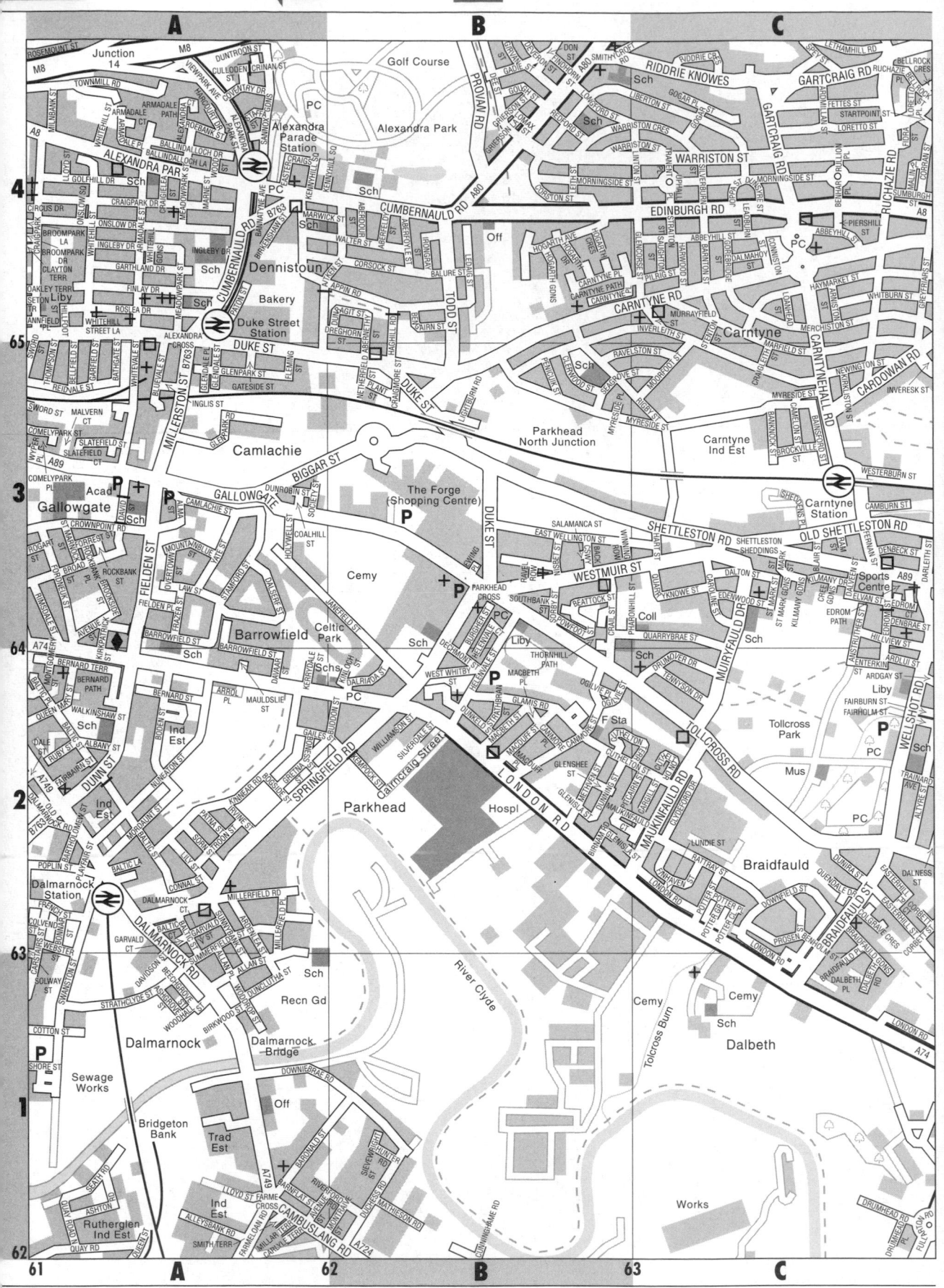

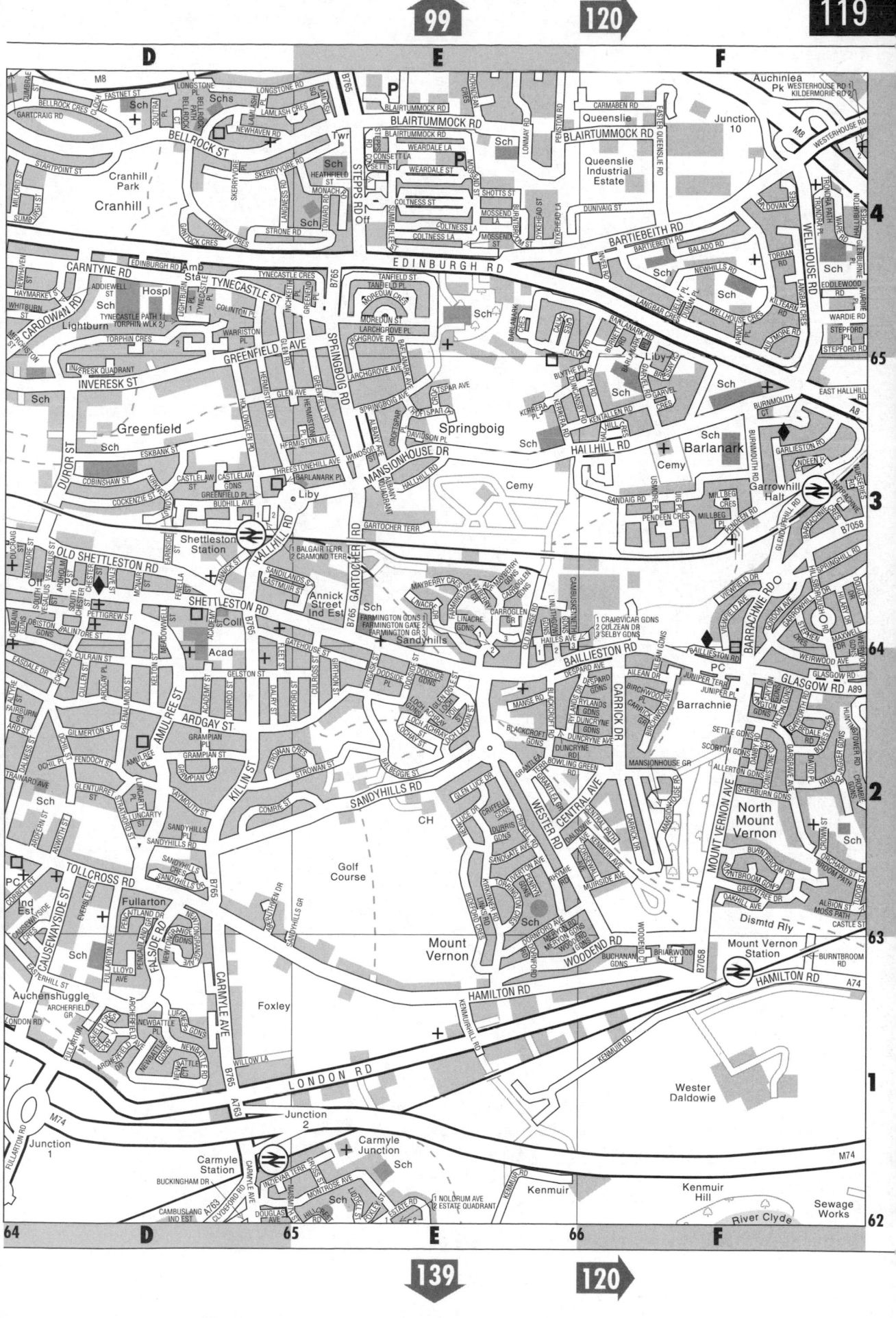

A   B   C

65

4

3

64

2

63

1

62

F Sta

Liby

WESTERHOUSE RD

Easterhouse

Sch

DUBTON ST

CAIRNBROOK IND EST

DRUMLANRIG AVE

DRUMLANRIG QUADRANT 1
DALILEA PATH 2
DRUMLANRIG PL 3

DUNPHAIL DR

Sch

Schs

Heatheryknowe

COMMON HEAD RD

Commonhead

Heatheryknowe Rd

HEATHERYKNOWE RD

M73

A752

West Maryston

DENMILNE RD

Netherhouse

Junction 9

SPRINGCROFT RD

EASTERHOUSE RD

ROGERFIELD RD

Easterhouse Station

Rhindmuir Cres

Junction 8

MANSE RD

MELROSE AVE

A89

Springhill

HALL HILL RD

SPRINGCROFT AVE

SPRINGCROFT GDNS

1 MICKLEHOUSE PL
2 MICKLEHOUSE OVAL
3 MICKLEHOUSE WYND
4 THORNBRIDGE AVE
5 BARONY CT
6 BARONY WYND
7 QUEENSBY AVE
8 FORTEVIOT AVE

Swinton

DALREOCH PATH

ROSLYN DR

CAMPSIE VIEW

BRAESIDE CRES

WINDSOR PATH 1
PRINCESS DR 2
MINSTER WLK 3
CASTLE WAY 4

Garrowhill

BARRACHNIE RD

EDINBURGH RD

SPRINGHILL RD

BANNERCROSS GDNS 9
BANNERCROSS AVE 10
THORNBRIDGE GDNS 11

Sch

BENTS RD

SWINTON AVE

SWINTON CRES

GLASGOW AND EDINBURGH RD

COATBRIDGE RD

A8

MONKLAND VIEW CRES

ROSEBANK

Junction 2

Crosshill

BREDISHOLM RD

GLASGOW RD

Sch

HUNTINGTOWER RD

WILLOWDALE CRES

ROWANDALE AVE

ROSEDALE DR

LONGLEE

SANDFORD GDNS

CHURCH ST

MAIN ST

Liby

Off

Muirhead

ELLISMUIR PL

BREDISHOLM TERR

Ellismuir Farm

THORNYBURN DR RD

BRACADALE DR

GLASGOW AND EDINBURGH RD

A8

Baillieston

SOUTH SCOTT ST

MUIRHEAD RD

DRUMPELLIER AVE

CALDERWOOD AVE

Sch

Ellismuir

Baillieston Station

BOGHALL RD

North Calder Water

Newlands Glen

1 BLAIR CRES
2 KELBURNE GDNS
3 ORCHARD ST
4 CALDERWOOD GDNS
5 BROOM PATH
6 MOSS PATH

Broomhouse

Dismantled Railway

A74

DALDOWIE RD

BAILLIESTON RD

CALDERPARK AVE

LUSSHILL TERR

PC

Glasgow Zoo

Woodhead Farm

Calderbraes Golf Course

Newlands Farm

M73

Calderbraes

1 CALDERBRAES AVE
2 CATHKIN RD
3 CATHKIN GDNS
4 DECHMONT RD

ATHOLL TERR 5
BROOMFIELD TERR 6
LAIDLAW GDNS 7
MONROE PL 8
MELROSE GDNS 9

HAMILTON RD

PC

P

P

ROUNDKNOWE RD

Calder Bridge

CH

Junction 1

GLASGOW RD

A74

OLD EDINBURGH RD

Birkenshaw

Sch

Sewage Works

M74

Junction 3

M74

NEWLANDS RD

B7001

67   A   68   B   69   C

119 **140**

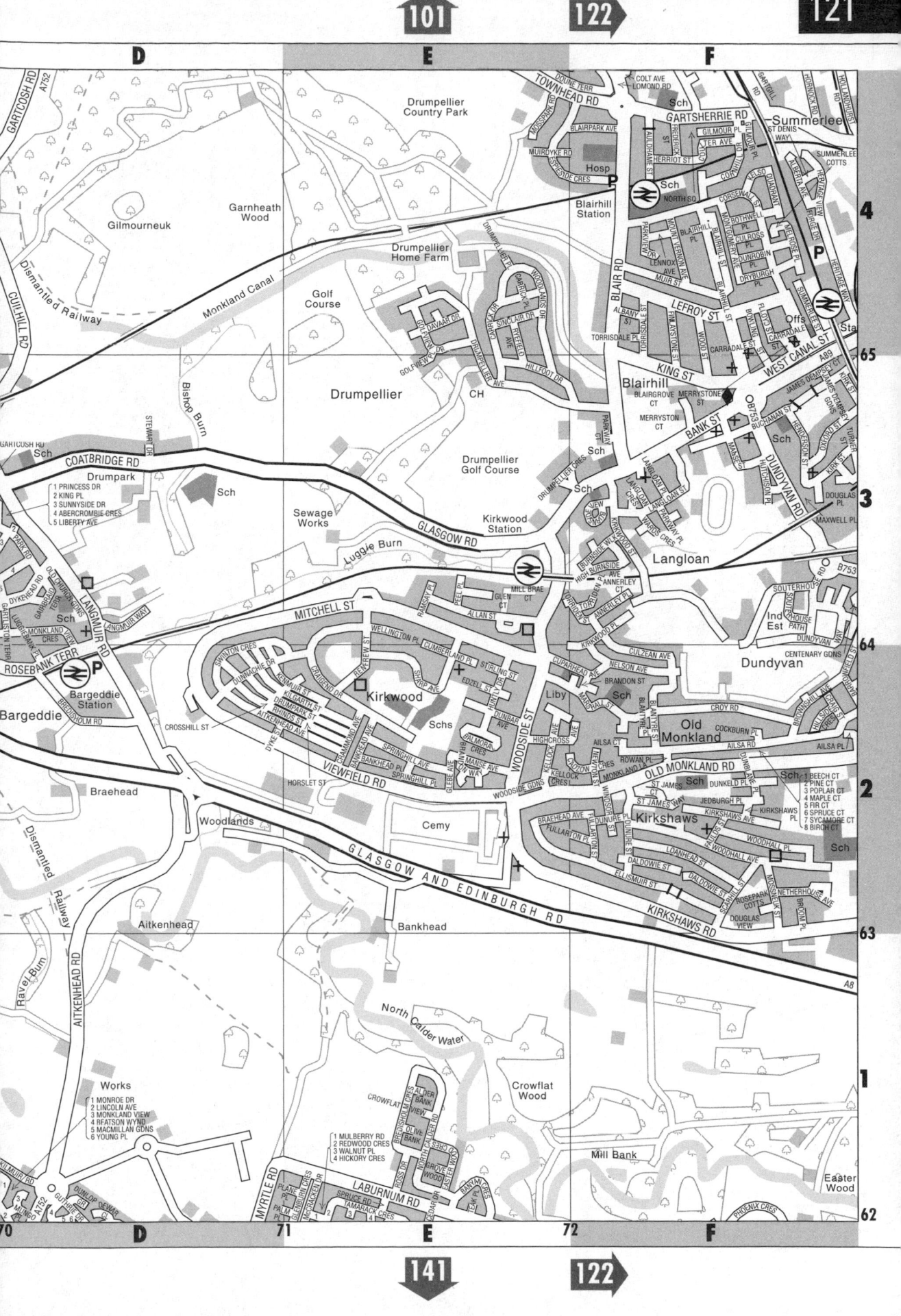

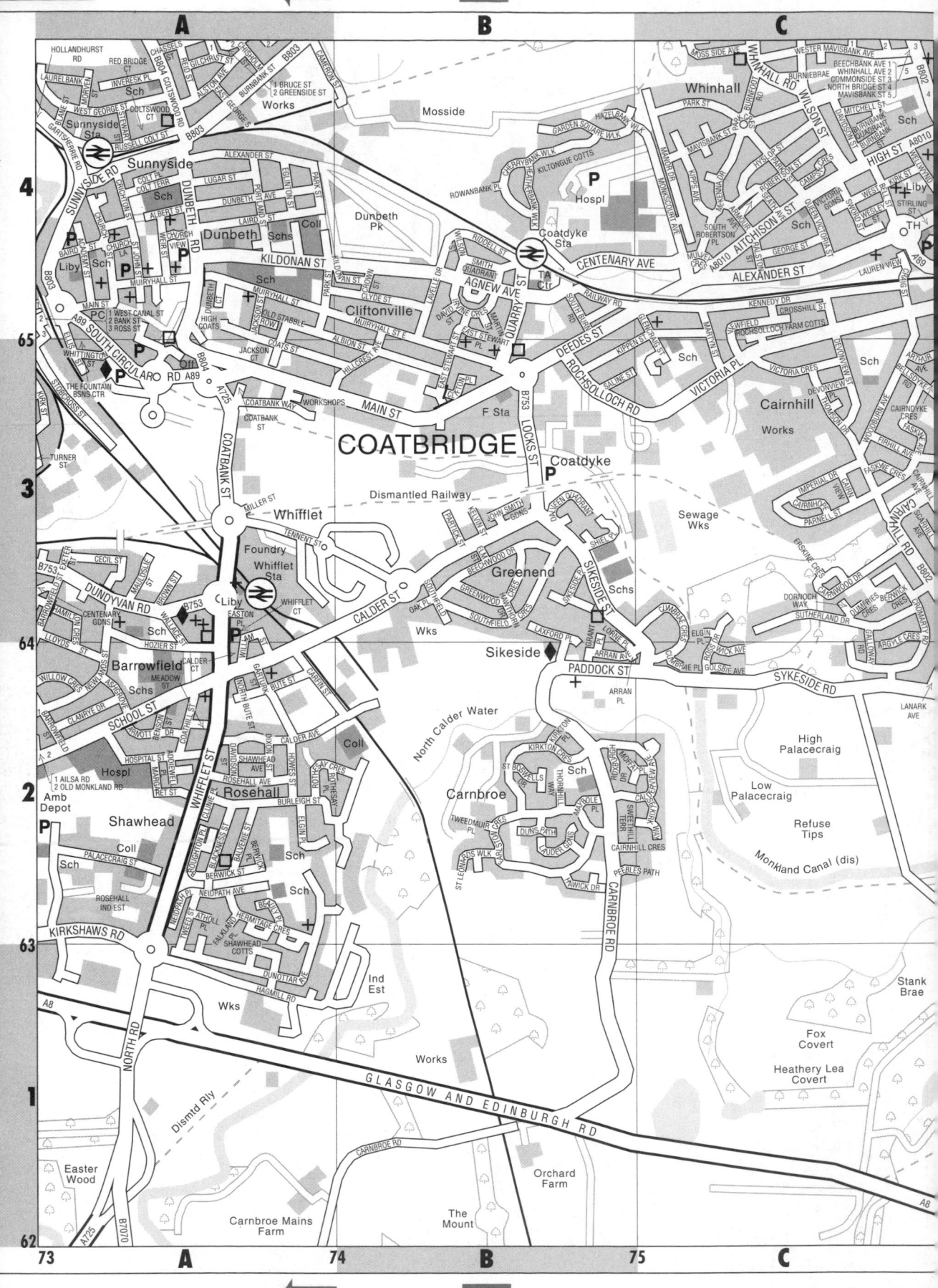

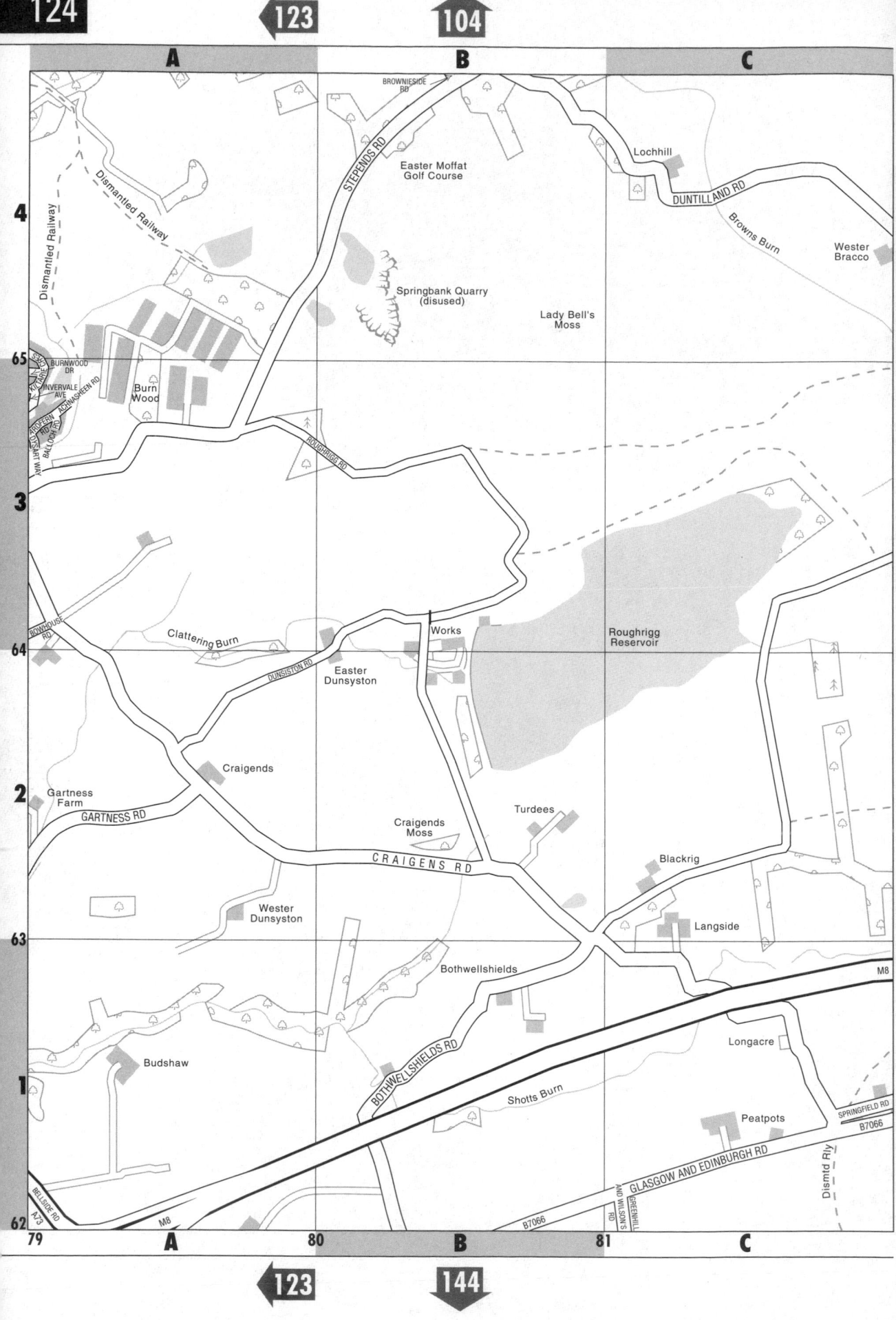

BROWNSIDE RD

STEPENDS RD

Easter Moffat
Golf Course

Lochhill

DUNTILLAND RD

Browns Burn

Wester
Bracco

Dismantled Railway

Dismantled Railway

Springbank Quarry
(disused)

Lady Bell's
Moss

4

BURNWOOD DR

INVERVALE AVE

ACHNASHEEN RD

BALLOCH RD

CROFFERN RD

DESART WAY

Burn
Wood

65

ROUGHRIGG RD

3

BRAWHOUSE RD

Clattering Burn

Works

Roughrigg
Reservoir

DUNSISTON RD

Easter
Dunsyston

64

Craigends

Turdees

Blackrig

2

Gartness
Farm

GARTNESS RD

Craigends
Moss

Langside

CRAIGENS RD

Wester
Dunsyston

63

Bothwellshields

M8

Longacre

Budshaw

BOTHWELLSHIELDS RD

Shotts Burn

Peatpots

SPRINGFIELD RD

B7066

1

GLASGOW AND EDINBURGH RD

GREENHILL RD

AND WILSON'S RD

Dismtd Rly

BELLSIDE RD

A73

M8

B7066

62

79   A   80   B   81   C

Watch Moss

Black Hill

Torrance

Tipperdavio

Television
Station

Mast

Dun Daugh

Tod Holes

Forrestburn Water

Mountcow

Well Knowe

DUNTILLAND RD

Duntilland Hill

Dismantled Railway

Duntilland Farm

Duntilland Quarry

M8

Dismantled Railway

Sewage
Works

Shotts Burn

B7066

SCHOOL RD

Sch

HIRST RD

BOGFOOT RD

Kirk of
Shotts

CROSSART
ST

REID ST

DAVID ST

MUIRHALL TERR

GIBSON ST

MAIN ST

BLACKCROFT TERR

MUIRHEAD
GDNS

KIRKVIEW
AVE

Threeprig

Salsburgh

SPRINGFIELD RD

LORNE
GDNS

CARSDALE
AVE

DUNTILLAND AVE

CARVALE AVE

Manse

Glebe
Farm

MANSE RD

NEWMILL AND CANTHILL RD

MARGARET AVE 1
SIGHTHILL TERR 2
BERTRAM DR 3

Roundknowe
Wood

Canthills
Plantation

Riven Loch

Spoil
Tip

125
106

Baads

Forrestburn Water

Works

Blairmuckhole and Forrestdyke Rd

Forrestburn Holding

Bridgehill

Forrestburn Water

Works

Papperthill Craigs

4

Forrest Water

FORREST RD

Bentfoot

Forrestburn Reservoir

Blairmuckhole

65

3

Dewshills

Blairmains

M8

64

Mine (dis)

Llynallan Rd

B7066

DREWSHILL COTTS

Junction 5

South Blair

TV Station

Mast

HOUSE O' MUIR RD

North Hirst

Welleslea

M8

2

Shotts Burn

HIRST RD

SOUTH HIRST RD

B7057

HIRSTRIGG COTTS

South Hirst

Easter Hassockrigg

Resr

Wester Hassockrigg

SHOTTSBURN RD

B7066

63

SHOTTS RD

River Almond

1

Cant Hills

FORTISSET RD

Opencast Workings

B717

NEWMILL AND CANTHILL RD

WEST BENHAR RD

B7057

BENHAR RD

B717

Easter Baton

62

85   A   86   B   87   C

125
146

D E F

Blairhill
Quarry

Forrestburn Water

Hill Farm

Dismtd Rly

Loan Farm

B718

Dismtd Rly

4

Blairmuckhill

Netherton Farm

Knowehead

M8

65

Service Area

Sewage Works

WESTCRAIGS RD

WHYTE ST

BURNBRAE RD

VIEWFIELD

Treebanks

Service Area

HOWBURN RD

MILLER ST

MILLER DR

MOLLISON

YOUNG CRES

POLKEMMET

MURDOS

Sch

POLKEMMET LA

POLKEMMET RD

BURNS CRES

3

How Burn

HOWBURN CRES

HAWTHORN DR

MAINS RD

LOAN PL

DUNN TERR

EAST MAIN ST

GREENRIGG COTTS

AIRMUCKHOLE AND FORRESTDYKE RD

NETHERTON ST

GIBBSHILL PL

PAXSTONE DR

PAXSTONE CRES

BANK RD

FORREST PL

RIG WAY

B7066

MOSSBURN AVE

WEST MAIN ST

Works

Hall

Sch

P

B718

STEWART GR

Harthill

Tam's Loup Quarry

Eastfield

Bertram St

BROOMHILL ST

BIRCH TERR

BAIRD TERR

ALMOND TERR

CHURCH ST

B717

OLD EASTFIELD ST

CUNNINGHAM TR

COVENANTER RD

FLAX MILL RD

MILL RD

VICTORIA ST

VICTORIA RD

ALBERT RD

BALBAKIE RD

STOEHEAD

PEDEN ST

MINTHILL PL

ORR TERR

Sch

MUIRHEAD PL

LIVINGSTONE QUADRANT

Paxtane

64

LLYNALLAN RD

HIRST RD

B711

B711

West Benhar

WEST BENHAR RD

Works

River Almond

2

Active Workings

Spoil Heap

63

Dismtd Rly

1

Brownhill Farm

Dismtd Rly

62

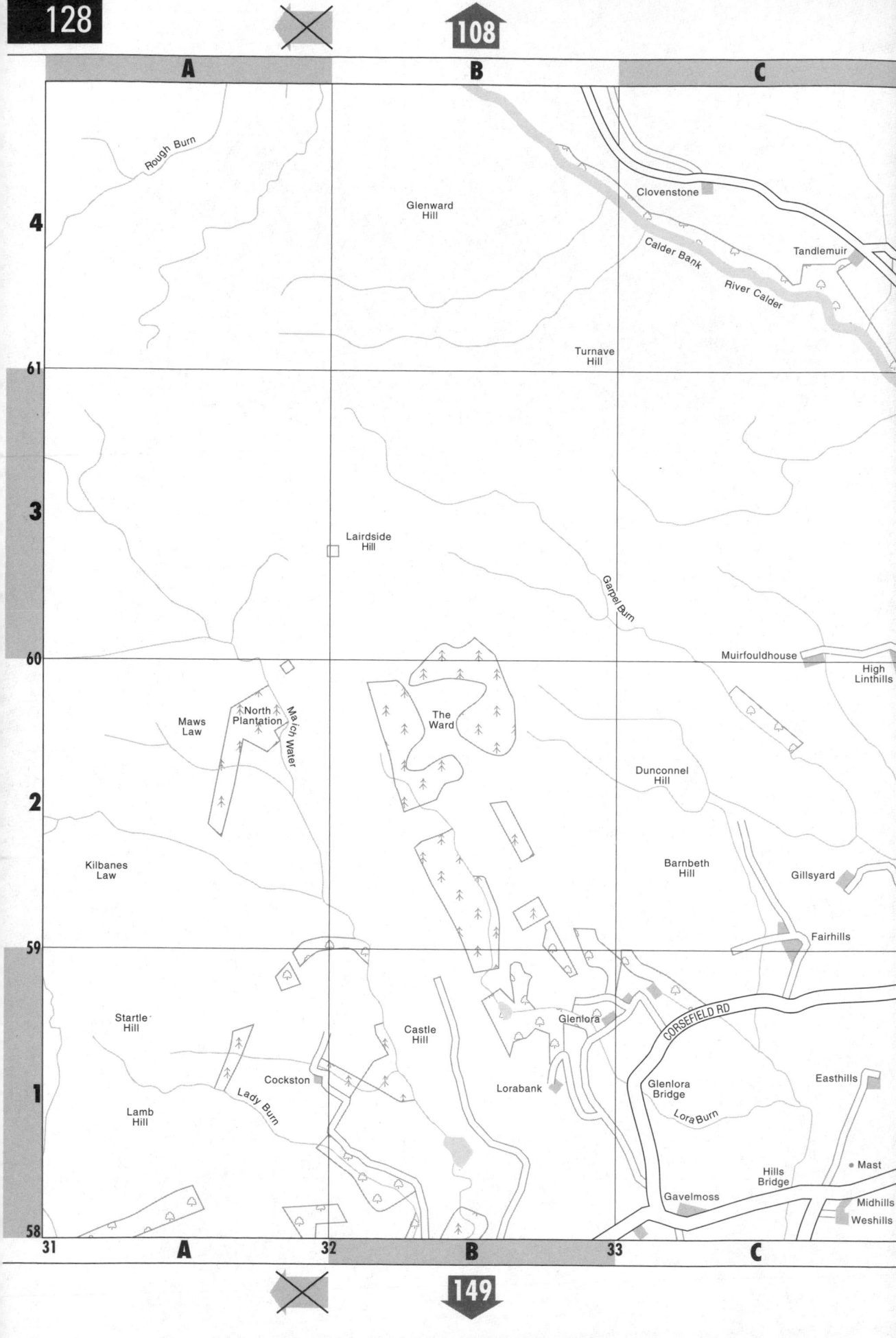

Rough Burn

Glenward
Hill

Clovenstone

Calder Bank

Tandlemuir

River Calder

4

Turnave
Hill

61

3

Lairdside
Hill

Garpel Burn

Muirfouldhouse

High
Linthills

60

North
Plantation

Maich Water

Maws
Law

The
Ward

Dunconnel
Hill

Kilbanes
Law

Barnbeth
Hill

Gillsyard

2

Fairhills

59

Startle
Hill

Castle
Hill

Glenlora

CORSEFIELD RD

Cockston

Lady Burn

Lorabank

Glenlora
Bridge

Easthills

1

Lamb
Hill

Lora Burn

Hills
Bridge

• Mast

Gavelmoss

Midhills

Weshills

58

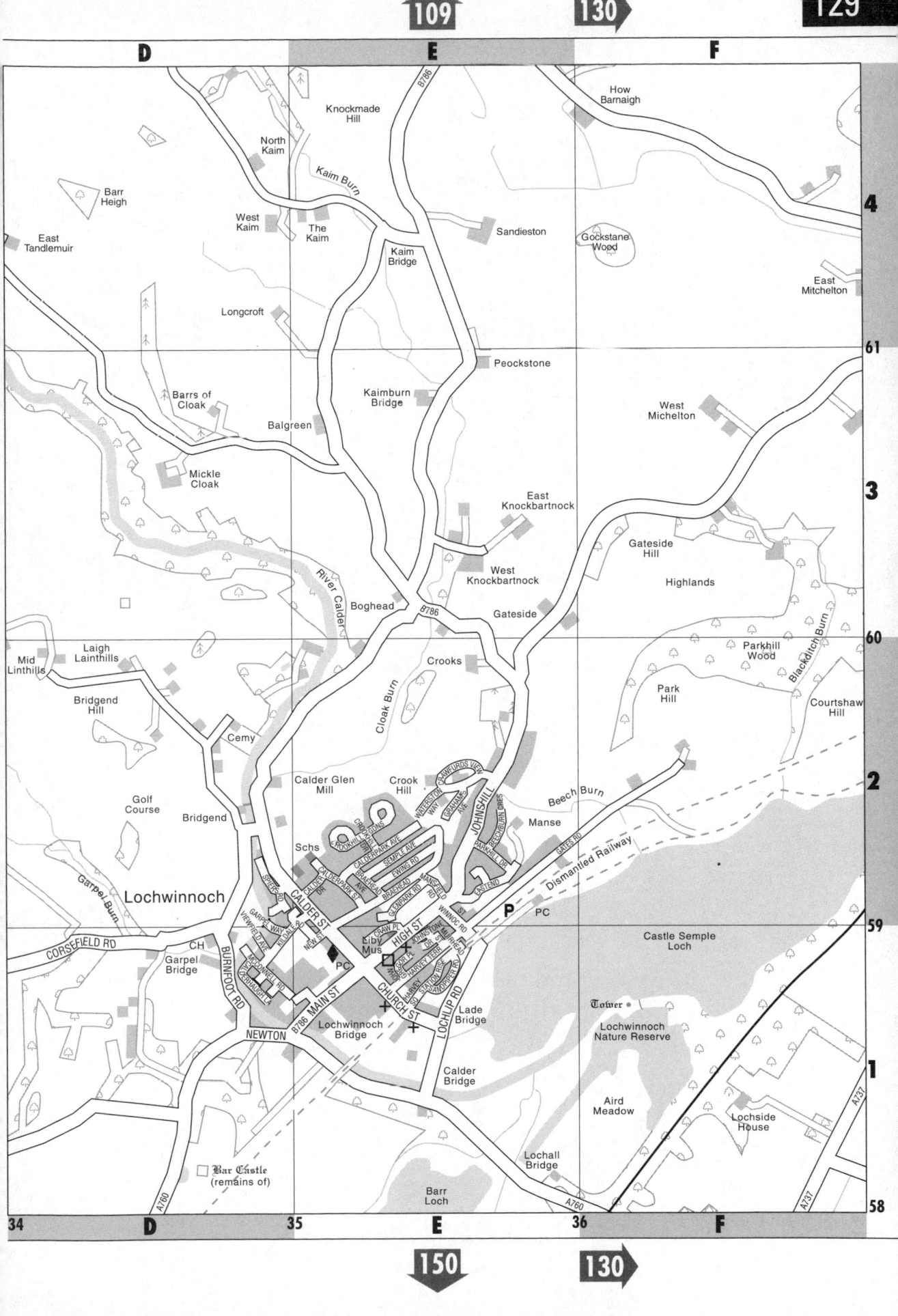

D
E
F

Knockmade
Hill

North Kaim

Kaim Burn

Barr
Heigh

West
Kaim

The
Kaim

Sandieston

How
Barnaigh

Gockstane
Wood

East
Mitchelton

4

East
Tandlemuir

Kaim
Bridge

Longcroft

Peockstone

61

Barrs of
Cloak

Balgreen

Kaimburn
Bridge

West
Michelton

Mickle
Cloak

East
Knockbartnock

Gateside
Hill

Highlands

3

River Calder

Boghead

B786

West
Knockbartnock

Gateside

Mid
Linthills

Laigh
Lainthills

Crooks

Parkhill
Wood

Blackditch Burn

60

Bridgend
Hill

Cemy

Cloak Burn

Park
Hill

Courtshaw
Hill

Golf
Course

Bridgend

Calder Glen
Mill

Crook
Hill

CRAWFURDS VIEW

WATERSTON WAY

JOHNSHILL

Beech Burn

Dismantled Railway

2

Garpel Burn

Lochwinnoch

Schs

CALDERPARK AVE
CROOKHILL GDNS
CALDERPARK ST
BRAEHEAD
SEMPLE AVE
EWING RD
MANSFIELD
BRAEPARK RD
GLENPARK AVE

SEAPARK
PARKHILL DR
CASTEND

Manse

P

PC

Castle Semple
Loch

59

CORSEFIELD RD

CH

Garpel
Bridge

BURNFOOT RD

SPIERS RD
GARPEL WAY
KILMALE PL
MCDOWALL RD
VIEWFIELD AVE
NETHERHAUGH LA

MAIN ST

B786

CALDER ST

NEW ST
CRAW PL
Liby
Mus
PC

HIGH ST
JOHNSTONE DR
NIMMO ST
MANSEFIELD

HARVEY TERR
STATION RD

CHURCH ST

LOCHLIP RD

Lade
Bridge

Tower

Lochwinnoch
Nature Reserve

Lochside
House

A737

1

NEWTON

Lochwinnoch
Bridge

Calder
Bridge

Aird
Meadow

□ Bar Castle
(remains of)

A760

Lochall
Bridge

Barr
Loch

A760

A737

58

34
D
35
E
36
F

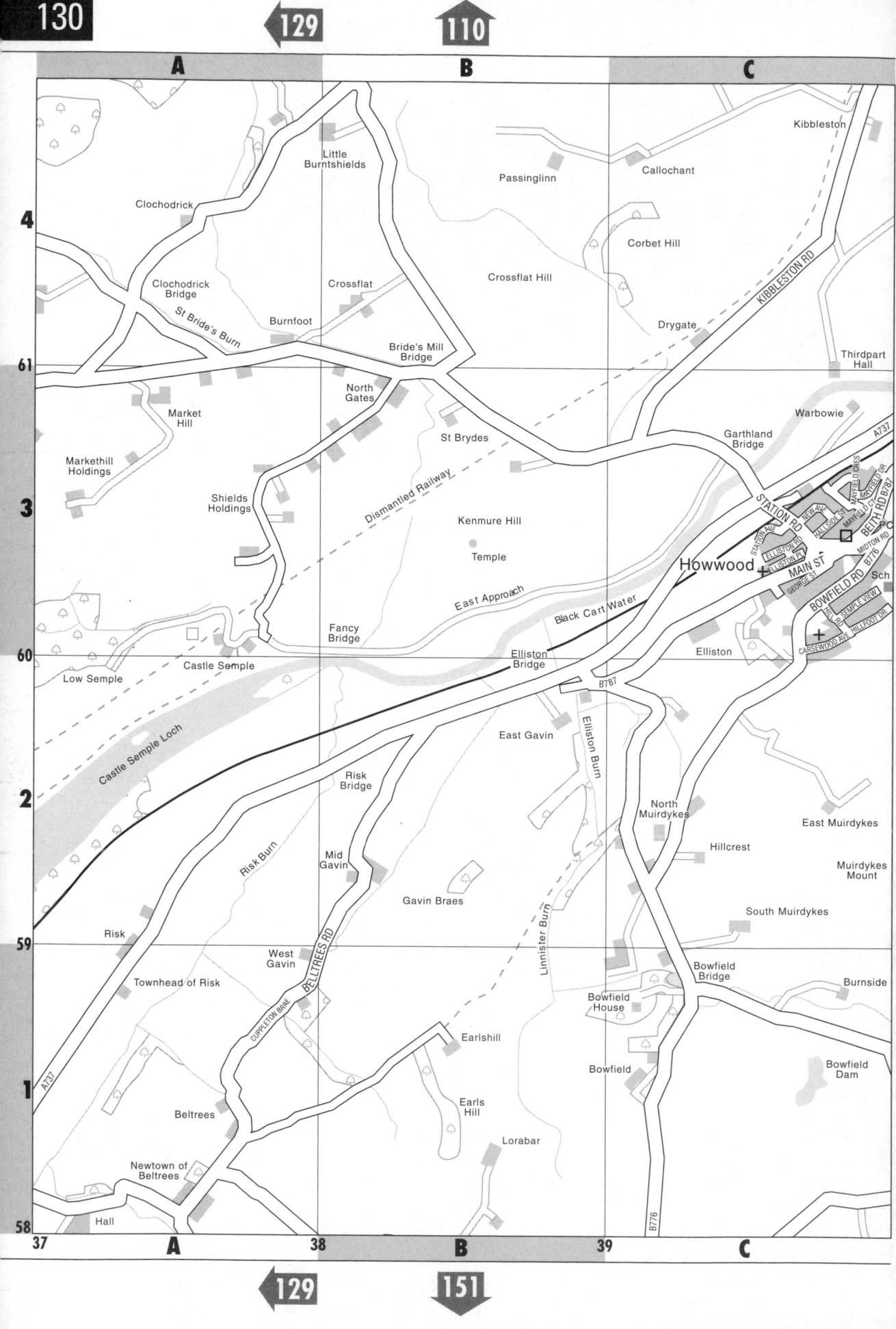

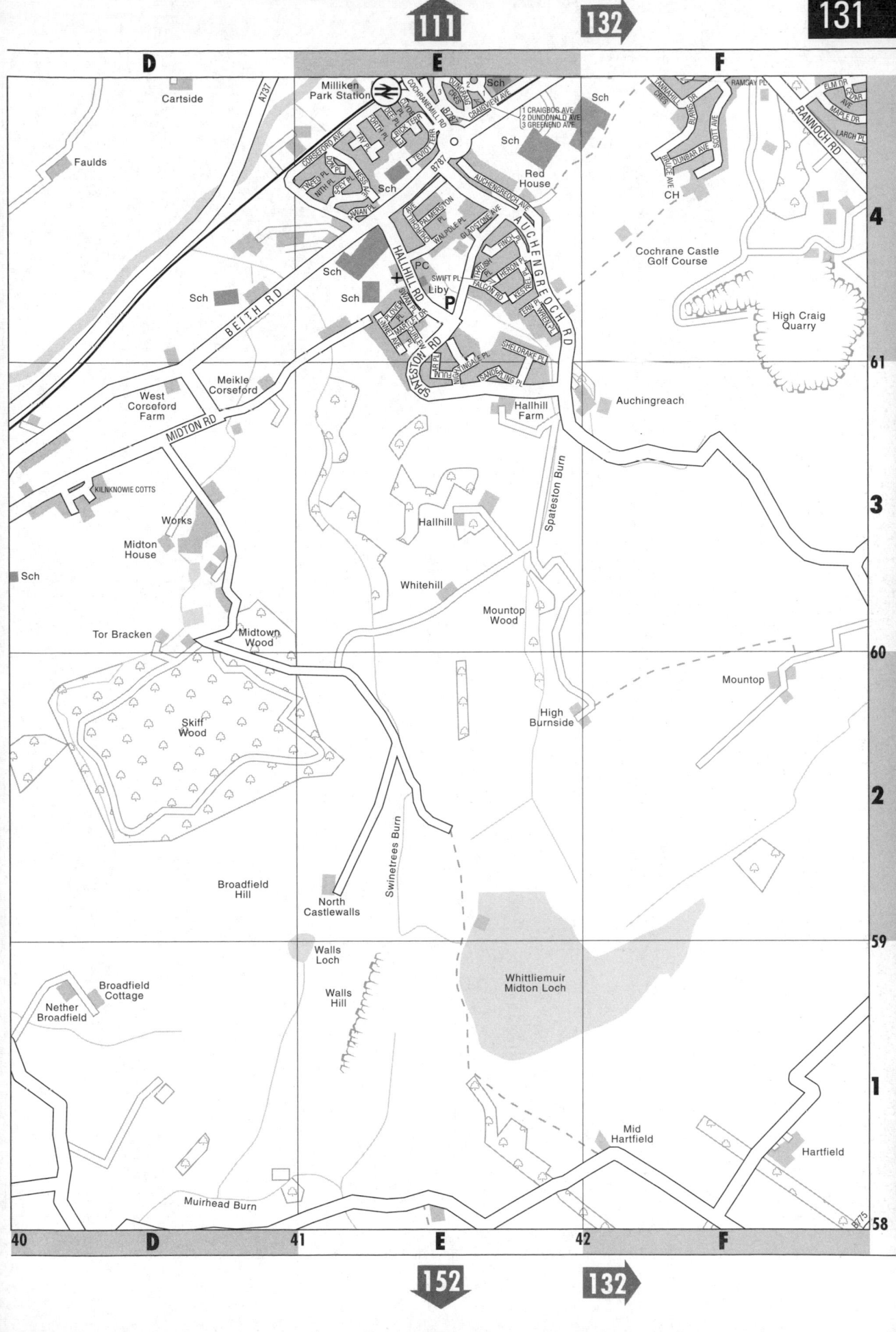

D   E   F

Cartside

Faulds

Milliken
Park Station

1 CRAIGBOS AVE
2 DUNDONALD AVE
3 GREENEND AVE

Sch

Sch

Red House

Cochrane Castle
Golf Course

High Craig
Quarry

4

RANNOCH RD

CH

Sch

Sch

BEITH RD

Sch

PC
Liby
P

Sch

HALLHILL RD

AUCHENGREOCH RD

SPATESTON RD

SWIFT PL

FALCON RD

SHELDRAKE PL

Hallhill
Farm

Auchingreach

61

West
Corseford
Farm

Meikle
Corseford

MIDTON RD

Spateston Burn

KILNKNOWIE COTTS

Works

Hallhill

3

Midton
House

Whitehill

Mountop
Wood

Sch

Tor Bracken

Midtown
Wood

Mountop

60

High
Burnside

Skiff
Wood

2

Swinetrees Burn

Broadfield
Hill

North
Castlewalls

Walls
Loch

59

Broadfield
Cottage

Nether
Broadfield

Walls
Hill

Whittliemuir
Midton Loch

1

Mid
Hartfield

Hartfield

Muirhead Burn

B775

58

40   D   41   E   42   F

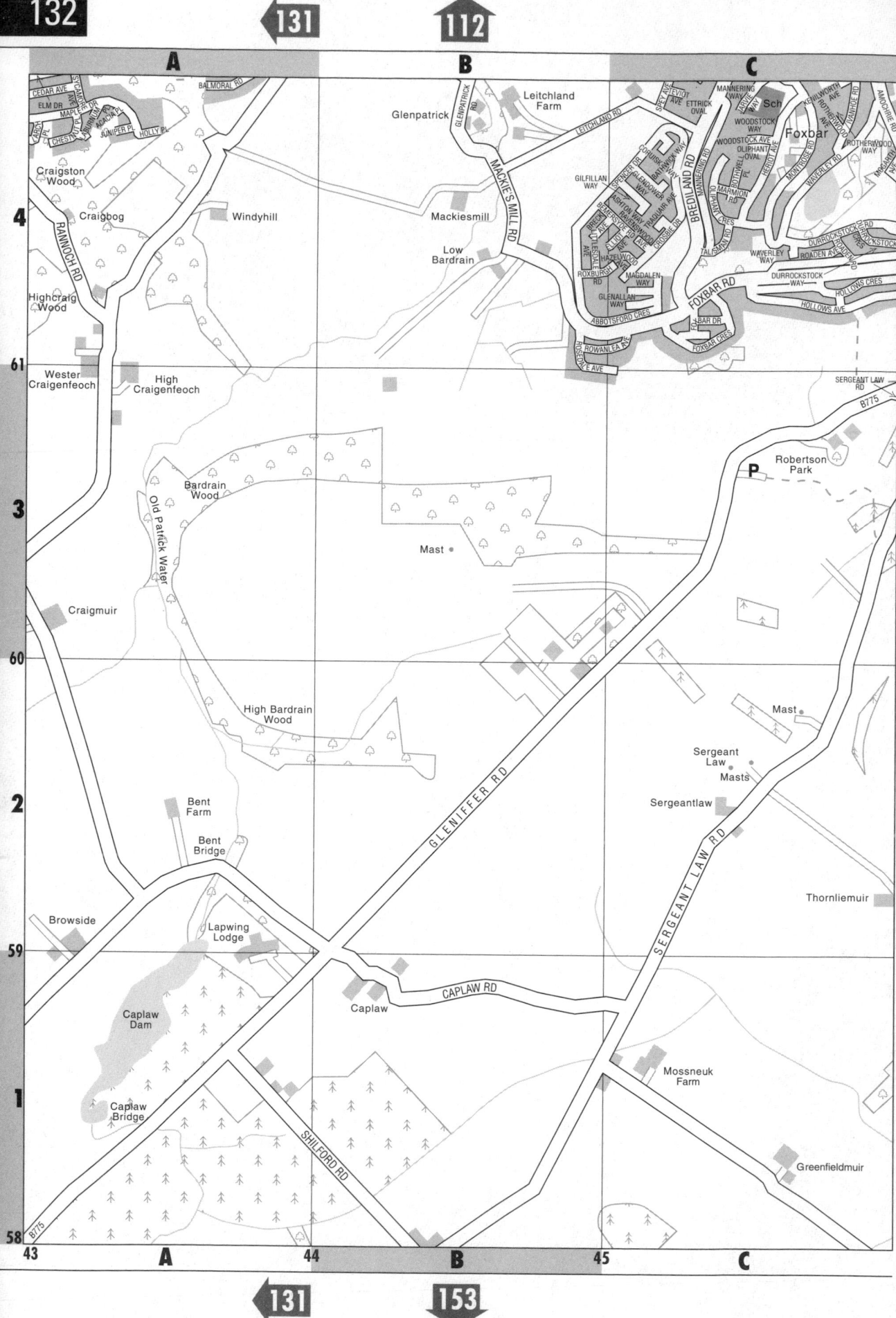

A B C

4

61

3

60

2

59

1

58

43 44 45

A B C

Balmoral Rd
Glenpatrick
Leitchland Farm
Glenpatrick Rd
Leitchland Rd
Mackie's Mill Rd
Mackiesmill
Low Bardrain
Foxbar
Sch
Woodstock Way
Woodstock Ave
Oliphant Oval
Bredland Rd
Mannering Rd
Rotherwood Way
Kenilworth Ave
Ivanhoe Rd
Amochrie Rd
Gilfillan Way
Marmion
Waverley Rd
Durrockstock Rd
Durrockstock
Waverley Way
Roaden Ave
Durrockstock Way
Hollows Cres
Hollows Ave
Foxbar Rd
Foxbar Dr
Foxbar Cres
Abbotsford Cres
Rowanlea Ave
Rosedale Ave
Sergeant Law Rd
B775

Craigston Wood
Craigbog
Windyhill
Rannoch Rd
Highcraig Wood
Wester Craigenfeoch
High Craigenfeoch

Robertson Park
P

Bardrain Wood
Old Patrick Water
Mast
Craigmuir
Mast

High Bardrain Wood
Sergeant Law
Masts
Sergeantlaw
Sergeant Law Rd
Gleniffer Rd

Bent Farm
Bent Bridge
Thornliemuir

Browside
Lapwing Lodge

Caplaw Dam
Caplaw
Caplaw Rd
Mossneuk Farm

Caplaw Bridge
Shilford Rd
Greenfieldmuir
B775

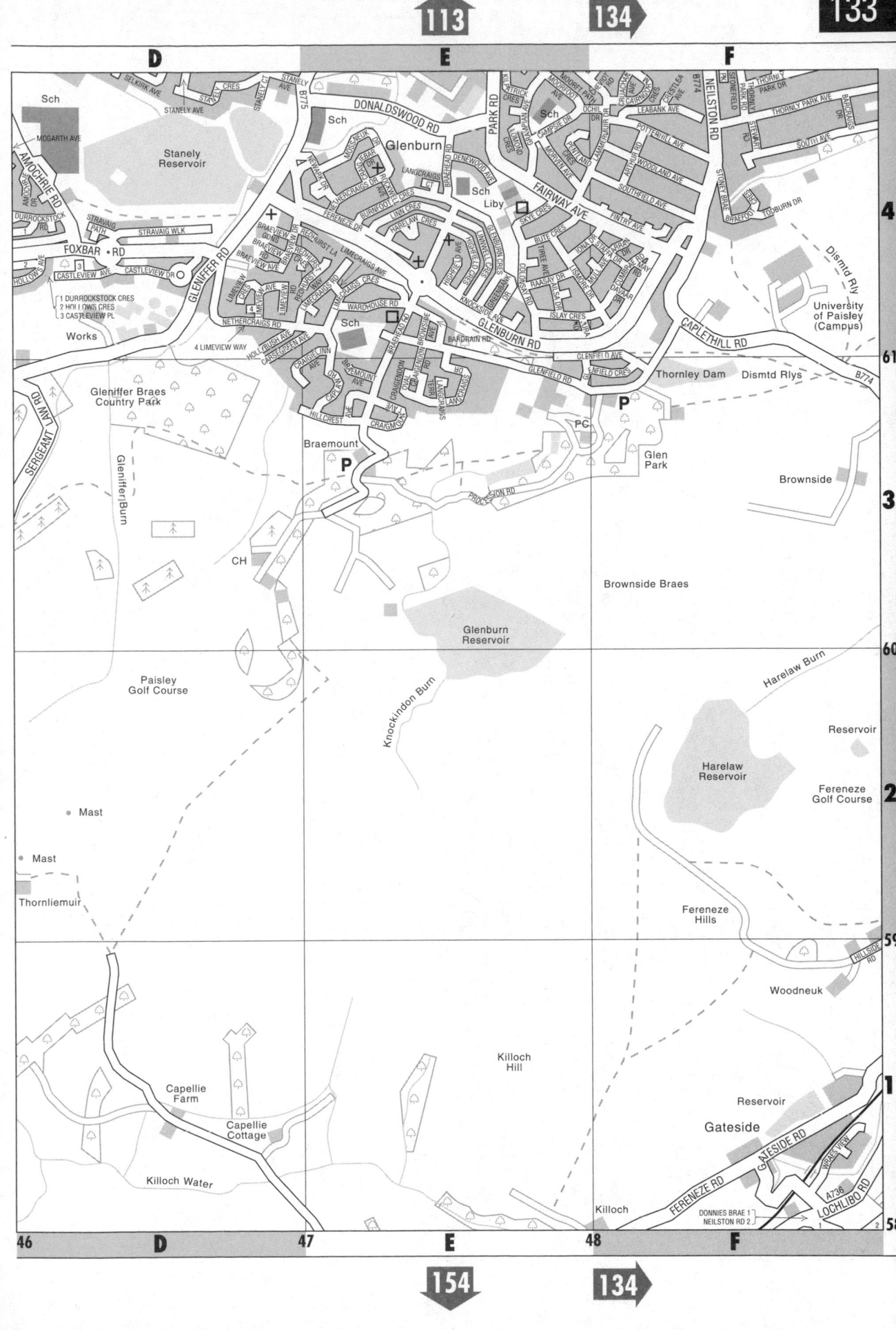

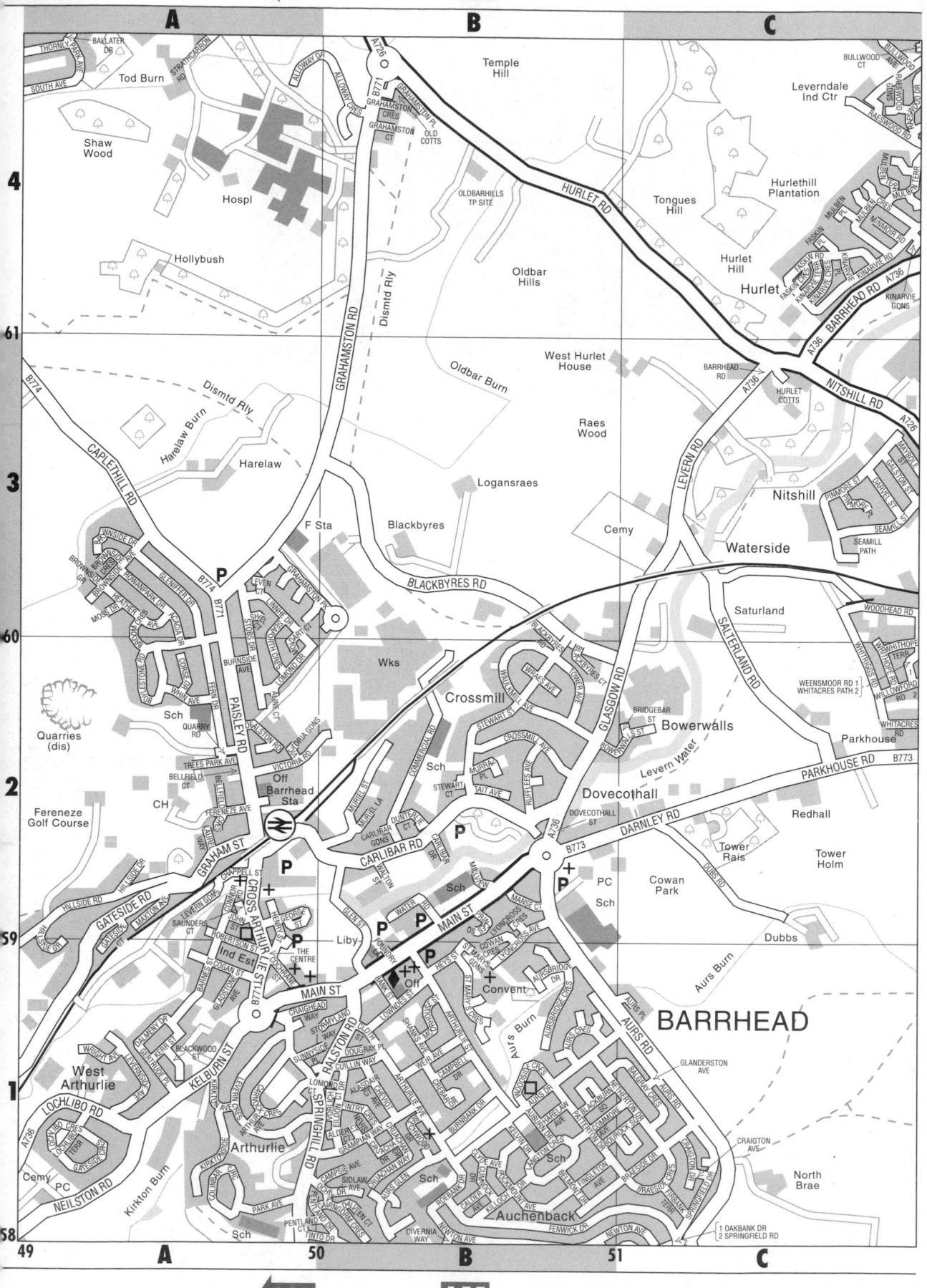

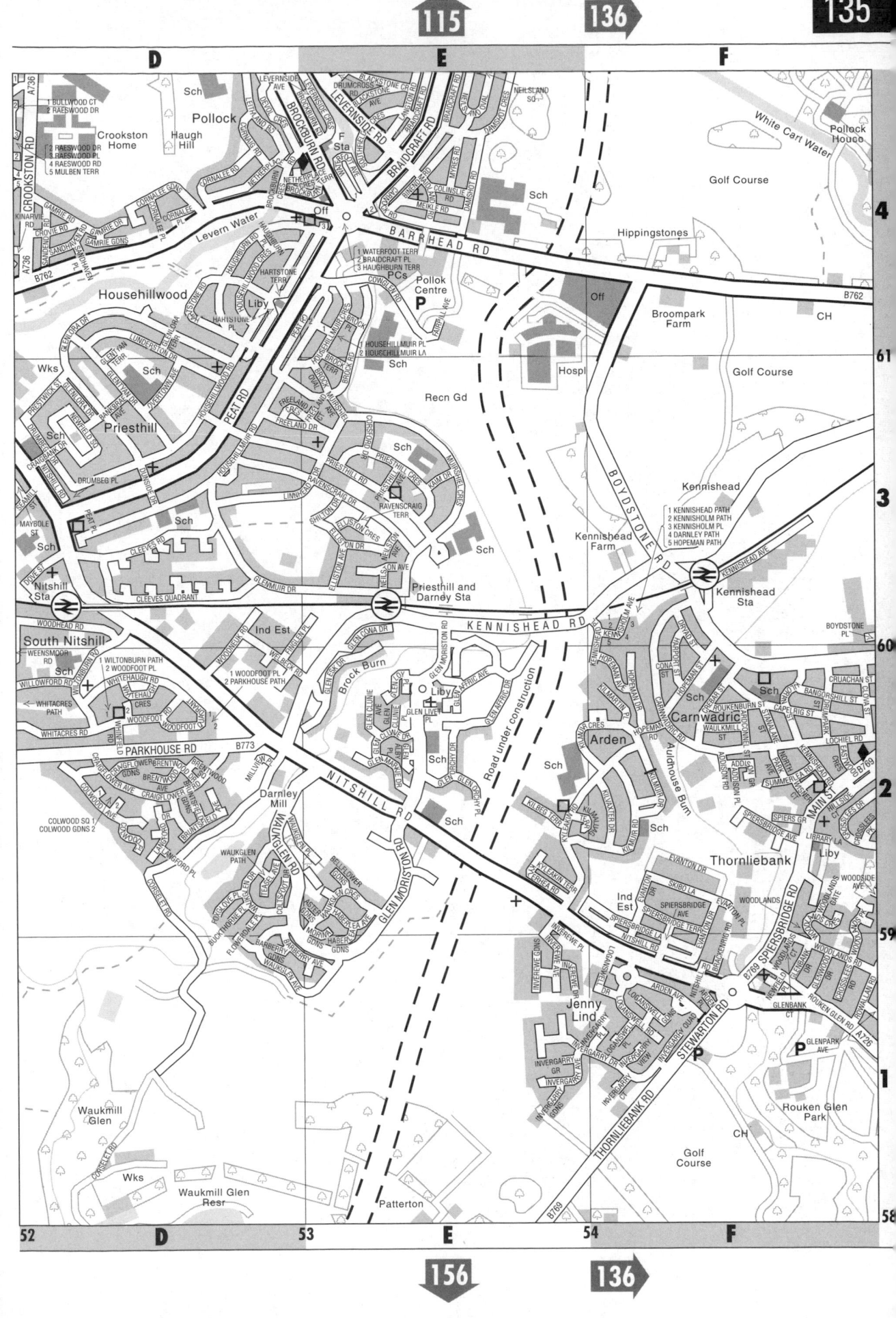

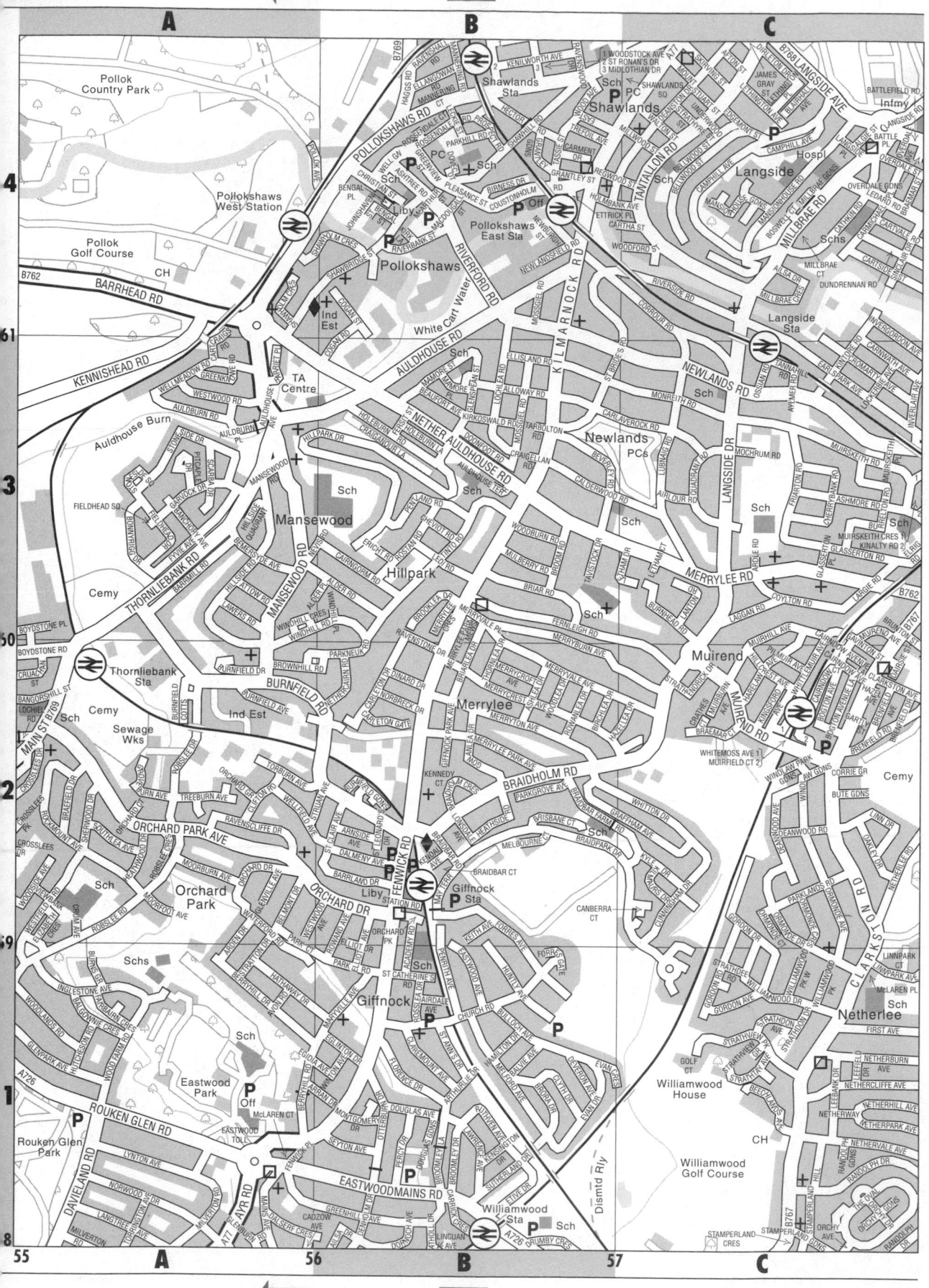

A B C

Pollok
Country Park

Pollokshaws
West Station

Pollok
Golf Course

CH

B762

BARRHEAD RD

KENNISHEAD RD

Auldhouse Burn

FIELDHEAD SQ

Cemy

THORNLIEBANK RD

Thornliebank
Sta

Cemy

Sewage
Wks

Sch

Ind Est

MAIN ST B769

BOYDSTONE RD
BOYDSTONE PL

Crosslees
Pk

ORCHARD PARK AVE

Orchard
Park

Sch

Schs

Eastwood
Park

P
Off
McLaren Ct

ROUKEN GLEN RD

Rouken Glen
Park

DAVIELAND RD

AYR RD
A77

EASTWOODMAINS RD

Giffnock

Sch

EASTWOOD
TOLL

TA
Centre

AULDHOUSE RD

Mansewood

Sch

Hillpark

MANSEWOOD RD

NETHER AULDHOUSE RD

Sch

BURNFIELD RD

Merrylee

BRAIDHOLM RD

FENWICK RD

Liby
P
Giffnock
Sta

ORCHARD DR

Sch

Sch

White Cart Water

Ind
Est

Pollokshaws

POLLOKSHAWS RD

RIVERFORD RD

Shawlands
Sta

Shawlands

P
PC

Pollokshaws
East Sta

KILMARNOCK RD

Newlands
PCs

NEWLANDS RD

LANGSIDE DR

MERRYLEE RD

Muirend

MUIREND RD

B762

Williamwood
House

Williamwood
Golf Course

Dismtd Rly

Williamwood
Sta

Sch

LANGSIDE AVE

Shawlands

P
PC

Langside
Hosp

TANTALLON RD

MILL BRAE RD

Langside

Langside
Sta

Newlands

Schs

Sch

Sch

Cemy

Netherlee

CLARKSTON RD

Williamwood
House

CH

Battlefield
Infmy

LANGSIDE RD

B767

STAMPERLAND

A726

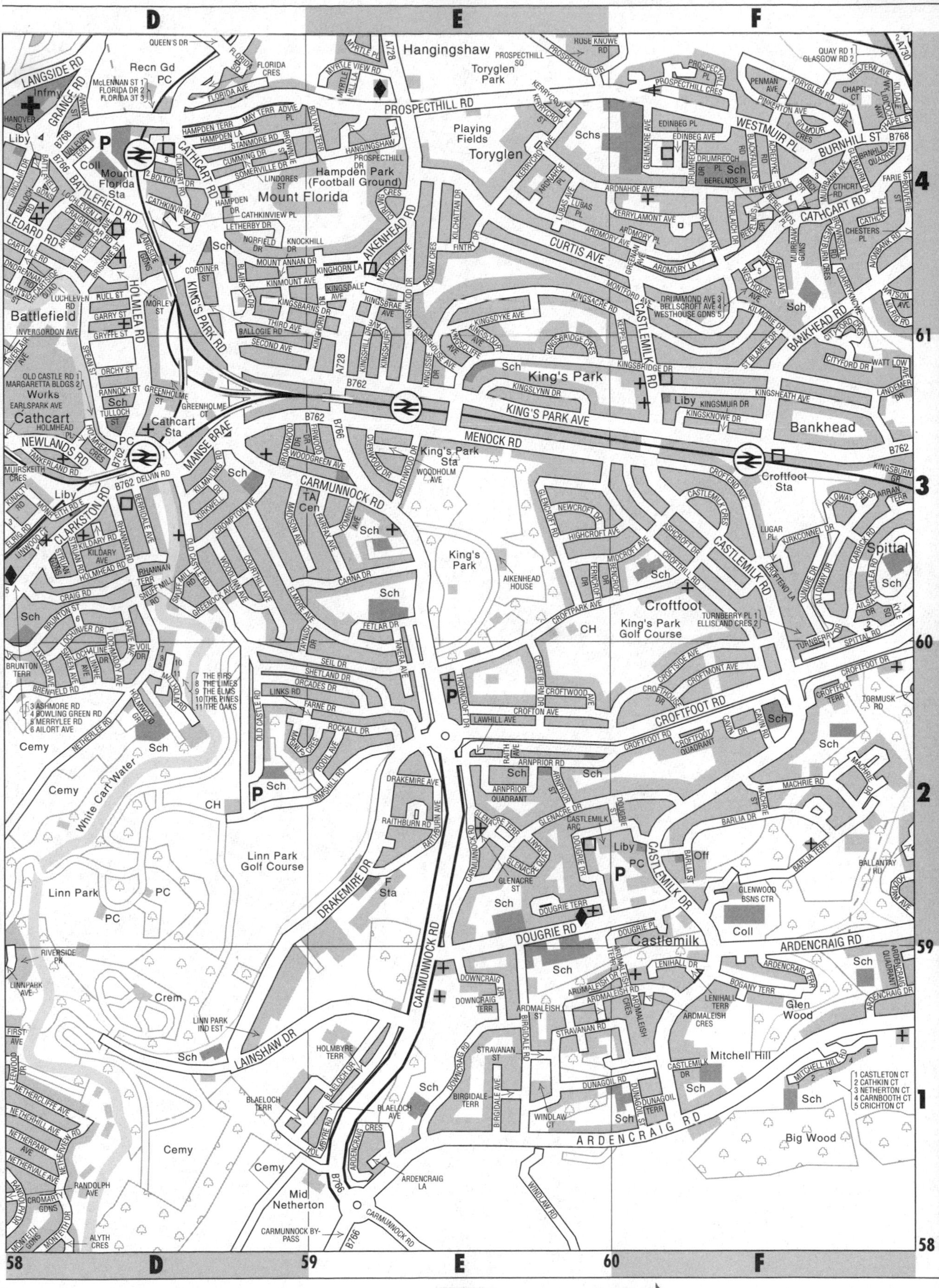

137
 118

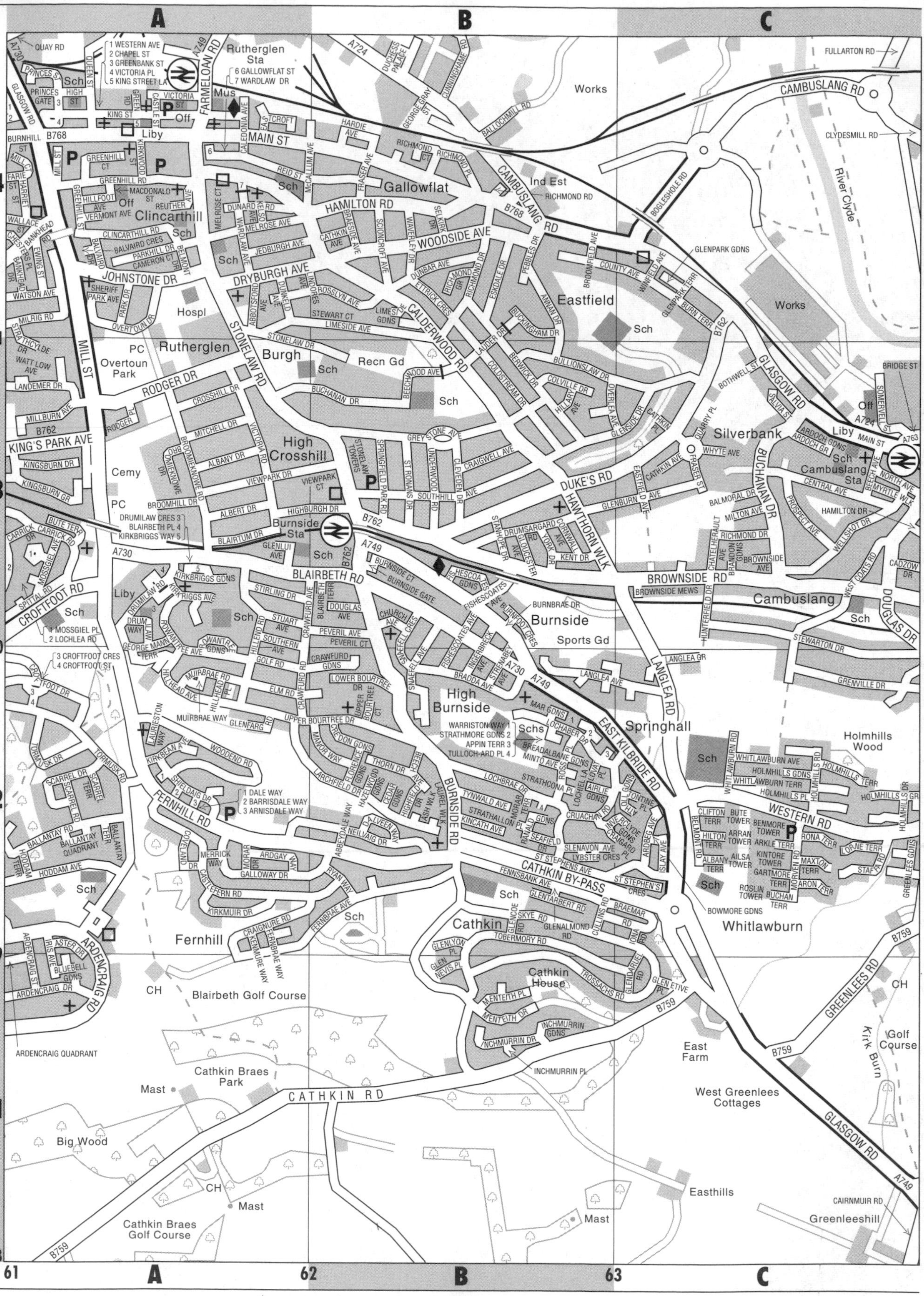

A B C

1 WESTERN AVE
2 CHAPEL ST
3 GREENBANK ST
4 VICTORIA PL
5 KING STREET LA
6 GALLOWFLAT ST
7 WARDLAW DR

Rutherglen Sta

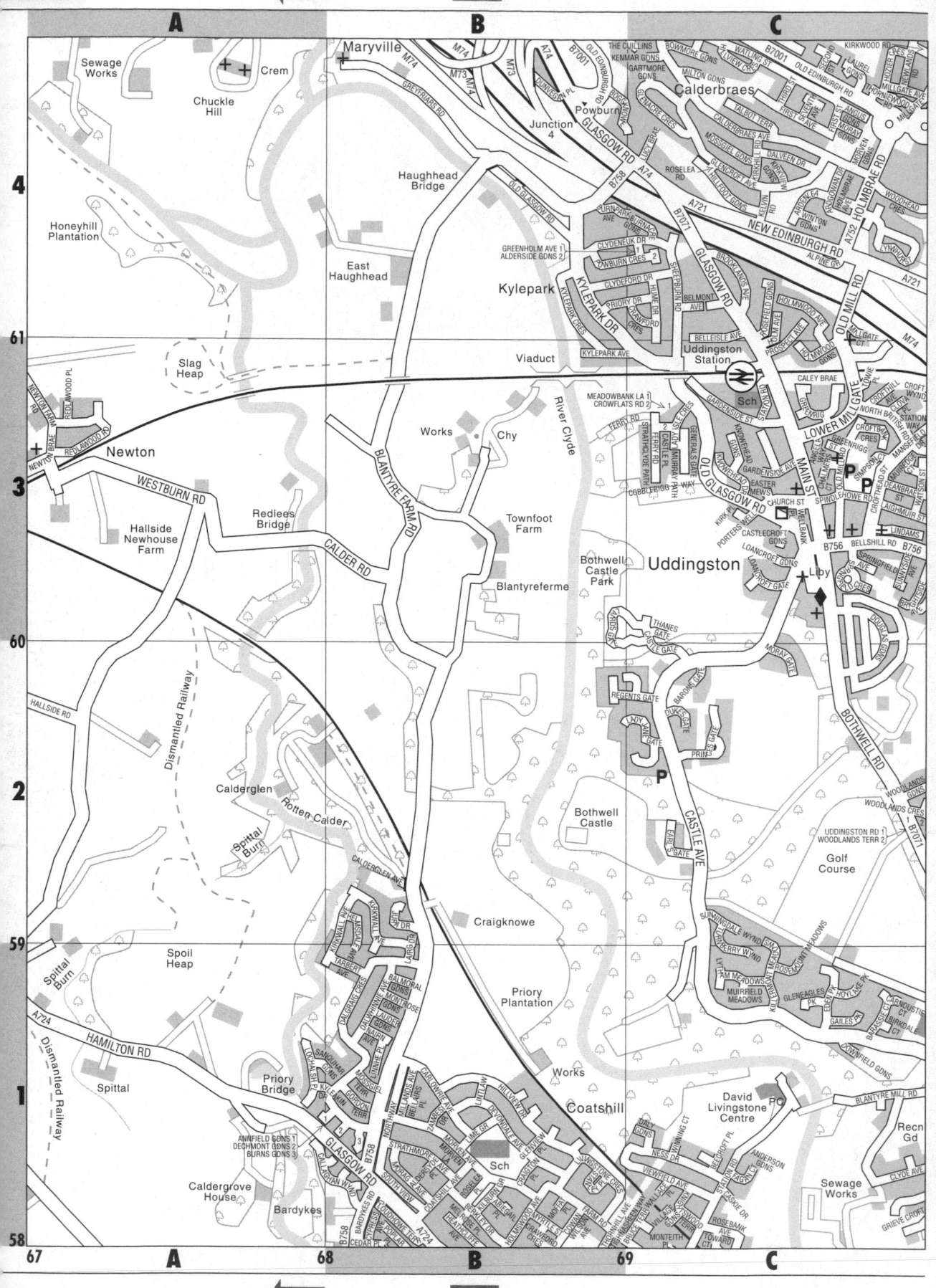

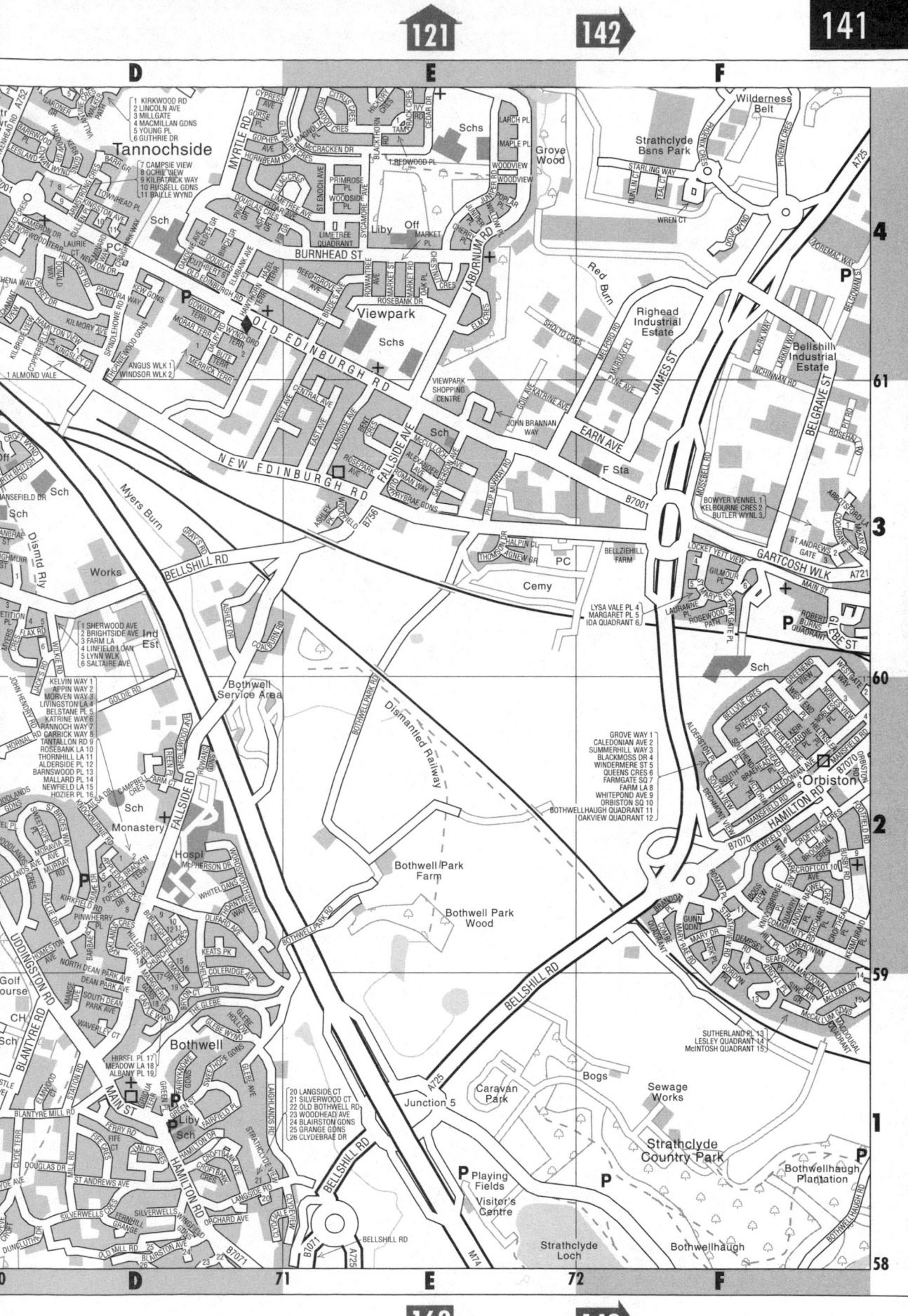

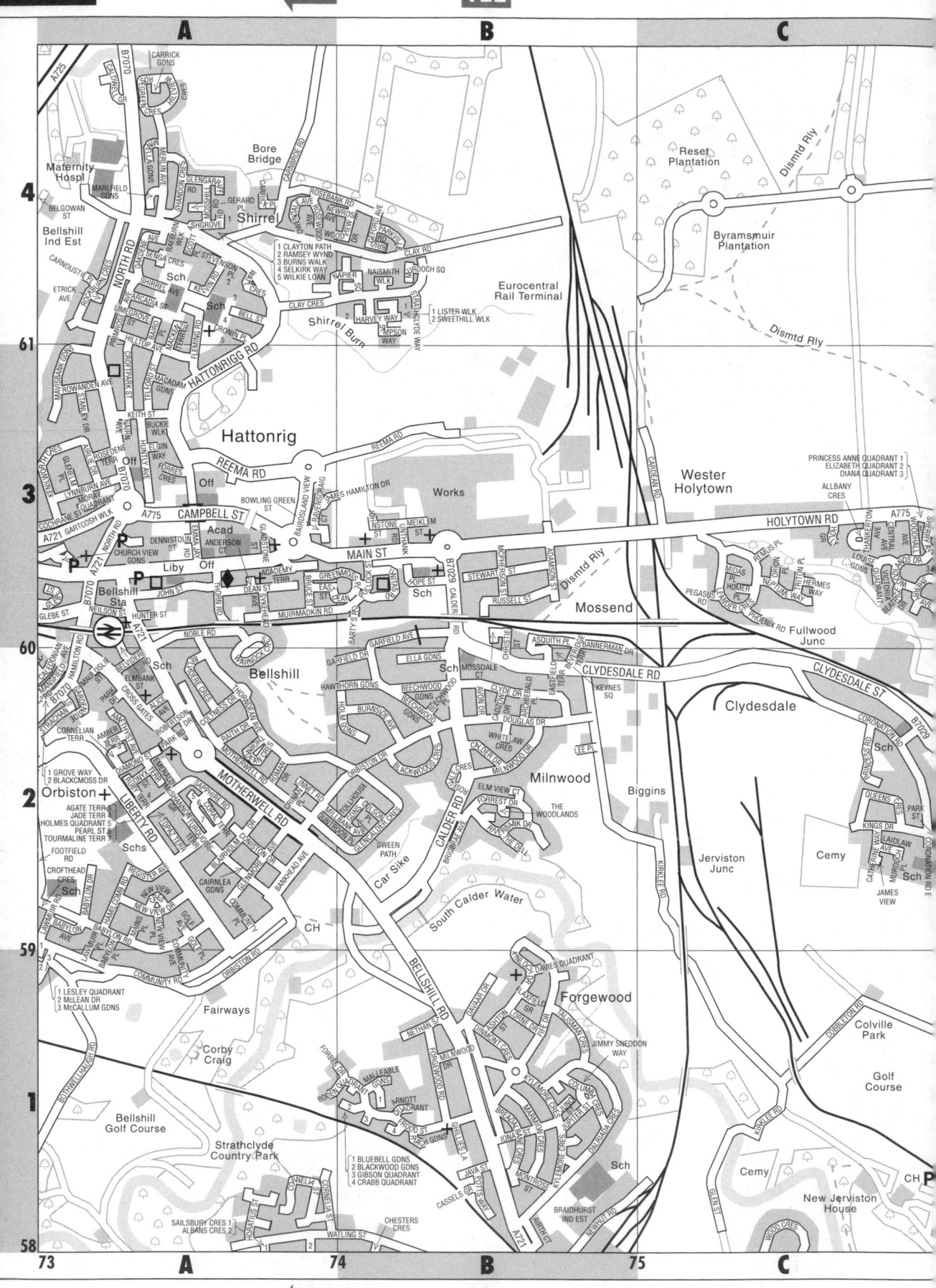

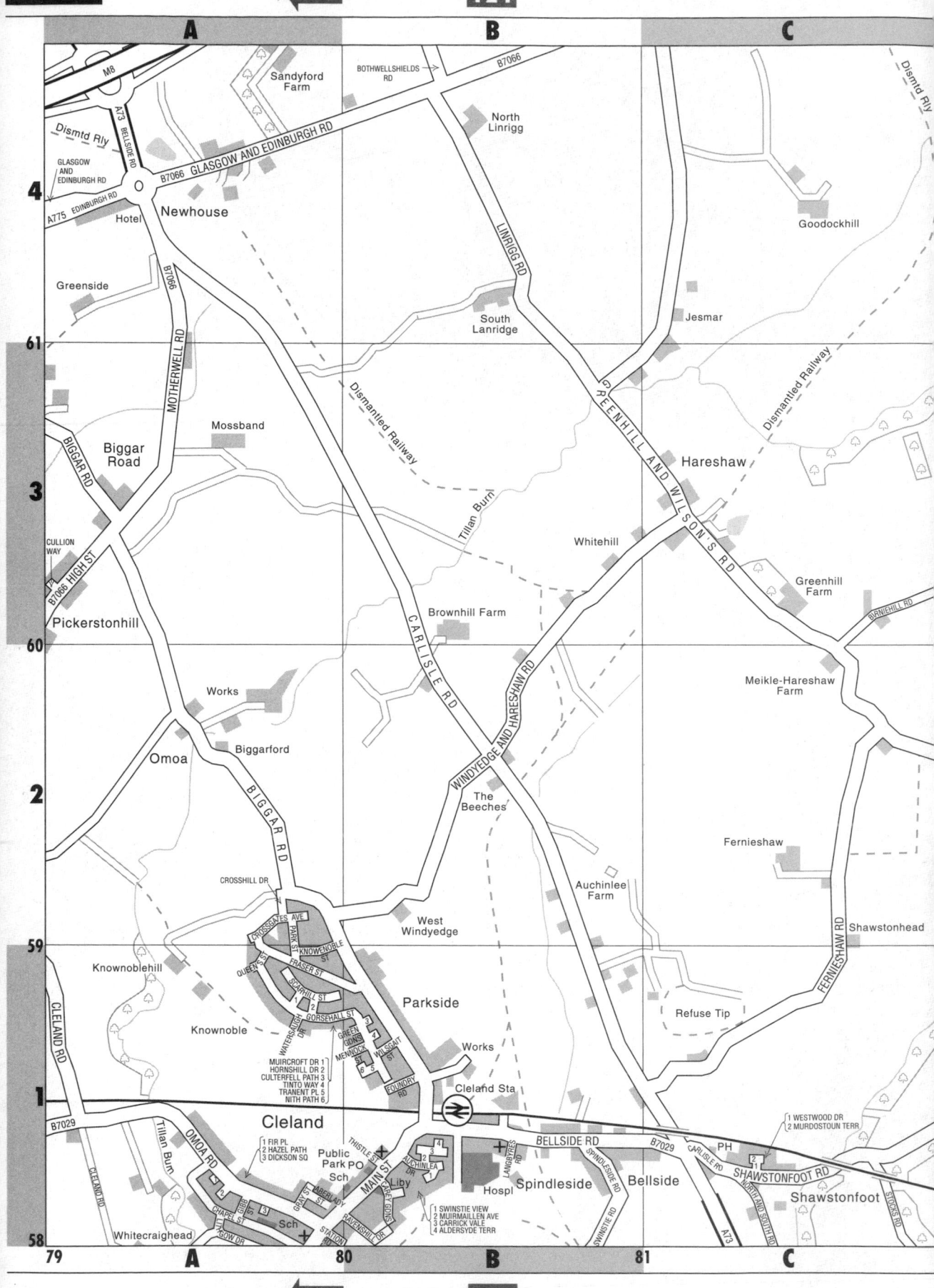

A   B   C

M8

A73

Dismtd Rly

BELLSIDE RD

GLASGOW AND EDINBURGH RD

Sandyford Farm

BOTHWELLSHIELDS RD

B7066

North Linrigg

B7066 GLASGOW AND EDINBURGH RD

GLASGOW AND EDINBURGH RD

A775 Edinburgh Rd

Hotel

Newhouse

4

Greenside

B7066

MOTHERWELL RD

LINRIGG RD

South Lanridge

Goodockhill

Jesmar

61

Mossband

Dismantled Railway

Dismantled Railway

GREENHILL AND WILSON'S RD

Hareshaw

BIGGAR RD

Biggar Road

3

CULLION WAY

B7066 HIGH ST

Tillan Burn

Whitehill

Greenhill Farm

BURNIEHILL RD

Pickerstonhill

60

Brownhill Farm

Works

CARLISLE RD

Meikle-Hareshaw Farm

Biggarford

WINDYEDGE AND HARESHAW RD

Omoa

2

BIGGAR RD

The Beeches

Fernieshaw

CROSSHILL DR

West Windyedge

Auchinlee Farm

Shawstonhead

CROSSGATES AVE

PARK ST

KNOWENOBLE ST

FRASER ST

FERNIESHAW RD

59

Knownoblehill

QUEEN'S ST

SCARHILL ST

GORSEHALL ST

Parkside

Knownoble

WATERSMEETH DR

GREEN GDNS

MENNOCK ST

WILSGATE ST

Refuse Tip

MUIRCROFT DR 1
HORNSHILL DR 2
CULTERFELL PATH 3
TINTO WAY 4
TRANENT PL 5
NITH PATH 6

FOUNDRY RD

Works

CLELAND RD

1

B7029

Cleland

Tillan Burn

OMOA RD

1 FIR PL
2 HAZEL PATH
3 DICKSON SQ

Cleland Sta

BELLSIDE RD

B7029

CARLISLE RD

PH

1 WESTWOOD DR
2 MURDOSTOUN TERR

SHAWSTONFOOT RD

Public Park PO Sch

THISTLE ST

MAIN ST

AUCHINLEA DR

Liby

LANGBYRES RD

Hospl

Spindleside

SWINSTIE RD

SPINDLESIDE RD

Bellside

NORTH AND SOUTH RD

STOCKS RD

A73

Shawstonfoot

CHAPEL ST

GIBB ST

Sch

GRAY ST

ABERLADY ST

CRG GDNS

RAVENSHILL DR

STATION RD

GLASGOW DR

1 SWINSTIE VIEW
2 MUIRMAILLEN AVE
3 CARRICK VALE
4 ALDERSYDE TERR

Whitecraighead

58

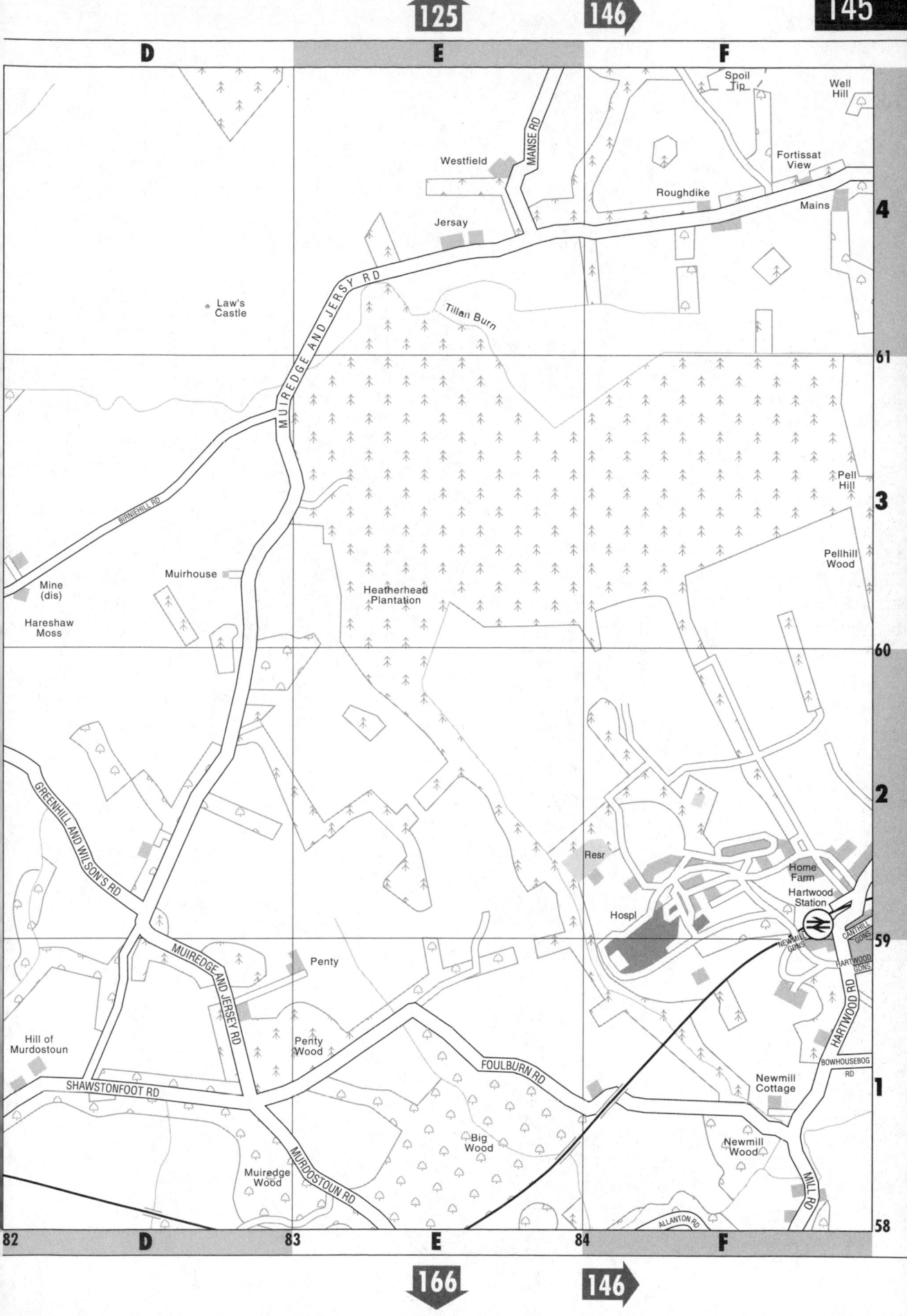

Spoil Tip
Well Hill

Westfield
Fortissat View
Roughdike
Mains
Jersay

MANSE RD

MUIREDGE AND JERSY RD

Law's Castle

Tillan Burn

Pell Hill

BIRNIEHILL RD

Pellhill Wood

Mine (dis)

Muirhouse

Heatherhead Plantation

Hareshaw Moss

GREENHILL AND WILSON'S RD

Resr

Home Farm
Hartwood Station

Hospl

CANTHILL GDNS

Newmill GDNS
HARTWOOD GDNS

MUIREDGE AND JERSEY RD

Penty

HARTWOOD RD

Hill of Murdostoun

Penty Wood

BOWHOUSEBOG RD

Newmill Cottage

SHAWSTONFOOT RD

FOULBURN RD

Newmill Wood

Big Wood

Muiredge Wood

MURDOSTOUN RD

MILL RD

ALLANTON RD

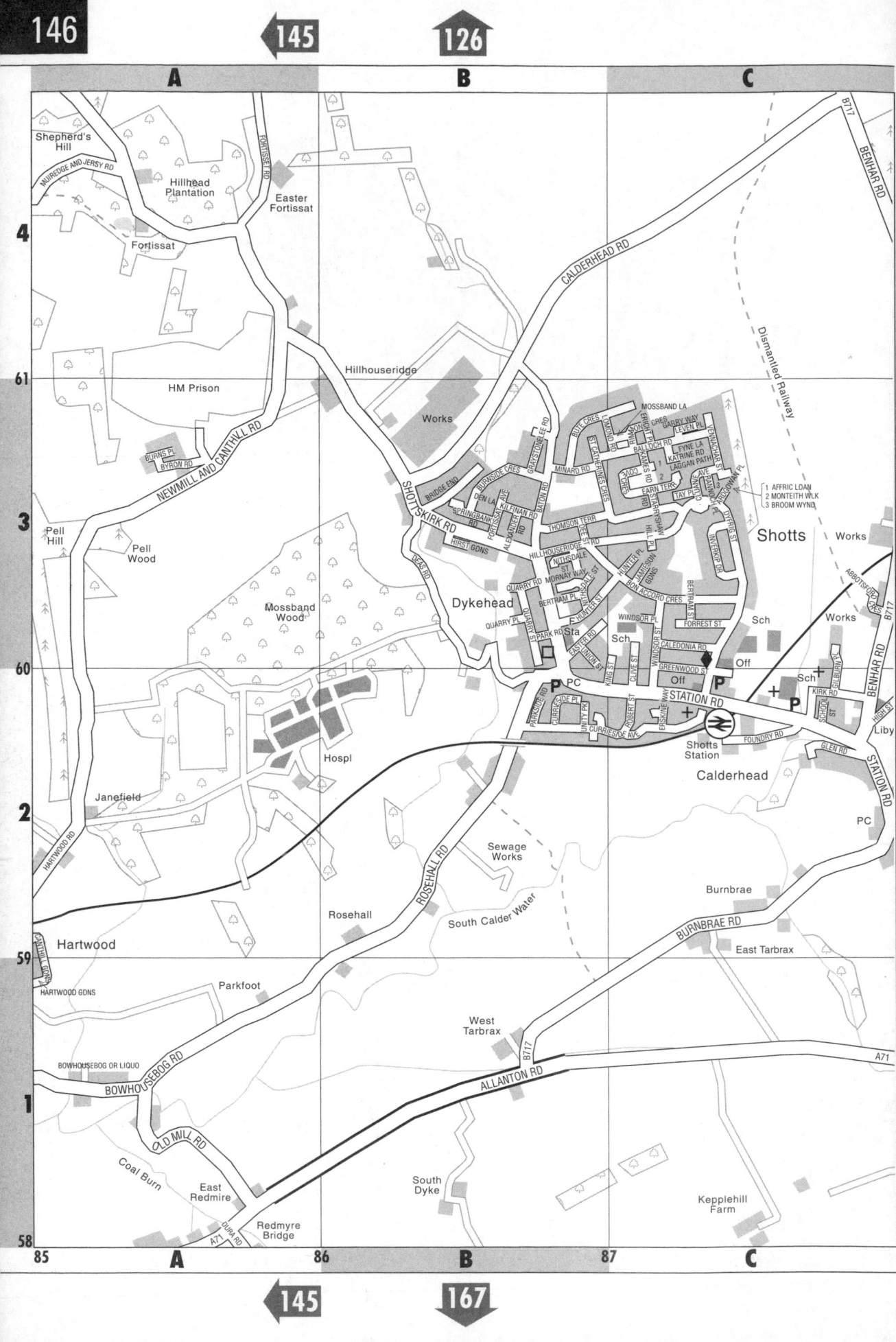

D E F

4

Fauldhouse

61

3

Golf Course

CH

Amb Sta

BENHAR RD

B717

Starryshaw Farm

South Calder Water

Spoil Heap

Stanebent

Cairneyhead

Torbothie

Stane

STABLE RD

GRAY ST

HIGH ST

60

CHARLES ST

TORBOTHIE RD

CLYDE DR

KENTIDE DR

HAWTHORN DR

CALDER DR

SOUTHFIELD RD

SOUTHFIELD CRES

SOUTHFIELD AVE

Torbothie

PC

ULG WAY

GAIR WYND

Sch

+

CEMETERY RD

MAINS RD

CHARLOTTE ST

NEVIS PL

GARTEN DR

Cemy

1 ETIVE WAY
2 TILG WAY
3 GAIR WYND
4 BOWMORE WLK
5 TORRIN LOAN
6 DORNIE WYND
7 MORAR WAY
8 COIRE LOAN
9 SUNA PATH
10 SALEN LOAN

2

B7010

MAIN ST

SANDYVALE AVE

SOUTHHILL

LEHANS RD

Sandyvale PL

LOCHABER CRES

TULLOCH RD

APPIN TERR

RETFORD AVE

WYLIE PL

DINGHY PL

LAGGAN AVE

MAVISBANK

SHIELDS PL

Stane

BLINNY CT 1
TARBRAX PATH 2

BRIDGE PL

KNOLL CROFT RD

LANSDOWNE CRES

HUNTLY TERR

B7010

SPRINGHILL RD

BLACKHALL ST

BROWN ST

BEECHMOUNT CT

BEBRYHILL

Springhill

SPRINGHILL AND LEADLOCH RD

B7010

59

STANE RD

Works

BELMONT DR

MILLDOWN TERR

LARCHFIELD LA

NORTHFIELD AVE

ELMWOOD RD

Springhill

Knowton Farm

B715 HEADLESSCROSS RD B715

Dismantled Railway

Lingore Linn

A71

Works

1

Dismtld Rly

58

88 D 89 E 90 F

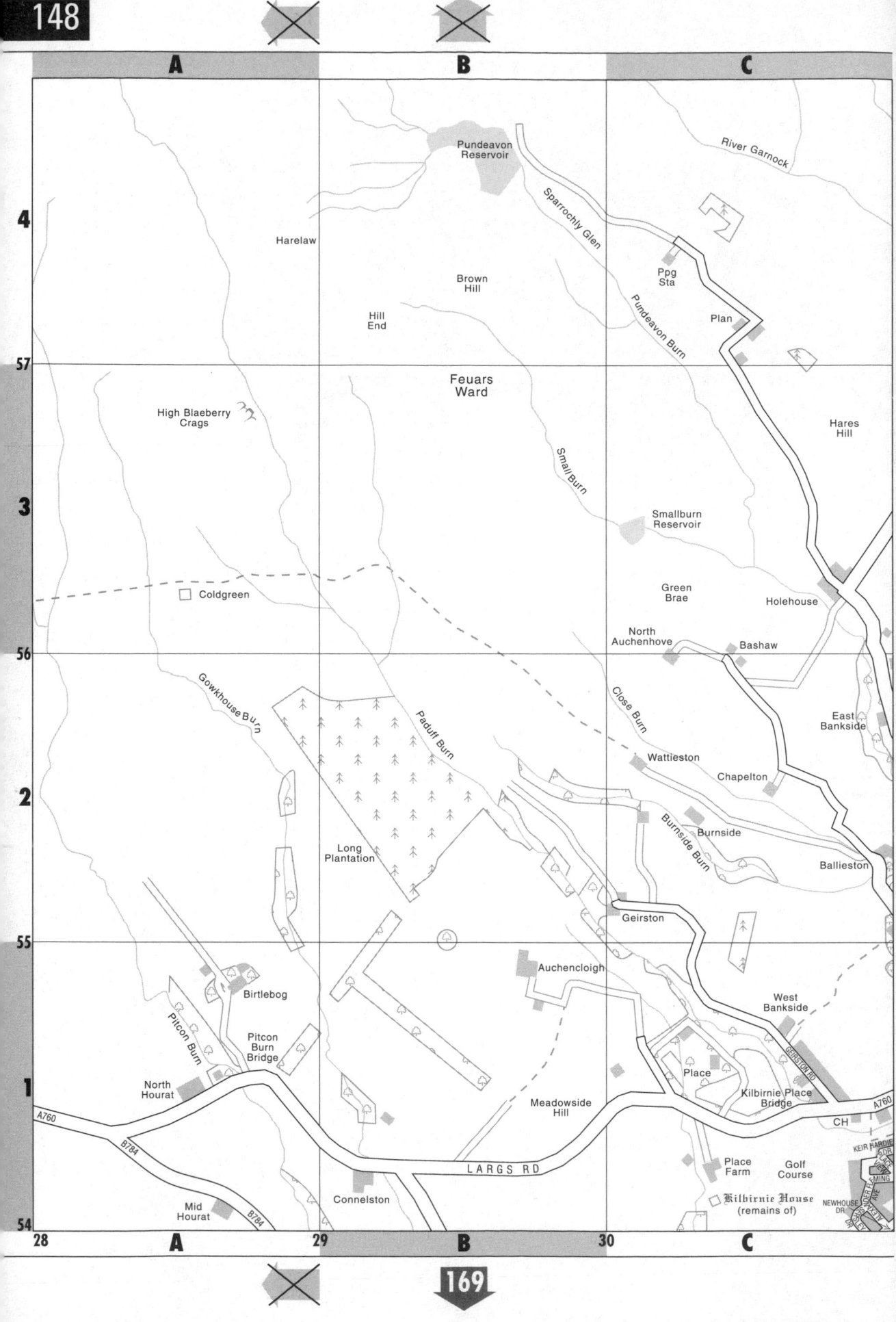

River Garnock

Pundeavon
Reservoir

Sparrochly Glen

Harelaw

Brown
Hill

Ppg
Sta

Plan

Pundeavon Burn

Hill
End

4

57

Feuars
Ward

High Blaeberry
Crags

Hares
Hill

Small Burn

Smallburn
Reservoir

3

Green
Brae

Holehouse

Coldgreen

North
Auchenhove

Bashaw

56

Gowkhouse Burn

Paduff Burn

Close Burn

East
Bankside

Wattieston

Chapelton

2

Burnside Burn

Burnside

Long
Plantation

Ballieston

Geirston

55

Birtlebog

Auchencloigh

West
Bankside

Pitcon Burn

Pitcon
Burn
Bridge

GEIRSTON RD

Place

Kilbirnie Place
Bridge

North
Hourat

CH

A760

A760

B784

Meadowside
Hill

KEIR HARDIE

NEWHOUSE
DR

1

LARGS RD

Place
Farm

Golf
Course

Connelston

Kilbirnie House
(remains of)

Mid
Hourat

B784

54

28   **A**   29   **B**   30   **C**

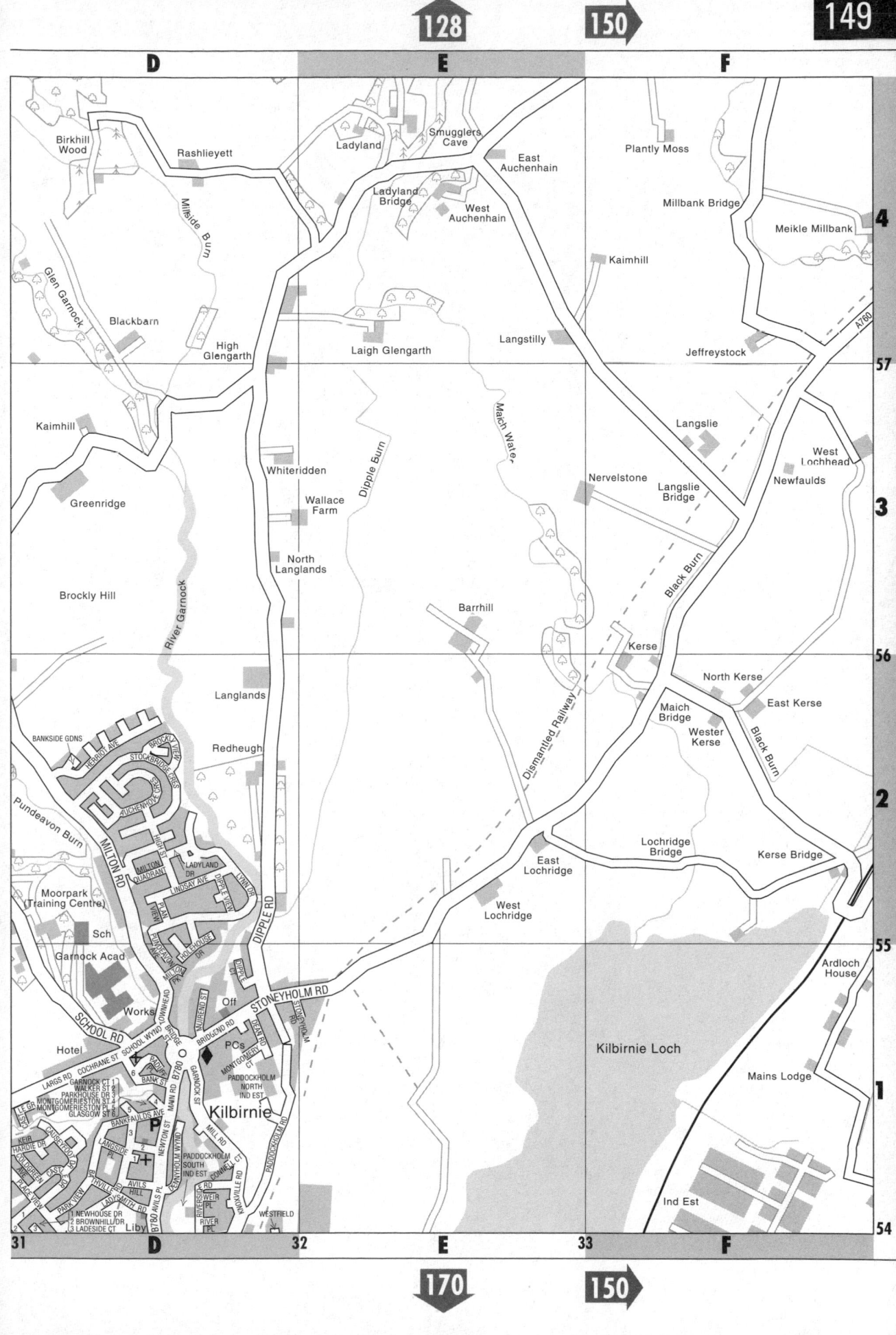

D   E   F

Birkhill Wood

Rashlieyett

Ladyland

Smugglers Cave

East Auchenhain

Plantly Moss

Ladyland Bridge

West Auchenhain

Millbank Bridge

Meikle Millbank

4

Millside Burn

Glen Garnock

Blackbarn

High Glengarth

Laigh Glengarth

Langstilly

Kaimhill

Jeffreystock

A760

57

Kaimhill

Whiteridden

Wallace Farm

Dipple Burn

Maich Water

Langslie

Nervelstone

Langslie Bridge

West Lochhead

Newfaulds

3

Greenridge

North Langlands

Brockly Hill

River Garnock

Barrhill

Black Burn

Kerse

56

Langlands

North Kerse

East Kerse

BANKSIDE GDNS

Redheugh

Dismantled Railway

Maich Bridge

Wester Kerse

Black Burn

2

Pundeavon Burn

MILTON RD

Moorpark (Training Centre)

Sch

Garnock Acad

East Lochridge

West Lochridge

Lochridge Bridge

Kerse Bridge

55

Works

Off

STONEYHOLM RD

Ardloch House

Hotel

SCHOOL RD

PCs

Kilbirnie Loch

Mains Lodge

1

Kilbirnie

P

Ind Est

Liby

WESTFIELD

31   D   32   E   33   F   54

A   B   C

A760

Hole

Dismantled Railway

Meikle
Millbank

4

A760

East
Lochhead

Barr
Loch

Yardfoot

A760

Mossend
Farm

Lochwinnoch
Station

A760

ROADHEAD

Roadhead
Bridge

A737

High
Barfod

East
Auchengowan

Nether
Barfod

Mid
Auchengowan

Yardfoot Burn

57

Mid
Lochhead

West
Netherhouses

East
Netherhouses

Bourtrees

West
Auchengowan

Dubbs Water

Knowes

3

Woodside
Meadows

Barrodger

Barrodger
Cottage

Knowes
Mill

Boydstone

56

Roebank
Bridge

Park

Clark's
Bridge

Boydstone

Mill of
Beith Bridge

Mill of
Beith

Davies o'
the Mill

Loanhead

MUIRBURN RD

Roebank Burn
Roebank Glen

2

Knowes

Woodside

Southridgehill

Badmany

Loanhead
Quarry
(Whinstone)

Gateside of
Fullwoodhead

CH

Golf
Course

55

Mains Burn

LOMOND CRES

WOTHERSPOON DR

THORNTREE AVE

CYPRESS AVE

CHERRYWOOD DR

AULDLEA RD

Knowehead

Bigholm

THREEPWOOD RD

High
Fullwoodhead

Cemy

BEECH AVE

ARRAN CRES

ROEBANK RD B7049

Grangehill

Low
Fullwoodhead

1

Bath Burn

SYCAMORE AVE

ASH DR

SYCAMORE
CT

MAPLE
DR

WOODSIDE
RD

BARRINGTON AVE

BY PASS RD

WILSON ST

Bigholm

Crummock

Mid
Bogside

LAIGH CT 1
MEDINE CT 2
SOMERVILLE CT 3
KING'S CT 4

JANEFIELD
PL

KING'S RD

LAIGH RD

TRINITY ST

CRUMMOCK ST

TRINITY
CRES

Beith

PO

Sta

HAWTHORN AVE

BLACKTHORN AVE

MAINS AVE

MID RD

ELBA PL

MURPARK RD

ST B7049

REFORM
ST

MITCHELL
ST

NEW ST

A737

MAINS ST

Hill of
Beith

Bog
Hall

54

CEDAR AVE

ROBERT BURNS CT

WEE
CL

BELTRE

P

Mast

34   A   35   B   36   C

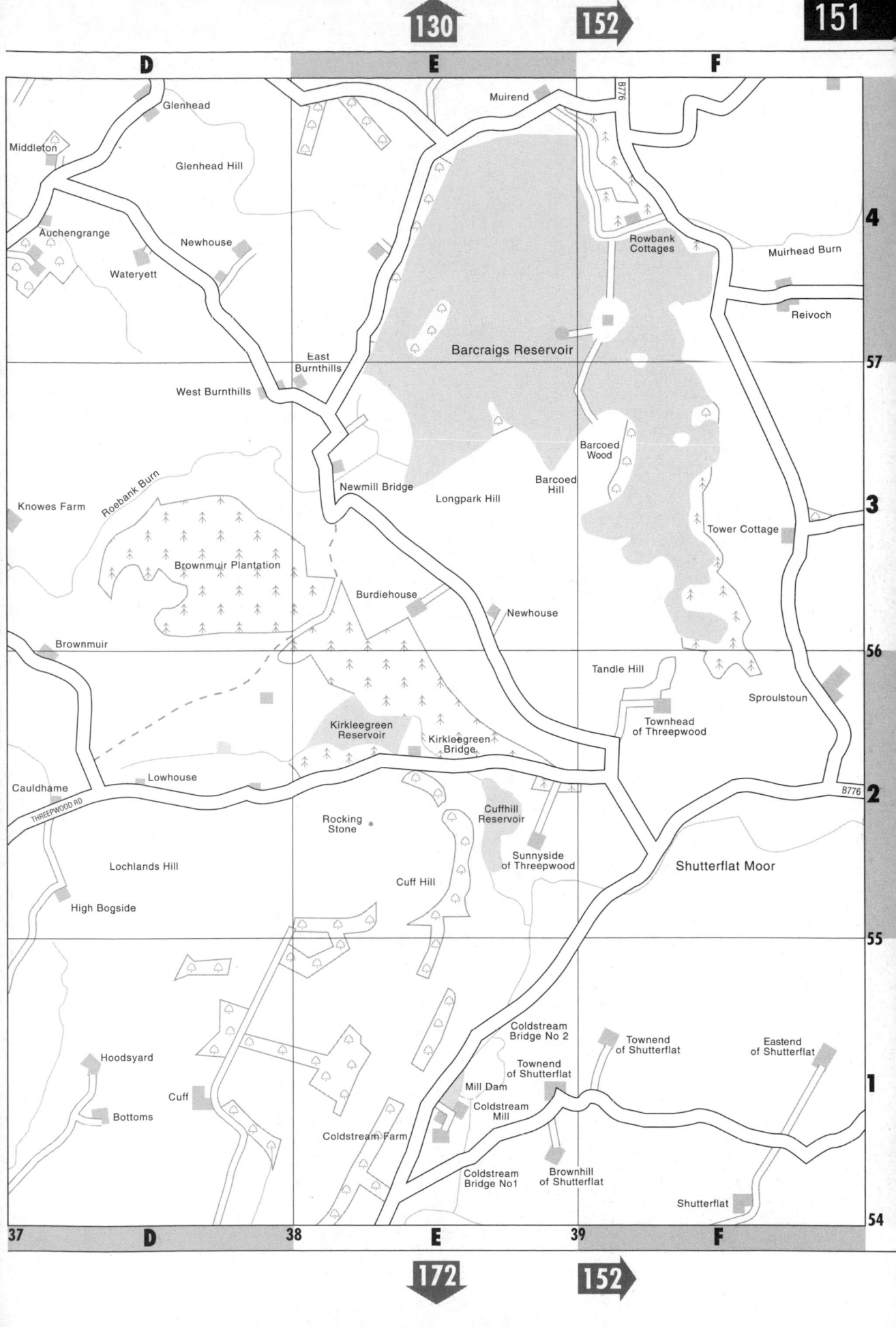

Middleton
Glenhead
Glenhead Hill
Auchengrange
Newhouse
Wateryett

Muirend

B776

Rowbank
Cottages

Muirhead Burn

Reivoch

East
Burnthills
West Burnthills

Barcraigs Reservoir

Knowes Farm

Roebank Burn

Brownmuir Plantation

Newmill Bridge

Longpark Hill

Barcoed
Wood

Barcoed
Hill

Tower Cottage

Brownmuir

Burdiehouse

Newhouse

Tandle Hill

Sproulstoun

Cauldhame

Lowhouse

Kirkleegreen
Reservoir

Kirkleegreen
Bridge

Townhead
of Threepwood

THREEPWOOD RD

Rocking
Stone

Cuffhill
Reservoir

Sunnyside
of Threepwood

B776

Lochlands Hill

Cuff Hill

Shutterflat Moor

High Bogside

Coldstream
Bridge No 2

Townend
of Shutterflat

Eastend
of Shutterflat

Hoodsyard

Cuff

Townend
of Shutterflat

Mill Dam

Coldstream
Mill

Bottoms

Coldstream Farm

Coldstream
Bridge No1

Brownhill
of Shutterflat

Shutterflat

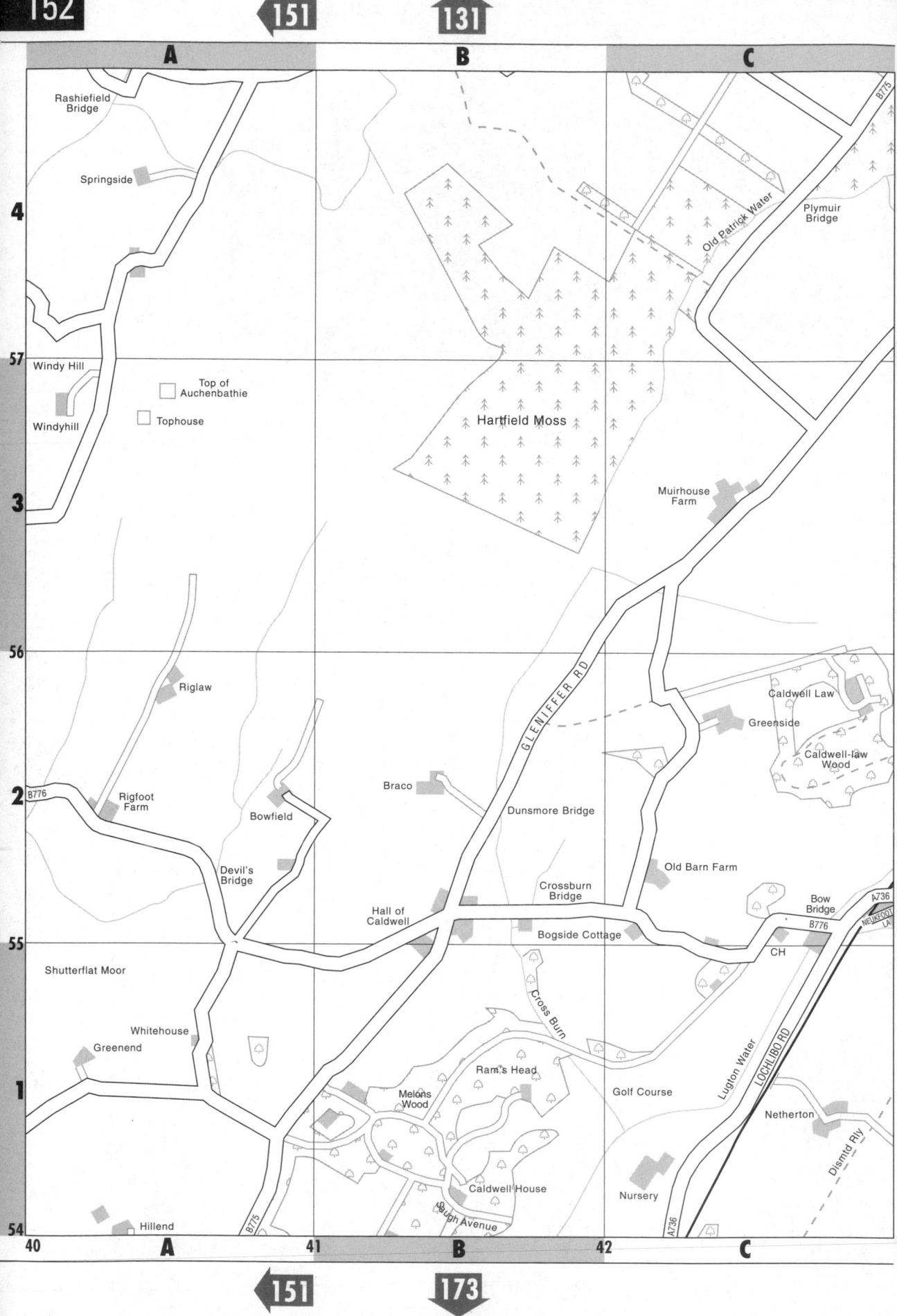

A B C

Rashiefield Bridge

Springside

4

Old Patrick Water

Plymuir Bridge

57 Windy Hill

Top of Auchenbathie

Tophouse

Windyhill

Hartfield Moss

Muirhouse Farm

3

56

Riglaw

Caldwell Law

Greenside

Caldwell-law Wood

B776 Braco

GLENIFFER RD

Dunsmore Bridge

2 Rigfoot Farm

Bowfield

Old Barn Farm

Devil's Bridge

Crossburn Bridge

Bow Bridge

A736

NEUKFOOT LA

B776

Hall of Caldwell

Bogside Cottage

CH

55

Shutterflat Moor

Cross Burn

Lugton Water

LOCHLIBO RD

Whitehouse

Greenend

Ram's Head

Golf Course

Netherton

1

Melons Wood

Dismtd Rly

Caldwell House

Nursery

Hillend

ugh Avenue

54

40 A 41 B 42 C

B775 A736

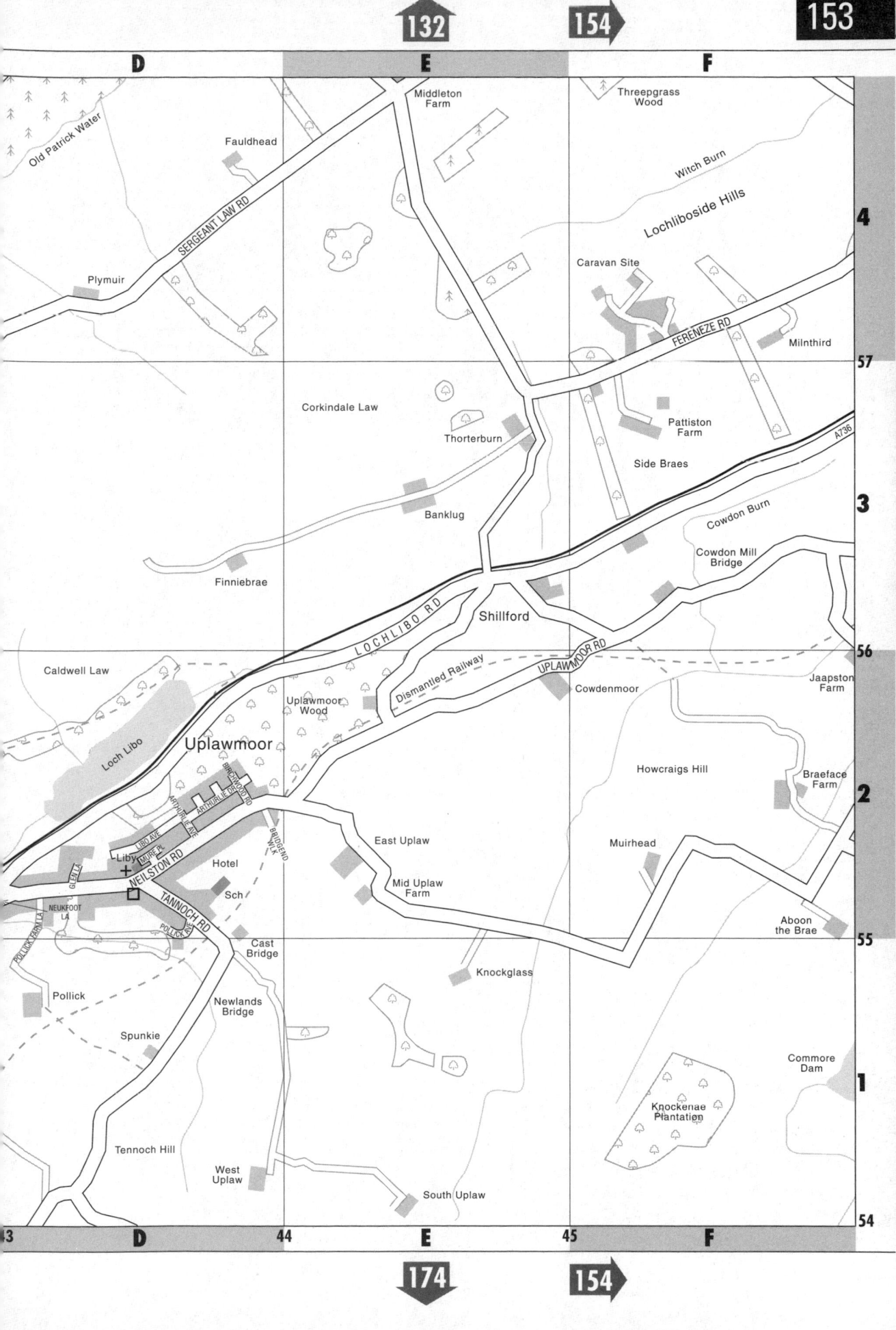

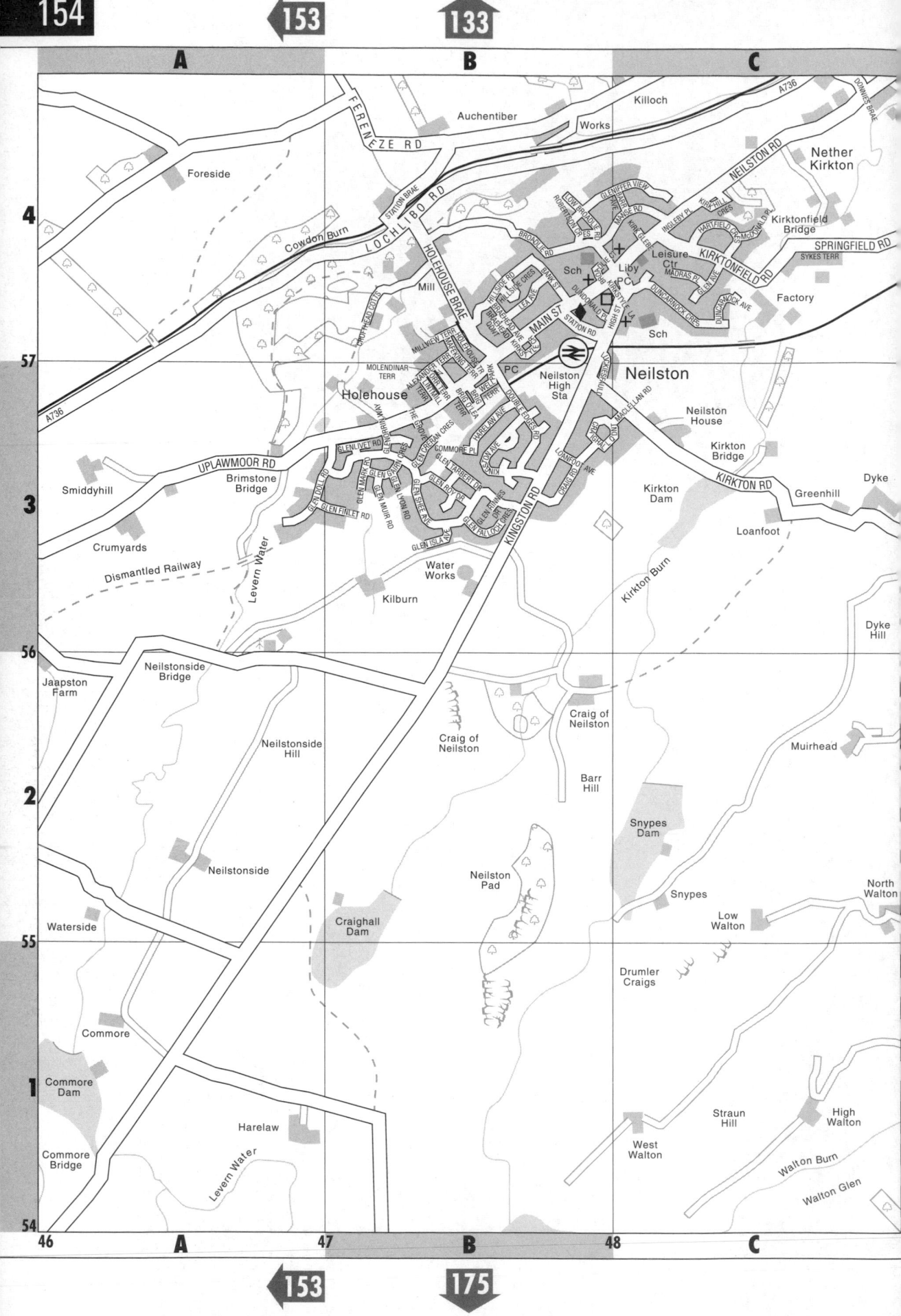

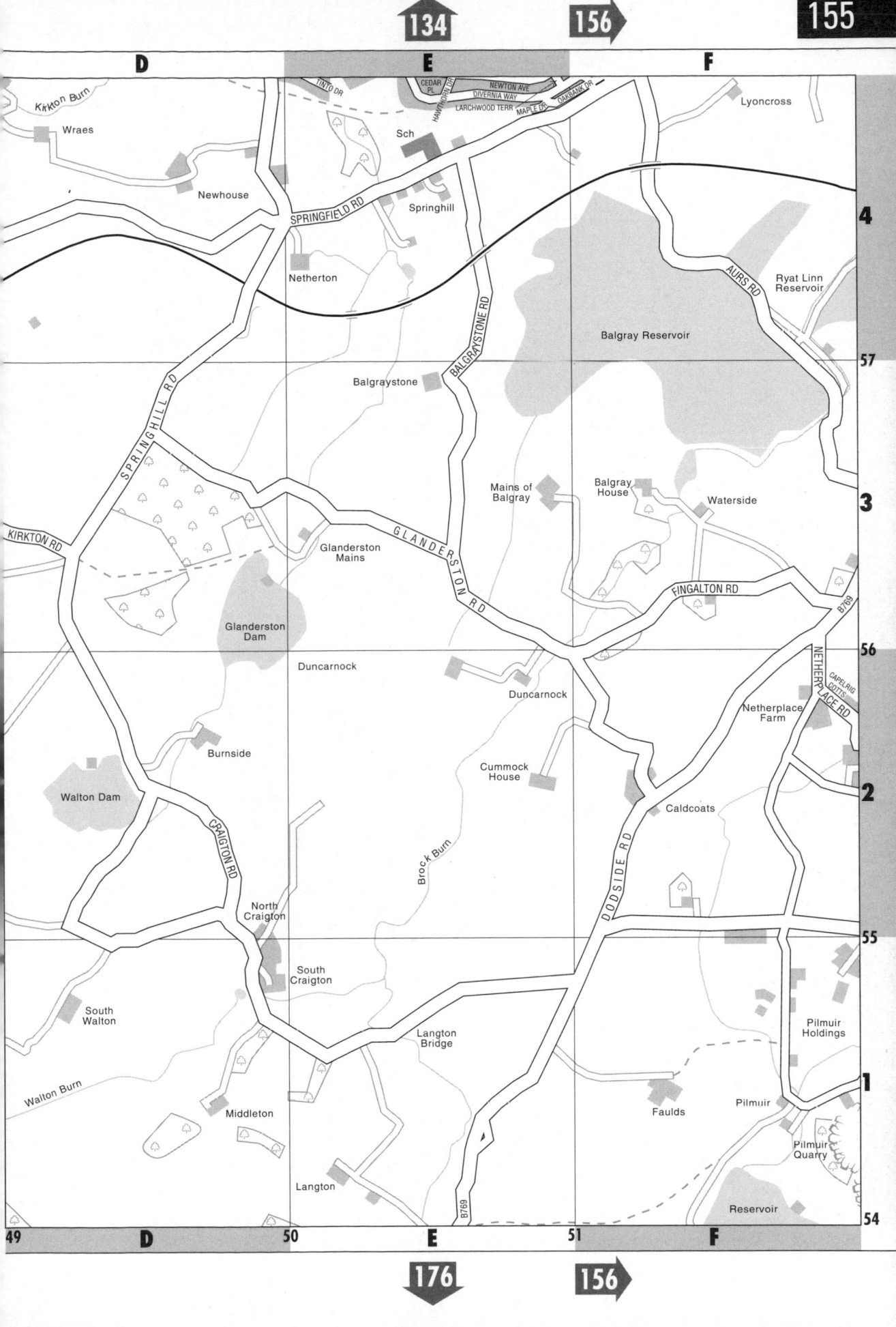

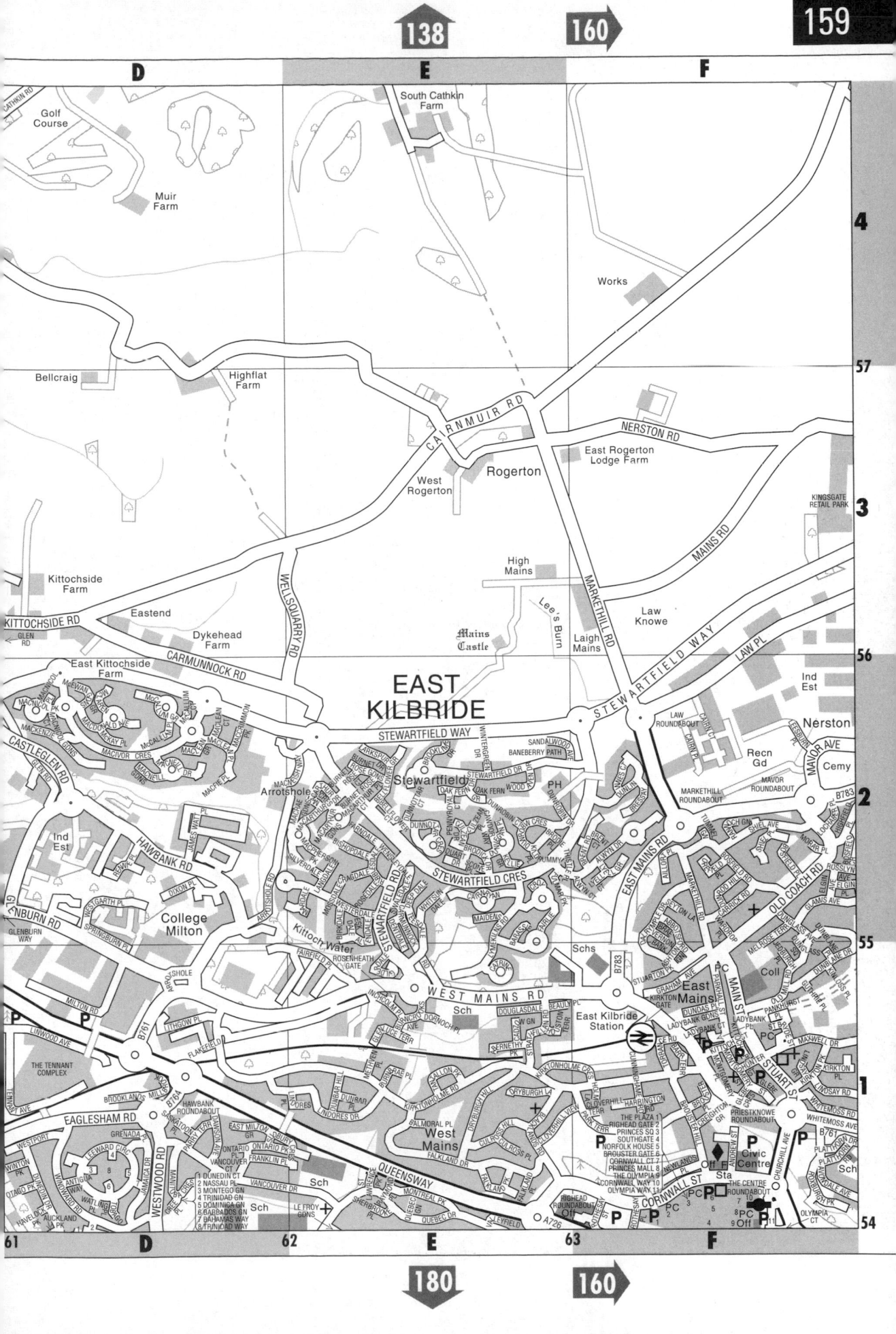

D E F

4

57

3

South Cathkin Farm

Golf Course

Muir Farm

Works

Bellcraig

Highflat Farm

CAIRNMUIR RD

NERSTON RD

West Rogerton

Rogerton

East Rogerton Lodge Farm

KINGSGATE RETAIL PARK

Kittochside Farm

Eastend

KITTOCHSIDE RD

GLEN RD

Dykehead Farm

CARMUNNOCK RD

WELLSQUARRY RD

High Mains

Lee's Burn

Mains Castle

Laigh Mains

MARKETHILL RD

Law Knowe

MAINS RD

STEWARTFIELD WAY

LAW PL

56

Ind Est

East Kittochside Farm

EAST KILBRIDE

STEWARTFIELD WAY

Law Roundabout

Nerston

CASTLEGLEN RD

Arrotshole

Stewartfield

SANDALWOOD BANEBERRY PATH

PH

MARKETHILL ROUNDABOUT

Recn Gd

MAVOR AVE

Cemy

MAVOR ROUNDABOUT

B783

2

Ind Est

HAWBANK RD

College Milton

Kittoch Water

ROSENHEATH GATE

STEWARTFIELD CRES

STEWARTFIELD RD

Schs

B783

East Mains

Coll

55

GLENBURN RD

GLENBURN WAY

ARROTSHOLE

FAIRFIELD PL

WEST MAINS RD

Sch

Douglasdale

East Kilbride Station

Kirkton Gate

EAST MAINS RD

MAIN ST

OLD COACH RD

P P

MILTON RD

B761

THE TENNANT COMPLEX

EAGLESHAM RD

B76A

HAWBANK ROUNDABOUT

EAST MILTON GR

WESTWOOD RD

West Mains

QUEENSWAY

Sch

A726

CORNWALL ST

PRIESTKNOWE ROUNDABOUT

Civic Centre

THE CENTRE ROUNDABOUT

OLYMPIA CT

1

1 DUNEDIN CT
2 NASSAU PL
3 MONTEGO GN
4 TRINIDAD GN
5 DOMINICA GN
6 BARBADOS GN
7 BAHAMAS WAY
8 TRINIDAD WAY

1 THE PLAZA
2 RIGHEAD GATE
3 PRINCES SQ
4 SOUTHGATE
5 NORFOLK HOUSE
6 BROUSTER GATE
7 CORNWALL CT
8 PRINCES MALL
9 THE OLYMPIA
10 CORNWALL WAY
11 OLYMPIA WAY

54

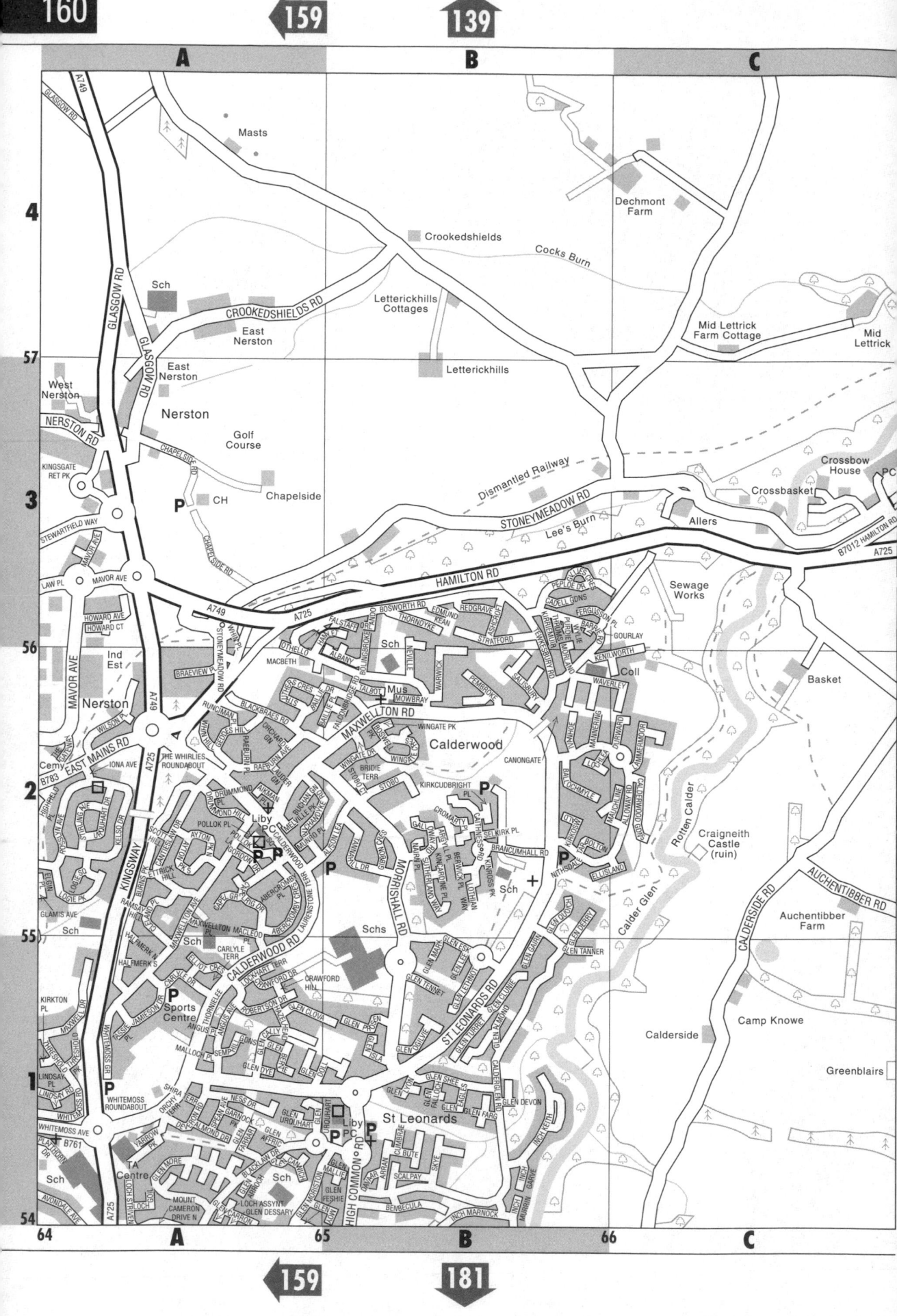

159
139

A B C

4

Masts

Dechmont Farm

Crookedshields

Cocks Burn

Crookedshields Cottages

CROOKEDSHIELDS RD

Mid Lettrick Farm Cottage

Mid Lettrick

Sch

East Nerston

Letterickhills Cottages

57

East Nerston

Letterickhills

West Nerston

GLASGOW RD

Nerston

NERSTON RD

Golf Course

KINGSGATE RET PK

CHAPELSIDE RD

Dismantled Railway

Crossbow House

PC

Crossbasket

Stewartfield Way

P CH

Chapelside

STONEYMEADOW RD

Lee's Burn

Allers

B7012 HAMILTON RD

A725

3

LAW PL

MAVOR AVE

HOWARD AVE

HOWARD CT

HAMILTON RD

Sewage Works

Basket

A749

A725

Ind Est

56

Nerston

MAVOR AVE

A749

BRAEVIEW

STONEYMEADOW RD

OTHELLO

MACBETH

BOSWORTH RD

THORNDYKE

EDMUND KEAN

REDGRAVE

STRATFORD

FERGUSSON PL

CADELL GDNS

GOURLAY

Coll

FALSTAFF

ALBANY

Sch

NEVILLE

WARWICK

PEMBROKE

SALISBURY

WAVERLEY

KENILWORTH

BOLINGBROKE

ALBOT

Mus

MOWBRAY

MAXWELLTON RD

WINGATE PK

Calderwood

CANONGATE

Rotten Calder

Craigneith Castle (ruin)

EAST MAINS RD

Cemy

IONA AVE

THE WHIRLIES ROUNDABOUT

B783

HIGHFIELD

STIRLING AVE

URQUHART

KELSO CT

2

RUNCIMAN

BLACKBRAES DR

RAEBURN PL

ORCHART

RAEBURN RD

WINGATE DR

WINGATE

BRIDIE TERR

STOBO

KIRKCUDBRIGHT

P

CROMARTY

THE KIRK PL

BRANCUMHALL RD

P

Sch

KINGSWAY

AIRMAN

DRUMMOND PL

DRUMMOND HILL

POLLOK PL

AYTON

Liby

P PC

GORDON

NAIRN

TANNARY

MORRISHALL RD

BERWICK LOTHIAN

SUTHERLAND WAY

BALLOCHMYLE

ALLOWAY

BOLTON

ELLISLAND

NITHSDALE

P

AUCHENTIBBER RD

CALDERSIDE RD

55

WHIN PL

ETTRICK HILL

CARLYLE TERR

MACLEOD

ABERCROMBY

CALDERWOOD RD

LAURENSTONE

Sch

Schs

Crawford Hill

GLEN ESK

GLEN MALLIE

Calder Glen

Auchentibber Farm

Sch

MAXWELLTON

HALFMERK N

LOCKHART

CRANFORD DR

ROBERTSON DR

GLEN CLOVA

ST LEONARDS RD

GLEN LEE

GLEN TENNET

GLEN TANNER

Calderside

Camp Knowe

P Sports Centre

THORNLEE

ANGUS PL

GLEN NEVIS

MALLOCH PL

GLEN DYE

GLEN SHEE

GLEN URR

GLEN FEN

Greenblairs

1

KIRKTON PL

LINDSAY RD

P

WHITEMOSS ROUNDABOUT

SHIRA

ORCH TERR

NESS DR

GLEN URQUHART

Liby

P PC

St Leonards

GLEN FARG

GLEN DEVON

INCH KEITH

WHITEMOSS AVE

B761

TA Centre

PLATTHORN

Sch

MOUNT CAMERON DRIVE N

LOCH ASSYNT

GLEN DESSARY

GLEN FESHIE

BENBECULA

SCALPAY

BUTE

SKYE

INCH MARNOCK

MUIRIN

GARVE

INCH FELL

54

A725

64

A

65

B

66

C

D E F

4

57

3

56

2

55

1

54

PEITER PL 10
CAERLAVEROCK PL 11
SANDALE PATH 12
MALVAIG LA 13
MAVIS BANK 14
MAPLE WAY 15
ETTERICK WYND 16
TRAQUAIR WYND 17
DRYBURGH WAY 18
BARNETT PATH 19
CAUSEYSTANES 20
ROXBURGH PL 21
GREENBANK 22
LIBERTY PATH 23
LOCHABER PATH 24
MADISON PATH 25
TOURNAI PATH 26

Barnhill

Malcolmwood

Wheatlands

Blantyre Station
5 TOWARD CT
6 ROSEBANK AVE
River Clyde

1 TIGHNASHEEN WAY
2 MAREE WAY
3 YARROW WAY
4 MONTEITH PL

Public Park

Works

Clydeview Shopping Ctr

Glasgow Rd

Blantyre

Sch

Rotten Calder

Dismtd Rly

Hamilton Rd

Craigmuir Gdns

High Blantyre

1 AUCHENTIBBER CT
2 ATHOLL CT
3 ARDGOUR CT
4 CHIRNSIDE CT
5 RANNOCH CT

Hillhouse Rd

Loanfoot Rd
Cemy

Hamilton International
Technology Park

Main St

Ind Est

Udston Rd

Udston

Hospl

Craigmuir

Newhouse

Sydes Brae

Dismantled Railway

John Knox La

Hillhouse

St Ninian's Pl

Liby

Ind Est

Park Farm

Red Burn

Park House

Blantyre Park Farm

Clyde Cottage

Udston Cottage

Auchentibber Rd

Auchentibber

Meml

Dykehead

Parkneuk

Dykehead House

Earnock Rd

Wellhall Rd

Broomhouse

Parkneuk Rd

Park View

Newfield

Braehead Cottage

Newhousemill Rd

MAUCHLINE CT 1
MAYBOLE GDNS 2
LENDALFOOT GDNS 3

Earnock

Sherry Dr

Muirmains

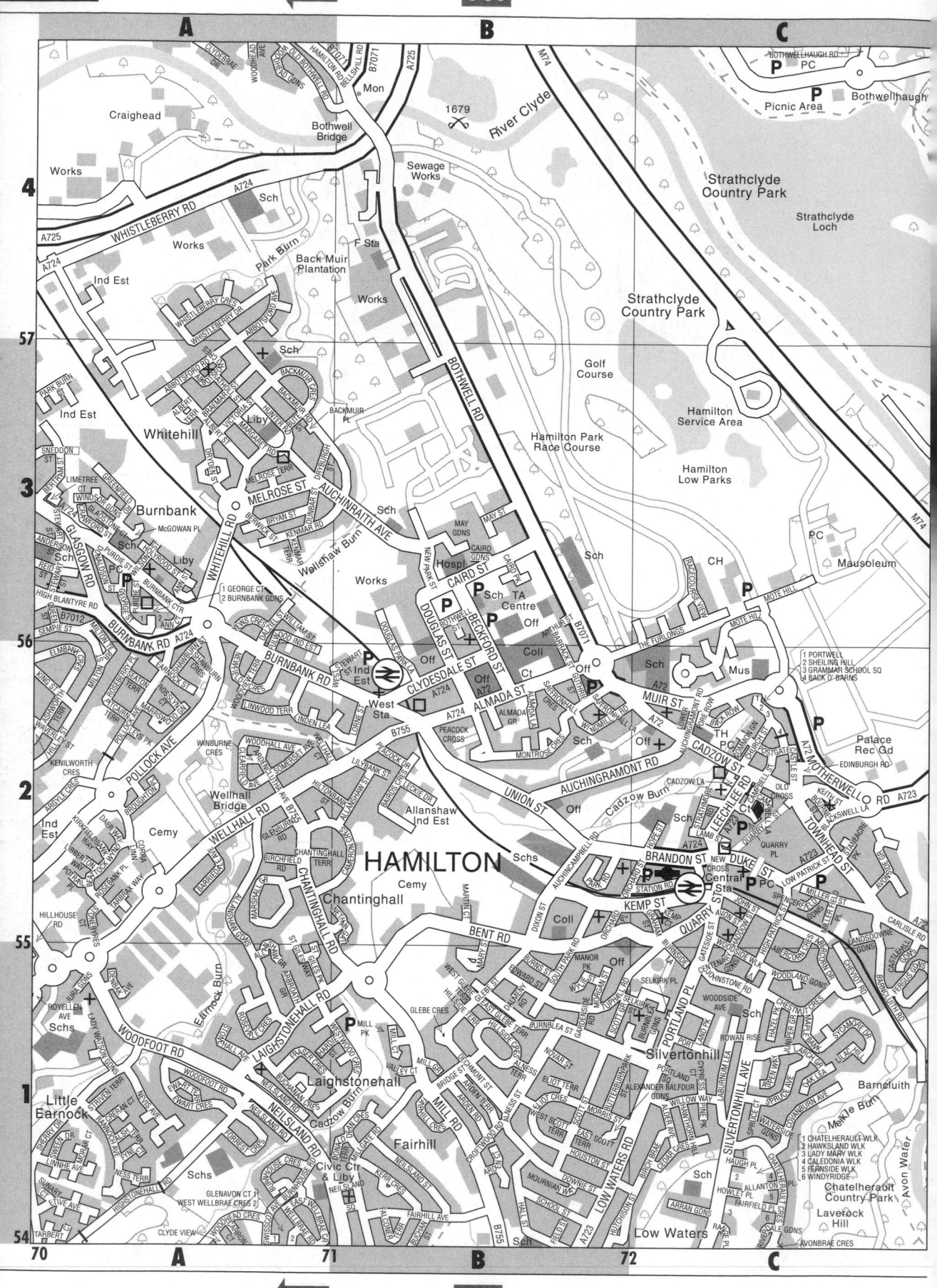

MOTHERWELL

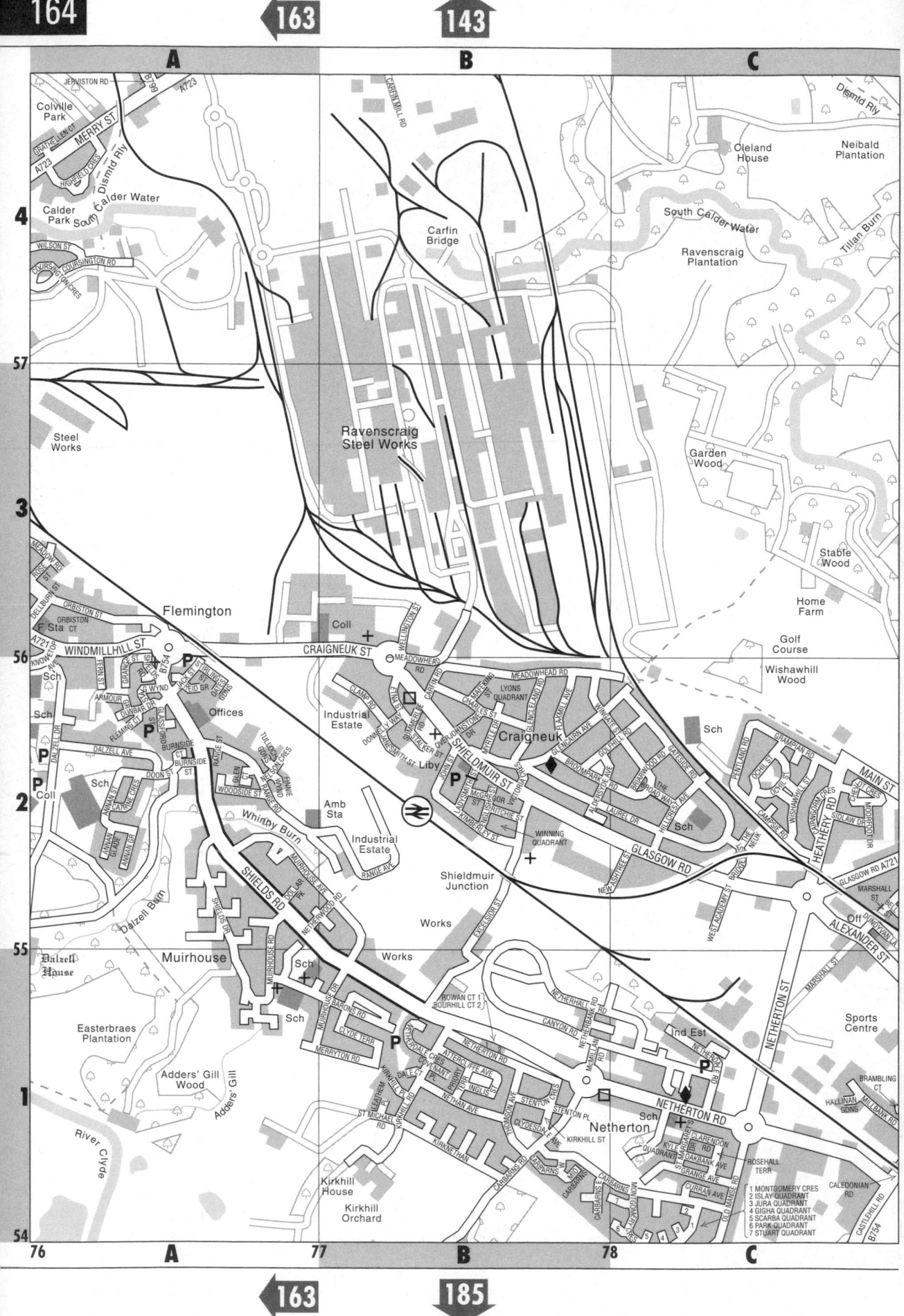

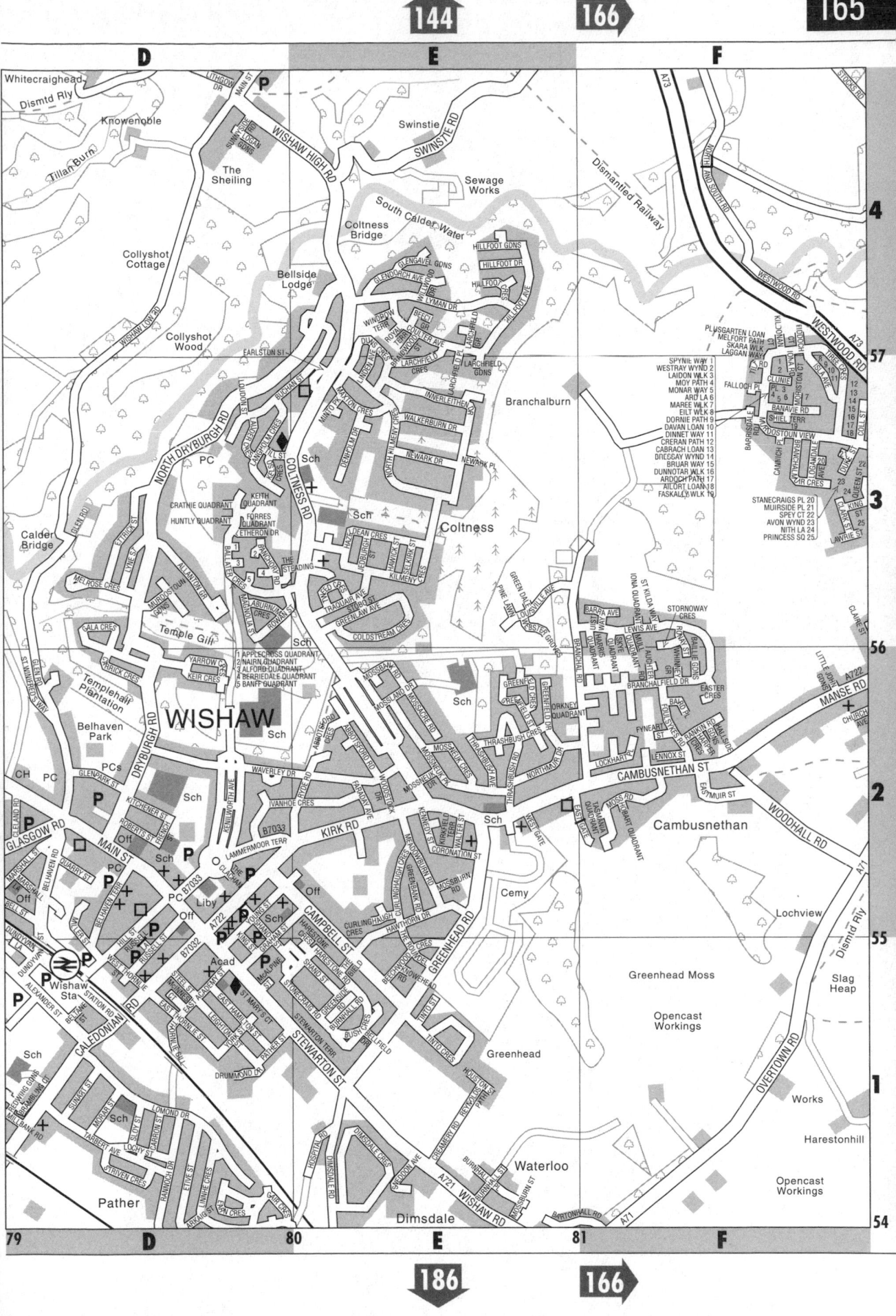

165
145

A   B   C

Mill

ALLANTON RD
MILL RD
A71

Mill

WOOD
VIEW CALDER RD
AUCHTERBURN RD
COLTNESS AVE

Brucefield

Easterhouse

MURDOSTOUN RD

Murdostoun
Castle

Mill

MILL RD

LANARK ST

Crosshill

WILSON RD

Kennel Knowe
Wood

4

South Calder Water

Murdostoun
Bridge

ALLANTON RD

Bonkle

CHURCH RD
CARFIN PL

57

A73

East
Crindledyke
CALDER AVE
KILMICHAEL AVE

WOODSIDE CRES

MEADOWFIELD PL
BROWNHILL VIEW

Sharnothshield
Small Holdings

Calkers
Wood

EASTWOOD DR
NORTHWOOD DR

ABERNETHYN RD

FIRTREE RD
FIRTREE PL
ALCATH RD

Crindledyke

LINWOOD RD
HAWTHORN AVE

Gallow Hill

MURDOSTOUN
PL VIEW
LEWDEN
PL VIEW

BAILLIESMUIR

MUIRHOUSE AVE

BONKLE RD

AUCHTER ST

Sharnothshield

KING'S ST
WEST PL ST
STEWART CRES

CRINDLEDYKE CRES
BONKLE GDNS
GODDARD PL

BRAEDALE PL
BRAEDALE CRES

Cathburn
Holdings

WESTWOOD RD

PARK DR

Sch

NEWTON DR
PARK VIEW

Sch

CATHBURN RD

MILL RD

Newmains

56

MANSE RD
Liby
A722
HOPE ST
CLAIRE ST
PARKSIDE ST
Sch
CHURCH AVE
SCHOOL RD

A71

A73

Morningside
Farm

BROWN ST

Works

Watstonfoot

VICTORIA ST

SCHOOL RD

Sch

Woodside
Farm

MORNINGSIDE RD

Morningside

Dismantled Railway

2

Works

A71
OVERTOWN RD

Watstonmids

Auchter Water

WOODHALL RD

55

MAIN ST

Slag
Heap

Chapel

CHAPEL RD

Dismantled Railway

1

Harestonhill

Holmhill

Watstonheads

Herdshill

A73

Bogside
Farm

54

82   A   83   B   84   C

165
187

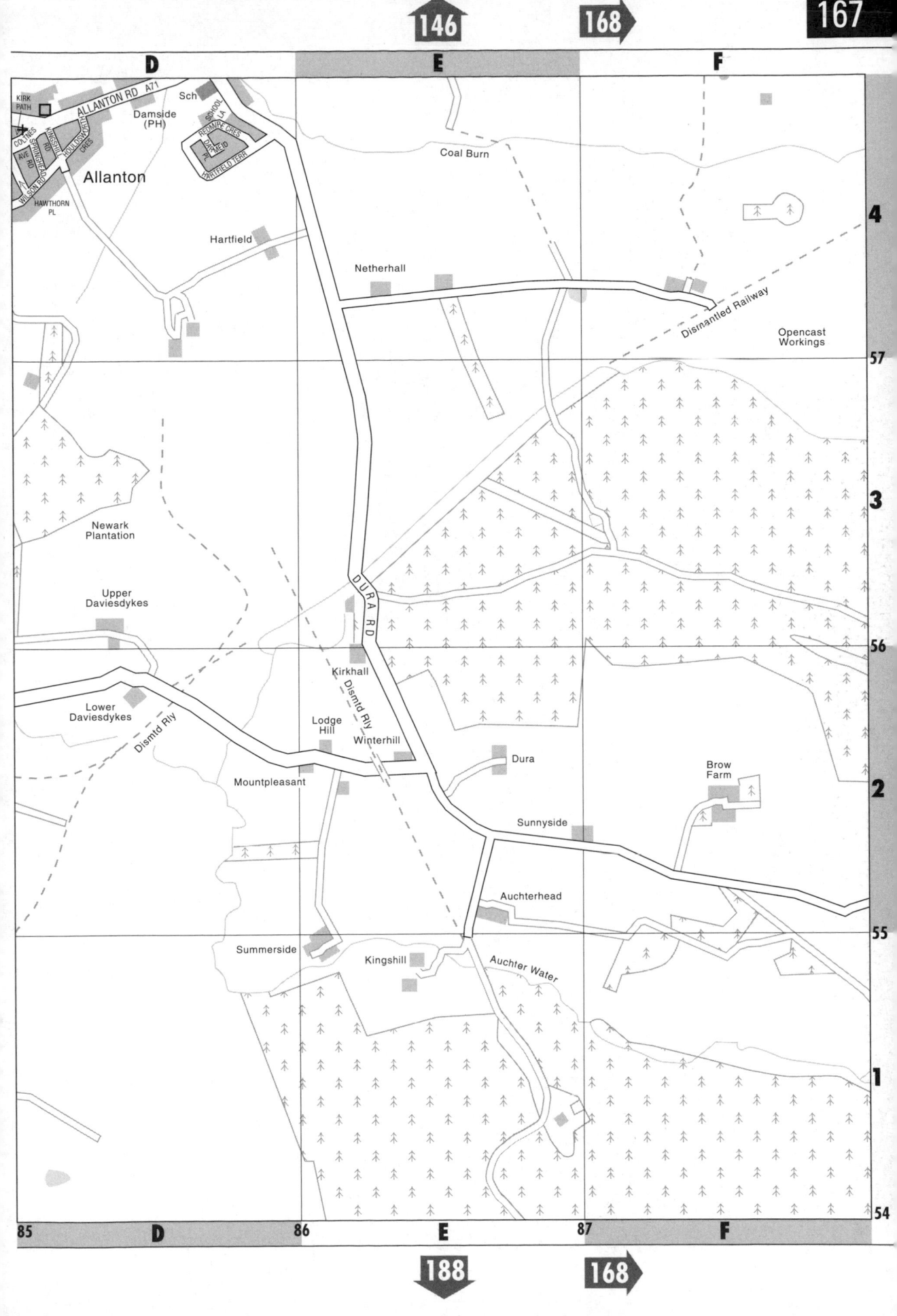

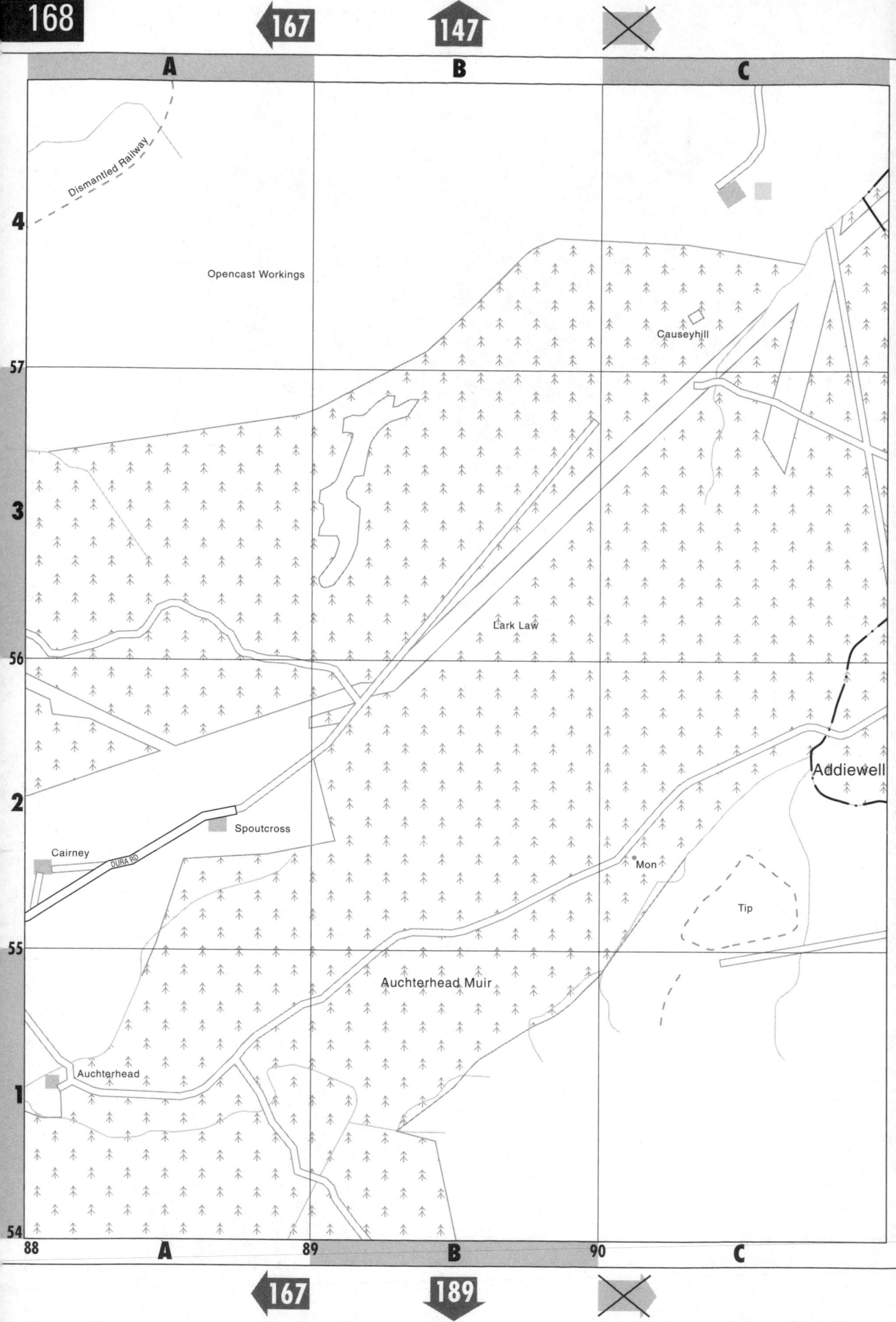

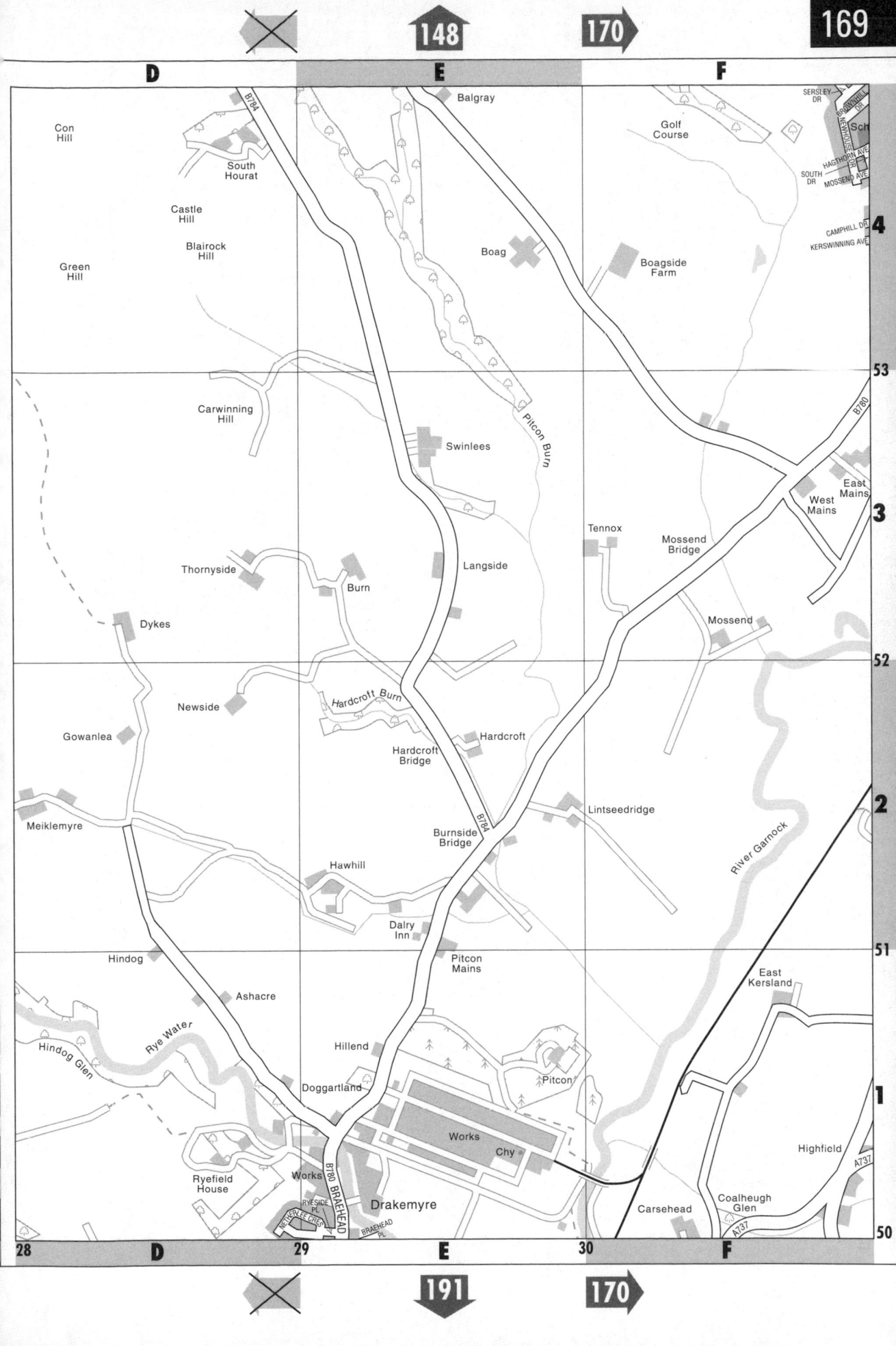

D E F

Con Hill

South Hourat

Castle Hill

Blairock Hill

Green Hill

SERSLEY DR
BROWNHILL DR
NEWHOUSE
Sch
HAGTHORN RD
SOUTH DR
MOSSEND AVE

Golf Course

Balgray

Boag

Boagside Farm

CAMPHILL DR
KERSWINNING AVE

4

B780

53

Carwinning Hill

Swinlees

Pitcon Burn

East Mains

West Mains

3

Thornyside

Burn

Langside

Tennox

Mossend Bridge

Dykes

Mossend

52

Newside

Hardcroft Burn

Hardcroft

Gowanlea

Hardcroft Bridge

Meiklemyre

B784

Lintseedridge

River Garnock

2

Hawhill

Burnside Bridge

Hindog

Dalry Inn

Pitcon Mains

East Kersland

51

Ashacre

Rye Water

Hillend

Pitcon

Hindog Glen

Doggartland

Highfield

A737

1

Ryefield House

Works

B780 BRAEHEAD

Works

Drakemyre

Chy

Carsehead

Coalheugh Glen

A737

RYESIDE PL
WEDDERLEE CRES
BRAEHEAD PL

50

28 D 29 E 30 F

169 149

A   B   C

1 BROWNHILL DR
2 BAILLIESTON AVE
3 KERSWINNING AVE

PADDOCKHOLM
Sch
F'D Sta
Amb Sta
WESTFIELD
AVILS PL
PC
HOLMHEAD
B777
DALRY RD
WESTERN CRES
CENTRAL AVE
EASTERN CRES
KIRKLAND RD
Cemy
Manse
Brierysink
BRIERY CT
SOUTH NEUK
SUNDERLAND CT
ST BRENNANS CT
Sch
LOADINGBANK CT
LOADINGBANK
B780
BALGRAY RD
GRAHAMSTON AVE
MAIN ST
HOLMS RD
BURNSIDE ST
KERSLAND RD
GARNOCK

Kilbirnie Loch

Industrial Estate

WILLOWYARD RD

GLENGARNOCK WORKSHOPS

LOCHSHORE EAST IND EST

Lochshore South Ind-Est

Willowyard Ind Est
KILBURN RD
BEECHFIELD RD
OLD WILLOWYARD RD
LOCHVIEW RD
B777

53

Dismantled Railway

Glengarnock Station

Glengarnock
PH
Kersland House
DAISYBANK
BEITH RD
SMITH AVE
Mc PHERSON AVE
Longbar
LONGBAR AVE
B777

Crawfield

Whitestanes

A737

3

River Garnock

Auchengree Bridge

Little Auchengree

Meikle Auchengree

Works

Sidehouse

Powgree Burn

Brackenhills Bridge
Dismd Riv

Davidshill

Maulside Mains

52

Brownhill

Langmuir of Auchengree

Maulside

Coalburn

Barcosh

Davidshill

2

Brownhill House

Glenhead

Todhills

Hareshaw
CROSSROADS
PH
The Den

51

West Muirhouse

East Muirhouse

Little Barkip

Barkip Plantation

1

Birkentop Cottage

Easter Highfield

High Swindridgemuir

Wheatyfauld

A737

Bombo Burn

East Middlebank

Highfield

Highfield

West Middlebank

50

169   192

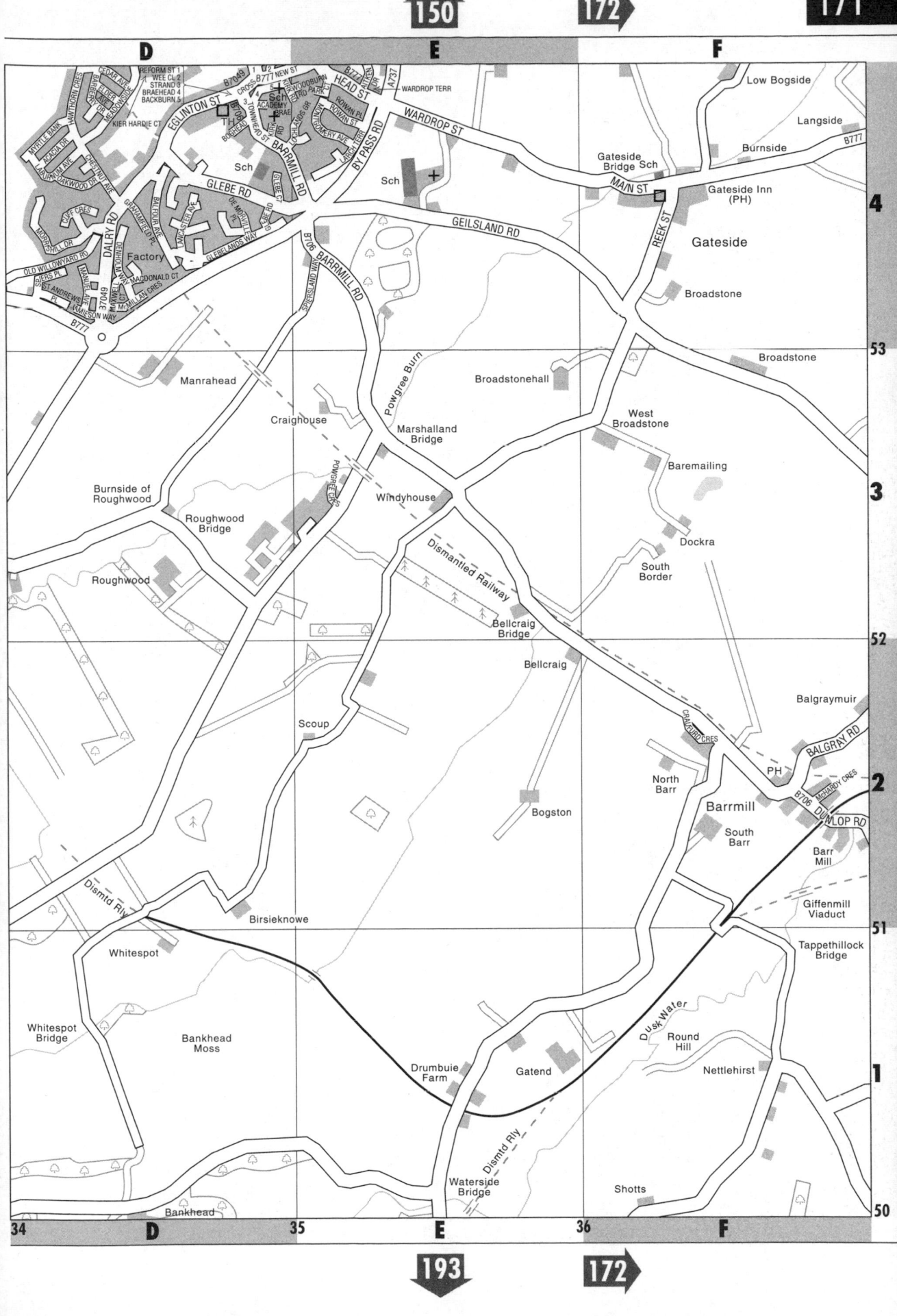

D   E   F

REFORM ST 1
WEE CL 2
STRAND 3
BRAEHEAD 4
BACKBURN 5

CEDAR AVE
HAWTHORN CRES
EGLINTON ST
B7049
CROSS
NEW ST
B777
HEAD ST
A737
WARDROP TERR
WARDROP ST

MYRTLE BANK
ACACIA DR
LAUREL
ELM AVE
OAKWOOD DR
CHESTNUT AVE
KIER HARDIE CT
B7049
THE
BOGHEAD
TOWNHEAD ST
ACADEMY
BRAE
Sch
WOODBURN PL
PARK
ROWAN ST
BAKERY AVE
Sch
BY PASS RD
BARRMILL RD

Low Bogside

Langside

Burnside

B777

DALRY RD
MARSHALL DR
SIERS PL
ST ANDREWS PL
MAXWELL
MCMILLAN CRES
KILWINNING
B7049
OLD WILLOWYARD RD
Factory
GLEBE RD
LANCASTER AVE
BALFOUR RD
GRAHAMFIELD PL
DR MOFFAT
DR JERG
GLEBELANDS WAY
MACDONALD CT
B777
BARRMILL RD

Gateside
Bridge Sch
MAIN ST
Gateside Inn
(PH)

Gateside

4

GEILSLAND RD
Sch
Broadstone

53

Manrahead
Craighouse
Powgree Burn
Broadstonehall
Broadstone

West
Broadstone

Marshalland
Bridge
Windyhouse
Baremailing

Burnside of
Roughwood
Roughwood
Bridge
POWGREE CRES
Dockra

Roughwood
South
Border

3

Dismantled Railway
Bellcraig
Bridge

52

Bellcraig
CRAIGURD CRES
Balgraymuir
BALGRAY RD

Scoup
North
Barr
PH
MCHARDY CRES
B706 DUNLOP RD
2

Bogston
Barrmill
South
Barr
Barr
Mill

Giffenmill
Viaduct

Dismtd Rly
Birsieknowe

51

Whitespot
D Usk Water
Tappethillock
Bridge

Whitespot
Bridge
Bankhead
Moss
Round
Hill
Nettlehirst

1

Drumbuie
Farm
Gatend
Shotts

Waterside
Bridge
Bankhead
Dismtd Rly

50

34   D   35   E   36   F

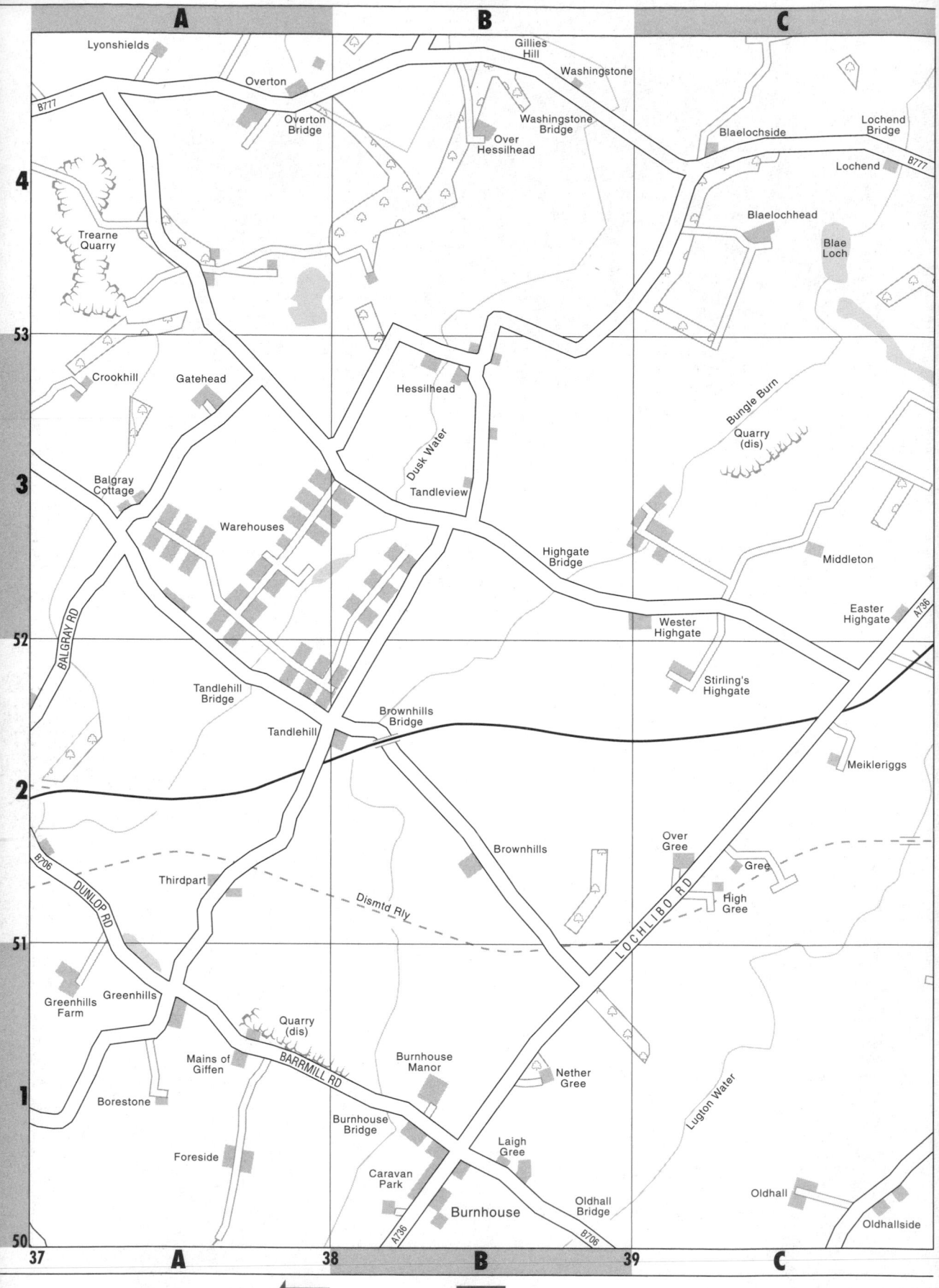

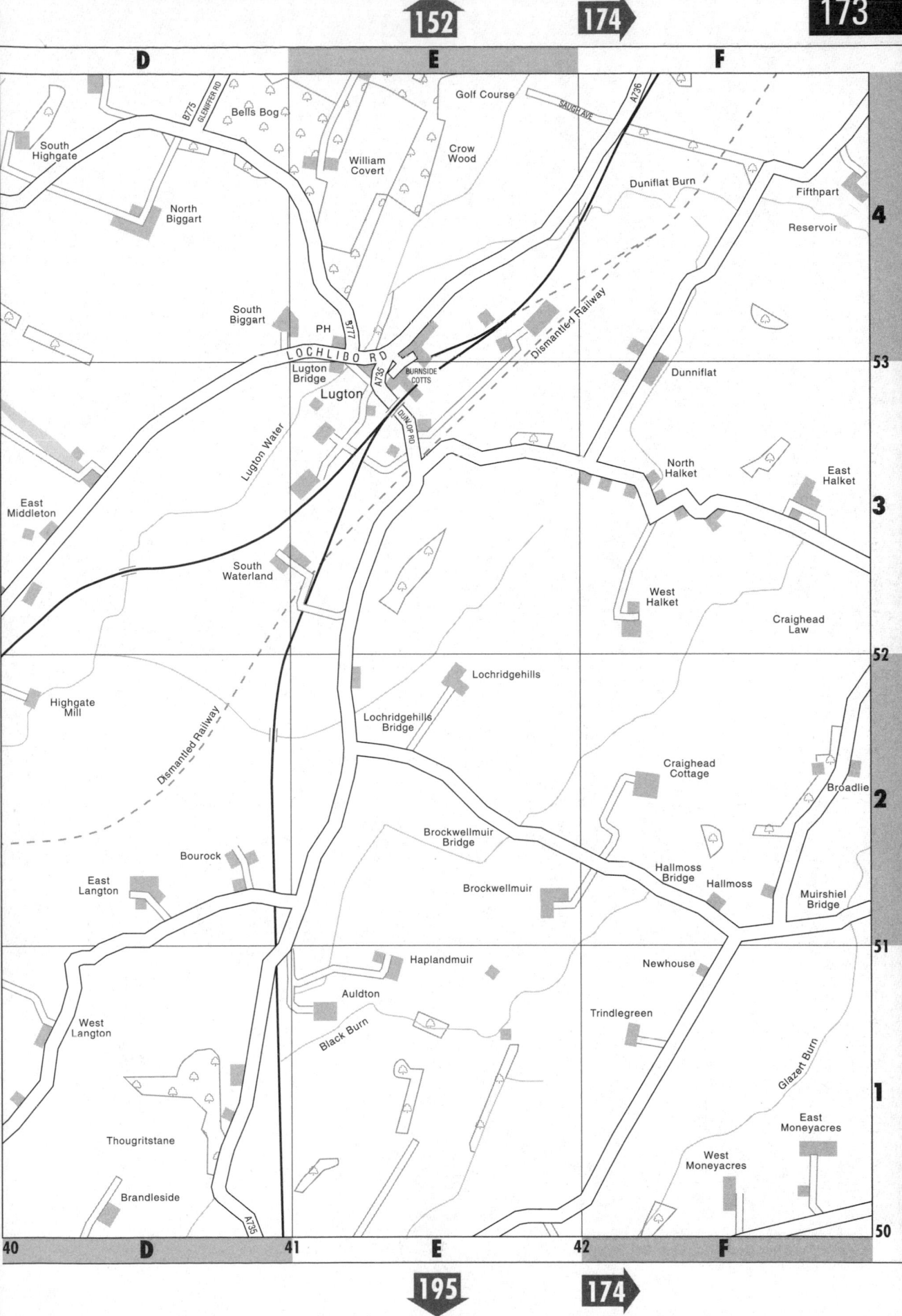

D
E
F

4

53

3

52

2

51

1

50

South Highgate

North Biggart

Bells Bog

William Covert

Golf Course

Crow Wood

SAUGH AVE

A736

Duniflat Burn

Fifthpart

Reservoir

GLENIFFER RD

B775

South Biggart

PH

B777

LOCHLIBO RD

A735

Lugton Bridge

Lugton

BURNSIDE COTTS

DUNLOP RD

Dismantled Railway

Dunniflat

North Halket

East Halket

East Middleton

Lugton Water

South Waterland

West Halket

Craighead Law

Highgate Mill

Dismantled Railway

Lochridgehills

Lochridgehills Bridge

Craighead Cottage

Broadlie

Bourock

Brockwellmuir Bridge

Brockwellmuir

Hallmoss Bridge

Hallmoss

Muirshiel Bridge

East Langton

Haplandmuir

Newhouse

West Langton

Auldton

Black Burn

Trindlegreen

Glazert Burn

Thougritstane

East Moneyacres

West Moneyacres

Brandleside

A735

40
41
42

D
E
F

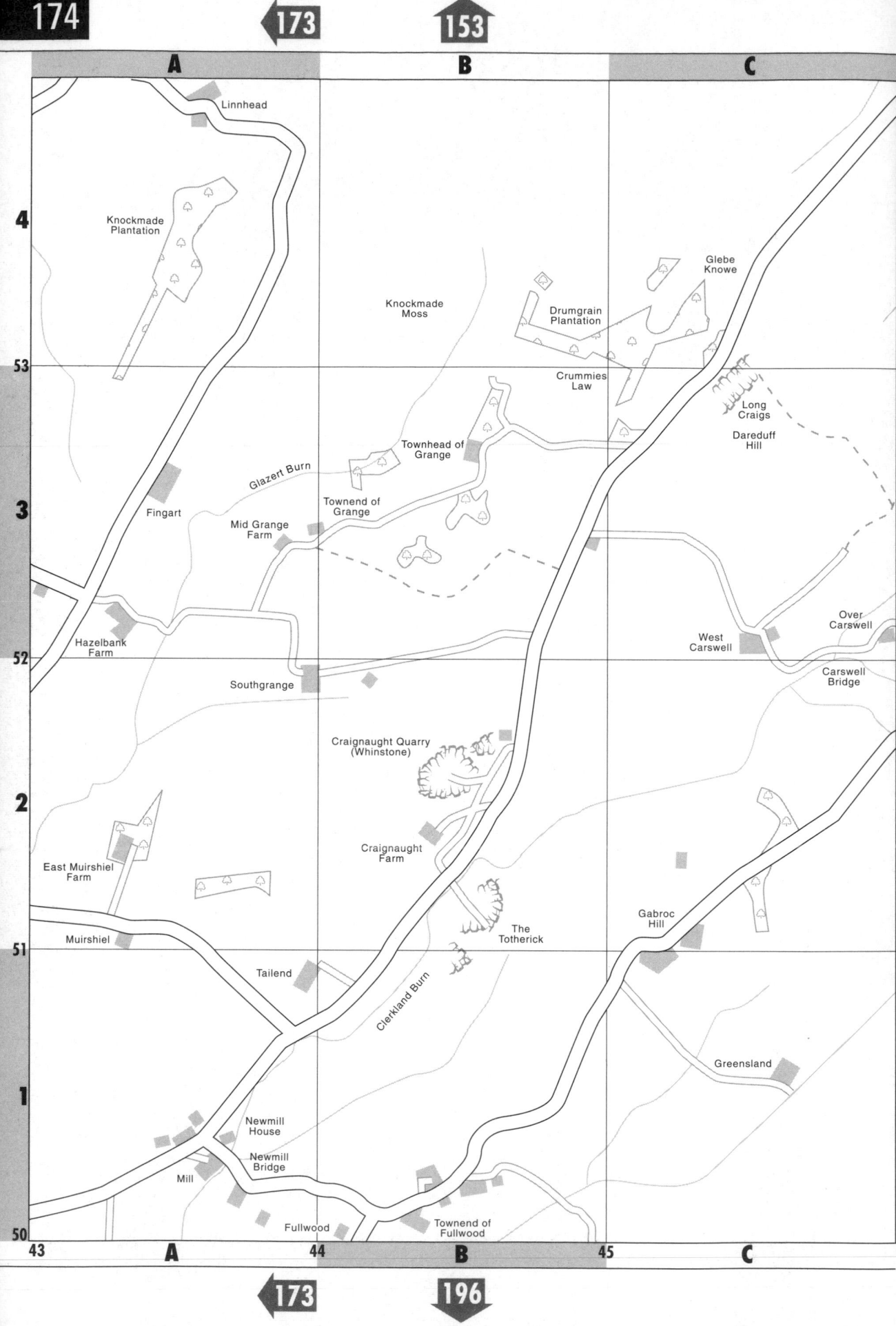

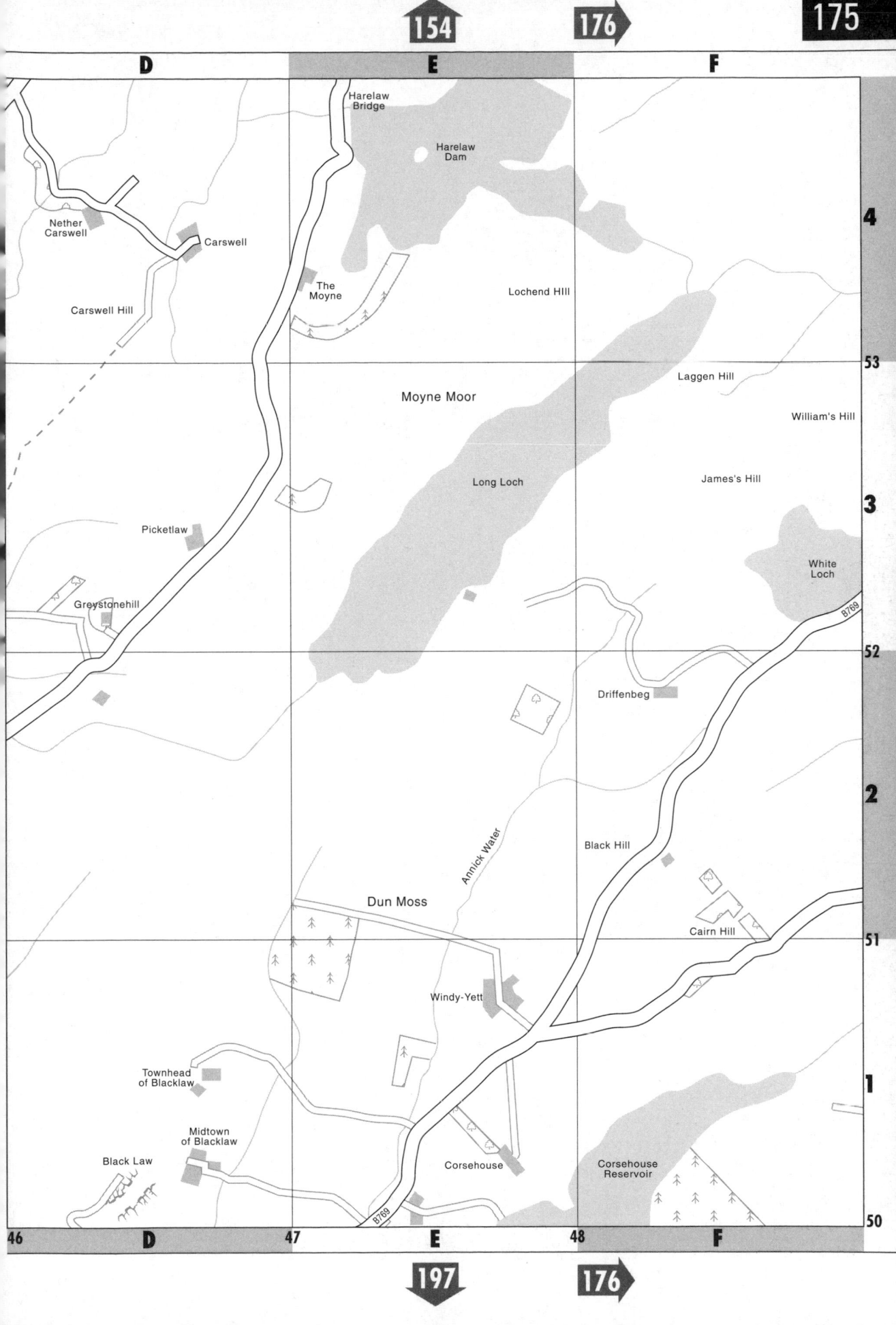

D

Nether
Carswell

Carswell

Carswell Hill

Harelaw
Bridge

Harelaw
Dam

The
Moyne

Lochend Hill

Moyne Moor

Long Loch

Laggen Hill

William's Hill

James's Hill

White
Loch

Picketlaw

Greystonehill

B769

Driffenbeg

Annick Water

Black Hill

Dun Moss

Cairn Hill

Windy-Yett

Townhead
of Blacklaw

Midtown
of Blacklaw

Black Law

Corsehouse

B769

Corsehouse
Reservoir

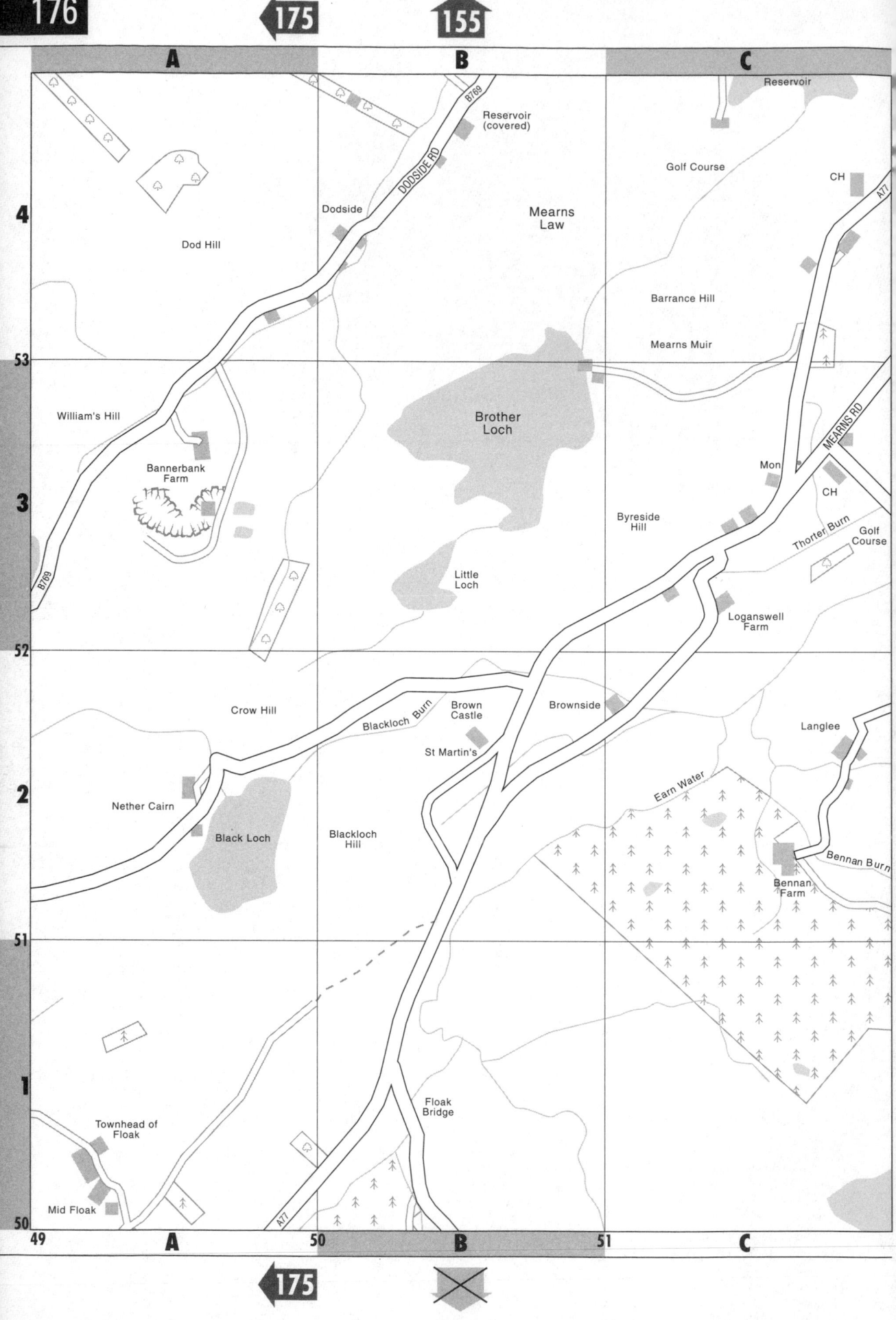

A B C

4

53

3

52

2

51

1

50

49 A 50 B 51 C

Reservoir (covered)

DODSIDE RD

B769

Dodside

Dod Hill

Mearns Law

Reservoir

Golf Course

CH

A77

Barrance Hill

Mearns Muir

William's Hill

Bannerbank Farm

Brother Loch

Byreside Hill

Little Loch

Mon

CH

MEARNS RD

Thorter Burn

Golf Course

Loganswell Farm

B769

Crow Hill

Blackloch Burn

Brown Castle

Brownside

St Martin's

Langlee

Earn Water

Nether Cairn

Black Loch

Blackloch Hill

Bennan Burn

Bennan Farm

Townhead of Floak

Floak Bridge

A77

Mid Floak

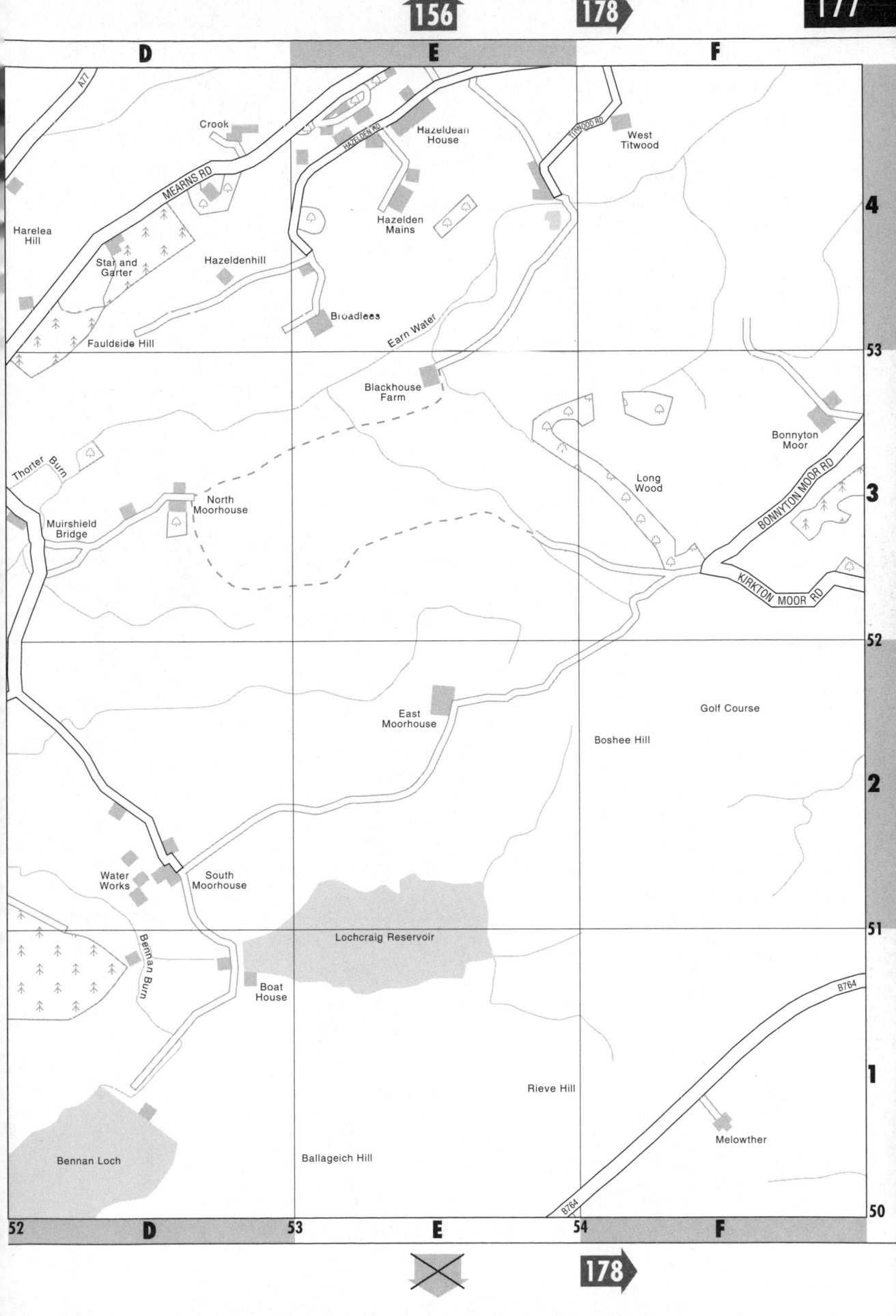

A77

Crook

Hazeldean
House

HAZELDEN RD

West
Titwood

TITWOOD RD

MEARNS RD

Harelea
Hill

Star and
Garter

Hazeldenhill

Hazelden
Mains

Fauldside Hill

Broadlees

Earn Water

Blackhouse
Farm

Bonnyton
Moor

Thorter Burn

Long
Wood

BONNYTON MOOR RD

Muirshield
Bridge

North
Moorhouse

KIRKTON MOOR RD

East
Moorhouse

Golf Course

Boshee Hill

Water
Works

South
Moorhouse

Bennan Burn

Lochcraig Reservoir

B764

Boat
House

Rieve Hill

Melowther

B764

Bennan Loch

Ballageich Hill

A   B   C

Bogside

FLOORS RD

Brackenrig Burn

BONNYTON MOOR RD

Bonnyton

Castlehill
House

HUMBIE RD

Castlehill
Wood

Castlehill

Crosslees
Wood

Crosslees

Borland Burn

Low
Borland

GLASGOW RD

B767

BRACKENRIG
CRES

BARLAE AVE

RIVERSIDE RD

Stoneside

White Cart Water

Holehouse

HOLEHOUSE RD

Cemy

CRAIGBANK
DR

ABRAHAM CRES

Mid
Borland

High
Borland

Resr

Eaglesham

LYNN DR

ALEXANDER AVE

KIRKTON DR

POLLOCK AVE

GLAZERT DR

BALFEARN DR

POLBAE CRES

TARFF AVE

AIRYLIGG DR

WOODLAND CRES

COO LA

BRANNOCK DR

1 MANSEVIEW TERR
2 BORLAND CRES

PARK CRES

Liby

POLNOON
DR

PCs

EAGLESHAM RD

B764

GILMOUR ST

B767

CHEAPSIDE ST

P

BONNYTON DR

GLENDUNNING
PL

QUARRY
LA

POLNOON ST

Common

MID RD

PH

MONTGOMERY SQ

MONTGOMERY ST

MONTGOMERY CT 1
KIRKTON CT 2

MOOR RD

ALNWICK DR

2

1

BROWNMUIR AVE

STRATHAVEN RD

Sch

EGLINTON ST

BRANKTON AVE

EGLINTON WLK

HILL O DR

EASTLANDS
PL

Brownmuir
Holding

KIRKTON MOOR RD

North
Kirktonmoor

CH

Golf Course

South
Kirktonmoor

Picketlaw
Reservoir

Picketlaw

Low Hill

High Dam

High Hill

B764

Woodhouse

Enoch Burn

East
Revoch

Park
Farm

West
Revoch

55   A   56   B   57   C

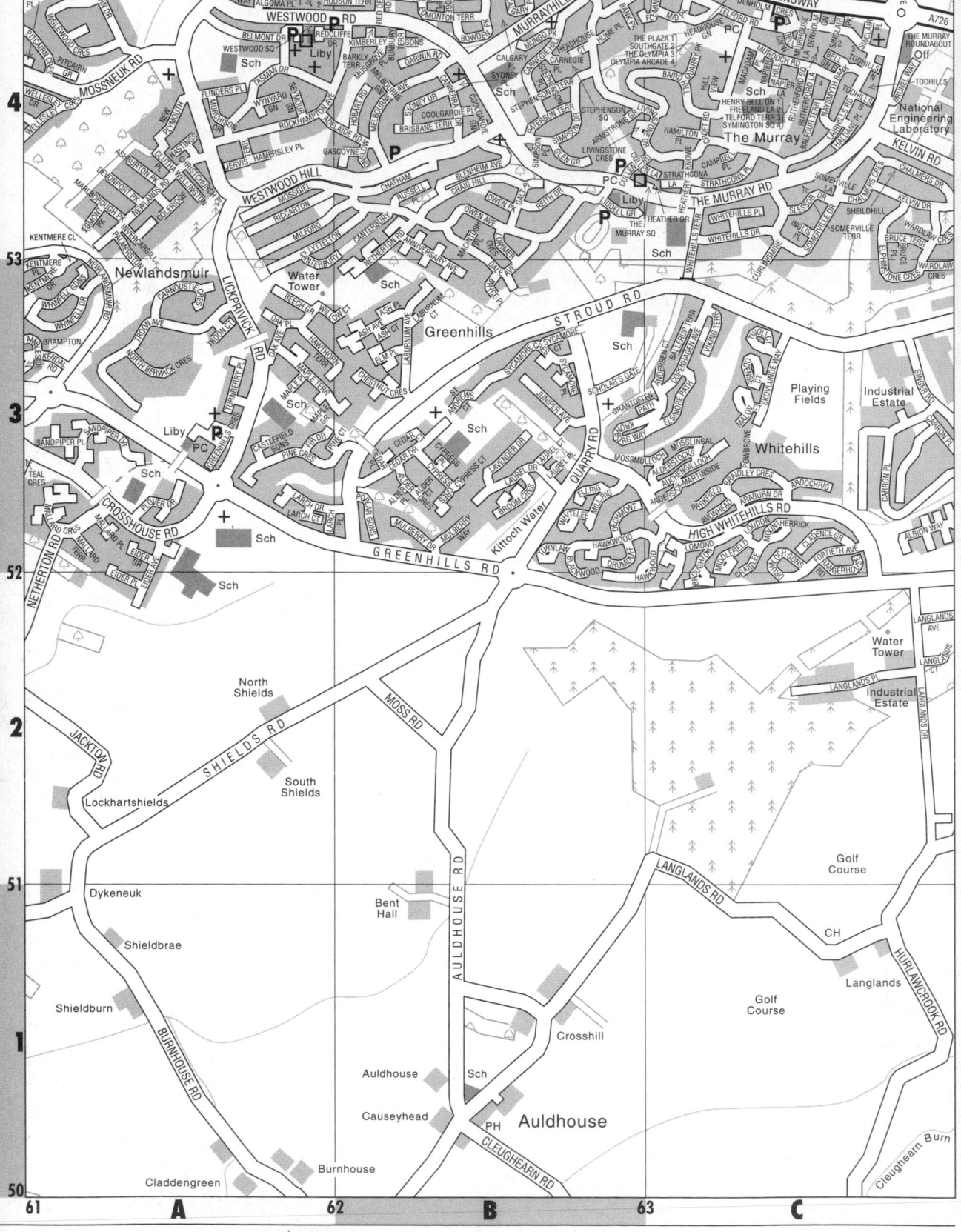

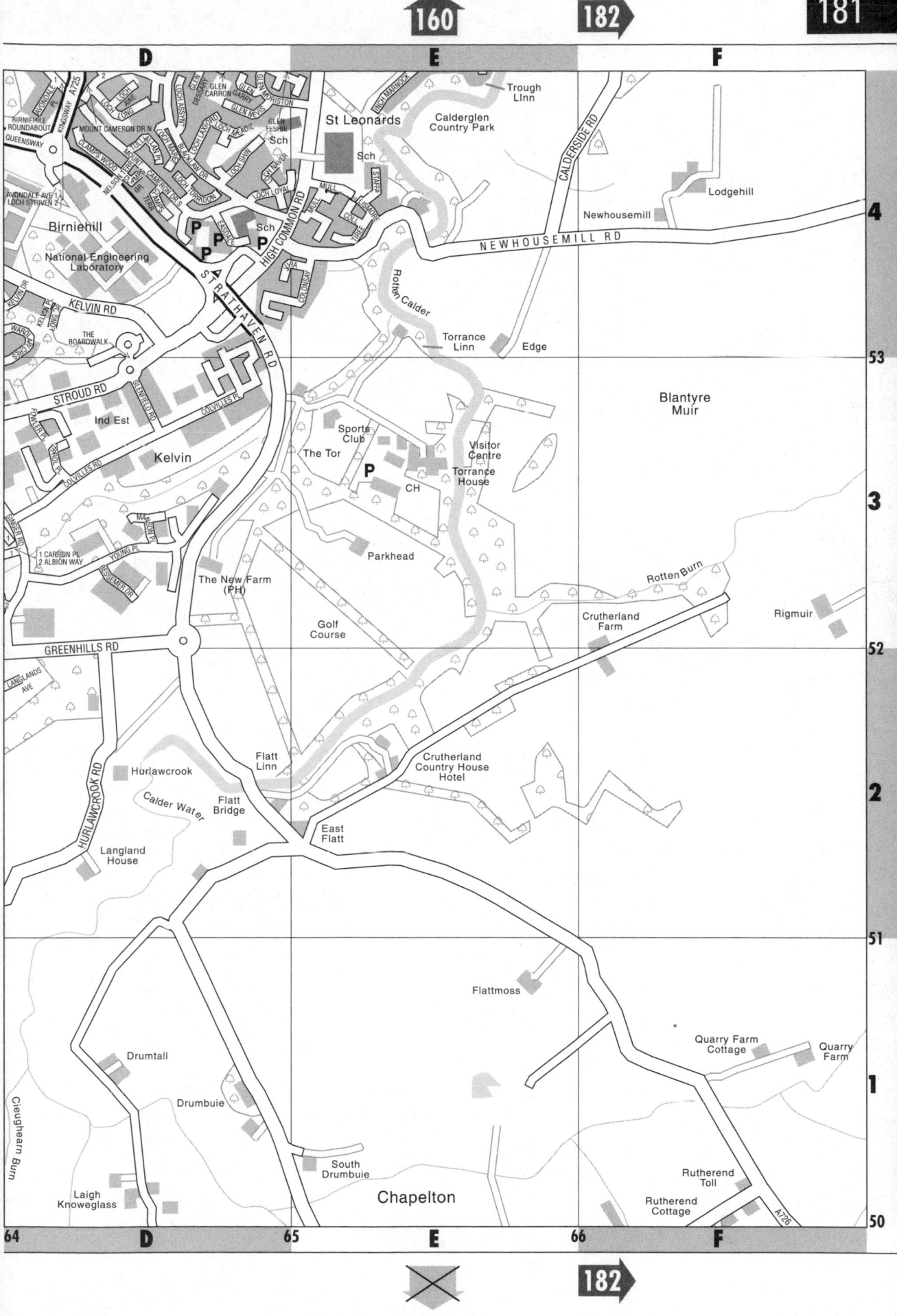

D
E
F

Trough Linn
St Leonards
Calderglen Country Park
CALDERSIDE RD
Lodgehill
Newhousemill
4
NEWHOUSEMILL RD

Birniehill
AVONDALE AVE 1
LOCH STRIVEN 2
National Engineering Laboratory
KELVIN RD
KELVIN DR
STRATHAVEN RD
HIGH COMMON RD

Rotten Calder
Torrance Linn
Edge
53

Blantyre Muir

THE BOARDWALK
STROUD RD
GLENFIELD RD
COLVILLES PL
Ind Est
Kelvin
COLVILLES RD
FOXLEA PL
Sports Club
The Tor
Visitor Centre
P
CH
Torrance House
3

1 CARRON PL
2 ALBION WAY
MANSON PL
YOUNG PL
BESSEMER DR
Parkhead
Rotten Burn
Rigmuir
Crutherland Farm

The New Farm (PH)
Golf Course
52

GREENHILLS RD
LANGLANDS AVE

HURLAWCROOK RD
Hurlawcrook
Flatt Linn
Crutherland Country House Hotel
2
Calder Water
Flatt Bridge
Langland House
East Flatt

51
Flattmoss

Cleughearn Burn
Drumtall
Quarry Farm Cottage
Quarry Farm
1
Drumbuie

South Drumbuie
Chapelton
Rutherend Toll
Laigh Knoweglass
Rutherend Cottage
A726
50

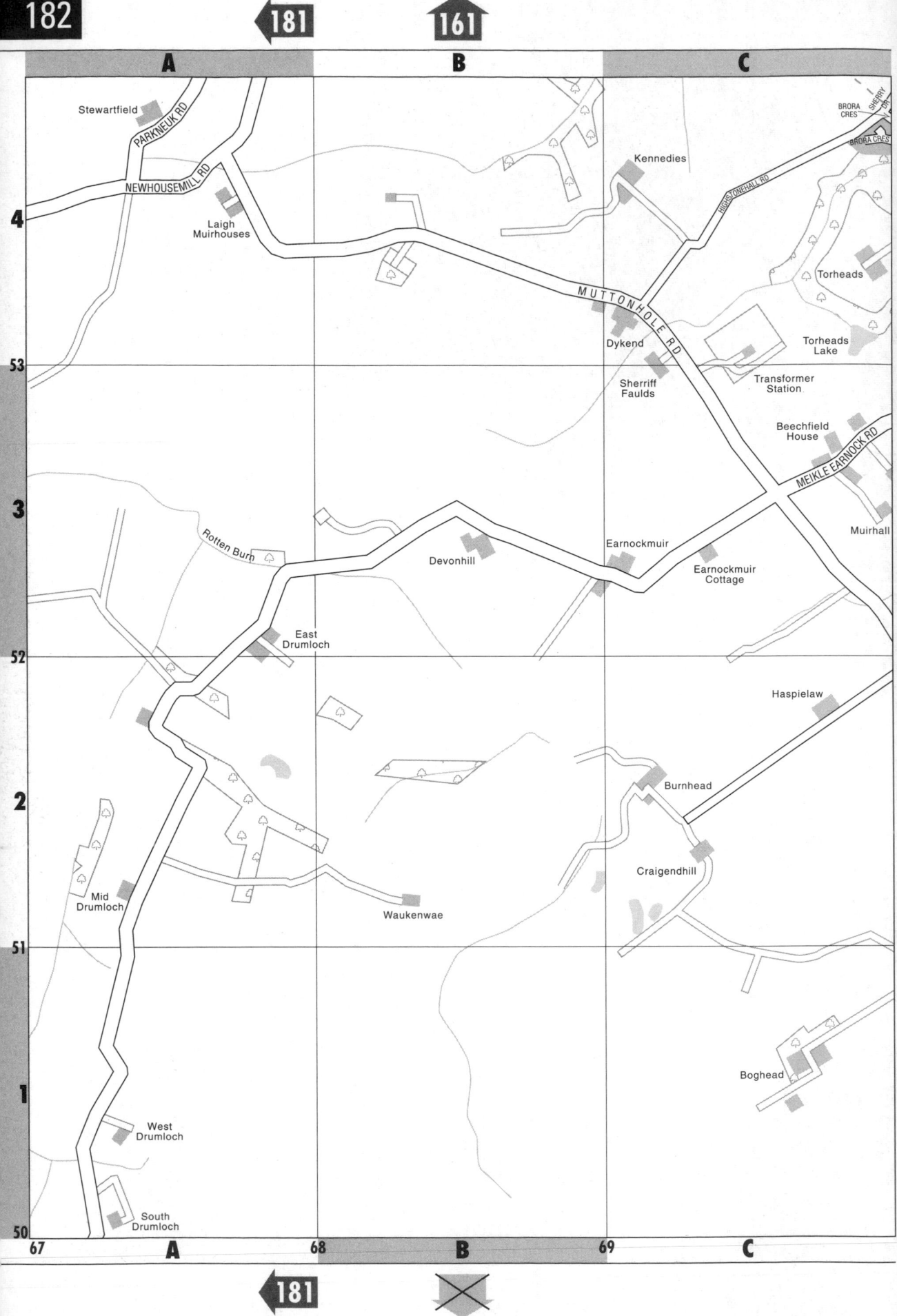

A B C

BRORA CRES
SHERRY DR
BRORA CRES

Stewartfield

PARKNEUK RD

NEWHOUSEMILL RD

Kennedies

HIGHSTONEHALL RD

Torheads

Laigh
Muirhouses

MUTTONHOLE RD

Dykend

Torheads
Lake

4

Sherriff
Faulds

Transformer
Station

53

Beechfield
House

MEIKLE EARNOCK RD

Rotten Burn

Devonhill

Earnockmuir

Muirhall

3

Earnockmuir
Cottage

East
Drumloch

52

Haspielaw

Burnhead

2

Craigendhill

Mid
Drumloch

Waukenwae

51

Boghead

1

West
Drumloch

South
Drumloch

50

67 A 68 B 69 C

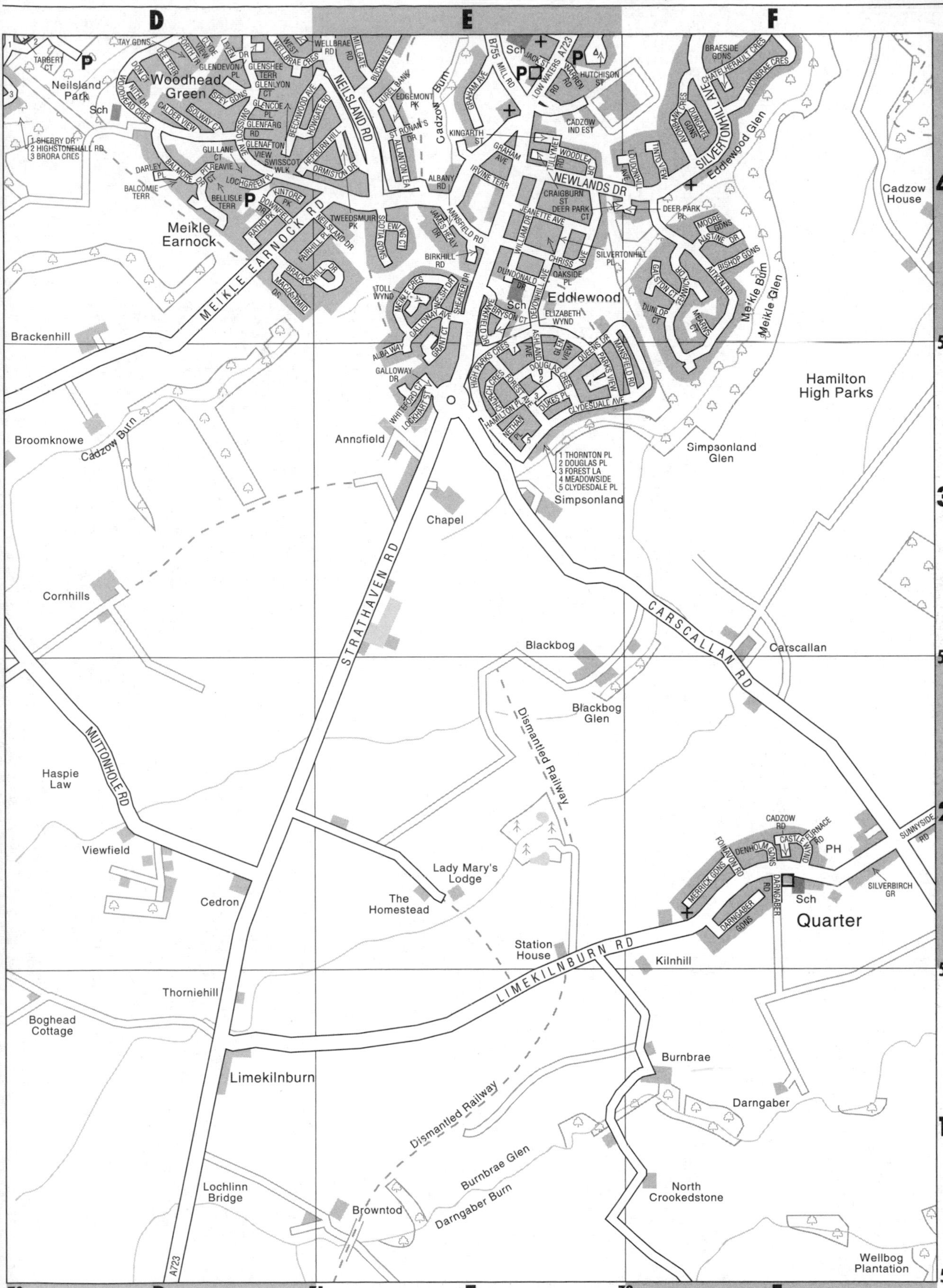

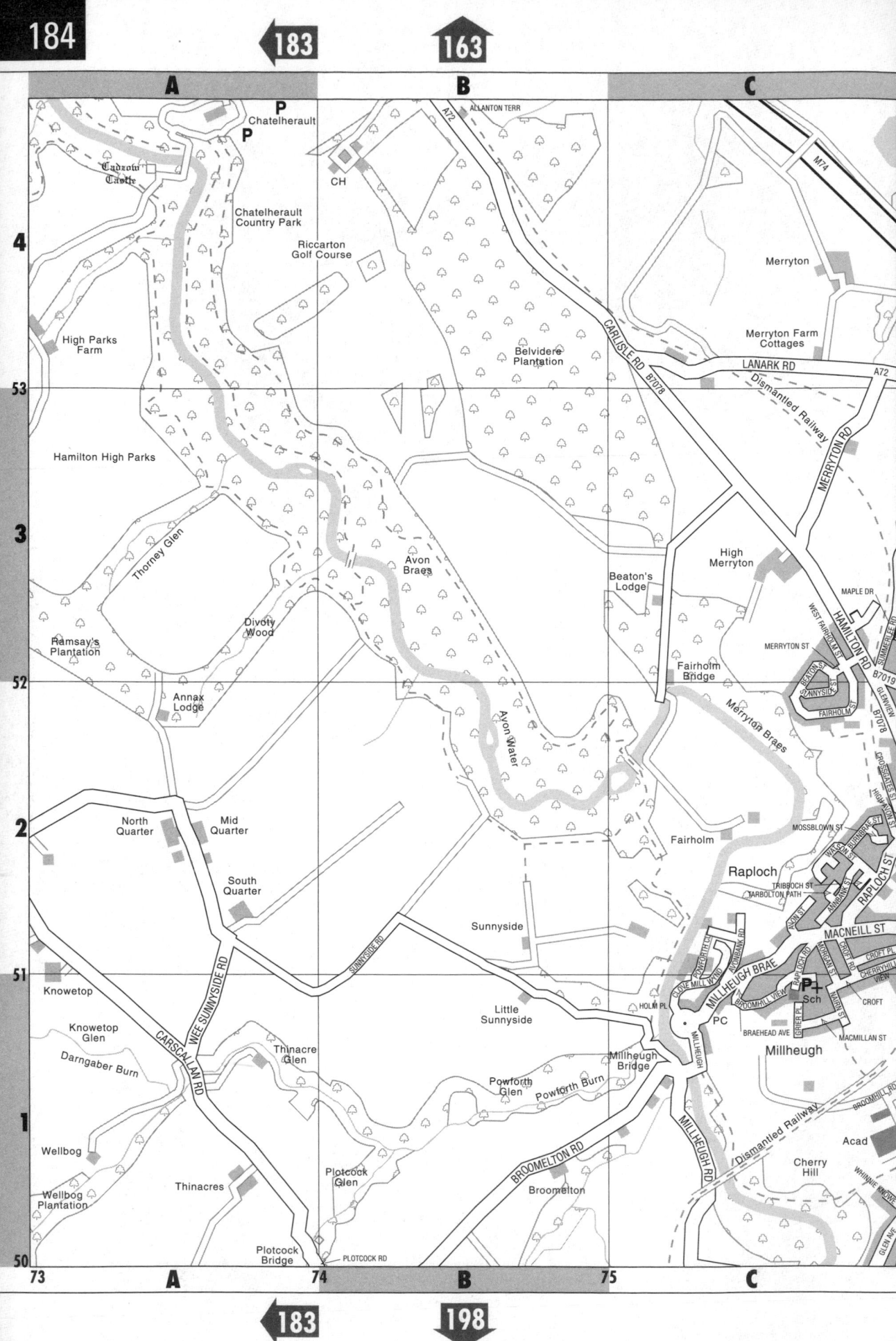

A · B · C

P
Chatelherault
P

Cadzow Castle
CH

Chatelherault Country Park

Riccarton Golf Course

Belvidere Plantation

ALLANTON TERR

A72

CARLISLE RD
B7078

LANARK RD
A72

Merryton

Merryton Farm Cottages

MERRYTON RD

Dismantled Railway

High Parks Farm

Hamilton High Parks

4

53

Thorney Glen

Avon Braes

Divoty Wood

High Merryton

MAPLE DR

WEST FAIRHOLM ST
HAMILTON RD
B7019

Beaton's Lodge

MERRYTON ST

Ramsay's Plantation

Annax Lodge

Fairholm Bridge

FAIRHOLMS

BEATON
SUNNYSIDE ST

GLENVIEW
B7078
CROSSGATES ST
HIGH PATRICK ST

3

52

Avon Water

Fairholm Braes

Fairholm

MOSSBLOWN ST
RANNOCH ST
MUIRBRAE ST

North Quarter

Mid Quarter

South Quarter

Raploch

TRIBBOCH ST
TARBOLTON PATH

AYRBANK ST
AYR ST

MACNEILL ST

RAPLOCH ST

CROFT PL
CHERRYHILL VIEW
CROFT

2

51

Knowetop

WEE SUNNYSIDE RD

SUNNYSIDE RD

Sunnyside

CLYDE MILL WYND
POWFORTH CL
NAISMITH RD

MILLHEUGH BRAE
BROOMHILL VIEW

P
Sch

BRAEHEAD AVE
MACMILLAN ST

Millheugh

Knowetop Glen

Darngaber Burn

CARSCALLAN RD

Thinacre Glen

Little Sunnyside

Powforth Glen

Powforth Burn

Millheugh Bridge

HOLM PL

PC

MILLHEUGH

1

Wellbog

Thinacres

Plotcock Glen

Broomelton

BROOMELTON RD

MILLHEUGH RD

Dismantled Railway

BROOMHILL RD

Acad

Cherry Hill

WHINNIE KNOWE
GLEN AVE

Wellbog Plantation

Plotcock Bridge

PLOTCOCK RD

50

73 · A · 74 · B · 75 · C

D   E   F

Sewage Works   Randalls Orchard   Carbarns Orchard
CALA SONA CT   OLD MARSE RD   GIGHA QUADRANT
ALLERSHAW TOWER 1   BIRKSHAW TOWER 2   CAPLAW TOWER 3
B754   ALLERSHAW RD
MONTGOMERY CRES   North Lodge   CASTLEHILL RD   B754
Carbarnswood   Lower Carbarns   Castlehill
CAP LAW PL   ALLERSHAW PL
4
LINGHOPE PL
Carbarns Wood
Hall Gill

Junction 7   Upper Carbarns   Cambusnethan House   Highmainshead Wood   **53**
Tammy's Burn
River Clyde

Prince's Lodge   LANARK RD
Highlees   Whittrick Burn   Nursery   **3**
SUMMERLEE RD   Skelly Gill

WILLOWBANK   Nursery   **52**
CHERRYTREE CRES   BROOM DR   BEECH DR   CHESTNUT GRV   MAPLE DR
Tilework Cottage   Sewage Works
Cemy   EAST STATION IND EST
LONDON ST   HAMILTON ST   DOUGLAS RD   CAZTONS   GLENVIEW NORTH   BRYCE GDNS   GLEN GLEBS   Skellyton Wood   Dismtd Rly   Skellyton   A72   **2**
GLENORAN LA   EASTWOOD WAY
P   WELLGATE ST   MONTGOMERY ST   PERCY ST   DRYGATE ST   Meadowhill   ANTRIM   RUSSELL   ASHBURTON   DUNCAN   CARRICK PL   1 GLENBURN WYND   2 PORTLAND WYND   3 SIGHTHILL LOAN   4 PARKNOOK WAY   5 LOMOND WLK   6 HOZIER LOAN   7 CRAIGIE LA   8 GEORGE WAY   9 ALBANY WYND   10 CRAIGMORE WYND   11 BURNS LOAN   12 ABBEY WLK   13 BANK WAY   14 BRAESIDE LA
PC   Off   GORBALS CROSS   Liby   Larkhall   Golf Course   Millburn Glen
Off   KING ST   UNION ST   MUIR ST   HIGH PLEASANCE   LOW PLEASANCE   Sch   BURNSIDE PL   Milburn Cottage   CORNSILLOCH BRAE   A71
RAPLOCH ST   CALEDONIAN ST   CHARING CROSS   Sch   Burnhead   1 LOANING   2 DOON ST   3 LOVAT PATH   4 ALLOWAY ST   5 BALMORAL PATH   6 MILLBURN LA   7 MOSSGIEL LA   8 WINDSOR PATH   9 CARRICK ST   10 GILLBANK LA   11 CATRINE ST   12 LOCHLEE LOAN   Cornsilloch
MACNEILL ST   BOWMANFLAT   MARGARET ST   BURNHEAD RD   Mill Burn
ST DAVID S PL   CHURCH ST   MARGARET AVE   SUMMERHILL AVE   HILL ST   Sch   MANDORA   CH   Millburn   AYR RD   A71
CHERRYHILL VIEW   BROOMHILL CT   JOHN ST   MACHANHILL   LINKS VIEW   GOLF GDNS
Leisure Centre   CHARLOTTE PATH   HARELEESHILL RD   COVENANT   O'CORRIE WAY   WILKIE CRES   Shawsburn   B7019
Machan   JANE CT   ORCHARD GATE   Off   CLYDE ST   SCOTT ST   NEVISON ST   13 MAXWELL PATH   14 BRUCE'S LOAN   15 FLEMING WAY   16 ALOA WAY   17 ARRAN PATH   18 DALSERF PATH   19 LOCHNAGAR WAY   20 BLAIR ATHOLL DR   21 TRINITY WAY   22 GLEN FRUIN DR   23 ST ANDREWS PATH   24 LAWRIE WAY   25 KATRIONA PATH   26 CAMERON PATH   27 HAZELDENE LA   28 ROSEMOUNT LA   29 LAUREL LA   30 BRACKEN WAY   31 CAMERONIAN WAY   32 LAMMER WYND   **1**
HAWICK CRES   MACHAN RD   QUARRY ST   EAST MACHAN   WOODBURN TERR   Sch   ASHGILLHEAD RD   Nurseries   GARRION PL   Stewart Gill
MELROSE PL   GLEN AVE   Sch   LOCHPARK PL   BEECH TERR   Works
WHINNIE KNOWE   ROBERT SMILLIE CRES   WESTERTON AVE   KEIR HARDIE RD   Ind Est   GREENLOAN VIEW   REDHOLME   BERTRAM ST   Ashgillhead   MILLBURN RD   **50**
SHEARFORD LA   FERNDALE   ROBERT SMILLIE   DUNEATON WYND   **Hareleeshill**   Shawsrigg   M74   Shawsrigg   A71

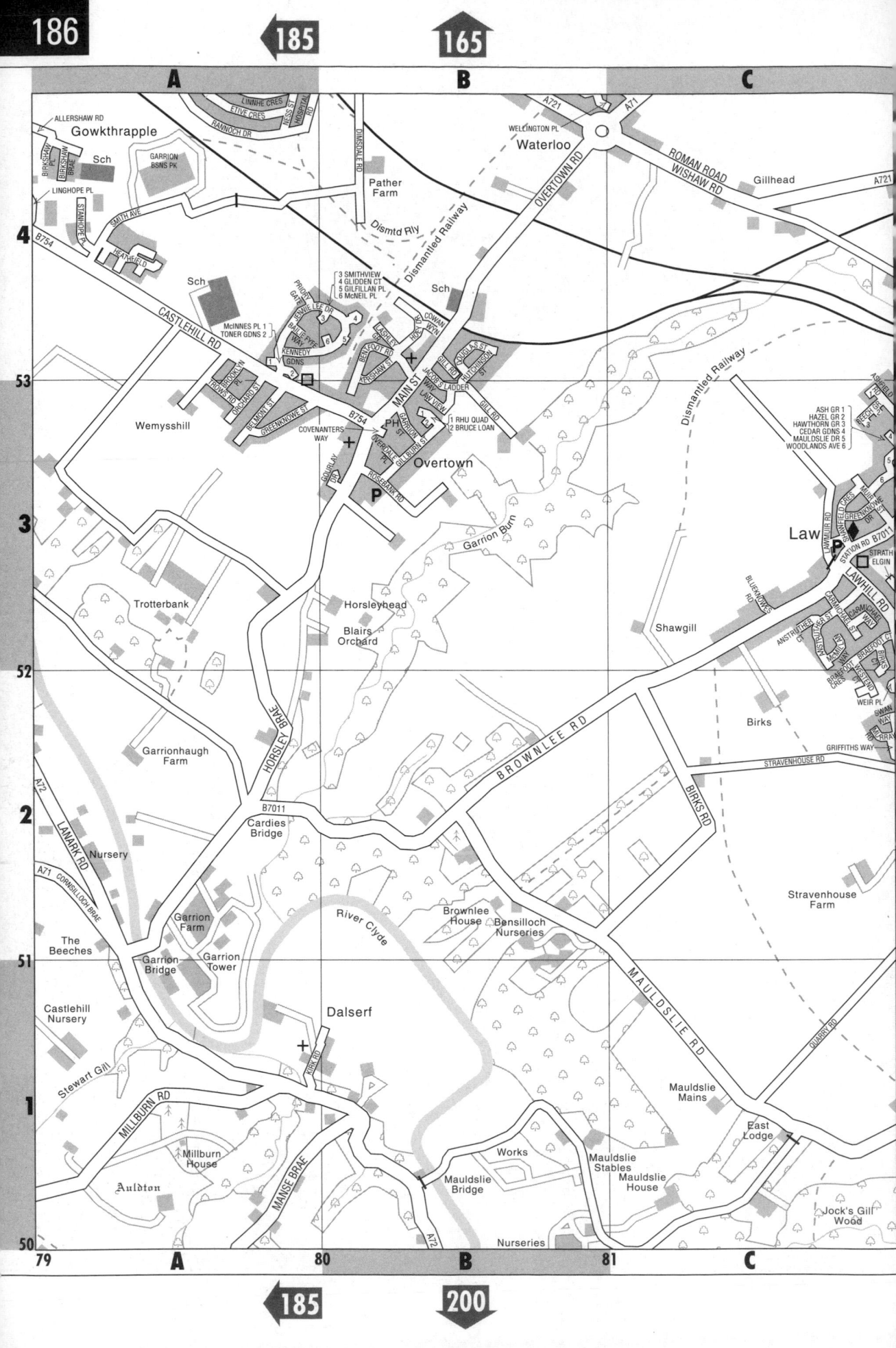

A   B   C

Gowkthrapple
ALLERSHAW RD
BIRKSHAW PL
LINNHE CRES
ETIVE CRES
RANNOCH DR
DIMSDALE RD
A721
A71
WELLINGTON PL
Waterloo
OVERTOWN RD
ROMAN ROAD
WISHAW RD
Gillhead
A721
Sch
GARRION BSNS PK
LINGHOPE PL
STANHOPE PL
SMITH AVE
HEATHFIELD
B754
Pather Farm
Dismtd Rly
Dismantled Railway
4
CASTLEHILL RD
Sch
Sch
3 SMITHVIEW
4 GLIDDEN CT
5 GILFILLAN PL
6 McNEIL PL
JENNIE LEE DR
PRIORY GATE
BAILLIE PYLE
McINNES PL 1
TONER GDNS 2
KENNEDY GDNS
LASHLEY
BENTFOOT RD
KERSHAW ST
COWAN
DOUGLAS ST
HUTCHINSON ST
GILL RD
Dismantled Railway
ASH GR 1
HAZEL GR 2
HAWTHORN GR 3
CEDAR GDNS 4
MAULDSLIE DR 5
WOODLANDS AVE 6
ASHFIELD
53
Wemysshill
TRIMS RD
BROOKLYN
BELMONT ST
ORCHARD ST
GREENKNOWE ST
B754
COVENANTERS WAY
PH
MAIN ST
GARRION ST
JACOB'S LADDER
LAW VIEW
GILL RD
1 RHU QUAD
2 BRUCE LOAN
GREENKNOWE DR
STATION RD
B7011
STRATH ELGIN
AVERCAL
GILLBURN PL
GOURLAY
ROSEBANK RD
Overtown
P
BLUEKNOWES RD
Law
P
LAWHILL RD
3
Trotterbank
Horsleyhead
Blairs Orchard
Garrion Burn
Shawgill
ANSTRUTHER ST
CARMICHAEL WAY
BRAEFOOT
BRAEFOOT CRES
WESTEND
WEIR PL
SWAN WAY
52
Garrionhaugh Farm
A72
LANARK RD
A71
CORNSILLOCH BRAE
HORSLEY BRAE
BROWNLEE RD
BIRKS RD
Birks
STRAVENHOUSE RD
GRIFFITHS WAY
2
Nursery
B7011
Cardies Bridge
Stravenhouse Farm
The Beeches
Garrion Farm
River Clyde
Brownlee House
Bensilloch Nurseries
MAULDSLIE RD
QUARRY RD
51
Garrion Bridge
Garrion Tower
Castlehill Nursery
Dalserf
KIRK RD
Mauldslie Mains
East Lodge
Stewart Gill
MILLBURN RD
MANSE BRAE
Works
Mauldslie Stables
Mauldslie House
1
Millburn House
Auldton
A72
Mauldslie Bridge
Nurseries
Jock's Gill Wood
50

79   80   81

D E F

Bogside

WISHAW RD
A721
A73

Lanniemuirs

Twelve Acre
Plantation

Mid
Hyndshaw

Hyndshaw

4

Wildmanbridge

Works
PH
Gillhead

B7011
WILDMAN RD

Wildman
Bridge

Hospl

Dismantled Railway

Bowridge
Bridge

53

STATION PL
Nursery
CEDAR GDNS
Nursery

Bowridge Burn

STATION RD

Waterlands

OLD WISHAW RD

Garrion Burn

Castlehill
Bridge

Castlehill

Castlehill
Farm

CASTLEHILL RD

Belstane
Place

3

Brackenhill

Works

Castlehill
Works

52

Sch

1 WATERLANDS PL
2 SWAN WAY
3 MURRAY RD
4 GRIFFITHS WAY
5 KINGSHILL VIEW

AIRDRIE RD

HEATHER ROW

KINTYRE WYND 1
KILMARTIN LA 2
DUNARD CT 3
PEACOCK LOAN 4
CAIRNBAIRN CT 5
KENMORE WAY 6
BARRS LA 7
KILMORY GDNS 8
BELSTANE PK 9
SHAND LA 10
STONEFIELD GDNS 11
REDHOUSE LA 12

HONEYBANK
CRES

2

Law Hill
Park
Regis

East Law

Law of
Mauldslie

LAWHILL RD

STRAVENHOUSE RD

QUARRY RD

WHITESHAW RD

Dismantled Railway

Works

Castlehill
Ind Est

Dismantled Railway

Hyndshaw RD

PARK DR

NEWBARNS ST

1

MAULDSLIE RD

CH

Hallcraig

GASWORKS RD

WESTERHOUSE
CT

LUGGIE RD

KIRK RD

STEWART ST

SANDY RD

51

Sch

Sta
P PC
P

A721

1 MOORSIDE ST
2 CAIRNHILL CT
3 CAIRNEYMOUNT RD

GREENBANK
TERR
MILLER ST
CARNWATH RD

P
P

KIRKTON ST

Liby

Sch

1

Mauldslie
Cottage

Golf Course

STATION RD

KENILWORTH
CT

ORCHARD ST

1 LAGAN RD
2 BENTY'S LA

A721
GLENEOCH

Sch

Jock's Gill

Jock's Burn

Jock's Gill

Carluke
Station

UNITAS CRES

A73

50

82 D 83 E 84 F

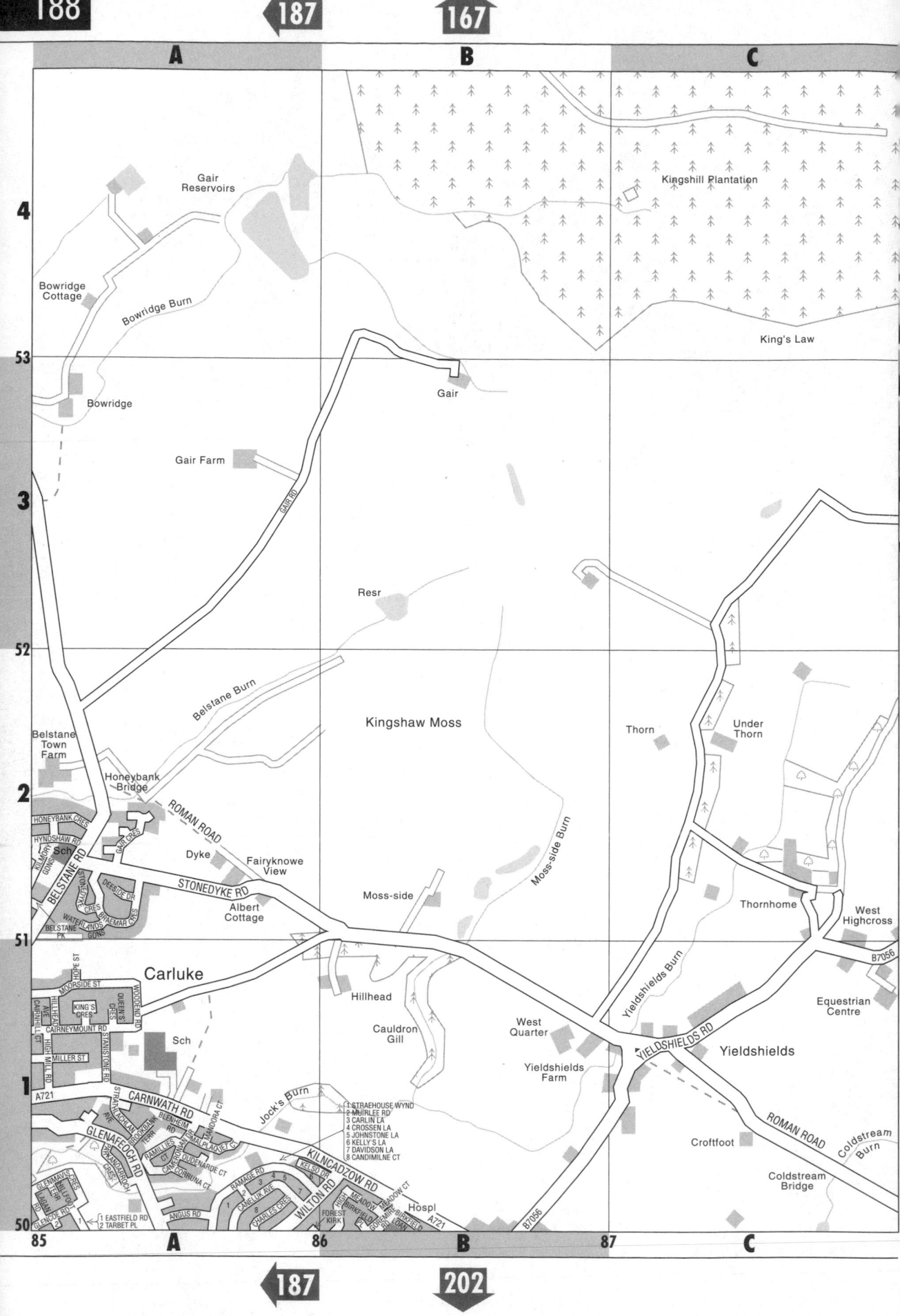

A   B   C

4

Gair
Reservoirs

Kingshill Plantation

Bowridge
Cottage

Bowridge Burn

King's Law

53

Bowridge

Gair

Gair Farm

GAIR RD

3

Resr

52

Belstane Burn

Kingshaw Moss

Thorn

Under
Thorn

Belstane
Town
Farm

Honeybank
Bridge

ROMAN ROAD

Moss-side Burn

HONEYBANK CRES

HYNDSHAW
GDNS

Dyke

Fairyknowe
View

GAIR CRES

2

KILMORY
GDNS

Sch

BELSTANE RD

DEESIDE DR

STONEDYKE RD

Moss-side

Thornhome

West
Highcross

YLOCHKORMOCH
CRES

BRAEMAR CRES

Albert
Cottage

Yieldshields Burn

WATERLANDS
GDNS

B7056

BELSTANE
PK

51

YIELDSHIELDS RD

Equestrian
Centre

Carluke

Hillhead

MOORSIDE ST

KING'S
CRES

Cauldron
Gill

West
Quarter

YIELDSHIELDS RD

Yieldshields

HOPE ST

QUEEN'S
CRES

WOODEND RD

Yieldshields
Farm

TILL HEAD

CARPHILL CT

CAIRNEYMOUNT RD

STANISTONE RD

Sch

HIGH MILL RD

MILLER ST

1 STRAHOUSE WYND
2 MUIRLEE RD
3 CARLIN LA
4 CROSSEN LA
5 JOHNSTONE LA
6 KELLY'S LA
7 DAVIDSON LA
8 CANDIMILNE CT

1

A721

CARNWATH RD

Jock's Burn

ROMAN ROAD

Coldstream
Burn

STRAHACHLAN
AVE

BLENHEIM
RD

CANDIMOORA CT

KELSO DR

Croftfoot

GLENAFEOCH RD

RAMILLIES
TERR

OUDENARDE CT

RAMSAE RD

KILNCADZOW RD

Coldstream
Bridge

GLENMAVIS
CRES

MILL
RD

CORUNNA CT

CANELUK AVE

CHARLES CRES

WILTON RD

MEADOW CT

Hospl

GLENCOE RD

ANGUS RD

FOREST
KIRK

A721

B7056

1 EASTFIELD RD
2 TARBET PL

50

85   A   86   B   87   C

168

D
E
F

Black Law

Birniehall

Forth

4

53

Netherton Burn

3

Thornmuir

Springfield
Reservoir

52

Hill of
Westerhouse

Middlehope
Farm

Easterseat

2

Springfield

B7056

Knowehead

Middlehouse

YIELDSHIELDS RD

Netherton Burn

Westerhouse

Damhead

East
Highcross

51

Coldstream Burn

Candymill Burn

1

ROMAN
ROAD

Mid
Coldstream

Craigend

50

38

D

89

E

90

F

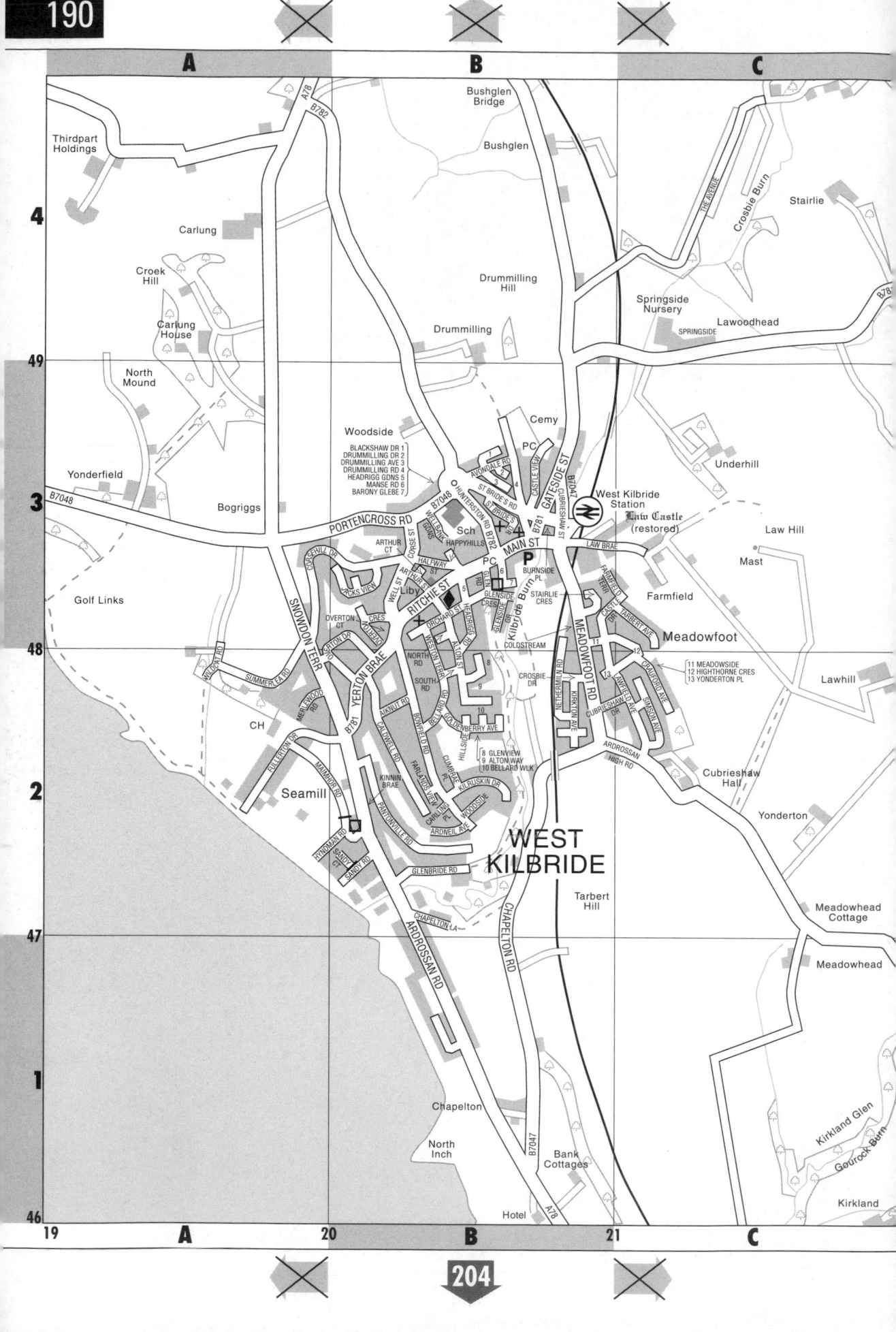

A B C

Thirdpart
Holdings

Bushglen
Bridge

Bushglen

Crosbie Burn

Stairlie

Carlung

Drummilling
Hill

The Avenue

Croek
Hill

Drummilling

Springside
Nursery

Lawoodhead

Carlung
House

SPRINGSIDE

North
Mound

Underhill

Yonderfield

Woodside

Cemy

PC

BLACKSHAW DR 1
DRUMMILLING DR 2
DRUMMILLING AVE 3
DRUMMILLING RD 4
HEADRIGG GDNS 5
MANSE RD 6
BARONY GLEBE 7

AVONDALE RD

CASTLE VIEW

GATESIDE ST

West Kilbride
Station

B7048

B7048

Bogriggs

PORTENCROSS RD

ST BRIDE'S RD

ST BRIDE ST

HUNTERSTON RD B782

WELLPARK
GDNS

B781

CUMSHINAN ST

Law Castle
(restored)

Law Hill

Sch

HAPPYHILLS

MAIN ST

LAW BRAE

Mast

Golf Links

ARTHUR
CT

CORSE ST

HALFWAY
ST

ARTHUR ST

WELL ST

Liby

RITCHIE ST

ORCHARD ST

GLENSIDE

PC

P

BURNSIDE
PL

Kilbride Burn

STAIRLIE
CRES

FAIRHAVEN
TERR

CASTLE TERR

Farmfield

CORSEHILL DR

BRACKS VIEW

CRES

Overton
CT

GLENSIDE
CRES

TARBERT AVE

Meadowfoot

SNOWDON TERR

YERTON BRAE

WESTON TERR

HEADRIGG RD

HALTON ST

North
RD

COLDSTREAM

CROSBIE
DR

NETHERMILL RD

MEADOWFOOT RD

CRAWFORD AVE

SINCLAIR AVE

11 MEADOWSIDE
12 HIGHTHORNE CRES
13 YONDERTON PL

Lawhill

WILDCAT RD

SUMMERLEA RD

MERLEWOOD
RD

SOUTH
RD

AKINUT RD

CALDWELL RD

BELL RD

GOLDENBERRY AVE

HILLSIDE

KIRKTON AVE

CUBRIESHAW
DR

CUBRIESHAW
RD

ARDROSSAN
HIGH RD

Cubrieshaw
Hall

CH

FULLERTON DR

MAMMOD RD

KINNIN
BRAE

FARLANDS VIEW

CUMBRAE
PL

KILRUSKIN DR

WOODSIDE

8 GLENVIEW
9 ALTON WAY
10 BELLARD WLK

Yonderton

Seamill

PLANTONVILLE RD

CAROLINE

ARDNEIL AVE

WEST
KILBRIDE

HYNDMAN RD

SANDY CT

SANDY RD

GLENBRIDE RD

CHAPELTON LA

ARDROSSAN RD

CHAPELTON RD

Tarbert
Hill

Meadowhead
Cottage

Meadowhead

Chapelton

North
Inch

B7047

Bank
Cottages

Kirkland Glen

Gourock Burn

Kirkland

Hotel

A78

D E F

Little Broadlie
Coalheughglen
Putyan
Burn
Cemy
Dalry
Stock Bridge
Carsehead Bridge
BEITH RD
B707
A737
1 NETHERLEE CRES
2 BRAEHEAD PL
Off
Rye Water
St PALLADIUS TERR
WINGFAULDS AVE
JAMES ST
3 REGAL CT
4 WATT CT
5 THE CROSS
JAMES ST
SHARON ST
WEST KILBRIDE RD
PC
Liby
PC
NEW ST
6 TOWNEND LA
7 AITKEN ST
Manse
East Kirkland
F Sta
Dalry Station
BLAIR RD
BRIDGEND
TOFTS
TOFTS CRES
STOOPHILL CRES
BLAIRLANDS DR
Peesweep Mount

4

Hindog Pl
Sch
Merksworth Ave
Lynn Ave
Kilwinning Rd
B780
Carswell Ct 1
Archibald Dr 2
Kittyshaw
High Lynn
Caaf Water
Lynn Glen
P
Lynn Bridge
Craigmill
Craighead
Pinnoch Point

Lynn Holms
River Garnock
Blairland
Stoopshill
Blair Bridge
Bombo Burn
Crow Grove
Blair
Dismantled Railway
Hillside Cotts

49

Caaf Bridge
Hillend

3

48

High Monkcastle
Monk Castle
Laigh Monkcastle
Monkcastle Bridge
Blair Park
Park Cottage
Blair Smithy
South Lodge

2

Monkcastle
Newhouse
Dusk Water
Dismantled Railway
Dusk Bridge

47

Broomhill
Lodge
Laigh Smithstone
Craighead
High Smithstown
Townhead of Dalgarven
Cockenzie
A737

1

46

28 D 29 E 30 F

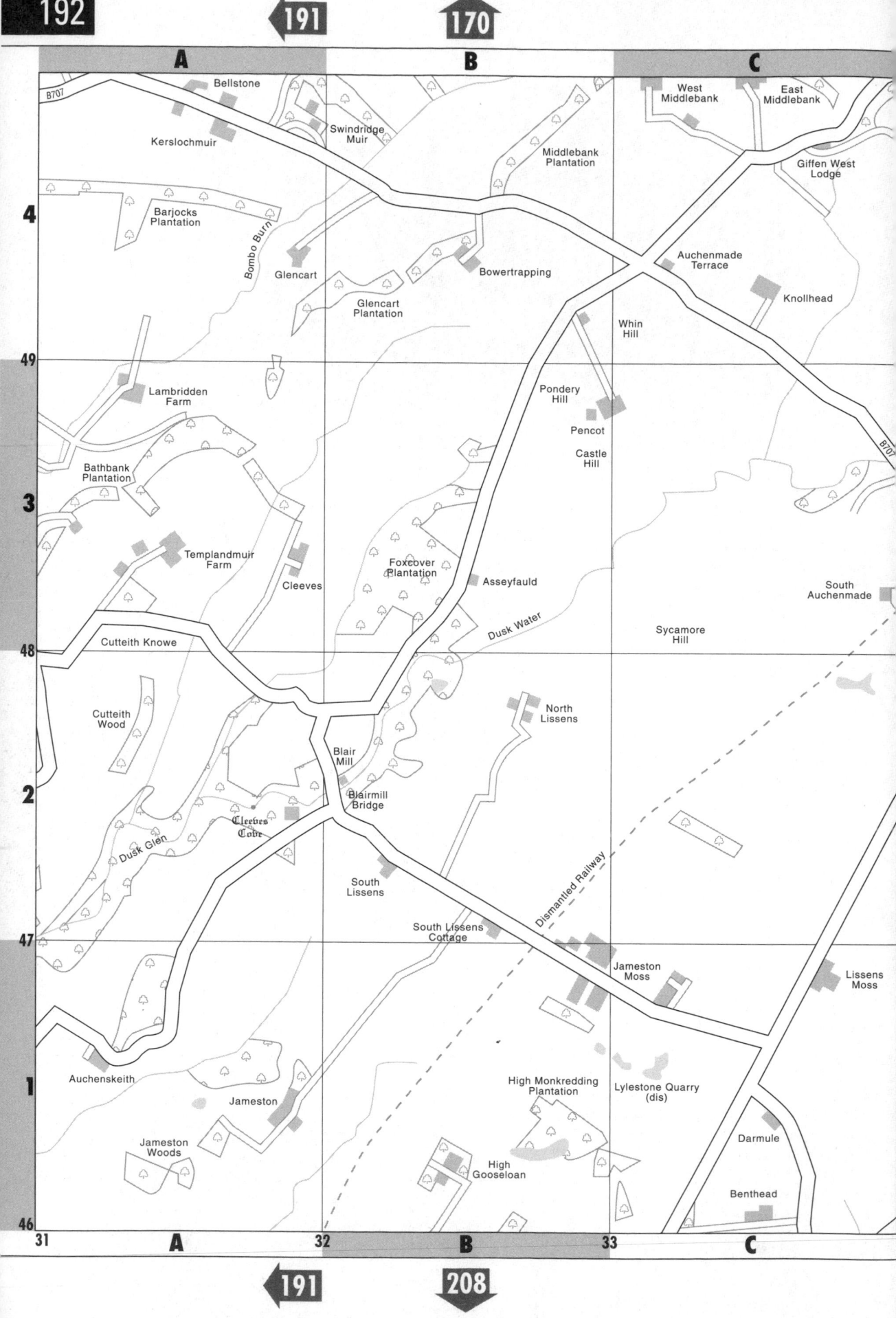

B707

A

Bellstone

Kerslochmuir

Swindridge
Muir

Middlebank
Plantation

West
Middlebank

East
Middlebank

Giffen West
Lodge

4

Barjocks
Plantation

Glencart

Bowertrapping

Auchenmade
Terrace

Knollhead

Glencart
Plantation

Whin
Hill

49

Lambridden
Farm

Pondery
Hill

Pencot

B707

Bathbank
Plantation

Castle
Hill

3

Templandmuir
Farm

Cleeves

Foxcover
Plantation

Asseyfauld

South
Auchenmade

Cutteith Knowe

Dusk Water

Sycamore
Hill

48

Cutteith
Wood

North
Lissens

Blair
Mill

2

Blairmill
Bridge

Cleeves
Cove

Dusk Glen

Dismantled Railway

South
Lissens

South Lissens
Cottage

47

Jameston
Moss

Lissens
Moss

1

Auchenskeith

Jameston

High Monkredding
Plantation

Lylestone Quarry
(dis)

Darmule

Jameston
Woods

High
Gooseloan

Benthead

46

31   A   32   B   33   C

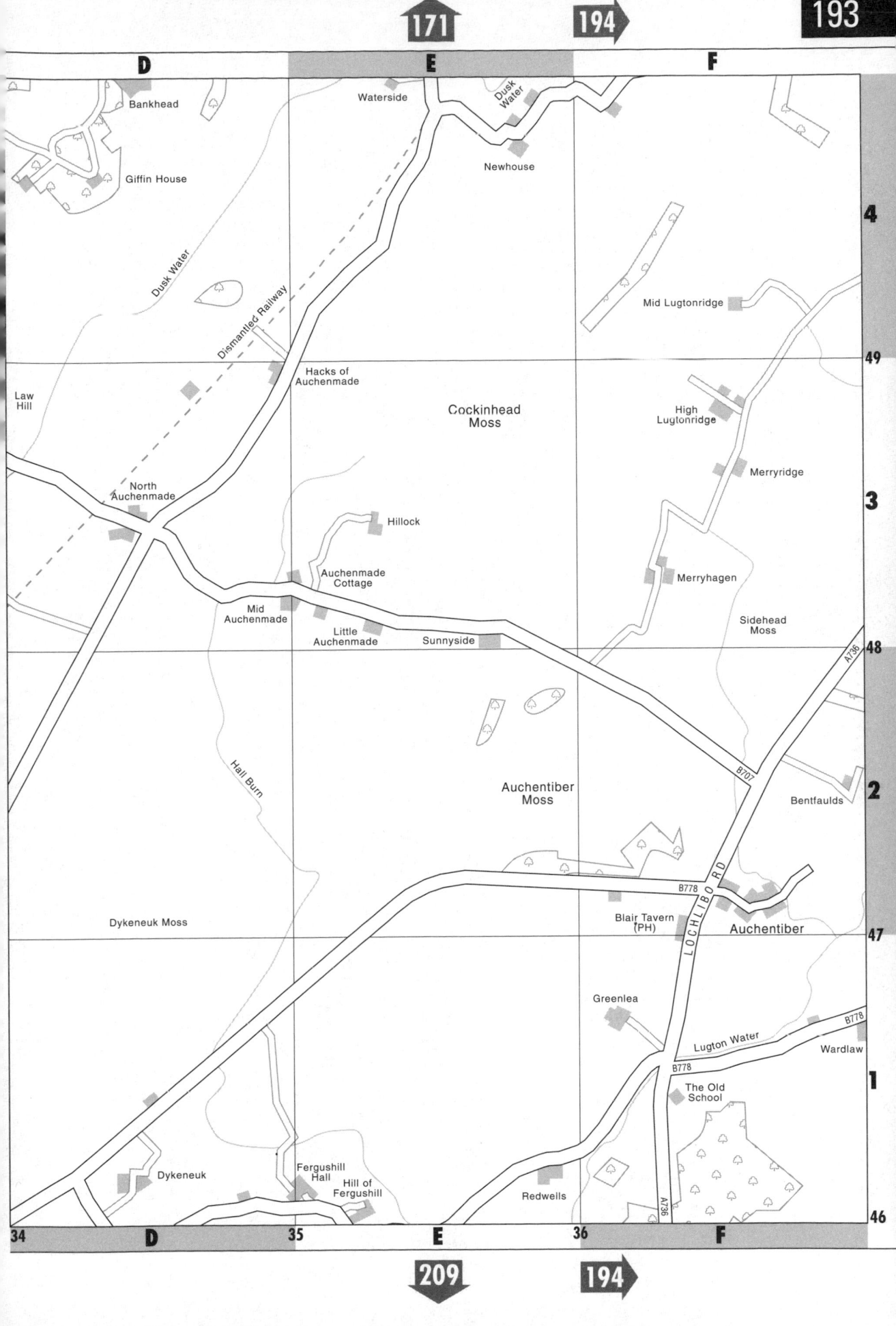

A **B** **C**

South Nettlehurst

Nettlehurst

4

Lugtonridge

Lugtonridge

East Lugtonridge

A736

LOCHLIBO RD

B706

Nether Oldhall

Oldhall
Murry Farm

Silverhill

North Borland

Newhall

Craigbank

Fox Covert

Overl Borland

49

Loanhead

Braehead

Aiket Castle

Borlandhills

Deepstone

Lugton Water

Low Borland

3

Sidehead

Leahead

Glazert Burn

Barr Hill

A736

Sydehead

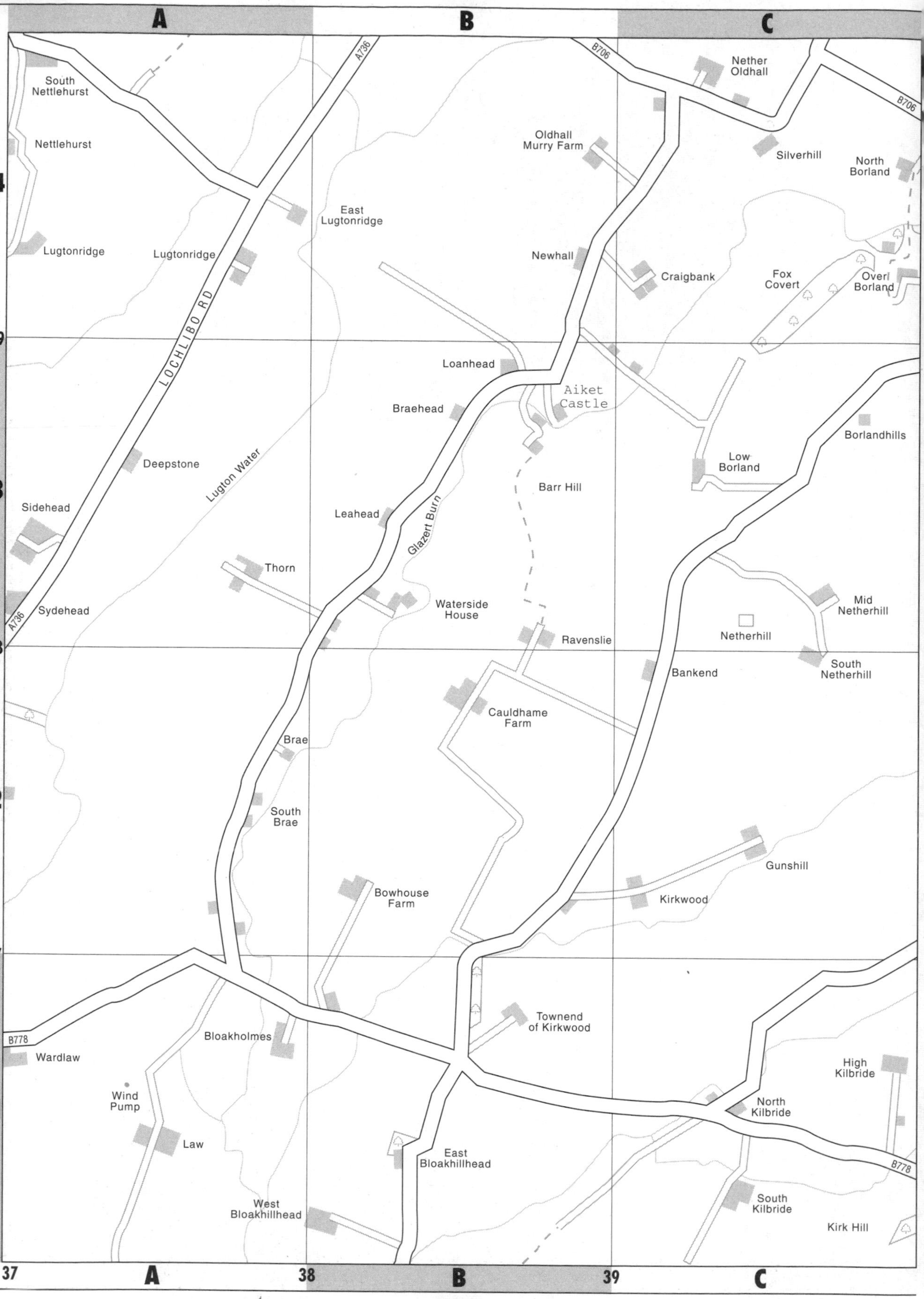

Thorn

Waterside House

Ravenslie

Netherhill

Mid Netherhill

48

Bankend

South Netherhill

Brae

South Brae

Cauldhame Farm

2

Gunshill

Bowhouse Farm

Kirkwood

47

B778

Wardlaw

Bloakholmes

Townend of Kirkwood

High Kilbride

1

Wind Pump

Law

North Kilbride

East Bloakhillhead

B778

West Bloakhillhead

South Kilbride

Kirk Hill

46

37 **A** 38 **B** 39 **C**

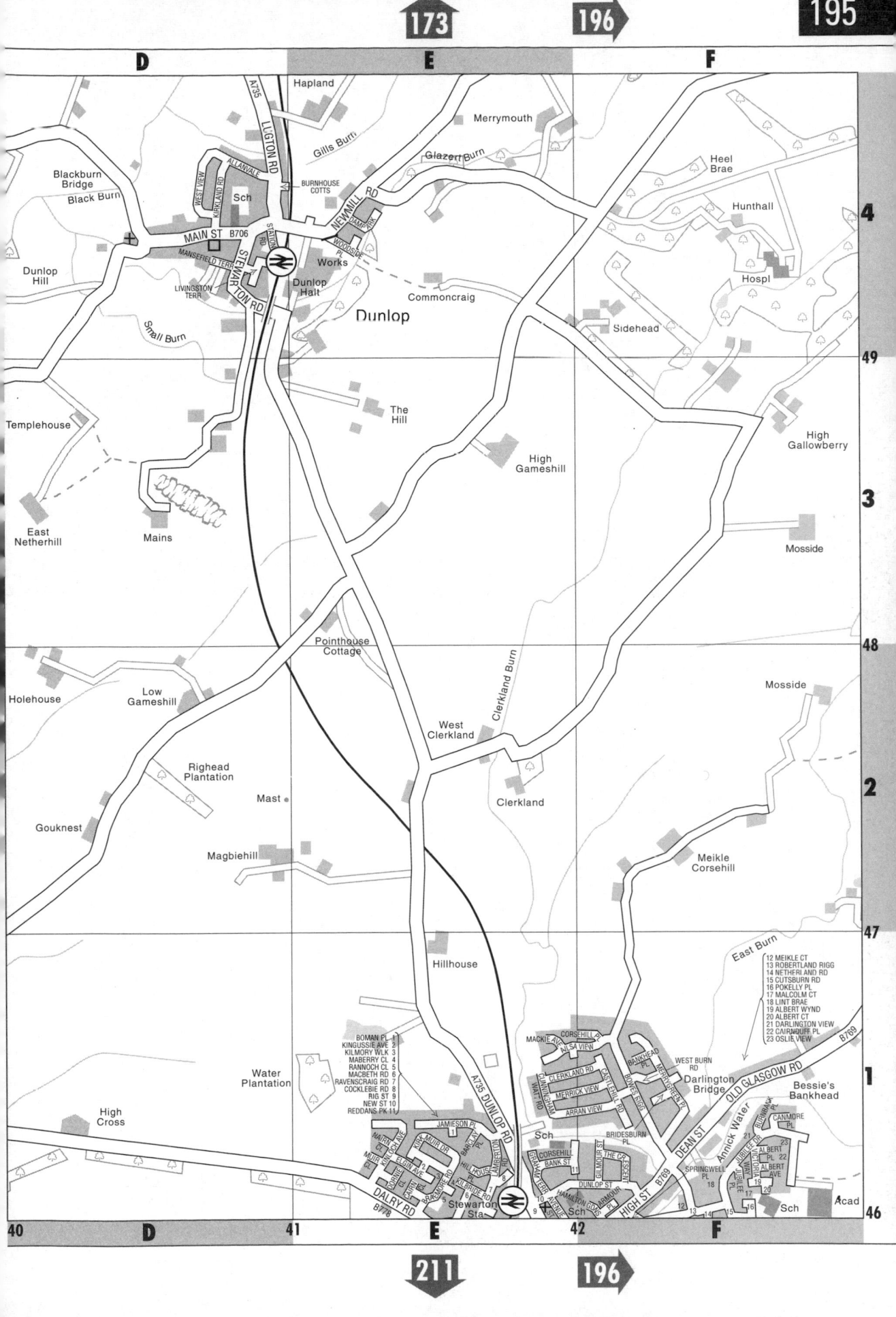

D E F

Hapland
Merrymouth
Blackburn Bridge
Black Burn
Gills Burn
Glazert Burn
Heel Brae
Hunthall
WEST VIEW
KIRKLAND RD
ALLANVALE
Sch
BURNHOUSE COTTS
NEWMILL RD
LIGTON RD
A735
MAIN ST B706
Dunlop Hill
MANSFIELD TERRACE
STATION RD
STEWARTON RD
LIVINGSTON TERR
Works
Dunlop Halt
Woodside
JAMPL
Hospl
4

Small Burn
Dunlop
Commoncraig
Sidehead
49

Templehouse
The Hill
High Gameshill
High Gallowberry
3

East Netherhill
Mains
Mosside

Pointhouse Cottage
48

Holehouse
Low Gameshill
West Clerkland
Clerkland Burn
Mosside

Righead Plantation
Mast
Clerkland
Meikle Corsehill
2

Gouknest
Magbiehill
47

East Burn
Hillhouse
12 MEIKLE CT
13 ROBERTLAND RIGG
14 NETHERLAND RD
15 CUTSBURN RD
16 POKELLY PL
17 MALCOLM CT
18 LINT BRAE
19 ALBERT WYND
20 ALBERT CT
21 DARLINGTON VIEW
22 CAIRNDUFF PL
23 OSLIE VIEW

BOMAN PL 1
KINGUSSIE AVE 2
KILMORY WLK 3
MABERRY CL 4
RANNOCH CL 5
MACBETH RD 6
RAVENSCRAIG RD 7
COCKLEBIE RD 8
RIG ST 9
NEW ST 10
REDDANS PK 11

Water Plantation
MACKIE AVE
CORSEHILL PL
AILSA VIEW
BANKHEAD PL
WEST BURN RD
Darlington Bridge
OLD GLASGOW RD
B769
Bessie's Bankhead
CANMORE PL

High Cross
JAMIESON PL
CHINNINGHAM
WATT RD
CLERKLAND RD
MERRICK VIEW
ARRAN VIEW
CASTLEHILL RD
BOWES RIGG
NEWGREEN PL
BRIDESBURN PL
DEAN ST
Sch
Annick Water
SPRINGWELL PL
ALBERT PL 22
JUBILEE PL
ALBERT WAY
VICTORIA WAY
ALBERT AVE
23
20

NAIRN AVE
MOIR CT
ELGIN AVE
DUBRIE AVE
MOIR AVE
CANT RD
BARSCUBE RD
HILLHOUSE
NUTBERRY AVE
KILBRIDE RD
BIRKMUIR
CORSEHILL BANK ST
BANK ST 11
THE CRESCENT
DUNLOP ST
GIL MOUR ST
HIGH ST B769
Sch
Acad
A735 DUNLOP RD
DALRY RD B778
Stewarton Sta
HAMILTON GDNS
BRIDGEND
9
10
12 13 14
16 17

40 D 41 E 42 F

195
174

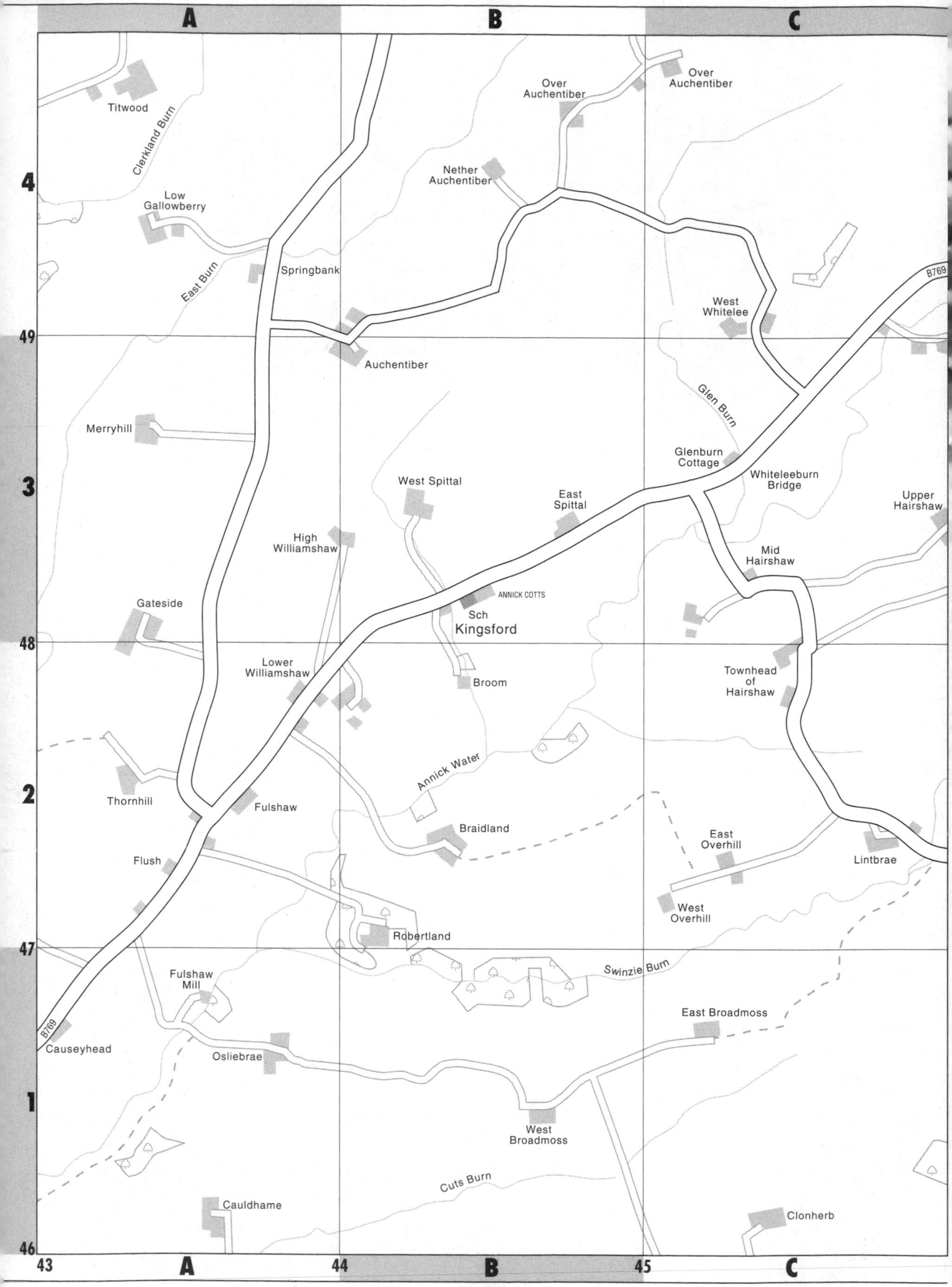

A

B

C

Titwood

Clerkland Burn

4

Over Auchentiber

Over Auchentiber

Low Gallowberry

Nether Auchentiber

East Burn

Springbank

B769

49

Auchentiber

West Whitelee

Glen Burn

Merryhill

Glenburn Cottage

Whiteleeburn Bridge

Upper Hairshaw

3

West Spittal

East Spittal

High Williamshaw

Mid Hairshaw

ANNICK COTTS

Gateside

Sch

Kingsford

48

Lower Williamshaw

Broom

Townhead of Hairshaw

Annick Water

2

East Overhill

Thornhill

Fulshaw

Braidland

Lintbrae

Flush

West Overhill

Robertland

47

Swinzie Burn

B769

Fulshaw Mill

East Broadmoss

Causeyhead

Osliebrae

1

West Broadmoss

Cuts Burn

Cauldhame

Clonherb

46

43

A

44

B

45

C

175

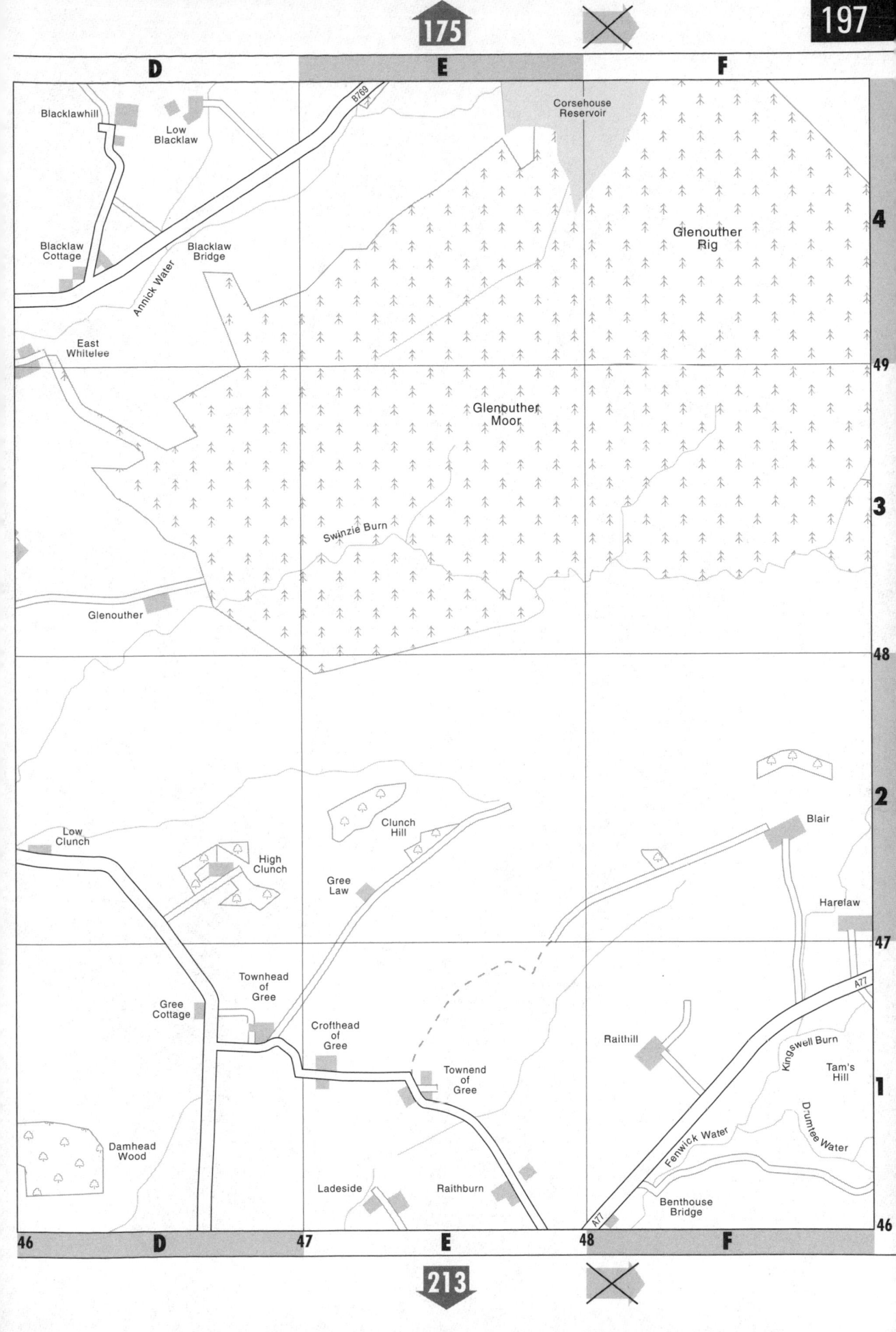

Blacklawhill

Low
Blacklaw

Corsehouse
Reservoir

Glenouther
Rig

Blacklaw
Cottage

Blacklaw
Bridge

Annick Water

East
Whitelee

Glenouther
Moor

Swinzie Burn

Glenouther

Low
Clunch

Clunch
Hill

Blair

High
Clunch

Gree
Law

Harelaw

Townhead
of
Gree

Gree
Cottage

Crofthead
of
Gree

Raithill

Kingswell Burn

Tam's
Hill

Townend
of
Gree

Damhead
Wood

Ladeside

Raithburn

Fenwick Water

Drumtee Water

Benthouse
Bridge

213

184

A　　　　　　B　　　　　　C

Thinacremuir
Lodge
Plotcock Glen
East
Thinacremuir

Thinacremuir
Muir

Newhouse Farm
Cottages
Newhouse

BROOMELTON RD

PLOTCOCK RD

Mafflat

Mafflat
Orchard

Corslet

Patrickholm

GLEN AVE
PRIMROSE AVE

Avon Water

Patrickbrae
Cottage

Dismantled Railway

Kittymuirhill

4

49

Longfaugh

Low
Kittymuir

Dismantled Railway

3

CRAIGTHORNHILL RD

Craigthornhill

Craigthorn

MILLHEUGH RD

Crofthead

Kittymuir

48

High East
Quarter

Howmains

East
Quarter

GLASSFORD RD

Glassford

Burnside

HUNTERLEES RD

Knowehead

Priest's Burn

Hunterlees

Holm

Avon Water

Linthaugh
Bridge

Linthaugh

Alexander Hamilton
Memorial Park

A71

2

47

Manse
Whitehill
Cottage

Cemy

Tapped
Hill

Whitehill

White
Hill

MUIRBURN RD

Braehead

Avonholm

MANSE RD

Manse

Cemy

East
Mains

Thorndale

East Mains
Holdings

West
Mains

Cemy

Dismantled Railway

Homeleigh

Dismtd Rly

Hospl

Industrial
Estate

LOCKHART ST

LAWRIE ST
GREEN ST
McLEAN GDNS
CROW RD
W HILL RD
W LIBRARY
NEW ST
MILLAR ST KIRK ST
QUEEN ST

VICARS RD

KING ST
ANGLE ST

1 TRONGATE
2 THE CROSS

PC

Stonehouse

CAMERNAN ST
MURRAY DR
WATSTONE RD
BOGHALL
ST

Sch

TOWNHEAD ST
UNION ST

SIDEHEAD
CALEDONIAN
AVE

STRATHAVEN RD
SPITAL RD

North
Lodge

Bankhead

1

46

73　　　　　A　　　　74　　　　B　　　　75　　　　C

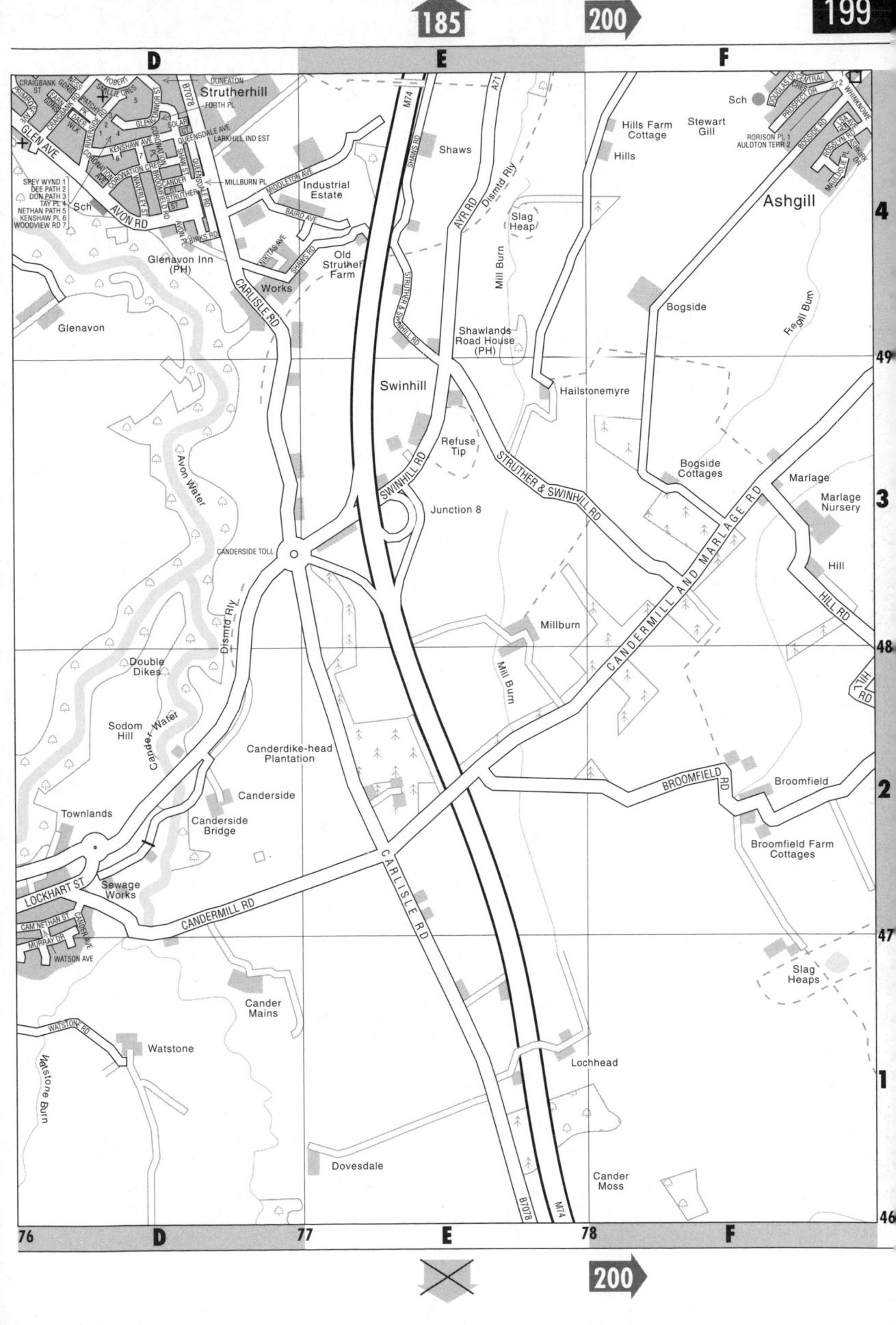

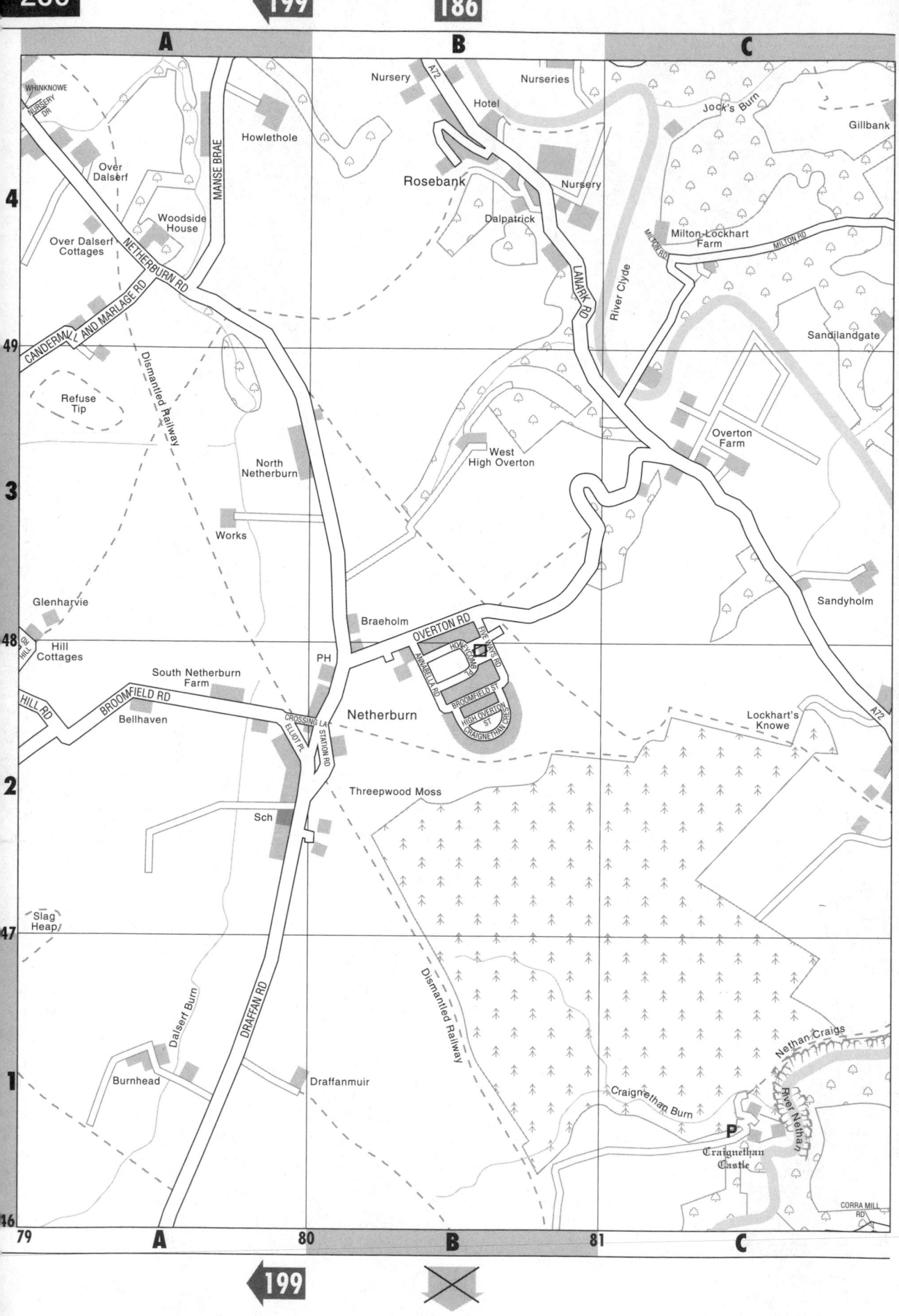

Whinknowe
NURSERY DR
Nursery
Nurseries
Jock's Burn
Gillbank
Over Dalserf
Howlethole
Hotel
MANSE BRAE
Rosebank
Nursery
Over Dalserf Cottages
Woodside House
Dalpatrick
Milton-Lockhart Farm
MILTON RD
MILTON RD
NETHERBURN RD
LANARK RD
River Clyde
CANDERMILL AND MARLAGE RD
Sandilandgate
Refuse Tip
Overton Farm
North Netherburn
West High Overton
Works
Glenharvie
Sandyholm
Braeholm
OVERTON RD
Hill Cottages
HILL RD
PH
Netherburn
Lockhart's Knowe
South Netherburn Farm
LANARKLLA RD
BROOMFIELD ST
HIGH OVERTON ST
CRAIGNETHAN RD
A72
FIVE WAYS RD
BROOMFIELD RD
Bellhaven
CROSSING LA
ELLIOT PL
STATION RD
Threepwood Moss
Sch
Slag Heap
Dismantled Railway
Dalserf Burn
DRAFFAN RD
Nethan Craigs
Craignethan Burn
River Nethan
Burnhead
Draffanmuir
P
Craignethan Castle
CORRA MILL RD

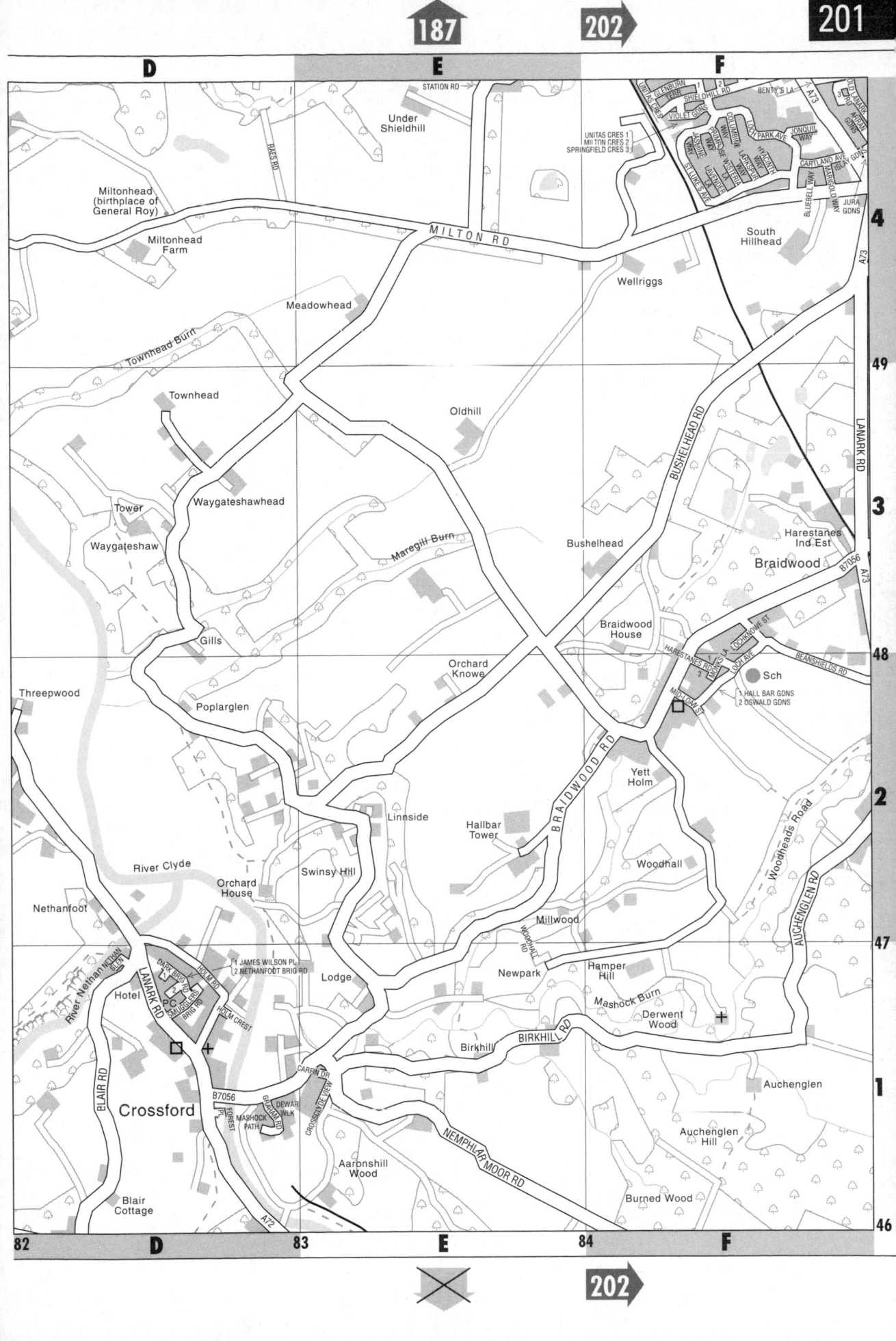

187
202

D E F

STATION RD

UNITAS CRES
GLENBURN
TERR
SHIELDHILL RD
BENTY'S LA
A73
OLD LANARK RD
CARRON GDNS

Under
Shieldhill

VIOLET GDNS
COLUMBINE WAY
JONQUIL WAY
BLUEBELL WAY
BROADLEY WAY
JURA GDNS

UNITAS CRES 1
MILTON CRES 2
SPRINGFIELD CRES 3

CARTLAND AVE

4

Miltonhead
(birthplace of
General Roy)

MILTON RD

South
Hillhead

Miltonhead
Farm

Wellriggs

A73

49

Meadowhead

Townhead Burn

LANARK RD

3

Townhead

Oldhill

BUSHELHEAD RD

Harestanes
Ind Est

Tower

Waygateshawhead

Maregill Burn

Bushelhead

Braidwood

B7056
A73

Waygateshaw

Gills

Braidwood
House

Harestanes RONK'S LA
LOCHKNOWE ST
LOCH AVE

Sch

BEANSHIELDS RD

48

Threepwood

Poplarglen

Orchard
Knowe

MID TOWN ST

1 HALL BAR GDNS
2 OSWALD GDNS

Linnside

Hallbar
Tower

BRAIDWOOD RD

Yett
Holm

Woodhall

Woodheads Road

AUCHENGLEN RD

2

River Clyde

Orchard
House

Swinsy Hill

Millwood

WOODHALL RD

Nethanfoot

River Nethan

NETHAN
GLEN

DARK BRIG RD

HOLM RD

1 JAMES WILSON PL
2 NETHANFOOT BRIG RD

Lodge

Newpark

Hamper
Hill

Mashock Burn

Derwent
Wood

47

Hotel

LANARK RD

PC
SMUGGLERS
BRIG RD

HOLM CREST

Birkhill

BIRKHILL RD

Auchenglen

1

BLAIR RD

Crossford

B7056

CARFIN DR

FOREST
PL

DEWAR
WLK

GRAHAM RD

CROSSFORD VIEW

MASHOCK
PATH

Aaronshill
Wood

NEMPHLAR MOOR RD

Auchenglen
Hill

Blair
Cottage

A72

Burned Wood

46

82 D 83 E 84 F

202

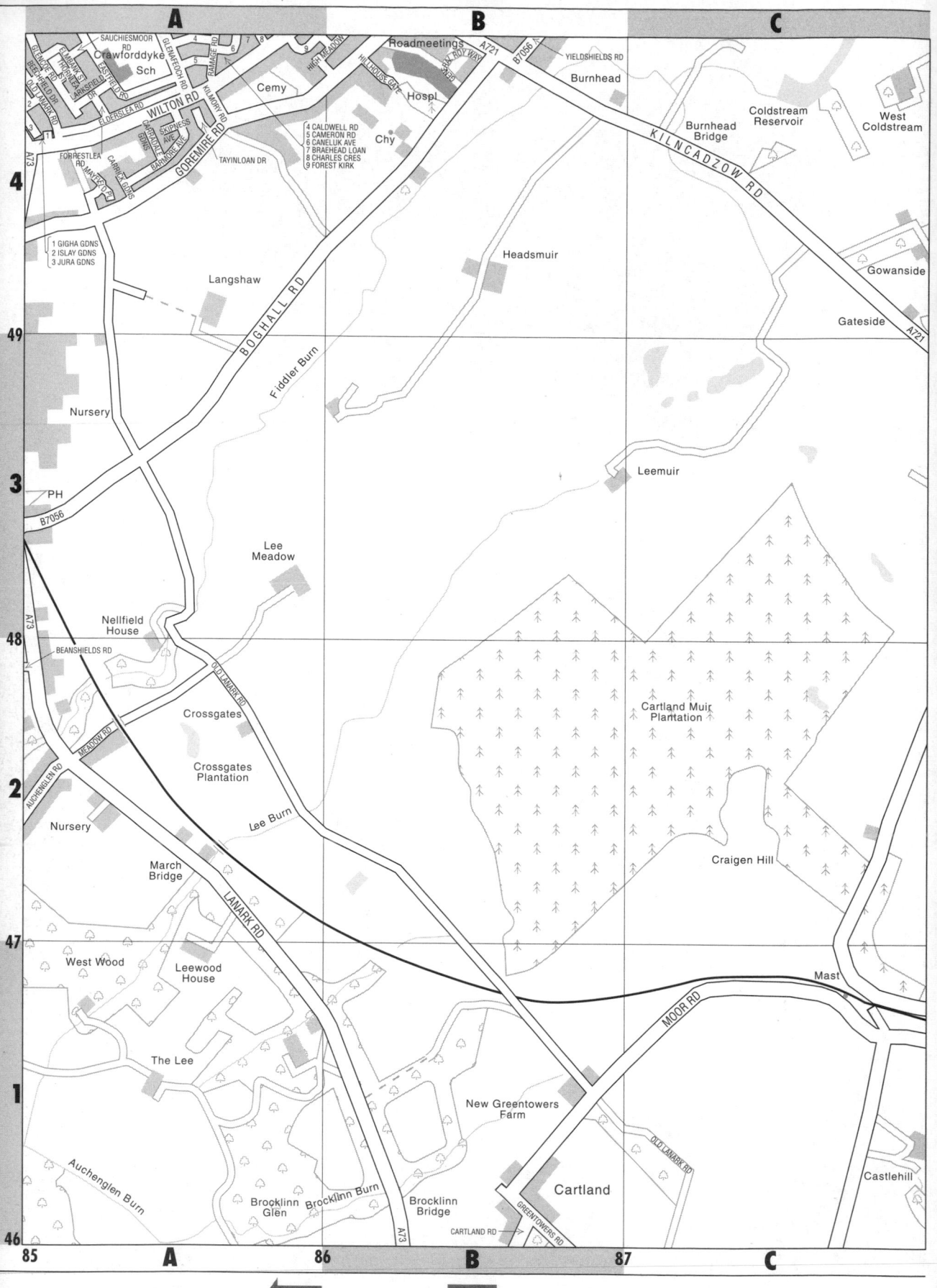

A B C

4

1 GIGHA GDNS
2 ISLAY GDNS
3 JURA GDNS

49

3

48

2

47

1

46

85 A 86 B 87 C

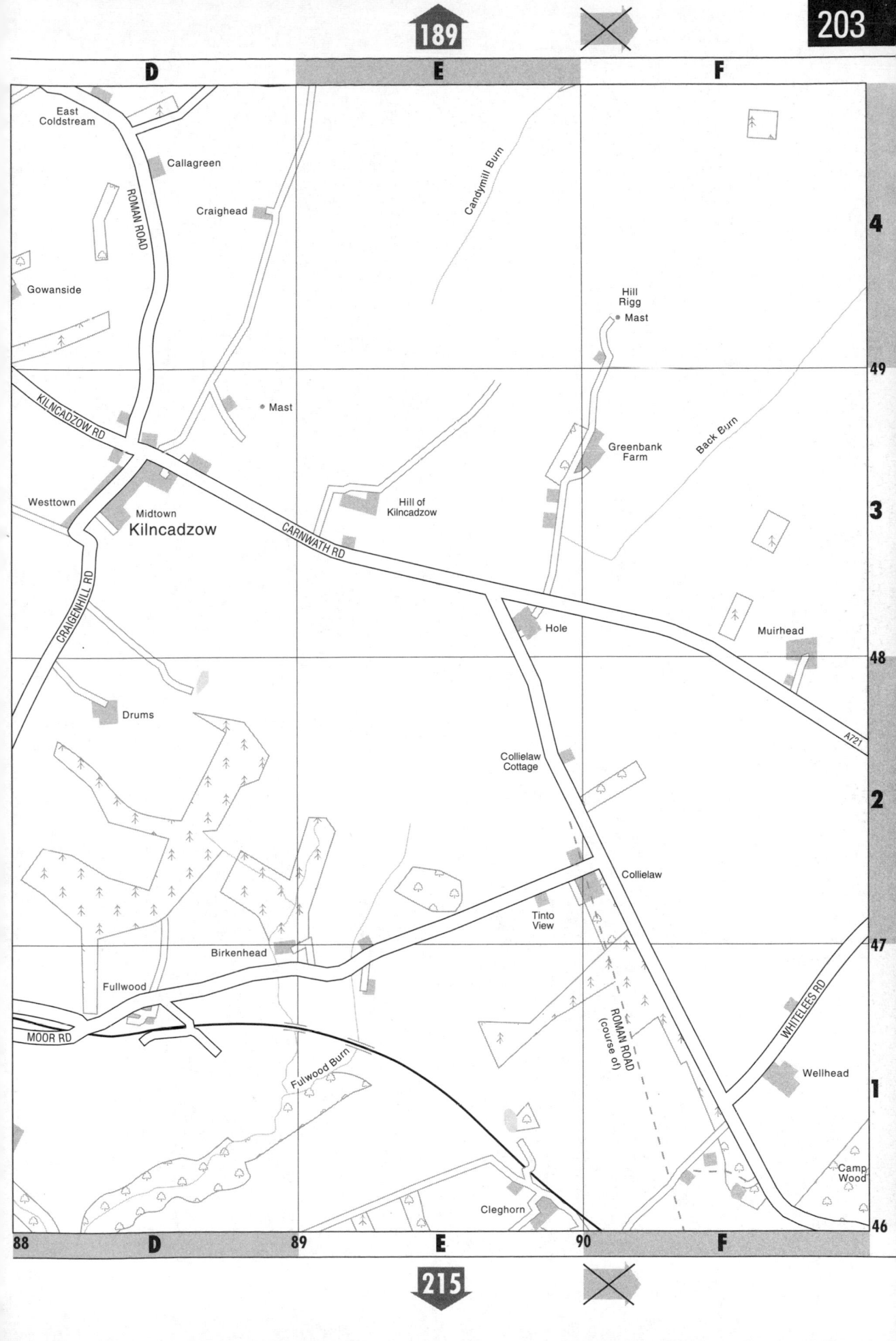

D   E   F

East
Coldstream

Callagreen

ROMAN ROAD

Craighead

Candymill Burn

4

Gowanside

Hill
Rigg
• Mast

49

KILNCADZOW RD

• Mast

Greenbank
Farm

Back Burn

Westtown

Hill of
Kilncadzow

Midtown
Kilncadzow

CARNWATH RD

3

CRAIGENHILL RD

Hole

Muirhead

48

Drums

A721

Collielaw
Cottage

2

Collielaw

Tinto
View

Birkenhead

47

Fullwood

WHITELEES RD

ROMAN ROAD
(course of)

Wellhead

MOOR RD

1

Fullwood Burn

Camp
Wood

Cleghorn

46

88   D   89   E   90   F

A **B** **C**

Glenhead

Kirkland

South
Inch

P

P

P

Gourock Burn

Glenfoot

4

45

Boydston
Braes

PC

Scart
Rock

Boydston
Shore

3

A78

44

2

North
Islet

43

East
Islet

Broad
Rock

Horse
Isle
(Nature Reserve)

1

North Bay

42

19   **A**   20   **B**   21   **C**

206

D E F

4

Busbie
Bridge

High
Boydstone

Little
Busbie

Meikle
Busbie

Craigspark
Plantation

Craigspark

Rashley

45

Low
Boydstone

Caravan
Park

Stanley Burn

Sorbie

3

Townhead

Montfode Burn

Mill Glen
Reservoir

Mill
Farm

Filter
Station

Montfode

Works

Whitlees

44

LONGCRAIGS
KINNAN PL

SOUTH ISLE RD

CHAPELHILL MOUNT

DALRY RD

BURN'S TERR

AFTON PL
MOSSGIEL RD

KIRKHALL RD

CRAIGSPARK

MONTFODE DR

DALRY LA

OAK RD

ASHGROVE RD

WHIT VIEW
WHITE CRAIG RD

CLYDE TERR

LAWSON DR

KNOCKRIOCH

2

HAUPLAND RD

ARDNEIL CT

CHURCHILL DR

MILL GLEN RD

ST MARY

ST NINIAN'S DR

LAIRD WEIR

GREENACRES

SORBIE RD

Sch

Sch

Sch

RASHLEY

ST ANDREWS

Sch

EGLINTON RD

Sch

NORTH CRESCENT RD

STANLEY RD

BEGGS CT

WHITLEES CT

Sch

PCs

CARRICK PL

CUMBRAE
TERR

QUEEN'S DR

CENTRAL AV

George
Aitken Ct

ELM PARK

Dykesmains

Sch

North
Bay

CENTRAL
QUADRANT

STRATHCLYDE AV

AILSA GDNS

CASTLE

PARK VIEW

43

McDOWALL

McDOWALL AVE

Stanley Burn

Cemy

Longfield PL

Sch

SIMPSON DR

ARDROSSAN

CALEDONIA RD

PAISLEY

SHELLBRIDGE WAY

HARBOUR
IND EST

PARK RD

KIRKHALL
GDNS

Dismtd Rly

NURSERY
PL

Acad

Longfield Ave

MID DYKES RD

KILBRANNAN
AVE

DYKESFIELD
PL

CATACOL
AVE
ROSS RD

F Sta

MONTGOMERIE ST

GLASGOW ST

HILL ST

Sch

PARKHOUSE RD

SORBIE RD

DYKESMAINS RD

McKILLOP

HIGH RD

1

Ardrossan
Harbour
Station

Town
Hall

PC Hall

Ardrossan
Town
Station

SOUTH BEACH RD

Acad

Ferry
Terminal

P

Harbour
Liby
Off

PC

Ardrossan
South Beach
Station

JACK'S RD

Breakwater

Harbour

HARBOUR RD 1
HARBOUR ST 2
HARBOUR PL 3
BUTE PL 4
INCHES RD 5

DOCK RD
A738

SOUTH CRESCENT RD

Promenade
South Beach

A78

WEST DOURA AVE

42

216 206

← **205**

A | B | C

4

Smithstone
Plantation

Quarry

Towerlodge

Littlelaught

AULD CLAY RD

Bankend

Meiklelaught

45

Lochwood

West Knockrivoch
Mount

East Knockrivoch
Mount

Knockrivoch

Diddup

3

Stevenston or
Ashgrove Loch

South Knockrivoch
Mount

The Craigs | Loch Craigs

44

Glen
Banks

Golf
Course

Lochcraigs

Ford

CH

Mast

Sharphill

Corsankell

Glen Burn

Filter
Station

Hillhead

2

SHARPHILL
IND EST

Middlepart

Fellie Hill

Greenhead
Holdings

CAIRRICK AVE
LOCHLEA
RD
MISSELL
ISLAND

FLEMING

HILLHEAD RD

HAWTHORN

43

DUFFY
BURNS AVE
DAVAAR
ROSS
WHEATLEY RD

MULGREW AVE
DALRY

KENILWORTH
DR

1 ISLAY CRES
2 KEIR HARDIE PL
3 JEAN ARMOUR PL
4 ABBOTSFORD PL
5 TALISMAN WLK
6 MUNRO WLK

MIDDLEPART

MAXWELL PL 1
CLEMENTS PL 2
OAKLAND DR 3
ARDCHOILLE DR 4
ASHGROVE AVE 5
KERELAW AVE 6

CAMBUSKEITH RD

ELMS RD
BURNLEA
GREENEND

CASTLE AVE
HAWTHORN

ARDCHOILLE

LANDSBOROUGH PL

HYSLOP
ST ANDREW'S PL
ST JOHN'S PL

Hawkhill

SANNOX DR

SHAW
PL
PRIMROSE

Schs

Quarrel Burn

Sch

Sch

DONALDSON AVE
CRAIGSIDE AVE
ROSS AVE

FORD

HAMILTON CRES
ST MONACH'S

Sch

ST STEPHEN'S
ST COLUMBA'S PL

1

NEW ENGLAND
RD
ANDERSON

GILFILLAN
AVE
FLECK

7 MIDDLEPART CRES
8 DUGUID DR
9 PROSPECTHILL RD
10 McNAY CRES
11 McKINNON PL
12 CLARK PL
13 ADAMS AVE
14 LOCHRANZA PL

Mayfield

Kerelaw
Mains

KERELAW RD

Stevenston Burn

McGREGOR AVE

ALEXANDER AVE

BURNS

LESLIE
MORRISON AVE

James
ST JAMES PL

Cemy

HAWKHILL DR

A78

HIGH RD
A78

Priest
Hill

DIDDUP DR

CUNINGHAME DR

MAYFIELD
GR

SINCLAIR ST

PATRICK ST

LOGGARD

GLENCAIRN ST
B752

Sch

WALLACE AVE

Cemy

KILWINNING RD

Sch

Caravar
Park

ST
LAWRENCE
PL

HIGH RD

MAYFIELD RD

HIGH RD

HIGH RD

MAYVILLE

1 JOHN BROGAN PL
2 MARY LOVE PL
3 CLYDE VIEW AVE
4 CAPONCRAIG AVE

THE RIGGS
GLEBE ST

SCHOOLWELL

AFTON
RD

Mount Pleasant

TOWNHEAD ST

MAIN ST

GARNOCK

KILWINNING RD
HIGHFIELD DR

HILLCRES

DUBBS RD
B752

Ardeer Mains

DUBBS RD

42

25 | A | 26 | B | 27 | C

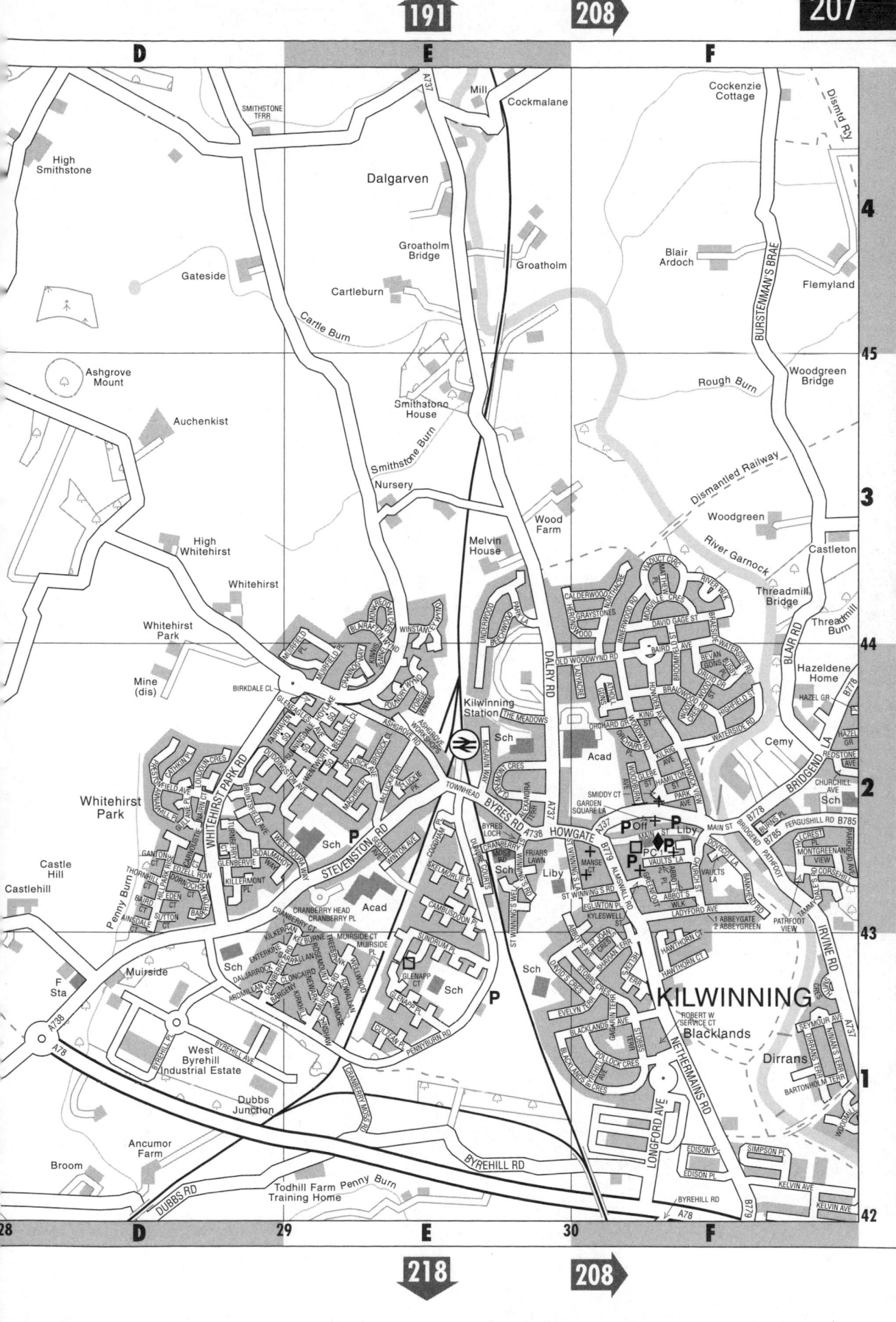

207
192

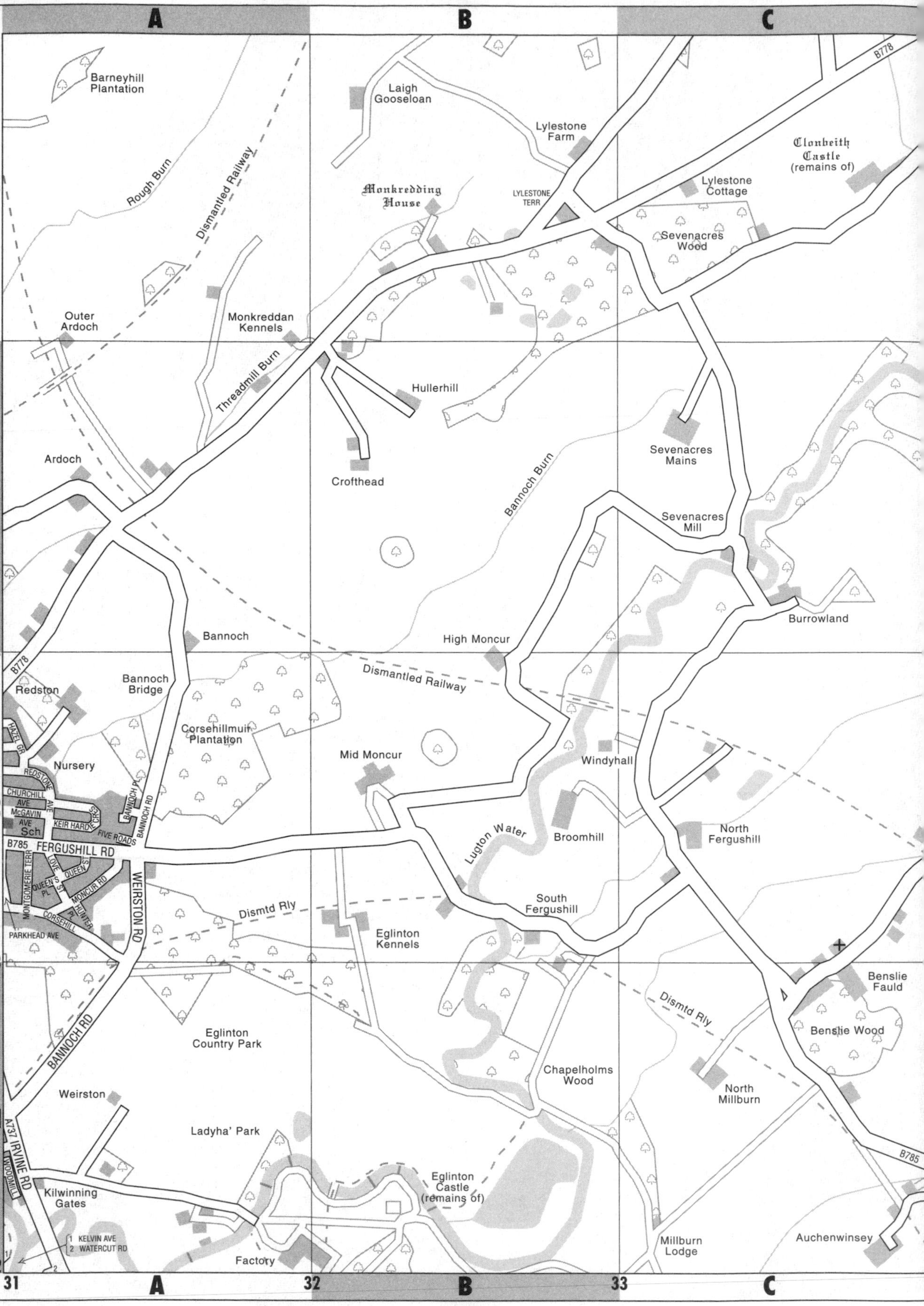

A | **B** | **C**

4

Barneyhill Plantation

Laigh Gooseloan

Lylestone Farm

Clonbeith Castle (remains of)

Rough Burn

Dismantled Railway

Monkredding House

LYLESTONE TERR

Lylestone Cottage

Sevenacres Wood

Outer Ardoch

Monkreddan Kennels

Threadmill Burn

Hullerhill

45

Ardoch

Crofthead

Bannoch Burn

Sevenacres Mains

Sevenacres Mill

3

Burrowland

Bannoch

High Moncur

44

Dismantled Railway

B778

Redston

Bannoch Bridge

Corsehillmuir Plantation

Mid Moncur

Windyhall

HAZEL GR

Nursery

REDSTON

CHURCHILL AVE

McGAVIN AVE

KEIR HARD Sch

FIVE ROADS

BANNOCH PL

BANNOCH RD

Lugton Water

Broomhill

North Fergushill

2

B785 FERGUSHILL RD

MONTGOMERIE TERR

QUEEN'S PL

FIVE QUEEN

MONCUR RD

CORSEHILL

HUNTER

WEIRSTON RD

Dismtd Rly

Eglinton Kennels

South Fergushill

PARKHEAD AVE

43

BANNOCH RD

Eglinton Country Park

Dismtd Rly

Chapelholms Wood

Benslie Fauld

Benslie Wood

Weirston

North Millburn

1

A737 IRVINE RD

WOODMILL

Ladyha' Park

Kilwinning Gates

Eglinton Castle (remains of)

Millburn Lodge

Auchenwinsey

B785

1 KELVIN AVE
2 WATERCUT RD

Factory

42

31 | **A** | **32** | **B** | **33** | **C**

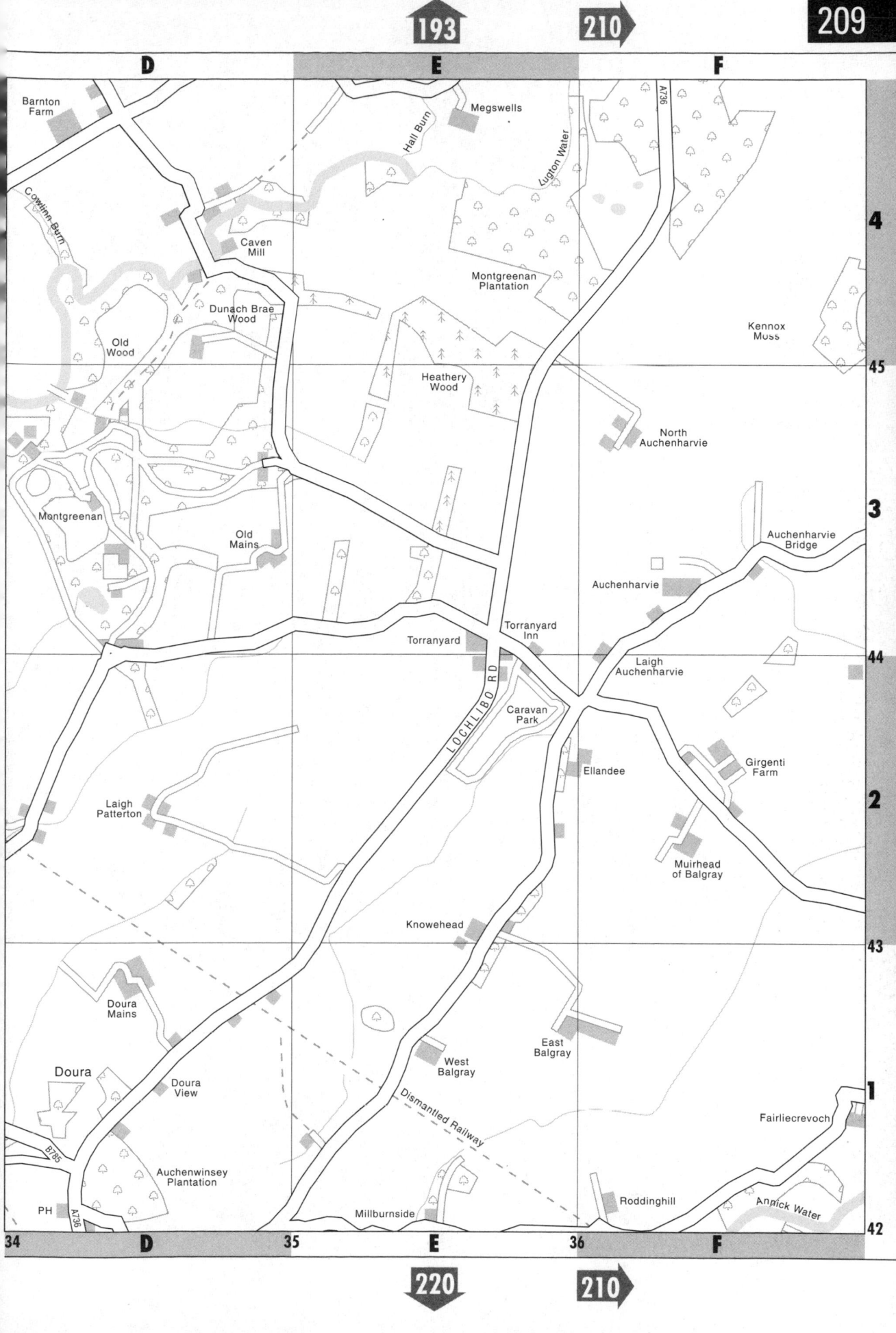

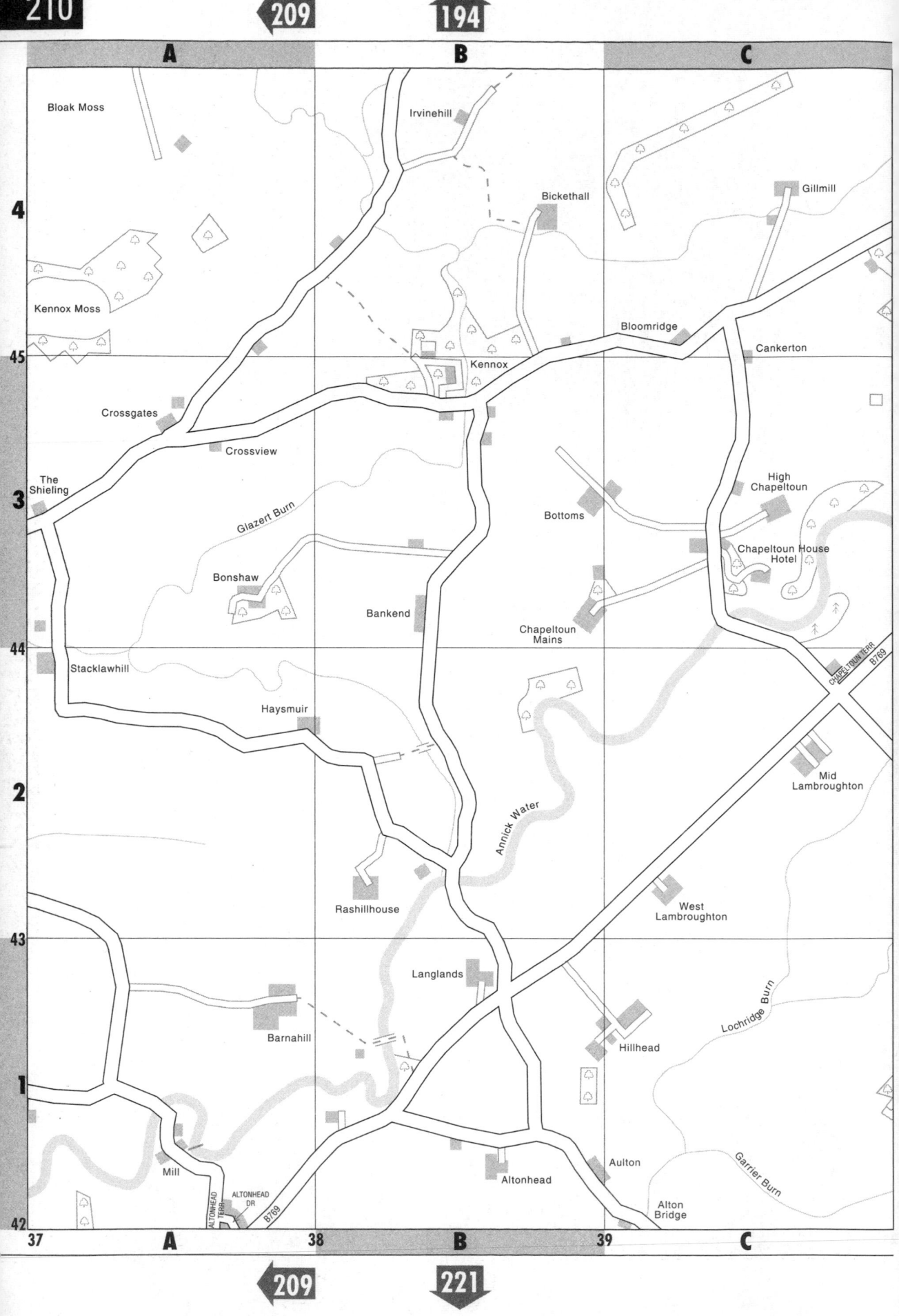

A
B
C

Bloak Moss

Irvinehill

Bickethall

Gillmill

4

Kennox Moss

Bloomridge

Cankerton

45

Kennox

Crossgates

Crossview

The
Shieling

High
Chapeltoun

3

Bottoms

Chapeltoun House
Hotel

Glazert Burn

Bonshaw

Bankend

Chapeltoun
Mains

44

Stacklawhill

Haysmuir

CHAPELTOUN TERR
B769

Mid
Lambroughton

2

Annick Water

Rashillhouse

West
Lambroughton

43

Langlands

Lochridge Burn

Barnahill

Hillhead

1

Mill

Aulton

Garrier Burn

ALTONHEAD
TERR

ALTONHEAD
DR

B769

Altonhead

Alton
Bridge

42

37

A

38

B

39

C

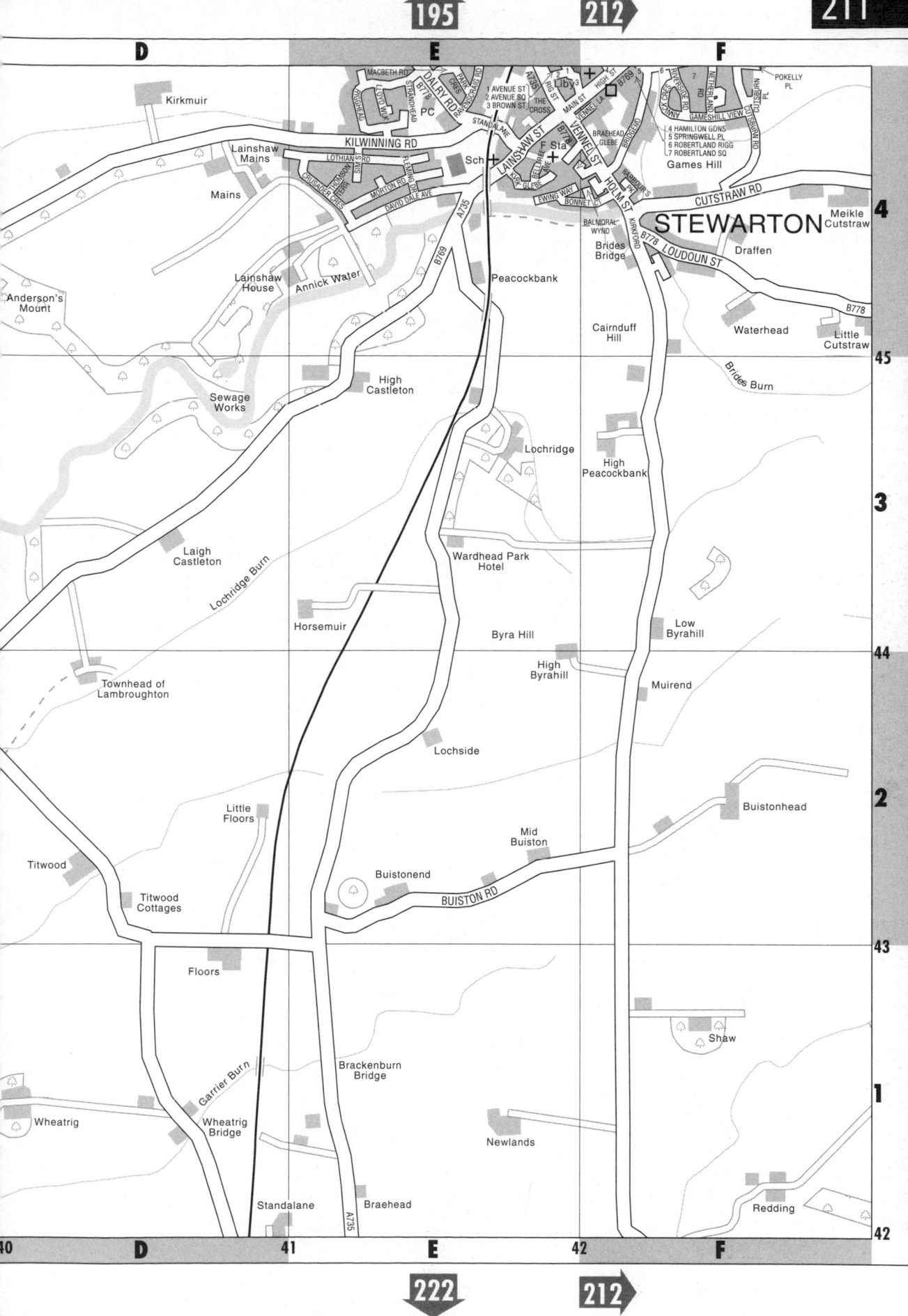

D   E   F

KIRKMUIR

MACBETH RD
DALRY RD
STRANDHEAD
KILWINNING RD
PC

Lainshaw
Mains
LOTHIAN RD
CRUSADER CRES
THOMSON TER
MORTON RD
DAVID DALE AVE
Mains
FLEMING DR

1 AVENUE ST
2 AVENUE SQ
3 BROWN ST
THE CROSS
MAIN ST
LAINSHAW ST
Sch
STANDALANE
F Sta
HOLM ST
VENNEL ST
BELL CRES
EWING WAY
BONNET
BALMORAL WYND
KIRKFORD
B769

4 HAMILTON GDNS
5 SPRINGWELL PL
6 ROBERTLAND RIGG
7 ROBERTLAND SQ
RIVERSIDE RD
NETHERLAND
GAMESHILL VIEW
CABURN RD
POKELLY PL
Games Hill

STEWARTON

Lainshaw
House
Annick Water
Anderson's
Mount

Peacockbank
Brides
Bridge
Cairnduff
Hill
LOUDOUN ST
Draffen
Waterhead
Meikle
Cutstraw
Little
Cutstraw
CUTSTRAW RD
B778

Sewage
Works
High
Castleton
Lochridge
High
Peacockbank
Brides Burn

4

45

Laigh
Castleton
Lochridge Burn
B769
Wardhead Park
Hotel
Low
Byrahill

3

Townhead of
Lambroughton
Horsemuir
Byra Hill
High
Byrahill
Muirend

44

Little
Floors
Lochside
Buistonhead

2

Titwood
Titwood
Cottages
Buistonend
Mid
Buiston
BUISTON RD

43

Floors
Shaw

Brackenburn
Bridge
Garrier Burn
Wheatrig
Wheatrig
Bridge
Standalane
A735
Braehead
Newlands
Redding

1

40   D   41   E   42   F   **42**

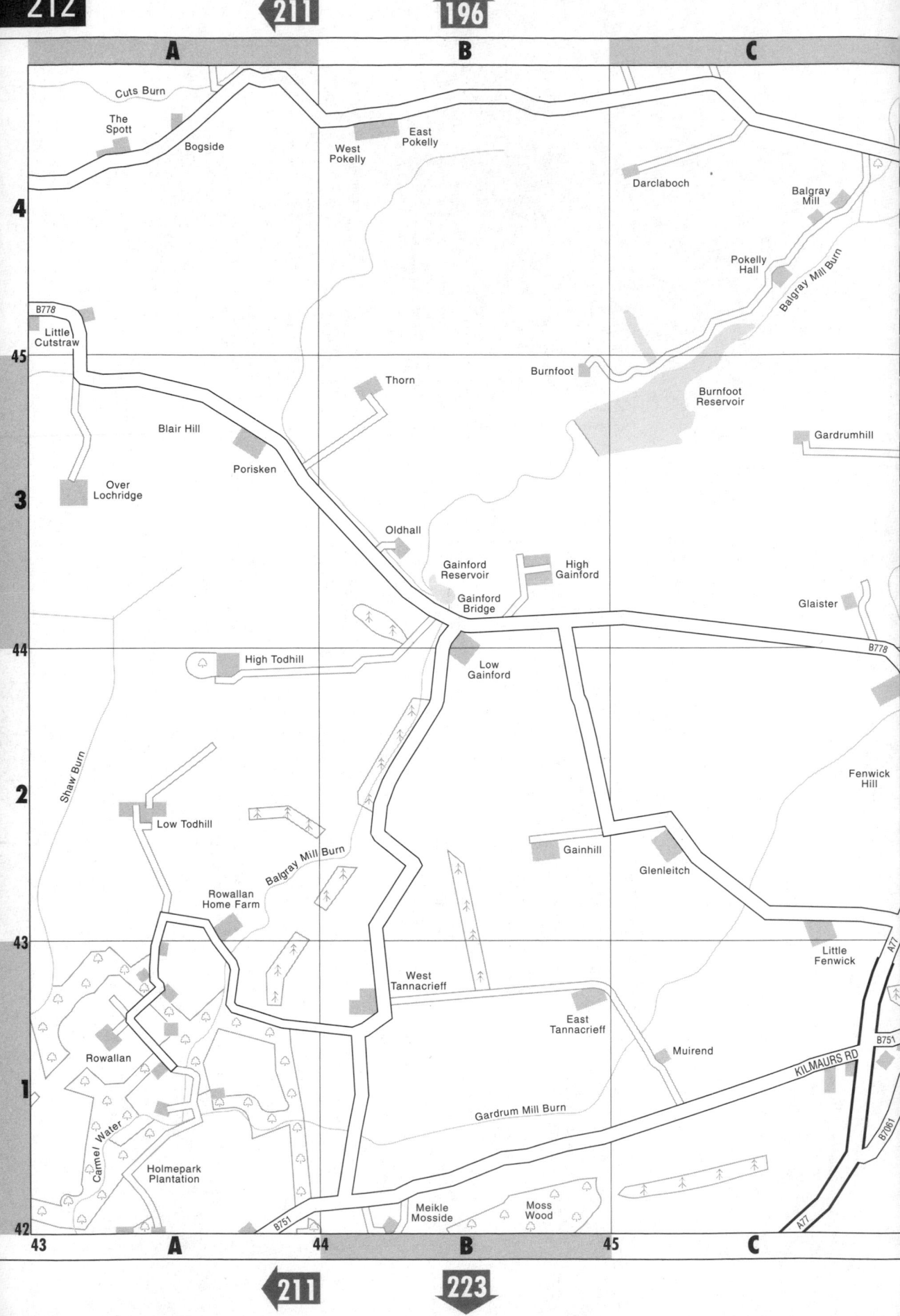

A
B
C

Cuts Burn
The Spott
Bogside
West Pokelly
East Pokelly
Darclaboch
Balgray Mill
4
Pokelly Hall
Balgray Mill Burn
B778
Little Cutstraw
45
Thorn
Burnfoot
Burnfoot Reservoir
Blair Hill
Gardrumhill
Porisken
Over Lochridge
3
Oldhall
Gainford Reservoir
High Gainford
Glaister
Gainford Bridge
44
High Todhill
Low Gainford
B778
Shaw Burn
Fenwick Hill
2
Low Todhill
Balgray Mill Burn
Gainhill
Glenleitch
Rowallan Home Farm
43
Little Fenwick
A77
West Tannacrieff
East Tannacrieff
Muirend
B751
Rowallan
KILMAURS RD
1
Gardrum Mill Burn
B7081
Carmel Water
Holmepark Plantation
Meikle Mosside
Moss Wood
A77
42
43
A
44
B
45
C

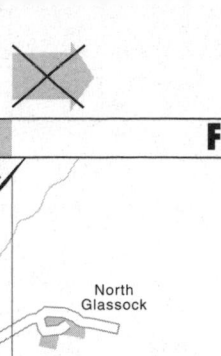

A   B   C

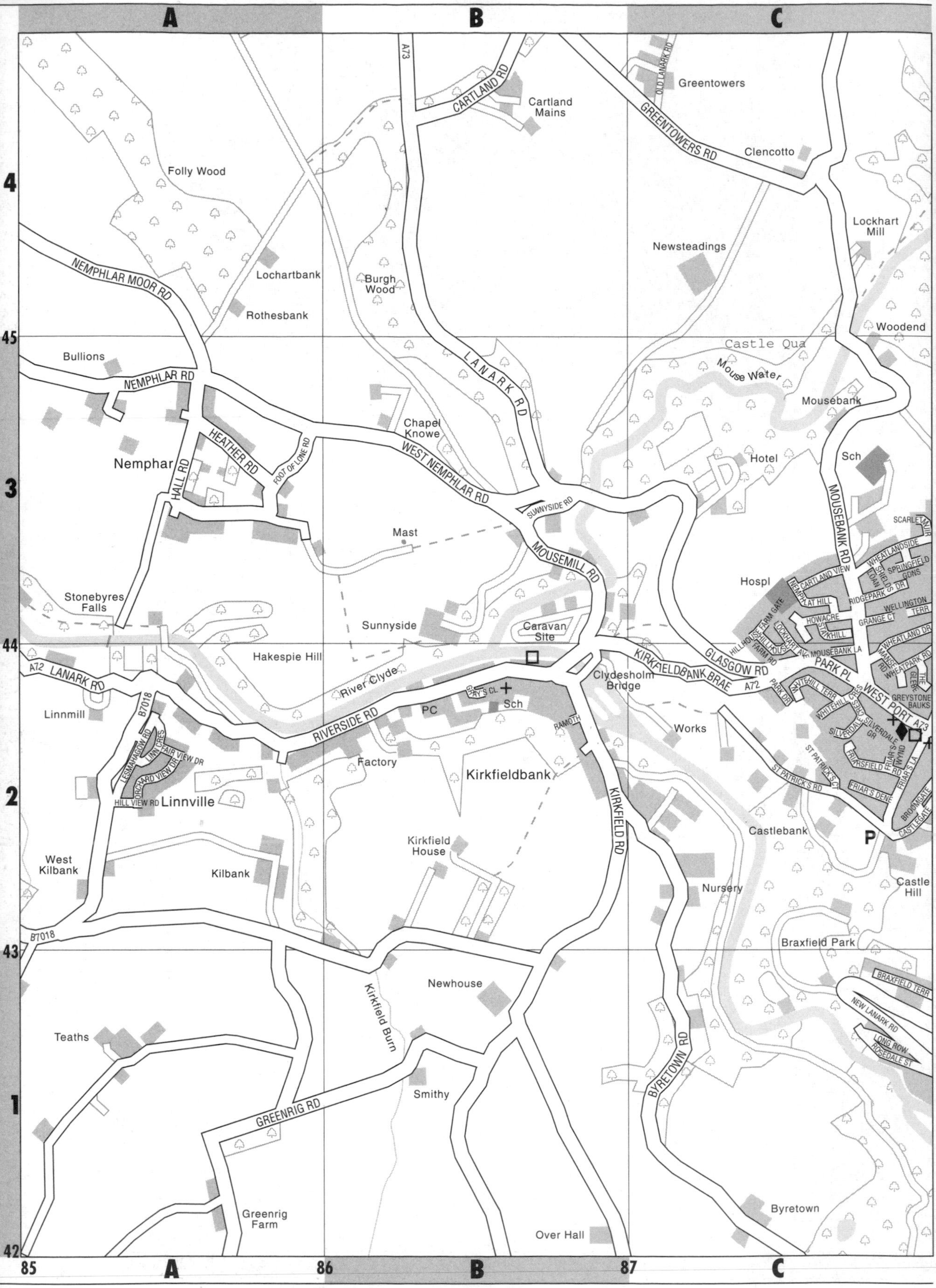

4

Folly Wood

Greentowers

OLD LANARK RD

GREENTOWERS RD

Clencotto

Newsteadings

Lochartbank

Burgh Wood

NEMPHLAR MOOR RD

Rothesbank

Lockhart Mill

Woodend

45

Bullions

NEMPHLAR RD

Castle Qua

Mouse Water

Mousebank

LANARK RD

Chapel Knowe

HEATHER RD

HALL RD

Nemphar

FOOT OF LONE RD

WEST NEMPHLAR RD

SUNNYSIDE RD

Hotel

Sch

MOUSEBANK RD

SCARLET MUIR

WHEATLANDSIDE

SPRINGFIELD GDNS

3

Mast

MOUSEMILL RD

Hospl

CARTLAND VIEW

FLAT HILL

HOWACRE

RIDGEPARK DR

GRANGE CT

WELLINGTON TERR

Stonebyres Falls

Sunnyside

Caravan Site

HILL HOUSE

MILL FARM

LOCKHART

MOUSEBANK LA

WHEATLAND DR

THE GREEN

44

LANARK RD

A72

Hakespie Hill

River Clyde

GRAY'S CL

KIRKFIELDBANK BRAE

GLASGOW RD

A72

Clydesholm Bridge

PARK PL

WEST PORT

A73

WHITEHILL

SILVERDALE GR

WHEATPARK PL

GREYSTONE BAUKS

Linnmill

B7018

RIVERSIDE RD

PC

Sch

RAMOTH

Works

SILVERDALE

WARD

FRIARSFIELD RD

FRIAR'S DENE

2

FERNLEIGH RD

ORCHARD VIEW DR

LINN CRES

FAIR VIEW DR

Factory

Kirkfieldbank

KIRKFIELD RD

ST PATRICK'S RD

FRIAR'S CT

CASTLEGATE

West Kilbank

HILL VIEW RD

Linnville

Kilbank

Kirkfield House

Castlebank

Castle Hill

43

B7018

Nursery

Braxfield Park

BRAXFIELD TERR

Teaths

Newhouse

Kirkfield Burn

BYRETOWN RD

NEW LANARK RD

LONG ROW

ROSEDALE ST

1

GREENRIG RD

Smithy

Byretown

42

Greenrig Farm

Over Hall

85   A   86   B   87   C

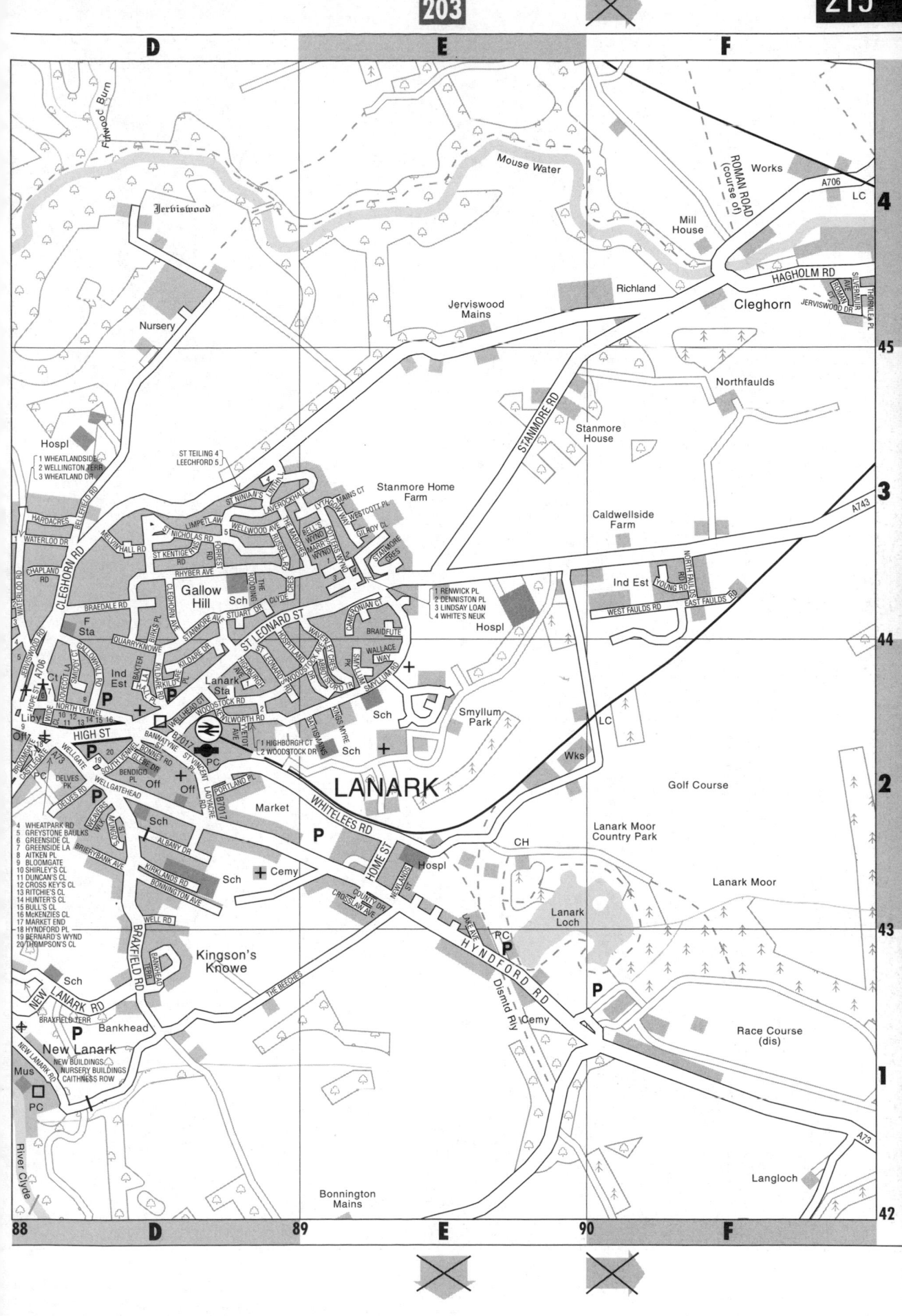

D E F

Finwood Burn

Mouse Water

ROMAN ROAD (course of)

Works

A706

LC

Jerviswood

Mill House

Jerviswood Mains

Richland

HAGHOLM RD

Cleghorn

SILVERMUIR AVE
THORNLEA PL
ROMAN PL
Jerviswood Dr

4

Nursery

45

Northfaulds

Hospl

1 WHEATLANDSIDE
2 WELLINGTON TERR
3 WHEATLAND DR

ST TEILING 4
LEECHFORD 5

STANMORE RD

Stanmore House

Stanmore Home Farm

Caldwellside Farm

A743

3

HARDACRES
BELLEFIELD RD
CLEGHORN RD
WATERLOO DR
CHAPLAND RD
BRAEDALE RD
WATERLOO RD
JERVISWOOD DR
A706

ST NINIAN'S
LIMPETLAW
ST NICHOLAS RD
MELVILHALL RD
ST KENTIGERN'S
RHYBER AVE
CLEGHORN AVE
QUARRYKNOWE
KIRKFIELD
BAXTER
BIRKS PL
KILDAR RD

LAVEROCKHALL
WELLWOOD AVE
THE MANSE
BELLS WYND
MARR WYND
RUSSELL RD
THE RODDING
CLYDE CRES
STUART DR
STANMORE AVE
KILDARE DR

WESTCOTT PL
GILROY PL
POTTERS WYND
STANMORE CRES
CAMERONIAN CT
BRAIDFUTE

Gallow Hill

Sch

F Sta

Ind Est

Lanark Sta

St LEONARD ST

WOODSTOCK RD
DILLWORTH RD

HIGHMUIR
HOSPITLAND DR
ST LEONARD ST
ABBOTSFORD RD
WAVERLEY CRES
SMYLLUM RD
KINGS MYRE
BRENTISMAINS
KINGS AVE
VICTORY AVE

1 RENWICK PL
2 DENNISTON PL
3 LINDSAY LOAN
4 WHITE'S NEUK

Hospl

Ind Est

NORTH FAULDS RD
YOUNG RD
WEST FAULDS RD
EAST FAULDS RD

44

Ct

PC
DOVECOT LA
SANDILANDS
NORTH VENNEL
HOPE ST
DELVES RD
A73
BROOMGATE
CASTLEGATE
WELLGATE
BLOOMGATE
BANNATYNE
ST VINCENT PL
ST VINCENT ST

1 HIGHBORGH CT
2 WOODSTOCK DR

WALLACE WAY

Smyllum Park

Sch

Sch

Sch

LC

Wks

LANARK

Golf Course

2

Lib

Off

HIGH ST

WELLHEAD LA

B7017

PC

Off

P

Off

P

Market

4 WHEATPARK RD
5 GREYSTONE BAULKS
6 GREENSIDE CL
7 GREENSIDE LA
8 AITKEN PL
9 BL BLOOMGATE
10 SHIRLEY'S CL
11 DUNCAN'S CL
12 CROSS KEY'S CL
13 RITCHIE'S CL
14 HUNTER'S CL
15 BULL'S CL
16 McKENZIES CL
17 MARKET END
18 HYNDFORD PL
19 BERNARD'S WYND
20 THOMPSON'S CL

PC
DELVES PK
WELLGATEHEAD
BENDIGO PL
PORTLAND PL
B7017
BRIERYBANK AVE
SOUTH VENNEL
GLEBE DR
SUNNYSIDE
WEAVERS WYND
KIRKLANDS RD
ALBANY DR
BONNINGTON AVE
WELL RD

Sch

P

WHITELEES RD

HOME ST

Sch

Cemy

Sch

COUNTY DR
CROSSLAW AVE
NEWLANDS ST

Hospl

Lanark Moor Country Park

CH

Lanark Moor

43

BRAXFIELD RD
PAINS HEAD
NEW LANARK RD

Kingson's Knowe

THE BEECHES

LANGLEA RD
HYNDFORD RD

Dismid Riv

RC

P

Lanark Loch

Cemy

P

Sch

Braxfield Terr

Bankhead

Race Course (dis)

New Lanark

NEW BUILDINGS
NURSERY BUILDINGS
CAITHNESS ROW

Mus

PC

1

River Clyde

Bonnington Mains

Langloch

A73

42

88 D 89 E 90 F

205

A   B   C

South Beach

Promenade

South Bay

SALTCOATS

SOUTH CRESCENT RD	1
BUTE TERR	2
STANLEY PL	3
GALLOWAY PL	4
LAIGHDYKES RD	5
HARLEY PL	6
BROWN PL	7
TAYLOR PL	8
O'CONNOR CT	9
BARNETT CT	10
WELLPARK LA	11
VICTORIA RD	12
BRAEHEAD PL	13
GLADSTONE RD	14
PARKEND RD	15
NINEYARD ST	16
FINDLAY'S BRAE	17
ERSKINE PL	18
BRADSHAW ST	19
QUAY ST	20
GREEN ST	21

Eagle Rock

West Shore

Harbour

Pav

Saltcoats Sta

PCs

4

41

3

40

2

39

1

38

22   A   23   B   24   C

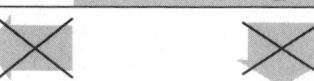

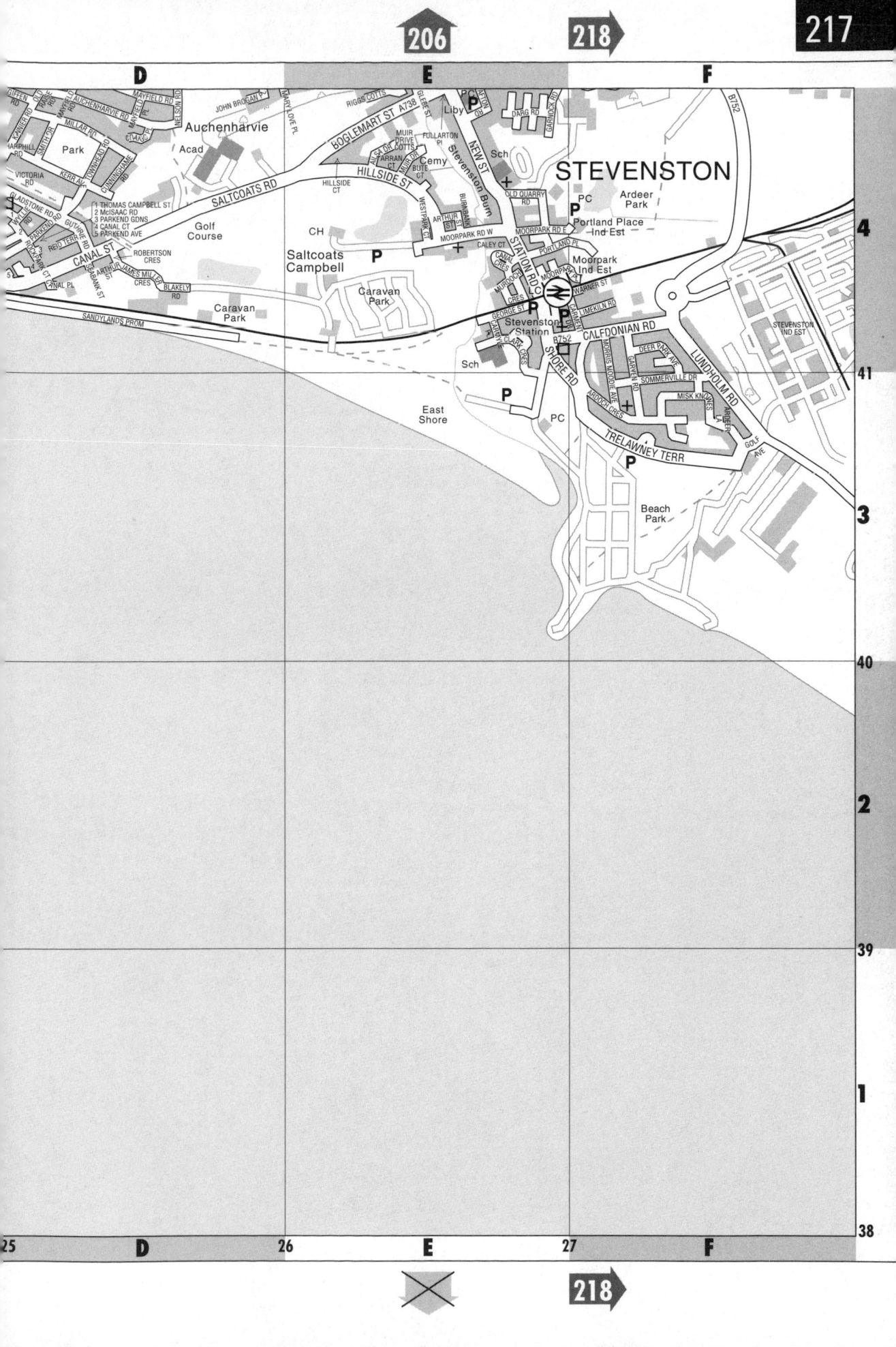

Auchenharvie
Acad

Park

Victoria
RD

1 THOMAS CAMPBELL ST
2 McISAAC RD
3 PARKEND GDNS
4 CANAL CT
5 PARKEND AVE

CANAL ST

GLADSTONE RD

JOHN BROGANT

MARYLOVE PL

BOGLEMART ST A738

HILLSIDE ST

HILLSIDE CT

RIGGS COTTS

MUIR DRIVE

CH

SALTCOATS RD

Golf
Course

Saltcoats
Campbell

ROBERTSON CRES

JAMES MILLER CRES

BLAKELY RD

Caravan
Park

P

Caravan
Park

SANDYLANDS PROM

East
Shore

P

PC

STEVENSTON

Ardeer
Park

PC

P

Portland Place
Ind Est

Moorpark
Ind Est

MOORPARK RD W

MOORPARK RD E

CALEY CT

Portland Pl

STATION RD

P

P

Stevenston
Burn

NEW ST

Liby

Cemy

Sch

OLD QUARRY
RD

P

P

B752

Stevenston
Station

Sch

CALEDONIAN RD

LIMEKILN RD

WARNER ST

DEER PARK AVE

MORRIS MOODIE AVE

GARVEN RD

SOMMERVILLE DR

MISK KNOWES

ARDOCH CRES

TRELAWNEY TERR

LUNDHOLM RD

GOLF AVE

P

Beach
Park

STEVENSTON
IND EST

B752

4

41

3

40

2

39

1

38

217
207

A B C

DUBBS RD

Penny Burn

BYREHILL RD

A78

B79

WATERCUT RD

Nethermains
Bridge

Refuse
Tip

4

41

P

3

P

PC

Works

Stevenston
Site

River Garnock

Hospl

Golf
Course

CH

40

Bogside

Bogside
Race Course
(disused)

Crooky's
Point

River Irvine

2

39

Bogside
Flats

1

Irvine
Harbour

River Irvine

HARBOUR ST

BEACH DR

P

Leisure
Centre

38

28 A 29 B 30 C

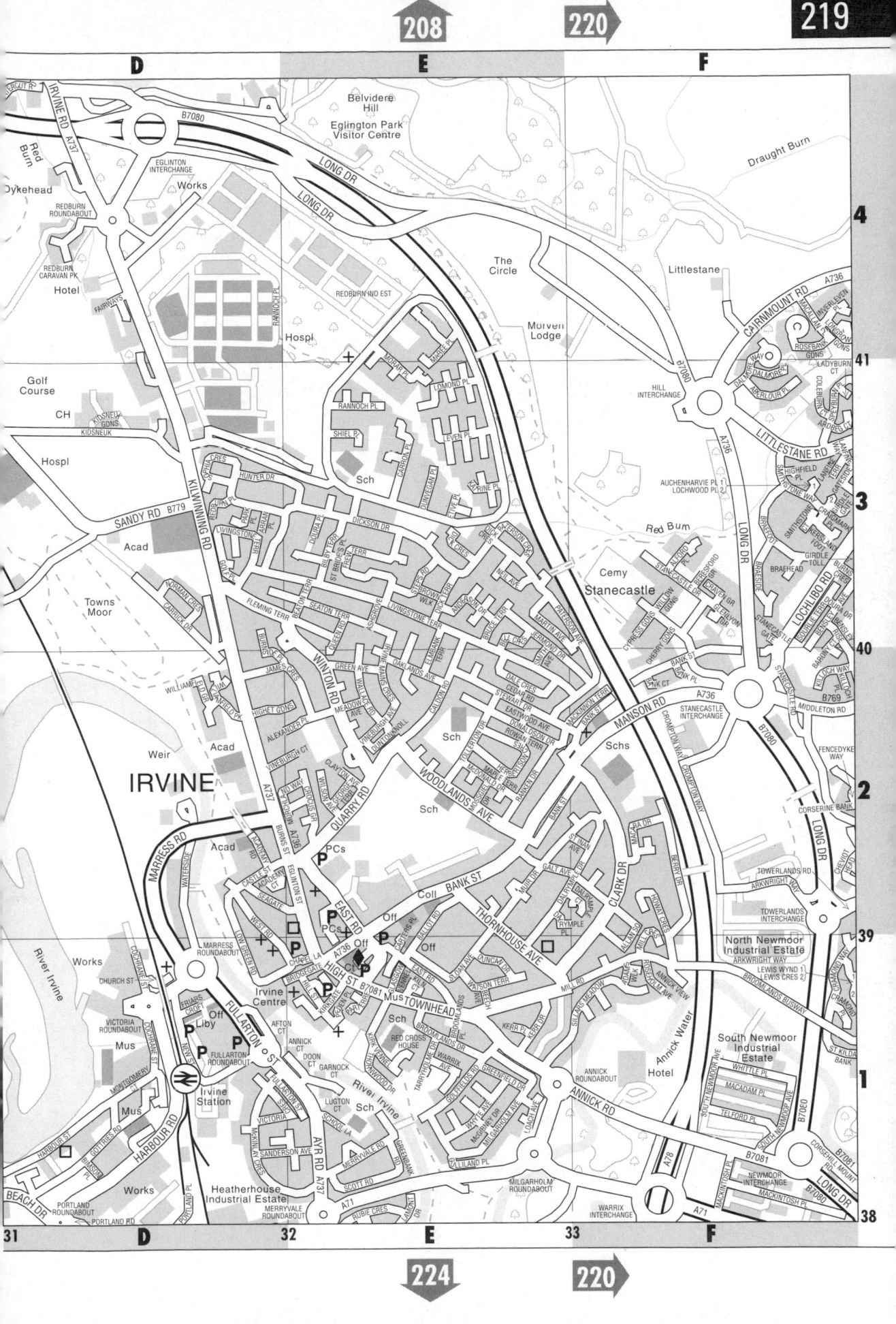

219
209

A   B   C

Dismtd Rly
Draught Burn
A736
High Armsheugh
Sourlie
West Wood
Annick Lodge
Dismtd Rly
Caravan Park
B769

4

Holehouse
Braehead

A736 CAIRNMOUNT RD
SOURLIE ROUNDABOUT
Lawthorn Plantation
Middleton

41

MILL BURN
LOCHLIBO RD
BRYCE KNOX
SPEYBURN
LINKWOOD
ABERFELDY TERR
CARDOW CRES
LITTLESTANE RISE
LITTLESTANE TERR
LONGROW GDNS
MADDINGTON GDNS
STRATHVIEW PK
LITTLESTANE ROUNDABOUT
LAWTHORN ROUNDABOUT
LAWTHORN
KAMES CT
Perceton House
Perceton Mains
Overton Farm

Girdle Toll
PERCETON ROUNDABOUT
Old Perceton
WARWICK HILL
EAST BOWHOUSE HEAD
THE PADDOCK

3

LITTLESTANE RD
MIDDLETON RD
West Bowhouse Workshops
BURNS CRES
NEWHOUSE WAY Schs
BENSLEY RISE
1 BONNYTON ROW
2 BONNYTON FOOT
3 SOUTHOOK ROW
4 NEWTONHEAD
5 BUSBIEHEAD
6 OVERTON PL
LANGMUIR WAY
LAMBERTON GDNS
DARNSHAW CL
Cheepy Neuk

40

B769
GREENSIDE
CHAPELGILL PL
WYVIS PL
LAWER PL
GRAMPIAN CT
LOMOND WAY
CRUACH CT
Annick Water
Muirhouses
Drummuir
Warwickdale

PERCETON ROW
CAPRINGSTONE BURN

2

DRUMELZIER CT
FENCEDYKE WAY
BIRKS HILL
WHITEWISP CT
WHITEHOPE GREEN
1 SHIELHOPE CT
2 GREENSIDE
3 MID RIG
1 CRAMALT CT
2 MILLFORE CT
3 BODESBECK CT
4 CROFTHEAD
5 NORTH VENNEL
6 CROFTHEAD CT
7 MOORFOOT PL
8 SOUTH VENNEL
9 KILSYTH WLK
Annick Water
Sch

Sch
CHEVIOT CT
LAMMERMUIR
BARRHILL
MOORFOOT CT
KILPATRICK CT
WINDLESTRAW
KILPATRICK PL
FINTRY TERR
FINTRY WLK
CAMPSIE AVE
KILSYTH CRES
CAMPSIE WAY
CHURCH PL
Sch
Capringstone
Sch
OVERTOUN RD
STATION DR
Sch
Springside
BANKHEAD AVE

39

DIAMOND WAY
LEWIS WYND
LEWIS RISE
MILL PL
STRONSAY CT
GIGHA WYND
PLADDA AVE
HEATHERSTANE BANK
HOPETOUN BANK
HEATHERSTANE WAY
LONGBAR AVE
CHAPMANS
CAIRNSGARROCH
SHALLOCH PL
DRAUGHT HILL
HILLDOWN PL
SHAFTO PL
HILLSHAW FOOT
Bourtreehill
Liby
KYLE AVE
GARRIER RD
STATION RD
KIRKLAND TERR
CROFT TERR
SPRINGHILL TERR

TOWERLANDS RD
BROOMLANDS
BUSHAY CT
GIGHA TERR
BARRA CRES
BARRA WYND
Dismtd Rly
SPRINGSIDE TERR
MAIN RD
CORSEHILL TERR
CRAIG VIEW
CORSE AVE
B7081

1

St KILDA CT
St KILDA BANK
Sch
Broomlands
EAST BROOMLANDS
GIGHA TERR
STATION BRAE
MAIN ST
Sch
Mon
Springside

DALMAILING AVE
MACROBERT AVE
B7081
F Sta
Acad
Cemy
Liby
TOWNFOOT
P
WOOD GR
BUTE CT
DUNDONALD RD
Sch
Dreghorn
RIVERSIDE RD
Corsehill

38

34   A   35   B   36   C

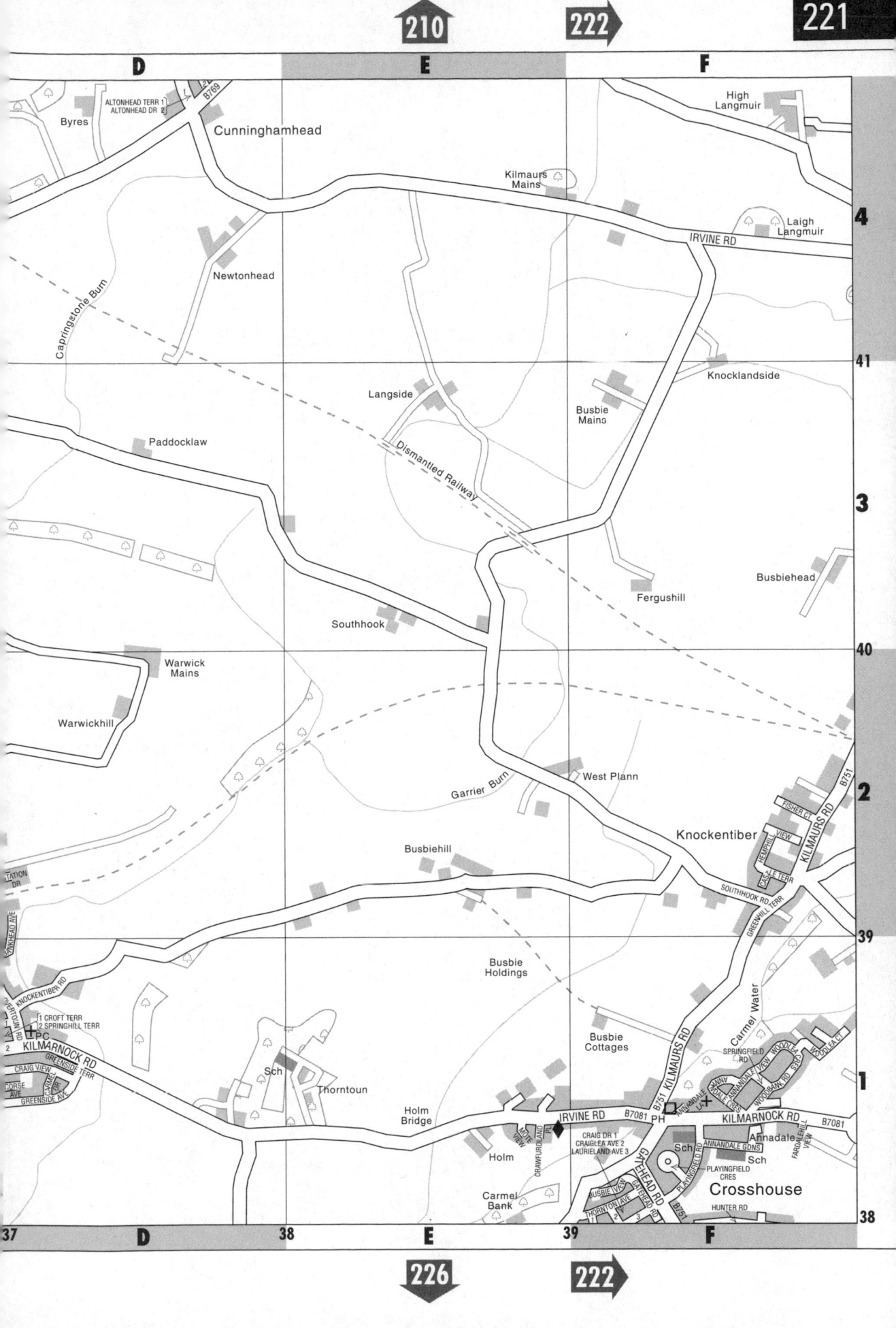

210

222

D E F

High
Langmuir

Byres
ALTONHEAD TERR 1
ALTONHEAD DR 2
B769

Cunninghamhead

Kilmaurs
Mains

Laigh
Langmuir

IRVINE RD

4

Newtonhead

Capringstone Burn

41

Langside

Knocklandside

Paddocklaw

Busbie
Mains

Dismantled Railway

3

Busbiehead

Fergushill

Southhook

40

Warwick
Mains

Warwickhill

West Plann

2

Garrier Burn

Knockentiber

B751

FISHER CT

KILMAURS RD

HEMPHILL VIEW

CASS... LE TERR

Busbiehill

SOUTHHOOK RD TERR

GREENHILL TERR

STATION
DR

39

Busbie
Holdings

Carmel Water

KNOCKENTIBER RD

NEWTON RD

1 CROFT TERR
2 SPRINGHILL TERR

PC

KILMARNOCK RD

GREENSIDE TERR

CRAIG VIEW

GORSE AVE

CAIRN...

GREENSIDE AVE

Sch

Thorntoun

Busbie
Cottages

KILMAURS RD

SPRINGFIELD
RD

CARMEL...

WOODEND...

ANNANDALE VIEW

WOODLEA CT

1

Holm
Bridge

CRAWFURDLAND PL

NOTE...

IRVINE RD

B7081

PH

KILMARNOCK RD

B7081

Holm

CRAIG DR 1
CRAIGLEA AVE 2
LAURIELAND AVE 3

GYTHEAD RD

Sch

ANNANDALE GDNS

Annandale

Sch

FARDALE...

PLAYINGFIELD
CRES

Crosshouse

Carmel
Bank

BUSBIE VIEW

THORNTON AVE

GREENAN RD

PLAYINGFIELD RD

B751

HUNTER RD

38

37 D 38 E 39 F 38

226

222

A · B · C

4

41

3

40

2

39

1

38

Habbie
Auld

WEST PARK DR
HABBIELAND RD
FOUR ACRES DR
HIGH VIALT
WEST PARK CRES
BENRIG AVE
BOYD ORR CRES
BEACHFIELD GDNS
McNAUGHT PL
EAST PARK DR
BELMONT CRES
VINE PARK AVE
VINE PARK
GLENCAIRN TERR
STANDALANE
TOWNHEAD
MAIN ST
LADESIDE RD
LADESIDE RD
ST MAURS GDNS
ST MAURS AVE
MILLHILL RD

IRVINE RD

Liby
Sch
Crofthead
CROFTHEAD RD
HAMILTON CT
YARDSIDE RD
SUNNYSIDE
TOWNEND
B751

Kilmaurs
Place

Kilmaurs

Shaw
Burn

Haghouse
Bridge

Shaw
Bridge

Bellsland

Kilmaurs Mill
Bridge

Braehead

Rowallan
Mill

Buntonhill

Buntonhill
Mount

Kilmaurs
Station

Towerhill

Ind
Est

BRAEHEAD TERR
TOWERHILL AVE
KIRKLAND GDNS
JOCKSTHORN TERR
FENWICK RD
MILL AVE
KILMARNOCK RD

Cemy

KIRKTON RD

Jocksthorn

Grassmillside

Carmel Water

CROSSHOUSE RD

Kirkland

The
Old Manse

Woodhill Burn

Altonhill

North
Woodhill

Bailiehill
Mount

South
Woodhill

GLASSOCK RD
BRINGAN RD
KIRKTON RD
GLENCRAIGS
DR
Sch

Onthank

MILLHILL TERR
NEWLANDS DR
NEWLANDS
PL
KNOCKINLAW
MOUNT
KNOCKINLAW RD
MACHRIE RD
GORDON DR
ASHDALE RD
AUCHINCLOY PL
KILMAURS RD
Knocklaw

Altonhill

WOODHILL RD
ARDGOUR RD
ARDGOUR PL
Longpark

West
Hillhead
ALTONHILL
AVE
ETTRICK PL 1
LEVEN AVE 2
Schs
FARM RD
HILLBANK
RD

B751

Greenhill

Greenhill
Smallholdings

Fardalehill

WESTERN RD

Ind
Est

Amb
Sta

Hillhead

WITCH RD

MONTGOMERY PL 1
HILLPARK DR 2
NORTHCRAIG RD 3
ORCHARD ST 4
DEAN ST 5
DEAN LA 6
FULTON'S LA 7
MORRIS LA 8
DEAN CT 9
BOYD ST 10

Hospl

SIMPSON ST
LISTER ST

Coll

B7081 KILMARNOCK RD

B7064

Bonnyton

Works

BELLEVUE GDNS 1
BONNYTON PL 2

BRODICK
SANNOX
CARMEL AVE
CARMEL
TERR

SOUTHHOOK RD

MUNRO AVE

BONNYTON RD

Bonnyton
Ind Est

NORTH
HAMILTON
PL

BURNS PREC 11
FOREGATE SQ 12
THE FOREGATE 13
THE CROSS 14
WEST GEORGE ST 15
LANGLANDS BRAE 16
JOHN DICKIE ST 17
GRANGE ST 18
WOODSTOCK PL 19

Sch

Kilmarnock
Sta

STIRLING CRES

IRVINE RD

PC

HOLLY PL 1
LOANFOOT AVE 2
GRANGE TERR 3

Annanhill
Golf Course

B7081

40 · A · 41 · B · 42 · C

D   E   F

Tannahill

Moss
Wood

Little
Mosside

Meiklewood

Dalmusternock

4

Craufurdland
Loch

Northcraig
Reservoir

Loch
Plantation

Wardknowe
Plantation

Northcraig

41

Southcraig
Holdings

Rushybog
Plantation

Craufurdland
Castle

Fenwick Water

Borland

Broombrae

Greenhead
Plantation

3

Borland
Bridge

Sch

GLASGOW RD

Craufurdland Water

Hotel

Bringan

Assloss
House

Ford

Assloss

WARDLAW RD

40

East
Wardlaw

ASSLOSS RD

Assloss
Bridge

Dean Castle
Country Park

Hillhouse

2

Dean
Castle

Dean

WESTERN RD

KNOCKINLAW RD

B7082

Grassyards
Interchange

Whinpark

Sch
FRASER WLK
DUNDAS WLK

DONALDSON RD

DEAN RD

BEANSBURN

Ford
Beansburn

GRASSYARDS RD

P

39

GILLSBURN
GDNS

Kilmarnock Water

SOUTH DEAN RD

Murray PL

Silverwood

Townholm

URQUHART
RD

DEAN ST

HARRIET RD

FORBES
WLK

New Farm
Loch

Newhouse

Willie Mair's
Brae

Acad

ARMSTRONG
RD

Sch

MORRISON
PL

GRAHAM
PL

STRAWBERRYBANK RD

P

1

Mon

MACALPINE PL

Cemy

MACKIE PL

Acad

P

MACALLISTER PL 1
MACINNES PL 2
MACINTOSH PL 3
MACDOUGALL DR 4
MACMILLAN DR 5
MACMILLAN PL 6
MACEWAN PL 7

Ralstonhill

Templetonburn

Burns
Mon & Mus

1 FULTON'S LA
2 MORRIS LA
3 UNION ST
4 SOULIS ST

Sch

KAY PARK TERR

PC

8 MACPHERSON WLK
9 MACPHERSON GDNS
10 MACDONALD GDNS
11 MACDONALD PL
12 MILTON AVE

Coll

MILTON RD

River Irvine

38

43   D   **44**   E   **45**   F

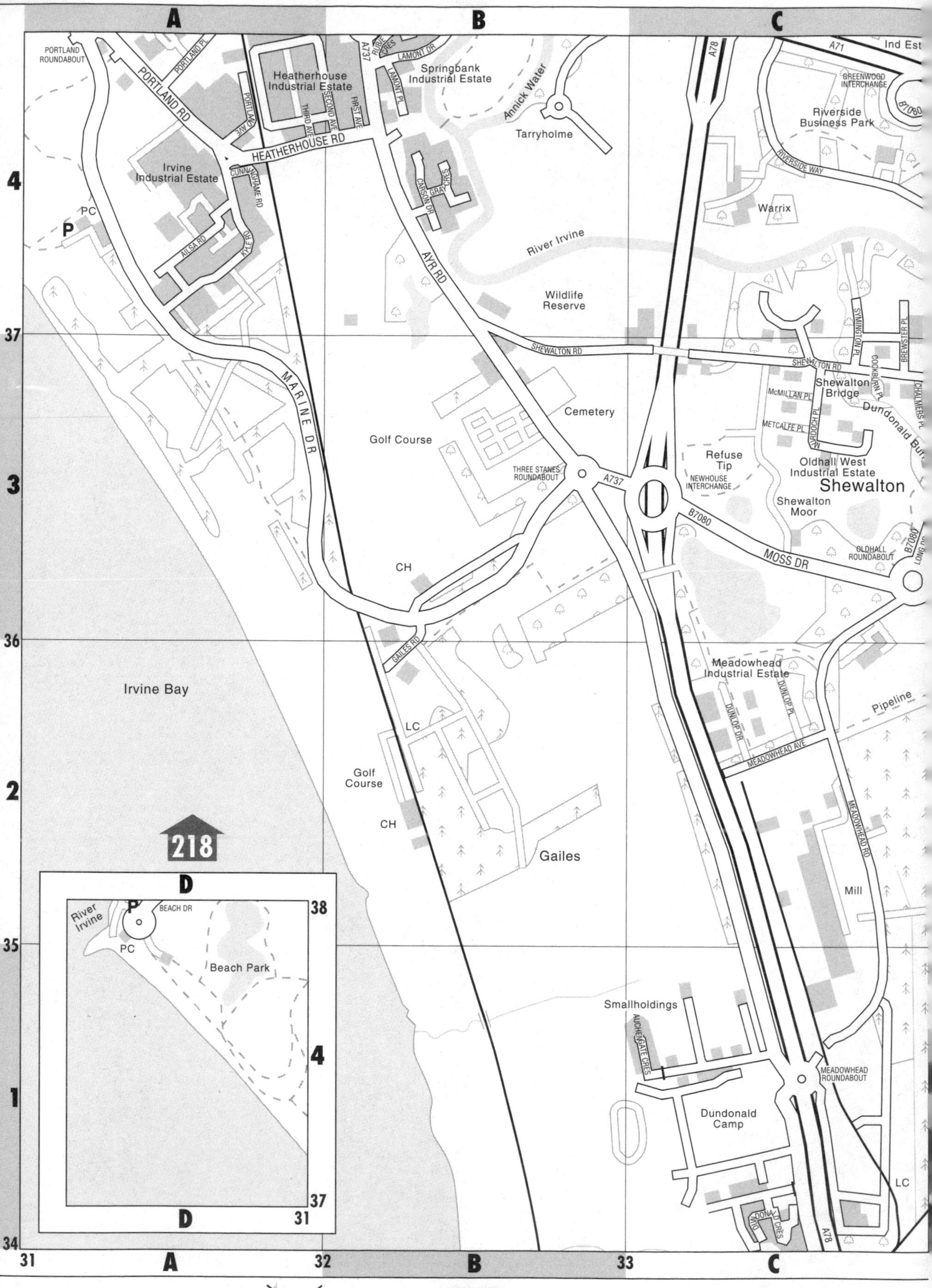

A **B** **C**

PORTLAND
ROUNDABOUT

PORTLAND RD
PORTLAND PL

A737

Heatherhouse
Industrial Estate

LAMONT DR

HUGHES CRES

Springbank
Industrial Estate

Annick Water

A71 Ind Est

GREENWOOD
INTERCHANGE

Riverside
Business Park

B7080

LAMONT PL

Tarryholme

RIVERSIDE WAY

HEATHERHOUSE RD

FIRST AVE

SECOND AVE

THIRD AVE

CONNACHRAME RD

AYR RD

A759

CARSON DR

GRAY

Irvine
Industrial Estate

PC

P

4

Warrix

River Irvine

Wildlife
Reserve

SYMINGTON PL

BREWSTER PL

COCKBURN PL

CHALMERS PL

37

MARINE DR

SHEWALTON RD

SHEWALTON RD

McMILLAN PL

MURDOCH PL

Shewalton
Bridge

Dundonald Burn

METCALFE PL

Golf Course

Cemetery

THREE STANES
ROUNDABOUT

A737

Refuse
Tip

NEWHOUSE
INTERCHANGE

Oldhall West
Industrial Estate

Shewalton

B7080

LONG DR

3

CH

B7080

Shewalton
Moor

OLDHALL
ROUNDABOUT

MOSS DR

OLDHALL
ROUNDABOUT

36

GAILES RD

Irvine Bay

Meadowhead
Industrial Estate

DUNLOP DR

DUNLOP PL

Pipeline

LC

MEADOWHEAD AVE

Golf
Course

218

CH

MEADOWHEAD RD

2

Gailes

Mill

D

P

BEACH DR

38

River
Irvine

PC

35

Beach Park

4

Smallholdings

AUCHENGATE CRES

MEADOWHEAD
ROUNDABOUT

1

Dundonald
Camp

LC

D

37

31

ALDONA CRES

A78

34

31 **A** **32** **B** **33** **C**

D   E   F

GREENWOOD INTERCHANGE

B7080

A71

CORSEHILL MOUNT

B7081 Sch

DUNLOP CRES

CAMPBELL PL

TOWNFOOT

RD TA Centre

CORSEHILL MOUNT RD

LISMORE

MONTGOMERYFIELD

THE GLEBE

GLEBE AVE

IONA WAY

SLAY CT

LISMORE WAY

TIREE

SKYE

BERTOMA

ERISKAY

JURA

HARRIS CT

MANOR

MANOR TERR

DUNDONALD RD

B7081

GLEB IRVINE

MORVILLE AVE

McLEAN DR

CORSEHILL

FORD AVE

SHARPE

B730

DUNDONALD RD

A71

CORSEHILL MOUNT ROUNDABOUT

Garrier Burn

Carmel Water

STEADMAN PL

LONG DR

RIVERSIDE WAY

Riverside Business Park

River Irvine

Holmsford Bridge

B730

Holms

Holm's Bridge

4

37

Pipeline

Works

SHEWALTON DR

GRIERS WLK

DREGHORN RD

Works

SHEWALTON RD

MAIN ST

STATION ROW

Drybridge

Girtridge

3

Pipeline

Dundonald Burn

Factory

Harperland Holdings

Ploughland Mount

Ploughland Holdings

Palmer Mount

36

Shewalton Moss

Refuse Tip

A759

2

CASTLEVIEW

B730

CASTLEVIEW

AUCHANS DR

COCHRANE DR

CASTLE DR

GILLILAND

NEWFIELD PL

STUART PL

DRYBRIDGE RD

FULLARTON AVE

Liby Sch

KILMARNOCK RD

B750

Guilliland

OLD AUCHANS VIEW

KILWOOD CRES

OATS PL

KANKNOLL

KINCAID DR

WILSON PL

Park

VERNON PL

PCs

WINEHOUSE YETT

MAIN ST

BRUCE

WALLACE AVE

RICHMOND TERR

MARY DR

WATT PL

35

Auchans

Beech Wood

Parkthorn

Dundonald Burn

Dundonald

Inn

Old Bank

TARBOLTON RD

AUCHESTON CT

B730

1

A759

Hillhouse Quarry (Whinstone)

34

D   E   F

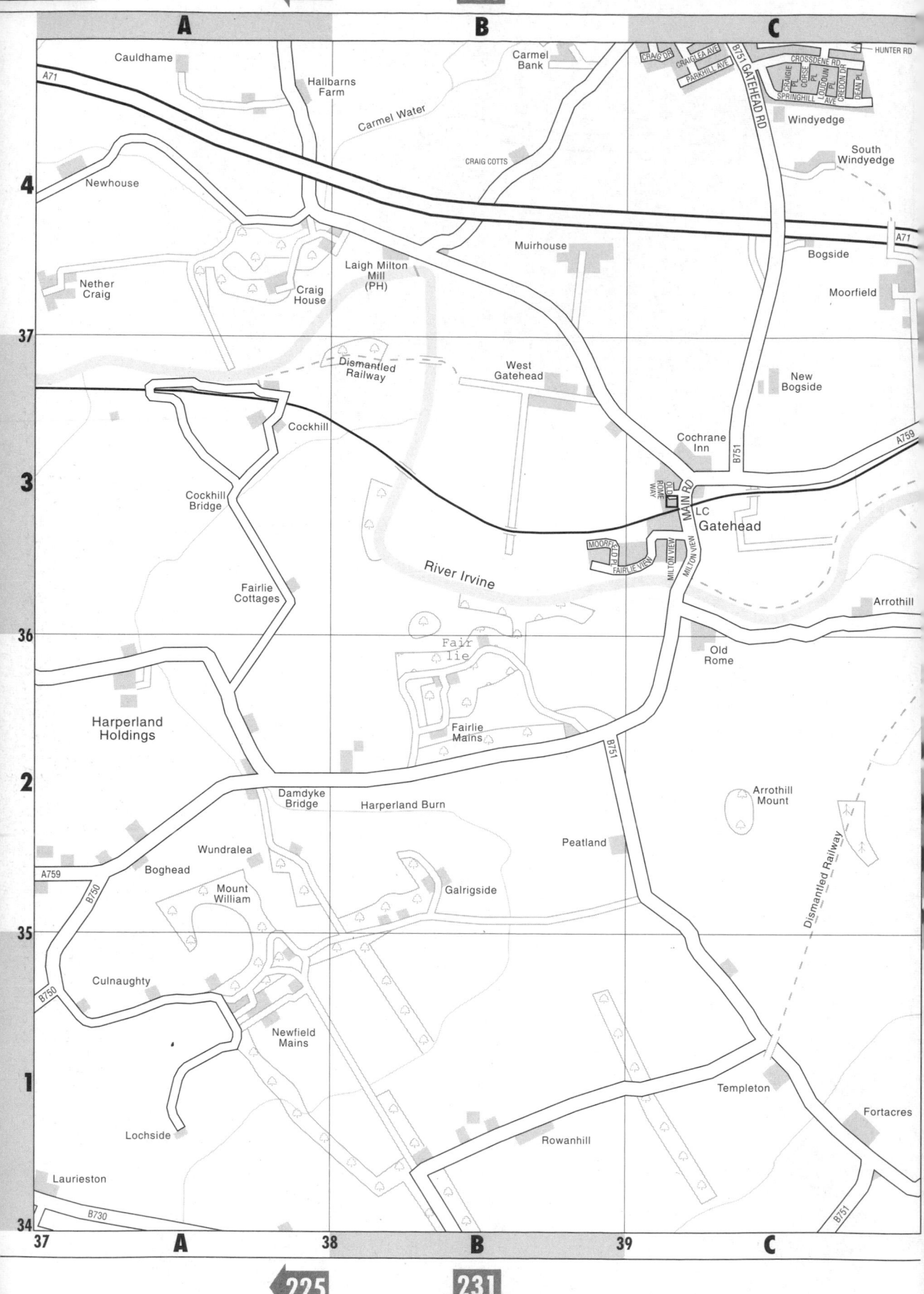

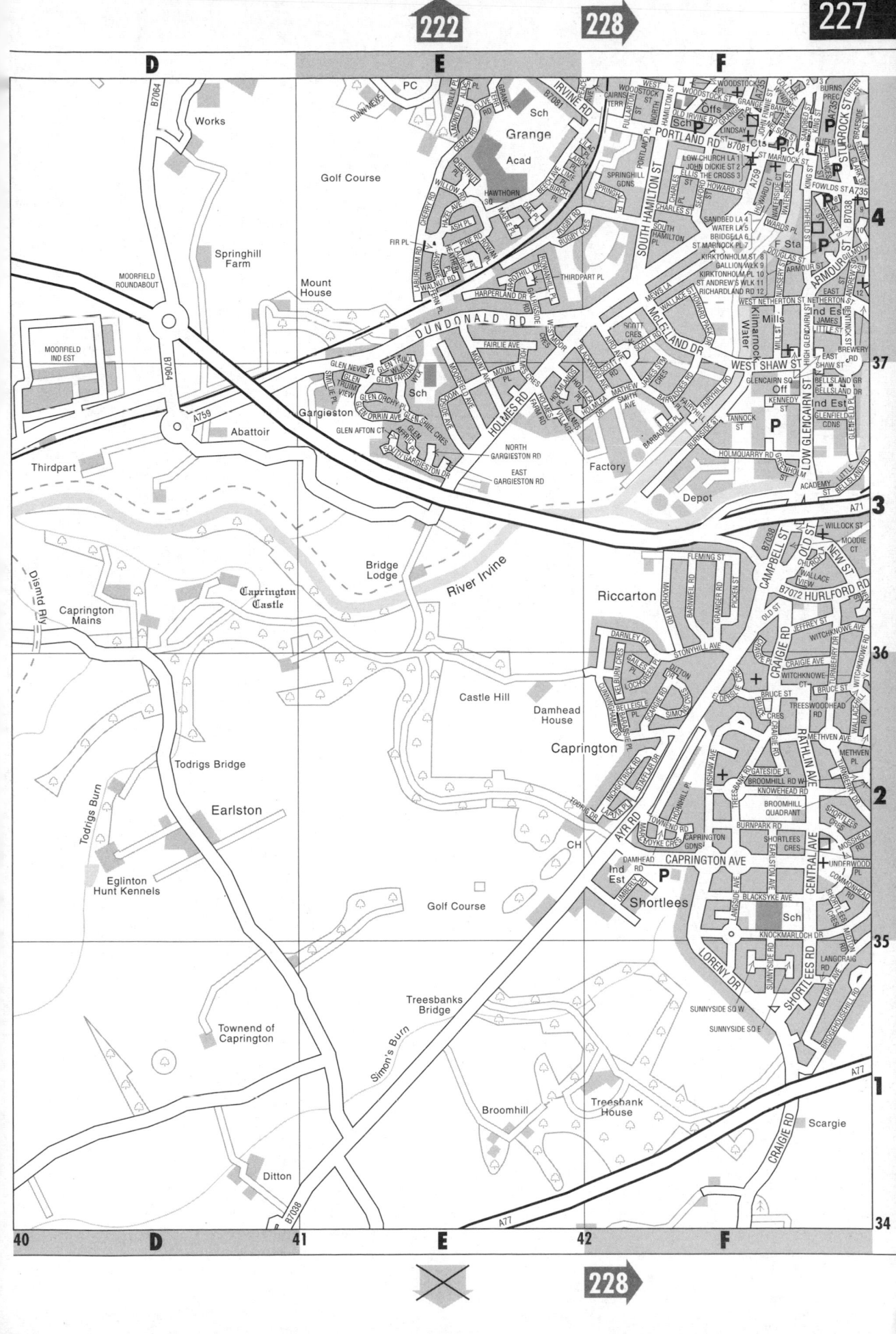

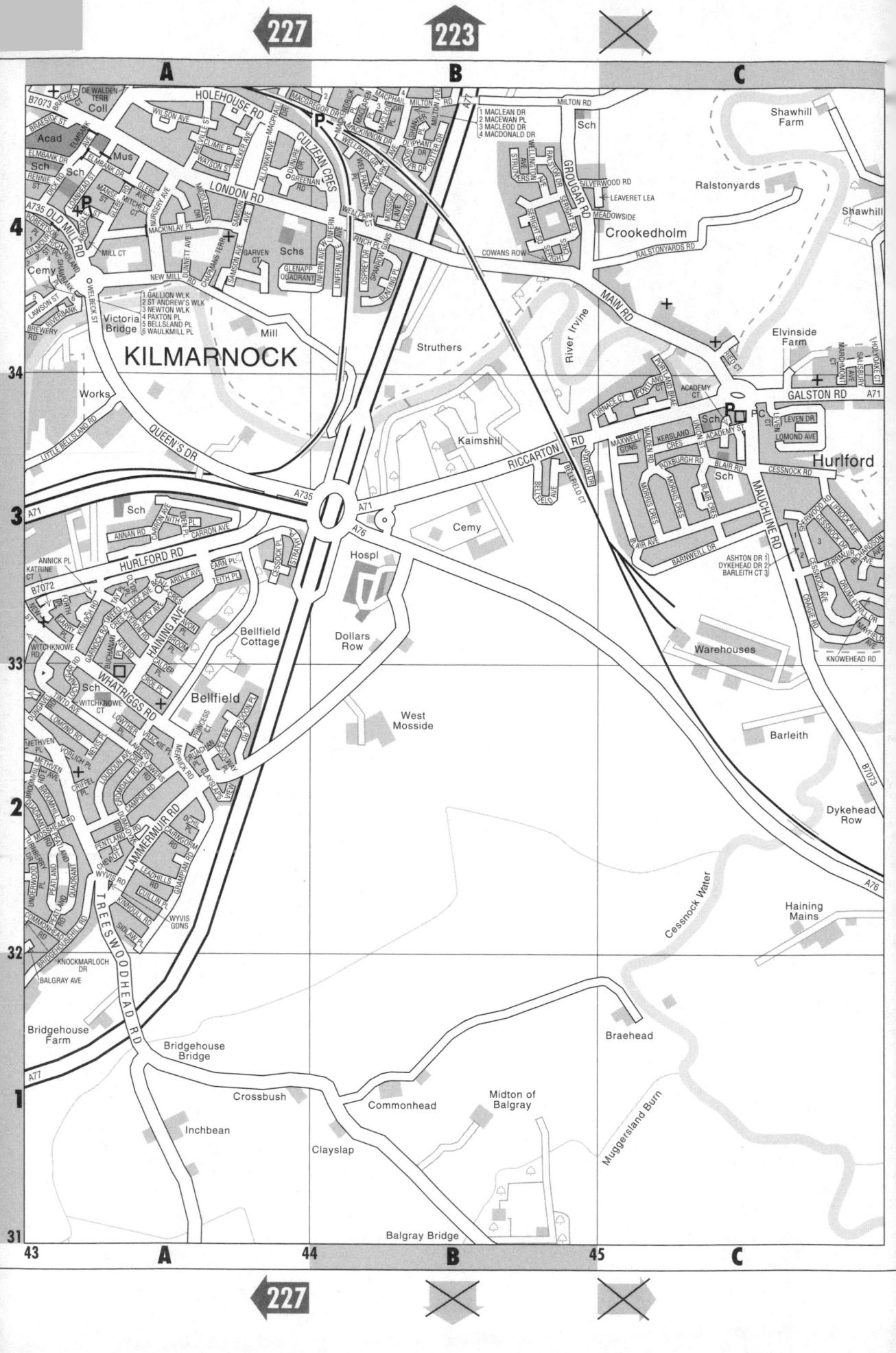

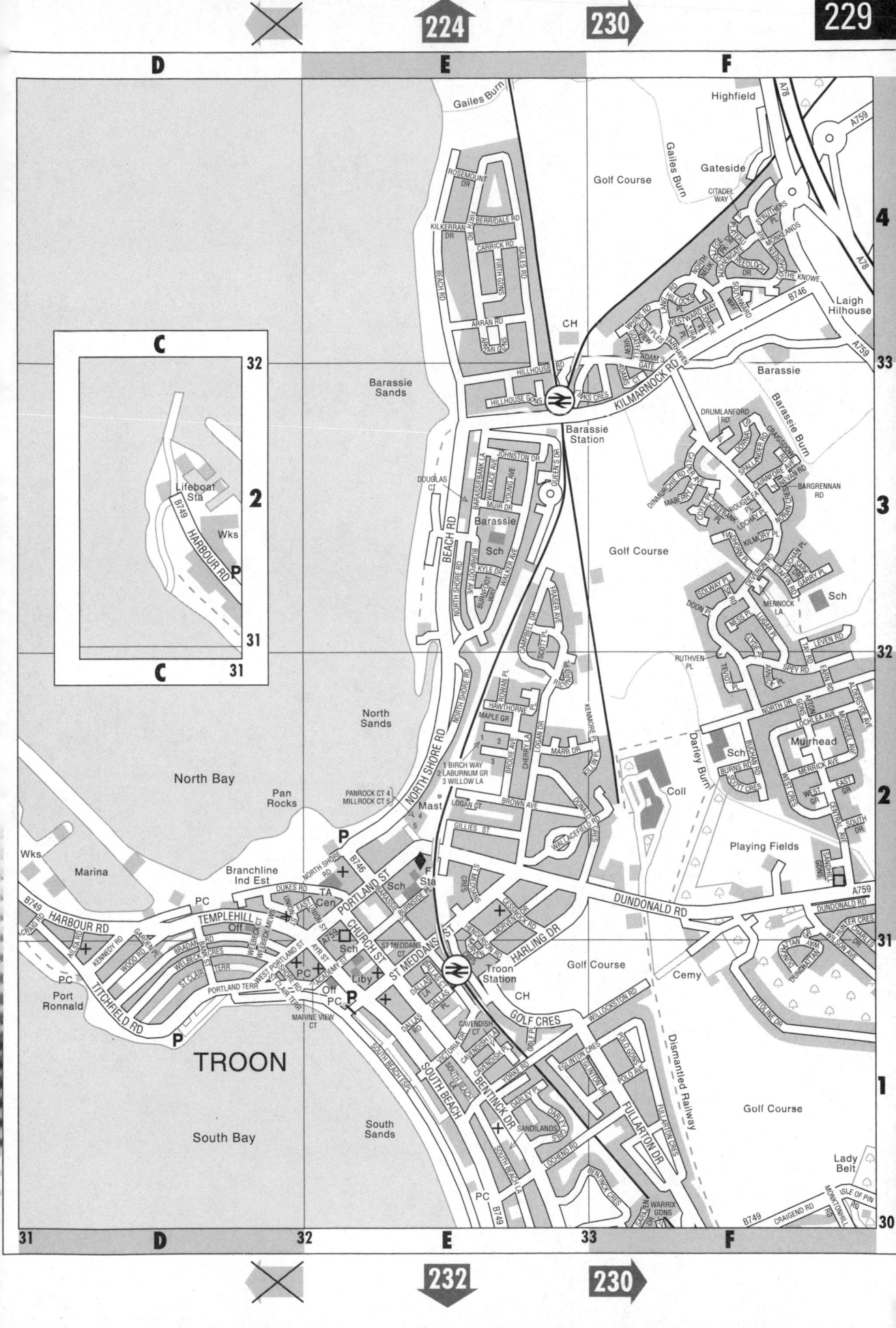

D

E

F

Highfield

Gailes Burn

Golf Course

Gailes Burn

Gateside

CITADEL WAY

4

A759

A78

A78

Laigh Hilhouse

B746

A759

ROSEMOUNT DR

KILKERRAN DR

BERRIDALE RD

FIRTH RD

CARRICK RD

GAILES RD

BEACH RD

ARRAN RD

ARRAN GV

CH

HILLHOUSE RD

HILLHOUSE GDNS

WKS CRES

KILMARNOCK RD

Barassie

33

Barassie Sands

Barassie Station

DRUMLANFORD RD

Barassie Burn

BARGRENNAN RD

C

32

DOUGLAS CT

JOHNSTON DR

WALLACE AVE

YOUNG AVE

MUIR DR

BARASSIEBANK LA

BEACH RD

NORTH SHORE RD

Barassie Sch

KYLE DR

WALKER DR

BURNSIDE WAY

CALDER AVE

MABERRY PL

DINMURCHIE RD

COLCREEBANK PL

DOUGHEAT DR

LOCHWAY PL

KILMORY PL

Sch

Lifeboat Sta

B749

HARBOUR RD

Wks

P

2

FRASER AVE

CAMPBELL DR

SCOTT PL

DOON PL

NESS PL

TAY PL

PEDEN PL

STIRLING PL

GARRY PL

Sch

MENNOCK LA

C

31

RUTHVEN PL

TEVIOT PL

SPEY RD

EARN RD

LEVEN RD

31

North Sands

ROWAN PL

HAWTHORNE

MAPLE GR

BROOM PL

CHERRY LA

LOGAN DR

MARR DR

KENMORE PL

KILN PL

Coll

North Drive

ASHGROVE

North Bay

Pan Rocks

PANROCK CT 4
MILLROCK CT 5

NORTH SHORE RD

1 BIRCH WAY
2 LABURNUM GR
3 WILLOW LA

LOGAN CT

BROWN AVE

GILLIES ST

WALLACEFIELD RD

DONALD TERR

Coll

DARLEY BURN

Sch

BURNS RD

SCOTT CRES

MERRICK AVE

Muirhead

LOCHLEA AVE

MOSSGIEL AVE

WEST CRES

WEST GR

EAST GR

CENTRAL AVE

SOUTH DR

2

Mast

Playing Fields

A759

Wks

Marina

Branchline Ind Est

PC

NORTH SHORE RD

B746

TA Cen

PORTLAND ST

Sch

F Sta

ST MEDDANS CRES

KELBURNE DR

MORVEN DR

RESINGER CT

HARLING DR

DUNDONALD RD

DUNDONALD RD

WINTER CRES

WILSON AVE

31

B749

HARBOUR RD

KENNEDY RD

DUKES RD

BRADAN CRES

WELBECK CRES

WELBECK MEWS

BIRCK MEWS

UNION ST

EAST RD

ST CLAIR

PORTLAND TERR

CLAIR TERR

TEMPLEHILL

Off

A759

AYR ST

ACADEMY ST

Sch

Liby

Off

PC

P

ST MEDDANS ST

DALLAS

DALLAS RD

CH

Troon Station

Golf Course

Cemy

RAYTAN AVM

DUNCHATTAN

31

PC

Port Ronnald

TITCHFIELD RD

WOOD RD

ALSA RD

PC

P

MARINE VIEW CT

CAVENDISH CT

CAVENDISH PL

GOLF CRES

WILLOCKSTON RD

Dismantled Railway

1

TROON

SOUTH BEACH ST

BENTINCK DR

VICTORIA DR

DARLEY PL

YORKE RD

CAVENDISH

SANDILANDS

EGLINTON CRES

POLO AVE

POLO GV

OTTOLINE DR

FULLARTON DR

Golf Course

South Bay

South Sands

SOUTH BEACH

B749

LOCHEND RD

BENTINCK CRES

SANDILANDS

DARLEY

POLO PL

FULLARTON CRES

Lady Belt

ISLE OF PIN

MONKTONHILL RD

B749

CRAIGEND RD

WARRIX GDNS

SARATH DR

30

D

E

F

4

33

3

32

2

31

1

30

Hillhouse Quarry

Hillhouse

Chapel Hill

Merkland Loch

Hallyards Quarry

Hallyards

Dundonald Burn

Highlees

Highlees Mount

Works

Aught Wood

Collenan Smallholdings

Wardlaw Hill

Harpercroft

• Mast

Works

Highgrove House

Clevance

Langholm

Old Loans Rd
SEAVIEW TERR
COLLENAN AVE
MAIN ST
CROSSBURN DR
CROSSBURN TERR
PH
CROSSBURN LA
BEECH RD
STABLE WYND
PADDOCK
HALL LA
CRAIKSLAND PL
Loans
KYLE CRES
TROON RD
FULLARTON PL
TROON RD
B746
Crossburn

Clevance Cottage

Craiksland

Corraith

Wester Croft

A759 DUNDONALD RD

HUNTERS WYND
CHARLES DR
LADY MARGARET LA
BALCOMIE CRES
WILSON AVE
COTTOLINE DR

Darley Burn

B746

Southside

Southside Cottages

High Wexford

Wexford Cottage

Darley Plantation

Golf Course

PC

Lady Belt

Crosbie House

ISLE OF PIN RD

FULLARTON CLYD

Fairlees

B746

A78

Rumbling Burn

KERRIX RD

Crookside

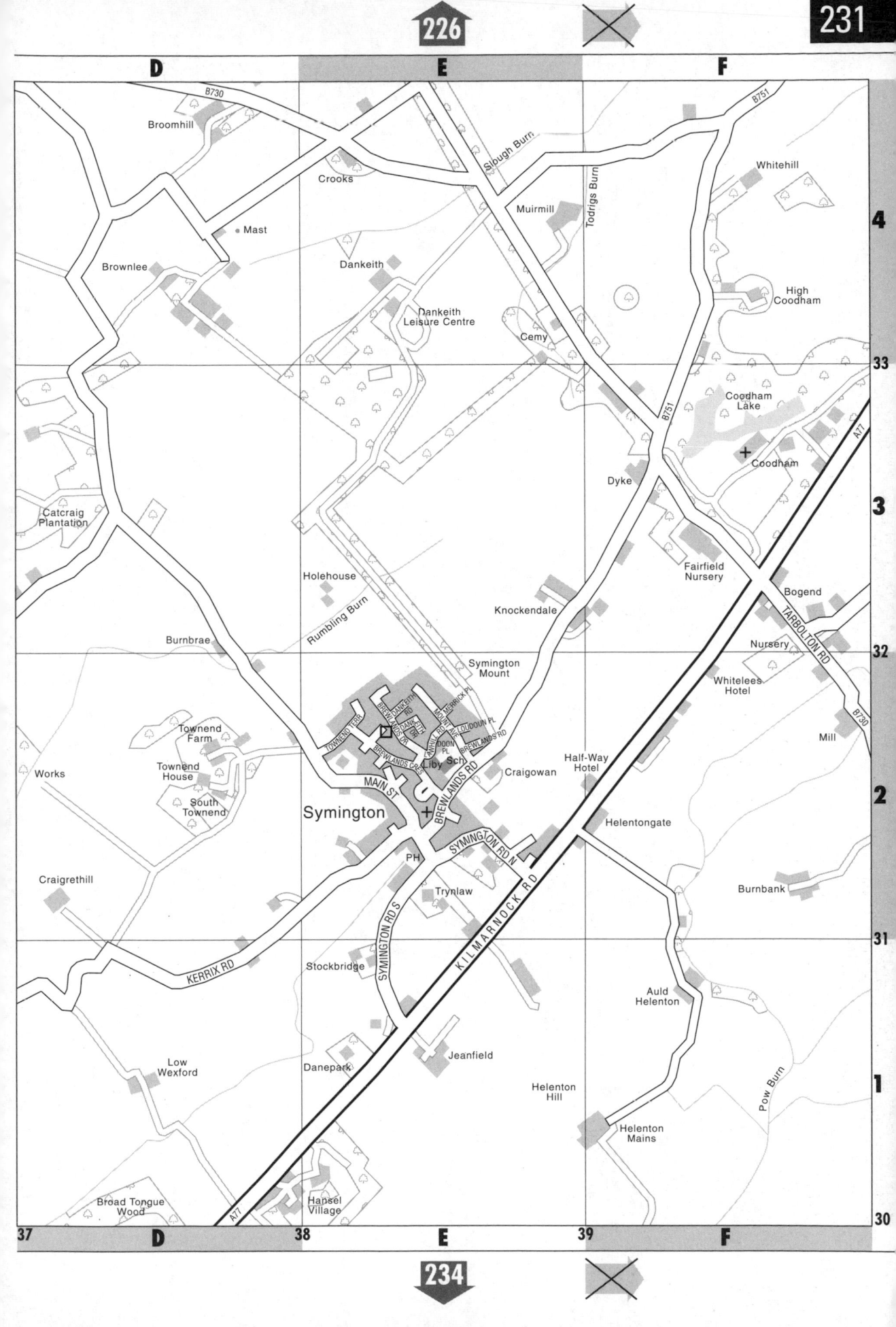

229

	A	B	C

SOUTH BEACH ESPL
B749 SOUTH BEACH
SOUTH BEACH CT
BENTINCK DR
BENTINCK CRES
SARAZEN DR
CRAIGEND RD
FULLARTON DR
Dismtd Rly
B749
B749
MONKTONHILL RD
SOUTHWOOD RD
B749

CH
CH
Hotel
Golf Course
Hotel
Golf Course
CROSBIE RD

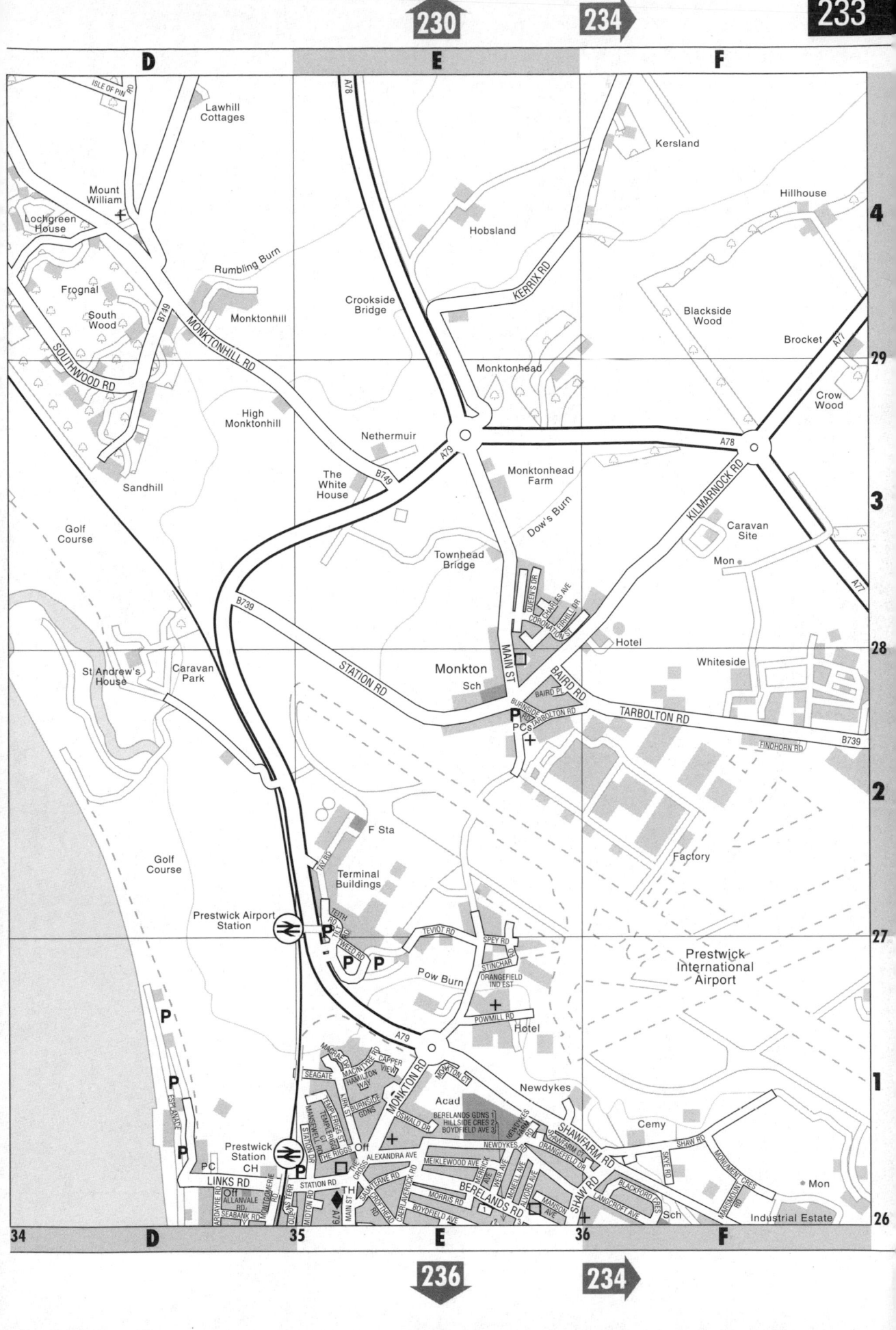

D
E
F

ISLE OF PIN RD

Lawhill
Cottages

A78

Kersland

Mount
William

Hillhouse

Lochgreen
House

4

Frognal

Rumbling Burn

Hobsland

KERRIX RD

Blackside
Wood

Brocket

A77

South
Wood

Monktonhill

Crookside
Bridge

B719

MONKTONHILL RD

29

SOUTHWOOD RD

Monktonhead

High
Monktonhill

Nethermuir

Crow
Wood

A78

A79

B749

KILMARNOCK RD

Sandhill

Golf
Course

The
White
House

Monktonhead
Farm

Dow's Burn

3

Caravan
Site

Mon

B739

Townhead
Bridge

QUEEN'S DR

CHARLES AVE

FIRHILL DR

CORONATION ST

Hotel

28

St Andrew's
House

Caravan
Park

STATION RD

Monkton
Sch

MAIN ST

BAIRD RD

Whiteside

Baird Pl

P

TARBOLTON RD

Golf
Course

BURNSIDE

PC
TARBOLTON RD

FINDHORN RD

B739

2

F Sta

TAY RD

Factory

Terminal
Buildings

TEVIOT RD

SPEY RD

Prestwick
International
Airport

Prestwick Airport
Station

TEITH RD

P

WEED RD

P
P

STINCHAR

Pow Burn

ORANGEFIELD
IND EST

27

P

Hotel

POWMILL RD

A79

P

Newdykes

1

MACRAE RD

MAGIN TREE RD

CAPPER

SEAGATE

HAMILTON WAY

MONKTON RD

Acad

SHAWFARM RD

Cemy

SHAW RD

BERELANDS GDNS 1
HILLSIDE CRES 2
BOYDFIELD AVE 3

P

NEWDYKES

SHAWFARM CT

LINK ST

BURNSIDE GDNS

OSWALD DR

ORANGEFIELD DR

SKYE RD

MONUMENT CRES

P

PC

Prestwick Station

CH

TEMPLE RIGGS

MANSEWELL RD

THE RIGGS

CROSS

Alexandra Ave

CAERNTERIE RD

MEIKLEWOOD AVE

ALVORD AVE

WHEAT LANE

Mon

STATION RD

LINKS RD

ARDAYRE RD

ESPLANADE

ALLANVALE RD

SEABANK RD

MONTGOMERIE

BOYDFIELD AVE

OLD ST TERR

MID ST

MAIN ST

STATION RD

A79

Off

TH

Morris RD

BERELANDS RD

MANSON AVE

LANGCROFT AVE

MASSONMUIR

Blackford CRES

Sch

Industrial Estate

26

34
D
35
E
36
F

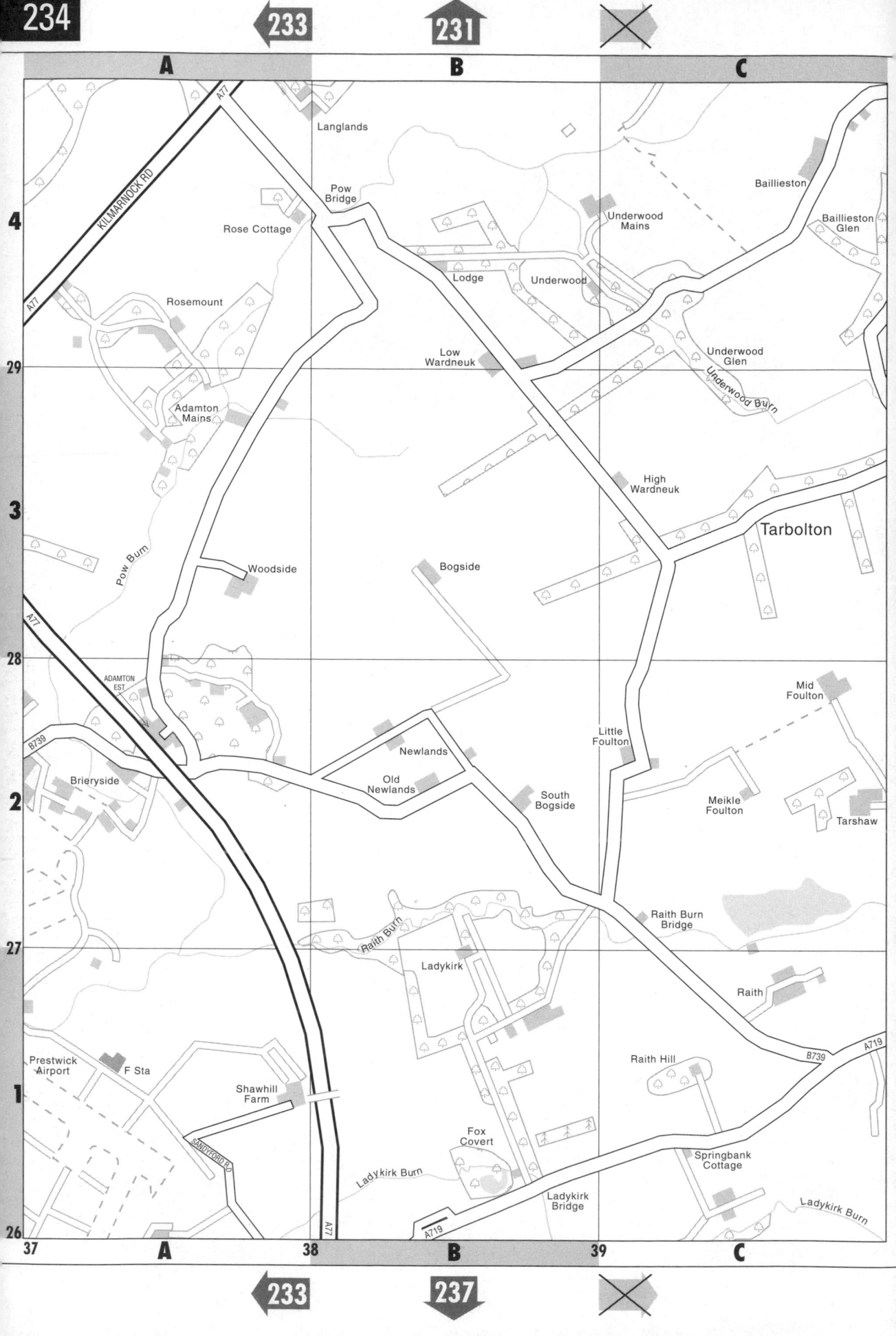

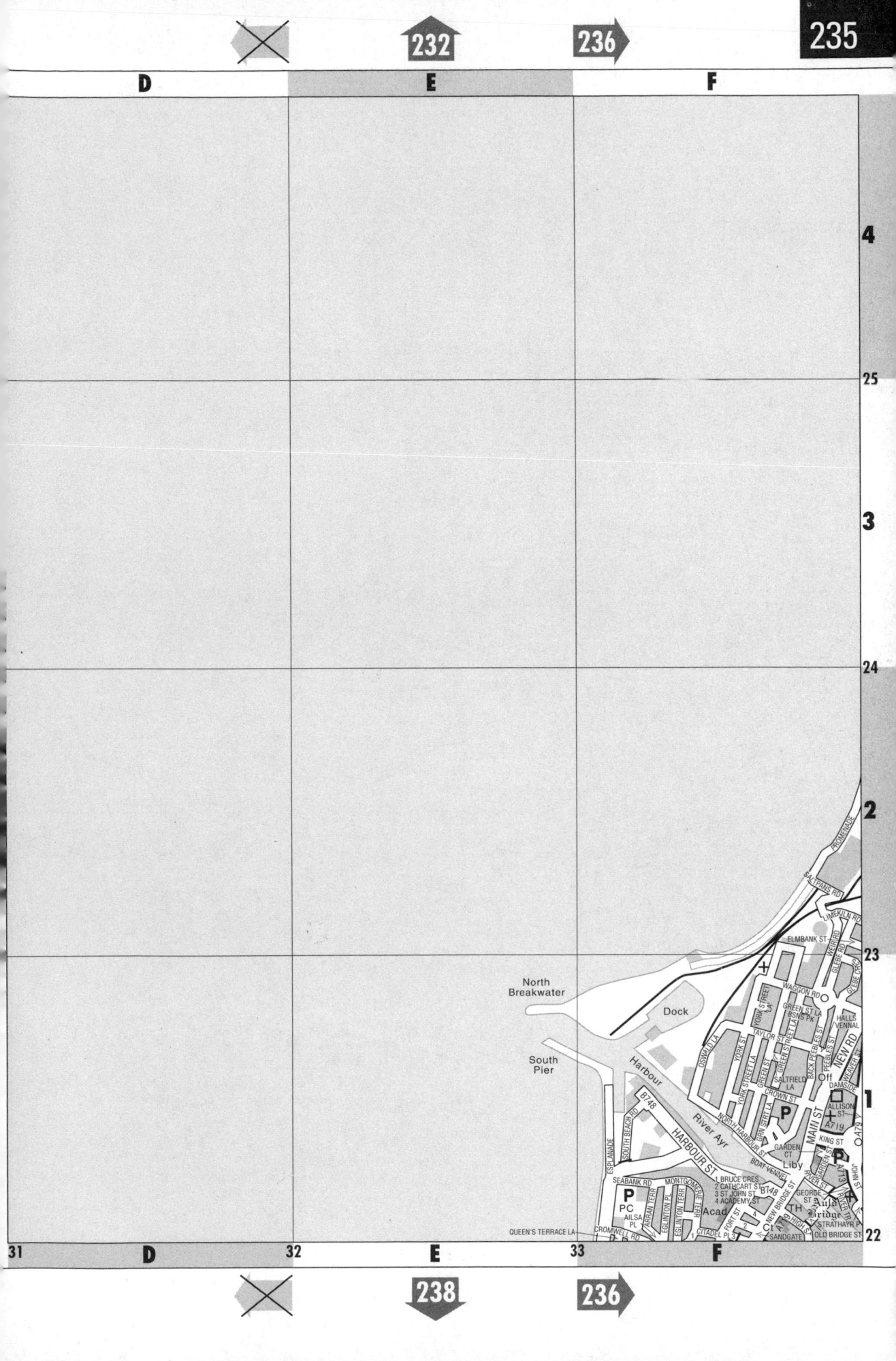

4

25

3

24

2

SALTPANS RD

PROMENADE

LIMEKILN RD

ELMBANK ST

23

North
Breakwater

GLEBE RD

WAGGON RD

Dock

GREEN ST LA

BSNS PK

HALLS
VENNAL

NEW RD

YORK STREET

TAYLOR

GREEN ST LA

OSWALD LA

YORK ST

PEEBLES ST

BACK PEEBLES ST

GREEN STREET LA

South
Pier

SALTFIELD
LA

Harbour

CROWN ST

Off

DAMSIDE

ALLISON
ST

1

RIVER TERR

SOUTH BEACH RD

B748

River Ayr

NORTH HARBOUR ST

P

GARDEN
CT

KING ST

MAIN ST

WALKER RD

P

A713

A719

Liby

ESPLANADE

SEABANK RD

HARBOUR ST

BOAT VENNEL

1 BRUCE CRES
2 CATHCART ST
3 ST JOHN ST
4 ACADEMY ST

B748

NEW BRIDGE ST

GEORGE

TH

A719

HIGH

Auld
Bridge

STRATHAYR

MONTGOMERIE TERR

Acad

RIVER ST

P

PC

AILSA
PL

ARRAN TERR

EGLINTON PL

EGLINTON TERR

FORT ST

SANDGATE

OLD BRIDGE ST

QUEEN'S TERRACE LA

CROMWELL RD

CITADEL PL

22

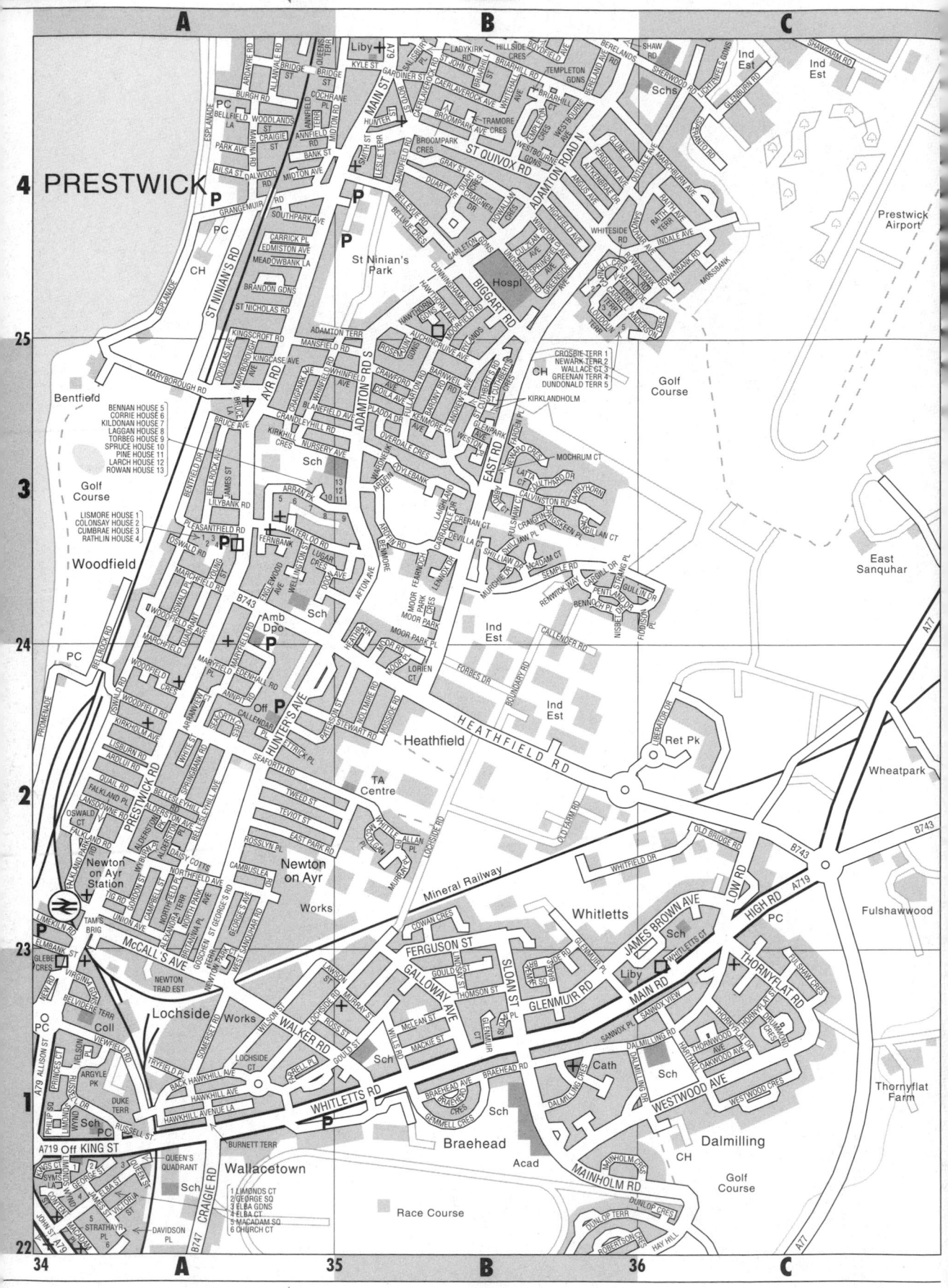

PRESTWICK

Bentfield

BENNAN HOUSE 5
CORRIE HOUSE 6
KILDONAN HOUSE 7
LAGGAN HOUSE 8
TORBEG HOUSE 9
SPRUCE HOUSE 10
PINE HOUSE 11
LARCH HOUSE 12
ROWAN HOUSE 13

Golf Course

LISMORE HOUSE 1
COLONSAY HOUSE 2
CUMBRAE HOUSE 3
RATHLIN HOUSE 4

Woodfield

CROSBIE TERR 1
NEWARK TERR 2
WALLACE CT 3
GREENAN TERR 4
DUNDONALD TERR 5

Golf Course

Prestwick
Airport

East
Sanquhar

Heathfield

Ind Est

Ind Est

Ret Pk

Wheatpark

Fulshawwood

Newton
on Ayr
Station

Newton
on Ayr

TA
Centre

Works

Mineral Railway

Whitletts

Lochside

Works

Braehead

Acad

Dalmilling

Golf
Course

Thornyflat
Farm

Wallacetown

1 LIMONDS CT
2 GEORGE SQ
3 ELBA GDNS
4 ELBA CT
5 MACADAM SQ
6 CHURCH CT

Race Course

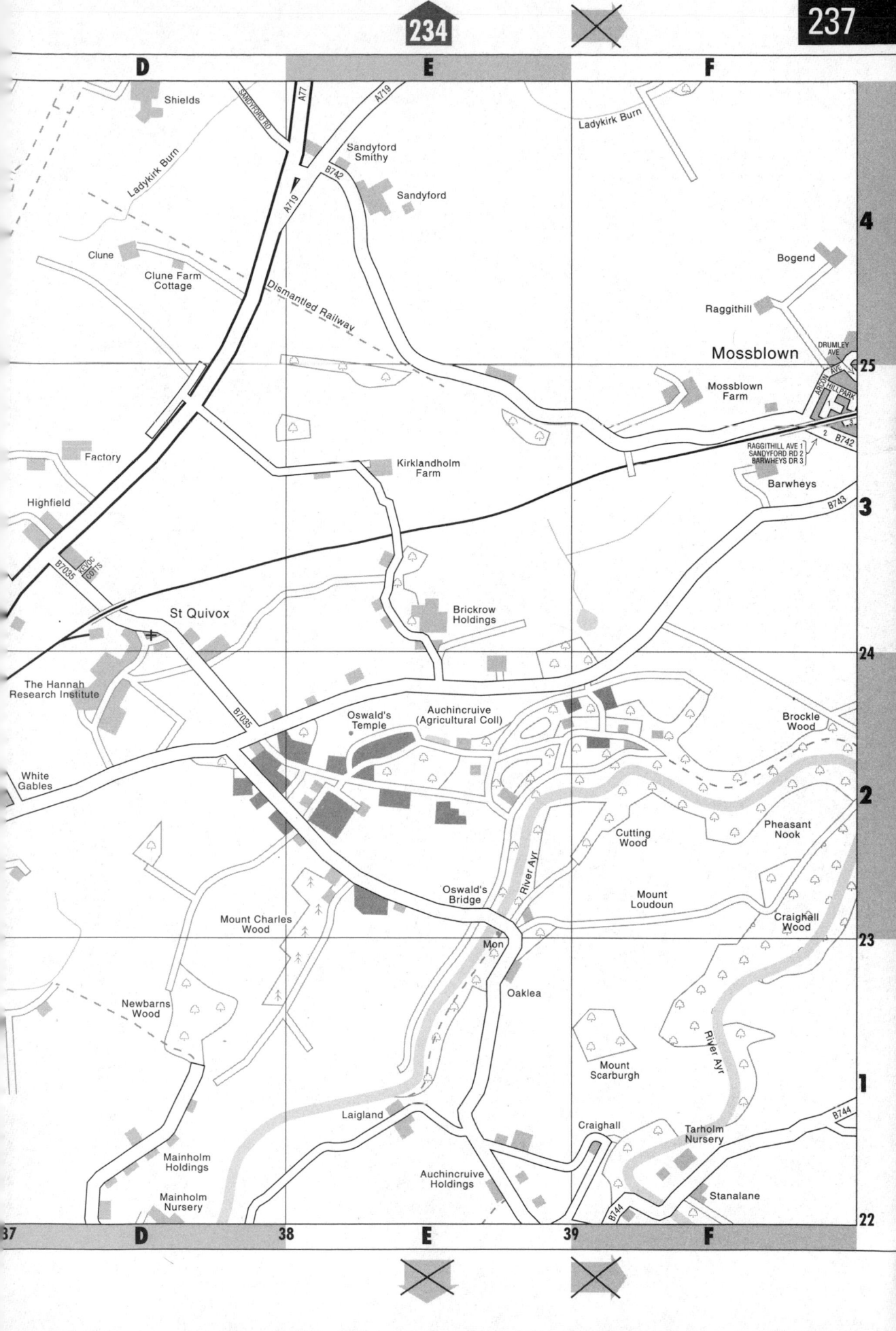

D   E   F

Shields

Ladykirk Burn

Sandyford
Smithy

Sandyford

Ladykirk Burn

4

Clune

Clune Farm
Cottage

Dismantled Railway

Bogend

Raggithill

DRUMLEY AVE

Mossblown

25

Mossblown
Farm

ARCON AVE

MILL PARK

Factory

Kirklandholm
Farm

RAGGITHILL AVE 1
SANDYFORD RD 2
BARWHEYS DR 3

Barwheys

B742

Highfield

KIRKO'
GOTTS

B7035

Brickrow
Holdings

B7035

St Quivox

3

B743

The Hannah
Research Institute

Oswald's
Temple

Auchincruive
(Agricultural Coll)

Brockle
Wood

24

White
Gables

Cutting
Wood

Pheasant
Nook

2

River Ayr

Mount
Loudoun

Craighall
Wood

Mount Charles
Wood

Oswald's
Bridge

Mon

Oaklea

23

Newbarns
Wood

Mount
Scarburgh

River Ayr

Laigland

Craighall

Tarholm
Nursery

B744

1

Mainholm
Holdings

Auchincruive
Holdings

Stanalane

Mainholm
Nursery

B744

22

A | B | C

QUEEN'S TERRACE LA 1
CROMWELL RD 2
AILSA PL 3
BRUCE CRES 4
DOUGLAS LA 5
DOUGLAS ST 6
HOPE ST 7
LORNE ARC 8
BLACKFRIARS WLK 9
KYLE CTR 10
BARNS TERRACE LA 11
DALBLAIR ARC 12

QUEEN'S TERR
CHARLOTTE ST
CHRLTTE ST LA
BATH PL
MEWS LA
WELLINGTON
SQ
Off
Off
NWMR KT 1
SANDGATE
KIRK PORT
FORT ST
A719
Off
PC
PC
Off
Off
NILE CT
HIGH ST
MILL WYND
BOSWELL ST
ARTHUR ST
CARRICK ST
SANDGATE

Low Green
ESPLANADE
FAIRFIELD PK
CRAIGWEIL PL
PC
PC
Sch
WELLINGTON LA
PARK TERR
ALLOWAY PK
FAIRFIELD RD
KILLOCH PL 13
BURNS STATUE SQ 14
SMITH ST 15
PARKHOUSE ST 16
SHIELING PK
ALLOWAY PL
BARNS ST
BARNS ST LA
BARNS PK
ALLOWAY
UNION ARC 12
ALLOWAY ST
KYLE'S
Off
DALBLAIR RD
MILLER RD
A70
PARK CIRCUS LA
PARK CIR
BERESFORD TERR
BEVERLEY CT
Off
A79
CARRICK ST LA
10

AYR

SAVOY PK
WHEATFIELD RD
CRAIGWEIL PL
SAVOY CT
BELLEVUE ST
BELLEVUE CRES
BELLEVUE LA
Sch
BELLEVUE RD
MRCHMNT RD
MARCHMONT
DORNOCH PK
SOUTH LODGE CT
SPRINGVALE RD
SPRINGVALE PK
BOWMAN RD
CARRICK RD
BALLANTINE DR

BLACKBURN DR
BLACKBURN RD
WESTFIELD RD
BENTFIELD AVE
CLARKE AVE
RONALDSHAW PK
WATTFIELD RD
SOUTHPARK RD
AIRLIE CT
VICTORIA PK
MIDTON RD
CARRICK AVE
CARRICK GDNS
BROOMFIELD RD
BROOMFIELD GDN
CHALMERS RD
CURTECAN PL
ST LEONARD'S RD
HARTFIELD RD
A79
Off
B7024

Sch

P

SEAFIELD RD
SEAFIELD CRES
SEAFIELD DR
ARROL PK
Seafield

RACECOURSE VIEW
ROSSBANK CRES
CORSEHILL RD
CORSEHILL PL
BELLEVALE QUADRANT
BELLEVALE PK
BELLEVALE AVE
ROSSLAND AVE

Playing Fields

CARWINSHOCH VIEW
AUCHENTYRE
AUCHENDRAIN

CHAPEL PARK RD

Golf Course
DOONFOOT RD
EWENFIELD RD
EWENFIELD AVE
EWENFIELD GDNS
WESTFIELD

Cunning Park
ABERCROMBY DR
CRAIGSHIELD
GEARHOLM RD
Belleisle Bridge
Slaphouse Burn
Slaphouse
Slaphouse Bridge

LONGBANK DR
LONGLANDS PK
KNOLL PK

Longhill Point
PC
P
Belleisle
Hotel
MONUMENT RD
Rozelle Park

CASTLE WLK
GREENAN PL
SCAUR O' DOON RD
NORTHCOUR
CUNNING PARK DR
BRUCE'S WELL RD
Belleisle Park
ROZELLE

P

GREENAN RD
Sch
LOCHPARK
GREENAN CRES
Rozelle PC
ST VINCENT CRES

Greenan
GREENAN GR
GREENAN PK
GREENAN WAY
ABBOTS WAY
Golf Course
GREENFIELD AVE
WRIGHTFIELD
ST VINCENT

ABBOTS CRES
ABBOTS WAY
KILBRANDON WAY
EARLS WAY
KNOWEHOLM
Nursery
Mill
MOOR
CHARLES CRES
STRATHDOON PL
Mus
BURNESS AVE
CARRICK
BURNS
CLOCHRANHILL
WELLPARK

High Greenan
Burton Smithy
DUNURE RD
SHALLOCH PK
Doonfoot
River Doon
Doonbank Farm
AIRLIE CRES
GREENFIELD AVE
CAMBUSDOON DR
ALLOWAY
The LOANING
WOODEND
CARSELOCH RD

CROSSBURN
BROWNCARRICK DR
LOCHBRAE PL
GLENMONT PL
NEWARK CRES
CORSBIE RD
AIRY RD
CORSEMORE DR
STRATHFIELD PK
GLENALLA CRES
BALMICHAEL PK
LAMFORD DR
CRAIGSTEWART CRES
POURTMARK AVE
LONGHILL AVE
Alloway
DOONHOLM PL
Sch
Liby
UPPER CROFTS
THE LOANING
WOODEND RD

Dismantled Railway
A719
B7024
Heritage Cen
MURDOCH'S LONE
P
Dismtd Rly
River Doon
DOONHOLM RD
LAIGH MOUNT

31 | 32 | 33

A | B | C

EXPLANATION OF THE STREET INDEX REFERENCE SYSTEM

Street names are listed alphabetically and show the locality, the page number and a reference to the square in which the name falls on the map page.

Example: Canal St. Pais..113 E2

Canal St   This is the full street name, which may have been abbreviated on the map.

Pais   This is the abbreviation for the town, village or locality in which the street falls.

113   This is the page number of the map on which the street name appears.

E2   The letter and figure indicate the square on the map in which the centre of the street falls..The square can be found at the junction of the vertical column carrying the appropriate letter and the horizontal row carrying the appropriate figure.

ABBREVIATIONS USED IN THE INDEX
Road Names

Approach	App	Green	Gn
Arcade	Arc	Grove	Gr
Avenue	Ave	Heights	Hts
Boulevard	Bvd	Industrial Estate	Ind Est
Buildings	Bldgs	Junction	Junc
Business Park	Bsns Pk	Lane	La
Business Centre	Bsns Ctr	North	N
Broadway	Bwy	Orchard	Orch
Causeway	Cswy	Parade	Par
Centre	Ctr	Park	Pk
Circle	Circ	Passage	Pas
Circus	Cir	Place	Pl
Close	Cl	Precinct	Prec
Common	Comm	Promenade	Prom
Corner	Cnr	Retail Park	Ret Pk
Cottages	Cotts	Road	Rd
Court	Ct	South	S
Courtyard	Ctyd	Square	Sq
Crescent	Cres	Stairs	Strs
Drive	Dr	Steps	Stps
Drove	Dro	Street,Saint	St
East	E	Terrace	Terr
Embankment	Emb	Trading Estate	Trad Est
Esplanade	Espl	Walk	Wlk
Estate	Est	West	W
Gardens	Gdns	Yard	Yd

Key to abbreviations of Town, Village and Rural locality names used in the index of street names.

Locality	Abbr	Page	Grid
Addiewell	Add	168	C2
Airdrie	Aird	123	D4
Airth	Air	14	B2
Alexandria	Alex	27	E3
Allanton	Alla	167	D4
Alloa	All	10	B3
Alva	Alva	5	D3
Arden	Arden	18	B3
Ardrossan	Ard	205	D1
Armadale	Arm	107	F4
Ashgill	Ash	199	F4
Auldhouse	Auld	180	B1
Avonbridge	Avon	87	F4
Ayr	Ayr	238	C2
Banknock	Bank	38	C2
Bannockburn	Bann	7	F1
Barrhead	Barr	134	C1
Bearsden	Bear	75	F3
Beith	Beith	150	A1
Bishopbriggs	Bish	78	B2
Bishopton	Bishop	72	A2
Blackridge	Blac	107	E2
Bonhill	Bonh	28	A2
Bonnybridge	Bon	40	A3
Bridge of Allan	B of A	2	A4
Bridge of Weir	B of W	110	C4
Calderbank	Calder	123	D2
Caldercruix	Cald	105	D3
California	Cali	66	C3
Cambus	Camb	9	D4
Cambusbarron	Cam	6	B3
Cardross	Card	48	A4
Carluke	Car	188	A1
Chapelhall	Chap	123	F1
Chapelton	Chapel	181	E1
Clackmannan	Clack	10	C2
Cleland	Cle	144	A1
Clydebank	Clyde	74	A1
Coatbridge	Coat	122	B3
Cowie	Cowie	12	B4
Coylton	Coy	239	F2
Crossford	Cro	201	D1
Crosshouse	Cross	221	F1
Cumbernauld	Cumb	62	B3
Dalry	Dalry	191	D4
Denny	Den	21	F1
Dumbarton	Dumb	49	F1
Dunblane	Dun	1	B4
Dundonald	Dund	225	F1
Dunipace	Duni	21	E2
Dunlop	Dunlop	195	E4
Duntocher	Dunt	74	A4
Eaglesham	Eagle	178	C3
East Kilbride	E Kil	159	E2
Eastfield	East	127	E2
Erskine	Ersk	73	D1
Falkirk	Falk	42	B3
Fallin	Fall	8	B2
Fauldhouse	Fau	147	F4
Fenwick	Fen	213	D2
Fishcross	Fish	5	F2
Forth	For	189	F3
Gartocharn	Gart	20	C4
Glasgow	Glasg	117	E3
Glassford	Glass	198	A2
Glenboig	Glen	101	F3
Glenmavis	Glenm	102	C2
Gourock	Gour	44	B4
Grangemouth	Gran	24	C2
Greengairs	Gree	83	F1
Greenock	Green	46	A3
Hamilton	Ham	162	B2
Harthill	Hart	127	F3
Hattonrig	Hat	142	A3
Helensburgh	Helen	16	A1
Holytown	Holy	143	D3
Houston	Hous	91	D1
Howwood	How	130	C3
Hurlford	Hurl	228	C3
Inchinnan	Inch	93	E3
Irvine	Irvine	219	D2
Johnstone	John	111	F1
Kilbarchan	Kilbar	111	D2
Kilbirnie	Kilb	149	D1
Kilmacolm	Kil	89	E4
Kilmarnock	Kilmk	228	A4
Kilmaurs	Kilm	222	B4
Kilncadzow	Kilnc	203	D3
Kilsyth	Kils	60	B4
Kilwinning	Kilw	207	F1
Kirkintilloch	Kirk	79	D1
Lanark	Lan	215	E2
Langbank	Lang	70	A4
Larbert	Larb	23	D2
Larkhall	Lark	185	D2
Laurieston	Laur	42	C2
Law	Law	186	C3
Lennoxtown	Lennox	57	E4
Linwood	Lin	112	A3
Lochwinnoch	Loch	129	D2
Menstrie	Men	3	F3
Milngavie	Miln	55	D2
Milton of Campsie	M of C	58	B3
Mossblown	Moss	237	F4
Motherwell	Mother	163	E4
Muirhead	Muir	100	B4
Neilston	Neil	154	C3
New Sauchie	N Sau	5	E1
Newmains	New	166	A3
Newton Mearns	Newt M	156	B2
Old Kilpatrick	O Kill	73	D3
Paisley	Pais	113	F1
Plains	Plains	104	A2
Plean	Plea	12	B2
Port Glasgow	P Glasg	47	F1
Prestwick	Pres	236	A4
Quarter	Quart	183	F2
Renfrew	Ren	94	C1
Rhu	Rhu	15	E3
Rosneath	Ros	15	D2
Salsburgh	Sals	125	E1
Saltcoats	Salt	216	B4
Shewalton	Shew	224	C3
Shieldhill	Shi	66	B3
Shotts	Shot	146	C3
Slamannan	Slam	86	A3
Springside	Spring	220	C1
Stenhousemuir	Sten	23	E2
Stepps	Stepps	99	E3
Stevenston	Steven	217	F4
Stewarton	Stew	211	F4
Stirling	Stir	7	E4
Stonehouse	Stone	198	C1
Strathblane	Strath	31	E2
Symington	Sym	231	E2
Tannochside	Tan	141	D4
Tarbolton	Tar	234	C3
Thorntonhall	Thorn	158	B2
Tillicoultry	Till	5	F4
Torwood	Tor	22	C3
Troon	Troon	229	D1
Tullibody	Tull	4	B2
Twechar	Twe	59	F2
Uddingston	Udd	140	C3
Uplawmoor	Uplaw	153	D2
West Kilbride	W Kil	190	B2
Westfield	West	87	F1
Wishaw	Wish	165	D2

Abbey Cl. Pais

Alloway Dr. Clyde

243
Alloway Dr. Cowie
Arran Ave. P Glasg

Alloway Dr. Cowie 12 B4
Alloway Dr. Glasg 137 F3
Alloway Dr. Kirk 59 D1
Alloway Dr. Newt M 157 D2
Alloway Dr. Pais 134 A4
Alloway Gdns. Ham 161 E1
Alloway Gdns. Kirk 59 D1
Alloway Gr. Kirk 58 C1
Alloway Pk. Ayr 238 C4
Alloway Pl. Ard 205 E2
Alloway Pl. Ayr 238 C4
Alloway Place La. Ayr 238 C4
Alloway Quadrant. Kirk 59 D1
Alloway Rd. E Kil 160 C2
Alloway Rd. Glasg 136 B3
Alloway St. Ayr 238 C4
Alloway St. Lark 185 E1
Alloway Terr. Kirk 58 C1
Alloway Wynd. Holy 143 F2
Alma La. Falk 42 A3
Alma St. Falk 42 A3
Alma St. Glasg 118 A3
Alma Terr. Falk 42 A3
Almada Gr. Ham 162 B2
Almada La. Ham 162 B2
Almada St. Ham 162 B2
Almond Ave. Ren 94 C1
Almond Cres. Pais 112 C1
Almond Ct. Stir 7 E3
Almond Dr. Bank 38 C1
Almond Dr. Bishop 72 A1
Almond Dr. E Kil 160 A1
Almond Dr. Kirk 79 D3
Almond Pl. Coat 101 E1
Almond Pl. Holy 143 D3
Almond Pl. Kilmk 227 E4
Almond Rd. Bear 75 E1
Almond Rd. Cumb 62 C2
Almond Rd. Stepps 99 E3
Almond St. Glasg 98 B1
Almond Terr. East 127 E3
Almond Vale. Tan 141 D4
Almond Way. Mother 163 F2
Almondbank. Plains 103 F2
Almswall Rd. Kilw 207 F2
Alness Cres. Glasg 115 F2
Alness St. Ham 162 B1
Alness Terr. Ham 162 B1
Alnwick Dr. Eagle 178 B2
Aloa Way. Lark 185 E1
Alpha Ctr. Clyde 94 B4
Alpine Gr. Tan 140 C4
Alsatian Ave. Clyde 74 B1
Alsh Terr. Ham 162 A1
Alston Ave. Coat 122 A4
Alston Gdns. Bear 75 D4
Altnacreag Gdns. Muir 81 D2
Altnock Pl. Dalry 191 D4
Alton Rd. Pais 114 B2
Alton St. W Kil 190 B3
Alton Way. W Kil 190 B2
Altonhead Dr. Spring 210 A1
Altonhead Terr. Spring 221 D4
Altonhill Ave. Kilmk 222 C2
Altry Pl. Ayr 238 A1
Altyre St. Glasg 118 C2
Aluclutha Ave. Dumb 50 A2
Alva Gate. Glasg 115 F2
Alva Gdns. Bear 75 E4
Alva Gdns. Glasg 115 F1
Alva Pl. Kirk 79 F2
Alva Terr. Green 45 D4
Alvord Ave. Pres 233 E1
Alwyn Ave. Hous 111 E4
Alwyn Ct. E Kil 159 F2
Alwyn Dr. E Kil 159 F2
Alyssum Cres. Mother 163 E4
Alyth Cres. Glasg 158 A4
Alyth Gdns. Glasg 115 F2
Alyth Gdns. Glasg 158 A4
Ambassador Way. Ren 94 B1
Amber Terr. Hat 142 A2
Ambleside. E Kil 180 A3
Amethyst Ave. Hat 142 A2
Amisfield St. Glasg 96 C3
Amlaird Rd. Kilmk 223 D3
Amochrie Dr. Pais 133 D4
Amulree Pl. Glasg 119 D2
Amulree St. Glasg 119 D2
Ancaster Dr. Glasg 95 F3
Ancaster La. Glasg 95 F3
Anchor Ave. Pais 114 A2
Anchor Cres. Pais 114 A2
Anchor Dr. Pais 114 A2
Anchor La. Glasg 117 E4
Anchor Wynd. Pais 114 A2
Ancroft St. Glasg 97 D2
Andersen Ct. E Kil 180 C3
Anderside. E Kil 180 C3
Anderson Ave. Kils 36 A1
Anderson Cres. Ayr 239 D2
Anderson Cres. Cali 66 C3
Anderson Cres. Kils 59 F4
Anderson Cres. Pres 236 C4
Anderson Ct. Hat 142 A3
Anderson Dr. Den 21 F1
Anderson Dr. Irvine 219 E3
Anderson Dr. Newt M 156 B2
Anderson Dr. Ren 94 B2
Anderson Dr. Salt 206 A1
Anderson Dr. Sten 24 A1
Anderson Gdns. Udd 140 C1
Anderson La. Aird 123 D4
Anderson Park Rd. Den 21 F1
Anderson Pl. Kilmk 223 E1
Anderson Pl. Stir 7 D2
Anderson Rd. Bishop 72 A2
Anderson St. Aird 123 D4
Anderson St. Bon 40 A3
Anderson St. Glasg 96 A1
Anderson St. Ham 161 F3
Anderson St. Mother 163 F3
Anderson St. P Glasg 47 E1
Anderson Terr. Ard 205 E1
Anderson Terr. Bank 39 D2
Anderston Quay. Glasg 116 C3
Andrew Ave. Kirk 79 E2
Andrew Ave. Ren 94 C2
Andrew Cres. Sten 23 E2
Andrew Dr. Clyde 94 B4
Andrew Pl. Car 187 F2
Andrew Sillars Ave. Glasg 139 E3
Andrew St. E Kil 159 F1
Andrew's La. Glasg 117 E3
Andrews St. Pais 113 F3
Anford Pl. Udd 161 F3
Angela Way. Udd 140 C3
Angle Gate. Glasg 95 E2
Angle St. Stone 198 C1
Angus Ave. Aird 123 D3
Angus Ave. Bish 78 B1
Angus Ave. E Kil 160 A1
Angus Ave. Glasg 115 E2
Angus Ave. Ham 163 D2
Angus Ave. Mother 163 E4
Angus Ave. Pres 236 B4
Angus Gdns. Tan 140 C4
Angus Oval. Glasg 115 D2
Angus Pl. E Kil 160 A1
Angus Pl. Glasg 115 D2
Angus Rd. Car 188 A1
Angus Rd. Gour 44 B2
Angus Rd. P Glasg 47 E1
Angus St. Alex 27 F2
Angus St. Clyde 94 C4
Angus St. Glasg 97 F2
Angus Wlk. Tan 141 D4
Ann Ct. Ham 162 A3
Ann St. Green 45 F2
Ann St. Green 45 F3
Ann St. Ham 162 A3
Ann St. John 112 A2
Annabella Rd. Ash 200 B2
Annan Ave. E Kil 179 F4
Annan Ct. Falk 42 B1
Annan Dr. Bear 75 E2
Annan Dr. Glasg 138 B4
Annan Dr. Pais 112 C1
Annan Glade. Mother 164 A2
Annan Gr. Mother 164 A2
Annan Pl. John 131 E4
Annan Rd. Kilmk 228 A3
Annan St. Glasg 137 D4
Annan St. Mother 164 A2
Annandale Cres. Cross 221 F1
Annandale Gdns. Cross 221 F1
Annandale. Gree 83 F1
Annandale La. Cross 221 F1
Annandale St. Glasg 117 D2
Annandale View. Cross 221 F1
Annandale Way. Irvine 220 A3
Annanhill Ave. Kilmk 222 B1
Annanhill Pl. Kilw 207 D2
Annbank St. Glasg 117 F3
Annbank St. Lark 184 C2
Anne Ave. Ren 94 B2
Anne Cres. Kirk 79 E2
Anne Dr. B of A 2 A3
Anne Dr. Sten 23 F2
Anne St. All 9 F4
Annerley Ct. Coat 121 F3
Annerley Pl. Coat 121 F3
Annes Ct. Glasg 117 F2
Annet Rd. Bank 39 E3
Annette St. Glasg 117 D1
Annfield Dr. Stir 7 E3
Annfield Gdns. Stir 7 D3
Annfield Gdns. Udd 140 B1
Annfield Glen Rd. Ayr 239 D2
Annfield Pl. Glasg 117 F4
Annfield Rd. Pres 236 A4
Annfield Terr. Pres 236 A4
Annick Cotts. Stew 196 B3
Annick Cres. Stew 211 F4
Annick Ct. Irvine 219 E1
Annick Dr. Bear 75 E1
Annick Dr. Irvine 220 A1
Annick Pl. Kilmk 228 A3
Annick Pl. Troon 229 F2
Annick Rd. Irvine 219 F1
Annick Rd. Irvine 220 A1
Annick Roundabout. Irvine 219 E1
Annick St. Glasg 119 D3
Annick St. Glasg 139 E3
Annick View. Irvine 219 F1
Anniesdale Ave. Stepps 99 E3
Annieshill View. Plains 104 A1
Anniesland Cres. Glasg 95 D3
Anniesland Ind Est. Glasg 95 F4
Anniesland Rd. Glasg 95 E3
Annieston. Twe 59 F2
Anniversary Ave. E Kil 180 B4
Annpit Rd. Ayr 236 A2
Annsfield Rd. Ham 183 E4
Ansdell Ave. Udd 161 E4
Anson Ave. Falk 41 F2
Anson St. Glasg 117 F2
Anson Way. Ren 94 B1
Anstruther Ct. Law 186 C3
Anstruther St. Glasg 118 C3
Anstruther St. Law 186 C3
Antermony Rd. M of C 58 C3
Antigua St. Green 46 A2
Antigua Way. E Kil 159 D1
Anton Cres. Kils 60 C4
Antonine Ave. Mother 163 E4
Antonine Gdns. Dunt 74 A3
Antonine Gdns. Falk 41 E3
Antonine Gr. Bon 39 F2
Antonine. Kirk 59 D1
Antonine Rd. Bear 75 D3
Antonine St. Falk 41 E3
Antrim La. Lark 185 D2
Anwoth St. Glasg 119 D2
Apollo Path. Holy 143 D3
Appin Ct. Kirk 59 D1
Appin Rd. Glasg 118 B4
Appin Terr. Glasg 138 B2
Appin Terr. Ham 161 F2
Appin Terr. Shot 147 D2
Appin Way. Glenm 102 C2
Appin Way. Udd 141 D2
Appleby Cl. E Kil 179 F3
Appleby St. Glasg 97 D2
Applecross Gdns. Muir 80 C2
Applecross Quadrant. Wish 165 D3
Applecross Rd. Kirk 59 D1
Applecross St. Glasg 97 D2
Appledore Cres. Udd 141 D2
Apsley La. Glasg 96 A1
Apsley St. Glasg 96 A1
Aqua Ave. Ham 161 F1
Aquila Way. Car 187 E1
Araburn Dr. E Kil 180 C3
Aranthrue Cres. Ren 94 B2
Aranthrue Dr. Ren 94 B2
Aray St. Glasg 96 B3
Arbroath Ave. Glasg 115 D2
Arbroath Cres. Stir 2 A2
Arbroath Gr. Ham 162 A1
Arbuckle Pl. Plains 104 A2
Arbuckle Rd. Cald 104 A2
Arbuckle Rd. Plains 104 A2
Arbuckle St. Kilmk 228 A4
Arbuthnot St. Falk 41 F3
Arcade. Stir 7 D4
Arcadia St. Glasg 117 F3
Arcadia St. Hat 142 A4
Arcan Cres. Glasg 75 D1
Arch Way. Kils 36 B1
Archerfield Ave. Glasg 119 D1
Archerfield Cres. Glasg 119 D1
Archerfield Dr. Glasg 119 D1
Archerfield Gr. Glasg 119 D1
Archerhill Ave. Glasg 95 D4
Archerhill Cotts. Glasg 95 D4
Archerhill Cres. Glasg 95 D4
Archerhill Rd. Glasg 95 D4
Archerhill Sq. Glasg 94 C4
Archerhill Terr. Glasg 95 D4
Archers Ave. Stir 7 E2
Archibald Dr. Dalry 191 D4
Archibald Terr. M of C 58 A3
Archiebald Pl. Hat 142 B2
Archray Rd. Cumb 82 A3
Arcon Ave. Moss 237 F3
Ard La. New 165 F3
Ard Loan. Holy 143 D3
Ard Rd. Ren 94 A2
Ard St. Glasg 119 D2
Ardardan Cotts. Card 25 F1
Ardargie Dr. Glasg 139 E4
Ardargie Gr. Glasg 139 E4
Ardargie Pl. Glasg 139 E4
Ardayre Rd. Pres 236 A4
Ardbeg Ave. Bish 78 B1
Ardbeg Ave. Glasg 138 C2
Ardbeg Ave. Kilmk 222 C2
Ardbeg Ct. Irvine 219 F3
Ardbeg La. Glasg 117 D1
Ardbeg Rd. Green 46 B1
Ardbeg St. Glasg 117 D1
Ardchoille Dr. Steven 206 C1
Ardchoille La. Steven 206 C1
Ardconnel St. Glasg 135 F2
Ardeer La. Steven 217 F3
Arden Ave. Glasg 135 F1
Arden Ct. Ham 162 B1
Arden Dr. Glasg 136 A2
Arden Gr. Kils 36 B1
Arden Hill. Rhu 15 E3
Arden Pl. Glasg 135 F1
Arden Rd. Green 46 B1
Arden Rd. Ham 162 B1
Arden St. Plains 104 A1
Arden Terr. Ham 162 B1
Ardencaple Dr. Helen 16 A1
Ardencaple Quadrant. Helen 16 A1
Ardenclutha Ave. Ham 162 A2
Ardenclutha Dr. P Glasg 47 D1
Ardenconnel Ho. Rhu 15 E3
Ardenconnel Way. Rhu 15 E3
Ardencraig Cres. Glasg 137 E1
Ardencraig Dr. Glasg 138 A1
Ardencraig La. Glasg 137 E1
Ardencraig Quadrant. Glasg 137 F1
Ardencraig Rd. Glasg 137 F1
Ardencraig Rd. Glasg 137 F2
Ardencraig St. Glasg 138 A1
Ardencraig Terr. Glasg 137 F1
Ardenlea St. Glasg 118 A2
Ardenlea. Tan 140 C4
Ardery St. Glasg 96 A1
Ardessie St. Glasg 76 B1
Ardfern Rd. Chap 124 A3
Ardfern St. Glasg 110 D2
Ardfin Ct. Pres 236 B3
Ardfin Rd. Pres 236 B3
Ardgare. Rhu 15 D4
Ardgay Pl. Glasg 119 D2
Ardgay St. Glasg 119 D2
Ardgay Way. Glasg 138 A2
Ardgour Ct. Ham 161 F3
Ardgour Dr. Lin 112 A3
Ardgour Par. Holy 143 E1
Ardgour Pl. Kilmk 222 C2
Ardgour Rd. Kilmk 222 C2
Ardgowan Ave. Pais 113 F2
Ardgowan Ct. Pais 114 A2
Ardgowan Dr. Tan 140 C4
Ardgowan Pl. Shot 146 C3
Ardgowan St. Green 45 F3
Ardgowan St. P Glasg 47 D1
Ardgowan St. Pais 113 F2
Ardgowan
Terrace La. Glasg 96 B1
Ardgryfe Cres. Hous 91 E1
Ardholm St. Glasg 119 D3
Ardhu Pl. Glasg 75 D2
Ardlamont Sq. Lin 112 B3
Ardlaw St. Glasg 115 F3
Ardle Ave. Kilmk 228 A3
Ardle Rd. Glasg 136 C3
Ardlui Gdns. Miln 54 B2
Ardlui Rd. Ayr 236 A2
Ardlui St. Glasg 118 C2
Ardmaleish Cres. Glasg 137 F1
Ardmaleish Dr. Glasg 137 E1
Ardmaleish Rd. Glasg 137 F1
Ardmaleish St. Glasg 137 E1
Ardmaleish Terr. Glasg 137 F1
Ardmay Cres. Glasg 137 E4
Ardmillan. Kilw 207 D1
Ardmillan St. Glasg 118 C4
Ardmore Ct. Irvine 220 A3
Ardmore Pl. Green 45 F2
Ardmore Rd. Green 46 B1
Ardmore Rd. P Glasg 47 E1
Ardmore Rd. P Glasg 68 B4
Ardmory Ave. Glasg 137 E4
Ardmory La. Glasg 137 F4
Ardmory Pl. Glasg 137 F4
Ardnahoe Ave. Glasg 137 F4
Ardnahoe Pl. Glasg 137 E4
Ardneil Ave. W Kil 190 B2
Ardneil Ct. Ard 205 D2
Ardneil Rd. Glasg 115 F3
Ardnish St. Glasg 115 F4
Ardo Gdns. Glasg 116 A3
Ardoch Cres. Dumb 49 E2
Ardoch Cres. Steven 217 F3
Ardoch Gdns. Glasg 138 C3
Ardoch Gr. Glasg 138 C3
Ardoch Path. New 165 F3
Ardoch Rd. Bear 76 A3
Ardoch St. Glasg 97 E2
Ardoch Way. Muir 80 C1
Ardochrig. E Kil 180 C3
Ardressie Pl. Glasg 96 B3
Ardrossan High Rd. W Kil 190 C2
Ardrossan Rd. Salt 216 C4
Ardrossan Rd. W Kil 190 B1
Ardshiel Rd. Glasg 115 F4
Ardsloy La. Glasg 95 D2
Ardsloy Pl. Glasg 95 D2
Ardtoe Cres. Stepps 99 F3
Ardtoe Pl. Stepps 99 F3
Arduthie Rd. Glasg 115 F4
Ardvreck Pl. Sten 24 A2
Ardwell Rd. Glasg 115 F2
Argosy Way. Ren 94 B1
Argus Ave. Chap 123 E1
Argyle Cres. Aird 122 C3
Argyle Cres. Ham 161 F2
Argyle Gdns. Lennox 57 F4
Argyle Pk. Ayr 236 A1
Argyle Pl. Kils 60 C4
Argyle Pl. Salt 216 C4
Argyle Rd. Bear 75 F4
Argyle Rd. Gour 44 C3
Argyle Rd. Salt 216 C4
Argyle St E. Helen 16 B1
Argyle St. Glasg 116 C4
Argyle St. Glasg 117 D4
Argyle St. Green 45 F3
Argyle St. Pais 113 E2
Argyle St. Stone 198 C1
Argyle St W. Helen 16 B1
Argyll Arc. Glasg 117 E4
Argyll Ave. Dumb 50 B2
Argyll Ave. Falk 42 B3
Argyll Ave. Inch 93 F1
Argyll Ave. Ren 94 A2
Argyll Ave. Stir 2 B1
Argyll Est. Alex 27 E4
Argyll Gdns. Lark 185 D2
Argyll Pl. All 10 B4
Argyll Pl. Dumb 50 B2
Argyll Pl. E Kil 160 B2
Argyll Pl. Hat 141 F1
Argyll Rd. Clyde 74 B1
Argyll Rd. Ros 15 D2
Argyll St. Alex 27 E4
Argyll St. All 10 B4
Arisaig Dr. Bear 76 A2
Arisaig Dr. Glasg 115 F2
Arisaig Pl. Glasg 115 F2
Arisdale Cres. Newt M 156 C3
Ark La. Glasg 117 F4
Arkaig Ave. Plains 103 F2
Arkaig St. Wish 165 D1
Arkle Terr. Glasg 138 C2
Arkleston Cres. Pais 114 A4
Arkleston Rd. Pais 114 A3
Arkleston Rd. Pais 114 B4
Arkleston Rd. Ren 114 A4
Arklet Rd. Glasg 115 F4
Arkwright Way. Irvine 219 F2
Arlington St. Glasg 96 C1
Armadale Ct. Glasg 118 A4
Armadale Path. Glasg 118 A4
Armadale Pl. Glasg 118 A4
Armadale Pl. Green 45 F2
Armadale Rd. Rhu 15 F2
Armadale St. Glasg 118 A4
Armine Path. Holy 143 E2
Armour Ave. Aird 122 C4
Armour Ave. Cowie 12 B4
Armour Ct. Kirk 59 D1
Armour Ct. Udd 161 D3
Armour Dr. Ayr 239 E3
Armour Dr. Kirk 59 D1
Armour Gdns. Kirk 59 D1
Armour Gr. Mother 164 A2
Armour Pl. Ard 205 E2
Armour Pl. Holy 143 E2
Armour Pl. John 112 A2
Armour Pl. Kirk 59 D1
Armour Pl. Lin 112 B3
Armour Pl. Stew 195 F1
Armour St. Glasg 117 F3
Armour St. John 112 A2
Armour St. Kilmk 227 F4
Armstrong Cres. Tan 141 D4
Armstrong Gr. E Kil 180 B4
Armstrong Rd. Helen 25 D4
Armstrong Rd. Kilmk 223 E1
Arnbrae Rd. Kils 36 A1
Arness Terr. Kilmk 222 C2
Arngask Rd. Glasg 115 F4
Arnhall Pl. Glasg 115 F2
Arnhem St. Glasg 139 E3
Arnholm Pl. Glasg 115 F2
Arnisdale Pl. Glasg 120 A4
Arnisdale Rd. Glasg 120 A4
Arnisdale Way. Glasg 138 A2
Arniston St. Glasg 118 C4
Arnol Pl. Glasg 119 F4
Arnold Ave. Bish 78 A1
Arnold St. Glasg 97 D3
Arnot St. Falk 42 B2
Arnothill Ct. Falk 41 F3
Arnothill. Falk 42 A2
Arnothill Gdns. Falk 42 A2
Arnothill La. Falk 41 F2
Arnothill Mews. Falk 42 A2
Arnott Dr. Coat 122 A2
Arnott Quadrant. Mother 142 B1
Arnott Way. Glasg 139 D3
Arnprior Gdns. Muir 80 C1
Arnprior Pl. Ayr 238 C1
Arnprior Quadrant. Glasg 137 E2
Arnprior Rd. Glasg 137 E2
Arnprior St. Glasg 137 E2
Arns Gr. All 9 F4
Arnside Ave. Glasg 136 B2
Arnswell. N Sau 5 E1
Arnum Gdns. Car 187 F1
Arnum Pl. Car 187 F1
Arnwood Dr. Glasg 96 A3
Aron Terr. Glasg 138 C2
Arondale Rd. Plains 103 F2
Aros Dr. Glasg 115 F1
Aros La. Glasg 115 E1
Aros Rd. Rhu 15 E3
Arran Ave. Coat 122 B2
Arran Ave. Dumb 49 E3
Arran Ave. Inch 93 F1
Arran Ave. Kilmk 223 D2
Arran Ave. P Glasg 69 D4

246

Bearsden Rd. Glasg | Birnam Cres. Bear

Bearsden Rd. Glasg 95 F4
Bearside Rd. Stir 7 D2
Beaton Ave. Bann 7 E1
Beaton Rd. Bonh 27 F4
Beaton Rd. Glasg 116 C1
Beaton St. Lark 184 C3
Beaton Terr. Irvine 219 E3
Beatrice Dr. Holy 142 C3
Beatrice Gdns. Hous 111 E4
Beattock St. Glasg 118 B3
Beattock Wynd. Ham 162 A2
Beatty Ave. Stir 2 A1
Beatty Pl. Helen 17 D1
Beatty St. Clyde 73 F2
Beauclerc St. Alva 5 D4
Beaufield Gdns. Kilm 222 A4
Beaufort Ave. Glasg 136 B3
Beaufort Dr. Klrk 79 D4
Beaufort Dr. Sten 24 A2
Beaufort Gdns. Bish 77 F1
Beauly Cres. Kil 89 E4
Beauly Cres. Kilmk 228 A3
Beauly Ct. Falk 42 B1
Beauly Dr. Pais 112 C1
Beauly Pl. Coat 122 A2
Beauly Pl. E Kil 159 E1
Beauly Pl. Glasg 96 B3
Beauly Pl. Holy 143 D3
Beauly Pl. Muir 80 B1
Beauly Rd. Glasg 120 A2
Beaumont Dr. Sten 24 A1
Beaumont Gate. Glasg 96 B2
Beckford St. Ham 162 B3
Beda Pl. Fall 8 B3
Bedale Rd. Glasg 119 F2
Bedcow View. Klrk 79 F4
Bedford Ave. Clyde 74 B1
Bedford Ct. All 10 A3
Bedford La. Glasg 117 D3
Bedford Pl. All 10 A3
Bedford St. Glasg 117 D3
Bedford St. Green 45 E4
Bedlay Ct. Muir 81 D2
Bedlormie Dr. Blac 107 E1
Beech Ave. B of W 90 B1
Beech Ave. Bear 76 A4
Beech Ave. Beith 150 A1
Beech Ave. Glasg 116 A2
Beech Ave. Glasg 120 A3
Beech Ave. Glasg 138 B2
Beech Ave. Glasg 138 C3
Beech Ave. Holy 143 D2
Beech Ave. Irvine 219 E1
Beech Ave. John 112 B1
Beech Ave. Kilmk 227 E4
Beech Ave. Lark 185 E1
Beech Ave. Newt M 156 C2
Beech Ave. Pais 114 A1
Beech Ave. Plea 12 B2
Beech Cres. Duni 21 E2
Beech Cres. Holy 143 E4
Beech Cres. Lar 41 E4
Beech Cres. Newt M 156 C2
Beech Ct. Coat 121 F2
Beech Dr. Cald 104 C2
Beech Dr. Clyde 74 A3
Beech Gdns. Glasg 120 A3
Beech Gr. Ayr 239 E4
Beech Gr. E Kil 180 A3
Beech Gr. Law 186 C3
Beech Gr. Muir 101 D3
Beech Gr. Rhu 15 E3
Beech Gr. Wish 165 E4
Beech La. Stir 2 A2
Beech Pl. Bish 98 A4
Beech Pl. Gour 44 B3
Beech Pl. Udd 161 F4
Beech Rd. Bish 98 A4
Beech Rd. Holy 143 E4
Beech Rd. John 111 E1
Beech Rd. Klrk 79 E3
Beech Terr. Lark 185 D1
Beechbank Ave. Aird 102 C1
Beechburn Cres. Loch 129 E2
Beeches Ave. Dunt 73 F3
Beeches Rd. Dunt 73 F3
Beeches Terr. Dunt 74 A3
Beeches The. Hous 91 E1
Beeches The. Kilbar 111 E3
Beeches The. Lan 215 D1
Beeches The. Newt M 156 C3
Beechfield Dr. Car 202 A4
Beechfield Rd. Beith 170 C4
Beechgrove Ave. Tan 141 E4
Beechgrove. Muir 80 C1
Beechgrove Pl. Helen 25 C4
Beechgrove Quadrant. Holy 143 D3
Beechgrove St. Glasg 118 A1
Beechlands Ave. Glasg 136 C1
Beechlands Dr. Newt M 157 E3
Beechmount Ct. Shot 147 D1
Beechmount Rd. Klrk 79 E2
Beechtree Terr. M of C 58 B3
Beechwood Ave. Glasg 138 B3
Beechwood Ave. Ham 183 D4
Beechwood Ave. Lang 70 B4
Beechwood Ave. Newt M 157 E3
Beechwood Cres. Wish 165 E1
Beechwood Ct. Bear 75 F2
Beechwood Dr. Bonh 28 A1
Beechwood Dr. Coat 122 B3
Beechwood Dr. Glasg 95 F2
Beechwood Dr. Ren 94 B1
Beechwood Gdns. Hat 142 B2
Beechwood Gdns. Muir 80 C1
Beechwood Gr. Barr 134 B1
Beechwood. Kilw 207 E3
Beechwood La. Bear 75 F2
Beechwood. Lark 185 D3
Beechwood. N Sau 5 E1
Beechwood. N Sau 5 F1
Beechwood Paddock. Troon 230 A2
Beechwood Pl. Glasg 95 F2
Beechwood Pl. Hat 142 B2
Beechwood Rd. Cumb 82 C4
Beechworth Dr. Holy 143 E1
Beecroft Pl. Udd 140 C1
Begg Ave. Falk 41 F2
Beggs Terr. Ard 205 E2
Beil Dr. Clyde 94 C4
Beith Rd. Beith 170 B3
Beith Rd. Beith 191 F4
Beith Rd. Green 45 F1
Beith Rd. How 131 D4
Beith Rd. John 111 F1
Beith St. Glasg 96 A1
Beith St. Glasg 96 B1
Belgowan St. Hat 141 F4
Belgrave La. Glasg 96 C2
Belgrave St. Hat 141 F3
Belhaven Rd. Ham 161 F2
Belhaven Rd. Wish 165 D2
Belhaven St. P Glasg 47 D1
Belhaven Terr. Glasg 96 B2
Belhaven Terr W. Glasg 96 B2
Belhaven Terr. Wish 165 D2
Belhaven Terrace La. Glasg 96 B2
Belhaven Terrace West La. Glasg 96 B2
Bell Cres. Irvine 219 E3
Bell Gn E. E Kil 180 C4
Bell Gn W. E Kil 180 C4
Bell St. Aird 122 C4
Bell St. Clyde 94 B4
Bell St. Glasg 117 E3
Bell St. Green 46 C1
Bell St. Hat 142 A4
Bell St. Ren 94 B2
Bell St. Wish 165 D2
Bell Trees Rd. How 130 B1
Bell View Ct. Ren 94 B2
Bell's Wynd. Falk 42 A2
Bell's Wynd. Lan 215 E3
Bellahouston Dr. Glasg 115 F2
Bellairs Pl. Udd 140 B1
Bellard Rd. W Kil 190 B2
Bellard Wlk. W Kil 190 B2
Bellas Pl. Plains 104 A1
Bellcraig Ct. Thorn 158 A3
Belleaire Dr. Green 45 E4
Bellefield Rd. Lan 215 D3
Belleisle Ave. Udd 140 C4
Belleisle Cl. Kilw 207 E2
Belleisle Cres. B of W 110 B3
Belleisle Pl. Gour 44 A3
Belleisle Pl. Kilmk 227 F2
Belleisle St. Glasg 117 D1
Bellesleyhill Ave. Ayr 236 A2
Bellesleyhill Rd. Ayr 236 A2
Bellevale Ave. Ayr 239 D3
Bellevale Quadrant. Ayr 238 C3
Bellevue Ave. Klrk 79 D4
Bellevue Cres. Ayr 238 C4
Bellevue Gdns. Kilmk 222 B1
Bellevue La. Ayr 238 C4
Bellevue Rd. All 9 F3
Bellevue Rd. Ayr 238 C4
Bellevue Rd. Kilmk 222 B1
Bellevue Rd. Klrk 79 D4
Bellevue Rd. Pres 236 B4
Bellevue St. Ayr 238 C4
Bellevue St. Falk 42 B2
Bellfield Ave. Hurl 228 B3
Bellfield Cres. Barr 134 A2
Bellfield Ct. Barr 134 A2
Bellfield Ct. Hurl 228 B3
Bellfield Dr. Wish 165 E1
Bellfield La. Pres 236 A4
Bellfield Rd. Bann 7 F1
Bellfield Rd. Klrk 79 D4
Bellfield Rd. Stir 7 D3
Bellfield St. Glasg 118 A3
Bellflower Ct. E Kil 159 E2
Bellflower Gdns. Glasg 135 E2
Bellflower Gr. E Kil 159 E2
Bellgrove St. Glasg 117 F3
Bellisle Terr. Ham 183 D4
Bellrock Ave. Pres 236 A3
Bellrock Cres. Glasg 119 D4
Bellrock Ct. Glasg 119 D4
Bellrock Path. Glasg 119 D4
Bellrock Rd. Ayr 236 A2
Bellrock St. Glasg 119 D4
Bellscroft Ave. Glasg 137 F4
Bellsdyke Rd. Air 24 B3
Bellsdyke Rd. Aird 123 D3
Bellsdyke Rd. Lar 23 E2
Bellsdyke Rd. Sten 23 E2
Bellsfield Dr. Udd 161 F3
Bellshaugh Gdns. Glasg 96 B3
Bellshaugh La. Glasg 96 B3
Bellshaugh Pl. Glasg 96 B3
Bellshaugh Rd. Glasg 96 B2
Bellshill Rd. Hat 141 F2
Bellshill Rd. Mother 142 B1
Bellshill Rd. Tan 141 D3
Bellshill Rd. Tan 141 E1
Bellshill Rd. Udd 141 D3
Bellshill Rd. Udd 141 E1
Bellside Rd. Chap 123 F1
Bellside Rd. Chap 144 A4
Bellside Rd. Cle 144 B1
Bellsland Dr. Kilmk 227 F3
Bellsland Gr. Kilmk 227 F3
Bellsland Pl. Kilmk 228 A4
Bellsmeadow Rd. Falk 42 B2
Bellsmyre Ave. Dumb 50 A3
Belltree Ave. Stew 211 E4
Belltrees Cres. Pais 113 D2
Bellvue Cres. Hat 141 F2
Bellvue Cres. Pres 236 B4
Bellwood St. Glasg 136 C4
Bellziehill Farm. Tan 141 F3
Belman's Cl. Beith 150 A1
Belmont Ave. Ayr 239 D3
Belmont Ave. Shi 66 C4
Belmont Ave. Udd 140 C4
Belmont Cres. Ayr 239 D3
Belmont Cres. Glasg 96 C2
Belmont Cres. Kilm 222 A4
Belmont Ct. Klrk 79 E4
Belmont Dr. Ayr 239 D3
Belmont Dr. Barr 134 B1
Belmont Dr. E Kil 180 A4
Belmont Dr. Glasg 136 A2
Belmont Dr. Glasg 138 A4
Belmont Dr. Shot 147 D1
Belmont La. Glasg 96 C2
Belmont Pl E. Ayr 239 D3
Belmont Pl W. Ayr 239 D3
Belmont Rd. Ayr 239 D3
Belmont Rd. Glasg 97 F3
Belmont Rd. Glasg 138 C2
Belmont Rd. Kil 89 E4
Belmont Rd. Pais 114 A3
Belmont St. Clyde 74 A1
Belmont St. Coat 101 E1
Belmont St. Falk 42 B2
Belmont St. Glasg 96 C2
Belmont St. Kils 36 B1
Belmont St. Wish 186 A3
Belses Dr. Glasg 115 E3
Belstane Pk. Car 187 F2
Belstane Pl. Udd 141 D2
Belstane Rd. Car 188 A2
Belstane Rd. Cumb 82 C3
Belsyde Ave. Glasg 75 D1
Beltane St. Glasg 116 C4
Beltane St. Wish 165 D1
Beltrees Ave. Glasg 115 D1
Beltrees Cres. Glasg 115 D1
Beltrees Rd. Glasg 115 D1
Belvidere Cres. Bish 78 A1
Belvidere Cres. Hat 142 A2
Belvidere Rd. Hat 142 A2
Belvidere Terr. Ayr 236 A1
Belville Ave. Green 46 B2
Belville St. Green 46 A2
Belvoir Pl. Udd 161 E4
Bemersyde Ave. Glasg 136 A3
Bemersyde. Bish 78 B1
Bemersyde Pl. Lark 185 D1
Bemersyde Rd. Pais 132 C4
Ben Alder Dr. Pais 114 B1
Ben Bouie Dr. Helen 16 C1
Ben Buie Way. Pais 114 B1
Ben Hope Ave. Pais 114 B1
Ben Lawers Dr. Cumb 61 D1
Ben Lawers Dr. Pais 114 B1
Ben Ledi Ave. Pais 114 B1
Ben Ledi Cres. Cumb 61 D1
Ben Loyal Ave. Pais 114 B1
Ben Lui Dr. Pais 114 B1
Ben Lui Pl. Cumb 61 D1
Ben More Dr. Cumb 61 D1
Ben More Dr. Pais 114 B1
Ben Nevis Rd. Pais 114 B1
Ben Nevis Way. Cumb 61 D1
Ben Vane Ave. Pais 114 B1
Ben Venue Rd. Cumb 61 D1
Ben Venue Way. Pais 114 B1
Ben Wyvis Dr. Pais 114 B1
Benalder St. Glasg 96 B1
Benarty Gdns. Bish 78 A1
Benbain Pl. Irvine 220 A3
Benbecula. E Kil 160 B1
Benbecula Rd. Kilmk 223 D3
Bencleuch Pl. Irvine 220 A2
Bencloich Ave. Lennox 57 F4
Bencloich Cres. Lennox 33 F1
Bencloich Rd. Lennox 57 F4
Bencloich St. Lennox 33 F1
Benclutha. P Glasg 47 F1
Bencroft Dr. Glasg 137 F3
Bendigo Pl. Lan 215 D2
Benford Ave. Holy 143 E2
Benford Knowe. Holy 143 F2
Bengairn St. Glasg 118 B4
Bengal Pl. Glasg 136 B4
Bengal St. Glasg 136 B4
Benhar Pl. Glasg 118 C4
Benhar Rd. East 126 C1
Benhar Rd. Shot 147 D3
Benholm St. Glasg 118 C2
Benmore La. Gour 44 C2
Benmore. Pres 236 B3
Benmore Tower. Glasg 138 C2
Bennan House. Pres 236 A3
Bennan Sq. Glasg 117 E1
Bennoch Pl. Pres 236 B3
Benrig Ave. Kilm 222 A4
Bensley Ave. Irvine 219 F3
Bensley Rise. Irvine 219 F2
Benson St. Coat 122 A2
Benston Pl. John 111 F1
Benston Rd. John 111 F1
Bent Cres. Tan 141 E3
Bent Rd. Chap 123 E2
Bent Rd. Ham 162 B2
Bentfield Ave. Ayr 238 C3
Bentfield Dr. Pres 236 A3
Bentfoot Rd. Wish 186 B4
Benthall St. Glasg 117 E2
Bentheads. Bann 11 F4
Bentinck Cres. Troon 229 F1
Bentinck Dr. Troon 229 E1
Bentinck St. Glasg 96 C1
Bentinck St. Green 45 E4
Bentinck St. Kilmk 227 F4
Bents Rd. Glasg 120 A3
Benty's La. Car 201 F4
Benvie Gdns. Bish 78 A1
Benview Ave. P Glasg 68 C4
Benview. Bann 7 E1
Benview Rd. Newt M 157 F4
Benview Rd. P Glasg 68 C4
Benview St. Glasg 96 C2
Benview Terr. Fish 5 F2
Benview Terr. Pais 114 A1
Benvue Rd. Lennox 57 F4
Berchem Pl. Salt 216 C4
Bereland Ave. Pres 236 B4
Berelands Cres. Glasg 137 F4
Berelands Gdns. Pres 233 E1
Berelands Pl. Glasg 137 F4
Berelands Rd. Pres 233 E1
Beresford Ave. Glasg 95 F2
Beresford Gr. Irvine 219 F3
Beresford La. Ayr 238 C4
Beresford Terr. Ayr 238 C4
Berkeley St. Glasg 116 C4
Berkeley St. Stir 7 D2
Berkeley Terrace La. Glasg 116 C4
Berkley Dr. Udd 140 B1
Berl Ave. Hous 111 E4
Bernadette Ave. Holy 143 E1
Bernadette St. Holy 143 E2
Bernard Path. Glasg 118 A2
Bernard St. Glasg 118 A2
Bernard Terr. Glasg 118 A2
Bernard's Wynd. Lan 215 D2
Berneray St. Glasg 97 E4
Berridale Ave. Glasg 137 D3
Berridale Rd. Troon 229 E4
Berriedale Ave. Glasg 120 A2
Berriedale. E Kil 179 F4
Berriedale Quadrant. Wish 165 D3
Berry Dr. Irvine 219 F2
Berryburn Rd. Glasg 98 B2
Berryhill Ave. Irvine 220 A3
Berryhill. Cowie 12 C4
Berryhill Dr. Glasg 136 A1
Berryhill Pl. Shot 147 D1
Berryhill Rd. Cumb 61 F1
Berryhill Rd. Glasg 136 A1
Berryknowe Ave. Muir 100 B4
Berryknowe. Kirk 80 A4
Berryknowes Ave. Glasg 115 E3
Berryknowes La. Glasg 115 E3
Berryknowes Rd. Glasg 115 E3
Berryyards Rd. Green 45 F2
Bertram Dr. Sals 125 E1
Bertram Pl. Shot 146 B3
Bertram St. East 127 E3
Bertram St. Glasg 116 C1
Bertram St. Ham 162 A3
Bertram St. Lark 185 E1
Bertram St. Shot 146 C3
Bervie St. Glasg 115 F3
Berwick Cres. Aird 122 C3
Berwick Cres. Lin 111 F4
Berwick Dr. Glasg 115 D2
Berwick Dr. Glasg 138 B3
Berwick Pl. Coat 122 A2
Berwick Pl. E Kil 160 B2
Berwick Pl. Gour 44 B2
Berwick Rd. Gour 44 B2
Berwick Rd. P Glasg 47 E1
Berwick St. Coat 122 A2
Berwick St. Ham 162 A3
Bessemer Dr. E Kil 181 D3
Beta Ctr. Clyde 94 B4
Betula Dr. Clyde 74 A3
Bevan Ct. Ard 205 D2
Bevan Dr. Alva 5 E4
Bevan Gdns. Kilw 207 F2
Bevan Gr. John 111 F1
Beveridge Terr. Hat 142 B2
Beverley Rd. Glasg 136 B3
Bevin Ave. Clyde 74 B1
Bideford Cres. Glasg 119 E2
Bield The. Wish 165 E1
Biggar Rd. Chap 123 F1
Biggar Rd. Holy 143 F4
Biggar St. Glasg 118 A3
Biggart Rd. Pres 236 B4
Bigholm Rd. Beith 150 B1
Bigton St. Glasg 99 D1
Bilby Terr. Irvine 219 E3
Billings Rd. Mother 163 D3
Bilsland Dr. Glasg 97 D3
Bilsland Pl. Alex 27 E1
Bimson Pl. Irvine 219 D1
Binend Rd. Glasg 135 E4
Binnie La. Gour 44 C4
Binnie Pl. Glasg 117 F3
Binnie Pl. Gran 24 C1
Binnie St. Gour 44 C4
Binniehill Rd. Cumb 61 E1
Binniehill Rd. Slam 85 F2
Binns Rd. Glasg 99 E1
Birch Ave. Newt M 157 F3
Birch Ave. Stir 6 C3
Birch Brae. Ham 162 C1
Birch Cotts. Helen 16 B1
Birch Cres. John 112 A1
Birch Cres. Newt M 157 F3
Birch Ct. Coat 121 F2
Birch Dr. Glasg 139 E3
Birch Dr. Klrk 79 E3
Birch Gr. Lark 185 D3
Birch Gr. Tan 141 D4
Birch Knowe. Bish 98 A4
Birch Pl. Kilmk 227 E4
Birch Pl. Udd 161 E4
Birch Quadrant. Aird 123 E4
Birch Rd. Ayr 239 E2
Birch Rd. Clyde 74 A3
Birch Rd. Cumb 62 C2
Birch Rd. Dumb 49 F2
Birch St. Glasg 117 E2
Birch St. Holy 143 D3
Birch View. Bear 76 A3
Birch Way. Troon 229 E2
Birchfield Dr. Glasg 95 D2
Birchfield Rd. Ham 162 A2
Birchgrove. Hous 91 E1
Birchlea Dr. Glasg 136 B2
Birchview Dr. Thorn 157 F2
Birchwood Ave. Glasg 119 F2
Birchwood Dr. Pais 113 D1
Birchwood. N Sau 5 E1
Birchwood Pl. Glasg 119 F2
Birchwood Rd. Uplaw 153 D2
Birdsfield Ct. Ham 161 F3
Birdsfield Dr. Udd 161 F3
Birdsfield St. Ham 161 F3
Birdston Rd. Glasg 98 B3
Birdston Rd. M of C 58 B2
Birgidale Ave. Glasg 137 E1
Birgidale Rd. Glasg 137 E1
Birgidale Terr. Glasg 137 E1
Birkdale Cl. Kilw 207 E2
Birkdale Ct. Udd 140 C1
Birkdale. E Kil 159 E2
Birken Rd. Klrk 79 F2
Birkenburn Rd. Cumb 62 C3
Birkenshaw Rd. Glen 81 F1
Birkenshaw St. Glasg 118 A4
Birkenshaw Way. Pais 113 F4
Birkfield Loan. Car 188 B1
Birkfield Pl. Car 188 B1
Birkhall Ave. Glasg 115 D2
Birkhall Ave. Inch 93 E4
Birkhall Dr. Bear 75 F1
Birkhill Ave. Bish 78 A1
Birkhill Gdns. Bish 78 A1
Birkhill Rd. Cam 6 C3
Birkhill Rd. Car 201 E1
Birkhill Rd. Ham 183 E4
Birkhill Rd. Stir 6 C3
Birkmyre Ave. P Glasg 47 D1
Birkmyre Rd. Glasg 115 F3
Birks Ct. Law 186 C3
Birks Hill. Irvine 220 A2
Birks Pl. Lan 215 D3
Birks Rd. Lark 199 D4
Birks Rd. Law 186 C2
Birkscairn Pl. Irvine 220 B1
Birkscairn Way. Irvine 220 B1
Birkshaw Brae. Wish 186 A4
Birkshaw Pl. Wish 186 A4
Birkshaw Tower. Wish 185 F4
Birkwood St. Glasg 118 A1
Birmingham Rd. Ren 94 A1
Birnam Ave. Bish 78 A1
Birnam Cres. Bear 76 A3

247
Birnam Ct. Falk
Braehead Rd. Pais

Birnam Ct. Falk 24 B1
Birnam Gdns. Bish 78 A1
Birnam Pl. Ham 161 F2
Birnam Rd. Glasg 118 B2
Birness Dr. Glasg 136 B4
Birnie Ct. Glasg 98 B2
Birnie Rd. Glasg 98 B2
Birniehill Rd. Cle 145 D3
Birniehill Roundabout. E Kil 181 D4
Birniewell Rd. Slam 86 A3
Birnock Ave. Ren 94 C1
Birrell Rd. Miln 54 C2
Birrens Rd. Mother 163 E4
Birsay Rd. Glasg 97 D4
Bishop Gdns. Bish 77 F1
Bishop Gdns. Ham 183 F4
Bishop La. Glasg 117 D4
Bishopdale. E Kil 159 E2
Bishopmill Pl. Glasg 98 B2
Bishopmill Rd. Glasg 98 B2
Bishops Gate. Thorn 150 D2
Bishops Pk. Thorn 158 A2
Bishopsgate Dr. Bish 97 F4
Bishopsgate Gdns. Bish 97 F4
Bishopsgate Pl. Bish 97 F4
Bishopsgate Rd. Bish 97 F4
Bishpobriggs Ind Est. Bish 98 A4
Bisland Ct. Glasg 97 D3
Bissett Cres. Dunt 73 F3
Black O' Hill
Roundabout. Cumb 61 D1
Black St. Aird 103 D1
Black St. Glasg 97 E1
Blackadder Pl. E Kil 179 E4
Blackbog Rd. Glenm 82 C1
Blackbraes Rd. E Kil 160 A2
Blackburn Cres. Dumb 49 E2
Blackburn Cres. Kirk 80 A4
Blackburn Dr. Ayr 238 C3
Blackburn Pl. Ayr 238 C3
Blackburn Rd. Ayr 238 C3
Blackburn Sq. Barr 134 B1
Blackburn St. Glasg 116 C3
Blackbyres Ct. Barr 134 B2
Blackbyres Rd. Pais 134 B3
Blackcraig Ave. Glasg 75 D2
Blackcroft Ave. Chap 123 F3
Blackcroft Gdns. Glasg 119 E2
Blackcroft Rd. Glasg 119 E2
Blackcroft Terr. Sals 125 D1
Blackdyke Rd. Kirk 79 F4
Blackfarm Rd. Newt M 156 C2
Blackfaulds Dr. Fen 213 D2
Blackfaulds Gdns. Fen 213 D2
Blackfaulds Rd. Glasg 137 F4
Blackford Cres. Pres 233 F1
Blackford Rd. Pais 114 A2
Blackfriars St. Glasg 117 E4
Blackfriars Wlk. Ayr 238 C4
Blackhall Ct. Pais 114 A2
Blackhall La. Pais 113 F2
Blackhall St. Pais 114 A2
Blackhall St. Shot 147 D2
Blackhill Dr. Helen 16 B2
Blackhill Pl. Glasg 98 B1
Blackhill Rd. Blac 107 F2
Blackhill Rd. Glasg 76 C1
Blackhill St. Ayr 239 D3
Blackhill View. Law 187 D2
Blackhouse Ave. Newt M 156 C2
Blackhouse Gdns. Newt M 156 C2
Blackhouse Pl. Ayr 239 E4
Blackhouse Rd. Newt M 156 C2
Blackie St. Glasg 96 B1
Blacklands Ave. Kilw 207 F1
Blacklands Cres. Kilw 207 F1
Blacklands Pl. Kirk 79 F2
Blacklands Rd. E Kil 159 E1
Blacklaw Dr. E Kil 181 D4
Blacklaw La. Pais 113 F3
Blackmill Cres. Sten 24 A2
Blackmoor Pl. Holy 143 D2
Blackmoss Dr. Hat 142 A2
Blackmuir Pl. Tull 4 B2
Blackness St. Coat 122 A2
Blackshaw Dr. W Kil 190 B3
Blackstone Ave. Glasg 135 E4
Blackstone Cres. Glasg 115 E1
Blackstone Rd. Lin 113 D4
Blackstoun Ave. Lin 112 A3
Blackstoun Oval. Pais 113 D3
Blackstoun Rd. Pais 113 D3
Blackswell La. Ham 162 C2
Blacksyke Ave. Kilmk 227 F2
Blackthorn Ave. Beith 150 A1
Blackthorn Ave. Kirk 79 D3
Blackthorn Gr. Kirk 79 D3
Blackthorn Rd. Cumb 62 C2
Blackthorn Rd. Tan 141 E4
Blackthorn St. Glasg 97 F3
Blacktongue Farm Rd. Gree 83 F1
Blackwood Ave. Kilmk 227 F3
Blackwood Ave. Lin 112 A3
Blackwood Ave. Newt M 156 C2
Blackwood. E Kil 180 B3
Blackwood Gdns. Mother 142 B1
Blackwood Rd. Cumb 60 C1
Blackwood Rd. Miln 54 C2
Blackwood St. Barr 134 A1
Blackwood St. Glasg 95 F4
Blackwoods Cres. Hat 142 B2
Blackwoods Cres. Muir 80 C1
Bladda La. Pais 113 F2
Blades Ct. Muir 101 D3
Bladnoch Dr. Glasg 75 E1
Blaefaulds Cres. Den 39 E4
Blaeloch Ave. Glasg 137 E1
Blaeloch Dr. Glasg 137 E1
Blaeloch Terr. Glasg 137 D1
Blaeshill Rd. E Kil 179 F4
Blair Atholl Dr. Lark 185 E1
Blair Ave. Hurl 228 C3
Blair Cres. Glasg 120 A2
Blair Cres. Hurl 228 C3
Blair Dr. M of C 58 B3
Blair Gdns. Gour 43 F3
Blair Gdns. Lennox 57 D1
Blair House. Cumb 62 A2
Blair Linn View. Cumb 83 D3
Blair Path. Mother 163 F3
Blair Rd. Beith 191 F4
Blair Rd. Coat 121 F4
Blair Rd. Cro 201 D1
Blair Rd. Glasg 114 C3
Blair Rd. Hurl 228 C3
Blair Rd. Kilw 207 F3
Blair St. Glasg 118 C3
Blair St. Kilmk 222 C1
Blair Terr. Sten 24 A2
Blairafton Wynd. Kilw 207 E3
Blairatholl Ave. Glasg 96 A2
Blairatholl Gdns. Glasg 96 A2
Blairbeth Dr. Glasg 137 D4
Blairbeth Pl. Glasg 138 A3
Blairbeth Rd. Glasg 138 B3
Blairbeth Terr. Glasg 138 B3
Blairdardie Rd. Glasg 75 E1
Blairdenan Ave. Muir 81 D2
Blairdenon Cres. Falk 41 F2
Blairdenon Dr. Cumb 61 E2
Blairdenon Dr. N Sau 5 D1
Blairdenon Rd. Alva 4 C3
Blairdenon Way. Irvine 220 A1
Blairforkie Dr. B of A 1 C4
Blairgowrie Rd. Glasg 115 E2
Blairgrove Ct. Coat 121 F3
Blairhall Ave. Glasg 136 C4
Blairhill Ave. Kirk 80 A3
Blairhill Pl. Coat 121 F4
Blairhill St. Coat 121 F4
Blairholm Dr. Hat 142 A2
Blairlands Dr. Beith 191 F4
Blairlinn Rd. Cumb 82 C3
Blairlogie St. Glasg 99 D1
Blairmore Cres. Green 46 B1
Blairmore Rd. Green 46 B1
Blairmuckhole and
Forrestdyke Rd. Sals 126 C4
Blairpark Ave. Coat 121 F4
Blairquhomrie Cotts. Bonh 20 C1
Blairston Ave. Udd 141 D1
Blairston Gdns. Udd 141 D1
Blairtum Dr. Glasg 138 A3
Blairtummock Rd. Glasg 119 E4
Blairtummock Rd. Glasg 119 F4
Blake Rd. Cumb 62 A1
Blakely Rd. Salt 217 D4
Blane Ave. Strath 31 D2
Blane Cres. Strath 31 D2
Blane Dr. Miln 55 D2
Blane Pl. Strath 31 D2
Blane St. Coat 122 A4
Blanefield Ave. Pres 236 B3
Blaneview. Stepps 99 E2
Blantyre Cres. Dunt 73 F4
Blantyre Ct. Ersk 73 D2
Blantyre Dr. Bishop 72 A2
Blantyre Farm Rd. Udd 140 B3
Blantyre Gdns. Cumb 60 C1
Blantyre Mill Rd. Udd 141 D1
Blantyre Pl. Coat 121 F2
Blantyre Rd. Udd 141 D1
Blantyre St. Coat 121 F2
Blantyre St. Glasg 96 B1
Blaven Ct. Glasg 120 B2
Blaven Head. Irvine 220 A2
Blawarthill St. Glasg 94 C3
Bleachfield. Falk 42 A3
Bleachfield. Miln 55 D2
Bleeze Rd. Dalry 191 D4
Blenheim Ave. E Kil 180 B4
Blenheim Ave. Stepps 99 F3
Blenheim Ct. Kils 36 C1
Blenheim Ct. Pais 113 E3
Blenheim Pl. Sten 23 F3
Blenheim Rd. Car 188 A1
Blindwells. Alva 4 B2
Blinkbonnie Terr. Slam 86 A3
Blinkbonny Rd. Falk 41 F2
Blinny Ct. Shot 147 D2
Blochairn Rd. Glasg 98 A1
Bloomgate. Lan 215 D2
Bluebell Gdns. Glasg 138 A1
Bluebell Gdns. Mother 142 B1
Bluebell Way. Aird 102 C1
Bluebell Way. Car 201 F4
Bluebell Way. Lennox 57 F4
Bluebell Wlk. Holy 143 D2
Blueknowes Rd. Law 186 C3
Bluevale St. Glasg 118 A3
Blyth Rd. Glasg 119 F3
Blythe Pl. Glasg 119 E3
Blythswood Ave. Ren 94 B2
Blythswood Dr. Pais 113 F3
Blythswood Rd. Ren 94 B2
Blythswood Sq. Glasg 117 D4
Blythswood St. Glasg 117 D4
Bo'ness Rd. Chap 123 E1
Bo'ness Rd. Holy 143 E4
Boardwalk The. E Kil 181 D4
Boat Vennel. Ayr 235 F1
Boclair Ave. Bear 75 F2
Boclair Cres. Bear 76 A2
Boclair Cres. Bish 78 A1
Boclair Rd. Bear 76 B3
Boclair Rd. Bish 78 A1
Boclair Rd. Glasg 76 B3
Boclair St. Glasg 95 F4
Bodden Sq. Holy 143 F4
Boden Quadrant. Mother 142 B1
Boden St. Glasg 118 A2
Bodesbeck Ct. Irvine 220 A2
Bodmin Gdns. Muir 80 C2
Bog Rd. Bank 38 C2
Bog Rd. Falk 42 B3
Bog Rd. Falk 42 C2
Bogany Terr. Glasg 137 F1
Bogbain Rd. Glasg 120 A4
Bogend Rd. Bann 11 F4
Bogend Rd. Lar 23 D4
Bogend Rd. Tor 22 C4
Bogfoot Rd. Sals 125 D1
Boggknowe. Tan 140 B4
Boghall Rd. Car 202 A4
Boghall Rd. Glasg 120 A2
Boghall St. Glasg 99 D1
Boghall St. Stone 198 C1
Boghead Ave. Dumb 50 A2
Boghead. Beith 171 D4
Boghead Rd. Dumb 50 A2
Boghead Rd. Glasg 98 A2
Boghead Rd. Kirk 79 D3
Bogiewood Rd. P Glasg 47 D1
Bogle St. Green 46 A2
Boglemart St. Steven 217 E4
Bogleshole Rd. Glasg 138 C4
Boglestone Ave. P Glasg 68 C4
Bogmoor Rd. Glasg 95 E1
Bogmoor Rd. Glasg 115 E4
Bogs View. Hat 141 F2
Bogside Rd. Ash 199 F4
Bogside Rd. Kils 60 B4
Bogside Rd. P Glasg 68 C4
Bogside Rd. Stepps 99 D3
Bogside St. Glasg 118 A2
Bogston La. Green 46 C1
Bogstonhill Rd. Hous 91 D1
Bogton Ave. Glasg 136 C2
Bogton Avenue La. Glasg 136 C2
Bohun Ct. Bann 7 E2
Boleyn Rd. Glasg 116 C1
Bolingbroke. E Kil 160 B2
Bolivar Terr. Glasg 137 E4
Bolton Dr. Glasg 137 D4
Bolton Terr. Lennox 57 F4
Boman Pl. Stew 195 E1
Bon Accord Cres. Shot 146 C3
Bon Accord Rd. Newt M 157 F3
Bon Accord Sq. Clyde 94 A4
Bonar Cres. B of W 110 C4
Bonar La. B of W 110 C4
Bonar Law Ave. Helen 16 A1
Bonawe St. Glasg 96 C2
Boness St. Glasg 118 A2
Bonhill Rd. Dumb 50 A2
Bonhill St. Glasg 97 D2
Bonkle Gdns. New 166 A3
Bonkle Rd. New 166 A3
Bonnar St. Glasg 118 A2
Bonnaughton Rd. Bear 75 D3
Bonnet Ct. Stew 211 F4
Bonnet Rd. Lan 215 D2
Bonnhill View. Alex 27 F2
Bonnington Ave. Lan 215 D2
Bonnybridge Rd. Bank 39 F3
Bonnybridge Rd. Bon 39 F3
Bonnyfield Rd. Bon 39 F3
Bonnyhill Rd. Bon 40 D2
Bonnyhill Rd. Falk 41 D2
Bonnyholm Ave. Glasg 115 D2
Bonnyrigg Dr. Glasg 136 A3
Bonnyside Rd. Bon 40 A3
Bonnyton Dr. Eagle 178 B3
Bonnyton Foot. Irvine 220 A3
Bonnyton Moor Rd. Eagle 178 A4
Bonnyton Pl. Irvine 220 A3
Bonnyton Pl. Kilmk 222 B1
Bonnyton Rd. Cross 222 B1
Bonnyton Rd. Kilmk 222 B1
Bonnyton Row. Irvine 220 A3
Bonnyview Gdns. Bon 40 A3
Bonnywood Ave. Bon 40 A4
Bontine Ave. Dumb 49 E2
Bonyton Ave. Glasg 94 C3
Boon Dr. Glasg 75 D1
Booth Pl. Falk 42 A2
Boquhanran Pl. Clyde 74 A2
Boquhanran Rd. Clyde 73 F1
Boquhanran Rd. Clyde 74 A2
Borden La. Glasg 95 F3
Borden Rd. Glasg 95 F3
Border Ave. Salt 216 C4
Border Pl. Salt 216 C4
Border St. Green 46 B2
Border Way. Kirk 79 F4
Bore Rd. Aird 123 D4
Boreland Dr. Glasg 95 D3
Boreland Dr. Ham 161 F1
Boreland Pl. Glasg 95 D3
Borestone Ave. Kilb 170 A4
Borestone Cres. Stir 7 D2
Borestone Ct. Stir 7 D1
Borestone Pl. Stir 7 D1
Borgie Cres. Glasg 139 D3
Borland Cres. Eagle 178 C3
Borland Rd. Bear 76 A2
Borron St. Glasg 97 E2
Borrowdale. E Kil 179 F3
Borrowlea Rd. Stir 7 E4
Borrowmeadow Rd. Stir 7 F4
Borthwick Dr. E Kil 179 E4
Borthwick St. Glasg 99 D1
Bosfield Cnr. E Kil 159 F2
Bosfield Pl. E Kil 159 F2
Bosfield Rd. E Kil 159 F2
Boston Dr. Helen 16 C2
Boswell Ct. Glasg 136 C4
Boswell Dr. Udd 161 E4
Boswell Pk. Ayr 238 C4
Boswell Pk. E Kil 160 B2
Boswell Sq. Glasg 114 C4
Bosworth Rd. E Kil 160 A3
Botanic Cres. Glasg 96 B2
Botanic Crescent La. Glasg 96 B2
Bothkennar Rd. Air 24 C2
Bothkennar Rd. Sten 24 C2
Bothlin Dr. Stepps 99 E3
Bothlyn Ave. Kirk 79 F4
Bothlyn Cres. Muir 100 C4
Bothlyn Rd. Muir 100 B4
Bothwell La. Glasg 96 C1
Bothwell La. Glasg 117 D4
Bothwell Pl. Coat 121 F4
Bothwell Pl. Pais 132 C4
Bothwell Rd. Car 187 F2
Bothwell Rd. Ham 162 B3
Bothwell Rd. Udd 140 C2
Bothwell St. Glasg 117 D4
Bothwell St. Glasg 138 C3
Bothwell St. Ham 162 B3
Bothwellhaugh
Quadrant. Hat 141 F2
Bothwellhaugh Rd. Hat 142 A1
Bothwellpark Rd. Tan 141 E2
Bothwellshields Rd. Chap 124 B1
Boturich Dr. Bonh 19 F1
Boundary Rd. Pres 236 B2
Bourhill Ct. Wish 164 B1
Bourne Cres. Inch 93 E4
Bourne Ct. Inch 93 E4
Bourne St. Ham 162 C2
Bournemouth Rd. Gour 44 C3
Bourock Sq. Barr 134 C1
Bourtree Pk. Ayr 239 D4
Bourtree Rd. Ham 161 F1
Bouverie St. Clyde 94 C3
Bouverie St. Glasg 137 F4
Bouverie St. P Glasg 47 E1
Bow Rd. Green 45 E2
Bow St. Stir 7 D4
Bowden Dr. Glasg 115 D3
Bowden Pk. E Kil 180 B4
Bower St. Glasg 96 C2
Bowerwalls St. Barr 134 C2
Bowes Cres. Glasg 119 F2
Bowes Rigg. Stew 195 F1
Bowfield Ave. Glasg 114 C3
Bowfield Cres. Glasg 114 C3
Bowfield Dr. Glasg 115 D3
Bowfield Pl. Glasg 114 C3
Bowfield Rd. How 130 C3
Bowfield Rd. W Kil 190 B2
Bowhouse Gdns. All 10 A3
Bowhouse Rd. All 10 A3
Bowhouse Rd. Chap 123 F3
Bowhouse Rise. Irvine 220 A3
Bowhousebog
Or Liquo. Shot 146 A1
Bowhousebog Rd. Shot 146 A1
Bowhousebrae Rd. Chap 123 F3
Bowie St. Dumb 49 F2
Bowling Green La. Glasg 95 E2
Bowling Green Rd. Glasg 95 E2
Bowling Green Rd. Glasg 119 E2
Bowling Green Rd. Glasg 137 D3
Bowling Green Rd. Muir 100 B4
Bowling Green St. Hat 142 A3
Bowling Green View. Glasg 139 F2
Bowling St. Coat 121 F4
Bowman Rd. Ayr 238 C3
Bowman St. Glasg 117 D1
Bowmanflat. Lark 185 D2
Bowmont Hill. Bish 78 A2
Bowmont Pl. E Kil 179 E4
Bowmont Pl. Glasg 139 E3
Bowmont Terr. Glasg 96 B2
Bowmore Ct. Irvine 220 A3
Bowmore Gdns. Glasg 138 C2
Bowmore Gdns. Tan 140 C4
Bowmore Rd. Glasg 115 F3
Bowmore Wlk. Shot 147 D2
Bowmount Gdns. Glasg 96 B2
Bowyer Vennel. Hat 141 F3
Boyd Ct. Kilmk 223 D1
Boyd Dr. Mother 163 D4
Boyd Orr Cres. Kilm 222 A4
Boyd Orr Rd. Salt 206 A1
Boyd St. Falk 42 A3
Boyd St. Glasg 117 E1
Boyd St. Kilmk 223 D1
Boyd St. Pres 236 B4
Boydston Rd. Ard 205 E2
Boydstone Pl. Glasg 136 A3
Boydstone Rd. Glasg 135 F3
Boyle St. Clyde 94 B4
Boylestone Rd. Barr 134 A2
Boyndie St. Glasg 120 A4
Brabloch Cres. Pais 113 F3
Bracadale Dr. Glasg 120 B2
Bracadale Gdns. Glasg 120 B2
Bracadale Gr. Glasg 120 B2
Bracadale Rd. Glasg 120 B2
Bracco Rd. Cald 105 E1
Brachelston St. Green 45 E2
Bracken Pk. Ayr 239 E2
Bracken Rd. P Glasg 69 D4
Bracken St. Glasg 97 D3
Bracken St. Holy 143 D2
Bracken Terr. Udd 141 D2
Bracken Way. Lark 185 E1
Brackenbrae Ave. Bish 77 F1
Brackenbrae Rd. Bish 77 F1
Brackendene. Hous 91 E1
Brackenhill Ave. Kilmk 223 D3
Brackenhill Dr. Ham 183 E4
Brackenhill Rd. Law 187 D3
Brackenhirst Rd. Glenm 102 C4
Brackenhurst St. Dumb 50 B3
Brackenknowe Rd. Gree 83 E2
Brackenlees Rd. Air 24 C3
Brackenlees Rd. Gran 24 C2
Brackenrig Cres. Eagle 157 F1
Brackenrig Rd. Glasg 135 F1
Brackla Ave. Clyde 94 C4
Bradan Ave. Ayr 239 D1
Bradan Ave. Clyde 94 C4
Bradan Rd. Troon 229 D1
Bradbury St. Sten 24 A1
Bradda Ave. Glasg 138 B2
Bradfield Ave. Glasg 96 B3
Bradshaw Cres. Ham 161 F2
Bradshaw St. Salt 216 C4
Brady Cres. Muir 81 D2
Brae The. Bann 7 E1
Brae The. Cam 6 B3
Braedale Ave. Aird 123 E4
Braedale Ave. Mother 163 E3
Braedale Cres. New 166 A3
Braedale Pl. New 166 B3
Braedale Rd. Lan 215 D3
Braeface Rd. Cumb 61 F1
Braefield Dr. Glasg 136 A2
Braefoot Ave. Miln 76 A4
Braefoot Cres. Law 186 C3
Braefoot Cres. Pais 133 F4
Braefoot Ct. Law 186 C3
Braefoot. Irvine 219 F3
Braehead. All 4 B1
Braehead. Alva 5 D4
Braehead Ave. Ayr 236 B1
Braehead Ave. Coat 121 E2
Braehead Ave. Dunt 74 A4
Braehead Ave. Lark 184 C1
Braehead Ave. Loch 129 E2
Braehead Ave. Miln 54 C1
Braehead Ave. Neil 154 B4
Braehead Ave. Tull 4 B1
Braehead. Beith 171 D4
Braehead. Bonh 28 A2
Braehead Cres. Ayr 236 B1
Braehead Cres. Dunt 74 A4
Braehead Ct. Kilmk 223 D1
Braehead. Dalry 191 E4
Braehead Dr. Hat 141 F2
Braehead Glebe. Stew 211 F4
Braehead. Irvine 219 F3
Braehead Loan. Car 202 A4
Braehead. Loch 129 E2
Braehead Pl. Dalry 191 E4
Braehead Pl. Hat 141 F2
Braehead Pl. Rhu 15 F3
Braehead Pl. Salt 216 C4
Braehead Quadrant. Holy 143 E2
Braehead Quadrant. Neil 154 B4
Braehead Rd. Ayr 236 B1
Braehead Rd. Cumb 62 A2
Braehead Rd. Dunt 74 A4
Braehead Rd. Fen 213 D2
Braehead Rd. P Glasg 68 C4
Braehead Rd. Pais 133 E4

250

Caithness Rd. E Kil

Carrick Cres. Wish

Caithness Rd. E Kil 160 B2
Caithness Rd. Gour 44 B2
Caithness Row. Lan 215 D1
Caithness St. Glasg 96 C2
Caithness St. Udd 161 E3
Cala Sona Ct. Wish 185 F4
Calcots Path. Glasg 100 B1
Calcots Pl. Glasg 100 B1
Caldarvan St. Glasg 97 D2
Calder Ave. Barr 134 B1
Calder Ave. Cald 104 C2
Calder Ave. Coat 122 A2
Calder Ave. New 166 A3
Calder Ave. Troon 229 F3
Calder Ct. Coat 122 A2
Calder Ct. Stir 7 E3
Calder Dr. Glasg 139 D3
Calder Dr. Hat 142 B2
Calder Dr. Loch 129 E2
Calder Dr. Shot 147 D2
Calder Gate. Bish 77 F2
Calder Pl. Falk 42 B1
Calder Pl. Glasg 120 A2
Calder Pl. Kilmk 228 A3
Calder Rd. Alla 166 C4
Calder Rd. Hat 142 B3
Calder Rd. Pais 113 D3
Calder Rd. Udd 140 B3
Calder St. Calder 123 E1
Calder St. Coat 122 B3
Calder St. Glasg 117 D1
Calder St. Loch 129 E2
Calder St. Udd 161 E4
Calder Tower. Mother 163 F3
Calder View. Ham 183 D4
Calder View. Mother 163 F4
Calderbank Rd. Calder 123 D2
Calderbank Terr. Mother 163 F4
Calderbank View. Glasg 120 B2
Calderbraes Ave. Tan 140 C4
Caldercruix Rd. Cald 105 E4
Caldercuilt Rd. Glasg 76 B1
Calderglen Ave. Udd 140 B2
Calderglen Rd. E Kil 160 B1
Caldergrove. Mother 163 F4
Calderhaugh La. Loch 129 D1
Calderhead Rd. Shot 146 B4
Calderpark Ave. Glasg 120 A1
Calderpark Ave. Loch 129 E2
Calderpark Cres. Glasg 120 A1
Calderpark St. Loch 129 E2
Calderrigg Pl. Aird 123 F4
Calderside Rd. Ham 160 C2
Caldervale St. Chap 123 F2
Calderview Ave. Coat 122 C2
Calderwood Ave. Glasg 120 A2
Calderwood Dr. Glasg 120 A2
Calderwood Dr. Udd 161 E3
Calderwood Gdns. E Kil 160 C2
Calderwood Gdns. Glasg 120 A2
Calderwood. Kilw 207 F3
Calderwood Rd. E Kil 160 A1
Calderwood Rd. Glasg 136 B3
Calderwood Rd. Glasg 138 B4
Calderwood Sq. E Kil 160 A2
Caldon Rd. Irvine 219 E2
Caldwell Ave. Glasg 95 D3
Caldwell Ave. Lin 112 A3
Caldwell Gr. Hat 142 A4
Caldwell Pl. Rhu 15 F3
Caldwell Quadrant. Mother 163 E3
Caldwell Rd. Car 202 A4
Caldwell Rd. W Kil 190 B2
Caledon La. Glasg 96 B1
Caledon St. Glasg 96 B2
Caledonia Ave. Glasg 117 E2
Caledonia Ave. Glasg 138 A4
Caledonia Cres. Ard 205 E1
Caledonia Cres. Gour 44 C4
Caledonia Cres. Gour 45 D4
Caledonia Ct. Pais 113 E3
Caledonia Dr. Glasg 120 A2
Caledonia Dr. Holy 143 F2
Caledonia Rd. Ard 205 E1
Caledonia Rd. Ayr 239 E3
Caledonia Rd. Beith 150 A1
Caledonia Rd. Glasg 117 E2
Caledonia Rd. Glasg 120 A2
Caledonia Rd. Salt 216 C4
Caledonia Rd. Shot 146 C3
Caledonia St. Clyde 73 F2
Caledonia St. Glasg 117 E2
Caledonia St. P Glasg 47 E1
Caledonia St. Pais 113 E3
Caledonia Terr. Dumb 49 E2
Caledonia Way E. Inch 93 F1
Caledonia Way. Inch 93 E1
Caledonia Way W. Inch 93 E1
Caledonia Wlk. Ham 162 C1
Caledonian Ave. Hat 141 F2
Caledonian Ave. Stone 198 C1
Caledonian Cres. Glasg 96 C1
Caledonian Ct. E Kil 180 C4
Caledonian Gdns. All 9 F3
Caledonian Pl. Kilb 170 A4
Caledonian Rd. All 9 F3
Caledonian Rd. Kilb 170 B4
Caledonian Rd. Lark 185 D2
Caledonian Rd. Steven 217 F4
Caledonian Rd. Wish 165 D1
Caley Brae. Udd 140 C3
Caley Ct. Steven 217 E4
Calfhill Rd. Glasg 115 D1
Calfmuir Rd. Kirk 80 A3
Calgary Pk. E Kil 180 B4
Calgary Pl. E Kil 180 B4
Calgary St. Glasg 97 E1
California Terr. Cali 66 C3
Callaghan Wynd. Udd 140 B1
Callander Dr. Lar 41 E4
Callander St. Glasg 97 D2
Callendar Ave. Falk 42 A1
Callendar Pl. Ayr 236 A2
Callendar Rd. Falk 42 B2
Callendar Riggs. Falk 42 B2
Callender Bsns Pk. Falk 42 C2
Callender Rd. Chap 123 E1
Callender Rd. Pres 236 B3
Callieburn Rd. Bish 98 A4
Callon St. Aird 123 D4
Cally Ave. Glasg 75 D2
Calside Ave. Pais 113 F2
Calside. Pais 113 F2
Calton Cres. Stir 7 D2
Calton Entry. Glasg 117 F3
Calvay Cres. Glasg 119 E4
Calvay Rd. Glasg 119 F4
Calvinston Rd. Pres 236 B3
Cam'nethan St. Stone 198 C1
Cambourne Rd. Muir 80 C2
Cambridge Ave. Clyde 74 A2
Cambridge Ave. Gour 45 D4
Cambridge Rd. Gour 44 B2
Cambridge Rd. Ren 94 B1
Cambridge St. Glasg 117 D4
Camburn St. Glasg 118 C3
Cambus Pl. Glasg 99 E1
Cambusdoon Dr. Ayr 238 C1
Cambusdoon Pl. Kilw 207 E2
Cambusdoon Rd. Glasg 99 E1
Cambuskeith Rd. Steven 206 C2
Cambuskenneth
Gdns. Glasg 119 E3
Cambuskenneth Pl. Glasg 99 E1
Cambuslang Ind Est. Glasg 139 D4
Cambuslang Rd. Glasg 138 B4
Cambuslang Rd. Glasg 138 C4
Cambuslea Rd. Ayr 236 A2
Cambusmoon Terr. Gart 20 C4
Cambusnethan St. Wish 165 F2
Camden St. Glasg 117 E2
Camelon Cres. Udd 161 E4
Camelon Rd. Falk 41 F3
Camelon St. Glasg 118 C3
Cameron Ave. Bishop 72 A2
Cameron Cres. E Kil 158 C4
Cameron Cres. Ham 162 B2
Cameron Ct. Aird 123 F4
Cameron Ct. Glasg 138 A4
Cameron Dr. Alex 27 E4
Cameron Dr. Bear 76 A2
Cameron Dr. Kilmk 223 E1
Cameron Dr. Newt M 156 C4
Cameron Dr. Tan 141 D4
Cameron Path. Lark 185 E1
Cameron Pl. Sten 24 A1
Cameron Rd. Car 202 A4
Cameron Rd. Gree 83 E1
Cameron Sq. Dunt 74 B3
Cameron St. Clyde 94 B4
Cameron St. Coat 122 A4
Cameron St. Glasg 114 C4
Cameron St. Mother 163 E3
Cameron Terr. Gart 86 A2
Cameronian Ct. Lan 215 E3
Cameronian Dr. Car 188 A1
Cameronian Pl. Hat 141 F2
Cameronian St. Stir 7 D4
Cameronian Way. Lark 185 E1
Camis Eskan House. Card 25 E4
Camlachie St. Glasg 118 A3
Camp Rd. Glasg 117 F1
Camp Rd. Glasg 120 A3
Camp Rd. Mother 163 F2
Camp St. Mother 163 F3
Campbell Ave. Bishop 72 A2
Campbell Ave. Dumb 50 B2
Campbell Ave. Miln 55 D1
Campbell Ave. Salt 216 C4
Campbell Ave. Steven 206 B1
Campbell Cres. Alex 27 E4
Campbell Cres. Laur 42 C2
Campbell Cres. Newt M 156 C3
Campbell Cres. Udd 141 D2
Campbell Ct. Ayr 239 E4
Campbell Ct. Green 45 F4
Campbell Ct. Stir 6 C2
Campbell Dr. Barr 134 B1
Campbell Dr. Bear 75 E3
Campbell Dr. Dumb 50 B2
Campbell Dr. Helen 25 D4
Campbell Dr. Lar 23 D1
Campbell Dr. Troon 229 E3
Campbell La. Ham 162 C2
Campbell Pl. E Kil 180 C4
Campbell Pl. Irvine 225 D4
Campbell Pl. Lennox 57 D1
Campbell St. Ayr 236 A2
Campbell St. Bonh 27 F2
Campbell St. Glasg 96 C4
Campbell St. Green 45 F3
Campbell St. Ham 162 C2
Campbell St. Hat 142 A3
Campbell St. Helen 16 B2
Campbell St. John 111 F1
Campbell St. Kilmk 227 F3
Campbell St. Ren 94 B3
Campbell St. Wish 165 E1
Campbell Terr. Dumb 50 B2
Campbeltown Dr. Kilmk 222 C2
Camperdown Ct. Helen 17 D1
Campfield St. Falk 42 A3
Camphill Ave. Glasg 136 C4
Camphill Ave. Klrk 79 E4
Camphill Dr. Kilb 170 A4
Camphill Gdns. Bishop 72 B2
Camphill. Pais 113 E2
Camphill Pl. Ayr 239 D3
Campie Terr. Gran 24 C1
Campion Ct. Ayr 239 D2
Campion Rd. Mother 163 F4
Camps Cres. Ren 94 C1
Campsie Ave. Barr 134 B1
Campsie Ave. Irvine 220 A2
Campsie Cres. Aird 122 C4
Campsie Cres. Klrk 79 E3
Campsie Dene Rd. Strath 31 D2
Campsie Dr. Bear 75 F4
Campsie Dr. Inch 93 F1
Campsie Dr. Miln 55 D1
Campsie Dr. Pais 133 E4
Campsie Dr. Ren 114 A4
Campsie Gdns. Newt M 157 E4
Campsie Pl. Muir 100 B4
Campsie Rd. Kilmk 228 A2
Campsie Rd. Lennox 57 F1
Campsie Rd. Lennox 58 A1
Campsie Rd. M of C 58 A3
Campsie Rd. P Glasg 69 D3
Campsie Rd. Wish 164 C2
Campsie St. Glasg 98 A3
Campsie View. Coat 120 C3
Campsie View. Cumb 62 A2
Campsie View Dr. Strath 31 D2
Campsie View. Ham 161 F1
Campsie View. Klrk 79 D4
Campsie View. Muir 100 B4
Campsie View. Stepps 99 E2
Campsie View. Tan 141 D4
Campsie Way. Irvine 220 A2
Campsie Wlk. Irvine 220 A2
Campston Pl. Glasg 99 D1
Camsail Ave. Helen 16 A1
Camsaill Rd. Ros 15 D2
Camsbusmore Pl. Glasg 99 E1
Camsdale Ave. Sals 125 D1
Camstradden Dr E. Bear 75 E2
Camstradden Dr W. Bear 75 E2
Camus Pl. Glasg 74 C2
Canal Ave. John 112 A1
Canal Cres. Steven 217 E4
Canal Ct. Salt 217 D4
Canal La. Kirk 58 B1
Canal Pl. Salt 217 D4
Canal Rd. John 112 A1
Canal St. Falk 41 E3
Canal St. Falk 42 A4
Canal St. Glasg 97 E1
Canal St. John 112 A2
Canal St. John 112 B2
Canal St. Kirk 58 B1
Canal St. Pais 113 E2
Canal St. Ren 94 B2
Canal St. Salt 217 D4
Canal Terr. Pais 113 F2
Canavan Ct. Stir 7 E2
Canberra Ave. Clyde 73 E2
Canberra Ct. Glasg 136 C2
Canberra Dr. E Kil 180 B4
Cander Ave. Stone 199 D2
Cander Rigg. Bish 78 A2
Cander St. Lark 199 D4
Candermill &
Marlage Rd. Ash 199 F3
Candermill Rd. Ash 199 D2
Candermill Rd. Stone 199 D2
Canderside Toll. Ash 199 E3
Candimilne Ct. Car 188 A1
Candleriggs. All 10 A3
Candleriggs. Glasg 117 E4
Candren Rd. Lin 112 C3
Candren Rd. Pais 113 D2
Candren Rd. Pais 113 D3
Caneluk Ave. Car 188 A1
Cangillan Ct. Pres 236 B3
Canmore Cres. Green 45 D2
Canmore Dr. Sten 23 F2
Canmore Pl. Glasg 118 B2
Canmore Pl. Stew 195 F1
Canmore St. Glasg 118 B2
Cannerton Cres. M of C 58 A3
Cannich Dr. Pais 114 A1
Cannich Pl. New 165 F3
Canniesburn Rd. Bear 75 E2
Canniesburn Toll. Bear 75 F2
Cannons Way. Falk 24 A1
Canon Ct. Holy 143 E1
Canonbie St. Glasg 100 B1
Canongate. E Kil 160 B2
Canterbury. E Kil 180 B4
Canthill Gdns. Shot 146 A2
Cantieslaw Dr. E Kil 160 A2
Canton Way. Glasg 116 B4
Canyon Rd. Wish 164 B1
Capel Ave. Newt M 156 C3
Capel Gr. E Kil 160 A2
Capel Pl. Irvine 220 A1
Capelrig Cotts. Newt M 155 F2
Capelrig Dr. E Kil 160 A2
Capelrig Dr. Newt M 156 C4
Capelrig Rd. Newt M 156 C3
Capelrig St. Glasg 135 F2
Caplaw Pl. Wish 185 F4
Caplaw Rd. Pais 133 E3
Caplaw Rd. Uplaw 132 B1
Caplaw Tower. Wish 185 F4
Caplethill Rd. Barr 134 A3
Caplethill Rd. Pais 133 F4
Caponcraig Ave. Steven 206 B1
Capper View. Pres 233 E1
Cappielow Ind Est. Green 46 B2
Capringstone Foot. Irvine 220 A3
Caprington Ave. Kilmk 227 F2
Caprington Gdns. Kilmk 227 F2
Caprington St. Glasg 99 D1
Captain St. Green 45 F2
Cara Dr. Glasg 115 F4
Caravelle Way. Ren 94 B1
Carbarns E. Wish 164 B1
Carbarns Rd. Wish 164 B1
Carbarns W. Wish 164 B1
Carbarns. Wish 164 C1
Carberry Rd. Glasg 116 B1
Carbeth Rd. Miln 54 C1
Carbeth St. Glasg 97 D2
Carbisdale St. Glasg 97 F3
Carbost St. Glasg 76 B1
Carbrook Dr. Plea 12 B2
Carbrook St. Glasg 98 A1
Carbrook St. Pais 113 E2
Carcluie Cres. Ayr 239 D1
Cardarrach St. Glasg 98 A2
Cardean Rd. Holy 142 C3
Cardell Ave. Pais 113 D2
Cardell Cres. Chap 123 E1
Cardell Dr. Pais 113 D2
Cardell Rd. Pais 113 D2
Cardon Pl. Irvine 220 A1
Cardonald Dr. Glasg 115 D2
Cardonald Gdns. Glasg 115 D2
Cardonald Place Rd. Glasg 115 D2
Cardow Cres. Irvine 220 A3
Cardow Rd. Glasg 98 B2
Cardowan Dr. Stepps 99 F3
Cardowan Rd. Glasg 119 D4
Cardowan Rd. Stepps 99 F3
Cardrona St. Glasg 99 D2
Cardross Ave. P Glasg 68 C4
Cardross Cres. Green 46 B1
Cardross Ct. Glasg 117 F4
Cardross Pl. Green 46 B1
Cardross Rd. Alex 27 D1
Cardross Rd. Card 25 E2
Cardross Rd. Card 26 C1
Cardross Rd. Dumb 49 E2
Cardross Rd. Helen 25 D4
Cardross St. Glasg 117 F4
Cardrowan Rd. Plea 12 B1
Cardwell Rd. Gour 44 C4
Cardwell St. Glasg 117 D2
Cardyke St. Glasg 98 A2
Careloch Rd. P Glasg 68 C4
Careston Pl. Bish 78 B1
Carey Gdns. Cle 144 B1
Carey Rd. Salt 205 F2
Carfin Dr. Car 201 E1
Carfin Mill Rd. Holy 143 E1
Carfin Rd. Holy 143 E2
Carfin Rd. Mother 164 B2
Carfin St. Coat 122 A2
Carfin St. Glasg 117 D1
Carfin St. Holy 143 D2
Carfrae St. Glasg 116 B4
Cargil Ave. Kil 89 E4
Cargill Dr. Pres 236 B3
Cargill Sq. Bish 98 B4
Cargill St. Glasg 118 C2
Carham Cres. Glasg 115 E3
Carham Dr. Glasg 115 E3
Caribou Gn. E Kil 180 A4
Carillon Rd. Glasg 116 B3
Carisbrooke Cres. Bish 78 A2
Carlaverock Rd. Glasg 136 C3
Carleith Ave. Dunt 73 F3
Carleith Quadrant. Glasg 115 E4
Carleith Terr. Dunt 73 F3
Carleston St. Glasg 97 F2
Carleton Dr. Glasg 136 B2
Carleton Gate. Glasg 136 B2
Carleton Gdns. Pres 236 B4
Carlibar Ave. Glasg 94 C4
Carlibar Dr. Barr 134 B2
Carlibar Gdns. Barr 134 B2
Carlibar Rd. Barr 134 B2
Carlie Ave. B of A 2 A3
Carlile Pl. Pais 113 F3
Carlin La. Car 188 A1
Carlisle La. Aird 123 E4
Carlisle Rd. Aird 123 E3
Carlisle Rd. Ash 199 E2
Carlisle Rd. Chap 123 E3
Carlisle Rd. Chap 144 B3
Carlisle Rd. Cle 144 B1
Carlisle Rd. Ham 163 D1
Carlisle Rd. Lark 184 C4
Carlisle Rd. Lark 199 E2
Carlisle St. Glasg 97 E2
Carlowrie Ave. Udd 140 B1
Carlton Ct. Glasg 117 D3
Carlton Pl. Glasg 117 D3
Carlung Pl. W Kil 190 B2
Carlyle Ave. Glasg 114 C4
Carlyle Dr. E Kil 160 A1
Carlyle Terr. E Kil 160 A1
Carlyle Terr. Glasg 118 A1
Carmaben Rd. Glasg 119 F4
Carman Rd. Alex 27 E1
Carman Rd. Card 48 B4
Carmel Ave. Kilmk 222 B1
Carmel Dr. Spring 221 D1
Carmel Pl. Kilm 222 A4
Carmel Pl. Kilmk 222 B1
Carmel Terr. Kilmk 222 B1
Carmen View. Dumb 50 A3
Carment Dr. Glasg 136 B4
Carment Dr. Steven 217 F4
Carmichael Path. Glen 101 E3
Carmichael Pl. Glasg 136 C4
Carmichael St. Glasg 116 B3
Carmichael St. Green 45 E3
Carmichael St. Law 186 C3
Carmichael Way. Law 186 C3
Carmona Dr. Bonh 28 A4
Carmuirs Ave. Falk 41 E3
Carmuirs Dr. Falk 41 E3
Carmuirs St. Falk 41 E3
Carmunnock
By-Pass. E Kil 158 B4
Carmunnock Rd. E Kil 159 D2
Carmunnock Rd. E Kil 159 E2
Carmunnock Rd. Glasg 137 E3
Carmunnock Rd. Thorn 158 A3
Carmyle Ave. Glasg 139 D4
Carmyle Pl. Steven 217 E4
Carna Dr. Glasg 137 E3
Carnarvon St. Glasg 96 C1
Carnaughton Pl. Alva 4 C3
Carnbooth Ct. Glasg 137 F1
Carnbroe Rd. Coat 122 B2
Carnbroe Rd. Hat 122 B1
Carneddans Rd. Miln 54 B2
Carnegie Dr. Falk 41 E3
Carnegie Hill. E Kil 180 B4
Carnegie Pl. E Kil 180 B4
Carnegie Rd. Glasg 115 D3
Carnell Cres. Pres 236 B4
Carnell Terr. Pres 236 B4
Carnoch St. Glasg 76 B1
Carnock Cres. Barr 134 A1
Carnock Gdns. Miln 54 C1
Carnock Rd. Glasg 135 E4
Carnock St. Cowie 12 C4
Carnock St. Green 46 A2
Carnoustie Ave. Gour 44 A3
Carnoustie Cres. Bish 78 B1
Carnoustie Cres. E Kil 180 A3
Carnoustie Ct. Kilw 207 D2
Carnoustie Ct. Udd 140 C1
Carnoustie Pl. Glasg 116 C3
Carnoustie Pl. Hat 142 A4
Carnoustie St. Glasg 116 C3
Carntyne Path. Glasg 118 B4
Carntyne Pl. Glasg 118 B4
Carntyne Rd. Glasg 118 C4
Carntynehall Rd. Glasg 118 C3
Carnwadric Rd. Glasg 135 F2
Carnwath Ave. Glasg 136 C3
Carnwath Rd. Car 188 A1
Carnwath Rd. Kilnc 203 E3
Caroline Cres. Alva 4 C3
Caroline St. Glasg 118 C3
Carolside Ave. Newt M 157 F4
Carolside Dr. Glasg 75 D2
Carolside Gdns. Newt M 157 F4
Carradale Ave. Falk 41 E2
Carradale Cres. Cumb 81 F4
Carradale Dr. Pres 236 B3
Carradale Gdns. Bish 78 B1
Carradale Gdns. Car 202 A4
Carradale Pl. Lin 112 A3
Carradale St. Coat 121 F4
Carranbuie Rd. Car 187 F2
Carrbridge Dr. Glasg 96 B3
Carresbrook Ave. Kirk 80 A3
Carriagehill Ave. Pais 113 F1
Carriagehill Dr. Pais 113 F1
Carrick Ave. Ayr 238 C3
Carrick Ave. Salt 206 A2
Carrick Cres. Glasg 136 B1
Carrick Cres. Wish 165 D2

252

Cherry Pl. John

Colebrooke St. Glasg

Cherry Pl. John 112 A1
Cherry Pl. M of C 58 A2
Cherry Pl. Tan 141 E4
Cherry Rd. Kilmk 227 E4
Cherrybank Rd. Glasg 136 C3
Cherrybank Wlk. Aird 122 B4
Cherryhill View. Lark 184 C2
Cherrytree Cres. Lark 185 D3
Cherrywood Dr. Beith 150 B1
Cherrywood Rd. John 112 B1
Chester Rd. Gour 44 C2
Chester St. Glasg 119 D3
Chesterfield Ave. Glasg 96 A3
Chesters Cres. Mother 163 E4
Chesters Pl. Glasg 138 A4
Chesters Rd. Bear 75 E2
Chestnut Ave. Beith 171 D4
Chestnut Ave. Bishop 71 F3
Chestnut Ave. Cumb 62 C3
Chestnut Cres. Duni 21 E2
Chestnut Cres. E Kil 180 B3
Chestnut Cres. Ham 162 C1
Chestnut Cres. Tan 141 E4
Chestnut Ct. Cumb 62 C3
Chestnut Ct. M of C 58 A3
Chestnut Dr. Clyde 74 A3
Chestnut Dr. Klrk 79 D3
Chestnut Gr. Car 187 F1
Chestnut Gr. Glen 101 E3
Chestnut Gr. Lark 185 D3
Chestnut Gr. Mother 163 E2
Chestnut Gr. Sten 23 F2
Chestnut Gr. Udd 161 E4
Chestnut La. Miln 54 C1
Chestnut Pl. Cumb 62 C3
Chestnut Pl. John 132 A4
Chestnut Pl. Kilmk 227 E4
Chestnut Rd. Ayr 239 E3
Chestnut St. Glasg 97 E3
Cheviot Ave. Barr 134 B1
Cheviot Cres. Wish 164 C2
Cheviot Ct. Aird 103 D1
Cheviot Ct. Irvine 220 A2
Cheviot Dr. Newt M 156 B2
Cheviot Gdns. Bear 75 E4
Cheviot Head. Irvine 219 F2
Cheviot Pl. Kilmk 228 A2
Cheviot Rd. Glasg 136 B3
Cheviot Rd. Ham 162 C1
Cheviot Rd. Lark 185 E1
Cheviot Rd. Pais 113 F1
Cheviot St. Udd 161 E4
Cheviot Way. Irvine 220 A2
Chillin Pl. Lark 185 E1
Chirnside Ct. Ham 161 F3
Chirnside Pl. Glasg 115 D3
Chirnside Rd. Glasg 115 D3
Chisholm Ave. Bishop 72 B2
Chisholm Ave. Stir 2 A2
Chisholm Dr. Newt M 156 C3
Chisholm St. Coat 122 A4
Chisolm St. Glasg 117 E3
Chriss Ave. Ham 183 E4
Christchurch Pl. E Kil 180 A4
Christian St. Glasg 136 B4
Christie Gdns. Salt 216 C4
Christie La. Pais 113 F3
Christie St. Hat 142 B3
Christie St. Pais 113 F3
Christopher St. Glasg 98 A1
Chromars Pl. Green 45 F2
Chryston Rd. Kirk 80 B3
Chryston Rd. Muir 100 B4
Chryston Rd. Twe 80 B3
Chuckie La. Kilbar 111 E3
Church Ave. Card 48 A4
Church Ave. Glasg 138 B3
Church Ave. New 166 A2
Church Ave. Stepps 99 E3
Church Cres. Aird 103 F1
Church Cres. Ham 183 E3
Church Ct. Ayr 236 A1
Church Ct. Dumb 49 F2
Church Dr. Klrk 79 E3
Church Gr. N Sau 5 E1
Church Hill. Pais 113 F3
Church La. Car 187 F1
Church La. Coat 122 A4
Church La. Duni 21 E2
Church La. Kilmk 227 F3
Church La. Kils 60 B4
Church Pl. Cald 104 C2
Church Pl. Falk 42 A3
Church Pl. O Kill 73 D3
Church Pl. Rhu 15 E2
Church Pl. Salt 205 E1
Church Rd. B of W 110 C4
Church Rd. Cali 66 C3
Church Rd. Glasg 136 B1
Church Rd. Kil 89 F1
Church Rd. Muir 100 B4
Church Rd. New 166 B3
Church Rd. Newt M 157 F3
Church Rd. Rhu 15 E3
Church St. Alex 27 F2
Church St. All 10 A3
Church St. Bon 40 B2
Church St. Clyde 74 A2
Church St. Coat 122 A4
Church St. Dumb 49 F2
Church St. East 127 E3
Church St. Glasg 96 B1
Church St. Glasg 120 B2
Church St. Gour 44 C4
Church St. Ham 162 C2
Church St. Holy 143 F2
Church St. Irvine 219 D1
Church St. John 111 F2
Church St. Kilbar 111 D2
Church St. Kilmk 222 C1
Church St. Kils 60 B4
Church St. Kilw 207 F2
Church St. Lark 185 D1
Church St. Loch 129 E1
Church St. P Glasg 47 E1
Church St. Sten 23 F2
Church St. Sten 24 B1
Church St. Troon 229 E1
Church St. Udd 140 C3
Church St. Udd 161 F4
Church View. Coat 122 A4
Church View Ct. Lennox 33 E1
Church View Gdns. Hat 142 A3
Church View. Glasg 139 D4
Church Wlk. Den 21 F1
Churchill Ave. E Kil 159 F1
Churchill Ave. John 131 E4
Churchill Ave. Kilw 208 A2
Churchill Cres. Ayr 239 E4
Churchill Cres. Udd 141 D2
Churchill Dr. Ard 205 E2
Churchill Dr. B of A 2 A3
Churchill Dr. Bishop 72 A2
Churchill Dr. Glasg 96 A2
Churchill Pl. Kilbar 111 D2
Churchill Rd. Kil 89 E4
Churchill Sq. Helen 17 D1
Churchill St. All 9 F4
Churchill Way. Glasg 77 F1
Circus Dr. Glasg 117 F4
Circus Pl. Glasg 117 F4
Circus Place La. Glasg 117 F4
Citadel Pl. Ayr 235 F1
Citadel Pl. Mother 163 E4
Citadel Way. Troon 229 F4
Citizen La. Glasg 117 E4
Citrus Cres. Tan 141 E4
Cityford Cres. Glasg 137 F4
Cityford Dr. Glasg 137 F3
Civic St. Glasg 97 D1
Civic Way. Klrk 79 E4
Clachan Dr. Glasg 115 F4
Clachan Rd. Ros 15 D2
Clachan The. Wish 165 D2
Clackmannan Rd. All 10 B3
Claddens Pl. Klrk 79 F2
Claddens Quadrant. Glasg 97 E3
Claddens St. Glasg 97 D3
Claddoch Cotts. Card 25 E3
Cladence Gr. E Kil 180 C3
Clair Rd. Bish 78 B1
Claire St. New 166 A3
Clairinch Gdns. Ren 94 B1
Clairmont Gdns. Glasg 96 C1
Clamp Rd. Mother 164 B2
Clamps Gr. E Kil 181 D4
Clamps Terr. E Kil 181 D4
Clamps Wood. E Kil 181 D4
Clanrye Dr. Coat 122 A2
Clapperhow Rd. Holy 143 D1
Clare St. Glasg 98 A1
Claremont. All 9 F4
Claremont Ave. Klrk 79 D4
Claremont Cres. Kilw 207 E2
Claremont Dr. B of A 2 B4
Claremont Dr. Miln 55 D1
Claremont Gdns. Miln 55 D1
Claremont Pass. Glasg 96 C1
Claremont Pl. Glasg 96 C1
Claremont St. Bon 39 F3
Claremont St. Glasg 116 C4
Claremont Terr. Glasg 96 C1
Claremont Terrace La. Glasg 96 C1
Claremount Ave. Glasg 136 B1
Clarence Dr. Glasg 96 A2
Clarence Dr. Pais 114 A2
Clarence Gdns. Glasg 96 A2
Clarence La. Glasg 96 A2
Clarence St. Clyde 74 B2
Clarence St. Green 45 F3
Clarence St. Pais 114 A3
Clarendon Pl. Ayr 239 E3
Clarendon Pl. Glasg 97 D1
Clarendon Pl. Stir 7 D4
Clarendon Rd. Stir 7 D4
Clarendon Rd. Wish 164 C1
Clarendon St. Glasg 97 D1
Clarinda Ave. Falk 41 D3
Clarinda Cres. Kirk 59 D1
Clarinda Pl. Holy 143 E2
Clarion Cres. Glasg 95 D4
Clarion Rd. Glasg 95 D4
Clark Cres. Steven 217 E4
Clark Dr. Irvine 219 F2
Clark Pl. Lennox 78 B4
Clark Pl. Newt M 156 A2
Clark Pl. Salt 206 A1
Clark St. Aird 123 D4
Clark St. Clyde 73 F2
Clark St. John 111 F2
Clark St. Kilmk 227 F4
Clark St. New 165 F3
Clark St. Pais 113 E3
Clark St. Ren 94 A2
Clark St. Stir 7 D1
Clark Way. Hat 141 F4
Clarke Ave. Ayr 238 C3
Clarkston Ave. Glasg 136 C2
Clarkston Dr. Aird 123 E4
Clarkston Rd. Glasg 136 C2
Clarkwell Rd. Ham 161 F2
Clarkwell Terr. Ham 161 F2
Clathic Ave. Bear 76 A2
Claud Rd. Pais 114 A3
Claude Ave. Glasg 139 F2
Claude St. Lark 185 D2
Clavens Rd. Glasg 114 C3
Claverhouse Pl. Pais 114 A2
Claverhouse Rd. Glasg 114 C4
Clavering St E. Pais 113 E3
Clavering St W. Pais 113 E2
Clay Cres. Hat 142 B4
Clay Cres. Kilmk 222 C1
Clay Rd. Hat 142 B4
Clayhouse Rd. Stepps 99 F2
Claymore Dr. Bann 7 E2
Claymore Dr. Hous 111 E4
Claypotts Pl. Glasg 99 D1
Claypotts Rd. Glasg 99 D1
Clayslaps Rd. Glasg 96 B1
Clayslaps View. Kilmk 228 A2
Claythorn Ave. Glasg 117 F3
Claythorn Cir. Glasg 117 F3
Claythorn Ct. Glasg 117 F3
Claythorn Pk. Glasg 117 F3
Claythorn St. Glasg 117 F3
Claythorn Terr. Glasg 117 F3
Clayton Ave. Irvine 219 E2
Clayton Path. Hat 142 A4
Clayton Terr. Glasg 117 F4
Clearfield Ave. Ham 162 A2
Cleaves The. Tull 4 A1
Cleddans Cres. Dunt 74 B3
Cleddans Rd. Dunt 74 B3
Cleddans Rd. Kirk 58 C1
Cleddans View. Clyde 74 B2
Cleddans View. Glenm 102 C2
Cleddens Ct. Bish 78 A1
Cleeves Ave. Beith 191 F3
Cleeves Quadrant. Glasg 135 D3
Cleeves Rd. Glasg 135 D3
Cleghorn Ave. Lan 215 D3
Cleghorn Rd. Lan 215 D3
Cleghorn St. Glasg 97 D2
Cleish Ave. Bear 75 E4
Cleland La. Glasg 117 E3
Cleland Pl. E Kil 160 A2
Cleland Rd. Cle 144 A1
Cleland Rd. Holy 143 E1
Cleland Rd. Holy 144 A1
Cleland Rd. Wish 165 D2
Cleland St. Glasg 117 E3
Clelland Ave. Bish 98 A4
Clem Attlee Gdns. Lark 185 D1
Clements Pl. Steven 206 C1
Clerkland Rd. Stew 195 E1
Clerwood St. Glasg 118 B3
Cleuch Ave. Tull 4 A1
Cleuch Dr. Alva 4 C4
Cleuch Gdns. Newt M 157 E4
Cleughearn Rd. Auld 180 B1
Clevans Rd. B of W 110 B4
Cleveden Cres. Glasg 96 A3
Cleveden Crescent La. Glasg 96 A3
Cleveden Dr. Glasg 96 B2
Cleveden Dr. Glasg 138 B3
Cleveden Drive La. Glasg 96 B2
Cleveden Gdns. Glasg 96 B3
Cleveden La. Glasg 96 A3
Cleveden Pl. Glasg 96 A3
Cleveden Rd. Glasg 96 A3
Cleveden Rd. Glasg 96 B3
Cleveland La. Glasg 116 C4
Cleveland St. Glasg 116 C4
Cliff Rd. Glasg 96 C1
Clifford Gdns. Glasg 116 A3
Clifford La. Glasg 116 B3
Clifford Pl. Glasg 116 B3
Clifford Rd. Stir 7 D3
Clifford St. Glasg 116 B3
Clifton Pl. Coat 122 B3
Clifton Pl. Glasg 116 C4
Clifton Rd. Glasg 136 A2
Clifton St. Glasg 96 C1
Clifton Terr. Glasg 138 C2
Clifton Terr. John 112 A1
Climie Pl. Kilmk 228 A4
Clincart Rd. Glasg 137 D4
Clincarthill Rd. Glasg 138 A4
Clippens Rd. Lin 111 F4
Clippens Rd. Lin 112 A3
Clive St. Shot 146 C3
Cloak Rd. Kil 69 E2
Cloan Ave. Glasg 75 D1
Cloan Cres. Bish 78 A2
Clober Farm La. Miln 54 C2
Clober Rd. Miln 55 D1
Cloberfield Gdns. Miln 54 C2
Cloberfield. Miln 54 C2
Cloberhill Rd. Glasg 75 E1
Cloch Brae. Gour 44 A3
Cloch Rd. Gour 43 F3
Cloch St. Glasg 119 D4
Clochbar Ave. Miln 54 C2
Clochbar Gdns. Miln 54 C1
Clochoderick Ave. Kilbar 111 D1
Clochranhill Rd. Ayr 238 C1
Clockerhill Pl. Holy 143 F2
Cloister Ave. Aird 123 E2
Clonbeith St. Glasg 99 F1
Cloncaird. Kilw 207 E1
Closeburn St. Glasg 97 E3
Cloth St. Barr 134 B1
Clouden Rd. Cumb 62 A1
Cloudhowe Terr. Udd 140 B1
Clouston La. Glasg 96 C2
Clouston St. Glasg 96 C2
Clova Pl. Udd 140 C3
Clova St. Glasg 135 F2
Clove Mill Wynd. Lark 184 C1
Clover Leaf Path. Alex 27 F2
Cloverbank St. Glasg 98 A1
Clovergate. Bish 77 F1
Cloverhill. Ayr 239 E3
Cloverhill Pl. Muir 100 B4
Cloverhill Terr. E Kil 159 F1
Cloverhill View. E Kil 159 E1
Cloves The. Men 4 A3
Cluanie Ave. Shot 146 C3
Clune Brae. P Glasg 47 F1
Clune Dr. Pres 236 B4
Clune Park St. P Glasg 47 F1
Clunie Pl. Coat 122 A2
Clunie Pl. New 165 F3
Clunie Rd. Glasg 115 F2
Cluny Ave. Bear 76 A1
Cluny Ave. Dunt 74 B4
Cluny Dr. Bear 76 A1
Cluny Dr. Pais 114 A3
Cluny Dr. Sten 23 F2
Cluny Gdns. Glasg 95 F2
Cluny Gdns. Glasg 120 A2
Cluny Villas. Glasg 95 F2
Clutha Pl. E Kil 180 A4
Clutha St. Glasg 116 B3
Clyde Ave. Barr 134 B1
Clyde Ave. Ham 163 E1
Clyde Ave. Lennox 78 A4
Clyde Ave. Udd 140 C1
Clyde Cres. Lan 215 D3
Clyde Cres. Lar 23 D2
Clyde Ct. Clyde 73 F3
Clyde Ct. Dumb 49 F2
Clyde Dr. Hat 142 B2
Clyde Dr. Shot 147 D2
Clyde La. Holy 143 D2
Clyde Pl. Ard 205 E2
Clyde Pl. Glasg 117 D3
Clyde Pl. Glasg 139 E2
Clyde Pl. Holy 143 D2
Clyde Pl. John 131 E4
Clyde Pl. Kilmk 228 A3
Clyde Pl. Troon 229 F3
Clyde Rd. Gour 44 C3
Clyde Rd. Pais 114 A4
Clyde Shopping Ctr. Clyde 74 A1
Clyde Sq. Green 45 F3
Clyde St. Car 187 F1
Clyde St. Coat 122 B4
Clyde St E. Helen 16 C1
Clyde St E. Helen 25 C4
Clyde St. Falk 41 F3
Clyde St. Glasg 117 E3
Clyde St. Ren 94 B3
Clyde Terr. Ard 205 E2
Clyde Terr. Mother 164 B1
Clyde Terr. Udd 141 D1
Clyde Tower. Mother 163 F3
Clyde Valley Ave. Mother 163 F2
Clyde View Ave. Steven 206 B1
Clyde View Ct. O Kill 72 B4
Clyde View. Ham 162 A1
Clyde View. Pais 114 A1
Clyde Way. Pais 114 A4
Clyde Wynds. Green 45 E2
Clydebrae Dr. Udd 162 A4
Clydebrae St. Glasg 116 A4
Clydeford Dr. Glasg 118 C2
Clydeford Dr. Udd 140 C4
Clydeford Rd. Glasg 139 D4
Clydeholm Rd. Glasg 95 E1
Clydeholm Terr. Clyde 94 B4
Clydeneuk Dr. Udd 140 B4
Clydesdale Ave. Ham 183 E3
Clydesdale Ave. Ren 94 A1
Clydesdale Ave. Wish 164 B1
Clydesdale Pl. Ham 183 E3
Clydesdale Rd. Hat 142 B2
Clydesdale St. Ham 162 B2
Clydesdale St. Holy 142 C2
Clydesdale St. Lark 185 D2
Clydeshore Rd. Dumb 49 F2
Clydeside Expressway. Glasg 116 C4
Clydeside Ind Est. Glasg 95 F1
Clydeside Rd. Glasg 117 F1
Clydesmill Dr. Glasg 139 D4
Clydesmill Gr. Glasg 139 D4
Clydesmill Pl. Glasg 139 D4
Clydesmill Rd. Glasg 139 D4
Clydevale. Udd 141 D1
Clydeview. Dumb 49 F1
Clydeview Rd. Green 46 A1
Clydeview Rd. P Glasg 68 C4
Clydeview Shopping Ctr. Udd 161 F4
Clydeview Terr. Glasg 139 E4
Clydeview. Udd 141 E1
Clynder Rd. Green 46 B1
Clynder St. Glasg 116 A3
Clyth Dr. Glasg 136 B1
Co-Operative Terr. John 112 A2
Coach Cl. Kils 61 D4
Coach Pl. Kils 60 C4
Coach Rd. Kils 60 C4
Coal Wynd. Bann 7 E1
Coalburn Rd. Tan 141 D3
Coalburn St. Gree 83 F1
Coalgate. All 10 A3
Coalhall Ave. Holy 143 D1
Coalhill Pl. Ard 205 D2
Coalhill St. Glasg 118 A3
Coalpots Way. Fish 5 F2
Coatbank St. Coat 122 A3
Coatbank Way. Coat 122 A3
Coatbridge Rd. Aird 102 B2
Coatbridge Rd. Coat 101 D2
Coatbridge Rd. Coat 120 C3
Coatbridge Rd. Glasg 120 C3
Coatbridge Rd. Glen 101 F3
Coatbridge Rd. Glenm 102 B2
Coathill St. Coat 122 A2
Coats Cres. Glasg 120 A3
Coats Dr. Pais 113 D2
Coats Pl. Dund 225 F1
Coats St. Coat 122 A3
Coatshill Ave. Udd 140 B1
Cobbett Rd. Mother 163 D3
Cobblebrae Cres. Falk 24 A1
Cobblerigg Way. Udd 140 C3
Cobbleton Rd. Holy 142 C1
Cobden Rd. Glasg 97 F1
Cobden St. Alva 5 D3
Cobden St. Alva 5 D4
Cobham St. Green 46 C1
Cobington Pl. Glasg 99 D1
Cobinshaw St. Glasg 119 D3
Coblecrook Gdns. Alva 4 C3
Coblecrook La. Alva 4 C3
Coblecrook Pl. Alva 4 C3
Coburg St. Glasg 117 D3
Cochno Rd. Dunt 74 A4
Cochno St. Clyde 74 B1
Cochran St. Pais 113 F2
Cochrane Ave. Dund 225 F1
Cochrane Ave. Falk 42 A2
Cochrane Cres. Alva 4 C4
Cochrane Ct. Miln 76 B4
Cochrane Dr. Dund 225 F1
Cochrane Pl. Helen 17 D1
Cochrane Pl. Pres 236 A4
Cochrane St. Barr 134 A1
Cochrane St. Falk 42 A2
Cochrane St. Glasg 117 E4
Cochrane St. Hat 141 F3
Cochrane St. Irvine 219 D1
Cochrane St. Kilb 149 D1
Cochranemill Rd. John 111 E1
Cochranes The. Alva 5 D4
Cochrie Pl. Tull 4 B1
Cockburn Pl. Coat 121 F2
Cockburn Pl. Shew 224 C3
Cockburn St. Falk 42 A2
Cockels Loan. Ren 94 A1
Cockenzie St. Glasg 119 D3
Cocklebie Rd. Stew 195 E1
Cockmuir St. Glasg 98 A2
Cogan Rd. Glasg 136 B3
Cogan St. Barr 134 A1
Cogan St. Glasg 136 B4
Coila Ave. Pres 236 B3
Coire Loan. Shot 147 D2
Colbert St. Glasg 117 F2
Colbreggan Ct. Dunt 74 B3
Colbreggan Gdns. Dunt 74 B3
Colchester Dr. Glasg 96 A3
Coldgreen Ave. Kilb 149 D1
Coldingham Ave. Clyde 94 C3
Coldstream Cres. Wish 165 E3
Coldstream Dr. Glasg 138 B3
Coldstream Dr. Pais 113 D1
Coldstream Pl. Glasg 97 E2
Coldstream Rd. Clyde 74 A1
Coldstream St. Udd 161 E4
Coldstream. W Kil 190 B3
Colebrooke Pl. Glasg 96 C2
Colebrooke St. Glasg 96 C2
Colebrooke St. Glasg 139 D3

253
Colebrooke Terr. Glasg — Craigie La. Lark

Colebrooke Terr. Glasg 96 C2
Coleburn Ct. Irvine 219 F3
Coleridge Ave. Udd 141 D2
Coleridge. E Kil 180 A4
Colfin St. Glasg 100 B1
Colgrain St. Glasg 97 D3
Colgrave Cres. Glasg 118 C2
Colinbar Circ. Barr 134 A1
Colinslee Ave. Pais 113 F1
Colinslee Cres. Pais 113 F1
Colinslee Dr. Pais 113 F1
Colinslie Rd. Glasg 135 E4
Colinton Pl. Glasg 119 D4
Colintraive Ave. Glasg 98 C2
Colintraive Cres. Glasg 98 C2
Coll Ave. P Glasg 69 D4
Coll Ave. Ren 94 B1
Coll. E Kil 181 E4
Coll Gdns. Irvine 225 D4
Coll Pl. Glasg 98 A1
Coll St. Glasg 98 A1
Coll St. New 165 F3
Colla Gdns. Bish 78 B1
Collace Ave. B of W 110 B4
College Cres. Falk 42 B4
College La. Glasg 117 E4
College Pk. Troon 229 F4
College St. Dumb 49 F2
College St. Glasg 117 E4
College Way. Dumb 49 F2
College Wynd. Kilmk 227 F4
Collenan Ave. Troon 230 A2
Collessie Dr. Glasg 99 E1
Collier St. John 111 F2
Colliertree Rd. Aird 123 E4
Collina St. Glasg 96 B3
Collingwood Ct. Falk 41 F3
Collingwood Pl. Helen 17 D1
Collingwood Terr. Gour 44 C3
Collins Dr. Troon 230 A2
Collins Rd. Helen 25 D4
Collins St. Dunt 74 B3
Collins St. Glasg 117 F4
Collyland Rd. N Sau 5 E2
Collylinn Rd. Bear 75 F2
Colmonell Ave. Glasg 94 C4
Colonsay Ave. P Glasg 69 D4
Colonsay Ave. Ren 94 B1
Colonsay Dr. Newt M 156 A3
Colonsay. E Kil 181 E4
Colonsay House. Pres 236 A3
Colonsay Pl. Kilmk 223 D3
Colonsay Rd. Glasg 115 F3
Colonsay Rd. Pais 133 E4
Colonsay Terr. Falk 42 A1
Colquhoun Ave. Glasg 115 D4
Colquhoun Ct. Glasg 116 B2
Colquhoun Dr. Alex 27 F4
Colquhoun Dr. Bear 75 F3
Colquhoun. Dumb 50 A2
Colquhoun Rd. Dumb 50 C1
Colquhoun Rd. Kilmk 223 E1
Colquhoun Sq. Helen 16 B1
Colquhoun St. Dumb 50 A2
Colquhoun St. Helen 16 B1
Colquhoun St. Stir 7 E3
Colsnaur. Men 4 A3
Colson Pl. Hat 142 B2
Colston Ave. Bish 97 F4
Colston Dr. Bish 97 F4
Colston Gdns. Aird 123 E4
Colston Gdns. Bish 97 F4
Colston Path. Bish 97 F4
Colston Pl. Aird 123 E4
Colston Pl. Bish 97 F4
Colston Rd. Aird 123 E4
Colston Rd. Glasg 97 F4
Colston Terr. Aird 123 E4
Colt Ave. Coat 101 F1
Colt Pl. Coat 122 A4
Colt Terr. Coat 122 A4
Coltmuir Cres. Bish 97 F4
Coltmuir Dr. Bish 97 F4
Coltmuir Gdns. Bish 97 F4
Coltmuir St. Glasg 97 D3
Coltness Ave. Alla 166 C4
Coltness Dr. Hat 142 A2
Coltness La. Glasg 119 E4
Coltness Rd. Wish 165 E3
Coltness St. Glasg 119 E4
Coltpark Ave. Bish 97 F4
Coltpark La. Bish 97 F4
Coltsfoot Dr. Glasg 135 D2
Coltswood Ct. Coat 122 A4
Coltswood Rd. Coat 122 A4
Columba Cres. Mother 142 B1
Columba Path. Udd 161 E4
Columba St. Glasg 116 A4
Columba St. Green 45 E2
Columba St. Helen 16 B1
Columbia Pl. E Kil 180 A4
Columbia Way. E Kil 180 A4
Columbine Way. Car 201 F4
Colvend St. Glasg 117 F2
Colville Dr. Glasg 138 B3
Colvilles Pl. E Kil 181 D3
Colvilles Rd. E Kil 181 D3
Colwood Ave. Glasg 135 D2
Colwood Gdns. Glasg 135 D2
Colwood Pl. Glasg 135 D2
Colwood Sq. Glasg 135 D2
Colwyn Ct. Aird 103 D1
Colzium View. Kils 60 C4
Combe Quadrant. Hat 141 F2
Comedie Rd. Stepps 99 F2
Comely Bank. Ham 161 F2
Comely Park Terr. Falk 42 A2
Comely Pl. Falk 42 A2
Comelybank La. Dumb 49 E2
Comelybank Rd. Dumb 49 F2
Comelypark Pl. Glasg 118 A3
Comelypark St. Glasg 118 A3
Commerce St. Glasg 117 D3
Commercial Ct. Glasg 117 E3
Commercial Rd. Barr 134 B2
Commercial Rd. Glasg 117 E3
Common Gn. Ham 162 C2
Commonhead Ave. Aird 102 C1
Commonhead La. Aird 102 C1
Commonhead Rd. Coat 120 C4
Commonhead Rd. Glasg 120 C4
Commonhead Rd. Kilmk 228 A2
Commonhead St. Aird 102 C1
Commonside St. Aird 102 C1
Commore Ave. Barr 134 B1
Commore Dr. Glasg 95 D4
Commore Pl. Neil 154 B3
Community Ave. Hat 142 A1
Community Pl. Hat 142 A2
Community Rd. Hat 142 A1
Comrie Cres. Ham 161 F2
Comrie Rd. Stepps 99 E3
Comrie St. Glasg 119 D2
Cona St. Glasg 135 F2
Conan Ct. Glasg 139 E3
Condorrat
Interchange. Cumb 82 B4
Condorrat Rd. Cumb 82 A2
Condorrat Rd. Glen 82 A2
Condorrat Rd. Glenm 102 B3
Condorrat Ring Rd. Cumb 82 B4
Coneyhill Rd. B of A 2 A4
Coneypark Cres. Bank 38 B2
Coneypark Pl. Bank 38 B2
Coneypark. Stir 6 C3
Congress Rd. Glasg 116 B4
Conifer Pl. Kirk 79 D3
Coningsby Pl. All 10 A3
Conisborough Path. Glasg 99 F1
Conisborough Rd. Glasg 100 A1
Coniston Dr. Hat 142 A2
Coniston. E Kil 179 F3
Conistone Cres. Glasg 119 F2
Connal St. Glasg 118 A2
Connell Cres. Miln 55 E1
Connell Ct. Kilb 149 D1
Conner Ave. Falk 42 A4
Conniston St. Glasg 118 C4
Connor Rd. Barr 134 A2
Connor St. Aird 103 F1
Conon Ave. Bear 75 E2
Consett La. Glasg 119 E4
Consett St. Glasg 119 E4
Constable Rd. Stir 7 D3
Constarry Rd. Kils 60 C2
Container Way. Green 45 F3
Content Ave. Ayr 239 D4
Content St. Ayr 236 A1
Contin Pl. Glasg 96 B3
Convair Way. Ren 94 B1
Conval Way. Pais 113 E4
Conway Ct. Falk 41 F2
Coo La. Eagle 178 C3
Coodham Pl. Kilw 207 E2
Cook Rd. Bonh 28 A4
Cook St. Glasg 117 D3
Coolgardie Gn. E Kil 180 B4
Coolgardie Pl. E Kil 180 B4
Cooper's Well St. Glasg 96 B1
Cooperage La. Falk 42 A3
Copenhagen Ave. E Kil 180 C3
Copland Pl. Alva 4 C4
Copland Pl. Glasg 116 A3
Copland Quadrant. Glasg 116 A3
Copland Rd. Glasg 116 A3
Coplaw St. Glasg 117 D2
Copperfield La. Tan 141 D4
Coral Terr. Hat 142 A2
Coralmount Gdns. Kirk 79 F4
Coranbae Pl. Ayr 238 A1
Corbett Ct. Glasg 118 C2
Corbett St. Glasg 119 D2
Corbie Pl. Miln 54 B1
Corbiewood Dr. Bann 11 F4
Corbiston Way. Cumb 62 A1
Cordiner St. Glasg 137 D4
Corentin Ct. Falk 42 B2
Corkerhill Gdns. Glasg 115 F2
Corkerhill Pl. Glasg 115 F1
Corkerhill Rd. Glasg 115 E2
Corlaich Ave. Glasg 137 F4
Corlaich Dr. Glasg 137 F4
Corlic St. Green 46 A1
Corlic Way. Kil 89 E4
Cormack Ave. Lennox 57 E1
Cormorant Ave. Hous 111 E4
Corn Exchange Rd. Stir 7 D4
Corn St. Glasg 97 D1
Cornaig Rd. Glasg 135 D4
Cornalee Gdns. Glasg 135 D4
Cornalee Pl. Glasg 135 D4
Cornalee Rd. Glasg 135 D4
Cornelia St. Mother 142 A1
Cornelian Terr. Hat 142 A2
Cornhaddock St. Green 45 F2
Cornhill. Ayr 239 D2
Cornhill Cres. Stir 7 D2
Cornhill Dr. Coat 121 F4
Cornhill St. Glasg 98 A3
Cornock Cres. Clyde 74 A2
Cornock St. Clyde 74 A2
Cornsilloch Brae. Ash 186 A2
Cornton Cres. B of A 2 A3
Cornton Rd. B of A 2 A2
Cornton Rd. Stir 2 A2
Cornwall Ave. Glasg 138 B3
Cornwall Dr. E Kil 159 F1
Cornwall St. E Kil 159 F1
Cornwall St. Glasg 116 B3
Cornwall St S. Glasg 116 B3
Cornwall Way. E Kil 159 F1
Coronation Ave. Lark 199 D4
Coronation Cres. Lark 199 D4
Coronation Pl. Gran 24 C2
Coronation Pl. Lark 199 D4
Coronation Pl. Muir 100 C4
Coronation Rd E. Holy 142 C2
Coronation Rd. Holy 142 C2
Coronation St. Pres 233 E3
Coronation St. Wish 165 E2
Coronation Way. Bear 76 A1
Corpach Pl. Glasg 100 B1
Corporation St. Falk 42 B2
Corra Linn. Ham 162 A2
Corran Ave. Newt M 156 B3
Corran St. Glasg 118 C4
Correen Gdns. Bear 75 D4
Corrie Ave. Sten 23 F2
Corrie Brae. Kils 36 B1
Corrie Cres. Kilmk 222 C2
Corrie Cres. Salt 205 F1
Corrie Ct. Ham 161 F1
Corrie Dr. Mother 163 D4
Corrie Dr. Pais 114 C2
Corrie Gr. Glasg 136 C2
Corrie House. Pres 236 A3
Corrie Pl. Falk 41 E2
Corrie Pl. Helen 16 C2
Corrie Pl. Kirk 79 F2
Corrie Pl. Troon 229 F4
Corrie Rd. Kils 36 B1
Corrie View. Cumb 81 F4
Corrie Way. Lark 185 D1
Corrour Rd. Glasg 136 C4
Corrour Rd. Newt M 156 B3
Corruna Ct. Car 188 A1
Corse Ave. Spring 221 D1
Corse Dr. Barr 134 A2
Corse Pl. Cross 226 C4
Corse Rd. Glasg 114 C3
Corse St. W Kil 190 B3
Corsebar Ave. Pais 113 E1
Corsebar Cres. Pais 113 E1
Corsebar Dr. Pais 113 E1
Corsebar La. Pais 113 D1
Corsebar Rd. Pais 113 D1
Corsebar Way. Pais 113 E2
Corsefield Rd. Loch 128 C1
Corseford Ave. John 131 E4
Corsehill Dr. W Kil 190 A3
Corsehill. Kilw 208 A2
Corsehill Mount Rd. Irvine 225 D4
Corsehill Mount
Roundabout. Irvine 225 E4
Corsehill Pk. Ayr 238 C3
Corsehill Pk. Irvine 225 E4
Corsehill Pl. Ayr 238 C3
Corsehill Pl. Glasg 120 B4
Corsehill Pl. Stew 195 F1
Corsehill Rd. Ayr 238 C3
Corsehill St. Glasg 120 B4
Corsehill Terr. Spring 220 C1
Corsehillbank St. Stew 195 E1
Corselet Rd. Barr 135 D1
Corselet Rd. Glasg 135 D2
Corserine Bank. Irvine 219 F2
Corserine Rd. Ayr 238 A1
Corsewall Ave. Glasg 119 F2
Corsewall St. Coat 121 F4
Corsford Dr. Glasg 135 E3
Corsliehill Rd. Hous 90 C4
Corsock Ave. Ham 161 F1
Corsock St. Glasg 118 B4
Corston St. Glasg 118 B4
Cortachy Ave. Sten 24 A2
Cortachy Pl. Bish 78 B1
Coruisk Dr. Newt M 157 E4
Corunna St. Glasg 116 C4
Coshneuk Rd. Stepps 99 D2
Cosy Neuk. Lark 185 E1
Cottage Cres. Falk 41 F3
Cottar St. Glasg 96 C4
Cotter Dr. Kilmk 228 B4
Cotton Ave. Lin 112 A3
Cotton St. Glasg 118 A1
Cotton St. Pais 113 F2
Coulport Pl. Helen 16 A1
Coulter Ave. Coat 121 F4
Coulter Ave. Wish 165 E4
Coulthard Dr. Pres 236 B3
Countess St. Salt 216 C4
County Ave. Glasg 138 C4
County Dr. Lan 215 E2
County Pl. Pais 113 F3
County Sq. Pais 113 F3
Couper St. Glasg 97 E1
Coursington Cres. Mother 164 A4
Coursington Gdns. Mother 163 F4
Coursington Pl. Mother 163 F4
Coursington Rd. Mother 163 F4
Coursington Rd. Mother 164 A4
Court Rd. P Glasg 47 E1
Courthill. Alva 5 D4
Courthill Ave. Glasg 137 D3
Courthill. Bear 75 E3
Courthill Cres. Kils 60 C4
Courthill Pl. Dalry 191 E4
Courthill St. Dalry 191 E4
Courtrai Ave. Helen 16 A1
Coustonholm Rd. Glasg 136 B4
Couther Quadrant. Aird 103 D1
Covanburn Ave. Ham 162 C1
Cove Cres. Shot 146 C3
Cove Pl. Helen 16 A1
Cove Rd. Gour 44 C4
Coveland Dr. Glasg 138 A2
Covenant Cres. Lark 185 D1
Covenant Pl. Wish 164 B1
Covenanter Rd. East 127 E2
Covenanters Way. Wish 186 B3
Coventry Dr. Glasg 118 A4
Cow Wynd. Falk 42 A2
Cowal Cres. Gour 44 A3
Cowal Cres. Kirk 59 D1
Cowal Dr. Lin 112 A3
Cowal St. Glasg 96 B4
Cowal View. Gour 44 A3
Cowan Cres. Ayr 236 B2
Cowan Cres. Barr 134 B2
Cowan La. Glasg 96 C1
Cowan Rd. Cumb 61 E1
Cowan St. Bon 40 A3
Cowan St. Glasg 96 C1
Cowan Wilson Ave. Udd 161 E4
Cowan Wynd. Tan 141 D4
Cowan Wynd. Wish 186 B4
Cowane St. Stir 7 D4
Cowans Row. Hurl 228 B4
Cowcaddens Rd. Glasg 97 D1
Cowcaddens St. Glasg 117 E4
Cowden Dr. Bish 78 A2
Cowden St. Glasg 115 E4
Cowdenhill Cir. Glasg 95 E4
Cowdenhill Pl. Glasg 95 E4
Cowdenhill Rd. Glasg 95 E4
Cowdray Cres. Ren 94 B2
Cowgate. Kirk 79 E4
Cowglen Rd. Glasg 135 E4
Cowie Rd. Bann 12 A4
Cowiehall Rd. Cowie 12 B4
Cowlairs Ind Est. Glasg 97 E3
Cowlairs Rd. Glasg 97 F2
Coxdale Ave. Kirk 79 D4
Coxhill St. Glasg 97 E2
Coxithill Rd. Stir 7 D2
Coxton Pl. Glasg 99 E1
Coyle Pk. Troon 229 F3
Coylebank. Pres 236 B3
Coylton Cres. Ham 161 F1
Coylton Rd. Glasg 136 C3
Crabb Quadrant. Mother 142 B1
Cragdale. E Kil 159 E2
Craggan Dr. Glasg 95 D3
Crags Ave. Pais 113 F1
Crags Cres. Pais 113 F1
Crags Rd. Pais 113 F1
Cragwell Pk. E Kil 158 C4
Craig Ave. Alex 27 E4
Craig Ave. Dalry 191 D4
Craig Cotts. Cross 226 B4
Craig Cres. Kirk 80 A4
Craig Cres. Stir 2 B2
Craig Ct. B of A 2 A3
Craig Dr. Cross 226 C4
Craig Gdns. Newt M 156 B3
Craig Hill. E Kil 180 B4
Craig Pl. Newt M 156 A3
Craig Rd. Glasg 137 D3
Craig Rd. Lin 111 F4
Craig Rd. Neil 154 B3
Craig Rd. Troon 229 D2
Craig St. Aird 122 C4
Craig St. Blac 107 F2
Craig St. Coat 121 F2
Craig St. Udd 161 F4
Craig View. Spring 221 D1
Craigallian Ave. Glasg 139 E2
Craigallian Ave. Miln 55 D2
Craiganour La. Glasg 136 B3
Craigard Pl. Glasg 138 B2
Craigash Quadrant. Miln 54 C2
Craigash Rd. Miln 54 C2
Craigbank Cres. Eagle 178 C3
Craigbank Dr. Glasg 135 D3
Craigbank Gr. Eagle 178 C3
Craigbank. N Sau 5 E1
Craigbank Rd. Lark 199 D4
Craigbank St. Lark 185 D1
Craigbanzo St. Dunt 74 B4
Craigbarnet Ave. Lennox 78 A4
Craigbarnet Cres. Stepps 99 D2
Craigbarnet Rd. Miln 54 B1
Craigbet Ave. Kil 89 F1
Craigbet Cres. Kil 89 F1
Craigbet Pl. Kil 89 F1
Craigbo Ave. Glasg 76 B1
Craigbo Ct. Glasg 96 B4
Craigbo Dr. Glasg 76 B1
Craigbo Pl. Glasg 96 B4
Craigbo Rd. Glasg 76 B1
Craigbo St. Glasg 76 B1
Craigbog Ave. John 131 E4
Craigburn Ave. Hous 111 E4
Craigburn Cres. Hous 111 E4
Craigburn Ct. Ash 185 F1
Craigburn Ct. Falk 41 F1
Craigburn Pl. Hous 111 F4
Craigburn St. Ham 183 E4
Craigdene Dr. Steven 206 C1
Craigdhu Ave. Miln 54 C1
Craigdhu Rd. Bear 75 F4
Craigdhu Rd. Miln 54 C1
Craigdonald Pl. John 111 F2
Craigellan Rd. Glasg 136 B3
Craigelvan Ave. Cumb 81 F3
Craigelvan Ct. Cumb 81 F3
Craigelvan Dr. Cumb 81 F3
Craigelvan Gdns. Cumb 81 F3
Craigelvan Gr. Cumb 81 F3
Craigelvan Pl. Cumb 81 F3
Craigelvan View. Cumb 81 F3
Craigenbay Cres. Kirk 79 F3
Craigenbay Rd. Kirk 79 F3
Craigenbay St. Glasg 98 A2
Craigencart Ct. Dunt 73 F3
Craigend Cres. Miln 54 C1
Craigend Dr. Coat 121 E2
Craigend Dr W. Miln 54 C1
Craigend Pl. Glasg 95 F3
Craigend Rd. Auld 179 F1
Craigend Rd. Stir 7 D2
Craigend Rd. Troon 232 C4
Craigend St. Glasg 95 F3
Craigendmuir Rd. Stepps 99 F2
Craigendmuir St. Glasg 98 B1
Craigendon Oval. Pais 133 E3
Craigendon Rd. Pais 133 E3
Craigendoran Ave. Helen 25 C4
Craigends Ave. Kil 89 F2
Craigends Dr. Kilbar 111 D2
Craigends Pl. Kil 89 F2
Craigends Rd. Hous 111 F4
Craigends Rd. Kilb 170 A3
Craigenfeoch Ave. John 111 E1
Craigenhill Rd. Kilnc 203 D3
Craigenlay Ave. Strath 31 E2
Craigens Rd. Chap 124 B2
Craigfaulds Ave. Pais 113 D1
Craigfell Ct. Ham 161 F1
Craigfern Dr. Strath 31 E2
Craigfin Ct. Pres 236 B3
Craigflower Ave. Glasg 135 D2
Craigflower Gdns. Glasg 135 D2
Craigflower Rd. Glasg 135 D2
Craigford Dr. Bann 7 E1
Craigforth Cres. Stir 1 C1
Craighalbert Rd. Cumb 61 E2
Craighalbert
Roundabout. Cumb 61 E2
Craighalbert Way. Cumb 61 E2
Craighall Pl. Ayr 239 D1
Craighall Quadrant. Neil 154 B3
Craighall Rd. Glasg 97 D1
Craighall St. Stir 1 C1
Craighaw St. Dunt 74 B4
Craighead Ave. Glasg 98 B2
Craighead Ave. M of C 58 B3
Craighead Rd. Bishop 72 A1
Craighead Rd. M of C 58 B3
Craighead St. Aird 123 F4
Craighead Way. Barr 134 A1
Craighill Dr. Newt M 157 E3
Craighill Gr. Newt M 157 E3
Craighill View. Blac 107 F2
Craighirst Dr. Dunt 74 A4
Craighirst Rd. Miln 54 B1
Craighlaw Ave. Newt M 157 E1
Craighlaw Dr. Newt M 157 E1
Craigholm Rd. Ayr 239 E4
Craigholme. Hous 91 E1
Craighorn Dr. Falk 41 F1
Craighorn. Men 4 A3
Craighorn Rd. Alva 4 C3
Craighouse St. Glasg 99 D1
Craighton Gdns. Lennox 57 F4
Craigie Ave. Ayr 239 D4
Craigie Ave. Kilmk 227 F2
Craigie Ct. Lar 23 D1
Craigie Dr. Newt M 156 C2
Craigie La. Lark 185 D2

Craigie Lea. Ayr

Culzean Cres. Glasg

255

Culzean Cres. Kilmk Dewar Wlk. Car

Culzean Cres. Kilmk 228 B4
Culzean Cres. Newt M 157 D2
Culzean Dr. E Kil 159 E2
Culzean Dr. Glasg 119 E2
Culzean Dr. Gour 43 F3
Culzean. Glenm 102 C3
Culzean Pl. E Kil 159 E2
Culzean Pl. Kilw 207 E1
Culzean Pl. Sten 23 F2
Culzean Rd. Ayr 238 B2
Cumberland Arc. Glasg 117 E2
Cumberland Ave. Helen 16 A2
Cumberland Pl. Coat 121 E2
Cumberland Pl. Glasg 117 E2
Cumberland Rd. Gour 44 C2
Cumberland Rd. Rhu 15 E3
Cumberland St. Glasg 117 D3
Cumberland St. Glasg 117 E2
Cumberland Terr. Rhu 15 E3
Cumberland Wlk. Gour 44 C2
Cumbernauld Rd. Bank 39 D2
Cumbernauld Rd. Cumb 81 E2
Cumbernauld Rd. Glasg 118 B4
Cumbernauld Rd. Muir 81 D2
Cumbernauld Rd. Muir 100 B4
Cumbernauld Rd. Stepps 99 E3
Cumbrae Ave. P Glasg 69 D4
Cumbrae Cres. Aird 122 C3
Cumbrae Cres N. Dumb 49 E3
Cumbrae Cres S. Dumb 49 E3
Cumbrae Ct. Clyde 74 A1
Cumbrae Ct. Green 45 D3
Cumbrae Ct. Irvine 225 E4
Cumbrae Dr. Falk 41 E2
Cumbrae Dr. Kilmk 223 D3
Cumbrae Dr. Mother 163 E4
Cumbrae. E Kil 160 B1
Cumbrae House. Pres 236 A3
Cumbrae Pl. Aird 122 C2
Cumbrae Pl. Gour 44 B3
Cumbrae Pl. W Kil 190 B2
Cumbrae Rd. Pais 133 F4
Cumbrae Rd. Ren 94 B1
Cumbrae Rd. Salt 205 F1
Cumbrae St. Glasg 119 D4
Cumlodden Dr. Glasg 96 B4
Cumming Dr. Glasg 137 D4
Cumnock Dr. Barr 134 B1
Cumnock Dr. Ham 161 E1
Cumnock Rd. Glasg 98 C3
Cumroch Rd. Lennox 33 E1
Cunard St. Clyde 94 A4
Cuninghame Dr. Salt 206 A1
Cuninghame Rd. Ard 205 E2
Cuninghame Rd. Kilbar 111 D2
Cuninghame Rd. Salt 217 D4
Cunning Park Dr. Ayr 238 B2
Cunningair Dr. Mother 163 F2
Cunningham Cres. Ayr 239 E3
Cunningham Dr. Dunt 73 F3
Cunningham Dr. East 127 E3
Cunningham Dr. Glasg 136 C2
Cunningham Gdns. Falk 42 C3
Cunningham Pl. Ayr 239 E3
Cunningham Rd. Glasg 114 C4
Cunningham Rd. Sten 24 A2
Cunningham Rd. Stir 7 E4
Cunningham St. Mother 163 E3
Cunningham Watt Rd. Stew 195 E1
Cunninghame Dr. Kilmk 227 F2
Cunninghame Rd. E Kil 159 F1
Cunninghame Rd. Glasg 138 B4
Cunninghame Rd. Irvine 224 A4
Cunninghame Rd. Pres 236 B4
Cupar Dr. Green 44 C2
Cuparhead Ave. Coat 121 F2
Cuppleton Brae. How 130 A1
Curfew Rd. Glasg 75 E1
Curle St. Glasg 95 E1
Curlew Cres. Green 45 D2
Curlew La. Green 45 D2
Curlew Pl. John 131 E4
Curling Cres. Glasg 137 E4
Curlinghaugh Cres. Wish 165 E2
Curlingmire. E Kil 180 C4
Curran Ave. Wish 164 C1
Currie Ct. Ard 205 E1
Currie St. Glasg 96 C3
Currieside Ave. Shot 146 C2
Currieside Pl. Shot 146 B2
Curtecan Pl. Ayr 238 C3
Curtis Ave. Glasg 137 E4
Curzon St. Glasg 96 C3
Cushenquarter Dr. Plea 12 B2
Customhouse Pl. Green 46 A3
Custonhall Pl. Den 21 E1
Cuthbert Pl. Kilmk 223 D1
Cuthbert St. Tan 141 D4
Cuthbertson St. Glasg 117 D1
Cuthelton Dr. Glasg 118 C2
Cuthelton St. Glasg 118 B2
Cuthelton Terr. Glasg 118 B2
Cutsburn Pl. Stew 211 F4
Cutsburn Rd. Stew 211 F4
Cutstraw Rd. Stew 211 F4
Cuttyfield Pl. Sten 24 B2
Cypress Ave. Beith 150 B1
Cypress Ave. Tan 141 D4
Cypress Ave. Udd 140 B1
Cypress Cres. E Kil 180 B3
Cypress Ct. E Kil 180 B3
Cypress Ct. Ham 162 C1
Cypress Ct. Kirk 79 D3
Cypress Gdns. Irvine 219 F3
Cypress Pl. E Kil 180 B3
Cypress St. Glasg 97 E3
Cyprus Ave. John 112 A1
Cyril St. Pais 114 A2

Daer Ave. Ren 94 C1
Daer Way. Ham 162 A2
Daer Wlk. Lark 199 D4
Daffodil Way. Mother 163 F4
Dairsie Gdns. Bish 98 B4
Dairsie St. Glasg 136 C2
Daisy Cotts. Ayr 236 A2
Daisy St. Glasg 117 D1
Daisybank. Beith 170 B3
Dakota Way. Ren 94 B1
Dalbeth Pl. Glasg 118 C1
Dalbeth Rd. Glasg 118 C1
Dalblair Arc. Ayr 238 C4
Dalblair Rd. Ayr 238 C4
Dalcharn Pl. Glasg 120 A4
Dalcross St. Glasg 96 B1
Dalcruin Gdns. Muir 81 D2
Dalderse Ave. Falk 42 A3
Daldowie Ave. Glasg 119 E2
Daldowie Rd. Glasg 120 A1
Daldowie St. Coat 121 F2
Dale Ave. E Kil 180 B3
Dale Cres. Irvine 219 E2
Dale Ct. Wish 164 B1
Dale Dr. Holy 143 D2
Dale St. Glasg 117 F2
Dale St. Glasg 118 A2
Dale Way. Glasg 138 A2
Daleview Ave. Glasg 96 A3
Daleview Dr. Newt M 157 E3
Daleview Gr. Newt M 157 E3
Dalfoil Ct. Glasg 114 C2
Dalgain Ct. Irvine 220 A3
Dalgarroch Ave. Clyde 94 C4
Dalgleish Ave. Dunt 73 F3
Dalgleish Ct. Stir 7 D4
Dalgraig Cres. Udd 140 B1
Dalhousie Gdns. Bish 78 A1
Dalhousie La. Glasg 97 D1
Dalhousie Rd. Kilbar 111 D1
Dalhousie St. Glasg 97 D1
Dalilea Dr. Glasg 100 B1
Dalilea Path. Glasg 100 B1
Dalilea Pl. Glasg 100 B1
Dalintober St. Glasg 117 D3
Daljarrock. Kilw 207 D1
Dalkeith Ave. Bish 78 A2
Dalkeith Ave. Glasg 116 A2
Dalkeith Rd. Bish 78 A2
Dallas Ct. Troon 229 E1
Dallas La. Troon 229 E1
Dallas Pl. Troon 229 E1
Dallas Rd. Troon 229 E1
Dalmacoulter Rd. Aird 103 D2
Dalmahoy Cres. B of W 110 B3
Dalmahoy St. Glasg 118 C4
Dalmahoy Way. Kilw 207 D2
Dalmailing Ave. Irvine 220 A1
Dalmailington Ave. Irvine 220 A1
Dalmally St. Glasg 96 C2
Dalmally St. Green 46 C1
Dalmarnock Ct. Glasg 118 A2
Dalmarnock Rd. Glasg 118 A1
Dalmary Dr. Pais 114 A3
Dalmellington Ct. Ham 161 E1
Dalmellington Rd. Ayr 239 E2
Dalmeny Ave. Glasg 136 B2
Dalmeny Dr. Barr 134 A1
Dalmeny Rd. Ham 162 B1
Dalmeny St. Glasg 117 F1
Dalmilling Cres. Ayr 236 B1
Dalmilling Dr. Ayr 236 C1
Dalmilling Rd. Ayr 236 C1
Dalmoak Rd. Green 46 B1
Dalmonach Rd. Bonh 27 F2
Dalmore Cres. Helen 16 A2
Dalmore Dr. Alva 4 C3
Dalmore Pl. Irvine 219 F3
Dalmore Way. Irvine 219 F3
Dalmorglen Pk. Stir 6 C3
Dalnair Pl. Miln 54 B1
Dalnair St. Glasg 96 B1
Dalness St. Glasg 119 D2
Dalnottar Ave. O Kill 73 D3
Dalnottar Dr. O Kill 73 D3
Dalnottar Gdns. O Kill 73 D3
Dalnottar Hill Rd. O Kill 73 D3
Dalnottar Terr. O Kill 73 D3
Dalreoch Ave. Glasg 120 B3
Dalreoch Ct. Dumb 49 E2
Dalreoch Path. Glasg 120 B3
Dalriada Cres. Mother 142 B1
Dalriada Dr. Lennox 78 B4
Dalriada Rd. Gour 44 B2
Dalriada St. Glasg 118 B2
Dalry Gdns. Ham 161 E1
Dalry La. Ard 205 E2
Dalry Rd. Ard 205 E2
Dalry Rd. Beith 171 D4
Dalry Rd. Kilb 170 A4
Dalry Rd. Kilw 207 E2
Dalry Rd. Salt 206 A1
Dalry Rd. Stew 195 E1
Dalry Rd. Tan 141 D4
Dalry St. Glasg 119 D2
Dalrymple Ct. Irvine 219 F2
Dalrymple Dr. E Kil 159 F1
Dalrymple Dr. Irvine 219 F2
Dalrymple Dr. Newt M 157 D2
Dalrymple Pl. Irvine 219 E2
Dalrymple St. Green 45 F3
Dalrymple St. Green 46 A3
Dalserf Cres. Glasg 136 A1
Dalserf Path. Lark 185 E1
Dalserf St. Glasg 118 A3
Dalsetter Ave. Glasg 75 D1
Dalsetter Pl. Glasg 75 D1
Dalshannon Pl. Cumb 82 A4
Dalshannon Rd. Cumb 82 A4
Dalshannon View. Cumb 82 A4
Dalshannon Way. Cumb 82 A4
Dalsholm Rd. Glasg 96 A4
Dalskeith Ave. Pais 113 D3
Dalskeith Cres. Pais 113 D3
Dalskeith Rd. Pais 113 D3
Dalswinton St. Glasg 120 B4
Dalton Ave. Clyde 74 C1
Dalton Hill. Ham 161 F1
Dalton St. Glasg 118 C3
Dalvait Gdns. Bonh 27 F4
Dalvait Rd. Bonh 27 F4
Dalveen Ct. Barr 134 B1
Dalveen Dr. Tan 140 C4
Dalveen Quadrant. Aird 122 B3
Dalveen St. Glasg 118 C3
Dalveen Way. Glasg 138 B2
Dalwhinnie Ave. Udd 140 B1
Dalwood Rd. Pres 236 A4
Daly Gdns. Udd 140 C1
Dalzell Ave. Mother 164 A2
Dalzell Dr. Mother 164 A2
Dalziel Dr. Glasg 116 B2
Dalziel Rd. Glasg 114 C4
Dalziel St. Ham 162 A3
Dalziel St. Mother 163 F4
Damhead Rd. Kilmk 227 F2
Dampark. Dunlop 195 E4
Damshot Cres. Glasg 115 E1
Damshot Rd. Glasg 135 E4
Damside. Ayr 235 F1
Danby Rd. Glasg 119 F2
Danes Cres. Glasg 95 D3
Danes Dr. Glasg 95 E2
Danes La N. Glasg 95 E2
Danes La S. Glasg 95 E2
Daniel McLaughlin Pl. Kirk 58 C1
Dankeith Dr. Sym 231 E2
Dankeith Rd. Sym 231 E2
Darg Rd. Steven 217 E4
Dargarvel Ave. Glasg 116 A2
Dargavel Ave. Bishop 72 A2
Dargavel Rd. Bishop 72 B4
Dargavel Rd. Ersk 72 C1
Dark Brig Rd. Cro 201 D1
Darkwood Cres. Pais 113 D3
Darkwood Dr. Pais 113 D3
Darleith Rd. Card 26 A1
Darleith St. Glasg 118 C3
Darley Cres. Troon 229 E1
Darley Pl. Ham 183 D4
Darley Pl. Troon 229 E1
Darlington View. Stew 195 F1
Darluith Rd. Lin 111 F3
Darmeid Pl. Alla 167 D4
Darnaway Ave. Glasg 99 E1
Darnaway St. Glasg 99 E1
Darndaff Rd. Green 46 A1
Darngaber Gdns. Quart 183 F2
Darngaber Rd. Quart 183 F2
Darngavil Rd. Plains 103 F3
Darnick St. Glasg 98 A1
Darnley Cres. Bish 77 F2
Darnley Dr. Kilmk 227 F3
Darnley Gdns. Glasg 116 C1
Darnley Path. Glasg 135 F3
Darnley Pl. Glasg 116 C1
Darnley Rd. Barr 134 C2
Darnley Rd. Glasg 116 C1
Darnley St. Glasg 116 C2
Darnley St. Stir 7 D4
Darnshaw Cl. Irvine 220 B3
Darrach Dr. Duni 21 D1
Darroch Ave. Gour 44 C4
Darroch Dr. Ersk 72 C2
Darroch Dr. Gour 44 C4
Darroch Way. Cumb 62 A2
Dartford St. Glasg 97 D2
Dartmouth Ave. Gour 44 C3
Darvel Cres. Pais 114 C2
Darvel Dr. Newt M 157 D3
Darvel St. Glasg 134 C3
Darwin Pl. Clyde 73 E2
Darwin Rd. E Kil 180 B4
Dava St. Glasg 116 A4
Davaar Dr. Coat 121 E4
Davaar Dr. Kilmk 223 D3
Davaar Dr. Mother 142 B1
Davaar Dr. Pais 133 F4
Davaar. E Kil 160 B1
Davaar Pl. Newt M 156 B3
Davaar Rd. Gour 44 B2
Davaar Rd. Ren 94 B1
Davaar Rd. Salt 205 F1
Davaar St. Glasg 118 A2
Davan Loan. New 165 F3
Davarr Pl. Falk 41 E2
Daventry Dr. Glasg 96 A3
Davey St. Green 45 E3
David Dale Ave. Stew 211 E4
David Gage St. Kilw 207 F3
David Orr St. Kilmk 222 C1
David Pl. Glasg 119 F2
David Pl. Pais 114 A4
David St. Coat 122 B4
David St. Glasg 118 A3
David St. Sals 125 D1
David Way. Pais 114 A4
David's Cres. Kilw 207 E1
David's Loan. Falk 24 B1
Davidson Ave. Beith 170 B3
Davidson Cres. Twe 59 F2
Davidson Dr. Gour 44 C4
Davidson Gdns. Glasg 95 F2
Davidson La. Car 188 A1
Davidson Pl. Ayr 236 A1
Davidson Pl. Glasg 119 E3
Davidson Quadrant. Dunt 73 F4
Davidson Rd. Bonh 27 F4
Davidson St. Aird 122 C4
Davidson St. Bann 7 E1
Davidson St. Clyde 94 C4
Davidson St. Coat 122 A2
Davidson St. Glasg 118 A2
Davidston Pl. Kirk 79 F2
Davieland Rd. Glasg 136 A1
Davies Quadrant. Mother 142 B1
Davington Dr. Ham 161 E1
Daviot St. Glasg 115 E3
Dawsholm Ind Est. Glasg 96 A4
Dawson Ave. All 9 F4
Dawson Ave. E Kil 159 D1
Dawson Pl. Glasg 97 D2
Dawson Rd. Glasg 97 D2
Dawson St. Falk 42 A4
De Morville Pl. Beith 171 D4
De Walden Terr. Kilmk 223 D1
Deacons Rd. Kils 60 C4
Dealston Rd. Barr 134 A2
Dean Cres. Ham 162 B1
Dean Cres. Muir 80 B1
Dean Cres. Stir 2 B1
Dean Ct. Kilmk 222 C1
Dean La. Kilmk 223 D1
Dean Park Ave. Udd 141 D1
Dean Park Dr. Glasg 139 E2
Dean Park Rd. Ren 94 C1
Dean Pl. Cross 226 C4
Dean Rd. Kilb 149 D1
Dean Rd. Kilmk 223 D2
Dean St. Clyde 74 B1
Dean St. Hat 142 A3
Dean St. Kilmk 223 D1
Dean St. Stew 195 F1
Dean Terr. Kilmk 223 D2
Deanbrae St. Udd 140 C3
Deanfield Quadrant. Glasg 114 C3
Deanhill La. Kilmk 223 D2
Deanpark Gdns. Ren 94 C2
Deans Ave. Glasg 139 E2
Deanside Rd. Glasg 115 D4
Deanston Dr. Glasg 136 C4
Deanwood Ave. Glasg 136 C2
Deanwood Rd. Glasg 136 C2
Deas Rd. Shot 146 B3
Dechmont Ave. Glasg 139 E2
Dechmont Ave. Mother 163 E4
Dechmont Cotts. Glasg 139 F2
Dechmont. E Kil 180 B3
Dechmont Gdns. Udd 140 B1
Dechmont Pl. Glasg 139 E2
Dechmont Rd. Tan 120 C1
Dechmont St. Glasg 118 B2
Dechmont St. Ham 162 B1
Dechmont View. Hat 141 F2
Dechmont View. Tan 141 D4
Dee Ave. Kilmk 228 A2
Dee Ave. Pais 112 C1
Dee Ave. Ren 94 C2
Dee Dr. Pais 112 C1
Dee Path. Holy 143 D3
Dee Path. Lark 199 D4
Dee Pl. E Kil 179 F3
Dee Pl. John 131 E4
Dee St. Coat 101 E1
Dee St. Glasg 118 B4
Dee St. Green 45 D3
Dee St. Shot 146 B3
Dee Terr. Ham 183 D4
Deedes St. Aird 122 B3
Deep Dale. E Kil 159 E2
Deepdene Rd. Bear 75 E1
Deepdene Rd. Muir 80 C1
Deer Park Ave. Steven 217 F4
Deer Park Ct. Ham 183 E4
Deer Park Pl. Ham 183 F4
Deerdykes Ct N. Cumb 81 F3
Deerdykes Ct S. Cumb 81 F3
Deerdykes Pl. Cumb 81 F3
Deerdykes Rd. Cumb 81 F3
Deerdykes View. Cumb 81 E3
Deerpark. N Sau 5 F1
Deeside Dr. Car 188 A2
Delfie Dr. Green 45 D2
Delhi Ave. Clyde 73 E2
Dell The. Hat 142 B2
Dellburn St. Mother 164 A3
Dellingburn St. Green 46 A2
Delny Pl. Glasg 119 F4
Delph Rd. Tull 4 B1
Delphwood Cres. Tull 4 B1
Delves Pk. Lan 215 D2
Delves Rd. Lan 215 D2
Delvin Rd. Glasg 137 D3
Dempsey Rd. Hat 141 F2
Dempster St. Green 45 F2
Den La. Shot 146 B3
Denbak Ave. Ham 162 A1
Denbeck St. Glasg 118 C3
Denbrae St. Glasg 118 C3
Denewood Ave. Pais 133 E4
Denham St. Glasg 97 D2
Denholm Cres. E Kil 180 C4
Denholm Dr. Glasg 136 B1
Denholm Dr. Wish 165 E3
Denholm Gdns. Green 45 E3
Denholm Gdns. Quart 183 F2
Denholm Gn. E Kil 180 C4
Denholm St. Green 45 E3
Denholm Terr. Green 45 E3
Denholm Terr. Ham 161 F2
Denholm Way. Beith 171 D4
Denmark St. Glasg 97 E2
Denmark St. Glasg 97 E3
Denmilne Gdns. Glasg 120 B4
Denmilne Path. Glasg 120 B4
Denmilne Rd. Glasg 120 B4
Denmilne St. Glasg 120 B4
Denniston Pl. Lan 215 E3
Dennistoun Cres. Helen 25 D4
Dennistoun Rd. Lang 70 B4
Dennistoun St. Hat 142 A3
Denny Rd. Bank 39 F3
Denny Rd. Lar 23 D1
Denny Way. Alex 27 E1
Dennyholm Wynd. Kilb 149 D1
Denovan Rd. Duni 21 F2
Denovan Rd. Tor 21 F2
Dentdale. E Kil 159 E2
Deramore Ave. Newt M 157 D4
Derby St. Glasg 116 C4
Derby Terrace La. Glasg 116 C4
Deroran Pl. Stir 6 C3
Derrywood Rd. M of C 58 B3
Dervaig Gdns. Gree 84 B2
Derwent Ave. Falk 41 F2
Derwent Dr. Coat 101 E1
Derwent St. Glasg 97 D2
Derwentwater. E Kil 179 F3
Despard Ave. Glasg 119 F2
Despard Gdns. Glasg 119 F2
Deveron Ave. Glasg 136 B1
Deveron Cres. Ham 161 F2
Deveron Rd. Bear 75 E1
Deveron Rd. E Kil 160 A1
Deveron Rd. Holy 143 D3
Deveron Rd. Kilmk 228 A3
Deveron Rd. Troon 229 F3
Deveron St. Coat 101 E1
Deveron St. Glasg 98 B1
Devilla Ct. Pres 236 B3
Devlin Gr. Udd 161 F4
Devol Ave. P Glasg 47 D1
Devol Cres. Glasg 135 D4
Devol Rd. Kil 68 B3
Devol Rd. P Glasg 68 B3
Devon Ct. Tull 4 A1
Devon Dr. Bishop 72 B2
Devon Dr. Men 4 C2
Devon Gdns. Bish 77 F2
Devon Gdns. Car 187 F1
Devon Pl. Camb 4 A1
Devon Pl. Glasg 117 D2
Devon Rd. All 10 B3
Devon Rd. Gour 44 B2
Devon St. Glasg 117 D2
Devon Village. Fish 5 F2
Devon Way. Mother 163 D3
Devonbank. Fish 5 F2
Devondale Ave. Udd 140 B1
Devonhill Ave. Ham 183 E4
Devonport Pk. E Kil 180 A4
Devonshire
Gardens La. Glasg 96 A2
Devonshire Terr. Glasg 96 A2
Devonshire
Terrace La. Glasg 96 A2
Devonview Pl. Aird 122 C3
Devonview St. Aird 122 C3
Devonway. Clack 10 C3
Dewar Cl. Tan 121 D1
Dewar Wlk. Car 201 D1

Falkland Pk. E Kil

260

Forth St. Fall

George St. Bonh

Forth St. Fall 8 B2
Forth St. Glasg 116 C2
Forth St. Green 45 D3
Forth St. Stir 2 A1
Forth Terr. Ham 183 D4
Forth View. Stir 2 A1
Forthvale. Men 4 A3
Forthview. Bann 7 F1
Forthview Ct. Falk 41 F1
Forties Rd. Hous 111 E4
Fortieth Ave. E Kil 180 C3
Fortingale Ave. Glasg 96 B3
Fortingale Pl. Glasg 96 B3
Fortingall Rd. Ham 161 F3
Fortissat Ave. Shot 146 B3
Fortisset Rd. Sals 126 A1
Fortrose St. Glasg 96 A1
Fossil Gr. Kirk 59 D1
Foswell Pl. Glasg 74 C3
Fotheringay La. Glasg 116 C1
Fotheringay Rd. Glasg 116 C1
Fothringham Rd. Ayr 239 D4
Foulburn Rd. Cle 145 E1
Foulis La. Glasg 95 F3
Foulis St. Glasg 95 F3
Foulsykes Rd. Wish 165 F2
Foundry La. Barr 134 B1
Foundry Loan. Lar 23 D1
Foundry Rd. Bon 40 A3
Foundry Rd. Cle 144 B1
Foundry Rd. Shot 146 C2
Foundry St. Falk 42 A4
Foundry Wynd. Kilw 207 E2
Fountain Ave. Inch 93 D2
Fountain Cres. Inch 93 E3
Fountain Dr. Inch 93 E2
Fountain Rd. B of A 2 A4
Fountain
Bsns Ctr The. Coat 122 A3
Fountainwell Ave. Glasg 97 E2
Fountainwell Dr. Glasg 97 E1
Fountainwell Pl. Glasg 97 E2
Fountainwell Rd. Glasg 97 E1
Fountainwell Sq. Glasg 97 F1
Fountainwell Terr. Glasg 97 F1
Four Acres Dr. Kilm 222 A4
Four Windings. Hous 91 D1
Fourth Ave. Dumb 50 B1
Fourth Ave. Ren 94 B1
Fourth Ave. Stepps 79 E1
Fourth Ave. Stepps 99 D3
Fourth Gdns. Glasg 116 A2
Fourth St. Tan 120 C1
Fowlds St. Kilmk 227 F4
Fowler Pl. E Kil 181 D3
Fowlis Dr. Newt M 156 B3
Fox Gr. Mother 163 D4
Fox St. Glasg 117 D3
Fox St. Green 45 E4
Foxbar Cres. Pais 132 C4
Foxbar Dr. Glasg 95 D3
Foxbar Dr. Pais 132 C4
Foxbar Rd. Pais 132 C4
Foxes Gr. Klrk 79 F3
Foxglove Pl. Ayr 239 E2
Foxglove Pl. Glasg 135 D2
Foxhills Pl. Glasg 76 C1
Foxley St. Glasg 119 E1
Foyers Terr. Glasg 98 A2
Franchi Dr. Sten 23 F3
Francis St. Glasg 117 D2
Frankfield Rd. Stepps 99 F3
Frankfield St. Glasg 98 C1
Frankfort St. Glasg 116 C1
Franklin Pl. E Kil 159 D1
Franklin Rd. Salt 205 F1
Franklin St. Glasg 117 F2
Fraser Ave. Bishop 72 A2
Fraser Ave. Dumb 50 B2
Fraser Ave. Glasg 138 B4
Fraser Ave. John 112 A1
Fraser Ave. Newt M 156 C3
Fraser Ave. Troon 229 E3
Fraser Cres. Ham 162 A1
Fraser Ct. Aird 123 F4
Fraser Gdns. Klrk 79 D4
Fraser Pl. Stir 2 A2
Fraser St. Cle 144 A1
Fraser St. Glasg 138 C3
Fraser Wlk. Kilmk 223 E2
Frazer Ave. Helen 16 A2
Frazer St. Glasg 118 A3
Frederick St. Coat 121 F4
Freeland Cres. Glasg 135 D3
Freeland Ct. Glasg 135 E3
Freeland Dr. B of W 90 B1
Freeland Dr. Glasg 135 D3
Freeland Dr. Inch 93 E3
Freeland La. E Kil 180 C4
Freeland Pl. Kilw 79 E4
Freeland Rd. Inch 93 D4
Freelands Cres. Clyde 73 E3
Freelands Ct. Clyde 73 E2
Freelands Rd. Clyde 73 E2
Freesia Ct. Mother 163 F3
French St. Clyde 73 F2
French St. Glasg 117 F2
French St. Ren 94 A1
French St. Wish 165 D2
Freuchie St. Glasg 120 A4
Frew Terr. Irvine 219 E3
Friar Ave. Bish 78 A2
Friar's Dene. Lan 214 C2
Friar's La. Lan 214 C2
Friar's Wynd. Lan 214 C2
Friars Croft. Irvine 219 D1
Friars Croft. Klrk 79 F4
Friars Lawn. Kilw 207 E2
Friars Pl. Glasg 95 E4
Friars St. Stir 7 D4
Friars Way. Aird 123 E2
Friarscourt Ave. Glasg 95 E4
Friarscourt Rd. Muir 80 A1
Friarsfield Rd. Lan 214 C2
Friarton Rd. Glasg 136 C3
Friendship Gdns. Sten 24 B2
Friendship Way. Ren 94 B1
Frobisher Ave. Falk 41 F2
Frobisher Pl. Helen 17 D1
Frood St. Mother 142 B1
Fruin Ave. Newt M 156 C3
Fruin Rd. Glasg 74 C1
Fruin Rise. Ham 161 F1
Fruin St. Glasg 97 E2
Fudstone Dr. Kilb 170 A4
Fulbar Ave. Ren 94 B2
Fulbar Cres. Pais 112 C1
Fulbar Ct. Ren 94 B2
Fulbar Gdns. Pais 112 C1
Fulbar La. Ren 94 B2
Fulbar Rd. Glasg 115 E4
Fulbar Rd. Lin 112 C2
Fulbar St. Ren 94 B2
Fullarton Ave. Dund 225 F1
Fullarton Ave. Glasg 119 D1
Fullarton Cres. Troon 229 F1
Fullarton Dr. Troon 229 F1
Fullarton La. Glasg 119 D1
Fullarton Pl. Coat 121 F2
Fullarton Pl. Steven 217 E4
Fullarton Pl. Troon 230 A2
Fullarton Rd. Glasg 119 D1
Fullarton Rd. Pres 236 B3
Fullarton Rndabout. Irvine 219 D1
Fullarton St. Ayr 238 C4
Fullarton St. Coat 121 F2
Fullarton St. Irvine 219 D1
Fullarton St. Kilmk 222 C1
Fullers Gate. Dunt 74 B4
Fullerton Ctyd. Troon 230 A1
Fullerton Dr. W Kil 190 A2
Fullerton La. Green 46 C2
Fullerton Sq. Ard 205 E1
Fullerton St. Pais 113 E4
Fullerton Terr. Pais 113 F4
Fulmar Ct. Bish 97 F4
Fulmar Pk. E Kil 159 E2
Fulmar Pl. John 131 E3
Fulshaw Cres. Ayr 236 C1
Fulshaw Ct. Pres 236 B3
Fulton Cres. Kilbar 111 D2
Fulton Dr. Hous 111 F4
Fulton Gdns. Hous 111 F4
Fulton Rd. Miln 55 D1
Fulton St. Glasg 95 F4
Fulton's La. Kilmk 222 C1
Fulwood Ave. Glasg 94 C4
Fulwood Ave. Lin 112 A3
Fulwood Ind Est. Ham 162 A3
Fulwood Pl. Glasg 94 C4
Furlongs The. Ham 162 C3
Furnace Ct. Hurl 228 C3
Furnace Rd. Quart 183 F2
Fyfe Park Terr. P Glasg 47 F1
Fyfe Shore Rd. P Glasg 47 F1
Fyffe Park Rd. P Glasg 47 F1
Fyne Ave. Tan 141 F3
Fyne Ct. Ham 162 A1
Fyne La. Shot 146 C3
Fyne Way. Holy 143 D3
Fyneart St. Wish 165 F2
Fynloch Pl. Dunt 73 F4
Fyvie Ave. Glasg 136 A3

Golf Ct. Glasg 136 C1
Gaberston Ave. All 10 B4
Gabriel St. Green 46 A1
Gadie Ave. Ren 94 C1
Gadie St. Glasg 118 B4
Gadloch Ave. Stepps 79 E1
Gadloch Gdns. Klrk 79 E2
Gadloch St. Glasg 97 E3
Gadloch View. Stepps 79 E1
Gadsburn Ct. Glasg 98 B3
Gadshill St. Glasg 97 F1
Gael St. Green 45 E2
Gagarin Terr. Kilw 207 F1
Gailes Pk. Udd 140 C1
Gailes Pl. Kilmk 227 F2
Gailes Rd. Shew 224 B2
Gailes Rd. Troon 229 E4
Gailes St. Glasg 118 A2
Gain and
Shankburn Rd. Glen 82 B1
Gain and
Shankburn Rd. Glenm 82 B1
Gain Rd. Glen 82 A1
Gainburn Cres. Cumb 81 F3
Gainburn Ct. Cumb 81 F3
Gainburn Gdns. Cumb 81 F3
Gainburn Pl. Cumb 81 F3
Gainburn View. Cumb 82 A3
Gainford Pl. Kilmk 222 C2
Gainside Rd. Glen 101 E3
Gair Cres. Car 188 A2
Gair Cres. Wish 165 D1
Gair Rd. Car 188 A3
Gair Wynd. Shot 147 D2
Gairbraid Ave. Glasg 96 B3
Gairbraid Ct. Glasg 96 B3
Gairbraid Pl. Glasg 96 B3
Gairbraid Terr. Coat 121 D3
Gairdoch Dr. Sten 24 B2
Gairdoch St. Falk 42 A4
Gairloch Gdns. Kirk 59 D1
Gaitskell Ave. Alex 27 E4
Gala Ave. Ren 94 C1
Gala Cres. Wish 165 D3
Gala St. Glasg 98 C1
Galbraith Cres. Law 187 D3
Galbraith Dr. Glasg 115 F4
Galbraith Dr. Miln 75 F4
Galdenoch St. Glasg 99 D1
Gallacher Ave. Pais 113 D1
Gallacher Cres. Bonh 19 F1
Gallacher Ct. Pais 113 E3
Gallahill Ave. P Glasg 69 D4
Gallamuir Dr. Plea 12 B2
Gallamuir Rd. Plea 12 B3
Gallan Ave. Glasg 76 C1
Gallion Wlk. Kilmk 227 F4
Galloway Ave. Ayr 236 B1
Galloway Ave. Ham 183 E4
Galloway Dr. Glasg 138 A2
Galloway Dr. Ham 183 E3
Galloway Pl. Salt 216 C4
Galloway Rd. Aird 122 C2
Galloway Rd. E Kil 160 B2
Galloway St. Falk 42 A3
Galloway St. Glasg 97 F3
Gallowflat St. Glasg 138 A4
Gallowgate. Glasg 117 F3
Gallowhill Ave. Klrk 79 E3
Gallowhill Gr. Klrk 79 E4
Gallowhill. Lark 185 D1
Gallowhill Rd. E Kil 158 C4
Gallowhill Rd. Klrk 79 E3
Gallowhill Rd. Lan 215 D2
Gallowhill Rd. Pais 114 A3
Galrigside Rd. Kilmk 227 E4
Galston Ave. Newt M 157 D3
Galston Ct. Ham 183 F4
Galston Rd. Hurl 228 C3
Galston St. Glasg 134 C3
Galt Ave. Irvine 219 E2
Galt Pl. E Kil 180 B4
Galt St. Green 46 B2
Gameshill View. Stew 211 F4
Gamrie Dr. Glasg 135 D4
Gamrie Gdns. Glasg 135 D4
Gamrie Rd. Glasg 135 D4
Gannochy Dr. Bish 78 B1
Gantock Cres. Glasg 119 D4
Ganton Ct. Kilw 207 D2
Garden Ct. Ayr 235 F1
Garden Pl. Troon 229 D2
Garden Square La. Kilw 207 F2
Garden Square Wlk. Aird 122 B4
Garden St. Ayr 235 F1
Garden St. Falk 42 B3
Garden St. Kilmk 222 C1
Garden Terr. Falk 42 B3
Garden Veteran's Cotts. Ersk 72 C3
Gardenhall Ct. E Kil 179 F4
Gardenhall. E Kil 179 F4
Gardenside Ave. Glasg 139 D4
Gardenside Ave. Udd 140 C3
Gardenside Cres. Glasg 139 D4
Gardenside. Hat 142 A2
Gardenside Pl. Glasg 139 D4
Gardenside Rd. Ham 162 B1
Gardenside St. Udd 140 C3
Gardiner St. Pres 236 B4
Gardner Gr. Tan 141 D4
Gardner St. Glasg 96 A1
Gardrum Gdns. Shi 66 B4
Gardrum Pl. Kilmk 222 C2
Gardyne St. Glasg 100 A1
Gare Rd. Ros 15 D2
Garelet Pl. Irvine 220 A1
Gareloch Ave. Pais 113 D1
Gareloch Cres. Aird 102 C1
Gareloch La. P Glasg 68 B4
Gareloch Rd. Green 46 A2
Gareloch Rd. Helen 15 F2
Gareloch Rd. P Glasg 68 C4
Gareloch Rd. Rhu 15 F2
Garfield Ave. Hat 142 B3
Garfield Dr. Hat 142 B2
Garfield St. Glasg 118 A3
Garforth Rd. Glasg 119 F2
Gargrave Ave. Glasg 119 F2
Garion Dr. Glasg 95 D3
Garlieston Rd. Glasg 119 F3
Garmouth Ct. Glasg 116 A4
Garmouth Gdns. Glasg 116 A4
Garmouth St. Glasg 115 F4
Garnet St. Glasg 97 D1
Garnethill St. Glasg 97 D1
Garngaber Ave. Klrk 79 E3
Garngaber Ct. Klrk 79 F3
Garngrew Rd. Bank 38 C2
Garnhall Farm Rd. Cumb 62 C4
Garnie Ave. Inch 93 E4
Garnie La. Inch 93 E4
Garnie Oval. Ersk 73 E1
Garnie Pl. Ersk 73 E1
Garnieland Rd. Ersk 73 E1
Garnieland Rd. Inch 93 F4
Garnkirk La. Stepps 99 F3
Garnock Ct. Irvine 219 E1
Garnock Ct. Kilb 149 D1
Garnock Pk. E Kil 160 A1
Garnock Rd. Kilmk 228 A3
Garnock Rd. Steven 217 E4
Garnock St. Dalry 191 E4
Garnock St. Glasg 97 F1
Garnock St. Kilb 149 D1
Garnock View. Kilw 207 F2
Garnockside. Kilb 170 A3
Garpel Way. Loch 129 D1
Garrallan. Kilw 207 E1
Garrawy Rd. Helen 16 C1
Garrel Gr. Kils 36 B1
Garrell Ave. Kils 36 B1
Garrell Pl. Kils 60 B4
Garrell Rd. Kils 60 B4
Garrell Way. Cumb 61 F1
Garrell Way. Kils 60 B4
Garrier Pl. Kilmk 222 B1
Garrier Rd. Spring 220 C1
Garrioch Cres. Glasg 96 B3
Garrioch Dr. Glasg 96 B3
Garrioch Gate. Glasg 96 B3
Garrioch Quadrant. Glasg 96 B3
Garrioch Rd. Glasg 96 B3
Garriochmill Rd. Glasg 96 C2
Garrion Bsns Pk. Wish 186 A4
Garrion Pl. Ash 185 F1
Garrion St. Wish 186 B3
Garrison Pl. Falk 42 A3
Garrowhill Dr. Glasg 119 F3
Garry Ave. Bear 76 A1
Garry Dr. Pais 113 D1
Garry Pl. Falk 42 B1
Garry Pl. Kilmk 228 A3
Garry Pl. Troon 229 F3
Garry St. Glasg 137 D4
Garry Way. Shot 146 C3
Garryhorn. Pres 236 B3
Garscadden Rd. Glasg 75 D1
Garscadden Rd S. Glasg 94 C4
Garscadden Rd S. Glasg 95 D4
Garscadden View. Clyde 74 B2
Garscube Cross. Glasg 97 D1
Garscube Rd. Glasg 97 D1
Garshake Ave. Dumb 50 B3
Garshake Rd. Dumb 50 B3
Garshake Terr. Dumb 50 B3
Gartartan Rd. Glasg 114 C3
Gartcarron Hill. Cumb 61 E2
Gartcloss Rd. Coat 101 E1
Gartclush Gdns. Bann 11 F4
Gartconnell Dr. Bear 75 F3
Gartconnell Gdns. Bear 75 F3
Gartconnell Rd. Bear 75 F3
Gartconner Ave. Kirk 80 A4
Gartcosh Rd. Coat 101 D1
Gartcosh Rd. Coat 120 C3
Gartcosh Wlk. Hat 141 F3
Gartcows Ave. Falk 42 A2
Gartcows Cres. Falk 42 A2
Gartcows Dr. Falk 42 A2
Gartcows Gdns. Falk 41 F2
Gartcows Pl. Falk 42 A2
Gartcows Rd. Falk 42 A2
Gartcraig Rd. Glasg 118 C4
Garten Dr. Shot 147 D2
Gartferry Ave. Muir 80 C1
Gartferry Rd. Muir 80 C1
Gartferry St. Glasg 98 A2
Gartfield St. Aird 123 D3
Gartgill Rd. Coat 101 F1
Garth St. Glasg 117 E4
Garthamlock Rd. Glasg 99 F1
Garthill Gdns. Falk 42 A2
Garthill La. Falk 42 A2
Garthland Dr. Ard 205 E2
Garthland Dr. Glasg 118 A4
Garthland La. Pais 113 F3
Gartlea Ave. Aird 123 D4
Gartlea Rd. Aird 123 D4
Gartleahill. Aird 123 D3
Gartliston Rd. Glen 101 F2
Gartliston Terr. Coat 121 D3
Gartloch Rd. Glasg 99 D1
Gartloch Rd. Glasg 100 B2
Gartly St. Glasg 136 C2
Gartmore Gdns. Tan 140 C4
Gartmore La. Muir 81 D1
Gartmore Rd. Pais 114 B2
Gartmore Terr. Glasg 138 C2
Gartmorn Rd. N Sau 5 E1
Gartness Dr. Chap 124 F3
Gartness Rd. Chap 124 A2
Gartocher Rd. Glasg 119 E3
Gartocher Terr. Glasg 119 E3
Gartons Rd. Glasg 98 B2
Gartsherrie Ave. Glen 101 F3
Gartsherrie Rd. Coat 121 F4
Gartshore Cres. Twe 59 F1
Gartshore Gdns. Cumb 60 C1
Garturk St. Coat 122 A2
Garturk St. Glasg 117 D1
Garvald Ct. Glasg 118 A2
Garvald La. Den 21 E1
Garvald Rd. Bank 39 E4
Garvald St. Glasg 118 A2
Garvald St. Green 46 B2
Garvally Cres. All 10 A4
Garve Ave. Glasg 137 D3
Garvel Cres. Glasg 119 F3
Garvel Pl. Miln 54 B1
Garvel Rd. Glasg 119 F3
Garvel Rd. Miln 54 C1
Garven Ct. Kilmk 228 A4
Garven Rd. Steven 217 F3
Garvie Ave. Gour 44 C3
Garvock Dr. Glasg 136 A3
Garvock Dr. Green 45 E2
Garwhitter Dr. Miln 55 D1
Gas St. John 112 A2
Gascoyne. E Kil 180 B4
Gask Pl. Glasg 94 C4
Gaskin Path. Stepps 99 F3
Gasworks Rd. Car 187 E2
Gatehead Rd. Cross 221 F1
Gatehouse St. Glasg 119 E2
Gates Rd. Loch 129 E2
Gateshead Pl. Kilbar 111 D2
Gateside Ave. Bon 40 B3
Gateside Ave. Glasg 139 E3
Gateside Ave. Green 45 D2
Gateside Ave. Kils 60 A4
Gateside Cres. Aird 123 D4
Gateside Cres. Barr 134 A1
Gateside Gdns. Green 45 D2
Gateside Gr. Green 45 D2
Gateside. Irvine 219 F3
Gateside Pk. Kils 60 A4
Gateside Pl. Kilmk 227 F2
Gateside Rd. Barr 134 A1
Gateside Rd. Mother 164 C2
Gateside Rd. Stir 7 D2
Gateside St. Glasg 118 A3
Gateside St. Ham 162 C2
Gateside St. W Kil 190 B3
Gateway The. E Kil 160 A2
Gauldry Ave. Glasg 115 E2
Gauze St. Pais 113 F3
Gavell Rd. Kils 60 A4
Gavin Hamilton Ct. Ayr 239 E3
Gavin St. Mother 163 F3
Gavin's Mill Rd. Miln 55 D1
Gavinburn Gdns. O Kill 73 D4
Gavinburn Pl. O Kill 73 D4
Gavinburn St. O Kill 73 D4
Gavins Rd. All 4 C1
Gavins Rd. Dunt 74 A3
Gavinton St. Glasg 136 C3
Gayne Dr. Glen 101 E3
Gean Ct. Cumb 62 C2
Gean Rd. All 9 F4
Gearholm Rd. Ayr 238 B2
Geary St. Glasg 76 B1
Geddes Hill. E Kil 160 A2
Geddes Rd. Glasg 98 B4
Geelong Gdns. Lennox 33 E1
Geils Ave. Dumb 50 B1
Geils Quadrant. Dumb 50 B2
Geilsland Rd. Beith 171 E4
Geilston Pk. Card 48 A4
Geirston Rd. Kilb 148 C1
Gelston St. Glasg 119 D2
Gemini Gr. Holy 143 D3
Gemmel Pl. Newt M 156 B2
Gemmell Cres. Ayr 236 B1
Gemmell Way. Stone 198 C1
General Roy Way. Car 202 B4
Generals Gate. Udd 140 C3
Gentle Row. Dunt 73 F3
George Aitken Ct. Ard 205 E2
George Ave. Clyde 74 B2
George Cres. Clyde 74 B2
George Ct. Ham 162 A3
George Gray St. Glasg 138 B4
George La. Pais 113 F2
George Mann Terr. Glasg 138 A2
George Pl. Pais 113 F2
George Rd. Gour 44 C3
George Reith Ave. Glasg 95 F3
George Sq. Ayr 236 A1
George Sq. Glasg 117 E4
George Sq. Green 45 F3
George St. Aird 122 C4
George St. Alva 5 D3
George St. Ayr 235 F1
George St. Ayr 236 A1
George St. Barr 134 A2
George St. Bonh 27 F2

Glendevon Sq. Glasg

265
Hilltop Rd. Muir Invercloy Pl. Kilmk

Hilltop Rd. Muir 80 C1
Hillview Ave. Kils 60 C4
Hillview Ave. Lennox 57 F4
Hillview Cotts. Twe 59 F2
Hillview Cres. Hat 142 A4
Hillview Cres. Lark 185 D1
Hillview Cres. Tan 140 C4
Hillview Dr. B of A 2 A3
Hillview Dr. Helen 16 B2
Hillview Dr. Newt M 157 F4
Hillview Dr. Udd 140 B1
Hillview Gdns. Bish 98 B4
Hillview. Gree 83 F1
Hillview. Kils 37 E2
Hillview Pl. Fall 8 B2
Hillview Pl. Newt M 156 B2
Hillview Pl. Newt M 157 F4
Hillview Rd. B of W 110 C4
Hillview Rd. Bon 40 B2
Hillview Rd. John 112 B1
Hillview Rd. Lar 23 E2
Hillview St. Glasg 118 C3
Hillview Terr. All 10 B3
Hilton. Cowie 12 C4
Hilton Cres. All 10 B4
Hilton Ct. Bish 78 A2
Hilton Gdns. Glasg 95 F4
Hilton Pk. Bish 77 F2
Hilton Rd. All 10 B4
Hilton Rd. Bish 78 A2
Hilton Rd. Miln 54 C1
Hilton Terr. Bish 77 F2
Hilton Terr. Fall 8 B2
Hilton Terr. Glasg 95 F4
Hilton Terr. Glasg 138 C2
Hiltonbank St. Ham 162 A2
Hindog Pl. Dalry 191 D4
Hindsland Rd. Lark 185 D1
Hinshaw St. Glasg 97 D2
Hinshelwood Dr. Glasg 116 A3
Hinshelwood Pl. Glasg 116 A3
Hirsel Pl. Udd 141 D1
Hirst Gdns. Shot 146 B3
Hirst Rd. East 126 B2
Hirst Rd. Sals 126 B2
Hirstrigg Cotts. Sals 126 A2
Hobart Cres. Clyde 73 E3
Hobart Quadrant. Wish 165 F2
Hobart Rd. E Kil 180 B4
Hobart St. Glasg 97 D2
Hobden St. Glasg 98 A2
Hoddam Ave. Glasg 138 A2
Hoddam Terr. Glasg 138 A2
Hodge St. Falk 42 A2
Hoey Dr. Wish 186 B4
Hogan Ct. Dunt 73 F3
Hogarth Ave. Glasg 118 B4
Hogarth Ave. Salt 205 F1
Hogarth Cres. Glasg 118 B4
Hogarth Dr. Glasg 118 B4
Hogarth Gdns. Glasg 118 B4
Hogg Ave. John 111 F1
Hogg Rd. Chap 123 E2
Hogg St. Aird 123 D4
Hogganfield St. Glasg 98 B1
Holbourne Pl. Men 4 A4
Hole Farm Rd. Green 45 E2
Holeburn La. Glasg 136 B3
Holeburn Rd. Glasg 136 B3
Holehills Dr. Aird 103 D1
Holehills Pl. Aird 103 D1
Holehouse Brae. Neil 154 B4
Holehouse Dr. Glasg 95 D3
Holehouse Dr. Kilb 149 D2
Holehouse Rd. Eagle 178 C3
Holehouse Rd. Kilmk 228 A4
Holehouse Rd. Thorn 179 D4
Holehouse Terr. Neil 154 B4
Holland St. Glasg 117 D4
Hollandbush Ave. Bank 38 C2
Hollandbush Cres. Bank 38 C2
Hollandhurst Rd. Coat 101 F1
Hollinwell Rd. Glasg 76 B1
Hollow Pk. Ayr 239 D1
Hollowglen Rd. Glasg 119 D3
Hollows Ave. Pais 132 C4
Hollows Cres. Pais 132 C4
Holly Ave. M of C 58 A3
Holly Ave. Sten 23 F2
Holly Bank. Ayr 239 E3
Holly Dr. Dumb 49 D3
Holly Dr. Glasg 98 A2
Holly Gr. Bank 38 C1
Holly Gr. Holy 142 C3
Holly Pl. John 132 A4
Holly Pl. Kilmk 222 B1
Holly St. Aird 123 E3
Holly St. Clyde 74 A2
Hollybank Pl. Glasg 139 D2
Hollybank St. Glasg 98 A1
Hollybrook St. Glasg 117 D1
Hollybush Ave. Pais 133 D4
Hollybush Rd. Glasg 114 C3
Hollymount. Bear 75 F1
Holm Ave. Pais 113 F1
Holm Ave. Udd 140 C4
Holm Cres. Fen 213 D2
Holm Crest. Cro 201 D1
Holm Gdns. Hat 142 B2
Holm La. E Kil 159 F1
Holm Pl. Lark 184 C1
Holm Pl. Lin 112 A4
Holm Place. Lark 184 C1
Holm Rd. Cro 201 D1
Holm St. Car 187 F1
Holm St. Glasg 117 D4
Holm St. Holy 143 D2
Holm St. Stew 211 F4
Holmbank Ave. Glasg 136 B4
Holmbrae Ave. Tan 140 C4
Holmbrae Rd. Tan 140 C4
Holmbyre Rd. Glasg 137 E1
Holmbyre Terr. Glasg 137 E1
Holmes Ave. Ren 94 B1
Holmes Cres. Kilmk 227 E3
Holmes Farm Rd. Kilmk 227 E3
Holmes Quadrant. Hat 142 A2
Holmes Rd. Kilmk 227 E3
Holmes Village. Kilmk 227 E3
Holmfauld Rd. Glasg 95 F1
Holmfauldhead Dr. Glasg 115 F4
Holmfauldhead Pl. Glasg 115 F4
Holmfield. Kirk 79 F4
Holmhead Cres. Glasg 137 D3
Holmhead. Kilb 170 A4
Holmhead Pl. Glasg 137 D3
Holmhead Rd. Glasg 137 D3
Holmhill Ave. Glasg 139 D2
Holmhills Dr. Glasg 138 C2
Holmhills Gdns. Glasg 138 C2
Holmhills Gr. Glasg 138 C2
Holmhills Pl. Glasg 138 C2
Holmhills Rd. Glasg 138 C2
Holmhills Terr. Glasg 138 C2
Holmlands Pl. Kilmk 227 E3
Holmlea Dr. Kilmk 227 F3
Holmlea Pl. Kilmk 227 F3
Holmlea Rd. Glasg 137 D4
Holmpark. Bishop 72 A2
Holmquarry Rd. Kilmk 227 F3
Holms Ave. Irvine 220 B1
Holms Cres. Ersk 72 C1
Holms Pl. Muir 100 C4
Holms Rd. Kilb 170 A3
Holmscroft Ave. Green 45 F2
Holmscroft St. Green 45 F3
Holmscroft Way. Green 45 F2
Holmston Cres. Ayr 239 E4
Holmston Dr. Ayr 239 E3
Holmston Rd. Ayr 239 E4
Holmswood Ave. Udd 140 B1
Holmwood Ave. Udd 140 C4
Holmwood Gdns. Udd 140 C3
Holmwood Gr. Glasg 137 D2
Holton Cres. N Sau 5 E1
Holton Sq. N Sau 5 E1
Holyknowe Cres. Lennox 57 F4
Holyknowe Rd. Lennox 57 F4
Holyoake Ct. Hurl 228 C4
Holyrood Cres. Glasg 96 C1
Holyrood Pl. Sten 23 F2
Holyrood Quadrant. Glasg 96 C1
Holyrood St. Ham 162 A3
Holytown Rd. Holy 142 C3
Holywell St. Glasg 118 A3
Home Farm Cotts. Den 39 F3
Home Farm Rd. Ayr 239 D1
Home St. Lan 215 E2
Homer Pl. Holy 142 C3
Homesteads The. Stir 6 B4
Homeston Ave. Udd 141 D2
Honeybank Cres. Car 188 A2
Honeybog Rd. Glasg 114 C3
Honeycomb Pl. Ash 200 B2
Honeysuckle La. Bonh 27 F4
Honeysuckle Pk. Ayr 239 D1
Honeywell Cres. Chap 123 F1
Hood Ct. Helen 16 A1
Hood St. Clyde 74 B1
Hood St. Green 45 F3
Hookney Terr. Den 21 E1
Hope Ave. Kil 89 F1
Hope Cres. Lark 185 D2
Hope St. Ayr 238 C4
Hope St. Car 188 A1
Hope St. Falk 42 A3
Hope St. Glasg 117 D4
Hope St. Green 45 F2
Hope St. Ham 162 C2
Hope St. Hat 142 B3
Hope St. Helen 25 C4
Hope St. Lan 215 D2
Hope St. Mother 163 F4
Hope St. New 166 A2
Hope St. Stir 1 C1
Hopefield Ave. Glasg 96 B3
Hopehill Rd. Glasg 97 D2
Hopeman Ave. Glasg 135 F2
Hopeman Dr. Glasg 135 F2
Hopeman. Ersk 73 D2
Hopeman Path. Glasg 135 F3
Hopeman Rd. Glasg 135 F2
Hopeman St. Glasg 135 F2
Hopepark Terr. Bon 39 F3
Hopetoun Bank. Irvine 220 B1
Hopetoun Dr. B of A 2 A4
Hopetoun Pl. Glasg 76 C1
Hopkin's Brae. Kirk 58 B1
Horatius St. Mother 142 A1
Hornal Rd. Udd 141 D2
Hornbeam Dr. Clyde 74 A2
Hornbeam Rd. Cumb 62 C3
Hornbeam Rd. Tan 141 D4
Horndean Cres. Glasg 99 E1
Horndean Ct. Bish 78 A2
Horne St. Glasg 97 F3
Hornock Rd. Coat 101 F1
Hornshill Dr. Cle 144 A1
Hornshill Farm Rd. Stepps 99 F3
Hornshill St. Glasg 98 A2
Horsbrugh Ave. Kils 36 B1
Horsburgh St. Glasg 99 E1
Horse Shoe Rd. Bear 75 F2
Horsewood Rd. B of W 110 B4
Horslet St. Coat 121 E2
Horslethill Rd. Glasg 96 B2
Horsley Brae. Wish 186 A2
Horton Pl. Helen 17 D2
Hospital Rd. Wish 186 A4
Hospital St. Coat 122 A2
Hospital St. Glasg 117 D2
Hospitland Dr. Lan 215 E2
Hotspur St. Glasg 96 C2
Houldsworth Cres. Alla 167 D4
Houldsworth La. Glasg 116 C4
Houldsworth St. Glasg 116 C4
House O' Muir Rd. Sals 126 A2
Househillmuir Cres. Glasg 135 E4
Househillmuir La. Glasg 135 E4
Househillmuir Pl. Glasg 135 E4
Househillmuir Rd. Glasg 135 D3
Househillwood Cres. Glasg 135 D4
Househillwood Rd. Glasg 135 D3
Housel Ave. Glasg 95 D4
Houston Cres. Dalry 191 D4
Houston Pl. Glasg 116 C3
Houston Pl. John 112 B1
Houston Rd. B of W 90 B1
Houston Rd. Hous 91 D1
Houston Rd. Inch 92 B2
Houston Rd. Kil 89 F4
Houston St. Glasg 116 C3
Houston St. Green 45 F3
Houston St. Ham 162 B1
Houston St. Ren 94 B2
Houston St. Wish 165 E1
Houston Terr. E Kil 159 E1
Houstonfield
Quadrant. Hous 91 D1
Houstonfield Rd. Hous 91 D1
Houstoun Ct. John 111 F2
Houstoun Sq. John 111 F2
Howacre. Lan 214 C3
Howard Ave. E Kil 160 A3
Howard Ct. E Kil 160 A3
Howard Ct. Kilmk 227 F4
Howard Park Dr. Kilmk 227 F4
Howard St. Falk 41 F2
Howard St. Glasg 117 E3
Howard St. Kilmk 227 F4
Howard St. Lark 185 E1
Howard St. Pais 114 A2
Howat Cres. Irvine 219 F2
Howat St. Glasg 116 A4
Howatshaws Rd. Dumb 50 A3
Howburn Cres. East 127 F3
Howburn Rd. East 127 E3
Howden Ave. Holy 143 E4
Howden Ave. Kilw 207 F2
Howden Dr. Lin 112 A3
Howden Pl. Holy 143 D3
Howe Rd. Kils 60 B4
Howes St. Coat 122 A2
Howetown. Fish 5 E2
Howford Rd. Glasg 115 D2
Howgate Ave. Glasg 74 C2
Howgate. Kilw 207 E2
Howgate Rd. Ham 183 E4
Howie Bldgs. Newt M 157 F4
Howie Cres. Ros 15 D2
Howie St. Lark 185 D1
Howie's Pl. Falk 41 D2
Howieshill Ave. Glasg 139 D3
Howieshill Rd. Glasg 139 D3
Howlands Rd. Stir 7 D2
Howlet Pl. Ham 162 C1
Howletnest Rd. Aird 123 E3
Howson View. Mother 163 D4
Howth Dr. Glasg 95 F4
Howth Terr. Glasg 95 F4
Hoylake Pk. Udd 140 C1
Hoylake Pl. Glasg 76 C1
Hoylake Sq. Kilw 207 E2
Hozier Cres. Tan 140 C4
Hozier Loan. Lark 185 D2
Hozier Pl. Udd 141 D2
Hozier St. Car 187 F1
Hozier St. Coat 122 A2
Hudson Terr. E Kil 180 B4
Hudson Way. E Kil 180 B4
Hudspeth Ct. Alex 27 E4
Hugh Murray Dr. Glasg 139 E3
Hugh Watt Pl. Kilm 222 A4
Hughenden Dr. Glasg 96 A2
Hughenden Gdns. Glasg 96 A2
Hughenden La. Glasg 96 A2
Hughenden Rd. Glasg 96 A2
Hugo St. Glasg 96 C3
Hulks Rd. Gree 83 E2
Humbie Ct. Newt M 156 C1
Humbie Gate. Newt M 156 C1
Humbie Gr. Newt M 156 C2
Humbie Lawns. Newt M 156 C1
Humbie Rd. Eagle 178 B4
Humbie Rd. Newt M 156 C1
Hume Cres. B of A 2 A3
Hume Ct. B of A 2 A3
Hume Dr. Udd 140 C4
Hume Dr. Udd 141 D2
Hume Pl. E Kil 180 B4
Hume Rd. Cumb 62 A2
Hume St. Clyde 74 A1
Hunter Ave. Salt 205 E1
Hunter Cres. Troon 230 A1
Hunter Dr. Irvine 219 D3
Hunter Gdns. Den 21 E1
Hunter Pl. Kilbar 111 D1
Hunter Pl. Kilw 208 A2
Hunter Pl. Miln 54 C1
Hunter Pl. Shot 146 C3
Hunter Pl. Sten 24 A2
Hunter Rd. Cross 221 F1
Hunter Rd. Glasg 118 B1
Hunter Rd. Ham 162 A3
Hunter Rd. Miln 54 C1
Hunter St. Aird 103 D1
Hunter St. E Kil 159 F1
Hunter St. Glasg 117 F3
Hunter St. Glasg 117 F4
Hunter St. Hat 142 A3
Hunter St. Pais 113 F3
Hunter St. Pres 236 B4
Hunter St. Shot 146 B3
Hunter's Ave. Ayr 236 A2
Hunter's Ave. Dumb 50 B2
Hunter's Cl. Lan 215 D2
Hunterfield Dr. Glasg 138 C3
Hunterhill Ave. Pais 113 F2
Hunterhill Rd. Pais 113 F2
Hunterlees Rd. Glass 198 A2
Hunters Hill Ct. Glasg 97 F3
Hunters Pl. Green 45 F3
Huntersfield Rd. John 111 E1
Huntershill Rd. Bish 97 F4
Huntershill St. Glasg 97 F3
Hunterston Rd. W Kil 190 B3
Hunthill La. Udd 161 D3
Hunthill Pl. Thorn 158 A3
Hunthill Rd. Udd 161 D4
Hunting Lodge Gdns. Ham 163 D1
Huntingdon Rd. Glasg 97 F1
Huntingdon Sq. Glasg 97 F1
Huntingtower Rd. Glasg 119 F2
Huntley Cres. Stir 1 C1
Huntley Gdns. Glasg 96 B2
Huntly Ave. Glasg 136 B1
Huntly Ave. Hat 142 A3
Huntly Ct. Bish 98 A4
Huntly Ct. Kilmk 223 E2
Huntly Dr. Bear 75 F4
Huntly Dr. Coat 121 E2
Huntly Dr. Glasg 139 D2
Huntly Dr. Gour 44 C2
Huntly Path. Muir 81 D1
Huntly Pl. Kilmk 223 E1
Huntly Pl. P Glasg 47 D1
Huntly Quadrant. Wish 165 D3
Huntly Rd. Glasg 96 B2
Huntly Rd. Glasg 114 C4
Huntly Terr. P Glasg 47 D1
Huntly Terr. Pais 114 A1
Huntly Terr. Shot 147 D2
Hurlawcrook Rd. Chapel 180 C1
Hurlawcrook Rd. E Kil 181 D2
Hurlet Cotts. Glasg 134 C3
Hurlet Rd. Pais 134 B4
Hurlford Ave. Glasg 94 C4
Hurlford Rd. Kilmk 228 A3
Hurly Hawkin. Bish 98 B4
Hurworth St. Falk 41 F2
Hutcheson Rd. Glasg 136 A1
Hutcheson St. Glasg 117 E4
Hutchinson Pl. Glasg 139 F2
Hutchinson St. Wish 186 B4
Hutchinson Town Ct. Glasg 117 E2
Hutchison Dr. Bear 76 A1
Hutchison Pl. Coat 121 F3
Hutchison St. Ham 162 B1
Hutton Ave. Hous 111 E4
Hutton Dr. Glasg 115 F4
Hutton Pk. All 10 B4
Huxley St. Glasg 96 C3
Hyacinth Way. Car 201 F4
Hydepark St. Glasg 116 C4
Hyndal Ave. Glasg 115 E1
Hyndford Pl. Lan 215 D2
Hyndford Rd. Lan 215 E1
Hyndland Ave. Glasg 96 A1
Hyndland Rd. Glasg 96 A2
Hyndland St. Glasg 96 B1
Hyndlee Dr. Glasg 115 E3
Hyndman Rd. W Kil 190 B2
Hyndshaw Rd. Car 188 A2
Hyndshaw View. Law 187 D2
Hyslop Pl. Clyde 74 A2
Hyslop Rd. Steven 206 C1
Hyslop St. Aird 122 C4

Iain Dr. Bear 75 E3
Iain Rd. Bear 75 E3
Ian Smith Ct. Clyde 94 B4
Ibrox St. Glasg 116 B3
Ibrox Terr. Glasg 116 A3
Ibroxholm Ave. Glasg 116 A3
Ibroxholm Oval. Glasg 116 A3
Ibroxholm Pl. Glasg 116 A3
Ida Quadrant. Hat 141 F3
Iddesleigh Ave. Miln 55 D1
Ilay Ave. Glasg 96 A4
Ilay Ct. Glasg 96 A4
Ilay Rd. Glasg 96 A4
Imperial Dr. Aird 122 C3
Inch Garve. E Kil 160 B1
Inch Keith. E Kil 160 B1
Inch Marnock. E Kil 160 B1
Inch Murrin. E Kil 160 B1
Inchbrae Rd. Glasg 115 E2
Inchcolm Pl. E Kil 159 E1
Inchconnachan Ave. Bonh 19 F1
Inches Rd. Ard 216 A4
Inches Rd. Salt 205 E1
Inchfad Dr. Glasg 74 C2
Inchfad Rd. Bonh 19 F1
Inchgotrick Rd. Kilmk 227 F2
Inchgower Gr. Rhu 15 E3
Inchgreen St. Green 46 C1
Inchholm La. Glasg 95 F1
Inchholm St. Glasg 95 F1
Inchinnan Rd. Hat 141 F4
Inchinnan Rd. Pais 113 F4
Inchinnan Rd. Ren 94 A2
Inchkeith Pl. Falk 42 A1
Inchkeith Pl. Glasg 119 D4
Inchlee St. Glasg 95 F2
Inchlonaig Dr. Bonh 19 F1
Inchmurrin Ave. Kirk 80 A4
Inchmurrin Cres. Bonh 19 F1
Inchmurrin Dr. Glasg 138 B1
Inchmurrin Dr. Kilmk 223 D3
Inchmurrin Gdns. Glasg 138 B1
Inchmurrin Pl. Glasg 138 B1
Inchna. Men 4 A3
Inchneuk Rd. Glen 101 F3
Inchoch St. Glasg 99 F1
Inchrory Pl. Glasg 74 C2
Inchwood Ct. Cumb 82 A4
Inchwood Pl. Cumb 81 F4
Inchwood Rd. Cumb 82 A4
Incle St. Pais 113 F3
Indale Ave. Pres 236 C4
India Dr. Inch 93 E3
India St. Alex 27 F3
India St. Glasg 117 D4
Industry St. Kirk 79 E4
Inga St. Glasg 96 C4
Ingerbreck Ave. Glasg 138 B2
Ingleby Dr. Glasg 118 A4
Ingleby Pl. Neil 154 C4
Inglefield Ct. Aird 123 D4
Inglefield St. Glasg 117 D1
Ingleneuk Ave. Stepps 99 D3
Ingleside. Kirk 79 E3
Ingleston Ave. Duni 21 E3
Ingleston St. Green 46 A2
Inglestone Ave. Glasg 136 A1
Inglewood. All 9 F4
Inglewood Cres. E Kil 180 A4
Inglewood Rd. All 9 F4
Inglis Pl. E Kil 180 C4
Inglis St. Glasg 118 A3
Inglis St. Wish 164 B1
Ingliston Dr. Bishop 71 F2
Ingram Pl. Kilmk 223 D2
Ingram St. Glasg 117 E4
Inishail Rd. Glasg 99 E1
Inkerman Pl. Kilmk 222 C1
Inkerman Rd. Glasg 114 C3
Innellan Dr. Kilmk 222 C2
Inner City Trad Est. Glasg 97 E1
Innerleithen Dr. Wish 165 E3
Innermanse
Quadrant. Holy 143 F3
Innerpeffray Dr. Sten 24 A2
Innerwick Dr. Glasg 115 D3
Innerwood Rd. Kilw 207 F3
Innes Ct. E Kil 159 F2
International Ave. Ham 161 E2
Inver Ct. Falk 24 B1
Inver Rd. Glasg 119 F4
Inverallan Ct. B of A 1 C4
Inverallan Dr. B of A 1 C4
Inverallan Rd. B of A 1 C4
Inveraray Dr. Bish 78 A2
Inverary Dr. Sten 23 F3
Inveravon Dr. Mother 163 E3
Inverbervie. Ersk 73 D1
Invercanny Dr. Glasg 75 D2
Invercanny Pl. Glasg 75 D2
Invercargill. E Kil 180 A4
Invercloy Pl. Kilmk 222 C2

Inverclyde Gdns. Glasg | **Kelvinview Ave. Bank**

270

Lexwell Rd. Pais

Loganswell Rd. Glasg

Lexwell Rd. Pais 112 C1
Leyden Ct. Glasg 96 C3
Leyden Gdns. Glasg 96 C3
Leyden St. Glasg 96 C3
Leys Pk. Ham 162 A2
Leys The. Bish 78 A1
Libberton Way. Ham 162 A2
Liberator Dr. Pres 236 C2
Liberton St. Glasg 118 C4
Liberty Ave. Coat 121 D3
Liberty Path. Udd 161 E4
Liberty Rd. Cald 105 D3
Liberty Rd. Hat 142 A2
Libo Ave. Glasg 115 E1
Libo Ave. Uplaw 153 D2
Libo Pl. Ersk 72 C1
Library La. Glasg 135 F2
Lichtenfels Gdns. Pres 236 C4
Lickprivick Rd. E Kil 180 A3
Liddel Rd. Cumb 61 F1
Liddell Gr. E Kil 180 B4
Liddell St. Glasg 119 E1
Liddells Ct. Bish 98 A4
Liddesdale Pl. Bish 97 F4
Liddesdale Rd. Glasg 97 E4
Liddesdale Sq. Bish 97 F4
Liddesdale Terr. Bish 97 F4
Liddlesdale Pass. Glasg 97 E4
Liddoch Way. Glasg 137 F4
Liff Gdns. Bish 98 B4
Liff Pl. Glasg 100 B1
Lifnock Ave. Hurl 228 C3
Lightburn Pl. Glasg 119 D4
Lightburn Rd. Glasg 118 B3
Lightburn Rd. Glasg 139 F2
Lilac Ave. Clyde 73 E3
Lilac Ave. Cumb 62 C3
Lilac Cres. Tan 141 E4
Lilac Ct. Cumb 62 C3
Lilac Gdns. Bish 98 A4
Lilac Hill. Cumb 62 C3
Lilac Hill. Ham 162 C1
Lilac Pl. Cumb 62 C3
Lilac Pl. Kilmk 227 F4
Lilac Way. Holy 143 D3
Lillyburn Pl. Glasg 74 C3
Lily St. Glasg 118 A2
Lilybank Ave. Aird 103 D1
Lilybank Ave. Glasg 139 E2
Lilybank Ave. Muir 100 B4
Lilybank Ct. N Sau 5 E1
Lilybank Gardens La. Glasg 96 B1
Lilybank Gdns. Glasg 96 B1
Lilybank La. Glasg 96 B1
Lilybank Rd. P Glasg 47 D1
Lilybank Rd. Pres 236 A3
Lilybank St. Ham 162 B2
Lilybank Terr. Glasg 96 B1
Lilybank Terrace La. Glasg 96 B1
Lime Cres. Aird 123 E4
Lime Cres. Cumb 62 C2
Lime Gr. Klrk 79 E3
Lime Gr. Lar 23 E1
Lime Gr. Mother 163 F2
Lime Gr. Udd 140 B1
Lime La. Glasg 95 E2
Lime Loan. Holy 143 D2
Lime Pl. Kilmk 227 E4
Lime Rd. Dumb 49 F2
Lime Rd. Falk 41 D2
Lime St. Glasg 95 E2
Lime St. Green 45 F2
Limecraigs Ave. Pais 133 E4
Limecraigs Cres. Pais 133 E4
Limecraigs Rd. Pais 133 E4
Limegrove St. Hat 142 A4
Limekiln Rd. Ayr 236 A2
Limekiln Rd. Steven 217 F4
Limekilnburn Rd. Quart 183 E2
Limekilns Rd. Cumb 82 C3
Limekilns St. Dunt 74 B4
Limelands Quadrant. Cald 104 C2
Limes The. Glasg 137 D2
Limeside Ave. Glasg 138 B4
Limeside Gdns. Glasg 138 B4
Limetree Ave. Tan 141 E4
Limetree Cres. Newt M 156 B2
Limetree Ct. Ham 162 A3
Limetree Dr. Clyde 74 A2
Limetree Quadrant. Tan 141 E4
Limetree Wlk. M of C 58 A2
Limeview Ave. Pais 133 D4
Limeview Cres. Pais 133 D4
Limeview Rd. Pais 133 D4
Limeview Way. Pais 133 D4
Limonds Ct. Ayr 236 A1
Limonds Wynd. Ayr 236 A1
Limpetlaw. Lan 215 D3
Linacre Dr. Glasg 119 E3
Linacre Gdns. Glasg 119 E3
Linburn Pl. Glasg 115 D3
Linburn Rd. Ersk 72 C1
Linburn Rd. Glasg 114 C3
Linclive Interchange. Lin 112 B3
Linclive Terr. Lin 112 B3
Lincoln Ave. Glasg 95 E3
Lincoln Ave. Tan 120 C1
Lincoln Rd. Gour 44 B2
Lincuan Ave. Glasg 157 E4
Lindams. Udd 140 C3
Linden Ave. Duni 21 E2
Linden Ave. Stir 7 E3
Linden Ave. Wish 165 E3
Linden Dr. Bank 38 C1
Linden Dr. Dunt 74 A3
Linden Lea. Ham 162 A2
Linden Lea. M of C 58 A3
Linden Pl. Glasg 95 F4
Linden St. Glasg 95 F4
Linden Way. Glasg 95 F4
Lindores Ave. Glasg 138 B4
Lindores Dr. E Kil 159 E1
Lindores Pl. E Kil 159 E1
Lindores St. Glasg 137 D4
Lindrick Dr. Glasg 76 C1
Lindsay Ave. Kilb 149 D2
Lindsay Dr. Glasg 96 A3
Lindsay Dr. Kilmk 223 E2
Lindsay Dr. Stir 2 A2
Lindsay Gr. E Kil 159 F1
Lindsay Loan. Lan 215 E3
Lindsay Pl. E Kil 160 A1
Lindsay Pl. Glasg 96 A3
Lindsay Pl. John 112 A2
Lindsay Pl. Klrk 79 E2
Lindsay Quadrant. Bonh 28 A4
Lindsay Rd. E Kil 159 F1
Lindsay Rd. Salt 205 F1
Lindsay St. Ayr 236 B1
Lindsay St. Kilmk 227 F4
Lindsay Terr. Lennox 57 F4
Lindsaybeg Rd. Muir 80 A1
Lindston Pl. Ayr 239 D1
Lindum Cres. Mother 163 D4
Lindum St. Mother 163 D4
Lineside Wlk. Rhu 15 F3
Linfern Ave E. Kilmk 228 B4
Linfern Ave. Kilmk 228 B4
Linfern Ave W. Kilmk 228 B4
Linfern Pl. Ayr 239 D2
Linfern Rd. Glasg 96 B2
Linfield Loan. Udd 141 D3
Linghope Pl. Wish 185 F4
Lingley Ave. Aird 123 D3
Linhope Pl. E Kil 179 F4
Links Cres. Troon 229 F3
Links Rd. Glasg 119 E2
Links Rd. Glasg 137 E2
Links Rd. Pres 233 D1
Links Rd. Salt 205 F1
Links The. Cumb 62 A3
Links View. Lark 185 E1
Linksview Rd. Holy 143 D1
Linkwood Ave. Glasg 74 C2
Linkwood Cres. Glasg 75 D2
Linkwood Ct. Irvine 220 A3
Linkwood Dr. Glasg 75 D2
Linkwood Pl. Glasg 74 C2
Linkwood Pl. Irvine 220 A3
Linlithgow Gdns. Glasg 119 E3
Linlithgow Pl. Sten 23 F2
Linn Cres. Lan 214 A2
Linn Cres. Pais 133 E4
Linn Dr. Glasg 136 C2
Linn Gdns. Cumb 61 D1
Linn Glen. Lennox 57 F4
Linn Park Gdns. John 112 A1
Linn Park Ind Est. Glasg 137 D1
Linn Rd. Ard 205 E2
Linnburn Terr. Ard 205 D2
Linnet Ave. John 131 E4
Linnet Rd. Green 45 D2
Linnet Rd. Hat 142 A2
Linnhe Ave. Bish 78 A1
Linnhe Ave. Glasg 137 D2
Linnhe Ave. Ham 162 A1
Linnhe Cres. Wish 165 D1
Linnhe Dr. Barr 134 A3
Linnhe Pl. Ersk 72 C1
Linnhe Pl. Udd 140 B1
Linnhead Dr. Glasg 135 E3
Linnhead Pl. Glasg 95 D2
Linnpark Ave. Glasg 136 C1
Linnpark Ct. Glasg 136 C1
Linnwell Cres. Pais 133 E4
Linrigg Rd. Chap 144 B4
Linside Ave. Pais 114 A2
Lint Brae. Stew 195 F1
Lint Riggs. Falk 42 A3
Linthaugh Rd. Glasg 115 E2
Linthaugh Terr. Glasg 115 E1
Linthill. Lan 215 D3
Linthouse Bldgs. Glasg 115 F4
Linthouse Rd. Glasg 95 F1
Lintie Rd. Holy 143 E2
Lintlaw Dr. Glasg 115 D3
Lintlaw. Udd 140 B1
Lintmill Terr. Neil 154 B3
Linton St. Glasg 118 C4
Lintwhite Cres. B of W 110 C4
Linwood Ave. E Kil 159 D1
Linwood Ave. Newt M 157 F4
Linwood Ct. Glasg 137 D3
Linwood Rd. Lin 112 C2
Linwood Terr. Ham 162 A2
Lion Bank. Kirk 58 B1
Lionthorn Rd. Falk 41 F1
Lipney. Men 4 A3
Lisburn Rd. Ayr 236 A2
Lismore Ave. Mother 163 D4
Lismore Ave. P Glasg 69 D4
Lismore Ave. Ren 94 B1
Lismore Ct. Falk 42 A1
Lismore Dr. Irvine 225 D4
Lismore Dr. Lin 111 F3
Lismore Dr. Pais 133 E4
Lismore. E Kil 181 E4
Lismore Gdns. Kilbar 111 E1
Lismore Hill. Ham 161 E2
Lismore House. Pres 236 A3
Lismore Pl. Muir 81 D2
Lismore Pl. Newt M 156 A3
Lismore Rd. Glasg 96 A3
Lismore Way. Irvine 225 E4
Lister Ct. B of A 2 A3
Lister Gdns. Thorn 158 A3
Lister Pl. Glasg 115 D4
Lister Rd. Glasg 115 D4
Lister St. Cross 222 A1
Lister St. Glasg 97 E1
Lister Wlk. Hat 142 B4
Lithgow Ave. Klrk 79 F4
Lithgow Ave. Lang 70 A4
Lithgow Cres. Pais 114 A1
Lithgow Dr. Cle 144 A1
Lithgow Pl. E Kil 159 D1
Little Bellsland Rd. Kilmk 228 A3
Little Denny Rd. Den 21 E1
Little Dovehill. Glasg 117 E3
Little John Gdns. New 165 F2
Little St. Glasg 116 C4
Littlehill St. Glasg 98 A2
Littleholm Pl. Clyde 73 F2
Littlemill Ave. Cumb 60 C1
Littlesdale Ave. Pais 132 B4
Littlestane Rd. Irvine 220 A3
Littlestane Rise. Irvine 220 A3
Littlestane
Roundabout. Irvine 220 A3
Littleston Gdns. Ersk 72 C1
Littleton Dr. Glasg 76 B1
Littleton St. Glasg 76 B1
Livilands Ct. Stir 7 D3
Livilands Gate. Stir 7 D3
Livilands La. Stir 7 D3
Livingston Dr. Plains 104 A2
Livingston La. Udd 141 D2
Livingston Terr. Dunlop 195 D4
Livingstone Ave. Glasg 115 D4
Livingstone Bvd. Ham 161 E2
Livingstone Cres. E Kil 180 B4
Livingstone Cres. Falk 42 C3
Livingstone Cres. Udd 140 B1
Livingstone Ct. Kilmk 223 E2
Livingstone Dr. E Kil 180 C4
Livingstone Dr. Laur 42 C1
Livingstone Gdns. Lark 185 D2
Livingstone Pk. Kils 36 B1
Livingstone Pl. Aird 123 D4
Livingstone Quadrant. East 127 E2
Livingstone St. Clyde 74 B1
Livingstone St. Ham 161 F2
Livingstone Terr. Irvine 219 E3
Livinstone Pk. Kils 36 A1
Lloyd Ave. Glasg 119 D1
Lloyd Dr. Holy 143 D1
Lloyd St. Glasg 118 A1
Lloyd St. Glasg 118 A4
Lloyd St. Holy 143 D1
Lloyd Wlk. Stew 211 E4
Lloyds St. Coat 122 A2
Llynallan Rd. East 127 D3
Loach Ave. Irvine 219 E1
Loadingbank Ct. Kilb 170 A4
Loadingbank. Kilb 170 A4
Loan Lea Cres. Lark 185 D1
Loan Pl. East 127 F3
Loan The. Miln 54 B2
Loanbank Quadrant. Glasg 115 F4
Loancroft Ave. Glasg 120 B2
Loancroft Gate. Udd 140 C3
Loancroft Gdns. Udd 140 C3
Loancroft Pl. Glasg 120 A2
Loanend Cotts. Glasg 139 F1
Loanfoot Ave. Glasg 95 D4
Loanfoot Ave. Kilmk 222 B1
Loanfoot Ave. Neil 154 B3
Loanfoot Gdns. Plea 12 B2
Loanfoot Rd. Udd 161 E3
Loanhead Ave. Bank 39 E3
Loanhead Ave. Holy 143 E2
Loanhead Ave. Lin 112 A3
Loanhead Ave. Ren 94 B2
Loanhead Cres. Holy 143 E2
Loanhead La. Lin 112 A3
Loanhead Rd. Holy 143 E2
Loanhead Rd. Lin 112 A3
Loanhead Rd. Salt 205 E1
Loanhead St. Coat 121 F2
Loanhead St. Glasg 118 C4
Loanhead St. Kilmk 228 A4
Loaning. Lark 185 E1
Loaning The. Ayr 239 D1
Loaning The. Klrk 79 E4
Loaning The. Mother 163 E4
Loaning The. Newt M 157 D4
Loaninghead Dr. Dumb 50 A3
Lobnitz Ave. Ren 94 B2
Loccard Rd. Steven 206 B1
Loch Achray Gdns. Glasg 119 E2
Loch Achray St. Glasg 119 E2
Loch Assynt. E Kil 181 D4
Loch Ave. Car 201 F2
Loch Awe. E Kil 181 D4
Loch Dr. Helen 16 A1
Loch Goil. E Kil 160 A1
Loch Laidon St. Glasg 119 E2
Loch Laxford. E Kil 181 D4
Loch Lea. Kirk 58 C1
Loch Long. E Kil 181 D4
Loch Loyal. E Kil 181 D4
Loch Maree. E Kil 181 D4
Loch Meadie. E Kil 181 D4
Loch Naver. E Kil 181 D4
Loch Park Ave. Car 201 F4
Loch Park Pl. Lark 185 D1
Loch Pl. B of W 110 B4
Loch Rd. B of W 110 B4
Loch Rd. Chap 123 E1
Loch Rd. Klrk 79 F4
Loch Rd. Miln 55 D2
Loch Rd. Stepps 99 E2
Loch Shin. E Kil 181 D4
Loch St. Calder 123 D1
Loch Striven. E Kil 160 A1
Loch Torridon. E Kil 181 D4
Loch View. Cald 105 D3
Loch View. Calder 123 D1
Loch Voil St. Glasg 119 E2
Lochaber Cres. Shot 147 D2
Lochaber Dr. Glasg 138 B2
Lochaber Dr. Sten 23 F2
Lochaber Path. Udd 161 E4
Lochaber Pl. E Kil 159 F2
Lochaber Rd. Bear 76 A1
Lochaber Wlk. M of C 58 B4
Lochaline Ave. Pais 113 D1
Lochaline Dr. Glasg 137 D2
Lochalsh Cres. M of C 58 B4
Lochalsh Dr. Pais 113 D1
Lochalsh Pl. Udd 140 A1
Lochans The. Ros 15 D2
Lochar Cres. Glasg 115 E1
Lochar Pl. E Kil 179 F4
Lochard Dr. Pais 113 D1
Lochay Pl. Troon 229 F3
Lochay St. Glasg 119 E2
Lochbrae Dr. Glasg 138 B2
Lochbrae. N Sau 5 E1
Lochbridge Rd. Glasg 120 A4
Lochbroom Ct. Newt M 156 C3
Lochbroom Dr. Newt M 156 C3
Lochbroom Dr. Pais 113 D1
Lochbuie La. Glenm 102 C2
Lochburn Cres. Glasg 96 C4
Lochburn Pass. Glasg 96 C4
Lochburn Rd. Glasg 96 C4
Lochcraig Ct. Irvine 220 A2
Lochdochart Rd. Glasg 120 B4
Lochearn Cres. Aird 102 C1
Lochearn Cres. Pais 113 D1
Lochearnhead Rd. Stepps 99 E3
Lochend Ave. Muir 100 C4
Lochend Cotts. Gart 20 C2
Lochend Cres. Bear 75 E2
Lochend Dr. Bear 75 F2
Lochend Rd. Bear 75 F2
Lochend Rd. Coat 101 D1
Lochend Rd. Glasg 100 B1
Lochend Rd. Kilb 170 B4
Lochend Rd. Troon 229 E1
Lochend St. Mother 163 F3
Locher Ave. Hous 91 F1
Locher Cres. Hous 111 F4
Locher Gdns. Hous 111 F4
Locher Rd. Kilbar 110 C2
Locher Way. Hous 111 F4
Locherburn Ave. Hous 111 E4
Locherburn Gr. Hous 111 E4
Locherburn Pl. Hous 111 E4
Lochfauld Rd. Glasg 77 D1
Lochfield Cres. Pais 113 F1
Lochfield Dr. Pais 114 A1
Lochfield Rd. Pais 114 A1
Lochgilp St. Glasg 96 B4
Lochgoin Ave. Glasg 74 C2
Lochgreen Ave. Troon 229 F4
Lochgreen Pl. Coat 101 E1
Lochgreen Pl. Ham 183 D4
Lochgreen Pl. Kilmk 227 F2
Lochgreen Rd. Falk 41 F1
Lochgreen St. Glasg 98 B2
Lochhead Ave. Den 21 F1
Lochhead Ave. Lin 112 A3
Lochiel Dr. M of C 58 B3
Lochiel La. Glasg 138 B2
Lochiel Rd. Glasg 135 F2
Lochinvar Pl. Bon 40 B2
Lochinvar Rd. Cumb 82 C4
Lochinver Cres. Pais 113 D1
Lochinver Dr. Glasg 137 D3
Lochinver Gr. Glasg 139 D3
Lochknowe St. Car 201 F
Lochlands Gr. Beith 171 E
Lochlands Ind Est. Falk 41 D
Lochlea Ave. Clyde 74 B
Lochlea Ave. Troon 229 F
Lochlea Dr. Ayr 239 D
Lochlea. E Kil 160 B
Lochlea Rd. Cumb 62 B
Lochlea Rd. Glasg 136 B
Lochlea Rd. Glasg 137 F
Lochlea Rd. Newt M 157 F
Lochlea Rd. Salt 206 A
Lochlea Way. Holy 143 F
Lochlee Loan. Lark 185 E
Lochleven La. Glasg 137 D
Lochleven Rd. Glasg 137 D
Lochlibo Ave. Glasg 94 C
Lochlibo Cres. Barr 134 A1
Lochlibo Ct. Irvine 220 A
Lochlibo Rd. Barr 134 A1
Lochlibo Rd. Beith 172 C
Lochlibo Rd. Kilw 209 E2
Lochlibo Rd. Neil 154 C4
Lochlibo Rd. Stew 209 E2
Lochlibo Rd. Uplaw 152 C1
Lochlibo Terr. Barr 134 A1
Lochlie Pl. Steven 206 C1
Lochlip Rd. Loch 129 E1
Lochmaben Dr. Sten 23 F2
Lochmaben Rd. Glasg 114 C2
Lochmaddy Ave. Glasg 137 D2
Lochnagar Dr. Bear 75 D4
Lochnagar Rd. Kilmk 228 A2
Lochnagar Way. Lark 185 E1
Lochpark. Ayr 238 B2
Lochpark Pl. Den 21 F1
Lochranza Dr. Helen 16 C1
Lochranza Pl. Salt 206 A1
Lochridge Pl. Den 21 E1
Lochshore
East Ind Est. Kilb 170 B4
Lochside. Bear 75 F2
Lochside Ct. Ayr 236 A1
Lochside. Muir 100 C3
Lochside Rd. Ayr 236 A1
Lochside Rd. Slam 86 B1
Lochside St. Glasg 116 C1
Lochview Ave. Gour 45 D4
Lochview Cres. Glasg 98 C2
Lochview Dr. Glasg 98 C2
Lochview Gdns. Glasg 98 C2
Lochview Pl. Glasg 98 C2
Lochview Rd. Bear 75 F2
Lochview Rd. Beith 170 C4
Lochview Rd. Coat 101 E1
Lochview Rd. P Glasg 47 D1
Lochview Terr. Muir 100 C3
Lochwinnoch Rd. Kil 89 E4
Lochwood Gdns. Glasg 120 B4
Lochwood Loan. Muir 81 D2
Lochwood Pl. Irvine 219 F3
Lochwood St. Glasg 98 C1
Lochy Ave. Ren 94 C1
Lochy Gdns. Bish 78 A1
Lochy Pl. Ersk 72 C1
Lochy St. Wish 165 D1
Lock Sixteen. Falk 41 E3
Lockerbie Ave. Glasg 136 C3
Locket Yett View. Hat 141 F3
Lockhart Ave. Glasg 139 E3
Lockhart Ave. Lan 214 C3
Lockhart Dr. Glasg 139 E3
Lockhart Pl. Stone 198 C2
Lockhart Pl. Wish 165 F2
Lockhart St. Car 187 F1
Lockhart St. Glasg 98 A1
Lockhart St. Ham 183 E3
Lockhart St. Stone 199 D2
Lockhart Terr. E Kil 160 A1
Locks St. Coat 122 B3
Locksley Ave. Cumb 82 C4
Locksley Ave. Glasg 95 E4
Locksley Cres. Cumb 82 C3
Locksley Ct. Cumb 82 C3
Locksley Pl. Cumb 82 C3
Locksley Rd. Cumb 82 C3
Locksley Rd. Pais 112 C1
Lodge Cres. Kil 89 F4
Lodge Dr. Sten 23 F1
Lodge Gdns. Kil 69 F1
Lodge Gr. Kil 69 F1
Lodge Pk. Kil 69 F1
Logan Ave. Newt M 156 B3
Logan Ct. Troon 229 E2
Logan Dr. Cumb 61 E2
Logan Dr. Pais 113 E3
Logan Dr. Troon 229 E2
Logan Gdns. Cle 165 D4
Logan St. Glasg 117 E2
Logan St. Udd 161 F4
Logan Tower. Glasg 139 F2
Logandale Ave. New 165 F3
Loganlea Dr. Holy 143 D1
Logans Rd. Mozther 163 E4
Loganswell Dr. Glasg 135 F1
Loganswell Gdns. Glasg 135 F1
Loganswell Pl. Glasg 135 F1
Loganswell Rd. Glasg 135 F1

271
Logie Dr. Lar
Main St. Barr

Logie Dr. Lar 23 D2
Logie La. B of A 2 B4
Logie Pk. E Kil 160 A2
Logie Rd. Stir 2 B2
Logie Sq. E Kil 160 A2
Lomax St. Glasg 118 B4
Lomond Ave. Hurl 228 C3
Lomond Ave. P Glasg 68 C4
Lomond Ave. Ren 94 A1
Lomond Cres. Alex 27 E4
Lomond Cres. B of W 110 B4
Lomond Cres. Beith 150 B1
Lomond Cres. Cumb 82 B4
Lomond Cres. Pais 133 E4
Lomond Cres. Sten 23 F2
Lomond Cres. Stir 2 A2
Lomond Ct. All 10 B3
Lomond Ct. Barr 134 B1
Lomond Ct. Cumb 82 B4
Lomond Ct. Dumb 49 F2
Lomond Ct. Helen 16 C1
Lomond Dr. Aird 102 C1
Lomond Dr. Alex 27 E4
Lomond Dr. Bann 7 F1
Lomond Dr. Barr 134 A2
Lomond Dr. Bish 78 A2
Lomond Dr. Cumb 82 A4
Lomond Dr. Dumb 50 A3
Lomond Dr. Falk 24 B1
Lomond Dr. Newt M 156 B4
Lomond Dr. Udd 141 D2
Lomond Dr. Wish 165 D1
Lomond. E Kil 180 C3
Lomond Gdns. John 112 B1
Lomond Gr. Cumb 82 B4
Lomond Ind Est. Alex 27 F3
Lomond Pl. Coat 101 F1
Lomond Pl. Cumb 82 A4
Lomond Pl. Ersk 72 C1
Lomond Pl. Irvine 219 E3
Lomond Pl. Stepps 99 F2
Lomond Rd. Alex 27 E4
Lomond Rd. Bear 75 F1
Lomond Rd. Bonh 27 F4
Lomond Rd. Coat 101 E1
Lomond Rd. Green 46 A2
Lomond Rd. Kilmk 228 A2
Lomond Rd. Kirk 79 E3
Lomond Rd. Shot 146 C3
Lomond Rd. Tan 120 C1
Lomond St. All 4 C1
Lomond St. Glasg 97 D3
Lomond St. Helen 16 C1
Lomond View. Cumb 82 B4
Lomond View. Ham 161 F1
Lomond Way. Bank 39 E3
Lomond Way. Holy 143 D3
Lomond Way. Irvine 220 A2
Lomond Wlk. Holy 143 E2
Lomond Wlk. Lark 185 D2
Lomondside Ave. Newt M 157 E4
Lomondview Ind Est. John 111 F2
London Rd. Glasg 118 C1
London Rd. Glasg 119 E1
London Rd. Hurl 228 A4
London Rd. Kilmk 228 A4
London St. Lark 185 D2
London St. Ren 94 B3
Lonend. Pais 113 F2
Loney Cres. Den 39 F4
Long Crags View. Dumb 50 B3
Long Dr. E Kil 181 D4
Long Dr. Irvine 219 F2
Long Dr. Kilw 219 E4
Long Dr. Shew 225 D4
Long Row. Glasg 120 B3
Long Row. Lan 214 C1
Long Row. Men 4 A4
Longay Pl. Glasg 97 E4
Longay St. Glasg 97 E4
Longbank Dr. Ayr 239 D2
Longbank Rd. Ayr 239 D2
Longbar Ave. Beith 170 B3
Longcraigs Ave. Ard 205 E3
Longcroft Dr. Ren 94 B2
Longdales Ave. Falk 42 A4
Longdales Ct. Falk 42 A4
Longdales Pl. Falk 42 A4
Longdales Rd. Falk 42 A4
Longden St. Clyde 94 B4
Longdyke Pl. Sten 24 B2
Longfield Ave. Salt 205 F1
Longfield Pl. Salt 205 F1
Longford Ave. Kilw 207 F1
Longford St. Glasg 118 B4
Longhill Ave. Ayr 238 B1
Longlands Pk. Ayr 238 C2
Longlee. Glasg 120 A2
Longmeadow. John 111 E1
Longpark Ave. Kilmk 222 C1
Longriggend Rd. Cald 85 E1
Longrow Gdns. Irvine 219 F4
Longstone Pl. Glasg 119 D4
Longstone Rd. Glasg 119 D4
Longwill Terr. Cumb 62 A2
Lonmay Rd. Glasg 119 E4
Lonsdale Ave. Glasg 136 B2
Loom Wlk. Kilbar 111 D2
Lora Dr. Glasg 115 F2
Loreny Dr. Kilmk 227 F1
Loretto Pl. Glasg 118 C4
Loretto St. Glasg 118 C4
Lorien Ct. Pres 236 B2
Lorimar Pl. Sten 24 A1
Lorimer Cres. E Kil 180 B4
Lorn Ave. Muir 100 B4
Lorn Dr. Bonh 19 F1
Lorn Pl. Kirk 59 E1
Lorne Arc. Ayr 238 C4
Lorne Cres. Bish 78 B1
Lorne Dr. Lin 112 A3
Lorne Dr. Mother 142 B1
Lorne Gdns. Laur 42 C2
Lorne Gdns. Sals 125 D1
Lorne Pl. Coat 122 B3
Lorne Rd. Glasg 114 C4
Lorne Rd. Lar 23 E1
Lorne St. Glasg 116 B3
Lorne St. Ham 162 B2
Lorne St. Helen 16 B1
Lorne Terr. Glasg 138 C2
Lornshill Cres. All 9 F4
Lorraine Gardens La. Glasg 96 B2
Lorraine Gdns. Glasg 96 B2
Lorraine Rd. Glasg 96 B2
Lorraine Way. Bonh 27 F1
Loskin Dr. Glasg 97 D4
Losshill. Men 4 A3
Lossie Cres. Ren 94 C1
Lossie St. Glasg 98 B1
Lothian Cres. Pais 113 E1
Lothian Cres. Stir 2 B2
Lothian Dr. Newt M 157 E4
Lothian Gdns. Glasg 96 C2
Lothian Rd. Ayr 239 D4
Lothian Rd. Gour 44 B2
Lothian Rd. Stew 211 E4
Lothian St. Glasg 114 C4
Lothian Way. E Kil 160 B2
Louburn. Blac 107 E2
Louden St. Aird 123 D4
Loudens Wlk. Duni 21 E3
Loudon. E Kil 180 C3
Loudon Gdns. John 112 A2
Loudon Rd. Stepps 99 D2
Loudon St. Wish 165 D3
Loudon Terr. Bear 75 E4
Loudonhill Ave. Ham 183 F4
Loudoun Ave. Kilmk 228 A2
Loudoun Cres. Kilw 207 D2
Loudoun Pl. Cross 226 C4
Loudoun Pl. Sym 231 E2
Loudoun St. Stew 211 F4
Loudoun Terr. Pres 236 B4
Louise Gdns. Holy 142 C3
Louisville Ave. Wish 165 E3
Lounsdale Cres. Pais 113 D1
Lounsdale Dr. Pais 113 D1
Lounsdale House. Pais 113 D1
Lounsdale Pl. Glasg 95 D2
Lounsdale Rd. Pais 113 D1
Lourdes Ave. Glasg 115 E2
Lourdes Ct. Glasg 115 E2
Lovat Ave. Miln 75 F4
Lovat Dr. Kirk 79 D4
Lovat Path. Lark 185 E1
Lovat Pl. Glasg 138 B2
Love Ave. Kil 89 F1
Love St. Kilw 208 A2
Love St. Pais 113 F3
Lovers Loan. Alva 5 D4
Lovers Wlk. Stir 2 A1
Low Barholm. Kilbar 111 D1
Low Broadlie Rd. Neil 154 B4
Low Church La. Kilmk 227 F4
Low Craigends. Kils 60 C4
Low Cres. Clyde 94 C4
Low Flender Rd. Newt M 157 E3
Low Glencairn St. Kilmk 227 F3
Low Green Rd. Irvine 219 D1
Low Parksail. Ersk 93 E4
Low Patrick St. Ham 162 C2
Low Pleasance. Lark 185 D2
Low Rd. Ayr 236 C2
Low Rd. Pais 113 E2
Low Waters Rd. Ham 162 B1
Lower Auchingramont Rd. Ham 162 C2
Lower Bourtree Dr. Glasg 138 B2
Lower Bouverie St. P Glasg 47 E1
Lower Bridge St. Stir 2 A1
Lower Castlehill. Stir 2 A1
Lower Mill Rd. Newt M 157 F3
Lower Millgate. Udd 140 C3
Lower Stoneymollan Rd. Alex 27 E4
Lower Sutherland Cres. Helen 16 A2
Lowndes St. Barr 134 B1
Lowther Ave. Bear 75 F4
Lowther Bank. Irvine 220 B1
Lowther Pl. Kilmk 228 A2
Lowther Terr. Glasg 96 B2
Loyal Ave. Ersk 72 C1
Loyal Gdns. Bear 75 D4
Loyal Pl. Ersk 72 C1
Loyne Dr. Ren 94 C1
Luath St. Glasg 116 A4
Lubas Ave. Glasg 137 E4
Lubas Pl. Glasg 137 E4
Lubnaig Dr. Ersk 72 C1
Lubnaig Gdns. Bear 75 E4
Lubnaig Pl. Aird 102 C1
Lubnaig Rd. Glasg 136 C3
Lubnaig Wlk. Holy 143 D3
Luce Ave. Kilmk 228 A3
Luckenhill Dr. Gree 84 B2
Luckiesfauld. Neil 154 B3
Luckingsford Ave. Inch 93 E4
Luckingsford Dr. Inch 93 E4
Luckingsford Rd. Inch 93 E4
Lucy Brae. Tan 140 C4
Ludgate. All 10 A3
Ludovic Sq. John 111 F2
Luffness Gdns. Glasg 119 D1
Lugar Ave. Irvine 220 A3
Lugar Cres. Pres 236 A3
Lugar Dr. Glasg 115 F2
Lugar Pl. Glasg 137 F3
Lugar Pl. Troon 229 F3
Lugar St. Coat 122 A4
Luggie Rd. Car 187 F2
Luggie View. Cumb 82 A4
Luggiebank Pl. Coat 121 D2
Luggiebank Rd. Kirk 58 B1
Luggiebank Rd. Kirk 79 E4
Lugton Ct. Irvine 219 E1
Lugton Rd. Dunlop 195 D4
Luing. Aird 123 F3
Luing Rd. Glasg 115 F3
Lumloch St. Glasg 98 A2
Lumsden La. Glasg 96 B1
Lumsden Pl. Steven 206 C1
Lumsden St. Glasg 96 B1
Lunan Dr. Bish 98 B4
Lunan Pl. Glasg 115 F4
Luncarty Pl. Glasg 119 D2
Luncarty St. Glasg 119 D2
Lunderston Dr. Glasg 135 D4
Lundholm Rd. Steven 217 F4
Lundie Gdns. Bish 98 B4
Lundie St. Glasg 118 C2
Lurg St. P Glasg 68 B4
Luss Ave. Green 46 A1
Luss Brae. Ham 161 F1
Luss Pl. Green 46 A1
Luss Rd. Alex 27 E4
Luss Rd. Glasg 115 F4
Luss Rd. Helen 17 D3
Lusset Glen. O Kill 73 D3
Lusset Rd. O Kill 73 D3
Lusshill Terr. Glasg 120 A1
Lybster Cres. Glasg 138 B2
Lychgate Rd. Tull 4 A1
Lye Brae. Cumb 62 A1
Lyell Ct. E Kil 159 F2
Lyell Gr. E Kil 159 F2
Lyle Cres. Bishop 72 A2
Lyle Gr. Green 45 D4
Lyle Pl. Green 45 D4
Lyle Pl. Pais 113 F1
Lyle Rd. Aird 123 F4
Lyle Rd. Green 45 D4
Lyle Rd. Kil 89 E4
Lyle Sq. Miln 54 C1
Lyle St. Green 45 F2
Lyle St. Green 46 A2
Lylefoot Cres. Green 45 D4
Lylefoot Pl. Green 45 D4
Lylesland Ct. Pais 113 F1
Lylestone Terr. Kilw 208 B4
Lyman Dr. Wish 165 E4
Lymburn Pl. Ayr 239 D4
Lymburn St. Glasg 116 B4
Lymekilns Rd. E Kil 159 E2
Lyndale Pl. Glasg 96 B4
Lyndale Rd. Glasg 96 B4
Lyndhurst Gardens La. Glasg 96 C2
Lyndhurst Gdns. Glasg 96 C2
Lyne Croft. Bish 78 A2
Lyne St. Wish 165 D3
Lynedoch Cres. Glasg 96 C1
Lynedoch Crescent La. Glasg 96 C1
Lynedoch Ind Est. Green 46 A2
Lynedoch Pl. Glasg 96 C1
Lynedoch St. Glasg 96 C1
Lynedoch St. Green 45 F2
Lynedoch Terr. Glasg 96 C1
Lynmouth Pl. Gour 44 C3
Lynn Ave. Dalry 191 E4
Lynn Ct. Lark 185 D1
Lynn Dr. Eagle 178 C3
Lynn Dr. Kilb 149 D2
Lynn Dr. Miln 55 E1
Lynn Wlk. Bonh 27 F4
Lynn Wlk. Udd 141 D3
Lynnburn Ave. Hat 142 A3
Lynne Dr. Glasg 76 C1
Lynnhurst. Tan 140 C4
Lynnwood Rd. New 166 B3
Lynton Ave. Glasg 136 A1
Lyon Cres. B of A 2 A3
Lyon Rd. Ersk 72 C1
Lyon Rd. John 112 A2
Lyon Rd. Pais 112 C1
Lyoncross Ave. Barr 134 B2
Lyoncross Cres. Barr 134 B2
Lyoncross Rd. Glasg 115 D1
Lyons Quadrant. Mother 164 B2
Lysa Vale Pl. Hat 141 F3
Lysander Way. Ren 94 B1
Lytham Dr. Glasg 76 C1
Lytham Meadows. Udd 140 C1
Lythgow Way. Lan 215 E3
Lyttelton. E Kil 180 A4

Mabel St. Mother 163 F3
Maberry Cl. Stew 195 E1
Maberry Pl. Troon 229 F3
Macadam Gdns. Hat 142 A3
Macadam Pl. Ayr 236 A1
Macadam Pl. E Kil 180 C4
Macadam Pl. Irvine 219 F1
Macadam Pl. Kilmk 223 E1
Macadam Place. Falk 41 E3
Macadam Sq. Ayr 236 A1
Macallan Pl. Irvine 219 F4
Macallister Pl. Kilmk 223 E1
Macalpine Pl. Kilmk 223 E1
Macandrew Pl. Kilmk 223 E1
Macara Dr. Irvine 219 F2
Macarthur Ave. Glenm 102 B2
Macarthur Cres. E Kil 159 E2
Macarthur Ct. E Kil 159 E2
Macarthur Dr. E Kil 159 E2
Macarthur Gdns. E Kil 159 E2
Macaulay Pl. Helen 16 A1
Macauley Pl. Kilmk 223 E1
Macbeth Dr. Kilmk 223 E1
Macbeth. E Kil 160 A3
Macbeth Gdns. Kilmk 223 E1
Macbeth Pl. Glasg 118 B2
Macbeth Rd. Green 45 D3
Macbeth Rd. Stew 211 E4
Macbeth St. Glasg 118 B2
Maccabe Gdns. Lennox 57 F4
Maccallum Pl. Kilmk 223 E1
Maccrimmon Pk. E Kil 159 D2
Macdairmid Dr. Ham 183 D4
Macdonald Ave. E Kil 159 D2
Macdonald Cres. Twe 60 A2
Macdonald Ct. Beith 171 D4
Macdonald Dr. Kilmk 223 E1
Macdonald Dr. Stir 7 D2
Macdonald Gdns. Kilmk 223 E1
Macdonald Gr. Hat 141 F1
Macdonald Pl. Kilmk 223 E1
Macdonald St. Glasg 138 A4
Macdonald St. Mother 163 F3
MacDonald Wlk. Bonh 27 F4
Macdougal Quadrant. Hat 141 F1
Macdougall Dr. Kilmk 223 E1
Macdougall St. Glasg 136 B4
Macdougall St. Green 46 B2
Macdowall St. John 111 F2
Macdowall St. Pais 113 E3
Macduff. Ersk 73 D1
Macduff Pl. Glasg 118 B2
Macduff St. Glasg 118 B2
Mace Ct. Bann 7 E2
Mace Rd. Glasg 75 E1
Macewan Pl. Kilmk 228 B4
Macfarlane Cres. Falk 42 A3
Macfarlane Dr. Kilmk 223 E1
Macfarlane Rd. Bear 76 A2
Macfie Pl. E Kil 159 D2
Macgregor Dr. Kilmk 228 B4
Machan Ave. Lark 185 D2
Machan Rd. Lark 185 D1
Machanhill. Lark 185 D1
Machanhill View. Lark 185 D1
Machrie Ct. Falk 41 E2
Machrie Dr. Glasg 137 F2
Machrie Dr. Helen 16 C2
Machrie Dr. Newt M 156 C3
Machrie Pl. Kilw 207 E2
Machrie Rd. Glasg 137 F2
Machrie Rd. Kilmk 222 C2
Machrie Rd. Mother 163 D4
Machrie St. Glasg 137 F2
Macinnes Pl. Kilmk 223 E1
Macintosh Pl. E Kil 180 B4
Macintosh Pl. Kilmk 223 E1
Macintyre Pl. Kilmk 223 E1
Macintyre Rd. Pres 233 E1
Macintyre St. Glasg 116 C4
Macivor Cres. E Kil 159 D2
Macivor Pl. Kilmk 223 E1
Mack St. Aird 123 D4
Mackean St. Pais 113 E3
Mackeith St. Glasg 117 F2
Mackellar Pl. Kilmk 223 E1
Mackendrick Pl. Kilmk 228 B4
Mackenzie Dr. Kilbar 111 D1
Mackenzie Dr. Kilmk 223 D1
Mackenzie Gdns. E Kil 159 D2
Mackenzie St. Green 46 B2
Mackenzie Terr. Hat 142 A4
Mackie Ave. Green 46 C1
Mackie Ave. P Glasg 47 D1
Mackie Ave. Stew 195 E1
Mackie Pl. Kilmk 223 E1
Mackie St. Ayr 236 B1
Mackie's Mill Rd. John 132 B4
Mackinlay Pl. Kilmk 228 A4
Mackinlay St. Glasg 117 D2
Mackinnon Dr. Kilmk 228 B4
Mackinnon Terr. Irvine 219 F2
Mackintosh Pl. Irvine 219 F1
Maclachlan Ave. Den 21 E1
Maclachlan Pl. Helen 16 C2
Maclachlan Rd. Helen 16 C2
Maclaren Pl. Kilmk 228 B4
Maclaren Terr. Sten 24 A1
Maclay Ave. Kilbar 111 D1
Maclean Cres. Alva 5 E4
Maclean Ct. E Kil 159 D2
Maclean Ct. Stir 7 E2
Maclean Dr. Kilmk 223 D1
Maclean Gr. E Kil 159 D2
Maclean Pl. E Kil 159 D2
Maclean Sq. Glasg 116 C3
Maclean St. Clyde 94 C4
Maclean St. Glasg 116 B3
Maclean Terr. Blac 107 F2
Maclehose Rd. Cumb 62 B2
Maclellan Rd. Neil 154 C3
Maclellan St. Glasg 116 B3
Macleod Cres. Helen 16 A2
Macleod Dr. Helen 16 B2
Macleod Dr. Kilmk 228 B4
Macleod Pl. E Kil 160 A2
Macleod Pl. Kilmk 228 B4
Macleod St. Glasg 117 F4
Macmillan Dr. Gour 44 B3
Macmillan Dr. Kilmk 223 E1
Macmillan Gdns. Tan 121 D1
Macmillan Pl. Kilmk 223 E1
Macmillan St. Lark 184 C1
Macnab Pl. Kilmk 223 D1
Macnaughton Dr. Kilmk 223 E1
Macneil Pl. Kilmk 223 D1
Macneill Dr. E Kil 159 D2
Macneill Gdns. E Kil 159 D2
Macneill St. Lark 184 C2
Macneish Way. E Kil 159 E2
Macnicol Ct. E Kil 159 D2
Macnicol Pk. E Kil 159 D2
Macnicol Pl. E Kil 159 D2
Macnicol Pl. Kilmk 223 E1
Macphail Dr. Kilmk 223 E1
Macpherson Gdns. Kilmk 223 E1
Macpherson Pk. E Kil 159 E2
Macpherson Pl. Kilmk 223 E1
Macpherson Wlk. Kilmk 223 E1
Macphie Rd. Dumb 50 B2
Macrae Dr. Pres 233 E1
Macrae Gdns. E Kil 159 E2
Macrimmon Pl. E Kil 180 C4
Macrobert Ave. Irvine 220 A1
Mactaggart Rd. Cumb 82 C4
Madeira La. Green 45 E4
Madeira St. Green 45 E4
Madill Pl. Sten 23 F2
Madison Ave. Glasg 137 D3
Madison Path. Udd 161 E4
Madras Pl. Neil 154 C4
Madras St. Glasg 117 F2
Mafeking St. Glasg 116 A3
Mafeking St. Mother 164 B2
Mafeking Terr. Neil 154 B4
Magdalen Way. Pais 132 C4
Maggie Wood's Loan. Falk 41 F3
Magna St. Mother 163 D4
Magnolia Gdns. Holy 143 E2
Magnolia Pl. Tan 141 E4
Magnolia St. Wish 165 D3
Magnus Cres. Glasg 137 D2
Magnus Rd. Hous 111 E4
Mahon Ct. Muir 80 C1
Maid Morville Ave. Irvine 225 E4
Maidens Ave. Newt M 157 D3
Maidens. E Kil 159 E2
Maidland Rd. Glasg 135 E4
Mailerbeg Gdns. Muir 80 C2
Mailie Wlk. Holy 143 E2
Mailing Ave. Bish 78 B1
Mailings Rd. Kils 37 F2
Maimhor Rd. W Kil 190 B2
Main Rd. Ayr 236 C1
Main Rd. Card 48 A4
Main Rd. Cross 226 C3
Main Rd. Cumb 82 A4
Main Rd. Fen 213 D2
Main Rd. Fen 213 F2
Main Rd. Hurl 228 C4
Main Rd. John 112 B2
Main Rd. Kilb 149 D1
Main Rd. Lang 70 B4
Main Rd. Pais 113 E2
Main Rd. Ros 15 D2
Main Rd. Spring 220 C1
Main St. Air 14 B2
Main St. Alex 27 F2
Main St. Ayr 235 F1
Main St. B of W 110 B4
Main St. Bann 7 E1
Main St. Barr 134 B2

273
Maxwell St. Pais
Mill Brae Ct. Coat

Maxwell St. Pais 113 F3
Maxwell Terr. Glasg 116 C2
Maxwellton Ave. E Kil 160 A2
Maxwellton Pl. E Kil 160 A2
Maxwellton Rd. E Kil 160 B2
Maxwellton Rd. P Glasg 68 C3
Maxwellton Rd. Pais 113 D2
Maxwellton St. Pais 113 E2
Maxwelton Rd. Glasg 98 B1
Maxwood Pl. Irvine 220 A3
May Gdns. Ham 162 B3
May Rd. Pais 133 F4
May St. Ham 162 B3
May Terr. Glasg 136 B2
May Terr. Glasg 137 D4
Maybank La. Glasg 117 D1
Maybank St. Glasg 117 D1
Mayberry Cres. Glasg 119 E3
Mayberry Gdns. Glasg 119 E3
Mayberry Gr. Glasg 119 E3
Mayberry Pl. Udd 161 E4
Maybole Cres. Newt M 157 D2
Maybole Gdns. Ham 161 E1
Maybole Gr. Newt M 157 D2
Maybole Pl. Coat 122 B2
Maybole Rd. Ayr 239 D2
Maybole Rd. P Glasg 68 C3
Maybole St. Glasg 134 C3
Mayfield Ave. Hurl 228 C3
Mayfield Ave. Newt M 157 F4
Mayfield Cres. How 130 C3
Mayfield Cres. Steven 206 B1
Mayfield Ct. How 130 C3
Mayfield Ct. Stir 7 D2
Mayfield Dr. Bank 30 D2
Mayfield Dr. How 130 C3
Mayfield Gr. Steven 206 B1
Mayfield Mews. Falk 41 F2
Mayfield Pl. Car 202 A4
Mayfield Pl. Salt 217 D4
Mayfield Rd. Ham 161 F2
Mayfield Rd. Salt 206 B1
Mayfield Rd. Salt 217 D4
Mayfield Rd. Steven 206 B1
Mayfield St. Glasg 96 C3
Mayfield St. Stir 7 D2
Mayne Ave. B of A 2 A3
Mayville St. Steven 206 B1
Mc Donald Ave. John 111 F1
Mc Laurin Cres. John 111 E1
Mc Lelland Dr. Plains 104 A1
Mc Phail St. Green 46 B2
McAdam Ct. Pres 236 B3
McAlister Rd. Alex 27 F3
McAlley Ct. B of A 1 C4
McAllister Ave. Aird 123 E4
McAllister Ct. Bann 7 E1
McAlpine St. Glasg 117 D4
McAlpine St. Wish 165 D1
McArdle Ave. Mother 163 D4
McArthur Pk Kirk 79 E4
McArthur St. Glasg 136 B4
McAslin Ct. Glasg 117 E4
McAslin St. Glasg 117 F4
McAuslan Pl. Helen 16 C1
McCall's Ave. Ayr 236 A1
McCallum Ave. Glasg 138 A4
McCallum Cres. Gour 44 C4
McCallum Ct. E Kil 159 D2
McCallum Gdns. Hat 141 F1
McCallum Gr. E Kil 159 D2
McCallum Pl. E Kil 159 D2
McCallum Rd. Lark 185 D1
McCASH PL. Kirk 79 E4
McClue Ave. Ren 94 A2
McClue Rd. Ren 94 B2
Mcclurg Ct. Mother 163 F3
McColgan Pl. Ayr 236 B2
McColl Ave. Alex 27 E3
McColl Pl. Alex 27 E3
McConnell Rd. Loch 129 D1
McCormack Gdns. Holy 143 F2
McCracken Ave. Ren 94 A1
McCracken Dr. Tan 141 E4
McCreery St. Clyde 94 B4
McCulloch Ave. Tan 141 E3
McCulloch La. Alex 27 E4
McCulloch St. Glasg 116 C2
McDonald Cres. Clyde 94 B4
McDonald Dr. Irvine 219 E2
McDonald Pl. Holy 143 D3
McDonald Pl. Neil 154 C4
McDowall Ave. Ard 205 E1
McDowall Pl. Ard 205 E1
McEwan Dr. Helen 16 C2
McEwan Gdns. E Kil 159 D2
McEwans Way. Stone 198 B1
McFarlane Rd. Bonh 28 A4
McFarlane St. Glasg 117 F3
McFarlane St. Pais 113 E4
McGavin Ave. Kilw 208 A2
McGavin Way. Kilw 207 E2
McGhee St. Clyde 74 A2
McGibney Dr. Irvine 219 E1
McGillivray Ave. Salt 205 F1
McGowan Pl. Ham 162 A3
McGown St. Pais 113 E3
McGregor Ave. Aird 123 E4
McGregor Ave. Bonh 28 A4
McGregor Ave. Ren 94 A1
McGregor Ave. Steven 206 B1
McGregor Dr. Dumb 50 B2
Mcgregor Path. Glen 101 E3
McGregor Rd. Cumb 61 F1
McGregor St. Clyde 94 B4
McGregor St. Glasg 115 F3
McGregor St. Mother 164 B2
McGrigor Rd. Miln 54 C2
McGrigor Rd. Stir 7 D2
McHardy Cres. Beith 171 F2
McInnes Ct. Wish 165 D1
McInnes Pl. Wish 186 A4
McInnes St. Bonh 28 A4
McIntosh Ct. Glasg 117 F4
McIntosh Quadrant. Hat 141 F1
McIntosh St. Glasg 117 F4
McIntosh Way. Mother 163 E3
McIntyre Pl. Pais 113 F1
McIntyre Terr. Glasg 139 D3
McIsaac Rd. Salt 217 D4
McIver St. Glasg 139 F3
McKay Cres. John 112 A1
McKay Gr. Hat 141 F3
McKay Pl. E Kil 159 D2
McKechnie St. Glasg 116 A4
McKellar Ave. Ard 205 E1
McKenna Dr. Aird 122 C4
McKenzie Ave. Clyde 74 A2
McKenzie Dr. Bonh 19 F1
McKenzie St. Pais 113 E3
McKenzie's Cl. Lan 215 D2
McKerrell St. Pais 114 A3
McKillop Pl. Salt 205 F1
McKim Wlk. Alex 49 E4
McKinlay Ave. Bonh 20 A1
McKinlay Cres. All 10 B4
McKinlay Cres. Irvine 219 D1
Mckinnon Pl. Salt 206 A1
McKnight Ave. Fen 213 F2
McLachlan Ave. Stir 7 D1
McLachlan St. Lar 23 E1
McLaren Ave. Ren 94 B1
Mclaren Ct. Glasg 136 A1
McLaren Ct. Lar 23 E1
McLaren Gr. E Kil 159 D2
Mclaren Pl. Glasg 136 C1
McLaren Terr. Stir 7 D2
McLean Cres. Bonh 19 F1
McLean Dr. Hat 141 F1
McLean Dr. Irvine 225 E4
Mclean Gdns. Stone 198 C1
McLean Pl. Pais 113 E4
McLean St. Ayr 236 B1
McLees La. Mother 163 D4
McLelland Dr. Kilmk 227 F4
McLennan St. Glasg 137 D4
McLeod Rd. Dumb 50 B2
McLeod St. Green 46 B2
McLuckie Dr. Kilw 207 E2
McLuckie Pk. Kilw 207 E2
McMillan Cres. Beith 171 D4
McMillan Dr. Ard 205 D2
McMillan Pl. Shew 224 C3
McMillan Rd. Wish 164 B1
McMillan Way. Law 186 C3
McNair St. Glasg 119 D3
McNaught Pl. Alex 27 E1
McNaught Pl. Kilm 222 A4
McNay Cres. Salt 206 A1
McNeil Ave. Clyde 74 C1
McNeil Pl. Wish 186 B4
McNeil St. Glasg 117 E2
McNeill Ave. Pres 233 E1
McPhail St. Glasg 117 F2
McPhater St. Glasg 97 D1
McPherson Cres. Chap 123 F1
McPherson Dr. Gour 44 B4
McPherson Dr. Stir 2 A1
McPherson Dr. Udd 141 D2
McPherson La. Alex 27 E4
McPherson St. Hat 142 B3
McShannon Gr. Hat 142 A2
McVean Pl. Bank 39 D2
Meadow Ave. Irvine 219 E2
Meadow Ave. Udd 161 E3
Meadow Ct. Car 188 B1
Meadow Ct. Dumb 49 F3
Meadow Gn. N Sau 5 D1
Meadow La. Ren 94 B3
Meadow La. Udd 141 D1
Meadow Path. Chap 123 F1
Meadow Pk. Alva 5 D3
Meadow Pk. Ayr 239 D3
Meadow Pl. Stir 2 B1
Meadow Rd. Dumb 50 A2
Meadow Rd. Glasg 96 A1
Meadow Rd. Kilnc 202 A2
Meadow Rd. Mother 164 A3
Meadow St. Coat 122 A2
Meadow St. Falk 42 B2
Meadow View. Cumb 62 B2
Meadow View. Plains 104 A2
Meadow Way. Newt M 156 B3
Meadowbank La. Pres 236 A4
Meadowbank La. Udd 140 C3
Meadowbank Pl. Newt M 156 B3
Meadowbank St. Dumb 49 F2
Meadowburn Ave. Kirk 79 F3
Meadowburn Ave. Newt M 156 B3
Meadowburn. Bish 78 A2
Meadowburn Rd. Wish 165 E2
Meadowfield Pl. New 166 B3
Meadowfoot Rd. W Kil 190 B2
Meadowforth Rd. Stir 7 E4
Meadowhead Ave. Muir 80 C1
Meadowhead Ave. Shew 224 C2
Meadowhead Rd. Mother 164 B2
Meadowhead Rd. Plains 103 F1
Meadowhead Rd. Shew 224 C2
Meadowhead
Roundabout. Shew 224 C1
Meadowhill. Newt M 156 B3
Meadowhill St. Lark 185 D2
Meadowland Rd. B of A 2 A3
Meadowpark Dr. Ayr 239 D3
Meadowpark St. Glasg 118 A4
Meadows Ave. Lark 185 D2
Meadows The. Hous 91 F1
Meadows The. Kilw 207 E2
Meadowside Ave. John 112 B1
Meadowside. Beith 171 D4
Meadowside Gdns. Aird 123 E4
Meadowside. Ham 183 E3
Meadowside. Hurl 228 C4
Meadowside Pl. Aird 123 E4
Meadowside Rd. Kils 59 F4
Meadowside St. Glasg 96 A1
Meadowside St. Ren 94 B3
Meadowside. W Kil 190 B3
Meadowwell St. Glasg 119 D3
Meadside Ave. Kilbar 111 D2
Meadside Rd. Kilbar 111 D2
Mealkirk St. Dunt 74 B4
Mearns Ct. Ham 183 F4
Mearns Rd. Mother 163 E4
Mearns Rd. Newt M 156 B1
Mearns St. Green 45 F2
Mearns St. Green 45 F3
Mearns Way. Bish 78 B1
Mearnscroft Gdns. Newt M 156 C2
Mearnscroft Rd. Newt M 156 C2
Medine Ave. Beith 150 A1
Medine Ct. Beith 150 A1
Medlar Rd. Cumb 62 B1
Medrox Gdns. Cumb 81 F3
Medwin Ct. E Kil 179 F4
Medwin Gdns. E Kil 179 F4
Medwin St. Glasg 139 F3
Medwyn Pl. All 9 F3
Medwyn St. Glasg 95 E2
Medwyn St. Glasg 95 F1
Meek Pl. Glasg 139 D3
Meeks Rd. Falk 42 A3
Meetinghouse La. Pais 113 F3
Megan St. Glasg 117 F2
Meikle Ave. Ren 94 B1
Meikle Bin Brae. Lennox 57 F4
Meikle Cres. Gree 103 E4
Meikle Cres. Ham 183 E4
Meikle Ct. Stew 195 F1
Meikle Drumgray Rd. Gree 103 F4
Meikle Earnock Rd. Ham 183 D4
Meikle Rd. Glasg 135 E4
Meiklehill Ct. Kirk 58 C1
Meiklehill Rd. Kirk 58 C1
Meiklem St. Hat 142 B3
Meiklerig Cres. Glasg 115 E1
Meikleriggs Dr. Pais 133 D1
Meiklewood Ave. Pres 233 E1
Meiklewood Rd. Glasg 115 E3
Meiklewood Rd. Kilmk 222 C3
Melbourne Ave. Clyde 73 E3
Melbourne Ave. E Kil 180 B4
Melbourne Ct. Glasg 136 B2
Melbourne Gn. E Kil 180 B4
Melbourne Rd. Salt 216 C4
Melbourne St. Glasg 117 F3
Melbourne Terr. Salt 216 C4
Meldon Pl. Glasg 115 E4
Meldrum Gdns. Glasg 116 B1
Meldrum Mains. Glenm 102 C2
Meldrum St. Clyde 94 B4
Melford Ave. Glasg 136 B1
Melford Ave. Kirk 79 D4
Melford Ave. Shot 147 D2
Melford Gdns. John 111 E1
Melford Rd. Tan 141 F4
Melford Way. Pais 114 A4
Melfort Ave. Clyde 74 D2
Melfort Ave. Glasg 116 A2
Melfort Dr. Stir 7 D2
Melfort Path. New 165 F4
Melfort Quadrant. Holy 143 E2
Melfort Rd. Ham 161 F1
Mellerstain Dr. Glasg 94 C3
Mellock Gdns. Falk 41 F1
Melness Pl. Glasg 115 E4
Melrose Ave. Chap 123 E1
Melrose Ave. Coat 120 C3
Melrose Ave. Glasg 138 A4
Melrose Ave. Holy 143 D3
Melrose Ave. Lin 112 A3
Melrose Ave. Pais 113 D1
Melrose Cres. Wish 165 D3
Melrose Ct. Glasg 138 A4
Melrose Gdns. Glasg 96 C2
Melrose Gdns. Tan 120 C1
Melrose Gdns. Twe 59 F2
Melrose Pl. Coat 121 F4
Melrose Pl. Falk 42 A2
Melrose Pl. Lark 185 D1
Melrose Pl. Udd 140 B1
Melrose Rd. Cumb 82 C4
Melrose Rd. P Glasg 68 C4
Melrose St. Glasg 97 D1
Melrose St. Ham 162 A3
Melrose Terr. E Kil 159 F2
Melrose Terr. Ham 162 A3
Melvaig Pl. Glasg 96 B3
Melvick Pl. Glasg 115 E4
Melville Ct. Glasg 117 E3
Melville Dr. Mother 163 F3
Melville Gdns. Bish 78 A1
Melville Pk. E Kil 160 A2
Melville Pl. B of A 2 A4
Melville Pl. Car 187 F1
Melville St. Falk 42 A3
Melville St. Glasg 116 C2
Melville St. Kilmk 228 A4
Melville Terr. Stir 7 D3
Melvinhall Rd. Lan 215 D3
Memel St. Glasg 97 F3
Memus Ave. Glasg 115 E2
Mennock Ct. Ham 161 F1
Mennock Dr. Bish 78 A2
Mennock La. Troon 229 F3
Mennock St. Cle 144 B1
Menock Rd. Glasg 137 E3
Menstrie Pl. Men 4 A3
Menteith Ave. Bish 78 A1
Menteith Ct. All 10 B3
Menteith Dr. Glasg 138 B1
Menteith Gdns. Bear 75 E4
Menteith Loan. Holy 143 D3
Menteith Pl. Glasg 138 B1
Menteith Rd. Mother 163 F4
Menteith Rd. Stir 2 A2
Menzies Dr. Glasg 98 A3
Menzies Dr. Stir 2 A1
Menzies Pl. Glasg 98 A3
Menzies Rd. Glasg 98 A3
Merchant La. Glasg 117 E3
Merchants Cl. Kilbar 111 D2
Merchiston Ave. Falk 42 A4
Merchiston Ave. Lin 111 F3
Merchiston Gdns. Falk 42 A3
Merchiston Rd. Falk 42 A3
Merchiston Rd. Falk 42 A4
Merchiston St. Glasg 118 C4
Merchiston Terr. Falk 42 A4
Mercury La. Gour 44 B2
Meredith Dr. Sten 23 F2
Merino Rd. Green 45 F2
Merkins Ave. Dumb 50 A3
Merkland Ct. Glasg 96 A1
Merkland Ct. Kirk 59 D1
Merkland Dr. Falk 42 C1
Merkland Dr. Kirk 80 A4
Merkland Pl. Kirk 59 D1
Merkland Rd. Ayr 239 D1
Merkland Rd. Coat 101 E1
Merkland St. Glasg 96 A1
Merksworth Ave. Dalry 191 E4
Merksworth Way. Pais 113 F4
Merlewood Rd. W Kil 190 A2
Merlin Ave. Green 45 D3
Merlin Ave. Hat 142 A4
Merlin La. Green 45 D3
Merlin Way. Pais 114 A4
Merlinford Ave. Ren 94 C2
Merlinford Cres. Ren 94 C2
Merlinford Way. Ren 94 C2
Merrick Ave. Pres 233 E1
Merrick Ave. Troon 229 F2
Merrick Ct. Aird 103 D1
Merrick Gdns. Bear 75 E4
Merrick Gdns. Glasg 116 A3
Merrick Gdns. Quart 183 F2
Merrick Pl. Irvine 220 A1
Merrick Pl. Sym 231 E2
Merrick Rd. Kilmk 228 A2
Merrick Terr. Tan 141 D4
Merrick View. Stew 195 F1
Merrick Way. Glasg 138 A2
Merry St. Holy 143 D1
Merry St. Mother 163 F4
Merryburn Ave. Glasg 136 B2
Merrycrest Ave. Glasg 136 B2
Merrycroft Ave. Glasg 136 B2
Merryflats. Twe 59 F2
Merrygreen Pl. Stew 195 F1
Merryland Pl. Glasg 116 B4
Merryland St. Glasg 116 A4
Merryland St. Glasg 116 B4
Merrylee Ave. P Glasg 68 C4
Merrylee Cres. Glasg 136 B3
Merrylee Park Ave. Glasg 136 B2
Merrylee Park Mews. Glasg 136 B3
Merrylee Pk. Glasg 136 B3
Merrylee Rd. Glasg 136 C3
Merrylees Rd. Udd 161 E4
Merryston Ct. Coat 121 F3
Merrystone St. Coat 121 F4
Merryton Ave. Glasg 75 D2
Merryton Ave. Glasg 136 B2
Merryton Pl. Glasg 75 D2
Merryton Rd. Lark 184 C3
Merryton Rd. Mother 164 B1
Merryton St. Lark 184 C3
Merryvale Ave. Glasg 136 B2
Merryvale Pl. Glasg 136 B3
Merryvale Rd. Irvine 219 E1
Merryvale
Roundabout. Irvine 219 E1
Merton Dr. Glasg 115 D3
Merville Cres. Cali 66 C3
Merville Terr. Cali 66 C3
Meryon Gdns. Glasg 119 E1
Meryon Rd. Glasg 119 E2
Metcalfe Pl. Shew 224 C3
Methil Rd. P Glasg 68 C3
Methil St. Glasg 95 E2
Methlan Pk. Dumb 49 E1
Methuen Rd. Ren 93 F1
Methuen Rd. Ren 114 A4
Methven Ave. Bear 76 A3
Methven Ave. Kilmk 227 F2
Methven Pl. E Kil 159 E1
Methven Pl. Kilmk 227 F2
Methven Rd. Newt M 157 D4
Methven St. Clyde 73 F2
Methven St. Glasg 118 B2
Metropole La. Glasg 117 E3
Mews La. Ayr 238 C4
Mews La. Green 45 E4
Mews La. Kilmk 227 F4
Mews La. Pais 113 F4
Mharie Pl. Bonh 27 F1
Michael
McParland Dr. Lennox 78 A4
Michael Terr. Chap 123 E1
Micklehouse Oval. Glasg 120 A3
Micklehouse Pl. Glasg 120 A3
Micklehouse Rd. Glasg 120 A3
Micklehouse Wynd. Glasg 120 A3
Mid Ave. P Glasg 68 C4
Mid Barrwood Rd. Kils 60 C4
Mid Carbarns. Wish 164 B1
Mid Dykes Rd. Salt 205 F1
Mid Pk. E Kil 180 C4
Mid Rd. Beith 150 A1
Mid Rd. Cumb 82 C3
Mid Rd. Eagle 178 C2
Mid Rig. Irvine 220 A2
Mid-Loan St. Car 201 F2
Mid-Wharf St. Glasg 97 E1
Midas Pl. Holy 142 C3
Midcroft Ave. Glasg 137 F3
Midcroft. Bish 77 F2
Middle Pk. Pais 113 E1
Middle Ward St. Dunt 74 B4
Middlefield. E Kil 180 C3
Middlefield Rd. Falk 42 B3
Middlehouse Ct. Car 187 E1
Middlemass Ct. Falk 42 A3
Middlemass Dr. Kilmk 228 A4
Middlemuir Ave. Kirk 79 E3
Middlemuir Rd. Kirk 79 E3
Middlemuir Rd. Stir 7 E3
Middlepart Cres. Salt 206 A1
Middlepart. Steven 206 B1
Middlepenny Pl. Lang 70 A4
Middlepenny Rd. Lang 70 A4
Middlerigg Rd. Cumb 61 E1
Middlesex St. Glasg 116 C3
Middleton Ave. Lark 199 D4
Middleton Cres. Pais 113 D3
Middleton Dr. Helen 25 C4
Middleton Dr. Miln 55 E1
Middleton La. Helen 25 C4
Middleton. Men 4 A3
Middleton Pk. Irvine 220 A2
Middleton Rd. Irvine 220 A2
Middleton Rd. Lin 112 B4
Middleton Rd. Pais 113 D3
Middleton St. Alex 27 E3
Middleton St. Glasg 116 B3
Midland St. Glasg 117 D4
Midlem Dr. Glasg 115 E3
Midlem Oval. Glasg 115 E3
Midlock St. Glasg 116 B3
Midlothian Dr. Glasg 116 B1
Midthorn Cres. Falk 42 C3
Midton Ave. Pres 236 A4
Midton Rd. Ayr 238 C3
Midton Rd. How 131 D3
Midton Rd. Kilmk 227 F1
Midton Rd. Pres 236 B4
Midton St. Glasg 97 F2
Midtown. Men 3 F3
Migvie Pl. Glasg 96 B3
Milford. E Kil 180 A4
Milford St. Glasg 119 D4
Milgarholm Ave. Irvine 219 E1
Milgarholm
Roundabout. Irvine 219 E1
Mill Ave. Kilm 222 B4
Mill Brae. Ayr 239 D4
Mill Brae. B of W 110 B4
Mill Brae Ct. Coat 121 E3

274

Mill Cres. Glasg

Moravia Ave. Udd

Mill Cres. Glasg 117 F2
Mill Cres. Irvine 219 F2
Mill Cres. Lennox 57 E1
Mill Ct. Glasg 138 A4
Mill Ct. Ham 162 B1
Mill Ct. Kilmk 228 A4
Mill Gr. Ham 162 B1
Mill Hill. Cam 6 B3
Mill Loan. Aird 123 D4
Mill of Gryffe Rd. B of W 110 B4
Mill Pk. Dalry 191 E4
Mill Pk. Ham 162 B1
Mill Pl. Lin 112 A3
Mill Rd. Aird 103 D1
Mill Rd. All 10 A3
Mill Rd. Cam 6 B3
Mill Rd. Car 187 F1
Mill Rd. Card 26 A1
Mill Rd. Cle 145 F1
Mill Rd. Clyde 94 B4
Mill Rd. East 127 F3
Mill Rd. Glasg 139 E3
Mill Rd. Gree 83 D1
Mill Rd. Ham 162 B1
Mill Rd. Irvine 219 F1
Mill Rd. Kilb 149 D1
Mill Rd. Kils 37 E2
Mill Rd. Kils 59 F4
Mill Rd. Mother 163 F4
Mill Rd. New 166 C3
Mill Rd. Sten 24 A2
Mill Rd. Udd 141 D1
Mill Rig. E Kil 180 B3
Mill Rise. Klrk 79 E2
Mill St. All 10 A3
Mill St. Ayr 239 D4
Mill St. Cald 104 C3
Mill St. Glasg 117 F2
Mill St. Glasg 138 A3
Mill St. Green 45 F2
Mill St. Kilmk 227 F4
Mill St. Pais 113 F2
Mill Way. Kirk 80 A4
Mill Wynd. Ayr 238 C4
Millands Ave. Udd 140 B1
Millar Pl. Bon 40 A2
Millar Pl. Sten 24 A3
Millar Pl. Stir 2 B1
Millar Rd. Salt 217 D4
Millar St. Green 46 A1
Millar St. Pais 113 F3
Millar St. Stone 198 C1
Millar Terr. Glasg 118 A1
Millarbank St. Glasg 97 F2
Millars Pl. Klrk 79 E2
Millars Wynd. N Sau 5 E1
Millarston Ave. Pais 113 D2
Millarston Dr. Pais 113 D2
Millbank Ave. Hat 142 B2
Millbank Rd. P Glasg 68 B4
Millbank Rd. Wish 164 C1
Millbeg Cres. Glasg 119 F3
Millbeg Pl. Glasg 119 F3
Millbrae Ave. Muir 100 B4
Millbrae Cres. Clyde 94 B4
Millbrae Cres. Glasg 136 C4
Millbrae Ct. Glasg 136 C4
Millbrae Gdns. Glasg 136 C4
Millbrae Rd. Glasg 136 C4
Millbrix Ave. Glasg 95 D3
Millbrook. E Kil 159 D1
Millbrook Pl. Men 3 F3
Millburn Ave. Clyde 94 C4
Millburn Ave. Glasg 138 A3
Millburn Ave. Ren 94 C2
Millburn Cres. Dumb 50 A2
Millburn Ct. E Kil 179 F4
Millburn Dr. Kil 89 D4
Millburn Dr. Ren 94 C2
Millburn Gdns. E Kil 179 F4
Millburn La. Lark 185 E1
Millburn Pl. Lark 199 D4
Millburn Rd. Alex 27 E2
Millburn Rd. Ash 186 A1
Millburn Rd. Dumb 50 A2
Millburn Rd. P Glasg 68 B4
Millburn Rd. Ren 94 B2
Millburn St. Falk 42 B3
Millburn St. Glasg 98 A1
Millburn St. Lennox 57 F4
Millburn St. Mother 163 F4
Millburn Terr. Irvine 220 A3
Millburn Way. E Kil 179 F4
Millburn Way. Ren 94 C2
Millcroft Rd. Cumb 62 A1
Millcroft Rd. Glasg 117 F1
Millcroft Rd. Glenm 82 C2
Millcroft Rd. Glenm 83 D2
Milldam Rd. Dunt 74 B4
Milldown Pl. Irvine 220 B1
Miller Ct. Dumb 50 A2
Miller Field Pl. Ham 162 C2
Miller Pl. Air 14 C2
Miller Pl. Ard 205 D2
Miller Pl. East 127 F3
Miller Rd. Ayr 238 C4
Miller Rd. Bonh 27 F4
Miller St. Car 188 A1
Miller St. Clyde 74 A1
Miller St. Coat 122 A3
Miller St. Dumb 50 A2
Miller St. East 127 F3
Miller St. Glasg 117 E4
Miller St. Glasg 120 A2
Miller St. Ham 162 C2
Miller St. John 112 A2
Miller St. Lark 185 D2
Miller St. Wish 165 D2
Miller's Pl. Aird 123 D4
Millerfield Pl. Glasg 118 A2
Millerfield Rd. Glasg 118 A2
Millerslea Gdns. Helen 16 C1
Millersneuk Ave. Klrk 79 E2
Millersneuk Cres. Stepps 99 D3
Millersneuk Dr. Klrk 79 E2
Millersneuk Rd. Klrk 79 E2
Millerston St. Glasg 118 A3
Millfield Ave. Ersk 72 C1
Millfield Ave. Mother 163 F4
Millfield Cres. Ersk 73 D1
Millfield Dr. Ersk 73 D1
Millfield Gdns. Ersk 73 D1
Millfield Hill. Ersk 72 C1
Millfield La. Ersk 72 C1
Millfield Meadows. Ersk 72 C1
Millfield Pl. Ersk 72 C1
Millfield View. Ersk 72 C1
Millfield Wlk. Ersk 73 D1
Millfield Wynd. Ersk 72 C1
Millflats St. Falk 24 A1
Millford Dr. Lin 112 A3
Millfore Ct. Irvine 220 A2
Millgate Ave. Tan 140 C4
Millgate Ct. Udd 140 C4
Millgate Rd. Ham 162 B1
Millglen Pl. Ard 205 E2
Millglen Rd. Ard 205 E2
Millhall Rd. Eagle 179 E2
Millhall Rd. Stir 7 E3
Millheugh Brae. Lark 184 C1
Millheugh. Lark 184 C1
Millheugh Pl. Udd 161 E3
Millheugh Rd. Stone 198 C3
Millhill Ave. Kilm 222 B4
Millhill Terr. Kilmk 222 C2
Millholm Rd. Glasg 137 D2
Millhouse Cres. Glasg 96 B4
Millhouse Dr. Glasg 96 B4
Millichen Rd. Glasg 76 C3
Millig St. Helen 16 B2
Milliken Dr. Kilbar 111 E1
Milliken Park Rd. John 111 E1
Milliken Rd. Kilbar 111 E1
Millport Ave. Glasg 137 E4
Millport Rd. P Glasg 68 C3
Millroad Dr. Glasg 117 F3
Millroad Gdns. Glasg 117 F3
Millroad St. Glasg 117 F3
Millrock Ct. Troon 229 E2
Millstream Cres. Cald 105 D2
Millview. Barr 134 B2
Millview Pl. Glasg 135 D2
Millview Terr. Neil 154 B4
Millwood St. Glasg 136 C4
Milnbank St. Glasg 118 A4
Milncroft Pl. Glasg 99 D1
Milncroft Rd. Glasg 99 D1
Milndavie Cres. Strath 31 E2
Milndavie Rd. Strath 31 E1
Milnepark Rd. Bann 11 F4
Milner La. Glasg 95 F3
Milner Rd. Glasg 95 F3
Milngavie Rd. Bear 75 F2
Milngavie Rd. Bear 76 A3
Milngavie Rd. Strath 31 E1
Milnpark Gdns. Glasg 116 C3
Milnpark St. Glasg 116 C3
Milnwood Dr. Hat 142 B2
Milnwood Dr. Mother 142 B1
Milovaig Ave. Glasg 76 B1
Milovaig St. Glasg 76 B1
Milrig Rd. Glasg 138 A4
Milton Ave. Glasg 138 C3
Milton Ave. Kilmk 223 E1
Milton Brae. Dumb 50 C1
Milton Brae. Stir 7 D1
Milton Cl. Duni 21 E2
Milton Cres. Bann 7 E1
Milton Cres. Car 187 F1
Milton Cres. Irvine 220 B1
Milton Ct. Dumb 50 C1
Milton Ct. Irvine 220 B1
Milton Douglas Rd. Dunt 74 A3
Milton Dr. Bish 97 F4
Milton Dr. Kilmk 223 E1
Milton Est. Bonh 27 F3
Milton Gdns. Bann 7 D1
Milton Gdns. Tan 140 C4
Milton Hill. Dumb 50 C1
Milton Mains Rd. Clyde 74 A3
Milton Pk. Ayr 239 D2
Milton Pk. Kilb 149 D1
Milton Pl. Duni 21 E2
Milton Quadrant. Kilb 149 D2
Milton Rd. Bann 7 E1
Milton Rd. Car 201 E4
Milton Rd. E Kil 159 D1
Milton Rd. Hurl 223 F1
Milton Rd. Irvine 220 B1
Milton Rd. Kilb 149 D2
Milton Rd. Kilmk 228 B4
Milton Rd. Kirk 58 B1
Milton Rd. Lennox 57 F4
Milton Rd. P Glasg 68 C3
Milton Row. Duni 21 F2
Milton St. Aird 123 D4
Milton St. Car 187 F1
Milton St. Glasg 97 E1
Milton St. Ham 162 A2
Milton St. Mother 163 F4
Milton Terr. Bann 7 D1
Milton Terr. Ham 162 A3
Milton View. Cross 226 C3
Milverton Ave. Bear 75 E3
Milverton Rd. Glasg 136 A1
Mimosa Rd. B of W 110 B4
Minard Rd. Glasg 116 C1
Minard Rd. P Glasg 68 C4
Minard Rd. Shot 146 B3
Minard Way. Tan 141 D4
Minch Way. Aird 123 E3
Mincher Cres. Mother 163 F2
Mine Rd. B of A 2 A4
Minella Gdns. Hat 142 A4
Minerva La. Gour 44 B2
Minerva St. Glasg 116 C4
Minerva Terr. Gour 44 B2
Minerva Way. Glasg 116 C4
Mingarry La. Glasg 96 C2
Mingarry St. Glasg 96 C2
Mingulay Cres. Glasg 97 E4
Mingulay Pl. Bish 97 F4
Mingulay St. Glasg 97 E4
Minmoir Rd. Glasg 134 C4
Minster Wlk. Coat 120 C3
Minstrel Rd. Glasg 75 E1
Minthill Pl. East 127 E3
Minto Ave. Glasg 138 B2
Minto Cres. Glasg 115 F3
Minto Ct. Alva 5 D3
Minto Gdns. Alva 5 D3
Minto Pk. Wish 165 E3
Minto St. Glasg 115 F3
Minto St. Green 45 E2
Mireton St. Glasg 97 D3
Mirren Dr. Dunt 73 F4
Mirren's Shore. P Glasg 47 E1
Mirrlees Dr. Glasg 96 B2
Mirrlees La. Glasg 96 B2
Misk Knowes. Steven 217 F3
Mission La. Falk 42 A2
Mitchell Ave. Glasg 139 F3
Mitchell Ave. Ren 94 A1
Mitchell Cres. All 9 F4
Mitchell Ct. Kilmk 228 A4
Mitchell Dr. Card 48 A3
Mitchell Dr. Glasg 138 A3
Mitchell Dr. Miln 55 E1
Mitchell Hill Rd. Glasg 137 F1
Mitchell La. Glasg 117 D4
Mitchell Pl. Falk 41 F1
Mitchell Pl. Salt 205 F1
Mitchell Rd. Cumb 62 A2
Mitchell St. Aird 122 C4
Mitchell St. Beith 150 B1
Mitchell St. Coat 121 E3
Mitchell St. Glasg 117 D4
Mitchell St. Green 46 C1
Mitchell Way. Alex 27 F3
Mitchison Rd. Cumb 62 A2
Mitre Ct. Glasg 95 F2
Mitre La. Glasg 95 F2
Mitre La W. Glasg 95 E2
Mitre Rd. Glasg 95 F2
Moat Ave. Glasg 95 E4
Mochrum Ct. Pres 236 B3
Mochrum Rd. Glasg 136 C3
Modan Rd. Stir 7 D2
Moffat Ave. Sten 24 B2
Moffat Ct. E Kil 179 F4
Moffat Gdns. E Kil 179 F4
Moffat Pl. Coat 122 C2
Moffat Pl. E Kil 179 F4
Moffat Pl. Udd 140 B1
Moffat Rd. Aird 123 F4
Moffat St. Glasg 117 E2
Moffat St. Green 46 B2
Moffat View. Plains 104 A2
Moffathill. Chap 123 F3
Mogarth Ave. Pais 132 C4
Moidart Ave. Ren 94 A2
Moidart Cres. Glasg 115 F3
Moidart Ct. Barr 134 A2
Moidart Gdns. Kirk 59 D1
Moidart Gdns. Newt M 156 C3
Moidart Pl. Glasg 115 F3
Moidart Rd. Glasg 115 F3
Moidart Rd. P Glasg 68 C4
Moir St. All 10 A4
Moir St. Glasg 117 E3
Molendinar St. Glasg 117 E3
Molendinar Terr. Neil 154 B3
Mollanbowie Rd. Bonh 19 F1
Mollins Ct. Cumb 81 E3
Mollins Rd. Cumb 81 E3
Mollinsburn Rd. Glen 81 F1
Mollinsburn Rd. Glenm 102 B3
Mollinsburn St. Glasg 97 F2
Mollison Ave. East 127 F3
Monach Gdns. Irvine 225 D4
Monach Rd. Glasg 119 E4
Monach Rd. P Glasg 69 D4
Monaebrook Pl. Helen 25 C4
Monar Dr. Glasg 97 D2
Monar Pl. Glasg 97 D2
Monar St. Glasg 97 D2
Monar Way. New 165 F3
Monart Pl. Glasg 96 C2
Moncks Rd. Falk 42 B2
Moncreiff Gdns. Klrk 79 E3
Moncreiff Ave. Klrk 79 E3
Moncrieff St. Pais 113 F3
Moncrieffe Rd. Chap 123 E2
Moncur Rd. Kilw 208 A2
Moncur St. Glasg 117 F3
Moness Dr. Glasg 115 F2
Moniebrugh Cres. Kils 36 C1
Moniebrugh Rd. Kils 36 C1
Monifieth Ave. Glasg 115 E2
Monikie Gdns. Bish 78 B1
Monkcastle Dr. Glasg 139 D3
Monkland Ave. Klrk 79 E3
Monkland La. Coat 121 F2
Monkland St. Aird 123 D4
Monkland Terr. Glen 101 E3
Monkland View. Calder 123 D1
Monkland View Cres. Coat 121 D3
Monkland View. Tan 121 D1
Monklands. Troon 229 F4
Monkreddan Cres. Kilw 207 E3
Monks La. Car 201 F2
Monks Rd. Aird 123 E2
Monksbridge Ave. Glasg 75 E1
Monkscourt Ave. Aird 122 C4
Monkscroft Ave. Glasg 96 A1
Monkscroft Ct. Glasg 96 A1
Monkscroft Gdns. Glasg 96 A1
Monkton Ct. Pres 233 E1
Monkton Dr. Glasg 75 E1
Monkton Gdns. Newt M 157 D2
Monkton Pl. P Glasg 68 C4
Monkton Rd. Pres 233 E1
Monktonhill Rd. Pres 233 D4
Monktonhill Rd. Troon 233 D4
Monkwood Pl. Ayr 239 D1
Monmouth Ave. Glasg 96 A3
Monreith Ave. Bear 75 E1
Monreith Rd E. Glasg 137 D3
Monreith Rd. Glasg 136 C3
Monroe Dr. Tan 120 C1
Monroe Pl. Tan 120 C1
Montague La. Glasg 96 A2
Montague St. Glasg 96 C1
Montalto Ave. Holy 143 D1
Montclair Pl. Lin 112 A3
Montego Gn. E Kil 159 D1
Monteith Dr. Glasg 158 A4
Monteith Gdns. Glasg 157 F4
Monteith Pl. Glasg 117 F3
Monteith Pl. Udd 161 F4
Monteith Row. Glasg 117 F3
Monteith Wlk. Shot 146 C3
Montfode Ct. Ard 205 E2
Montfode Dr. Ard 205 D2
Montford Ave. Glasg 137 F4
Montfort Pl. Falk 42 A2
Montgomerie Cres. Salt 216 C4
Montgomerie Pier Rd. Ard 205 D1
Montgomerie Rd. Pres 233 D1
Montgomerie Rd. Salt 216 C4
Montgomerie St. Ard 205 E1
Montgomerie St. P Glasg 47 E1
Montgomerie Terr. Ayr 235 F1
Montgomerie Terr. Kilw 208 A2
Montgomerieston Pl. Kilb 149 D1
Montgomerieston St. Kilb 149 D1
Montgomery Ave. Beith 171 E4
Montgomery Ave. Coat 121 F4
Montgomery Ave. Pais 114 A4
Montgomery Cres. Wish 185 F4
Montgomery Ct. Eagle 178 C2
Montgomery Ct. Kilb 149 D1
Montgomery Dr. Glasg 136 B1
Montgomery Dr. Kilbar 111 D2
Montgomery Pl. E Kil 159 F1
Montgomery Pl. Kilmk 222 C1
Montgomery Pl. Lark 185 D1
Montgomery Rd. Pais 114 A4
Montgomery Sq. Eagle 178 C2
Montgomery St. E Kil 159 F1
Montgomery St. Eagle 178 C2
Montgomery St. Falk 42 C3
Montgomery St. Glasg 118 A2
Montgomery St. Glasg 139 F3
Montgomery St. Irvine 219 D1
Montgomery St. Kilmk 222 C1
Montgomery St. Lark 185 D2
Montgomery Terr. M of C 58 B3
Montgomery Way. Stir 2 A2
Montgomeryfield. Irvine 225 D4
Montgreenan View. Kilw 207 F2
Montraive St. Glasg 118 B1
Montrave St. Glasg 115 E2
Montreal Pk. E Kil 159 E1
Montrose Ave. Glasg 114 C4
Montrose Ave. Glasg 119 E1
Montrose Ave. P Glasg 68 C3
Montrose Cres. Ham 162 B2
Montrose Dr. Bear 75 F4
Montrose Gdns. Kils 36 B1
Montrose Gdns. Miln 55 D2
Montrose Gdns. Udd 140 B1
Montrose Pl. Lin 112 A3
Montrose Rd. Pais 132 C4
Montrose Rd. Stir 2 B2
Montrose St. Clyde 74 B1
Montrose St. Glasg 117 E4
Montrose St. Mother 142 B1
Montrose Terr. B of W 110 B4
Montrose Terr. Bish 98 B4
Monument Cres. Pres 233 F1
Monument Rd. Ayr 238 C2
Monymusk Gdns. Bish 78 B1
Monymusk Pl. Glasg 74 C3
Moodie Ct. Kilmk 227 F3
Moodiesburn St. Glasg 98 C1
Moor Park Cres. Pres 236 B3
Moor Park Pl. Pres 236 B3
Moor Pk. Pres 236 B3
Moor Pl. Pres 236 B2
Moor Rd. Eagle 178 B2
Moor Rd. Lan 202 C1
Moor Rd. Miln 55 D1
Moor Rd. Pres 236 B3
Moor Rd. Strath 31 E1
Moorburn Ave. Glasg 136 A2
Moorburn Pl. Lin 111 F3
Moorcroft Rd. Newt M 156 B2
Moore Dr. Bear 75 F2
Moore Dr. Helen 25 D4
Moore Gdns. Ham 183 F4
Moore St. Glasg 117 F3
Moore St. Holy 143 D2
Moorfield Ave. Kilmk 227 E3
Moorfield Ave. P Glasg 68 B4
Moorfield Ind Est. Cross 227 D4
Moorfield La. Gour 44 B3
Moorfield Pl. Cross 226 B3
Moorfield Rd. Gour 44 B4
Moorfield Rd. Pres 236 B4
Moorfield Rd. Udd 161 E3
Moorfield
Roundabout. Cross 227 D4
Moorfoot Ave. Glasg 136 A2
Moorfoot Ave. Pais 113 E1
Moorfoot. Bish 78 B1
Moorfoot Dr. Gour 44 B3
Moorfoot Dr. Wish 164 C2
Moorfoot Path. Pais 133 E4
Moorfoot Pl. Irvine 220 A2
Moorfoot St. Glasg 118 C3
Moorfoot Way. Bear 75 E4
Moorfoot Way. Irvine 220 A2
Moorhill Cres. Newt M 156 B2
Moorhill Rd. Newt M 156 B2
Moorhouse Ave. Glasg 94 C3
Moorhouse Ave. Pais 113 D1
Moorhouse St. Barr 134 B1
Moorpark Ave. Muir 100 B4
Moorpark Dr. Glasg 115 D3
Moorpark Pl. Steven 217 E4
Moorpark Rd E. Steven 217 E4
Moorpark Rd W. Steven 217 E4
Moorpark Sq. Ren 94 A1
Moorside St. Car 188 A1
Morag Ave. Udd 140 B1
Moraine Ave. Glasg 75 D1
Moraine Cir. Glasg 75 D1
Moraine Dr. Glasg 75 D1
Moraine Dr. Newt M 157 E4
Moraine Pl. Glasg 75 D1
Morar Ave. Clyde 74 A2
Morar Cres. Aird 102 C1
Morar Cres. Bish 77 F1
Morar Cres. Bishop 72 B1
Morar Cres. Clyde 74 A2
Morar Cres. Coat 101 E1
Morar Ct. Clyde 74 A2
Morar Ct. Cumb 82 A4
Morar Ct. Ham 162 A1
Morar Dr. Bear 76 A2
Morar Dr. Clyde 74 A2
Morar Dr. Cumb 82 A4
Morar Dr. Falk 24 B1
Morar Dr. Glasg 138 A2
Morar Dr. Lin 112 A3
Morar Dr. Pais 113 D1
Morar Pl. E Kil 159 F2
Morar Pl. Irvine 219 E3
Morar Pl. Newt M 156 B4
Morar Pl. Ren 94 A2
Morar Rd. Clyde 74 A2
Morar Rd. Glasg 115 F3
Morar Rd. P Glasg 68 C4
Morar St. Wish 165 D1
Morar Terr. Glasg 138 B2
Morar Terr. Tan 141 D4
Morar Way. Holy 143 E2
Morar Way. Shot 147 D2
Moravia Ave. Udd 141 D2

275

Moray Ave. Aird

Nairn St. Glasg

Moray Ave. Aird 123 D3
Moray Dr. Glasg 157 F4
Moray Dr. Lennox 57 D1
Moray Gate. Udd 140 C2
Moray Gdns. Cumb 61 F3
Moray Gdns. Glasg 157 F4
Moray Gdns. Tan 140 C4
Moray Pl. Bish 78 B1
Moray Pl. Glasg 116 C1
Moray Pl. Kirk 59 D1
Moray Pl. Lin 112 A3
Moray Pl. Muir 100 B4
Moray Pl. Udd 161 E3
Moray Quadrant. Hat 142 A3
Moray Rd. P Glasg 47 E1
Moray Way. Holy 143 D3
Mordaunt St. Glasg 118 A2
Moredun Cres. Glasg 119 E4
Moredun Rd. Pais 113 D1
Moredun St. Glasg 119 E4
Morefield Rd. Glasg 115 E4
Morgan Ct. Stir 7 E2
Morgan Mews. Glasg 117 D2
Morgan St. Ham 162 B1
Morgan St. Lark 184 C2
Morina Gdns. Glasg 135 E2
Morion Rd. Glasg 95 E4
Moriston Ct. New 165 F3
Morland. E Kil 160 B2
Morley Cres. Stir 7 D2
Morley St. Glasg 137 D4
Morna La. Glasg 95 F1
Mornay Way. Shot 146 B3
Morningside Rd. New 166 B2
Morningside St. Glasg 118 C4
Morrin Path. Glasg 97 F2
Morrin St. Glasg 97 F2
Morris Cres. Hurl 228 C3
Morris Cres. Udd 161 E4
Morris La. Kilmk 223 D1
Morris
Moodie Ave. Steven 217 F4
Morris Rd. Pres 233 E1
Morris St. Green 46 B2
Morris St. Ham 162 B1
Morris St. Lark 185 E1
Morris Terr. Stir 7 D4
Morrishall Rd. E Kil 160 B2
Morrishill Dr. Beith 171 D4
Morrison Ave. Bon 39 F3
Morrison Ave. Steven 206 C1
Morrison Dr. Bann 7 E1
Morrison Dr. Lennox 57 F4
Morrison Gdns. Ayr 239 D4
Morrison Gdns. Lennox 78 B4
Morrison Pl. Kilmk 223 E1
Morrison Quadrant. Clyde 74 C1
Morrison St. Dunt 73 F3
Morrison St. Glasg 117 D3
Morriston Cres. Ren 94 C1
Morriston Park Dr. Glasg 139 D3
Morriston St. Glasg 139 D3
Morten Gdns. Glasg 116 B1
Morton Ave. Ayr 239 D3
Morton Pl. Kilmk 222 C1
Morton Rd. Ayr 239 D3
Morton Rd. Stew 211 E4
Morton St. Mother 163 F4
Morven Ave. Bish 78 B1
Morven Ave. Kilmk 222 C2
Morven Ave. Pais 133 E4
Morven Ave. Udd 140 B1
Morven Cres. Troon 229 E1
Morven Ct. Aird 103 D1
Morven Ct. Falk 42 B1
Morven Dr. Lin 112 A3
Morven Dr. Newt M 157 E4
Morven Dr. Troon 229 E2
Morven Gdns. Tan 140 C4
Morven La. Udd 140 B1
Morven Rd. Bear 75 F3
Morven Rd. Glasg 138 C2
Morven St. Coat 122 A4
Morven St. Glasg 115 F3
Morven Way. Udd 141 D2
Morville Cres. Kilw 207 F3
Mosesfield St. Glasg 97 F3
Moss Ave. Cald 105 D3
Moss Ave. Lin 112 A3
Moss Dr. Barr 134 A3
Moss Dr. Inch 93 D4
Moss Dr. Shew 224 C3
Moss Heights Ave. Glasg 115 E3
Moss Knowe. Cumb 62 B1
Moss Path. Glasg 119 F2
Moss Rd. Aird 123 D3
Moss Rd. Auld 180 B2
Moss Rd. B of W 110 C4
Moss Rd. Card 25 E2
Moss Rd. Cumb 62 C2
Moss Rd. Fall 8 B2
Moss Rd. Glasg 115 E4
Moss Rd. Kil 89 E4
Moss Rd. Kirk 70 D3
Moss Rd. Kirk 80 A4
Moss Rd. Lin 112 B4
Moss Rd. Muir 100 B4
Moss Rd. P Glasg 68 C4
Moss Rd. Wish 165 F2
Moss Side Ave. Aird 122 C4
Moss St. Pais 113 F3
Moss-Side Ave. Car 187 E1
Moss-Side Rd. Glasg 116 C1
Mossacre Rd. Wish 165 E2
Mossband La. Shot 146 C3
Mossbank Ave. Glasg 98 C2
Mossbank Cres. Holy 143 F2
Mossbank Dr. Glasg 98 C2
Mossbank. E Kil 179 F4
Mossbank. Pres 236 C4
Mossbank Rd. Wish 165 E2
Mossbank. Udd 161 E3
Mossbell Rd. Hat 141 F3
Mossblown St. Lark 184 C2
Mossburn Ave. Bonh 19 F1
Mossburn Ave. East 127 E3
Mossburn Rd. Wish 165 E2
Mossburn St. Wish 165 E1
Mosscastle Rd. Glasg 99 E1
Mosscastle Rd. Slam 86 A4
Mossdale Ct. Hat 142 B3
Mossdale. E Kil 159 E2
Mossdale Gdns. Ham 161 F1
Mossend Ave. Helen 16 C1
Mossend Ave. Kilb 170 A4
Mossend La. Glasg 119 E4
Mossend Pl. Helen 16 C1
Mossend St. Glasg 119 E4
Mossgiel Ave. Cowie 12 B4
Mossgiel Ave. Glasg 138 A3
Mossgiel Ave. Kilmk 228 B4
Mossgiel Ave. Stir 2 A1
Mossgiel Ave. Troon 229 F2
Mossgiel Cres. Newt M 157 F3
Mossgiel Dr. Clyde 74 B2
Mossgiel Dr. Irvine 219 E2
Mossgiel. E Kil 180 A4
Mossgiel Gdns. Kirk 58 C1
Mossgiel Gdns. Tan 140 C4
Mossgiel La. Lark 185 E1
Mossgiel Pl. Ayr 239 D3
Mossgiel Pl. Glasg 138 A3
Mossgiel Pl. Steven 206 C1
Mossgiel Rd. Ard 205 E2
Mossgiel Rd. Ayr 239 D3
Mossgiel Rd. Cumb 62 A1
Mossgiel Rd. Glasg 136 B3
Mossgiel Rd. Glasg 136 B4
Mossgiel Rd. Salt 206 A2
Mossgiel St. Falk 41 D3
Mossgiel Terr. Udd 140 B1
Mossgiel Way. Holy 143 E2
Mosshall Gr. Holy 143 F2
Mosshall Rd. Holy 143 E4
Mosshall St. Holy 143 F2
Mosshead Rd. Bear 76 A4
Mosshead Rd. Kilmk 228 A2
Mosshill Rd. Hat 142 A4
Mosside Pl. Kilmk 222 C2
Mosside Rd. Ayr 236 B2
Mossland Dr. Wish 165 E2
Mossland Rd. Glasg 114 C4
Mosslands Rd. Pais 113 F4
Mosslingal. E Kil 180 C3
Mossmulloch. E Kil 180 C3
Mossneuk Ave. E Kil 179 F4
Mossneuk Cres. Wish 165 E2
Mossneuk Dr. E Kil 179 F4
Mossneuk Dr. Pais 133 E4
Mossneuk Dr. Wish 165 E2
Mossneuk Pk. Wish 165 E2
Mossneuk Rd. E Kil 180 A4
Mossneuk St. Coat 121 F2
Mosspark Ave. Glasg 115 F2
Mosspark Ave. Miln 55 D2
Mosspark Bvd. Glasg 115 F2
Mosspark Dr. Glasg 115 F2
Mosspark La. Glasg 115 F2
Mosspark Oval. Glasg 115 F2
Mosspark Rd. Coat 121 E4
Mosspark Rd. Miln 55 D2
Mosspark Sq. Glasg 115 F2
Mossvale Cres. Glasg 99 E1
Mossvale La. Pais 113 E3
Mossvale Path. Glasg 99 E2
Mossvale Rd. Glasg 99 E1
Mossvale Sq. Glasg 99 D1
Mossvale Sq. Pais 113 E3
Mossvale St. Pais 113 E4
Mossvale Terr. Muir 81 D2
Mossvale Way. Glasg 99 F1
Mossvale Wlk. Glasg 99 E1
Mossview Cres. Aird 123 D3
Mossview La. Glasg 115 E3
Mossview Quadrant. Glasg 115 E3
Mossview Rd. Stepps 99 F3
Mosswell Rd. Miln 55 D2
Mossyde Ave. P Glasg 69 D4
Mossywood Ct. Cumb 81 F4
Mossywood Pl. Cumb 81 F4
Mossywood Rd. Cumb 81 F4
Mote Hill. Ham 162 C3
Mote View. Cross 221 E1
Motehill Rd. Pais 114 A4
Motherwell Rd. Chap 144 A3
Motherwell Rd. Ham 163 D2
Motherwell Rd. Hat 142 A2
Motherwell Rd. Holy 143 E1
Motherwell St. Aird 123 E4
Moulin Cir. Glasg 115 D2
Moulin Pl. Glasg 115 D2
Moulin Rd. Glasg 115 D2
Moulin Terr. Glasg 115 D2
Mount Annan Dr. Glasg 137 D4
Mount Ave. Kilmk 227 E3
Mount Ave. Sym 231 E2
Mount Cameron Dr N. E Kil 181 D4
Mount Cameron Dr S. E Kil 181 D4
Mount Charles Cres. Ayr 238 B1
Mount Harriet Ave. Stepps 99 F3
Mount Harriet Dr. Stepps 99 F3
Mount Hope. B of A 2 B4
Mount Oliphant. Cowie 12 B4
Mount Oliphant Cres. Ayr 239 D3
Mount Oliphant Pl. Ayr 239 D3
Mount Pl. Kilmk 227 E3
Mount
Pleasant Cres. M of C 58 A3
Mount Pleasant Dr. O Kill 73 D3
Mount Pleasant St. Green 45 F2
Mount St. Glasg 96 C2
Mount Stewart St. Car 187 F1
Mount Stuart St. Glasg 136 C4
Mount The. Ayr 239 D2
Mount Vernon Ave. Coat 121 F4
Mount Vernon Ave. Glasg 119 F2
Mount View. Irvine 220 B1
Mount William. N Sau 5 F1
Mountainblue St. Glasg 118 A3
Mountblow Rd. Clyde 73 E3
Mountgarrie Rd. Glasg 115 E4
Mountherrick. E Kil 180 C3
Mournian Way. Ham 162 B1
Mousebank La. Lan 214 C2
Mousebank Rd. Lan 214 C3
Mousemill Rd. Lan 214 B3
Mowbray Ave. Muir 100 C3
Mowbray Ct. Bann 7 E2
Mowbray. E Kil 160 B2
Moy Path. New 165 F3
Moyne Rd. Glasg 115 D1
Muckcroft Rd. Muir 80 B2
Mudale Ct. Falk 42 B1
Mugdock Rd. Miln 55 D2
Muir Cl. Stew 195 E1
Muir Cres. Alex 27 E4
Muir Dr. Irvine 219 E2
Muir Dr. Steven 217 E4
Muir Dr. Troon 229 E3
Muir Drive Cotts. Steven 217 E4
Muir Rd. Dumb 50 B3
Muir St. Alex 27 E4
Muir St. Bish 78 A1
Muir St. Coat 121 F4
Muir St. Ham 162 C2
Muir St. Lar 23 E1
Muir St. Lark 185 D2
Muir St. Law 186 C3
Muir St. Mother 163 E4
Muir St. Ren 94 B2
Muir St. Udd 161 E3
Muir Terr. Pais 114 A4
Muiralehouse Rd. Bann 11 F4
Muirbank Ave. Glasg 137 F4
Muirbank Gdns. Glasg 137 F4
Muirbrae Rd. Glasg 138 A2
Muirbrae Way. Glasg 138 A2
Muirburn Ave. Glasg 136 C2
Muirburn Rd. Beith 150 A2
Muirburn Rd. Glass 198 A1
Muircroft Dr. Cle 144 A1
Muirdrum Ave. Glasg 115 E2
Muirdyke Ave. Sten 24 B2
Muirdyke Rd. Coat 121 E4
Muirdyke Rd. Glen 102 A3
Muirdykes Ave. Glasg 115 D3
Muirdykes Ave. P Glasg 68 B4
Muirdykes Cres. Pais 113 D3
Muirdykes Rd. Glasg 115 D3
Muirdykes Rd. Pais 113 D3
Muiredge
and Jersey Rd. Cle 145 D1
Muiredge
and Jersy Rd. Sals 145 E4
Muiredge Ct. Udd 140 C3
Muiredge Terr. Glasg 120 A2
Muirend Ave. Glasg 136 C3
Muirend Rd. Card 48 A4
Muirend Rd. Glasg 136 C2
Muirend Rd. Kilmk 222 C3
Muirend Rd. Stir 7 D3
Muirend St. Kilb 149 D1
Muirfield Cres. Glasg 76 C1
Muirfield Ct. Glasg 136 C2
Muirfield Meadows. Udd 140 C1
Muirfield Pl. Kilw 207 E2
Muirfield Rd. Cumb 62 A3
Muirfield Rd. Lar 23 F1
Muirhall Pl. Lar 23 E2
Muirhall Rd. Lar 23 E2
Muirhall Terr. Sals 125 D1
Muirhead Cotts. Kirk 80 A4
Muirhead Dr. Holy 143 F2
Muirhead Dr. Lin 112 A3
Muirhead Gdns. Glasg 120 B2
Muirhead Gdns. Sals 125 D1
Muirhead Pl. East 127 E2
Muirhead Rd. Glasg 120 A2
Muirhead Rd. Sten 23 F2
Muirhead St. Kirk 79 E4
Muirhead St. Loch 129 E1
Muirhead Terr. Mother 163 F2
Muirhead Way. Bish 78 B1
Muirhead-Braehead
Interchange. Cumb 62 A2
Muirhill Ave. Glasg 136 C3
Muirhill Cres. Glasg 95 D4
Muirhouse Ave. Mother 164 A2
Muirhouse Ave. New 166 A3
Muirhouse Dr. Mother 164 B1
Muirhouse La. E Kil 180 C4
Muirhouse Pk. Bear 75 E4
Muirhouse Rd. Mother 164 A1
Muirhouse St. Glasg 117 D2
Muirkirk Dr. Glasg 95 F4
Muirkirk Dr. Ham 161 E1
Muirlee Rd. Car 188 A1
Muirlees Cres. Miln 54 C1
Muirmadkin Rd. Hat 142 A3
Muirmaillen Ave. Cle 144 B1
Muirpark Ave. Ren 94 B1
Muirpark Dr. Bish 98 A4
Muirpark Dr. Shi 66 B3
Muirpark Gdns. Men 4 C2
Muirpark Rd. Beith 150 A1
Muirpark St. Glasg 96 A1
Muirshiel Ave. Glasg 135 E3
Muirshiel Cres. Glasg 135 E3
Muirshiel La. P Glasg 68 B4
Muirshiel Rd. P Glasg 68 B4
Muirshot Rd. Lark 185 D2
Muirside Ave. Glasg 119 F2
Muirside Ave. Kirk 80 A4
Muirside Ct. Kilw 207 E1
Muirside Pl. Kilw 207 E1
Muirside Pl. New 165 F3
Muirside Rd. Glasg 120 A2
Muirside Rd. Kilw 207 E1
Muirside Rd. Pais 113 D4
Muirside Rd. Tull 4 B2
Muirside St. Glasg 120 A2
Muirskeith Cres. Glasg 137 D3
Muirskeith Pl. Glasg 136 C3
Muirskeith Rd. Glasg 136 C3
Muirton Dr. Bish 77 F2
Muirton Rd. Fal 7 F3
Muiryfauld Dr. Glasg 118 C3
Muiryhall St. Coat 122 A4
Muiryhall St E. Coat 122 B4
Mulben Cres. Glasg 134 C4
Mulben Pl. Glasg 134 C4
Mulben Terr. Glasg 134 C4
Mulberry Dr. E Kil 180 B3
Mulberry Rd. Glasg 136 B3
Mulberry Rd. Tan 121 E1
Mulberry Way. E Kil 180 B3
Muldron Terr. Shot 147 D1
Mulgrew Ave. Salt 206 A1
Mull. Aird 123 E3
Mull Ave. P Glasg 69 D4
Mull Ave. Pais 133 F4
Mull Ave. Ren 94 B1
Mull Cres. Irvine 220 A1
Mull Ct. All 10 A3
Mull Ct. Irvine 220 A1
Mull. E Kil 181 E4
Mull Pl. Irvine 220 A1
Mull Quadrant. Wish 165 F3
Mull St. Glasg 98 A1
Mull Terr. Irvine 220 A1
Mullardoch St. Glasg 76 B1
Mulvey Cres. Aird 122 C4
Mungalend. Falk 42 A4
Mungalhead Rd. Falk 42 A4
Mungo Pk. E Kil 180 B4
Mungo Pl. Tan 121 D1
Munlochy Rd. Glasg 115 E4
Munnoch Cres. Ard 205 D3
Munro Ave. Kilmk 222 B1
Munro Ave. Stir 2 A2
Munro Ct. Dunt 73 F3
Munro Dr E. Helen 16 C2
Munro Dr. Kilb 170 A4
Munro Dr. M of C 58 A3
Munro Dr W. Helen 16 B2
Munro Gdns. Laur 42 C2
Munro La E. Glasg 95 F3
Munro La. Glasg 95 F3
Munro Pl. All 9 F3
Munro Pl. E Kil 160 A2
Munro Pl. Glasg 95 F3
Munro Pl. Kilmk 222 C1
Munro Pl. Salt 206 A1
Munro Rd. Fal 7 F3
Munro Rd. Glasg 95 F3
Munro St. Alex 27 F3
Munro St. Green 45 D2
Munro St. Sten 23 F2
Munro Wlk. Salt 206 A1
Murano St. Glasg 96 C2
Murchie Dr. Pres 236 B3
Murchison Dr. E Kil 180 A4
Murchison Rd. Hous 91 E1
Murchland Ave. Fen 213 D2
Murchland Way. Irvine 219 E2
Murdieston St. Green 45 E2
Murdoch Cres. Steven 217 E4
Murdoch Dr. Miln 76 B4
Murdoch Pl. Holy 142 C2
Murdoch Pl. Shew 224 C3
Murdoch Rd. E Kil 180 C4
Murdoch Sq. Hat 142 B4
Murdoch's Lone. Ayr 238 C1
Murdostoun Cres. East 127 F3
Murdostoun Gdns. Wish 165 D3
Murdostoun Terr. Cle 144 C1
Murdostoun View. New 165 F3
Mure Ave. Kilmk 223 D3
Mure Pl. Uplaw 153 D2
Muriel La. Barr 134 B2
Muriel St. Barr 134 B2
Murnin Ct. Stir 7 E2
Murnin Rd. Bon 40 A2
Murray Ave. Kils 60 B4
Murray Ave. Salt 205 F1
Murray Dr. Stone 198 C1
Murray Gdns. M of C 58 B3
Murray Gr. Bear 75 D4
Murray Path. Udd 140 C3
Murray Pl. Ayr 236 B2
Murray Pl. Barr 134 B2
Murray Pl. Cam 6 B3
Murray Pl. Dumb 50 B2
Murray Pl. Gour 44 C3
Murray Pl. Kilmk 223 E1
Murray Pl. Stir 7 D4
Murray Pl. Tan 141 F4
Murray Rd. Law 186 C2
Murray Rd The. E Kil 180 C4
Murray Rd. Udd 141 D2
Murray
Roundabout The. E Kil 180 C4
Murray Sq The. E Kil 180 C4
Murray St. Ayr 236 B1
Murray St. Green 45 E3
Murray St. Pais 113 E3
Murray St. Ren 94 B2
Murray Terr. Mother 163 D4
Murrayfield. Bish 78 A2
Murrayfield Dr. Bear 75 F1
Murrayfield Pl. Bann 7 E1
Murrayfield St. Glasg 118 C4
Murrayfield Terr. Bann 7 E1
Murrayhill. E Kil 180 B4
Murrayshall Rd. Stir 7 D2
Murrayside. Stone 198 B1
Murrin Ave. Bish 78 B1
Murroch Ave. Dumb 50 B3
Murroch Cres. Bonh 28 A1
Murroes Rd. Glasg 115 E4
Musgrove Pl. E Kil 180 B4
Muslin St. Glasg 117 F2
Muttonhole Rd. Ham 182 C4
Muttonhole Rd. Quart 183 D2
Mybster Pl. Glasg 115 E4
Myers Cres. Udd 141 D3
Mylne Pl. Sten 24 A1
Myothill Rd. Bank 39 E4
Myres Rd. Glasg 135 E4
Myreside Pl. Glasg 118 B3
Myreside St. Glasg 118 C3
Myreton Ave. Kil 89 E4
Myreton Dr. Bann 11 F4
Myreton. Men 4 A3
Myreton Way. Falk 41 F2
Myretoungate. Alva 4 C3
Myrie Gdns. Bish 78 A1
Myroch Pl. Glasg 100 B1
Myrtle Ave. Kirk 79 E3
Myrtle Bank. Beith 171 D4
Myrtle Dr. Holy 143 D3
Myrtle Dr. Mother 164 B2
Myrtle Hill La. Glasg 137 E4
Myrtle La. Lark 185 E1
Myrtle Pk. Glasg 117 E1
Myrtle Pl. Glasg 137 E4
Myrtle Rd. Clyde 73 E2
Myrtle Rd. Tan 141 D4
Myrtle Sq. Bish 98 A4
Myrtle St. Udd 140 B1
Myrtle View Rd. Glasg 137 E4
Myrtle Wlk. Glasg 138 C3
Myvot Ave. Cumb 82 A3
Myvot Rd. Cumb 82 A3

Nailer Rd. Falk 41 F3
Nailer Rd. Stir 7 D1
Nairn Ave. Hat 142 A3
Nairn Ave. Udd 140 B1
Nairn Cl. Stew 195 E1
Nairn Cres. Aird 123 D3
Nairn Ct. Falk 42 B1
Nairn Ct. Kilw 207 D2
Nairn Dr. Gour 44 B3
Nairn Pl. Clyde 73 F2
Nairn Pl. E Kil 160 B2
Nairn Quadrant. Wish 165 D3
Nairn Rd. Gour 44 B2
Nairn St. Clyde 73 F2
Nairn St. Glasg 96 B1

279
Plotcock Rd. Stone
Rannoch Dr. Bear

Plotcock Rd. Stone 198 B4
Plover Dr. E Kil 180 A3
Plover Pl. John 131 E4
Plusgarten Loan. New 165 F4
Plymouth Ave. Gour 44 C3
Poet's View. Kirk 79 F4
Poindfauld Terr. Dumb 50 A2
Pointhouse Rd. Glasg 116 B4
Pokelly Pl. Stew 195 F1
Polbae Cres. Eagle 178 C3
Poles Rd. Fen 213 D2
Polkemmet Dr. Hart 127 F3
Polkemmet La. Hart 127 F3
Polkemmet Rd. Hart 127 F3
Pollick Ave. Uplaw 153 D2
Pollick Farm La. Dunlop 153 D1
Pollock Ave. Eagle 178 C3
Pollock Ave. Ham 162 A2
Pollock Cres. Kilw 207 F1
Pollock Rd. Bear 76 A2
Pollock Rd. Newt M 156 B2
Pollock St. Hat 142 B3
Pollock St. Mother 163 F4
Pollok Ave. Glasg 136 A4
Pollok Dr. Bish 77 F1
Pollok La. E Kil 160 A2
Pollok Pl. E Kil 160 A2
Pollokshaws Rd. Glasg 116 C1
Pollokshaws Rd. Glasg 117 D2
Polmadie Ave. Glasg 117 E1
Polmadie Rd. Glasg 117 E1
Polmadie St. Glasg 117 E1
Polmaise Ave. Stir 7 D2
Polmaise Cres. Fall 8 B3
Polmaise Ct. Stir 7 D2
Polmaise Rd. Cam 6 C2
Polmaise Rd. Stir 6 C3
Polnoon Ave. Glasg 95 D3
Polnoon Dr. Eagle 178 C3
Polnoon St. Eagle 178 B2
Polo Ave. Troon 229 F1
Polo Gdns. Troon 229 F1
Polson Dr. John 111 F1
Polsons Cres. Pais 113 E1
Polwarth La. Glasg 96 A2
Polwarth St. Glasg 96 A2
Pomona Pl. Ham 161 F1
Pompee Rd. N Sau 5 D1
Poplar Ave. Bishop 72 A1
Poplar Ave. Glasg 95 F2
Poplar Ave. John 112 A1
Poplar Ave. Newt M 156 C2
Poplar Cres. Bishop 72 A1
Poplar Ct. Coat 121 F2
Poplar Dr. Clyde 73 F3
Poplar Dr. Kirk 79 D3
Poplar Dr. M of C 58 B3
Poplar Gdns. E Kil 180 B3
Poplar Pl. Gour 44 B3
Poplar Pl. Holy 143 D2
Poplar Pl. Tan 141 E4
Poplar Pl. Udd 140 B1
Poplar Rd. Dumb 49 F2
Poplar St. Aird 123 E4
Poplar St. Green 46 C1
Poplar Way. Ayr 239 E3
Poplars The. Bear 75 E4
Poplars The. Tull 4 A1
Poplin St. Glasg 118 A2
Porchester St. Glasg 99 E1
Port Dundas Ind Est. Glasg 97 E1
Port Dundas Pl. Glasg 117 E4
Port Dundas Rd. Glasg 97 E1
Port Glasgow Rd. Green 46 C2
Port Glasgow Rd. Kil 69 D1
Port St. Glasg 116 C4
Port St. Stir 7 D4
Portal Rd. Glasg 95 E4
Portdownie. Falk 41 E3
Portencross Rd. W Kil 190 B3
Porter St. Glasg 116 B3
Porterfield Rd. Kil 89 F4
Porterfield Rd. Ren 94 A2
Porters La. Chap 123 E1
Porters Well. Udd 140 C3
Portessie. Ersk 73 D1
Porthlethen. Ersk 73 D1
Portland Ave. Irvine 224 A4
Portland Brae. Hurl 228 C3
Portland Ct. Hurl 228 C3
Portland Pk. Ham 162 C1
Portland Pl. Ham 162 C1
Portland Pl. Irvine 224 A4
Portland Pl. Kilmk 227 F4
Portland Pl. Lan 215 D2
Portland Pl. Steven 217 E4
Portland Rd. Irvine 224 A4
Portland Rd. Kilmk 227 F4
Portland Rd. Pais 114 A2
Portland
Roundabout. Irvine 219 D1
Portland Sq. Ham 162 C1
Portland St. Coat 122 A4
Portland St. Kilmk 222 C1
Portland St. Troon 229 E2
Portland Terr. Troon 229 D1
Portland Wynd. Lark 185 D2
Portman St. Glasg 116 C3
Portmark Ave. Ayr 238 B1
Portmarnock Dr. Glasg 96 C4
Porton Pl. Bishop 72 A2
Portpatrick Rd. O Kill 72 C4
Portreath Rd. Muir 80 C2
Portree Terr. Gour 44 C2
Portsmouth Dr. Gour 44 C3
Portsoy Ave. Glasg 94 C4
Portsoy. Ersk 73 D1
Portsoy Pl. Glasg 94 C4
Portugal St. Glasg 117 D3
Portwell. Ham 162 C2
Possil Cross. Glasg 97 E2
Possil Rd. Glasg 97 D2
Postgate. Ham 162 C2
Posthill. N Sau 5 E1
Potassels Rd. Muir 100 B4
Potrail Pl. Ham 162 A2
Potter Cl. Glasg 118 C2
Potter Gr. Glasg 118 C2
Potter Pl. Glasg 118 C2
Potter Pl. Gran 24 C2
Potter St. Glasg 118 C2
Potterhill Ave. Pais 133 F4
Potterhill Rd. Glasg 115 D1
Potters Wynd. Lan 215 E3
Pottery Pl. Kilmk 222 C1
Pottery St. Green 46 C2
Pottis Rd. Bann 7 E2
Potts Way. Mother 142 B1
Powbrone. E Kil 180 C3
Powburn Cres. Udd 140 B4
Powfoot St. Glasg 118 B3
Powforth Cl. Lark 184 C2
Powgree Cres. Beith 171 E3
Powmill Rd. Pres 233 E1
Powrie St. Glasg 99 E2
Prentice Rd. Mother 163 D3
President Kennedy Dr. Plea 12 B2
Preston Pl. Glasg 117 D1
Preston Pl. Gour 44 B4
Preston St. Glasg 117 D1
Prestonfield Ave. Kilw 207 D2
Prestonfield. Miln 54 C1
Prestwick Pl. Newt M 157 D2
Prestwick Rd. Ayr 236 A2
Prestwick St. Glasg 135 D3
Pretoria Rd. Lar 23 D1
Priestfield St. Udd 161 E3
Priesthill Ave. Glasg 135 E3
Priesthill Cres. Glasg 135 E3
Priesthill Rd. Glasg 135 E3
Priestknowe
Roundabout. E Kil 159 F1
Prieston Rd. B of W 110 B4
Primrose Ave. Hat 142 A4
Primrose Ave. Lark 199 D4
Primrose Cres. Mother 163 F3
Primrose Ct. Glasg 95 E2
Primrose Pk. Ayr 239 E2
Primrose Pl. All 10 A3
Primrose Pl. Cumb 82 A3
Primrose Pl. Kilmk 222 B1
Primrose Pl. Salt 206 A1
Primrose Pl. Tan 141 E4
Primrose St. All 10 A4
Primrose St. Bon 40 A3
Primrose St. Glasg 95 E2
Primrose Way. Car 201 F4
Prince Albert Rd. Glasg 96 B2
Prince Albert Terr. Helen 16 B1
Prince Edward St. Glasg 117 D1
Prince of
Wales Gdns. Glasg 96 B4
Prince Pl. New 166 A3
Prince's Gdns. Glasg 96 A2
Prince's Pl. Glasg 96 B2
Prince's Terr. Glasg 96 B2
Princes Ct. Ayr 236 A1
Princes Gate. Glasg 138 A4
Princes Gate. Udd 140 C2
Princes Mall. E Kil 159 F1
Princes Pk. Ersk 72 C2
Princes Pl. Ard 205 D1
Princes Sq. Barr 134 B2
Princes Sq. E Kil 159 F1
Princes
Square Shop Ctr. Glasg 117 E4
Princes St. Ard 205 D1
Princes St. Cald 105 D3
Princes St. Cali 66 C3
Princes St E. Helen 16 C1
Princes St. Falk 42 A3
Princes St. Glasg 138 A4
Princes St. Green 45 F3
Princes St. Kilmk 227 F4
Princes St. Mother 163 F4
Princes St. P Glasg 47 E1
Princes St. Salt 216 B4
Princes St. Stir 7 D4
Princess
Anne Quadrant. Holy 142 C3
Princess Cres. Pais 114 A3
Princess Ct. Helen 16 B1
Princess Ct. Kilmk 228 A2
Princess Dr. Coat 121 D3
Princess Rd. Holy 142 C2
Princess Sq. New 165 F3
Princess St. Bon 40 A3
Princess Way. Ros 15 D2
Printers Land. Thorn 158 A3
Priory Ave. Pais 114 A4
Priory Dr. Udd 140 B4
Priory Gate. Wish 186 A4
Priory Pl. Cumb 60 C1
Priory Pl. Glasg 95 E4
Priory Rd. Glasg 95 E4
Priory St. Udd 161 E4
Priory Terr. Wish 164 B1
Procession Rd. Pais 133 E3
Professors' Sq. Glasg 96 B1
Progress Dr. Cald 105 D3
Promenade. Ayr 236 A2
Prosen St. Glasg 118 C2
Prospect Ave. Glasg 138 C3
Prospect Ave. Udd 140 C4
Prospect Ct. Ham 161 E3
Prospect Dr. Ash 199 F4
Prospect Rd. Cumb 61 E3
Prospect Rd. Glasg 136 B4
Prospect St. Falk 41 F3
Prospecthill Cir. Glasg 117 E1
Prospecthill Cres. Glasg 137 F4
Prospecthill Dr. Glasg 137 E4
Prospecthill Pl. Glasg 137 F4
Prospecthill Pl. Green 45 F2
Prospecthill Rd. Falk 42 A1
Prospecthill Rd. Glasg 137 E4
Prospecthill Rd. Salt 206 A1
Prospecthill Sq. Glasg 137 E4
Prospecthill St. Green 45 F2
Provan Rd. Glasg 118 B4
Provand Hall Cres. Glasg 120 A2
Provanhill St. Glasg 97 F1
Provanmill Rd. Glasg 98 C1
Provost Cl. John 111 F2
Provost Gate. Lark 185 D2
Provost
Hunter Ave. Alva 5 E4
Pullar Ave. B of A 2 A3
Pullar Ct. B of A 2 A3
Pundeavon Ave. Kilb 149 D2
Purdie. E Kil 160 B3
Purdie St. Ham 162 A3
Purdon St. Glasg 96 A1
Putyan Ave. Dalry 191 D4
Pyatshaw Rd. Lark 185 D1

Quadrant Rd. Glasg 136 C3
Quadrant The. Glasg 157 F4
Quail Rd. Ayr 236 A2
Quakerfield. Bann 7 F1
Quarrelton Rd. John 111 F1
Quarrier St. Green 46 B2
Quarrolhall Cres. Sten 24 A2
Quarry Ave. Glasg 139 F2
Quarry Dr. Kil 69 E1
Quarry Dr. Kirk 79 F4
Quarry Knowe. Bann 11 F4
Quarry Knowe. Dumb 49 E3
Quarry Knowe Pl. Hat 141 F2
Quarry Knowe. Rhu 15 F3
Quarry La. Dumb 49 F2
Quarry La. Eagle 178 B2
Quarry La. Lennox 33 E1
Quarry Pk. E Kil 180 C4
Quarry Pl. Dumb 49 E3
Quarry Pl. Glasg 138 C3
Quarry Pl. Ham 162 C2
Quarry Pl. N Sau 10 B4
Quarry Pl. Shot 146 B3
Quarry Rd. Aird 103 D1
Quarry Rd. Barr 134 A2
Quarry Rd. Cam 6 B3
Quarry Rd. E Kil 180 B3
Quarry Rd. Irvine 219 E2
Quarry Rd. Lark 185 D1
Quarry Rd. P Glasg 68 C4
Quarry Rd. Pais 113 F1
Quarry Rd. Shot 146 B3
Quarry St. Coat 122 B4
Quarry St. Ham 162 C2
Quarry St. Holy 143 D2
Quarry St. John 111 F1
Quarry St. Lark 185 D1
Quarry St. Shot 146 B3
Quarry St. Wish 165 D2
Quarrybank. Kilbar 111 E1
Quarrybrae Ave. Newt M 157 E4
Quarrybrae Gdns. Tan 141 E3
Quarrybrae St. Glasg 118 C3
Quarryknowe. Glasg 137 F4
Quarryknowe. Lan 215 D2
Quarryknowe St. Dunt 74 C4
Quarryknowe St. Glasg 118 C3
Quarryside St. Glenm 102 C2
Quarrywood Ave. Glasg 98 B2
Quarrywood Rd. Glasg 98 B2
Quay Pend. Dumb 49 F2
Quay Rd. Glasg 118 A1
Quay Road N. Glasg 118 A1
Quay St. Dumb 49 F2
Quay St. Salt 216 C4
Quebec Dr. E Kil 159 E1
Quebec Gn. E Kil 159 E1
Quebec Wynd. Glasg 139 E4
Queen
Elizabeth Ave. Glasg 114 C4
Queen Elizabeth Ct. Mother 163 E4
Queen Elizabeth Sq. Glasg 117 E2
Queen Margaret Dr. Glasg 96 C2
Queen Mary Ave. Clyde 74 B1
Queen Mary Ave. Glasg 117 D1
Queen Mary St. Glasg 118 A2
Queen Rd. Irvine 219 E3
Queen Sq. Glasg 116 C1
Queen St. Alex 27 E2
Queen St. All 10 A4
Queen St. Alva 5 D4
Queen St. Ayr 236 A1
Queen St. Bann 7 E1
Queen St. Falk 42 B3
Queen St. Fall 8 B2
Queen St. Glasg 117 E4
Queen St. Glasg 138 A4
Queen St. Ham 162 A3
Queen St. Helen 16 B2
Queen St. Kilmk 227 F4
Queen St. Kilw 208 A2
Queen St. Kirk 79 E4
Queen St. Mother 163 F4
Queen St. New 165 F3
Queen St. P Glasg 47 E1
Queen St. Pais 113 E2
Queen St. Ren 94 B2
Queen St. Stir 7 D4
Queen St. Stone 198 C1
Queen Victoria Dr. Glasg 95 E2
Queen
Victoria Gate. Glasg 95 E3
Queen Victoria St. Aird 122 C4
Queen's Ave. B of A 2 A3
Queen's Ave. Glasg 139 D3
Queen's Court. Helen 25 C4
Queen's Cres. Car 188 A1
Queen's Cres. Chap 123 E2
Queen's Cres. Coat 120 C3
Queen's Cres. Falk 41 F3
Queen's Cres. Glasg 97 D1
Queen's Ct. B of A 1 C4
Queen's Ct. Miln 76 A4
Queen's Dr. Alex 27 E2
Queen's Dr. Ard 205 E2
Queen's Dr. Cumb 61 F3
Queen's Dr. Glasg 117 D1
Queen's Dr. Kilmk 228 A3
Queen's Dr. Lar 23 E1
Queen's Dr. Pres 233 E3
Queen's Dr. Troon 229 E3
Queen's Drive La. Glasg 117 D1
Queen's Gate. Newt M 157 F4
Queen's Gdns. Glasg 96 B2
Queen's La. B of A 2 A4
Queen's Park Ave. Glasg 117 D1
Queen's Pl. Glasg 96 B2
Queen's Pl. Kilw 208 A2
Queen's Quadrant. Ayr 236 A1
Queen's Rd. John 112 B1
Queen's Rd. Stir 6 C4
Queen's St. Cali 66 C3
Queen's St. Cle 144 A1
Queen's Terr. Ayr 238 C4
Queen's Terrace La. Ayr 238 C4
Queens Cres. Hat 141 F2
Queens Cres. Holy 142 C2
Queens Dr. Bishop 72 B2
Queens Dr. Duni 21 F2
Queens Dr. Falk 41 F3
Queens Dr. Ham 183 E3
Queens Point. Rhu 15 D4
Queens Terr. Pres 233 D1
Queens Way. Alex 27 E2
Queens Way. Lennox 78 A4
Queensbank Ave. Muir 100 C4
Queensberry Ave. Bear 75 F4
Queensberry Ave. Newt M 157 F4
Queensborough
Gdns. Glasg 96 A2
Queensby Ave. Glasg 120 A3
Queensby Dr. Glasg 120 A3
Queensby Pl. Glasg 120 B3
Queensby Rd. Glasg 120 B3
Queensdale Ave. Lark 199 D4
Queensdale Rd. Lark 199 D4
Queensferry St. Glasg 117 F1
Queenshaugh Dr. Stir 2 B1
Queenside Cres. Ersk 72 C1
Queensland Ct. Glasg 115 E3
Queensland Dr. Glasg 115 E3
Queensland Gdns. Glasg 115 E3
Queensland La E. Glasg 115 E3
Queensland La W. Glasg 115 E3
Queenslie St. Glasg 98 B1
Queensway. E Kil 159 E1
Queensway. Gour 44 B3
Queenzieburn Ind Est. Kils 60 A4
Quendale Dr. Glasg 118 C2
Quentin St. Glasg 116 C1
Quinton Gdns. Glasg 120 A3

Raasay Cres. Aird 123 F3
Raasay Dr. Pais 13 3 E4
Raasay Gdns. Newt M 156 A3
Raasay Pl. Glasg 97 E4
Raasay St. Glasg 97 E4
Racecourse Rd. Ayr 238 C3
Racecourse View. Ayr 238 C3
Racecourse View. Ham 162 C3
Rachan St. Glasg 100 B1
Radnor St. Clyde 74 A2
Rae St. Sten 23 E2
Raeberry St. Glasg 96 C2
Raebog Cres. Aird 102 C1
Raebog Rd. Glenm 102 C2
Raeburn Ave. E Kil 160 A2
Raeburn Cres. Ham 161 F2
Raeburn Pl. E Kil 160 A2
Raeburn Wlk. Hat 142 A4
Raes Rd. Car 201 D4
Raeside Ave. Newt M 156 B2
Raeswood Dr. Glasg 134 C4
Raeswood Pl. Glasg 135 D4
Raeswood Rd. Glasg 134 C4
Raewell Cres. Hat 141 F2
Rafford St. Glasg 116 A4
Raggithill Ave. Moss 237 F3
Raglan St. Bonh 27 F2
Raglan St. Glasg 97 D1
Raglan Street La. Bonh 27 F2
Railway Rd. Aird 122 B4
Raise St. Salt 216 C4
Raith Ave. Glasg 137 E2
Raith Ave. Pres 236 C4
Raith Dr. Hat 142 A2
Raith Rd. Fen 213 D2
Raith Terr. Pres 236 C4
Raithburn Ave. Glasg 137 E2
Raithburn Ave. Kilmk 222 C2
Raithburn Rd. Glasg 137 E2
Raithhill. Ayr 239 D1
Raleigh Ct. Falk 41 F3
Ralston Ave. Glasg 114 C2
Ralston Ct. Glasg 114 C2
Ralston Dr. Glasg 114 C2
Ralston Dr. Hurl 228 B4
Ralston Path. Glasg 114 C2
Ralston Pl. Glasg 114 C2
Ralston Rd. Barr 134 B1
Ralston Rd. Bear 75 F3
Ralston St. Aird 122 C4
Ralston St. Pais 114 A2
Ralstonyards Rd. Hurl 228 C4
Ram St. Glasg 118 C3
Ramage Rd. Car 188 A1
Ramillies Ct. Car 188 A1
Ramoth. Lan 214 B2
Rampart Ave. Glasg 95 D4
Ramsay Ave. John 111 F1
Ramsay Ave. Laur 42 C2
Ramsay Cres. Kilbar 111 D1
Ramsay Ct. Newt M 156 C2
Ramsay Hill. E Kil 160 A2
Ramsay Pl. Coat 121 E3
Ramsay Pl. John 111 F1
Ramsay Pl. Stir 2 A1
Ramsay St. Clyde 73 F2
Ramsey Tullis Ave. Tull 4 B1
Ramsey Tullis Dr. Tull 4 B1
Ramsey Wynd. Hat 142 A4
Ramstane Pl. Irvine 220 B3
Ranald Gdns. Glasg 138 B2
Randolph Ave. Glasg 137 D1
Randolph Cres. Bann 7 E1
Randolph Ct. Stir 7 D3
Randolph Dr. Glasg 136 C1
Randolph Gdns. Den 21 E1
Randolph Gdns. Glasg 136 C1
Randolph La. Glasg 95 F2
Randolph Pl. Bann 7 E1
Randolph Rd. Glasg 95 F2
Randolph Rd. Glasg 96 A2
Randolph Rd. Stir 7 D3
Randolph Terr. Stir 7 D2
Randyford Rd. Falk 42 B3
Randyford St. Falk 42 C3
Ranfurly Ct. B of W 110 B4
Ranfurly Pl. B of W 110 B4
Ranfurly Rd. B of W 110 C3
Ranfurly Rd. Glasg 114 C3
Range Ave. Mother 164 B2
Range Pl. Ham 162 C1
Range Rd. Mother 164 A2
Range St. Mother 164 A2
Rangerhouse Rd. E Kil 180 C3
Ranken Dr. Irvine 219 E2
Rankin Cres. Gree 83 F1
Rankin Ct. Kilmk 223 E2
Rankin Dr. Newt M 156 B3
Rankin Rd. Wish 165 F2
Rankin St. Car 187 F1
Rankin St. Green 45 E2
Rankine Pl. John 111 F2
Rankine St. John 111 F2
Rannoch Ave. Bish 78 A1
Rannoch Ave. Coat 101 E1
Rannoch Ave. Ham 162 A1
Rannoch Ave. Newt M 156 B4
Rannoch Cl. Stew 195 E1
Rannoch Ct. All 10 B3
Rannoch Ct. Cumb 82 A3
Rannoch Ct. Ham 161 F3
Rannoch Dr. Bear 76 A2

282

Salisbury Ave. Hurl Shotts Rd. Sals

Salisbury Ave. Hurl 228 C3
Salisbury Cres. Mother 163 D4
Salisbury. E Kil 160 B2
Salisbury Pl. Clyde 73 E3
Salisbury Pl. Pres 236 B4
Salisbury St. Glasg 117 D2
Salkeld St. Glasg 117 D3
Salmon Dr. Falk 41 F1
Salmon St. Green 45 F3
Salmona St. Glasg 97 D2
Saltaire Ave. Udd 141 D3
Saltcoats Rd. Salt 217 D4
Saltcoats Rd. Steven 217 E4
Salterland Rd. Barr 134 C2
Saltfield La. Ayr 235 F1
Saltire Cres. Lark 185 E1
Saltmarket. Glasg 117 E3
Saltmarket Pl. Glasg 117 E3
Saltoun La. Glasg 96 B2
Saltoun St. Glasg 96 B2
Saltpans Rd. Ayr 235 F2
Salvia St. Glasg 138 C3
Samson Ave. Kilmk 228 A4
Sanda Pl. Kilmk 223 D3
Sanda Pl. Salt 205 F1
Sanda St. Glasg 96 C2
Sandaig Rd. Glasg 119 F3
Sandale Path. Udd 161 E3
Sandalwood Ave. E Kil 159 E2
Sandbank Ave. Glasg 96 B3
Sandbank Cres. Bonh 27 F3
Sandbank Cres. Glasg 96 B3
Sandbank Dr. Glasg 96 B4
Sandbank St. Glasg 96 B4
Sandbank Terr. Glasg 96 B4
Sandbed La. Kilmk 227 F4
Sandbed St. Kilmk 227 F4
Sandend. Ersk 73 D2
Sandend Rd. Glasg 135 D4
Sanderling Pl. John 131 E3
Sanderling Rd. Pais 113 F4
Sanderson Ave. Irvine 219 D1
Sanderson Ave. Tan 141 E3
Sandfield Ave. Miln 55 D2
Sandfield Rd. Pres 236 B4
Sandfield St. Glasg 96 C3
Sandford Gdns. Glasg 120 A3
Sandgate Ave. Glasg 119 E2
Sandgate. Ayr 238 C4
Sandhaven Pl. Glasg 135 D4
Sandhaven Rd. Glasg 135 D4
Sandhill Gdns. Troon 229 F2
Sandholes Rd. Kilbar 111 E3
Sandholes St. Pais 113 E2
Sandholm Pl. Glasg 94 C3
Sandholm Terr. Glasg 94 C3
Sandiefield Rd. Glasg 117 E2
Sandielands Ave. Inch 93 E4
Sandilands Cres. Mother 163 D3
Sandilands St. Glasg 119 E3
Sandilands. Troon 229 E1
Sandmill St. Glasg 98 A1
Sandpiper Dr. E Kil 180 A3
Sandpiper Pl. E Kil 180 A3
Sandpiper Rd. Loch 129 E1
Sandra Rd. Bish 78 B1
Sandray Ave. P Glasg 69 D4
Sandringham Ave. Newt M 157 D3
Sandringham Ct. Newt M 157 D3
Sandringham Dr. John 112 A1
Sandringham La. Glasg 96 B2
Sandringham Terr. Green 45 F4
Sandwood Cres. Glasg 115 D3
Sandwood Rd. Glasg 115 D3
Sandy Ct. W Kil 190 B2
Sandy Rd. Car 187 F1
Sandy Rd. Glasg 96 A1
Sandy Rd. Irvine 219 D3
Sandy Rd. Ren 94 B1
Sandy Rd. W Kil 190 B2
Sandyfaulds Sq. Glasg 117 E2
Sandyfaulds St. Glasg 117 E2
Sandyford Ave. Holy 143 E4
Sandyford Pl. Glasg 116 C4
Sandyford Pl. Holy 143 E4
Sandyford Place La. Glasg 116 C4
Sandyford Rd. Holy 143 E4
Sandyford Rd. Pres 234 A1
Sandyford Rd. Ren 114 A4
Sandyford St. Glasg 116 B4
Sandyhill Ave. Shot 147 D2
Sandyhill Terr. Coy 239 F3
Sandyhills Cres. Glasg 119 D2
Sandyhills Dr. Glasg 119 D2
Sandyhills Gr. Glasg 119 D1
Sandyhills Pl. Glasg 119 D2
Sandyhills Rd. Glasg 119 E2
Sandyknowes Rd. Cumb 83 D4
Sandylands Cres. Mother 163 E3
Sandylands Prom. Salt 217 D4
Sandyvale Pl. Shot 147 D2
Sannox Dr. Mother 163 D4
Sannox Dr. Salt 206 A1
Sannox Gdns. Glasg 118 A4
Sannox Pl. Ayr 236 B1
Sannox Pl. Helen 16 C2
Sannox Rd. Kilmk 222 B1
Sannox View. Ayr 236 C1
Sanquhar Ave. Pres 236 B4
Sanquhar Gdns. Udd 140 A1
Sapphire Rd. Hat 142 A2
Saracen Head Rd. Glasg 117 F3
Saracen St. Glasg 97 E2
Sardinia La. Glasg 96 B2
Sark Dr. Troon 229 F3
Saskatoon Pl. E Kil 159 D1
Saucel Hill Terr. Pais 113 F2
Saucel St. Pais 113 F2
Sauchie Ct. Bann 7 F1
Sauchiehall La. Glasg 117 D4
Sauchiehall St. Glasg 117 D4
Sauchiesmoor Rd. Car 202 A4
Saugh Ave. Uplaw 173 E4
Saughs Ave. Glasg 98 C3
Saughs Dr. Glasg 98 C3
Saughs Gate. Glasg 98 C3
Saughs Pl. Glasg 98 C3
Saughs Rd. Glasg 98 C3
Saughs Rd. Glasg 99 D3
Saughs Rd. Stepps 99 D3
Saughton St. Glasg 118 C4
Saughtree Ave. Salt 205 F1
Saunders Ct. Barr 134 A2
Saunterne Rd. Pres 233 E1
Savoy Ct. Ayr 238 C4
Savoy Pk. Ayr 238 C4
Savoy St. Glasg 117 F2
Sawers Ave. Den 21 E1
Sawmill Rd. Glasg 95 F1
Sawmillfield St. Glasg 97 D1
Saxon Rd. Glasg 95 E4
Scadlock Rd. Pais 113 D3
Scalpay. E Kil 160 B1
Scalpay Pl. Glasg 97 E4
Scalpay Pl. Kilmk 223 D3
Scalpay St. Glasg 97 E4
Scamadale Rd. Gree 84 B2
Scapa St. Glasg 96 C4
Scaraway Dr. Glasg 97 E4
Scaraway Pl. Glasg 97 E4
Scaraway St. Glasg 97 E4
Scaraway Terr. Glasg 97 E4
Scarba Dr. Glasg 136 A3
Scarba Quadrant. Wish 164 C1
Scarffe Ave. Lin 111 F3
Scargie Rd. Kilmk 227 F2
Scarhill Ave. Aird 122 C3
Scarhill La. Aird 123 D3
Scarhill St. Cle 144 A1
Scarhill St. Coat 121 F2
Scarletmuir. Lan 214 C3
Scarlow St. P Glasg 47 E1
Scarrel Dr. Glasg 138 A2
Scarrel Rd. Glasg 138 A2
Scarrel Terr. Glasg 138 A2
Scaur O' Doon Rd. Ayr 238 B2
Schaw Ct. Bear 75 F3
Schaw Ct. N Sau 5 E1
Schaw Dr. Bear 75 F3
Schaw Dr. Dunt 74 C4
Schaw Rd. Pais 114 A3
Schawpark Ave. N Sau 5 E1
Schiltron Way. Bann 7 E2
Scholar's Gate. E Kil 180 B3
School Ave. Glasg 139 D3
School La. Alla 167 D4
School La. Car 187 F1
School La. Dumb 49 E2
School La. Irvine 219 E1
School La. Lennox 57 E4
School La. M of C 58 B3
School La. Men 4 A4
School Quadrant. Aird 102 C1
School Rd. Glasg 114 C3
School Rd. Kilb 149 D1
School Rd. Lennox 57 E1
School Rd. New 166 A2
School Rd. Newt M 156 B2
School Rd. Rhu 15 E3
School Rd. Sals 125 E2
School Rd. Stepps 99 F3
School Rd. Tull 4 A1
School St. Chap 123 E1
School St. Coat 122 A2
School St. Ham 162 B1
School St. Shot 146 C2
School Wlk. Sten 23 E2
School Wynd. Kilb 149 D1
School Wynd. Pais 113 F3
Schoolhouse La. Udd 161 E3
Schoolwell St. Steven 206 B1
Scioncroft Ave. Glasg 138 B4
Sclandersburn Rd. Den 39 E4
Scone Pl. E Kil 159 E2
Scone St. Glasg 97 E2
Sconser St. Glasg 76 C1
Scorton Gdns. Glasg 119 F2
Scotia Cres. Lark 185 D1
Scotia Gdns. Ham 183 E4
Scotia Pl. Falk 42 B3
Scotia St. Mother 163 E4
Scotland St. Glasg 116 C3
Scotland St W. Glasg 116 C3
Scotsblair Ave. Klrk 79 E4
Scotsburn Rd. Glasg 98 B2
Scotstoun Rd. Cowie 12 C4
Scotstoun St. Glasg 95 E2
Scott Ave. John 131 F4
Scott Ave. M of C 58 B3
Scott Ave. O Kill 72 B4
Scott Cres. All 10 A3
Scott Cres. Cumb 82 B4
Scott Cres. Kilmk 227 F4
Scott Cres. Troon 229 F2
Scott Ct. Helen 16 B1
Scott Dr. Bear 75 E3
Scott Dr. Cumb 82 B4
Scott Gr. Ham 162 B1
Scott Hill. E Kil 160 A2
Scott House. Cumb 62 A2
Scott Pl. Hat 142 A4
Scott Pl. Salt 205 F1
Scott Pl. Troon 229 E3
Scott Rd. Glasg 114 C4
Scott Rd. Irvine 219 E1
Scott Rd. Kilmk 227 F4
Scott St. Bonh 27 F2
Scott St. Clyde 73 F2
Scott St. Glasg 97 D1
Scott St. Glasg 120 A2
Scott St. Green 46 A2
Scott St. Ham 162 B1
Scott St. Lark 185 D1
Scott St. Mother 163 F4
Scott St. Stir 2 A1
Scott's Pl. Aird 123 D4
Scott's Rd. Pais 114 B2
Seabank Rd. Ayr 235 F1
Seabank St. Salt 217 D4
Seabegs Cres. Bon 40 A2
Seabegs Pl. Bon 39 F2
Seabegs Rd. Bon 39 F2
Seafar Rd. Cumb 61 F1
Seafield Ave. Bear 75 F4
Seafield Cottage La. Green 45 E4
Seafield Cres. Ayr 238 C3
Seafield Cres. Cumb 60 C1
Seafield Ct. Ard 205 D2
Seafield Ct. Falk 41 F1
Seafield Dr. Ard 205 E2
Seafield Dr. Ayr 238 B3
Seafield Dr. Glasg 138 B2
Seafield Rd. Ayr 238 C3
Seaford St. Kilmk 227 F4
Seaforth Cres. Ayr 236 A2
Seaforth Cres. Barr 134 A2
Seaforth La. Muir 81 D1
Seaforth Pl. Hat 141 F2
Seaforth Pl. Stir 7 D4
Seaforth Rd. Ayr 236 A2
Seaforth Rd. Clyde 74 A1
Seaforth Rd. Falk 24 B1
Seaforth Rd. Glasg 115 D4
Seaforth Rd N. Glasg 115 D4
Seaforth Rd S. Glasg 115 D4
Seagate. Irvine 219 D2
Seagate. Pres 233 E1
Seagrove St. Glasg 118 B3
Seamill Path. Glasg 134 C3
Seamill St. Glasg 134 C3
Seamore St. Glasg 97 D1
Seath Ave. Aird 122 C4
Seath Ave. Lang 70 B3
Seath Rd. Glasg 118 A1
Seath St. Glasg 117 E1
Seaton Pl. Falk 42 B2
Seaton Terr. Ham 162 A2
Seaton Terr. Irvine 219 E3
Seaview Rd. Salt 216 C4
Seaview Terr. Troon 230 A2
Seaward La. Glasg 116 C3
Seaward St. Glasg 116 C3
Second Ave. Bear 76 A2
Second Ave. Bonh 27 F3
Second Ave. Clyde 74 A2
Second Ave. Dumb 50 B1
Second Ave. Glasg 137 D3
Second Ave. Irvine 224 B4
Second Ave. Ren 94 B1
Second Ave. Stepps 79 E1
Second Ave. Stepps 99 D2
Second Ave. Tan 120 C1
Second Gdns. Glasg 116 A2
Second Rd. Ham 161 F3
Second St. Tan 140 C4
Seedhill. Pais 113 F2
Seedhill Rd. Pais 114 A2
Seggielea La. Glasg 95 E3
Seggielea Rd. Glasg 95 E3
Segton Ave. Kilw 207 E2
Seil Dr. Glasg 137 E2
Selborne Pl. Glasg 95 F3
Selborne Place La. Glasg 95 F3
Selborne Rd. Glasg 95 F3
Selby Gdns. Glasg 119 E3
Selby Pl. Coat 101 E1
Selby St. Coat 101 E1
Selkirk Ave. Glasg 115 E2
Selkirk Ave. Pais 133 D4
Selkirk Dr. Glasg 138 B4
Selkirk Pl. E Kil 160 B2
Selkirk Pl. Ham 162 C1
Selkirk Rd. P Glasg 68 B4
Selkirk St. Ham 162 B1
Selkirk St. Udd 161 E4
Selkirk St. Wish 165 E3
Selkirk Way. Coat 122 C2
Selkirk Way. Hat 142 A4
Sella Rd. Bish 78 B1
Selvieland Rd. Glasg 114 C3
Semphill Gdns. E Kil 160 A1
Sempie St. Ham 161 F2
Sempill Ave. Ersk 72 C1
Semple Ave. Bishop 72 A2
Semple Ave. Loch 129 E2
Semple Pl. Lin 112 A4
Semple Rd. Pres 236 B3
Semple View. How 130 C3
Senga Cres. Hat 142 A4
Seres Rd. Newt M 157 E4
Sergeant Law Rd. Pais 132 C2
Sergeant Law Rd. Uplaw 132 D3
Sergeant Law Rd. Uplaw 153 D4
Seright Cres. Hurl 228 B4
Seright Sq. Hurl 228 B4
Serpentine Wlk. Green 46 B2
Sersley Dr. Kilb 148 C1
Service St. Lennox 33 E1
Seton Dr. Stir 7 E2
Seton La. Ard 205 E1
Seton St. Ard 205 E1
Seton Terr. Glasg 117 F4
Settle Gdns. Glasg 119 F2
Seven Sisters. Klrk 79 F3
Seventh Ave. Tan 140 C4
Seventh Rd. Ham 161 F3
Severn Rd. E Kil 179 F4
Seymour Ave. Kilw 207 F1
Seymour Gn. E Kil 180 A4
Seyton Ave. Glasg 136 B1
Seyton La. E Kil 159 F2
Shaftesbury St. All 10 A4
Shaftesbury St. Glasg 116 C4
Shafton Pl. Glasg 95 F4
Shafton Rd. Glasg 95 F4
Shaftsbury Ave. Clyde 73 F1
Shaftsbury Cres. Holy 143 E2
Shakespeare Ave. Clyde 73 F2
Shakespeare St. Glasg 96 C3
Shalloch Pk. Ayr 238 B1
Shalloch Pl. Irvine 220 A1
Shamrock St. Glasg 97 D1
Shamrock St. Klrk 79 E4
Shand La. Car 187 F2
Shand St. Wish 165 E1
Shandon Brae. Bonh 27 F4
Shandon Cres. Bonh 27 F4
Shandon Cres. Hat 142 A4
Shandon Pl. Green 46 B1
Shandon Terr. Ham 161 F2
Shandwick St. Glasg 120 A4
Shankland La. Green 46 C1
Shankland Rd. Green 46 C1
Shanks Ave. Barr 134 B1
Shanks Ave. Den 39 F4
Shanks Cres. John 111 F1
Shanks Ct. Kilmk 222 C1
Shanks St. Aird 103 D1
Shanks St. Glasg 96 C3
Shannon Dr. Falk 41 F2
Shannon St. Glasg 96 C3
Shanter Pl. Kilmk 228 B4
Shanter Way. Ayr 238 C1
Shapinsay St. Glasg 97 E4
Sharon St. Dalry 191 D4
Sharp Ave. Coat 121 E2
Sharp St. Gour 44 C4
Sharp St. Mother 163 D4
Sharpe Ave. Irvine 220 B1
Sharphill Ind Est. Salt 206 A2
Shavian Terr. Kilw 207 F1
Shavin Brae. Ayr 239 E3
Shaw Ave. Bishop 72 B2
Shaw Ct. Ersk 72 C2
Shaw Pl. Dalry 191 D4
Shaw Pl. Green 45 F3
Shaw Pl. Lin 112 A3
Shaw Pl. Salt 206 A1
Shaw Rd. Miln 76 A4
Shaw Rd. Newt M 156 C2
Shaw Rd. Pres 233 F1
Shaw St. Glasg 116 A4
Shaw St. Lark 199 D4
Shawbank Pl. Kilmk 228 A4
Shawbridge St. Glasg 136 B4
Shawburn Cres. Ham 162 A2
Shawburn St. Ham 162 A2
Shawfarm Ct. Pres 233 E1
Shawfield Ave. Ayr 239 D2
Shawfield Cres. Law 186 C3
Shawfield Dr. Glasg 117 F1
Shawfield Rd. Glasg 117 F2
Shawhead Ave. Coat 122 A2
Shawhead Cotts. Coat 122 A2
Shawhill Cres. Newt M 156 C2
Shawhill Rd. Glasg 136 B4
Shawholm Cres. Glasg 136 A4
Shawlands Cross. Glasg 116 C1
Shawlands Sq. Glasg 136 C4
Shawmoss Rd. Glasg 116 B1
Shawpark St. Glasg 96 C3
Shawrigg Rd. Lark 185 E1
Shaws Rd. Lark 199 E4
Shawstonfoot Rd. Cle 145 D1
Shawwood Cres. Newt M 156 C2
Shearer Dr. Ham 183 E4
Shearer Quadrant. Bonh 28 A4
Sheddens Pl. Glasg 118 C3
Sheena Dr. Bonh 27 F1
Sheepburn Rd. Udd 140 C4
Sheila St. Glasg 98 C2
Sheildhill. E Kil 180 C4
Sheiling Hill. Ham 162 C2
Sheldaig Rd. Glasg 97 D4
Sheldrake Pl. John 131 E3
Shellbridge Way. Ard 205 E1
Shelley Ct. Glasg 96 A3
Shelley Dr. Clyde 74 A2
Shelley Dr. Udd 141 D1
Shelley Rd. Glasg 96 A3
Shells Rd. Kirk 58 C1
Sherbrooke Ave. Glasg 116 B2
Sherbrooke Dr. Glasg 116 B2
Sherbrooke Pl. E Kil 159 E1
Sherburn Gdns. Glasg 119 F2
Sherdale Ave. Chap 123 E1
Sheriff Park Ave. Glasg 138 A4
Sheriffmuir Rd. B of A 2 B4
Sheriffmuirlands. Stir 2 B2
Sherriff La. Sten 23 F2
Sherry Dr. Ham 162 A1
Sherwood Ave. Pais 114 A3
Sherwood Ave. Udd 141 D3
Sherwood Dr. Glasg 136 A2
Sherwood Pl. Glasg 75 D2
Sherwood Rd. Hurl 228 C3
Sherwood Rd. Pres 236 C4
Shetland Ct. All 10 A3
Shetland Dr. Glasg 137 E2
Shettleston Rd. Glasg 119 D3
Shettleston
Sheddings. Glasg 118 C3
Shewalton Dr. Shew 225 E3
Shewalton Rd. Shew 224 B3
Shewalton Rd. Shew 225 D3
Shiel Ave. E Kil 159 F2
Shiel Ct. Barr 134 A3
Shiel Gdns. Falk 24 B1
Shiel Gdns. Shot 147 D2
Shiel Hill. Ayr 239 D1
Shiel Pl. Aird 122 B3
Shiel Pl. E Kil 159 F2
Shiel Pl. Irvine 219 E3
Shiel Rd. Bish 78 A1
Shiel Terr. New 165 F3
Shielbridge Gdns. Glasg 76 C1
Shieldaig Dr. Glasg 138 A2
Shieldburn Rd. Glasg 115 E4
Shieldhall Gdns. Glasg 115 E4
Shieldhall Rd. Glasg 115 E4
Shieldhill Rd. Car 201 F4
Shieldmuir St. Mother 164 B2
Shields Dr. Mother 164 A2
Shields Loan. Lan 214 C3
Shields Rd. Auld 180 A2
Shields Rd. Glasg 116 C2
Shields Rd. Mother 164 A2
Shielhope Ct. Irvine 220 A2
Shieling Pk. Ayr 238 C4
Shilford Ave. Glasg 95 D4
Shilford Rd. Uplaw 132 B1
Shillay St. Bish 97 F4
Shilliaw Dr. Pres 236 B3
Shilliaw Pl. Pres 236 B3
Shillinghill. All 10 A3
Shillingworth Pl. B of W 110 B3
Shilton Dr. Glasg 135 E3
Shilton La. Ersk 72 C2
Shinwell Ave. Clyde 74 B1
Shipbank La. Glasg 117 E3
Shiphaugh Pl. Stir 2 B1
Shira Terr. E Kil 160 A1
Shire Way. All 9 F3
Shirley Quadrant. Mother 163 E2
Shirley's Cl. Lan 215 D2
Shirra's Brae Rd. Stir 7 E2
Shirrel Ave. Hat 142 A4
Shirrel Rd. Holy 143 D2
Shirva Lea. Twe 59 F2
Shiskine Dr. Glasg 96 B4
Shiskine Dr. Kilmk 222 C2
Shiskine Pl. Glasg 96 B4
Shiskine Pl. Helen 16 C1
Shiskine St. Glasg 96 B4
Sholto Cres. Tan 141 E4
Shore Rd. Air 14 B2
Shore Rd. Steven 217 E4
Shore Rd. Stir 7 D4
Shore Rd. Troon 229 D1
Shore St. Glasg 118 A1
Shore St. Gour 44 C4
Shore St. P Glasg 47 D1
Shore The. All 10 A3
Shortlees Cres. Kilmk 227 F2
Shortlees Rd. Kilmk 227 F1
Shortridge St. Glasg 96 C3
Shortroods Ave. Pais 113 F4
Shortroods Cres. Pais 113 F4
Shortroods Rd. Pais 113 E4
Shotts Rd. Sals 126 C1

Thornton Ave. Bon

287
Valeview Terr. Glasg
Wellhall Ct. Ham

Valeview Terr. Glasg 137 D4
Vallantine Cres. Tan 141 D4
Vallay St. Glasg 97 E4
Valley Ct. Ham 162 B1
Valley View. Glasg 139 E3
Valleybank. Kils 37 E2
Valleyfield Dr. Cumb 60 C1
Valleyfield. E Kil 159 E1
Valleyfield. M of C 58 A3
Valleyfield Pl. Stir 7 E3
Valleyfield St. Glasg 97 F2
Valleyview Dr. Falk 42 A4
Vancouver Ct. E Kil 159 D1
Vancouver Dr. E Kil 159 D1
Vancouver La. Glasg 95 E2
Vancouver Pl. Clyde 73 E2
Vancouver Rd. Glasg 95 E2
Vanguard St. Clyde 74 B1
Vanguard Way. Ren 94 B1
Vardar Ave. Newt M 157 E4
Varna La. Glasg 95 F2
Varna Rd. Glasg 95 F2
Varnsdorf Way. Aird 123 F3
Vasart Pl. Glasg 96 C2
Vaults La. Kilw 207 F2
Veir Terr. Dumb 49 F2
Veitch Pl. Lennox 57 E4
Veitches Ct. Dunt 74 A3
Vennachar St. Shot 146 C3
Vennacher Rd. Ren 94 A2
Vennal St. Dalry 191 D4
Vennard Gdns. Glasg 116 C1
Vennel La. Stew 211 F4
Vennel St. Stew 211 F4
Vennel The. Den 21 F1
Vermont Ave. Glasg 138 A4
Vermont St. Glasg 116 C3
Vernon Bank. E Kil 159 F2
Vernon Dr. Lin 112 A3
Vernon Pl. Dund 225 F1
Vernon St. Salt 216 C4
Verona Ave. Glasg 95 E2
Verona La. Glasg 95 E2
Vesalius St. Glasg 119 D3
Viaduct Circ. Kilw 207 F3
Viaduct Rd. Newt M 157 F4
Vicar St. Falk 42 A3
Vicarfield St. Glasg 116 A4
Vicarland Pl. Glasg 139 D2
Vicarland Rd. Glasg 139 D3
Vicars Rd. Stone 198 C1
Vicars Wlk. Glasg 139 D3
Vickers St. Mother 163 D4
Victor St. Plains 104 A1
Victoria Ave. Car 187 F1
Victoria Cir. Glasg 96 B2
Victoria Cres. Aird 122 C3
Victoria Cres. Irvine 219 E1
Victoria Cres. Kils 60 A4
Victoria Cres. Mother 164 B2
Victoria Cres. Newt M 157 F4
Victoria Crescent La. Glasg 96 B2
Victoria Crescent Pl. Glasg 96 B2
Victoria Crescent Rd. Glasg 96 B2
Victoria Cross. Glasg 117 D1
Victoria Dr E. Ren 94 B1
Victoria Dr. Troon 229 E1
Victoria Dr W. Ren 94 A2
Victoria Gdns. Aird 122 C4
Victoria Gdns. Barr 134 A2
Victoria Gdns. Kil 69 E1
Victoria Gdns. Pais 113 E1
Victoria Park Cnr. Glasg 95 E2
Victoria Park Dr N. Glasg 95 F2
Victoria Park Dr S. Glasg 95 F2
Victoria Park Gdns N. Glasg 95 F2
Victoria Park Gdns S. Glasg 95 F2
Victoria Park La N. Glasg 95 E2
Victoria Park La S. Glasg 95 E2
Victoria Park St. Glasg 95 E2
Victoria Pk. Ayr 238 C3
Victoria Pk. Kils 60 A4
Victoria Pl. Aird 122 C3
Victoria Pl. Glasg 138 A4
Victoria Pl. Hat 141 F2
Victoria Pl. Kils 60 B4
Victoria Pl. Miln 55 D1
Victoria Pl. Stir 7 D4
Victoria Quadrant. Holy 142 C3
Victoria Rd. Barr 134 A2
Victoria Rd. Cumb 61 E3
Victoria Rd. East 127 F3
Victoria Rd. Falk 42 B3
Victoria Rd. Glasg 117 D2
Victoria Rd. Glasg 138 A3
Victoria Rd. Gour 44 B4
Victoria Rd. Helen 16 C1
Victoria Rd. Kilbar 111 E3
Victoria Rd. Klrk 79 E2
Victoria Rd. Lar 23 D1
Victoria Rd. Pais 113 E1
Victoria Rd. Salt 217 D4
Victoria Rd. Stepps 99 E3
Victoria Rd. Stir 7 D4
Victoria Roundabout. Irvine 219 D1
Victoria Sq. Stir 7 D4
Victoria St. Alex 27 F2
Victoria St. All 10 A4
Victoria St. Ayr 236 A1
Victoria St. Dumb 50 A2
Victoria St. East 127 F3
Victoria St. Glasg 138 A4
Victoria St. Ham 162 A3
Victoria St. Klrk 79 E4
Victoria St. Lark 185 D2
Victoria St. New 166 A2
Victoria St. Udd 161 E4
Victoria Terr. Cumb 61 E3
Victoria Terr. Men 4 A4
Victoria Way. Stew 195 F1
Victory Dr. Kilbar 111 D2
Victory Way. Glasg 120 A2
Viewbank Ave. Calder 123 D1
Viewbank. Glasg 136 A2
Viewbank St. Glen 101 F3
Viewfield. Aird 122 C4
Viewfield Ave. Bish 97 F4
Viewfield Ave. Glasg 119 F3
Viewfield Ave. Klrk 79 E3
Viewfield Ave. Loch 129 D1
Viewfield Ave. M of C 58 A3
Viewfield Ave. Udd 140 C1
Viewfield Dr. Alva 4 C3
Viewfield Dr. Bish 97 F4
Viewfield Dr. Glasg 119 F3
Viewfield La. Glasg 96 C1
Viewfield Rd. Ayr 236 A1
Viewfield Rd. Bank 38 B2
Viewfield Rd. Bish 97 F4
Viewfield Rd. Coat 121 E2
Viewfield Rd. Hat 141 F2
Viewfield St. East 127 F3
Viewfield St. Stir 7 D4
Viewmount Dr. Glasg 96 B4
Viewpark Ave. Glasg 118 A4
Viewpark Ct. Glasg 138 B3
Viewpark Dr. Glasg 138 A3
Viewpark. Miln 55 D1
Viewpark Pl. Mother 163 E3
Viewpark Rd. Mother 163 E3
Viewpark
Shopping Ctr. Tan 141 E3
Viewpoint Pl. Glasg 97 F3
Viewpoint Rd. Glasg 97 F3
Viking Cres. Hous 111 E4
Viking Rd. Aird 123 D3
Viking Terr. E Kil 180 C3
Viking Way. Ren 94 B1
Villa Bank. Den 21 F1
Villafield Ave. Bish 78 A2
Villafield Dr. Bish 78 A2
Villafield Loan. Bish 78 A2
Village Gdns. Udd 140 C1
Village Rd. Glasg 139 F2
Vine Park Ave. Kilm 222 A4
Vine Park Dr. Kilm 222 A4
Vine St. Glasg 96 A1
Vineburgh Ave. Irvine 219 E2
Vineburgh Ct. Irvine 219 D2
Vinicombe La. Glasg 96 B2
Vinicombe St. Glasg 96 B2
Vintner St. Glasg 97 E1
Viola Pl. Lennox 78 B4
Violet Gdns. Car 201 F4
Violet Pl. Holy 143 D3
Violet St. Pais 114 A2
Virginia Ct. Glasg 117 E4
Virginia Gdns. Ayr 236 A1
Virginia Gdns. Miln 76 B4
Virginia Pl. Glasg 117 E4
Virginia St. Glasg 117 E4
Virginia St. Green 46 A2
Viscount Ave. Ren 94 B1
Vivian Ave. Miln 54 C1
Voil Dr. Glasg 137 D2
Voil Rd. Stir 2 A2
Vorlich Ct. Barr 134 B1
Vorlich Dr. Shi 66 C4
Vorlich Gdns. Bear 75 E4
Vorlich Pl. Kilmk 228 A2
Vorlich Pl. Stir 2 A2
Vorlich Wynd. Holy 143 E2
Vrackie Pl. Kilmk 228 A2
Vulcan St. Glasg 97 F2
Vulcan St. Mother 163 F4

W Lodge Gdns. All 9 F4
Waddell Ave. Glenm 102 B2
Waddell Ct. Glasg 117 E3
Waddell Ct. Kilmk 222 C2
Waddell St. Aird 103 D1
Waddell St. Glasg 117 E2
Waddell St. Sten 24 B1
Waggon Rd. Ayr 235 F1
Waggon Rd. Falk 42 A4
Waid Ave. Newt M 156 B3
Waldemar Rd. Glasg 95 E4
Walden Rd. Hurl 228 C3
Waldo St. Glasg 95 F4
Walk The. All 10 A3
Walker Ave. Kilmk 228 A4
Walker Ave. Troon 229 E3
Walker Ct. Glasg 96 A1
Walker Dr. John 112 B1
Walker Path. Tan 141 D4
Walker Rd. Ayr 236 A1
Walker St. Glasg 96 A1
Walker St. Green 45 E3
Walker St. Kilb 149 D1
Walker St. Pais 113 E2
Walkerburn Dr. Wish 165 E3
Walkerburn Rd. Glasg 115 D2
Walkinshaw Cres. Pais 113 D3
Walkinshaw Rd. Inch 93 E2
Walkinshaw St. Glasg 118 A2
Walkinshaw St. John 112 A2
Wall Gdns. Falk 41 E3
Wall St. Falk 41 E3
Wallace Ave. Bishop 72 A2
Wallace Ave. Dund 225 F1
Wallace Ave. John 112 B1
Wallace Ave. Steven 206 B1
Wallace Ave. Troon 229 E3
Wallace Cres. Den 21 E1
Wallace Cres. Plea 12 B2
Wallace Ct. Pres 236 B4
Wallace Ct. Stir 2 A1
Wallace Dr. Lark 185 E1
Wallace Gdns. Lennox 57 D1
Wallace Gdns. Stir 2 B2
Wallace Pl. Cam 6 B3
Wallace Pl. Falk 42 B3
Wallace Pl. Fall 8 B2
Wallace Pl. Green 45 F3
Wallace Pl. Ham 163 D1
Wallace Pl. Udd 140 C1
Wallace Rd. Holy 143 D1
Wallace Rd. Irvine 219 E2
Wallace Rd. Ren 94 A1
Wallace St. All 10 B4
Wallace St. Bann 7 F1
Wallace St. Clyde 74 A1
Wallace St. Coat 122 A3
Wallace St. Dumb 50 A2
Wallace St. Falk 42 B3
Wallace St. Glasg 117 D3
Wallace St. Glasg 138 A4
Wallace St. Green 45 E2
Wallace St. Kilmk 227 F4
Wallace St. Mother 163 E4
Wallace St. P Glasg 47 F1
Wallace St. Pais 113 F3
Wallace St. Plains 104 A1
Wallace St. Stir 2 A1
Wallace View. Kilmk 227 F3
Wallace View. Shi 66 B4
Wallace View. Tull 4 B2
Wallace Way. Lan 215 E2
Wallacefield Rd. Troon 229 E2
Wallacehill Rd. Kilmk 227 F2
Wallacewell Cres. Glasg 98 A3
Wallacewell Pl. Glasg 98 A3
Wallacewell
Quadrant. Glasg 98 B3
Wallacewell Rd. Glasg 98 B3
Wallbrae Rd. Cumb 83 D4
Wallneuk Rd. Pais 113 F3
Walls St. Glasg 117 E4
Wallstale Rd. Stir 7 D2
Walmer Cres. Glasg 116 B3
Walnut Cres. Glasg 97 E3
Walnut Cres. John 112 A1
Walnut Ct. M of C 58 A3
Walnut Dr. Klrk 79 D3
Walnut Pl. Glasg 97 E3
Walnut Pl. Tan 121 E1
Walnut Rd. Glasg 97 E3
Walnut Rd. Kilmk 227 E4
Walpole Pl. John 131 E4
Walter St. Glasg 118 B4
Walter St. Wish 165 E2
Walton Ave. Newt M 156 B3
Walton St. Barr 134 B2
Walton St. Glasg 136 C4
Wamba Ave. Glasg 95 F4
Wamphray Pl. E Kil 179 E4
Wandilla Ave. Clyde 74 B1
Ward St. All 10 A3
Warden Rd. Glasg 95 E4
Wardend Rd. Lennox 57 D1
Wardhill Rd. Glasg 98 A3
Wardhouse Rd. Pais 133 E4
Wardie Pl. Glasg 119 F4
Wardie Rd. Glasg 120 A4
Wardlaw Ave. Glasg 138 A4
Wardlaw Cres. E Kil 181 D4
Wardlaw Dr. Glasg 138 A4
Wardlaw Rd. Bear 75 F1
Wardlaw Rd. Fen 223 F3
Wardneuk Dr. Kilmk 223 D2
Wardneuk. Pres 236 B3
Wardpark Ct. Cumb 62 B3
Wardpark Pl. Cumb 62 B3
Wardpark Rd. Cumb 62 B3
Wardrop Pl. E Kil 159 F2
Wardrop St. Beith 171 E4
Wardrop St. Glasg 116 A4
Wardrop St. Pais 113 F2
Wardrop Terr. Beith 171 E4
Wards Cres. Coat 121 F3
Wards Pl. Kilmk 227 F4
Ware Rd. Glasg 120 A4
Warilda Ave. Clyde 74 B1
Warlock Dr. B of W 90 B1
Warlock Rd. Hous 90 B2
Warly Dr. Dund 225 F1
Warly Pl. Dund 225 F1
Warner St. Steven 217 E4
Warnock Cres. Hat 142 A2
Warnock Rd. Newt M 156 B4
Warnock St. Glasg 117 F4
Warren Rd. Ham 183 E4
Warren St. Glasg 117 D1
Warren Wlk. Lennox 57 F4
Warriston Cres. Glasg 118 C4
Warriston Pl. Glasg 119 D4
Warriston St. Glasg 118 C4
Warriston Way. Glasg 138 B2
Warrix Ave. Irvine 219 E1
Warrix Gdns. Troon 232 C4
Warrix Interchange. Irvine 219 F1
Warroch St. Glasg 116 C4
Warwick. E Kil 160 B2
Warwick Gr. Ham 161 F3
Warwick Hill. Irvine 220 A3
Warwick Rd. Gour 44 C2
Warwickhill Rd. Kilmk 222 B1
Washington Rd. Klrk 79 D4
Washington Rd. Pais 113 F4
Washington St. Glasg 117 D4
Watchmeal Cres. Dunt 74 B4
Water La. Kilmk 227 F4
Water Rd. Barr 134 B2
Water Row. Glasg 116 A4
Water St. P Glasg 47 E1
Waterbank Rd. E Kil 158 B3
Watercut Rd. Irvine 218 C4
Watercut Rd. Kilw 219 D4
Waterfoot Ave. Glasg 135 E4
Waterfoot Rd. Newt M 157 D2
Waterfoot Row. Newt M 157 E2
Waterfoot Terr. Glasg 135 E4
Waterford Rd. Glasg 136 A2
Waterlands Gdns. Car 188 A2
Waterlands Pl. Law 187 D2
Waterloo Dr. Lan 215 D3
Waterloo Gdns. Kirk 58 B1
Waterloo La. Glasg 117 D4
Waterloo Rd. Lan 215 D3
Waterloo Rd. Pres 236 A3
Waterloo St. Glasg 117 D4
Watermill Ave. Klrk 79 E2
Watersaugh Dr. Cle 144 A1
Watersedge Ct. Rhu 15 E2
Waterside Ave. Newt M 156 B2
Waterside Ct. Kilmk 227 F4
Waterside Dr. Newt M 156 B2
Waterside Gdns. E Kil 158 B4
Waterside Gdns. Ham 162 C1
Waterside. Irvine 219 D2
Waterside Rd. E Kil 158 B4
Waterside Rd. Kilw 207 F2
Waterside Rd. Klrk 79 F4
Waterside Rd. Thorn 158 B3
Waterside St. Glasg 117 E2
Waterside St. Kilmk 227 F4
Waterslap. Fen 213 D1
Waterston Way. Loch 129 E2
Wateryetts Dr. Kil 69 E1
Watling Ave. Falk 41 E3
Watling Dr. Falk 41 E3
Watling Gdns. Falk 41 E3
Watling Pl. E Kil 159 D1
Watling St. Falk 41 E3
Watling St. Mother 142 B1
Watling St. Tan 140 C4
Watson Ave. Glasg 138 A4
Watson Ave. Lin 112 A3
Watson Ave. Stone 199 D2
Watson Cres. Kils 60 C4
Watson Pl. Bank 39 E2
Watson Pl. Udd 161 D4
Watson St. Falk 42 A3
Watson St. Glasg 117 E3
Watson St. Kilmk 228 A4
Watson St. Lark 184 C2
Watson St. Mother 163 F3
Watson St. Udd 140 C3
Watson St. Udd 161 E4
Watson Terr. Irvine 219 E1
Watsonville Pk. Mother 163 F3
Watstone Rd. Stone 199 D1
Watt Cres. Hat 142 A4
Watt Ct. Dalry 191 E4
Watt Gdns. Falk 41 F3
Watt La. B of W 110 C4
Watt Low Ave. Glasg 137 F3
Watt Pl. Green 46 A3
Watt Pl. Miln 54 C2
Watt Rd. B of W 110 B4
Watt Rd. Glasg 115 D4
Watt St. Aird 103 E1
Watt St. Glasg 116 C3
Watt St. Green 45 F3
Wattfield Rd. Ayr 238 C3
Waukglen Ave. Glasg 135 D1
Waukglen Cres. Glasg 135 E2
Waukglen Dr. Glasg 135 D2
Waukglen Path. Glasg 135 D2
Waukglen Pl. Glasg 135 D2
Waukglen Rd. Glasg 135 D2
Waulking Mill Rd. Dunt 74 B4
Waulkmill Ave. Barr 134 B2
Waulkmill Pl. Kilmk 228 A4
Waulkmill St. Glasg 135 F2
Waverley Ave. Helen 25 D4
Waverley Ave. Kilmk 222 B1
Waverley Cres. Bon 40 A2
Waverley Cres. Cumb 82 B4
Waverley Cres. Ham 161 F2
Waverley Cres. Klrk 79 E4
Waverley Cres. Lan 215 E2
Waverley Cres. Stir 2 B1
Waverley Ct. Helen 16 B1
Waverley Ct. Udd 141 D1
Waverley Dr. Aird 103 D1
Waverley Dr. Glasg 138 B4
Waverley Dr. Wish 165 D2
Waverley. E Kil 160 B2
Waverley Gdns. Glasg 116 C1
Waverley Gdns. John 112 B1
Waverley Pl. Salt 205 F1
Waverley Rd. Lar 23 E1
Waverley Rd. Pais 132 C4
Waverley St. Coat 102 A1
Waverley St. Falk 42 A4
Waverley St. Glasg 116 C1
Waverley St. Green 45 E2
Waverley St. Ham 161 F2
Waverley St. Lark 199 D4
Waverley Terr. Dumb 49 D2
Waverley Terr. Lar 23 E1
Waverley Terr. Udd 161 E3
Waverley Way. Pais 132 C4
Weardale La. Glasg 119 E4
Weardale St. Glasg 119 E4
Weaver Ave. Newt M 156 B4
Weaver Cres. Aird 123 D3
Weaver La. Kilbar 111 D2
Weaver Pl. E Kil 179 F4
Weaver Row. Stir 7 D2
Weaver St. Ayr 235 F1
Weaver St. Glasg 117 E4
Weaver Terr. Pais 114 A2
Weavers Ave. Pais 113 D2
Weavers Rd. Pais 113 D2
Weavers Way. Stone 198 C1
Weavers Wlk. Lan 215 D2
Webster Ave. Sten 24 A2
Webster Groves. Wish 165 E3
Webster St. Clyde 94 C4
Webster St. Glasg 118 A2
Wedderlea Dr. Glasg 115 D3
Wee Cl. Beith 171 D4
Wee Row. Falk 42 A3
Wee Sunnyside Rd. Quart 184 A1
Weensmoor Rd. Glasg 134 C2
Weeple Dr. Lin 112 A3
Weighhouse Cl. Pais 113 F2
Weighhouse Rd. Car 187 F2
Weir Ave. Barr 134 B1
Weir Ave. Pres 233 E1
Weir Dr. Fall 8 B2
Weir Pl. Kilb 149 D1
Weir Pl. Law 186 C2
Weir Rd. Ard 205 E2
Weir Rd. Ayr 235 F2
Weir St. Coat 122 A4
Weir St. Falk 42 B3
Weir St. Green 46 B1
Weir St. Pais 113 F3
Weir St. Stir 1 C1
Weirston Rd. Kilw 208 A2
Weirwood Ave. Glasg 120 A3
Weirwood Gdns. Glasg 119 F2
Welbeck Cres. Troon 229 D1
Welbeck Ct. Troon 229 D1
Welbeck Mews. Troon 229 D1
Welbeck Rd. Glasg 135 D2
Welbeck St. Green 45 E4
Welbeck St. Kilmk 228 A4
Weldon Pl. Kils 60 C2
Welfare Ave. Glasg 139 E2
Well Gn. Glasg 136 B4
Well La. Lennox 57 E4
Well Rd. B of A 2 A4
Well Rd. Kilbar 111 D2
Well Rd. Lan 215 D2
Well St. Pais 113 E3
Well St. W Kil 190 B3
Welland Pl. E Kil 179 F4
Wellbank Gdns. W Kil 190 B3
Wellbank Pl. Udd 140 C3
Wellbrae. Lark 185 D1
Wellbrae Rd. Ham 162 A1
Wellbrae. Stone 198 C1
Wellbrae Terr. Muir 80 C1
Wellcroft Pl. Glasg 117 D2
Wellcroft Rd. Ham 161 F2
Wellcroft Terr. Ham 161 F2
Wellesley Cres. E Kil 179 F4
Wellesley Dr. E Kil 179 F4
Wellfield Ave. Glasg 136 A2
Wellfield St. Glasg 97 F2
Wellgate Dr. B of A 2 B4
Wellgate. Lan 215 D2
Wellgate St. Lark 185 D2
Wellgatehead. Lan 215 D2
Wellgreen. Stir 7 D3
Wellhall Ct. Ham 162 A2

Wellhall Rd. Ham

William St. P Glasg

289
William St. Pais
York St. Wish

William St. Pais 113 E2
Williamfield Ave. Stir 7 D2
Williamfield Gr. Irvine 219 D2
Williamfield Pk. Irvine 219 D2
Williamsburgh Terr. Pais 114 A3
Williamson Ave. Dumb 50 A2
Williamson Ave. Falk 24 A1
Williamson Dr. Helen 16 C1
Williamson Pl. Falk 42 B4
Williamson Pl. John 112 A1
Williamson St. Clyde 74 A2
Williamson St. Falk 42 A2
Williamson St. Glasg 118 B2
Williamwood Dr. Glasg 136 C1
Williamwood Pk. Glasg 136 C1
Williamwood Pk W. Glasg 136 C1
Willie Mair's Brae. Kilmk 223 D1
Willie Ross Pl. Kilmk 223 E2
Willison's La. P Glasg 47 E1
Willock St. Kilmk 227 F3
Willockston Rd. Troon 229 F1
Willoughby Dr. Glasg 95 F3
Willoughby La. Glasg 95 F3
Willow Ave. Bish 98 A4
Willow Ave. John 112 B1
Willow Ave. Klrk 79 F3
Willow Cres. Coat 122 A2
Willow Ct. E Kil 180 A3
Willow Dr. Aird 123 E4
Willow Dr. Bank 38 C1
Willow Dr. John 112 A1
Willow Dr. M of C 58 B3
Willow Dr. Udd 161 E4
Willow Gdns. Irvine 219 F3
Willow Gr. Holy 143 D3
Willow La. Glasg 119 D1
Willow La. Troon 229 E2
Willow Pk. Ayr 239 E2
Willow Pl. John 112 A1
Willow Pl. Tan 141 E4
Willow Rd. Kilmk 227 E4
Willow St. Glasg 95 F4
Willow Way. Ham 162 C1
Willowbank Cres. Glasg 96 C1
Willowbank Gdns. Klrk 79 E4
Willowbank. Lark 185 D3
Willowbank St. Glasg 96 C1
Willowburn Rd. Beith 170 C4
Willowdale Cres. Glasg 120 A2
Willowdale Gdns. Glasg 120 A2
Willowford Rd. Glasg 135 D2
Willows The. E Kil 158 C4
Willows The. Tull 4 A1
Willowyard Rd. Beith 170 C4
Wills Rd. Ayr 236 B1
Willwood Dr. Wish 165 E4
Wilmot Rd. Glasg 95 E3
Wilsgait St. Cle 144 B1
Wilson Ave. Den 21 E1
Wilson Ave. Falk 41 E3
Wilson Ave. Irvine 219 E2
Wilson Ave. Kilmk 228 A4
Wilson Ave. Lin 112 A3
Wilson Ave. Troon 230 A1
Wilson Dr. Bann 7 E1
Wilson Dr. Falk 41 E3
Wilson Gdns. Falk 41 E3
Wilson Pl. Bon 40 B2
Wilson Pl. Dund 225 F1
Wilson Pl. E Kil 160 A2
Wilson Pl. Newt M 156 B2
Wilson Rd. Alla 167 D4
Wilson Rd. Falk 41 E3
Wilson St. Aird 122 C4
Wilson St. Alex 27 F3
Wilson St. Ayr 236 A1
Wilson St. Beith 150 B1
Wilson St. Coat 122 B4
Wilson St. Glasg 117 E4
Wilson St. Ham 162 A3
Wilson St. Lark 185 D1
Wilson St. Mother 163 F4
Wilson St. P Glasg 47 E1
Wilson St. Pais 113 E2
Wilson St. Ren 94 B2
Wilton Crescent La. Glasg 96 C2
Wilton Dr. Glasg 96 C2
Wilton Rd. Car 202 A4
Wilton St. Coat 101 E1
Wilton St. Glasg 96 C2
Wiltonburn Path. Glasg 135 D2
Wiltonburn Rd. Glasg 135 D2
Wilverton Rd. Glasg 95 F4
Winburne Cres. Ham 162 A2
Winchester Ave. Den 21 F2
Winchester Dr. Glasg 96 A3
Windelstraw Ct. Irvine 220 A2
Winderemere St. Hat 141 F2
Windermere. E Kil 179 F3
Windhill Cres. Glasg 136 A3
Windhill Pl. Glasg 136 B3
Windhill Rd. Glasg 136 B3
Windlaw Ct. Glasg 137 E1
Windlaw Gdns. Glasg 136 C2
Windlaw Park Gdns. Glasg 136 C2
Windlaw Rd. E Kil 158 B4
Windlaw Rd. Glasg 137 E1
Windmill Rd. Ham 162 B2
Windmill St. Salt 216 C4
Windmillhill St. Mother 163 F3
Windrow Terr. Wish 165 E4
Windsor Ave. Falk 41 F2
Windsor Ave. Newt M 156 C3
Windsor Cres. Clyde 74 A2
Windsor Cres. Falk 41 F2
Windsor Cres. John 112 A1
Windsor Cres. Pais 114 A3
Windsor Ct. Car 187 F1
Windsor Dr. Duni 21 E2
Windsor Dr. Falk 41 F2
Windsor Dr. Glenm 102 C2
Windsor Gdns. All 9 F4
Windsor Gdns. Falk 41 F2
Windsor Gdns. Ham 162 A3
Windsor Path. Lark 185 E1
Windsor Pl. Shot 146 C3
Windsor Pl. Stir 7 D4
Windsor Quadrant. Car 187 F1
Windsor Rd. Falk 41 F2
Windsor Rd. Holy 143 D3
Windsor Rd. Ren 94 B1
Windsor St. Coat 121 F2
Windsor St. Glasg 97 D1
Windsor St. Glasg 119 E3
Windsor St. Men 3 F3
Windsor St. Shot 146 C3
Windsor Terr. Glasg 97 D1
Windsor Wlk. Tan 141 D4
Windward Pk. Ayr 239 D1
Windward Rd. E Kil 159 D1
Windy Yetts. Twe 59 F2
Windyedge
and Hareshaw Rd. Chap 144 B2
Windyedge Cres. Glasg 95 E3
Windyedge Pl. Glasg 95 E3
Windyhill Pk. Eagle 157 F1
Windyridge. Ham 162 C1
Windyridge Pl. Udd 161 E4
Winehouse Yett. Dund 225 F1
Winfield Ave. Glasg 138 C4
Wingate Ave. Dalry 191 D4
Wingate Cres. E Kil 160 B2
Wingate Dr. E Kil 160 B2
Wingate Pk. E Kil 160 B2
Wingate St. Mother 164 C2
Wingfaulds Ave. Dalry 191 D4
Wingfield Gdns. Udd 141 D1
Winifred St. Glasg 98 B2
Winning Ct. Udd 140 C1
Winning Quadrant. Mother 164 B2
Winning Row. Glasg 118 B3
Winnipeg Dr. E Kil 180 A4
Winstanley Wynd. Kilw 207 E3
Winston Ave. Pres 236 B4
Winston Cres. Lennox 57 E4
Winston Rd. Helen 17 D1
Wintergreen Dr. E Kil 159 E2
Winton Ave. Eagle 178 C2
Winton Ave. Glasg 136 B1
Winton Ave. Kilw 207 E2
Winton Cir. Salt 216 C4
Winton Cres. Udd 161 E4
Winton Ct. Ard 205 E1
Winton Dr. Glasg 96 B3
Winton Gdns. Tan 140 C4
Winton La. Ard 205 E1
Winton La. Glasg 96 B3
Winton Pk. E Kil 159 D1
Winton Pl. Ard 205 E1
Winton Rd. Irvine 219 E3
Winton St. Ard 205 E1
Winton St. Salt 216 C4
Wirran Pl. Clyde 94 C4
Wishart Ave. Dunt 74 B4
Wishart Dr. Stir 7 E2
Wishart St. Glasg 117 F4
Wishaw High Rd. Cle 165 E4
Wishaw Low Rd. Cle 165 D4
Wishaw Rd. Wish 186 C4
Wishawhill St. Wish 164 C2
Wisner Ct. Glasg 135 F2
Wisteria La. Car 201 F4
Wiston St. Glasg 139 F3
Witch Rd. Kilmk 222 C1
Witches Linn. Ard 205 D2
Witchhill Pl. Kilmk 222 C1
Witchknowe Ave. Kilmk 227 F3
Witchknowe Ct. Kilmk 227 F2
Witchknowe Rd. Kilmk 227 F3
Witchwood Ct. Coat 101 E1
Woddrop St. Glasg 118 A1
Wolcott Dr. Udd 161 E4
Wolfe Ave. Newt M 156 B4
Wolfe Rd. Falk 42 B2
Wolseley St. Glasg 117 E2
Wood Aven Dr. E Kil 159 E2
Wood Avens. Tull 4 B1
Wood Cres. Kilw 207 F2
Wood Cres. Mother 142 C1
Wood Farm Rd. Glasg 136 A1
Wood Gr. Irvine 220 B1
Wood La. Bish 98 B4
Wood Pk. Ayr 239 D2
Wood Pl. Strath 31 D2
Wood Quadrant. Clyde 94 C4
Wood Rd. Troon 229 D1
Wood St. Aird 103 E1
Wood St. Coat 121 F4
Wood St. Glasg 118 A4
Wood St. Green 45 E4
Wood St. Kilw 207 F2
Wood St. Mother 163 F4
Wood St. Pais 114 A2
Wood View. Alla 166 C4
Wood View. Holy 143 D3
Woodbank Cres. John 111 F1
Woodbank Cres. Newt M 157 F3
Woodbank Ct. Alex 27 E4
Woodbank Gdns. Alex 27 E4
Woodbank Rd. Cross 221 F1
Woodburn Ave. Aird 122 C3
Woodburn Ave. Bonh 28 A4
Woodburn Ave. Kilw 207 F2
Woodburn Ave. Newt M 157 F3
Woodburn Ave. Udd 161 F4
Woodburn Cres. Bon 39 F2
Woodburn Dr. All 4 C1
Woodburn Gdns. Falk 42 C3
Woodburn Pl. Hous 111 F4
Woodburn Rd. Beith 171 E4
Woodburn Rd. Falk 42 B3
Woodburn Rd. Glasg 136 B3
Woodburn Rd. Holy 143 E4
Woodburn St. Falk 42 C3
Woodburn St. Mother 163 F4
Woodburn Terr. Lark 185 E1
Woodburn Way. Alva 5 D3
Woodburn Way. Cumb 61 E1
Woodburn Way. Miln 55 D1
Woodcroft Ave. Glasg 95 F2
Wooddale. Mother 163 E2
Woodend Ct. Glasg 119 F1
Woodend Dr. Glasg 95 F3
Woodend Dr. Pais 114 B2
Woodend Gdns. Glasg 119 E1
Woodend La. Glasg 95 F3
Woodend Oval. Coy 239 F1
Woodend Pl. John 112 A1
Woodend Rd. Ayr 239 D1
Woodend Rd. Car 188 A1
Woodend Rd. Glasg 119 F1
Woodend Rd. Glasg 138 A2
Woodend St. Helen 16 A1
Woodfield Ave. Ayr 236 A3
Woodfield Ave. Bish 98 A4
Woodfield Cres. Ayr 236 A2
Woodfield Dr. Aird 103 E1
Woodfield Rd. Ayr 236 A2
Woodfield. Tan 141 E3
Woodfoot Pl. Glasg 135 D2
Woodfoot Quadrant. Glasg 135 D2
Woodfoot Rd. Glasg 135 D2
Woodfoot Rd. Ham 162 A1
Woodford Pl. Lin 112 A3
Woodford St. Glasg 136 C4
Woodgreen Ave. Glasg 137 E3
Woodhall Ave. Calder 123 D1
Woodhall Ave. Coat 121 F2
Woodhall Ave. Ham 162 A2
Woodhall Ave. Holy 142 C3
Woodhall
Cottage Rd. Calder 123 E1
Woodhall Mill Rd. Calder 123 D1
Woodhall Pl. Coat 121 F2
Woodhall Rd. Calder 123 D1
Woodhall Rd. Car 201 E1
Woodhall Rd. New 165 F2
Woodhall Rd. Wish 165 F2
Woodhall St. Chap 123 E1
Woodhall St. Glasg 118 A1
Woodhall Terr. P Glasg 69 D4
Woodhead Ave. Cumb 81 F4
Woodhead Ave. Klrk 79 E4
Woodhead Ave. Udd 141 D1
Woodhead Cres. Ham 183 D4
Woodhead Cres. Tan 140 C4
Woodhead Ct. Cumb 81 F4
Woodhead Gdns. Ham 162 A4
Woodhead Gr. Cumb 81 F4
Woodhead Pl. Cumb 81 F4
Woodhead Rd. Cumb 81 F4
Woodhead Rd. Glasg 135 D3
Woodhead Rd. Muir 100 A3
Woodhead Terr. Muir 100 A4
Woodhead View. Cumb 81 F4
Woodhill Cres. Irvine 220 A3
Woodhill Gr. Bish 98 B4
Woodhill Pl. Kilm 222 A3
Woodhill Rd. Blac 107 D2
Woodhill Rd. Glasg 98 A3
Woodhill Rd. Kilmk 222 C2
Woodholm Ave. Glasg 137 E3
Woodhouse Ct. Thorn 158 A3
Woodhouse St. Glasg 95 F4
Woodilee Cotts. Kirk 79 F3
Woodilee Rd. Holy 143 F2
Woodilee Rd. Klrk 79 F3
Woodland Ave. Aird 123 E2
Woodland Ave. Klrk 79 D4
Woodland Ave. Pais 133 F4
Woodland Cres. Eagle 178 B3
Woodland Cres. Glasg 139 E2
Woodland Gdns. E Kil 158 B4
Woodland Gdns. Ham 162 C1
Woodland Pl. Ard 205 E2
Woodland Terr. Lark 185 E1
Woodland Way. Cumb 62 A2
Woodland Way. Den 39 E4
Woodlands Ave. Irvine 219 E2
Woodlands Ave. Law 187 D3
Woodlands Ave. Muir 100 C3
Woodlands Ave. Udd 141 D2
Woodlands Cres. Ayr 239 D2
Woodlands Cres. Falk 42 A2
Woodlands Cres. Glasg 135 F2
Woodlands Cres. Udd 141 D2
Woodlands Ct. Alex 27 E4
Woodlands Ct. Glasg 135 F1
Woodlands Dr. Coat 121 E4
Woodlands Dr. Glasg 96 C1
Woodlands Dr. Holy 142 C3
Woodlands Gate. Glasg 96 C1
Woodlands Gate. Glasg 135 F2
Woodlands Gdns. Udd 141 D2
Woodlands. Glasg 135 F2
Woodlands Gr. Kilmk 220 D2
Woodlands Gr. Miln 55 D2
Woodlands. N Sau 5 F1
Woodlands Pk. Glasg 135 F2
Woodlands Pl. Kilmk 223 D2
Woodlands Rd. Glasg 96 C1
Woodlands Rd. Glasg 135 F1
Woodlands Rd. Holy 143 E4
Woodlands Rd. Mother 163 F2
Woodlands St. Miln 55 D1
Woodlands St. Mother 163 F2
Woodlands St. Pres 236 A4
Woodlands Terr. Glasg 96 C1
Woodlands Terr. Udd 141 D2
Woodlands The. Hat 142 B2
Woodlea Ave. Aird 123 E2
Woodlea Cres. Cross 221 F1
Woodlea Ct. Cross 221 F1
Woodlea Dr. Glasg 136 B2
Woodlea Dr. Ham 183 E4
Woodlea Pk. N Sau 10 A4
Woodlea Pl. Aird 103 E1
Woodlea Pl. Ayr 239 D1
Woodlinn Ave. Glasg 137 D3
Woodmill Dr. Lennox 57 E1
Woodmill Gdns. Cumb 81 F3
Woodmill. Kilw 207 F1
Woodneuk La. Muir 100 C3
Woodneuk Rd. Glasg 135 D3
Woodneuk Rd. Muir 100 C3
Woodneuk St. Chap 123 E1
Woodneuk Terr. Muir 100 C3
Woodrow Ave. Holy 143 D1
Woodrow Ave. Kil 69 E1
Woodrow Cir. Glasg 116 B2
Woodrow Pl. Glasg 116 B2
Woodrow Rd. Glasg 116 B2
Woods La. Ren 94 B2
Woodside Ave. B of W 90 B1
Woodside Ave. Glasg 136 A2
Woodside Ave. Glasg 138 B4
Woodside Ave. Ham 162 C1
Woodside Ave. Kilmk 227 E3
Woodside Ave. Kils 60 C4
Woodside Ave. Klrk 79 E3
Woodside Cres. Barr 134 B1
Woodside Cres. Bonh 27 F3
Woodside Cres. Glasg 96 C1
Woodside Cres. New 166 A3
Woodside Cres. Pais 113 E2
Woodside Ct. Cam 6 B3
Woodside Dr. Calder 123 D1
Woodside Dr. Newt M 157 E1
Woodside Gdns. Coat 121 E2
Woodside Gdns. E Kil 158 B4
Woodside Gdns. Newt M 157 E4
Woodside. Hous 91 E1
Woodside La. Kilbar 111 E3
Woodside Pl. Dunlop 195 E4
Woodside Pl. Fall 8 B2
Woodside Pl. Glasg 96 C1
Woodside Pl. Tan 141 E4
Woodside Place La. Glasg 96 C1
Woodside Rd. All 4 C1
Woodside Rd. Beith 150 A1
Woodside Rd. Cald 106 A2
Woodside Rd. E Kil 158 B4
Woodside Rd. Kilbar 111 E3
Woodside Rd. Stir 2 A2
Woodside Rd. Tull 4 A1
Woodside St. Chap 123 E1
Woodside St. Coat 121 E2
Woodside St. Holy 143 D2
Woodside St. Mother 164 A2
Woodside Terr. Clack 10 C2
Woodside Terr. Falk 42 A2
Woodside Terr. Glasg 96 C1
Woodside Terrace La. Glasg 96 C1
Woodside. W Kil 190 B2
Woodside Wlk. Ham 162 C1
Woodstock Ave. Glasg 116 B1
Woodstock Ave. Klrk 70 F4
Woodstock Ave. Lan 215 E2
Woodstock Ave. Pais 132 C4
Woodstock Dr. Lan 215 D2
Woodstock Dr. Wish 165 E2
Woodstock Pl. Kilmk 222 C1
Woodstock Rd. Green 45 E2
Woodstock Rd. Lan 215 D2
Woodstock St. Kilmk 227 F4
Woodstock Way. Pais 132 C4
Woodstone Ct. Rhu 15 F2
Woodvale Ave. Aird 123 E2
Woodvale Ave. Bear 76 A1
Woodvale Ave. Glasg 157 D4
Woodvale Dr. Pais 113 D3
Woodview Dr. Aird 123 D3
Woodview Dr. Hat 142 B4
Woodview La. Aird 123 D3
Woodview Rd. Lark 199 D4
Woodview. Tan 141 E4
Woodview Terr. Ham 162 A2
Woodville Pk. Glasg 116 A3
Woodville St. Glasg 116 A3
Woodwynd. Kilw 207 F2
Woodyard Rd. Dumb 49 F2
Woodyett Pk. Thorn 157 F3
Woodyett Rd. Thorn 157 F3
Wooer St. Falk 42 A2
Wordsworth Way. Udd 141 D2
Works Ave. Glasg 139 F3
Workshops. Coat 122 A3
Worsley Cres. Newt M 156 B4
Wotherspoon Dr. Beith 150 A1
Wraes Ave. Barr 134 B2
Wraes View. Barr 133 F1
Wraisland Cres. Bishop 71 F2
Wrangholm Cres. Holy 143 D2
Wrangholm Dr. Holy 143 D2
Wren Ct. Tan 141 F4
Wren Pl. John 131 E4
Wren Rd. Green 45 D2
Wright Ave. Barr 134 A1
Wright St. Falk 42 A3
Wright St. Ren 94 A1
Wright Way. Holy 143 D2
Wrightfield Pl. Ayr 238 C1
Wrightlands Cres. Inch 93 F4
Wyburn Pl. Ayr 236 A2
Wye Cres. Coat 101 E1
Wykeham Pl. Glasg 95 E3
Wykeham Rd. Glasg 95 E3
Wylie Ave. Alex 27 E2
Wylie Ave. Newt M 156 B4
Wylie. E Kil 160 B3
Wylie St. Ham 162 B1
Wyllie Rd. Salt 217 D4
Wynd Beatson. Tan 121 D1
Wynd The. Alva 5 D4
Wynd The. Cumb 62 A3
Wyndford Dr. Glasg 96 B3
Wyndford Pl. Glasg 96 B3
Wyndford Rd. Cumb 62 B4
Wyndford Rd. Glasg 96 B3
Wyndford Terr. Tan 141 D4
Wyndham St. Glasg 96 B2
Wynyard Gn. E Kil 180 A4
Wyper Pl. Glasg 118 A3
Wyvil Ave. Glasg 75 F1
Wyvis Ave. Bear 75 E4
Wyvis Ave. Glasg 94 C4
Wyvis Gdns. Kilmk 228 A2
Wyvis Pl. Glasg 94 C4
Wyvis Pl. Irvine 220 A2
Wyvis Pl. Shot 147 D2
Wyvis Quadrant. Glasg 94 C4
Wyvis Rd. Kilmk 228 A2

Yair Dr. Glasg 115 D3
Yardley Pl. Falk 24 A1
Yardside Rd. Kilm 222 A4
Yarrow Cres. Bishop 72 B1
Yarrow Cres. Wish 165 D2
Yarrow Ct. Glasg 139 F3
Yarrow Gardens La. Glasg 96 C2
Yarrow Gdns. Glasg 96 C2
Yarrow Pk. E Kil 160 A1
Yarrow Rd. Bish 78 A2
Yarrow Way. Udd 161 F4
Yate St. Glasg 118 A3
Yerton Brae. W Kil 190 B2
Yetholm St. Glasg 94 C3
Yetholm Terr. Ham 161 F2
Yett Rd. Holy 143 E2
Yetts Ave. Kil 69 E1
Yetts Cres. Klrk 79 F4
Yetts Hole Rd. Glen 102 A3
Yetts The. Cam 6 B3
Yew Dr. Glasg 90 A2
Yew Pl. John 111 F1
Yews Cres. Ham 162 A3
Yieldshields Rd. Car 189 E2
Yoker Ferry Rd. Glasg 94 C3
Yoker Mill Gdns. Clyde 94 C4
Yoker Mill Rd. Glasg 94 C4
Yokerburn Terr. Clyde 94 B4
Yonderton Pl. W Kil 190 B2
York Dr. Falk 42 B3
York Dr. Glasg 138 B3
York Rd. Gour 44 C3
York St. Ayr 235 F1
York St. Clyde 74 B1
York St. Falk 42 B3
York St. Glasg 117 D4
York St. Wish 165 D1

York Street La. Ayr

Zetland Rd. Glasg

STREET ATLASES ORDER FORM

COLOUR EDITIONS

	HARDBACK	SPIRAL	POCKET	£ Total
	Quantity @ £12.99 each	Quantity @ £9.99 each	Quantity @ £5.99 each	
OXFORDSHIRE	☐ 0 540 07512 4	☐ 0 540 07513 2	☐ 0 540 07514 0	➤ ☐
WEST YORKSHIRE	☐ 0 540 06329 0	☐ 0 540 06327 4	☐ 0 540 06328 2	➤ ☐
	Quantity @ £14.99 each	Quantity @ £9.99 each	Quantity @ £5.99 each	£ Total
LANCASHIRE	☐ 0 540 06440 8	☐ 0 540 06441 6	☐ 0 540 06443 2	➤ ☐

BLACK AND WHITE EDITIONS

	HARDBACK	SOFTBACK	POCKET	£ Total
	Quantity @ £10.99 each			
WARWICKSHIRE	☐ 0 540 05642 1	—	—	➤ ☐
	Quantity @ £12.99 each	Quantity @ £9.99 each	Quantity @ £4.99 each	£ Total
BRISTOL AND AVON	☐ 0 540 06140 9	☐ 0 540 06141 7	☐ 0 540 06142 5	➤ ☐
CARDIFF, SWANSEA & GLAMORGAN	☐ 0 540 06186 7	☐ 0 540 06187 5	☐ 0 540 06207 3	➤ ☐
CHESHIRE	☐ 0 540 06143 3	☐ 0 540 06144 1	☐ 0 540 06145 X	➤ ☐
DERBYSHIRE	—	☐ 0 540 06138 7	☐ 0 540 06139 5	➤ ☐
EDINBURGH & East Central Scotland	☐ 0 540 06180 8	☐ 0 540 06181 6	☐ 0 540 06182 4	➤ ☐
EAST ESSEX	☐ 0 540 05848 3	☐ 0 540 05866 1	☐ 0 540 05850 5	➤ ☐
WEST ESSEX	☐ 0 540 05849 1	☐ 0 540 05867 X	☐ 0 540 05851 3	➤ ☐
NOTTINGHAMSHIRE	—	☐ 0 540 05859 9	☐ 0 540 05860 2	➤ ☐
STAFFORDSHIRE	☐ 0 540 06134 4	☐ 0 540 06135 2	☐ 0 540 06136 0	➤ ☐
	Quantity @ £12.99 each	Quantity @ £9.99 each	Quantity @ £5.99 each	£ Total
GLASGOW & West Central Scotland	☐ 0 540 06183 2	☐ 0 540 06184 0	☐ 0 540 06185 9	➤ ☐

Post to: Philip's Direct,
27 Sanders Road,
Wellingborough, Northants,
NN8 4NL

◆ Free postage and packing

◆ All available titles will normally be dispatched within 5 working days of receipt of order but please allow up to 28 days for delivery

◆ Please tick this box if you do not wish your name to be used by other carefully selected organisations that may wish to send you information about other products and services

Registered Office: 25 Victoria Street, London SW1H 0EX.

Registered in England number: 3396524

I enclose a cheque / postal order, for a **total** of ☐
made payable to *Reed Book Services*, or please debit my
☐ Access ☐ American Express ☐ Visa ☐ Diners
account by ☐

Account no
☐☐☐☐ ☐☐☐☐ ☐☐☐☐ ☐☐☐☐

Expiry date ☐☐ ☐☐

Signature..

Name..

Address..

....

....

....POSTCODE

STREET ATLASES ORDER FORM

All Street Atlases contain Ordnance Survey mapping and provide the perfect solution for the driver who needs comprehensive, detailed regional mapping in a choice of compact and easy-to-use formats. They are indispensable and are ideal for use in the car, the home or the office.

The series is available from all good bookshops or by mail order direct from the publisher. Before placing your order, please check by telephone that the complete range of titles are available. Payment can be made in the following ways:

By phone Phone your order through on our special Credit Card Hotline on 01933 443863 (Fax: 01933 443849). Speak to our customer service team during office hours (9am to 5pm) or leave a message on the answering machine, quoting your full credit card number plus expiry date and your full name and address.

By post Simply fill out the order form (you may photocopy it) and send it to: **Philip's Direct, 27 Sanders Road, Wellingborough, Northants** NN8 4NL.

COLOUR EDITIONS

	HARDBACK	SPIRAL	POCKET	£ Total
	Quantity @ £10.99 each	Quantity @ £8.99 each	Quantity @ £4.99 each	£ Total
BERKSHIRE	☐ 0 540 06170 0	☐ 0 540 06172 7	☐ 0 540 06173 5	➤ ☐
MERSEYSIDE	☐ 0 540 06480 7	☐ 0 540 06481 5	☐ 0 540 06482 3	➤ ☐
	Quantity @ £12.99 each	Quantity @ £8.99 each	Quantity @ £4.99 each	£ Total
SURREY	☐ 0 540 06435 1	☐ 0 540 06436 X	☐ 0 540 06438 6	➤ ☐
	Quantity @ £12.99 each	Quantity @ £9.99 each	Quantity @ £4.99 each	£ Total
BUCKINGHAMSHIRE	☐ 0 540 07466 7	☐ 0 540 07467 5	☐ 0 540 07468 3	➤ ☐
DURHAM	☐ 0 540 06365 7	☐ 0 540 06366 5	☐ 0 540 06367 3	➤ ☐
HERTFORDSHIRE	☐ 0 540 06174 3	☐ 0 540 06175 1	☐ 0 540 06176 X	➤ ☐
EAST KENT	☐ 0 540 07483 7	☐ 0 540 07276 1	☐ 0 540 07287 7	➤ ☐
WEST KENT	☐ 0 540 07366 0	☐ 0 540 07367 9	☐ 0 540 07369 5	➤ ☐
EAST SUSSEX	☐ 0 540 07306 7	☐ 0 540 07307 5	☐ 0 540 07312 1	➤ ☐
WEST SUSSEX	☐ 0 540 07319 9	☐ 0 540 07323 7	☐ 0 540 07327 X	➤ ☐
TYNE AND WEAR	☐ 0 540 06370 3	☐ 0 540 06371 1	☐ 0 540 06372 X	➤ ☐
SOUTH YORKSHIRE	☐ 0 540 06330 4	☐ 0 540 06331 2	☐ 0 540 06332 0	➤ ☐
	Quantity @ £12.99 each	Quantity @ £9.99 each	Quantity @ £5.50 each	£ Total
GREATER MANCHESTER	☐ 0 540 06485 8	☐ 0 540 06486 6	☐ 0 540 06487 4	➤ ☐
	Quantity @ £12.99 each	Quantity @ £9.99 each	Quantity @ £5.99 each	£ Total
NORTH HAMPSHIRE	☐ 0 540 07471 3	☐ 0 540 07472 1	☐ 0 540 07473 X	➤ ☐
SOUTH HAMPSHIRE	☐ 0 540 07476 4	☐ 0 540 07477 2	☐ 0 540 07478 0	➤ ☐